THE SHORT WORKS OF JOHN HABRAKEN

This book offers, for the first time, access to the chronological arc of John Habraken's writing in a single collection.

Few architects or scholars have so consistently and patiently pursued such a humane and culturally vital set of radical questions related to the behaviour of the built environment as N. John Habraken. From the publication of his first book in 1960, he has quietly helped redraw the map of architectural research, education, practice, design methods and theory. His insights lead us to a better understanding of how the built field works, contributing to the development of methods enabling professionals to contribute to its coherence and resilience.

Following an introductory essay by the editors, placing Habraken's work in context, this collection is organized in two sections and further organized around a number of specific themes: The Built Field; Role of the Architect; Control; Sharing Forms; Examples of WAYS OF DOING; Open Building; Tools; and Cultivating the Built Environment. A series of interviews with the author enable him to reflect on his journey of inquiry, research, advocacy and teaching – and the relationship between WAYS OF SEEING and WAYS OF DOING.

Offering theoretical perspectives and methodological ways forward, this book will be of interest to architects, planners and urban designers tackling the challenges of the contemporary built environment that Habraken identifies, as well as educators and students.

Open Building

The Routledge Open Building Series is a library of titles addressing the Open Building approach to architecture and urban design. It offers an international perspective, providing theory, design methods, examples of construction techniques, manufactured products and many realized projects. These titles augment a growing literature in sustainability and resilience in the built environment by focusing on the fourth dimension.

Open Building advocates separation of design tasks: the design of what is shared and what will last, and the design of what belongs to individual occupancies and is expected to change more quickly. This is both a social/political and a design skills issue. Urban design projects, office buildings, shopping centers and laboratories are examples of separation of design tasks. The same should become the norm in multi-unit housing, healthcare and educational facilities, mixed-use and other project types making up our everyday world. The Open Building approach addresses how to establish the boundary between what is shared and what is decided independently; how to separate the distribution of utility lines between the two; how to evaluate a building's or urban design's capacity to accommodate a variety of interventions initially and over time; and what shared patterns, types and systems help designers cultivate coherent variety. More generally, Open Building helps design professionals work with change and to cooperate in the flowering of everyday environment.

This series, including the titles below, provides answers to these questions, and more, and is designed to be the go-to resource for anyone seeking to understand and practice Open Building.

The Appearance of the Form
Seven Essays on the Position Designing takes Between People and Things (Routledge Revivals)
N. John Habraken

Supports
An Alternative to Mass Housing (Routledge Revivals)
N. John Habraken

Healthcare Architecture as Infrastructure
Open Building in Practice
Edited by Stephen H. Kendall

Residential Architecture as Infrastructure
Open Building in Practice
Edited by Stephen H. Kendall

For more information about this series, please visit: www.routledge.com/Open-Building/book-series/OB

In Praise of *The Short Works of John Habraken*

"This book makes a significant contribution to the design and transformation of the built environment by changing our perceptions and understanding and therefore our ways of practicing architecture."

Professor Dietmar Eberle
Baumschlager Eberle Architects

"Professor Habraken's insights into the principles that make up cities and architecture, particularly his studies on the relationship between occupants, other stakeholders and the environment, have continued to have a profound influence on many projects and policies in Japan, including Japanese legislation to promote long-life housing."

Kazunobu Minami, PhD
Professor Emeritus, Shibaura Institute of Technology, Tokyo

"Habraken's oeuvre centers on a lifelong quest to sort out and restore the relationship between dwelling and the built environment that scaffolds everyday lives and rituals. Toward that end, there remains much to discover throughout this long-awaited collection."

Jonathan Teicher
writer, architect, urban designer and editor of several of Habraken's books

"John Habraken is a restless thinker. While the full depth of his theories can be read in his seminal books – *Supports* and *The Structure of the Ordinary* – in his short essays, we are privy to his thinking in process and his mind at work. *The Short Works of John Habraken* is an extraordinary contribution to the literature of people-based architecture, open-building, and thematic design through the texts of one of architecture's most influential philosophers and theorists."

Andrés Mignucci FAIA, Distinguished Professor ACSA
Arts & Literary Arts Scholar in Residence Rockefeller Foundation Bellagio Center

"One can never comprehend the behavior of everyday built environment without grasping the laws of its existence and transformations, that is its rules, regulations, agreements and conventions, i.e. control. The interplay of control and built form cannot be understood without Habraken's theories."

Dr Jamel Akbar, Professor of Architecture
Fatih Sultan Mehmet Vakıf University, Istanbul, Turkey

"John Habraken's contributions are in the field of mass housing, and the integration of citizens into the design process. The result is an architecture and urbanism of lively variety and greater meaning. Habraken is a hero of building and urban design."

Douglas Kelbaugh
Dean Emeritus, University of Michigan

"The impact of John Habraken's thinking on shaping a resilient built environment in our denser and more connected communities is immeasurable."

Farooq Ameen AIA, RIBA
Principal, City Design Studio, Los Angeles, CA

"This timely and excellent publication celebrates John Habraken's contribution to our better understanding of the physical and social structure of the built environment, and the need to re-define the roles and responsibilities of Architects. The impact of his work on teaching and practice continues to be profound."

Nabeel Hamdi
Former Director of the Centre for Development and Emergency Planning; Emeritus Professor, Oxford Brooks University, UK

"I heartily recommend this book. The theory proposed by Professor Habraken will prove to be of major significance and of a surprisingly wide scope for solving the housing problems in the Netherlands and far beyond."

Professor Jo Coenen, JCAU Architects and Urbanists
Former Government Architect of the Netherlands

THE SHORT WORKS OF JOHN HABRAKEN
WAYS OF SEEING/WAYS OF DOING

Edited by
STEPHEN H. KENDALL AND JOHN R. DALE

LONDON AND NEW YORK

Routledge
OPEN BUILDING SERIES

Cover image: N. John Habraken from Habraken's competition entry for the Amsterdam Town Hall
(1967: The Leaves and The Flowers)

First published 2023
by Routledge
4 Park Square, Milton Park, Abingdon, Oxon OX14 4RN

and by Routledge
605 Third Avenue, New York, NY 10158

Routledge is an imprint of the Taylor & Francis Group, an informa business

© 2023 selection and editorial matter, Stephen H. Kendall and John R. Dale; individual essays, reports and writings, N. John Habraken

The right of Stephen H. Kendall and John R. Dale to be identified as the authors of the editorial material, and of N. John Habraken for the individual essays, reports and writings, has been asserted in accordance with sections 77 and 78 of the Copyright, Designs and Patents Act 1988.

All rights reserved. No part of this book may be reprinted or reproduced or utilised in any form or by any electronic, mechanical, or other means, now known or hereafter invented, including photocopying and recording, or in any information storage or retrieval system, without permission in writing from the publishers.

Trademark notice: Product or corporate names may be trademarks or registered trademarks, and are used only for identification and explanation without intent to infringe.

British Library Cataloguing-in-Publication Data
A catalogue record for this book is available from the British Library

Library of Congress Cataloging-in-Publication Data
Names: Habraken, N. J., author. | Kendall, Stephen H., editor. | Dale, John R., editor.
Title: The short works of John Habraken : ways of seeing/ways of doing / edited by Stephen H. Kendall and John R. Dale.
Description: Abingdon, Oxon : Routledge, 2023. | Includes bibliographical references and index.
Identifiers: LCCN 2022035195 | ISBN 9780367820077 (hardback) | ISBN 9781003011385 (ebook)
Subjects: LCSH: Architecture.
Classification: LCC NA27 .H25 2023 | DDC 720—dc23/eng/20220920
LC record available at https://lccn.loc.gov/2022035195

ISBN: 978-0-367-82007-7 (hbk)
ISBN: 978-1-003-01138-5 (ebk)

DOI: 10.4324/9781003011385

Typeset in Minion Pro
by Apex CoVantage, LLC

"All work is as seed sown; it grows and spreads and sows itself anew."

– John Carlyle

CONTENTS

Preface xii
Introduction xiii
Attitudes Towards the Built Field; My Credo, Offered to Students of Architecture xxi

Introduction to WAYS OF SEEING 1

PART I
WAYS OF SEEING

Beginning
1965 Man and Matter 9

1968 Housing: the Act of Dwelling 14

2001 What Use Theory?: Questions of Purpose and Practice 20

Intermezzo by the editors

The Built Field
1964 The Tissue of the Town: Some Suggestions for Further Scrutiny 29

1971 You Can't Design the Ordinary 42

1979 General Principles about the Way Built Environments Exist 45

1984 The General from the Local 58

1988 Lives of Systems 63

2003 Making Urban Fabric Fine Grained – A Research Agenda 74

Control
1968 Supports, Responsibilities and Possibilities 83

1972 Playing Games 88

1972 Involving People in the Housing Process 90

1972 Control Hierarchies in Complex Artifacts 102

1987	Control Relations in the Built Environment	113
2004	Change and the Distribution of Design	117

Sharing Forms

1997	Forms of Understanding: Thematic Knowledge and the Modernist Legacy	125
1998	The Power of the Conventional	145

Intermezzo by the editors

Role of the Architect

1975	The Limits of Professionalism	153
1980	Notes of a Traveler	165
1980	Around the Black Hole	172
1999	Notes on a Network Profession	181
2002	Memories of a Lost Future	187
2006	Questions that Will Not Go Away: Some Remarks on Long-Term Trends in Architecture and Their Impact on Architectural Education	191
2013	Methodology and Ideology in Architecture	198

PART II
WAYS OF DOING

Introduction to WAYS OF DOING	207

Examples of WAYS OF DOING

1963	"Grondslagen" – Basic Principles for the Building of Supports and the Production of Support Dwellings	213
1967	The leaves and the Flowers	231
1987	Shell-Infill House	243
1994	The Samarkand Competition Submission	266

Intermezzo by the editors

The Open Building Approach

1964	Quality and Quantity: The Industrialization of Housing	279
1992	An Efficient Response to Users' Preferences	296
1994	NEXT21 in the Open Building Perspective	308
2003	Open Building as a Condition for Industrial Construction	317

Intermezzo by the editors

Contents   xi

Tools

Year	Title	Page
1965	SAR: Rules for Design: A Summary	329
1988	Type as a Social Agreement	336
1988	The Uses of Levels	346
1988	Concept Design Games	357
2003	Emergent Coherent Behavior of Complex Configurations Through Automated Maintenance of Dominance Relations	368
2008	Design for Flexibility: Towards a Research Agenda	374

Intermezzo by the editors

Cultivating Built Environment

Year	Title	Page
1978	Build as Before	383
1987	Control of Complexity	397
1994	Cultivating the Field: About an Attitude When Making Architecture	408
2004	Change and the Distribution of Design	418
2007	To Tend a Garden: Thoughts on the Strengths and Limits of Studio Pedagogy	424
2012	Cultivating Built Environment	429

Intermezzo by the editors

Summing Up

Year	Title	Page
2013	Methodology and Ideology in Architecture	437
2016	Cultivating Complexity: The Need for a Shift in Cognition	443
2017	Back to the Future	454
2018	The Lure of Bigness	460
2021	Open Building: a Professional Challenge	465
2022	Open Building and Government: Lessons Learned	471
	Short Works: Conclusions	474
	WAYS OF SEEING/WAYS OF DOING – A Timeline	475
	Complete List of Experience, Honors and Writings of John Habraken	479
	Editors' Biographies	485
	Index	487

PREFACE

Having launched the Council on Open Building in 2017, we decided to assemble under one cover many of John Habraken's short works, reminding practitioners and educators of his significant contributions and providing critical context to this ongoing endeavor. Our aim at that time was to foster what we believed to be a needed change in perspective among those responsible for stewarding the transformation of our built environment. Along with the needed shift in 'WAYS OF SEEING' was an urgent need to find new 'WAYS OF DOING or working' in the face of multiple, daunting challenges, both social and environmental.

We believe that this collection will prove to be very important to professionals responsible for the stewardship of the 'built field.' John Habraken has been a prolific writer. We have counted more than 60 published and unpublished works produced between 1963 and 2022 paralleling his many books. His entire oeuvre can be found at the end of the book. Together, his books and articles – published and unpublished – represent a singular and continually relevant body of work of great value to the environmental design professions and those who invest in the built field's sustenance.

Francesca Ford, Senior Publisher and our editor at Routledge, also encouraged us to undertake this work as part of the Routledge Open Building Series. Routledge had already published or reissued several important books by Habraken (*Palladio's Children*, *Conversations with the Form*, and revivals of *SUPPORTS* and *The Appearance of the Form*). Others were forthcoming. The *Structure of the Ordinary: Form and Control in the Built Environment*, Habraken's seminal treatise, had been published by the MIT Press in 1998.

The book is organized in parts that can be read individually in any sequence. We hope it adds to the broad international discussions now taking place among practitioners and educators: how can we balance the demands of large projects for efficient and rapid implementation with fine-grained user control; how can we design with change in mind; how can we learn to cooperate more effectively in large project implementation; how can we avoid making a choice between tradition and innovation or between mindless conformity and ultimately exhausting self-expression; and how can we and our allies in the building industry take advantage of new capabilities in computational tools, data management, logistics, and organizational systems. These expanding capabilities are now strongly influencing how we make and transform our everyday built environment, to make it adaptable and sustainable and of the highest quality.

Note on the use of the male pronoun

Habraken wrote recently: "Readers are asked to excuse me for the almost exclusive use of the male pronoun, a convention at the time of my earlier writing, which, of course, I no longer advocate."

INTRODUCTION

This collection reveals the remarkable dedication to a few key insights and questions that have occupied Nicholas John Habraken over almost seven decades. As such, these selected works – from a much larger opus including a sizable number of books published in several languages – reflect the rigorous detachment of a keen observer, the activism of building and sharing new design methods, the dedication of an architect and architectural educator, as well as a humanist's recognition of the pulse of everyday life. We see John Habraken as a sort of paragon of a unique kind of architect and educator, above all his willingness to think deeply about a problem or a question without ceasing. Throughout these published and unpublished essays, reports, design studies, design competitions and notes is a consistent belief in the possibility of a renewal of the design professions as stewards of the quality of everyday environment. This belief is accompanied by a commitment to a continuing renewal of our professional knowledge base. Both remain compelling and vital today. Also evident is his life-long commitment to finding ways of teaching architecture students congruent with his continually evolving understanding of how architects can and in fact must cooperate with one another, while recognizing that each has their own responsibility for the designs they're working on.

John Habraken served as Founding Director of the SAR (Foundation for Architects Research) in the Netherlands (1965–75) and was Founding Chair and Professor of the Department of Architecture and Urban Design at Eindhoven Technical University. He served as Professor and Head of the Department of Architecture at MIT (1975–81) and continued to teach there for a decade after that; he is now Professor Emeritus. He was made an honorary member of the Architectural Institute of Japan and was recognized by the Association of Collegiate Schools of Architecture in the US for his contributions to architectural education and received a number of prestigious Dutch awards for excellence in architecture. He has authored numerous books, published in many languages, about the form and distribution of control of built environment. These books include *Supports, An Alternative to Mass Housing* (In Dutch in 1961; In English by Praeger, 1972; Urban International Press, 1999; Routledge Revivals Open Building Series, 2019); *The Structure of the Ordinary: Form and Control in the Built Environment* (MIT Press, 1998); *Palladio's Children* (Taylor and Francis, 2007); and *Conversations with Form: A Workbook for Students of Architecture* (coauthored by Andres Mignucci and Jonathan Teicher; Routledge, 2014). His early pamphlet articulating the "two spheres of decision-making" in housing, *The ABC's of Housing* (1964, Scheltema & Holkema), and *The Appearance of the Form: Four Essays on the Position Designing Takes Between People and Things* (Awater Press, 1988) are available as e-books and in the Revivals Open Building Series by Routledge. Readers will find a comprehensive list of publications and awards at the end of the book.

The purpose of this book

Our intention is to take readers on an ordered and comprehensive journey of discovery of the original and independent thinking embodied in Habraken's work, calling on the unique ability of our colleagues in the environmental design fields to observe and act when faced with new challenges.

To get the most out of his work, readers are urged to suspend disbelief and follow Habraken's path of reasoning and exploration. After some travel, we believe the journey will offer much to reflect on, to value and to incorporate into practice.

This edited collection of some of John Habraken's most important works is a personal undertaking for the editors. Both studied under his mentorship at MIT. John Dale was enrolled in the post-professional research oriented SMArchS program from 1983–86. Habraken had inaugurated the program in 1978, one of the very first such degrees in an American school of architecture. John moved on to professional practice in Los Angeles, working for several major design firms and was only in touch with his professor occasionally until, in 2012, he reconnected when he was asked by Habraken to provide illustrations for a book and to contribute to his Thematic Design website (www.thematicdesign.org). Stephen Kendall, having left professional practice to enter the academic community, came to MIT to do a PhD in Design Theory and Methods under Habraken's direction, and was in residence there from 1985–87, completing the degree in 1990. He has known John Habraken from a first meeting in 1972 at a Design Methods conference in London and has remained in close contact since. In 1990, just when his PhD was accepted, he was invited to take part in the first full-fledged installation of the Matura Infill system in an emptied apartment in Voorburg, the Netherlands, a development Habraken was part of and is presented in several of the papers in this collection. More recently they jointly authored an unpublished essay "Base Building: A New Infrastructure" and a book *Open Building for Architects* (Routledge, Open Building Series, 2023).

What has led us to assemble this collection? Another authoritative book (*Housing for the Millions: John Habraken and the SAR*, NAI Publishers, 2000) offers a comprehensive historical view of John Habraken, seeking to put his work in a larger, and international, professional milieu. Our motivation is different. In 2017, we launched the Council on Open Building (www.councilonopenbuilding.org) to bring together the professional community of architects and engineers, public agencies and private developers across North America. The goal of the Council is to foster designing for change under conditions of distributed control – a central preoccupation of Habraken's thinking, research and writing. In this context, we see an urgent need to make available some of his most important but hard to access work to an audience of practicing architects, engineers, urban designers, clients and policy makers. This is no easy task because these professions tend to be practice-oriented as opposed to research-oriented or reflective. The professions and their clients shaping the built environment are understandably focused on obtaining and completing contracts where habits among all participants are entrenched and hard to change. Reading and taking seriously writings that challenge conventional WAYS OF SEEING and WAYS OF DOING takes focused effort and dedication.

The sometimes daunting realities of the way the built environment comes into being and incrementally transforms requires us to step back and think, and to then act in new ways. The challenges of these times – everywhere in the world – include the increased size of projects; the complexity of the teams charged with their design; the fast pace of work; the imperative to be efficient yet allow for variety and vicissitudes in the marketplace; and the inevitability that what is built will change later at the hands of other designers, for different investors, and through the agency of everyday citizens. We need Habraken's insights to help us meet these challenges with knowledge, imagination, skills and methods. We believe that there is no better time to carefully study what he has to offer – for the health of everyday built environment and for the cultivation of the shared knowledge base architects and urban designers depend on.

What imperative kept him going across almost seven decades of research, teaching and writing? Is his formulation of 'the natural relationship' (the act of dwelling without which, he believes, built environment would be forever alien) actually a recognition of a more fundamental need of humankind to reconnect with the material world in a time of mass consumption, anonymous and large commercial forces, and industrial production? Does his sustained focus on design methodology actually present a barrier to more widespread appreciation of his independent mind's work because of the suspicion that methods will somehow undermine creativity? Which of his works helps give access to the breadth and depth of his evolving thinking? Perhaps especially, why is his work not better known, especially in North America where one might expect a receptive audience for his commitment to empowering the individual and 'small-scale' players in the housing process and the cultivation of the everyday environment?

While we do not have definitive answers to these and other similar questions, we attempt to address them through recorded dialogues with Habraken and commentary distributed in 'intermezzos' throughout the book.

About John Habraken, the author

It is important to say that John Habraken, while a prolific writer, researcher, teacher and lecturer, was not a journalist, critic or conventional polemicist. His writings were addressed to other architects and educators and to students, not the general public. In his quest to convey the fundamental principles of the questions he was exploring, there was no time to comment on or criticize other architects or writers and he generally left the 'popularization' of his thinking to others. The main exception to this was his involvement with the co-invention and development of the Matura Infill system, reported on in a number of papers included here.

He was loath to introduce new words, so, except for a few terms such as "supports," "control," "urban tissue," "infill systems" and "levels" that he carefully defined, he used the most ordinary language familiar to most professionals involved in shaping the built environment. He also scrupulously avoided showing designs reflecting his ideas, with a few exceptions that we include in this collection. He wrote in the preface of the 2019 edition of SUPPORTS

> The book purposely avoided showing pictures, because I believed that **the most important points were not about architectural design per se, but about distribution of decision-making.** I believed, and evidence since demonstrates, that many different architectures would flower once this new way of making decisions would be adopted, so I should not show any examples to avoid opening myself to favoring one design over another.

Habraken did his early thinking and writing in the tumultuous 1960s and 70s, the time of youth revolt, communes, 'liberation theology,' deep international tensions and war, counterculture movements and widespread skepticism of 'the hegemony of the professional classes.' In a certain way, his thinking ignored these movements, although being inside the academic world during those years – first in Eindhoven (1965–75) and then at MIT (1975–89), it would have been hard to ignore the swirling debates that produced many manifestos, conferences, books and brought changes in architectural education, if not practice. His steadfast focus and almost stubborn refusal to be distracted from figuring out the questions that occupied him did set him apart in some ways from the turmoil. He sought out those people and writings, contemporaneous and historical, that could shed light on the questions he pursued, and mainly filtered out the rest which was more often than not just noise to him. Yet, he was always a voracious reader in literature, the sciences, history, the arts and the professions, and maintained an extensive international network of colleagues.

Habraken is at heart a methodologist, who insists that good methods, while certainly not assuring excellence, are critical to enabling architects to participate and cooperate in making a vibrant yet coherent built environment and, equally important, to support a robust and effective profession in tune with its times. This was a defiantly deviant perspective at a time when most architects – then as now – spend their energy trying to differentiate themselves from their peers. Habraken's focus was to build the common knowledge base that he believed must be constantly renewed and nurtured. He wrote:

> For the methodologist whose position is inevitably academic, what happens in the field is of fundamental importance. It is our primary source of knowledge: the inescapable reality where habits and conventions make work possible and where new trends of working appear under the pressure of changing technology and evolving demographic and social forces. The observation of this real world invites clarification of what is emerging, raises new questions to be answered, and opens the possibility of generalization and extrapolation that, in turn, must be tested against what is actually happening on the drafting tables, in the management meetings and on the building site.

This view was also notably at odds with most academic colleagues as well as practitioners who would come to MIT to lecture and engage in seminars or to teach. It's fair to say that the dominant attitude was, and remains, deeply skeptical of Habraken's commitment to studying and identifying regularities (laws) in the way that built environment comes into being and transforms. Most would, on being pressed, explain that efforts to formulate general principles of this sort are sheer folly. When Habraken would declare that we professionals need to learn the skills of designing for change, saying "We should not try to forecast what will happen, but try to make provision for what cannot be foreseen," the response would often be a retreat to the tired statement that no one has a crystal ball. Such attitudes represent a missed opportunity to engage and test Habraken's insights and contributions.

John Habraken has something of a scientist's detachment: he is a student of the man-made environment – what he refers to as the 'built field.' This stance mirrors students of the natural world and the social sciences. He believes that, as in the fields of the law and medicine, environmental design must forever adopt new principles from life, and always retain old ones from history (paraphrasing Oliver Wendell Holmes, the great American jurist). In that sense, he has been quietly, patiently and intensely focused on observing and understanding how the ordinary built environment of the past and the present works. One of his key points of view concerns 'the natural relationship,' an idea he formulated in his first book *SUPPORTS and the PEOPLE* (the title of the original Dutch edition). He writes: "The relation between user and dwelling is an iterative relation that makes the dwelling a living cell in the organic existence of a built environment."

This perspective – actually more of a conviction – drove his early work as Director of the Foundation for Architects Research (SAR), where his initial focus was on WAYS OF WORKING, – how to enable architects to participate in the 'housing process' in which he and the SAR supporters felt architects were being marginalized. The question the SAR group explored was straightforward but new: how can architects design buildings if the floor plans are not known, will be decided by others, must nevertheless meet client standards, and are expected to change?

During his decade leading the SAR, Habraken and his colleagues not only made proposals for WAYS OF WORKING (design methods for housing and urban tissues) but also raised conceptual questions about WAYS OF SEEING. In post–Second World War Europe, he opened himself to criticism for suggesting not just tools for designing but what some would call theories – that is, how things work. Many of his observations were not on the conventional map (see his essay "Notes of a Traveler"). His proposals were not easily understood by those who were, in his view – and ours – trapped by obsolete WAYS OF SEEING and therefore were immune to the new ways of working he put forward and demonstrated in his teaching, practical work and writing. In later years, he dedicated much of his writing to explaining both the WAYS OF DOING and SEEING the built environment that arose from his focus on the design methods needed to empower architects in the face of new realities.

John Habraken is, according to Nabeel Hamdi, Emeritus Professor at Oxford Brooks University and one of his colleagues at MIT, one of two seminal thinkers addressing the question of mass housing in the 20th century. Along with John Turner, who first recognized the vital role of individual households in the housing processes in developing countries, Habraken's contributions stand out as clearly the most influential, if largely unrecognized contribution to housing theory and practice. The many hundreds if not thousands of residential, educational, healthcare and urban design 'open building' projects around the world are a testament to the underlying strength and influence of his insights and contributions. More are discovered every year, and, Habraken likes to point out, many are not identified by those implementing them as 'open building' at all. This tells him, and us, that he did not invent something new but that he was perhaps the first to recognize and name a phenomenon that had a life of its own and needed recognition and cultivation to flourish.

The short works in this collection are evidence therefore of his propositions in both WAYS OF SEEING (conceiving) and WAYS OF DOING (working) in all their reciprocal richness. The essays eschew moral indignity or urgency, yet each advances the same basic arguments. Over all these years, John Habraken has been consistent in his advocacy of an enlarged professional knowledge base that is synchronous with new realities of the built environment, and in particular his conviction that 'the responsive or independent units of occupancy' such as dwellings in large projects – the result of separation of design tasks – is key to a regenerative and sustainable built environment.

Introduction

Understanding Habraken's writing and theories

Contemporary critics were often harsh in their assessment of John Habraken's writings. In 1972, shortly after the first English language edition of his first book SUPPORTS was published, a British architect writing in *The Architects' Journal* titled his review of the book in this way: "One Grows Wary of Ultimate Solutions." Another critic wrote: "Complete Freedom Neither Realistic nor Wanted;" and yet another stated: "I'm Sure it Will Go Away." In a scathing review of Habraken's book, a well-known American scholar titled a book review of SUPPORTS: "Simple-Minded Utopianism and Autocratic Nonsense" (Gutman, Robert in *Landscape Architecture*, January 1973).

Habraken once exclaimed "some criticize my work as pointing to socialism; others thought that what I was advocating was just a way to magnify the power of capitalists."

Again, we believe that these critics completely missed the points Habraken was making.

It is an understatement to say that Habraken has often been misunderstood both in the Netherlands and elsewhere, both inside the academic community and in the design professions. When, in 1998, he published what should be recognized as his magnum opus – *The Structure of the Ordinary: Form and Control in the Built Environment* (MIT Press, Cambridge, 1998) – no one could place it among the standard Library of Congress categories. It wasn't architecture, or urban planning; nor did it fit in the fields of geography or archeology. The book has defied categorization in the context of today's siloed world and, as a result is not broadly recognized. A similar fate has befallen his other books.

Some of the key ideas summarized in the following paragraphs figure prominently in the writings found in this collection.

Habraken's ideas about 'participation' are not aligned with most 'user participation' advocates. He has always thought that there is an imbalance in the distribution of **control** in the housing process – the user has been systematically eliminated from a decision-making role. This was his central argument in SUPPORTS and in the work of the SAR. Instead of advocating 'citizen's participation,' as many were doing at the time, he has argued instead that architects need to learn to participate in an ongoing process that continues with or without architects' help. (see The "Limits of Professionalism") He has written that if architects want to play in 'the built-environment game,' (see "Playing Games") they need to know the rules of the game (which exist independently from the professions) and to rethink their skills and adopt new attitudes or else get to work with others to change the rules. He has often pointed out that, without naming it, architects and their design teams have already been adjusting to the new realities, if only to stay in business. He has argued that naming what was going on in the 'field' would allow the design professions to methodically improve their capabilities ("Practice and Everyday Environment").

Habraken has also argued for the importance of and power of implicitly understood conventions – as an antidote to a dominant professional emphasis on uniqueness, invention and individual expression. ("The Power of the Conventional" and "Conventional Form") He believes that architects must work within a broader continuum of creativity that involves collaboration at many different levels. He argues that, in order to be successful in practice, architects need to develop a deep appreciation of conventions (shared knowledge) and develop new techniques of communication and cooperation across professional boundaries, as a springboard for finding new solutions.

He has asserted that the distribution of control or power plays a key role in the shaping of built environment and that patterns of control need to be studied carefully and addressed with care in practice ("Control Relations in the Built Environment" among others).

Habraken's research has led to a deeper and more nuanced understanding of the artificial dichotomy between public and private territory within the built environment. His careful study of territorial hierarchy and 'gates' as ever-present realities in all cultures has led to rethinking of the definition and control of public and private space. Ignorance of this hierarchy impoverishes built environment where many actors are involved in making decisions and do so in a hierarchically structured context. ("The Control of Complexity").

His analysis of the building industry reveals the frequent misunderstandings of the difference – and yet the complementarity – of the act of building (construction) and industrialized production. He has argued that the true power of industrial processes in the building sector lie in cultivating and harnessing demand by individual users. This is the basis for his advocacy of an infill industry serving the responsive or independent dwelling ("An Infill Industry; Open Building as a Condition for Industrial Construction").

He has unhesitatingly sought out the immutable laws of form and control in the making and transformation of built environment, distinguishing these laws from questions of 'meaning.' (*The Structure of the Ordinary: Form and Control in the Built Environment*, MIT Press, 1998) He has identified and named inherent hierarchies that order professional work – while leading to rich and satisfying environmental complexity ("The Uses of Levels").

This has drawn him into methodology – not formulas or recipes but ways of working ("Methodology and Ideology in Architecture").

Although Habraken has scrupulously refused to write or speak negatively about others in his field, he has never failed to point out the shortcomings of modernism. He has always been critical of architectural education ("Around the Black Hole"), while never failing to suggest and experiment with what he thought were better ways of teaching. Even while he was immersed in, lectured at and held leadership positions in several universities, he never stopped challenging his academic colleagues to examine the "Questions That Will Not Go Away." At the same time, over the course of four decades, a growing international network has evolved in support of Habraken's theoretical and methodological insights. Many of his advocates work outside the popular mainstream of practice and education but continue their work with energy and diligence, remaining connected through informal international networks and the Thematic Design website (www.thematicdesign.org).

Habraken's contribution to a theory of the built field

In his seminal book of theory – *The Structure of the Ordinary: Form and Control in the Built Environment* (MIT Press, 1998) – Habraken (paraphrasing from the dust cover of the book) shows that

> the intimate and unceasing interaction between people and the forms they inhabit uniquely defines built environment. This book, the culmination of decades of environmental observation and design research, is a recognition and analysis of everyday environment as the wellspring of urban design and formal architecture. The author's central argument is that built environment is universally organized by the Orders of Form, Place and Understanding. These three fundamental, interwoven principles correspond roughly to physical, biological and social domains.
>
> Historically, "ordinary" environment was the background against which architects built the "extraordinary." Drawing upon extensive examples from historical and contemporary sites worldwide, Habraken illustrates profound recent shifts in the structure of everyday environment. One effect of these transformations, he argues, has been the loss of implicit common understanding that previously enabled architects to formally enhance and innovate while still maintaining environmental coherence. Consequently, architects must now undertake a study of the ordinary environment as the fertile common ground in which form and place-making are rooted. In focusing on the built environment as an autonomous entity distinct from the societies and natural environments that jointly create it, this book lays the foundation for a new dialogue on methodology and pedagogy, in support of a more informed approach to professional intervention.

In *Palladio's Children: Seven Essays on Everday Environment and the Architect* (Taylor and Francis, 2005), Habraken critically examines the role of the architect as a professional descendent of Palladio, and as an heir to his architectural legacy. Seven innovative and carefully crafted essays explore a widening ideological gap. He points out the divide between today's architects whose core values, identity and education remain rooted in the Renaissance legacy of creating artful "masterpieces," and the practical demands on the profession. That book opens a new forum of debate across design theory, professional practice and academic issues. Moving from a historical perspective, Habraken shows how architects are increasingly involved in the design of everyday buildings. This must lead to a reassessment of architects' identities, values and education, and the contribution of the architect in the shaping of the built environment.

In 2014, he coauthored a book for students of architecture: *Conversations with Form: A Workbook for Students of Architecture* (Routledge, 2014) with Andres Mignucci and Jonathan Teicher. It offers a series of design exercises, accompanied by observational studies, examples and applied theory, aimed to improve designers' understanding and dexterity in making form. It specifically focuses on the skills needed to succeed in the everyday context in which the vast majority of architects will ultimately design and build, wherein no one designs in isolation and existing conditions never represent a tabula rasa.

And in 2023, a book written in collaboration with one of us (Kendall) was scheduled for publication, titled *Open Building for Architects* (Routledge, 2022). Using numerous built examples from around the world, the book goes on to identify basic attitudes and characteristics of everyday environment the Open Building approach designs for. It shows that the basic design skill for Open Building has to do with the DISTRIBUTION OF DESIGN TASKS in a HIERARCHY of levels of intervention. This is not a technical issue so much as it is an issue of control: who controls what, when. The approach is inevitably political. Of course, since architects deal with buildings and neighborhoods, the approach involves the fundamental decisions design professionals make every day about built form, technical systems and spaces.

The book focuses attention on the attitudes and skills needed for achieving good relations between designers who understand the place distribution of design tasks plays in our professional work. These skills help designers working on any large project relate to each other, because we inevitably look in three directions at the same time: we must honor the limitations offered by a higher-level design; we should be stimulating and generous to lower level design which is subject to what we did, and we must be able to share architectural values with other designers who work on the same level as we do. In all cases we need to be familiar with the judicious distribution of design tasks.

Clients of new projects of whatever scale, or adaptive reuse projects as well, rightfully demand cost control and efficiency. But they also want to meet the natural variety and vicissitudes in demand, in regulations, building and energy efficiency standards, and in financing, not only initially but over time. Designing for these changes is how expensive real property assets gain value over time. Experience by practitioners around the world is demonstrating the efficacy of the Open Building approach in meeting these challenges.

The challenge of implementing Habraken's ideas today

There is some basis for saying that, in the intellectual and professional communities of continental Europe, there is a tendency to first formulate concepts and then try to solve problems inside those concepts. This is akin to the civil law tradition. Laws are codified. In contrast, in the US and UK, the tendency is to say, well, if we have a problem, we will try to muddle through and solve it incrementally. The latter is the common law tradition, based on precedents.

This cultural difference may help to explain why, despite otherwise compelling reasons why freedom-loving and individualistic Americans should gravitate toward the SUPPORT/INFILL approach in which individual inhabitants have control over their direct living environment, this approach has never been recognized in the United States. Even after more than 10 years at MIT, Habraken's ideas about housing never took root in the American academic community or in practice. Nor, really, has his methodological thinking in general found a ready audience. On the other hand, it is only in recent years that a new generation of architects in Europe has found his recommendations to be relevant. Meanwhile, important work in the Netherlands, Finland, Japan and recently in China, Korea and in the Global South builds on his theories and methods. Only in the last few years has a network of design professionals and clients emerged in the United States advocating the principles of Open Building (The Council on Open Building) and in the Netherlands (Openbuilding.co).

Few architect/scholars have so consistently and patiently pursued such a humane and professionally vital viewpoint relating to the stewardship of the built environment as John Habraken has. From the publication of his first book in 1960, Habraken has quietly helped redraw the map of architectural research, education, practice, design methods and theory. His record of accomplishments, and their seminal value, is remarkable and without match. Today, we are witnessing an expanding worldwide recognition of his work.

John Habraken's insights are leading us to a better understanding of how the built environment works. His work in methodology is enabling professionals to contribute to its coherence and resilience. His writing, always scrupulously objective, postulates a theoretical perspective and methodological alternative and way forward beyond the current incoherence and dis-function in the built field's production and management.

The growing worldwide emphasis on built environment sustainability and resiliency make his insights and proposals more important than ever.

Organization of the book and how to use it

Two themes – WAYS OF SEEING and WAYS OF DOING – reveal themselves in many guises and from numerous vantage points in this collection. It is important to note that these WAYS OF SEEING did not remain in the realm of concepts. Habraken has always been interested in grounding new design methods – WAYS OF DOING – in these theoretical insights.

The book is thus organized in two main groupings: **WAYS OF SEEING and WAYS OF DOING**. Each group is further organized according to subject areas that reflect the evolution of Habraken's thinking over the years. Drawing on interviews the editors conducted with John Habraken in his home in the winter of 2018 and since, intermezzos reflecting our recent dialogues with him are interspersed among the chapters.

ATTITUDES TOWARDS THE BUILT FIELD; MY CREDO, OFFERED TO STUDENTS OF ARCHITECTURE

Editors' Note: *This Credo was initially published as the conclusion to the authors' essay "Cultivating the Field: About an Attitude when Making Architecture," published in PLACES, Vol. 9, Number 1, 1994.*

Study the built field,
It will be there without you,
But you can contribute to it.

Study the field as a living organism.
It has no form, but it has structure.
Find its structure, and form will come.

The field has continuity,
merge with it and others will join you.

Because the field has continuity no job is large or small;
All you do is adding to the field.

Nobody builds alone:
When you do something large, leave the small to others.
When you do something small, enhance the large.

Respond to those before you:
When you find structure, inhabit it;
When you find type, play with it;
When you find patterns, seek to continue them.

Be hospitable to those after you;
Give structure as well as form.

The more you seek to continue what was done by others already,
The more you will be recognized for it,
The more others will continue what you did.

Cooperate:
When you can borrow from others, borrow, and praise them for it.
When you can steal from others, steal, and admit it freely.
No matter what you do, your work will be your own.

Avoid style: leave it to the critics and historians.
Choose method: It is what you share with your peers.

Forget self-expression, it is a delusion.
Whatever you do will be recognized by others as your expression;
Don't give it a thought.
Do what the field needs.

INTRODUCTION TO WAYS OF SEEING

Habraken once explained to us how his intellectual and professional journey has moved back and forth between trying to understand some phenomenon in the way the built environment works and proposing tools based on that understanding. He is not sure how he came to the insight about 'the natural relationship' but speculates that it may have roots in his childhood growing up in Indonesia, where his father worked as an engineer. There, he could observe the kampong (informal) environments and how individual agency, balanced by social cohesion, was crucial for their well-being and improvement. Going to Holland for his university education made him face the rigid uniformity of mass housing that was spreading across the continent in the post–Second World War years. The contrast must have been unsettling. The SUPPORTS book was the result.

Intermezzo by the editors

JH: *I remember that the mass housing was going on in the Netherlands, after the war. They were putting up all those concrete blocks. I didn't like that at all.*

SK/JD: *Because of your experience in Indonesia?*

JH: *It was very different in the summer. In the hot weather, we rented in the mountains. We had a house. My father had built a house, which was also a good experience for me because again, it reinforced my decision to be an architect. In my free time on vacation, I walked through the kampongs. And I think in retrospect, it is a theory, I cannot prove it, but that experience made a difference.*

SK/JD: *The kampongs, the informal indigenous environments . . .*

JH: *They built their own houses in wood and lifted up on stilts, so the chickens were down below. And I remember that it was always very green, and very well organized and quiet. So, these were not slums. They were settlements. People lived there for generations. Then of course, the contrast with the mass housing in the Netherlands was big.*

JK/JD: *A huge contrast.*

Habraken engaged in the work of the SAR, with a highly disciplined focus on how architects could work under new circumstances they had never before been confronted with. He instinctively moved back and forth between the methodological work and larger questions. This led him to ask: "how can we see this work in a larger perspective?" What does it mean? What concepts (WAYS OF SEEING) are really needed to make these tools understood as practical tools.

These larger questions began to occupy Habraken's thinking and his writings of the time reflect the reciprocity between these two modes of thought. The selections that follow are a window into this search.

DOI: 10.4324/9781003011385-1

The work in **WAYS OF SEEING** is organized into a series of themes. The organizing themes are as follows:

Beginning
The built field
Control
Sharing forms
Role of the architect

Under each of these themes, Habraken's papers are arranged chronologically. They span from the very beginning of his career until 2021. We touch on a selection of them here to underline his major areas of focus in studying and interpreting built environment. These published and unpublished papers illustrate his incisive, consistent, methodical and iterative approach that has remained a constant across decades of observation, research, teaching and practice. They also reveal his ability to apply different voices, considering the application and context of each piece of writing. As you read through these essays, published articles and reports, these voices are remarkably varied: at times he is the sensitive but objective observer; at others he is the polemicist and advocate. At other times, we experience the scientist deeply immersed in a logical progression and sometimes, we experience the words of a poet, musing on his life experiences and causes.

While consistent and somewhat self-contained in his approach, Habraken nevertheless is deeply aware of historic precedent, parallel contemporary thought and the impact and influence of the great 20th-century modernists. Throughout this writing, he challenges contemporary norms and calls on his colleagues, students and the profession as a whole to look more deeply, develop coherent theories that can be shared as a common body of knowledge and develop new shared approaches to reflect social needs and more effectively shape the everyday environment.

The Tissue of the Town, written in 1964 is as relevant in its concerns in 2022 as it was when it was written. Habraken, the observer, uses his keen awareness of the historic urban environment around him to redefine the needs and priorities of contemporary city planning. He calls for deeper investigation and understanding – recognizing the presence of a fine-grained urban tissue that reflects the act of dwelling, as the reflection of the structure of a community – a tissue that is often being obliterated as cities grow huge and the scale and speed of growth requires interventions that often threaten the fine-grained tissue Habraken writes about.

You Can't Design the Ordinary, 1971, is written as the advocate, sharing with and engaging his readers. He uses the pronoun "We" to draw his audience to his point of view – as he underlines the problem of architects attempting to turn the fabric of the everyday into monuments and, as a result, the urban fabric becomes undifferentiated and disconnected from social experience.

Around the Black Hole, written in 1980 at a pivotal point in his tenure as Head of the Department of Architecture at MIT, Habraken is the polemicist, directly challenging and critiquing his profession and architectural education. He decries the lack of interest in understanding the human condition; the absence of common techniques for teaching and research; the major – yet ignored – problems facing professional practice, and the over-emphasis on individual expression versus the development of common methods for collaboration.

Control Relations in the Built Environment, dating from 1987 illustrates the scientist and logician at work, abstracting what he observes and analyzing it in terms of fundamental relationships. Through a precise, step by step set of graphic and written notations that for the uninitiated are challenging in their depth and intricacy, he shares his inner process, seeking to understand the behavior of the built environment as a series of configurations reflecting different patterns of control.

Memories of a Lost Future, 2002 is an almost surprising departure that presents his ongoing dialectic as free form poetry. In this fascinating piece, he expresses a thorough knowledge of the heroes of modern architecture and their influence on the shaping of built environment but also unleashes a diatribe against the monumentalizing of the everyday. He ends with the image of a river, with a call for shared knowledge, collaboration and a new WAY OF SEEING and DOING.

Change and Distribution of Design, 2004 is a wonderful example about how Habraken applies his theories to the analysis of historic precedents, describing well known spaces and places with new insight – clarifying spatial organizations and separated design tasks through the lens of territorial control and different levels of intervention.

Back to the Future, written in 2017, brings the reader full circle. Here is the seasoned and still enthusiastic expert assuming an educated and aware audience. This time he is pointing to successful contemporary precedents that are beautifully fulfilling his lifelong development of coherent theories and methods for the creation of a living, vital built environment.

Finally, **Open Building – A Professional Challenge**, written in 2021, is a testament to his clear thinking about the need for an evolving profession, again citing recent case studies. Habraken's ideas remain fresh, coherent and relevant in the face of our quickly evolving communities.

The following dialogue between the editors and the author recalls the beginning of Habraken's journey of seeing and doing.

SK/JD: So, when you began writing Supports, there was a big leap to start thinking about how the dweller could be involved in the design of their own houses. I mean, this is very early on in your career. What led you into that thinking? Because that was a big leap.

JH: You're right. Looking back at it, I think that, I did not know it at the time, but I was fascinated by urban fabrics. Because, typology was there in my mind, but I didn't know the word for it to describe it at all. I do remember that we went on an excursion to Italy.

JH: It was a tour organized by a student society . . .
we started a department for Interschool Design at Delft through Italy, and I organized it as chairman of the student body. And I went along with professor MARINUS JAN GRANPRE MOLIERE. And what struck me on that excursion was that we, of course, went to all the famous buildings. For instance, we started in the town and we walked through the town. But we were always talking about other things. And I was fascinated by the fabric. And I noticed that people just stopped talking and listening when we stopped in front of the famous building that was on the list. I thought it was a stupid way to go through the country like that. I was fascinated by this fabric. I think it was a result of my studies of fabrics. I started collecting maps of them and looking at them.

SK/JD: So, you were living right in the town and you were seeing, you were observing there. Obviously, cities were built densely, and with a certain continuity in all the fabric. There were the unwritten rules which were shaping, you know, you knew where the front door needed to be or how to get inside of the block and you saw that repeated with endless variations.

JH: I discovered that because of the maps. It was fascinating.

PART I

WAYS OF SEEING

BEGINNING

1965
MAN AND MATTER

Editors' Note: *This essay was published in Forum, Volume XVIX, No. 1, 1965. The author was Editor of Forum, International Magazine for architecture, Amsterdam, from 1964–66.*

We still take it too much for granted that creativity pertains to the exceptional achievements of certain gifted individuals. By only looking at it in this light, it remains shrouded in the haze of romanticism which is a relic of a previous generation. The result is that in thinking of social problems, we leave human creativity as an all-embracing influence out of account. For creativity is to be found in all people and we continually come across it in all its aspects. Its importance as a common phenomenon is equaled by our ignorance of it. Human creativity is something we may find in all manifestations of life. In achievements bespeaking great talent we may perceive it in a large dose. But to understand it and to assess its true value, we had better turn to everyday life.

That this is so is proved by looking into the way towns come into being and stay in existence. In itself, a town is a striking example of man's creative ability. But a town is not a self-contained piece of human creative work. It is made up of a great many interdependent but separately recognizable elements: buildings, streets, squares, canals, sewers, bridges, tramlines, harbors, factories, etc. Things which can be recognized as separate entities, together forming one whole which is more than the sum of its parts.

The creation of this whole is a never-ending process. A town is never finished. It is ever nascent. Therefore, it is not the result of a creative act, but of a creative process that never comes to an end as long as the town exists. This process is the process of man housing himself in the widest sense of the word. It is a very complicated process which in fact has not been properly studied yet. And whoever attempts to do so will soon perceive that it can only be understood if the part played by the ordinary people is seen as an inseparable part of it. In fact, a town can hardly be said to be the result of a process. A town is a process. Let me try to make this clear in a few words. A town does not only consist of matter shaped by man. The concept 'town' embraces the animate as well as the inanimate town – man and material environment together. A town without people is inconceivable.

Neither is a somewhat complex and varied community conceivable without a town. So, building a town is equivalent to establishing a community. A town is never finished because a human community never finds its final shape. After all, a community 'lives.' Therefore, a town is a 'living thing' in the literal sense of this paradoxical expression.

If a town consists of a community, a community in its turn consists of inter-human relations. For are not our inter-relations made to man, too? I even think that therefore, they are preeminently characteristic of man. Man's creativity in its most sublime form is to be found in the harmonious human relations he creates. There are animals which make their own material environment. But this making is automatic. It springs from the predestined and practically unalterable mode of existence of the animal. Man, however, continually remakes his patterns of life, as the circumstances change or as he wishes to change the circumstances.

Here too it is a continuous process. And these ever-changing human relations are reflected in the ever-changing shape of our material environment.

Therefore, man's ability to create is not limited to any field or sphere. Even in this concise survey, we cannot limit it without stating this beforehand. If we speak of our creativity with regard to our material environment, we must, therefore, also speak of our spiritual environment and our interrelations which are bound up with both. Creativity is the human capacity which has the remarkable quality that its sphere of action imperceptibly changes from the spiritual into the material and vice-a-versa. I would even say that creativity is somehow linked up with this continual merging of spirit and matter (if we may retain these opposites for arguments sake), that it may even be defined by this merging.

But if there is no special sphere of action there can be no specialist either. Then there are no people who, on account of their profession or knowledge, have the exclusive right of doing creative work. If this is so we may wonder what creativity is. If creativity cannot be defined by the mere fact that it gives rise to material forms, if it can neither be said to be restricted to the work of certain people, if it is also manifest in the form of a community, in the pattern of interrelations and in the shape we give to our entire environment, how then can we get a grasp on our theme?

After all, not all our making is creative. Of course, creativity has always something to do with 'making.' But it is possible to make something without a jot of creativity. The machine is the extreme example of this: it makes a great deal, but it is merely 'making.' I think that creativity is a capacity enabling us to do the right thing even under novel circumstances. In this sense, creativity is man's ability to create new relations between himself and his environment, whenever the need arises. In saying environment, I mean man's material environment as well as his social milieu and his spiritual life. Man sees his environment after all as an indivisible whole. And he is creative because he must always help to create his relation to what whole. Creating is therefore establishing a relation. This many result in all kinds of forms, in material forms, in patterns of thought, in modes of life and in many other things. Man is creative in that he gives shape to the relations between himself and the world by which he is surrounded. He does so by means of his language, gestures, ceremonies, legislation or via the shape given to a material thing.

. . . I should like to enter more deeply into the part played by the ordinary people in the creative process which gives rise to towns. For by doing so I hope to illustrate how our ignorance of the fact that human creativity is a common, almost trivial but all-penetrating element in life, may endanger our society. For it can be proved that our housing problem stems directly from this lack of insight.

Setting out from the above-mentioned attitude, I should like to enter more deeply into the part played by the ordinary people in the creative process which gives rise to towns. For by doing so I hope to illustrate how our ignorance of the fact that human creativity is a common, almost trivial but all-penetrating element in life, may endanger our society. For it can be proved that our housing problem stems directly from this lack of insight. In saying housing problem, I of course do not merely mean the so-called housing shortage. This shortage is only a symptom. The disease is the entire problem of a community that enjoys an ever-increasing material prosperity and yet is 'homeless.' A lack of understanding as to what is possible and what is impossible for human creativity spells danger for a world wielding ever greater technical power. In order to create this understanding in so small a compass I must state things very briefly without being able to analyze them or support them with arguments. Whoever may think this too flimsy should read the book in which I deal more elaborately with the processes giving rise to towns[1]. How does this process which gives rise to towns work? Or, put differently, what is the interaction between society and material environment?

However large the population of a town may be, the smallest independent unit in it will be the family, which in this argument is also taken to include the household formed by one person. This is the unit out of which our society is built up. Consequently, the smallest unit in a town is the dwelling. The cell constituting the organism of the town is the dwelling with the family in it. So, the relation between the dweller and his dwelling touches naturally on the complex relation between community and town. This latter relation is largely formed by the sum of the points of contact between the two relations. Therefore, it may be assumed that only if the relation between dweller and dwelling is a sound and active one, we may be assured that the town as a whole is a living and sound organism. You might say that the process which we call town will function better as the relation between dweller and dwelling functions better.

At present, this direct relation has stopped functioning altogether. That is not difficult to understand. In order that this relation should be possible the dwelling must somehow also be the creation of the dweller. In other words: it must be possible for the dweller to be instrumental in the building of his dwelling. Which means to say that he must share in the responsibility for the existence and the aspect of his dwelling. Today this is impossible. People are now housed by forces which are outside their control. Actually, there is at present no process at all, only a well- meant drive towards large-scale organized barracking.

If we therefore wish to get a harmonious relation between man and his material environment, between dweller and dwelling and between community and town, we must look for means of getting the above-mentioned process going again. How must we build without drifting into barracking? This is a technical problem, or rather it is a problem for which a technical solution must be found. We must find a way of building which makes the dweller responsible again for his dwelling and for the aspect it bears, so that he may identify himself with that dwelling in order that there may again be points of contact, making it possible for the process of the relation between community and matter to get going again. Formulated in this way the housing problem is quite different from what it is generally taken to be. The main issue is not that we must produce as much as possible. The crucial problem is: What is the way of producing which will yield a creative process?

At present, the relation between the dweller and dwelling which has proved to be desirable, is impossible because the dwelling today is practically always part of a bigger building. So the dwelling is not an independent unit and becomes literally unwieldy. A relation is not possible if one of the partners is immovable. So, if we wish to restore the process, we must give the dwelling a certain measure of independence. We must then build in such a way that the dwelling, whether constructed on the ground or high up in a structure, can be built, altered, or demolished irrespective of the dwellings surrounding it.

This is the reason why I have advocated the building of supporting structures, so called 'Supports,' in which a building industry can construct dwellings in keeping with the personal needs of the dwellers. If we adopt this way of building, the result will be an urban tissue built up of independent, living cells, which, like the cells of a living organism, can resuscitate themselves continually.

The method suggested here is especially suited for a very intensive industrialization. The industrial machinery we have at our command is much better suited for the construction of dwellings which can be mounted in a supporting structure than for making the housing blocks we produce today. It is not for nothing that for years, they have attempted to industrialize the conventional way of building. The reader who is interested in this line of argument can read more about it in an earlier publication[2]. I only mention the great scope for industrialization because I cannot help drawing a moral. For by first determining how (making the dwelling independent), by basing oneself on considerations which spring from the relation between man and matter and not on commercial considerations, it suddenly becomes clear that industrialization will be possible. Which means to say that we shall be able to build dwellings in great numbers. The housing shortage is indeed a symptom which will disappear when the disease itself is cured. There I come to the crucial point of my article. I have tried to outline a feasible way of building and producing which has two attractive aspects. On the one hand, it becomes possible for the dweller himself to become instrumental in shaping his dwelling. On the other hand, it becomes possible to make full use of the possibilities offered by industrial production.

My point now is: if evidently this system has advantages for the dweller and for the productive machinery, why then was it not adopted long ago?

The answer is quite simple. Because all trends of thought now influencing housing are based on the maxim that the dweller's interference is unnecessary, annoying, useless and disrupting. Because we set out from the idea that in this field the ordinary people cannot play a creative part. In thinking about the relations between man and his material environment (if any thought is given to it) we simply leave no room for the idea that the active relation between the ordinary person and his everyday dwelling might be the chief cornerstone of all creative work in the field of housing and town planning.

We have an unshakable faith in specialists. We believe that building is something technical and therefore something for specialists. We believe that towns are created by professional specialists who, after many years of study, will see to it that we get the towns we deserve. That belief makes it impossible for us to recognize that, thought specialists can produce and organize a great many things (and must do so), if all is well, there must be a point at which their work is finished by non-specialists. Unfortunately, we believe that creative ability is a specialization. The technical man believes it. The non-technical specialist believes it. The layman believes it. It was because of this that some non-technical people could assure me that they thought my ideas very attractive, confessing at the same time that they could not imagine how things could work if everybody had a say. They forget that our society is founded on the admission that everybody must have a say in all really important things in life. We think it quite normal that everybody has a say in the education of his children, in the politics of his country, in his relation to God, in the way he feeds and dresses, in his own social behavior. We all agree that ultimately this is part of the responsibility of the individual.

For all these important things, we have specialists today. But whatever they do, must in the end be passed to common man. And that is as it should be. Society can only benefit from those things that are everyday creations, that get their final shape in everyday life. The theologian knows that he does not decide the relation between man and God. The sociologist knows that he does not decide the relation between man and man. The politician knows that he is only the helmsman steering forces sprung from everyday life.

They can all do creative work as long as the layman has his share in it. At least that is our Western opinion. Strange as it may be, this insight disappears as soon as it is a matter of handling and shaping matter. Then suddenly the myth of the specialists springs up, of the magician, the priest of our marvelous and frightening 'modern technology.' The man who makes and designs for the sake of man but without consulting man. At worst a disturbing influence, generating frightening forces. At best, a patriarchal specialist who has decided 'that this is the only possible way' and that we must submit to a 'technical necessity.'

The opinion that housing and town planning are the exclusive domain of specialists is strengthened by the fact that today, producing things has indeed become a job of specialists. If we think that creativity is synonymous with the making of material things, there is indeed little room for the ordinary people. The things by which we are surrounded are all made in workshops and factories which the average person does not normally see. And in the factories, they are increasingly made by machines, without being touched by human hands. This is the very reason why it is important that it be realized that creating our material environment does begin with the production of material forms but needs something else to finish it. Let us for instance take a normal domestic establishment. All things in it are made by a productive machinery outside the dwelling. The furniture, the curtains and carpets, the fittings and appliances, the clothes, the books, the toys, even to an ever-larger extent the food. But the household itself is created by the family. The members of the family have assembled these things, they have arranged them and have chosen them. They use them in such a way that the small community of the family and the material environment of that community form a unity; that together they are a continuous creation, taking place every day again. Here the creative ability of man is active in that it ever again nourishes and recreates a harmonious relation between man and man and between man and his material environment. Here too is a constant merging of two relations.

The pattern of relations we call household influences the production of the things that are part of the household. The specialist who produces expends a great deal of thought and money to discover what people desire for their household. This is in his own commercial interest. There is an active interaction between consumer and producer. Therefore, also the things produced outside the household are partly created by the consumer.

A town is a household. Therefore, the dwelling is a product which must spring from a relation with the consumers. In this way a town can, in all its details, be created by ordinary people and everyday relations. But in order to achieve this we must build in such a way that a real household gets going and that we do not merely supply housing.

Industrialization gives us an enormous productive capacity. So enormous that even the specialist cannot compute how great the material abundance will be that will flood the world in the near future. This does not imply that there is nothing left for the common man to make. On the contrary, it means that the everyday community needs an ever-greater creative ability. For everything produced by the industries must be incorporated in the human household. Whatever the industries make, must be won in a creative process, incorporating it organically in our lives, giving it its right and undisputed place. If we cannot do this the things surrounding us become hostile things – foreign objects which hinder us and control us and make us feel more and more helpless and unhappy.

In the future, an ever-greater demand will be made upon our ability to create our own environment, that it may belong to us. The weak spot in the human household is no longer the inability to produce enough but the inability to establish a harmonious relation between ourselves and our environment. We shall have to learn how to live with our prosperity. We shall have to learn how to create. And we must begin at the beginning. Which is the dwelling. The common dwelling for the common man. Therefore, it is not utopian to say that shortly everybody will be able to construct his own dwelling in close cooperation with the producer. It is necessary that this come about as soon as possible. Not because that would be so pleasant for the dweller, but because then the foundation is laid for a civilized community that is fully alive, which is to say, for a flourishing human household. The independent dwelling constructed by the independent person is a vital necessity for our society that is getting richer and richer. Because our factories with the machines and computers can make so much, the making of our material environment has become everybody's concern, also of the nontechnical specialist. We are all familiar with the caricature of the criminal technical specialist who invents all sorts of things without being bothered about the human consequences. There should also be a caricature of the specialist in man, so the man who occupies himself with man: the physician, the theologian, the psychiatrist, the sociologist, the administrator. The caricature of the 'man-specialist' who only too often sees man as a phenomenon without environment. Who does not see how man is formed by his material environment, which in its turn is made by him. The specialist who in thinking of man divorces him from the material environment and does not realize that the people of the future will to a large extent be the product of their relations with their environment, the environment made by themselves.

I have the impression that our future relation with our material environment only offers a problem to those who have been technically trained. This is understandable, for they are the first to see what is up. But as long as they think that they are the persons who will also have to solve this problem for the community, we are facing a dangerous future. And this attitude is fairly general, also among the technical people who are aware of the problems, for they are naturally inclined to look for a technical solution to every problem.

It has everybody's approval that science students are also taught the humanities. It is realized to what an extent their work will influence man's life. But this is only a half-measure which springs from the idea that it is exclusively up to the men of science to reconcile man with his growing productive capacity. It is everybody's task. The primary requirement being insight. Insight into the relation between man and the things he makes. It is about time the students at the universities and also at the secondary schools are taught something about the phenomenon of man the producer and creator. And that they learn that a large productive capacity requires a great creative ability touching on all aspects of human life. In all our schools, we have made a difference between those who study science and those who study the humanities. In all our trained thoughts we have differentiated between the relations man-man and man-matter. Man's creativity, however, is based on the fact that these relations merge continually. Our mode of thought will have to be adapted to this. The sooner the better.

1968
HOUSING
The act of dwelling

Editors' note: *This technical study was published in The Architects' Journal Information Library, 22 May 1968, 1187–1192. It is taken from the authors book De Dragers en de Mensen (Frameworks for living), published by Scheltema & Holkema NV, Amsterdam, 1961, and later published in English in several editions as Supports: An Alternative to Mass Housing.*

By saying that we wish to give our environment the form which fits society best, we tacitly assume that society is a palpable phenomenon whose environmental needs we can, by observation and design, translate into brick and concrete. This concept is wide open to criticism. It assumes that town and population are two separate entities which can take shape independently of one another and yet it also maintains that it is possible to mold the town after the 'shape' of the population. In fact, of course it is neither possible to conceive a population without a town nor a town without a population.

In order to arrive at a different approach, we must first refuse to divorce population from town – for the shape of each is determined by the other and together they include animate and inanimate material. The idea that one can speak of two separate entities has arisen only because it fits in with the way of thinking inherent in the large-scale urban development project, for if a town is planned for an unknown population, the fatal division becomes unavoidable.

Any town which is a true unity of man and matter is conceivable only as the outcome of a process in which the 'natural relationship' [1] is at work, for then the population and the town possess each other in all respects, and it is possible for society (via the individual) to reflect itself in the shape of the town (via the dwelling). The relationship of population to town will then be that of a hand kneading a lump of clay. A town is, if the 'natural relationship' is active, an organism which is never quite finished, but which renews itself continually so that matter gains some of the mobility of life, and life receives some of the permanence of matter. By regarding the town as a unity, it becomes an active part in the process of housing man.

Unfortunately, this concept of urban structure is not generally accepted. The processes of thought which underlie the development project create an urban image molded to correspond to a static concept of society. The development project mentality sees town and society as two separate, static entities. This does not imply that no attempt is made to reckon with the future; only that the method guarantees failure.

There is no getting away from the fact that the housing development project must be tied down to facts known at the time of planning. The development project wants to anticipate change, but it must do so before building begins and therefore it cannot cope with the unforeseen. To get a clear picture of the detrimental results of the absence of the 'natural relationship' the project must be judged not solely in relation to planning, but as a living phenomenon which is continually changing. To do this it is necessary to view the development project in the mirror of the progress of time.

If today for instance it has become possible to construct gigantic architectural projects in which entire populations could be housed this is in itself no reason why such projects should be realized. The question we must ask ourselves is how such enormous things would evolve after completion. How will they maintain themselves? How are new devices and changed ideas going to fit in to the existing structure? The vitality of a town lies in its ability to change and assimilate to alter part after part *and yet to keep its identity*, ensuring for itself and its inhabitants of existence free of continuous upheaval.

The contemporary large-scale development project cannot easily be changed in detail because each individual dwelling is not only a part of a larger element, but the larger elements themselves have often been arranged in such a way that they form part of a bigger series. This makes it difficult, if not impossible, for the whole area to hold its' own as an organic unity. No new conceptions of living can touch it unless the area as a whole is again tackled as another big redevelopment project. Because the actual tenants of, for example, public sector dwellings are never *directly* allowed to advise, little can be altered to meet their desires. It does not matter whether they wish to enrich their lives or are able to improve their social status. The dwellings are renewed only when they decay. Not when they have become old-fashioned nor when they no longer come up to generally accepted standards, nor when their occupants feel deprived of what proves to be possible elsewhere. Only when structural soundness has deteriorated to such a degree that the occupants' health is endangered is redevelopment proposed. None of the stimuli which emanate from the 'natural relationship' operate.

The modem town or city (in contrast to a healthy body which is equally old in all its members) is therefore split into parts which are all at different stages of repair or dilapidation. The various parts always have a pronounced difference in value and status. When an area has sunk to its lowest ebb it can, with redevelopment, become almost overnight the most modern area. This implies that the standard of comfort enjoyed by the occupants of a town depends on the area in which they live. The needs of the dweller are unrelated to the cycle of the development project, so there is always a housing crisis in some part of the town in the process of being remedied by a big redevelopment project. Thus, the development system, which was in origin an emergency measure, is itself instrumental in causing a perpetual state of emergency.

This state of affairs may have been acceptable in the past, under rigorous class systems, when wealthy town dwellers went to live in new parts of the town, leaving the old quarters to the middle classes; who in turn left them to the working people. But how does this fit in with a society in which class distinctions in this sense of the word are rapidly disappearing, and in which a high overall standard of housing is desirable? A society moreover in which people with the same income do not by any means belong to the same class.

Under the regime of the development project there are at present old and new dwellings of all types for very big families, elderly couples, bachelors, career women, artists, laborers, shopkeepers, the middle classes and whatever other subdivisions statistics have made possible. New dwellings will be of their time as regards technical devices and finish, but old ones will be outdated beyond remedy because the development concept inhibits in-situ modification and growth. In each of the social groups into which development project statistics divides society there will be people who live in new and people who live in antique dwellings: the occupants are either lucky or not, and if not, little can be done about it. Whether one is rich or poor, willing to spend money on one's own dwelling or not, the development project will see to it that there is a graduation in the standard of living within the group one belongs to. The only thing the occupant can do is try to move into a better dwelling. The system is an invitation to a continuous game of musical chairs.

So much so that in the eyes of the authorities the standard of housing can be high only in recently developed areas. This implies that when a certain structural improvement is possible for instance better insulated wails or a new kind of heating. The improvement can be incorporated only in those areas that happen to be under redevelopment at that moment.

At a time when technical progress is exceptionally rapid this state of affairs cannot be tolerated, hampering as it does technical improvement in housing. Current public sector practice tends to assort that the life of a dwelling should be influenced by new technical possibilities but depend entirely on the planned time allotted to the entire structure to fall into disrepair. An individual person can substitute something better for something good in his own dwelling (a possibility which has caused the rapid evolution of the motorcar), but many of the social groups which housing projects manipulate, cannot do so. In this fashion the development project totters from one disruptive renewal to the next, in an everlasting feverish pursuit of finality, ever groping and seeking, theorizing and rationalizing in a stubborn endeavor to trap action into configuration.

The present-day nomad

The inertia of the development project means that the occupants must move if they can: each redevelopment thus causes a migration. The better dwelling is always in another part of the town. Fortunate people migrate to new virgin areas, leaving the old quarters in a state of disrepair, like primitive people who exhaust the soil and then migrate to other regions. Now that all available space in towns has been used for building and the first development areas of the tum of the century are due for redevelopment we are embarking on a second cycle which will no doubt effectively prevent real communities from being formed. The conditions most favorable for development of communities which are more than collections of families and individuals are fully worth investigation. These days we may be able to stock an aquarium with plants and animals in such a way that a biological balance is obtained, but we have hardly gone into the conditions for development of social harmony in urban area. We have only the vague idea that it must be a matter of organization.

The first prerequisite of such an organization must be freedom of association; as little as possible must be pre-determined as regards the kind of families to be housed and the way in which they should be juxtaposed. Unfortunately, it is becoming increasingly difficult in our society to realize this condition. Statistics produced by the proponents of the development project make any free association virtually impossible. Seen in an extreme form they demand that a person should move at each stage of his life; ie whenever there is a change in the structure of his family. The second prerequisite must be that the environment of the occupant must be renewable. This is the core of our criticism of the public sector development project. The indifference of the standard dwelling unit to the individuality and initiative of its occupants prevents them from ever taking full responsibility for it. They can at best, only adapt themselves to what is offered.

The last prerequisite is time. The forming of a community can be estimated but not rushed. There is no doubt that it requires more than one generation for a community to become at one with its environment and to bring that environment, in its turn, into harmony with its people. It is often said that new housing cannot be habitable in one day – it requires years. But if we allow the years to have their effect on a housing project, we generally see only increasing disuse and decay. Time is needed for the 'natural relationship' to embellish and complete the basic outline. People need more time to grow into a community than mass housing estates need to become dilapidated. An area which today has 'character' is always from the point of view of the planner a slum area. We feel almost instinctively that character and individuality go hand in hand with a certain degree of dilapidation and the melancholy called forth by age.

. . . we must make possible urban areas which can be old without being outdated and modern without losing their history; areas in which people can live for generations and which at the same time allow the substance but not the identity to change.

For this reason, we must make possible urban areas which can be old without being outdated and modern without losing their history; areas in which people can live for generations and which at the same time allow the substance but not the identity to change. This is quite the opposite of what the development project offers. The modern urban life dweller is a nomad divorced from the growth of his environment; he is thus not responsible for its decay. He *undergoes* his town as an external phenomenon and finds possibilities of self-expression more in keeping with his nomadic life – in his motorcar. We have, strayed far from the image of man which we visualized in the beginning; man who creates his own environment to be in harmony with himself, man of the 'natural relationship.'

If we accept the consequence of what has been said, it becomes necessary to revise not only the form of our urban structures, but also our whole way of thinking about building and dwelling, To make such a revision possible we must accept the fact that the large-scale development project has failed. Having admitted this a great deal will become possible after all, the current situation has resulted from the interaction of a system of forces, from which one force is missing, the 'natural relationship.' It is important to try to reintroduce this missing force. Such an attempt can hardly be called negative or destructive. The existing forces (our organizing ability, technical and constructive skill, capacity for research and experimentation and rational approach to concrete problems), the abilities on which we pride ourselves and which we apply with so little success to the development project need in no way be impaired. On the contrary they must be stimulated to become more active and effective, by the reintroduction of the 'natural relationship' which can then act as a catalyst.

Increasing need for a restoration of the 'natural relationship'

The decision to reintroduce the 'natural relationship' in housing is to some extent justified by the contemporary social-evolutionary trend towards increased individuality. This democratic evolution cannot be reconciled with a housing system which in its dealings and forms shows more resemblance to what we see in totalitarian states. It was not without justification that in 1918 H. P. Berlage's workers showed an instinctive and fierce opposition to the then nascent plans for drastic large scale government- financed housing projects, They demanded the rights enjoyed by other social classes; but to such little effect that today everyone has cause for complaint because all classes are increasingly housed in the same fashion.

The problem is more than a matter of the rights of the free individual; it is also a matter of responsibility. To increase the rights of a free citizen, his responsibilities must also increase. It is doubtful whether any society can any longer afford to take the responsibility for housing away from the individual.

The problem is more than a matter of the rights of the free individual; it is also a matter of responsibility. To increase the rights of a free citizen, his responsibilities must also increase. It is doubtful whether any society can any longer afford to take the responsibility for housing away from the individual. Just as responsibility for the upbringing of his children cannot be taken away from the individual without causing democracy great harm, housing responsibilities cannot be painlessly transferred to a technical, organizing body. Just as the ultimate responsibility for the education of the child rests with the parents (with the help of schools, social institutes or foundations), the chief responsibility for the housing process must rest with them too. It is perfectly right for the state to help people in this, but the 'natural relationship' is a necessary key to personal responsibility. This relationship presupposes that the individual takes possession of his environment; does not this mean precisely that he accepts responsibility for it?

It is therefore clear that the idea of the development project is inconsistent with many of the underlying principles of our society. Those who defend the centralized development project from conviction unavoidably come into conflict with these principles and should acknowledge the fact. If we take as our starting point the statement that we wish to strengthen the role of the individual in our society, this unavoidably implies that the relationship between man and dwelling must become more intensive. It is necessary to put the development project into reverse. The entire population should no longer be obliged to live in an institutional fashion, but the relationship between man and dwelling which formerly was the privilege of the rich should now be made available to all. Through increased wealth and leisure, the broad masses of our population today develop activities and interests which until recently were only for the few. It therefore is becoming more and more difficult to construct meaningful behavioral models to fit all the members of one income group. Unhappily the mass housing concept needs group patterns to be effective and therefore continually ignores the impossibility of getting an accurate picture of the behavior and desires of particular groups. The 'average working-class family' is something which no longer exists in terms of housing. It is therefore an illusion to think that by the crude expedient of the mass housing project, 'final' types of dwellings can be determined without impairing social evolution. Within the same income group are families with very different percentage, background, ambition and ways of life. How is the mass housing-project to take account of this – except by ignoring it?

The paradox is this: we now see that at the very moment when our technology is at the beginning of a great evolutionary leap; when for the first time in history it should be possible to make the 'natural relationship' function better than even before, our energies are diverted into an entirely different direction. Now that a massive organizational expertise has been developed, and no structural problem seems too great or too complicated, solving the problem of the 'natural relationship', which for centuries was solved with wholly inadequate resources is now seen as so impossible that it is not even considered. Blind faith in organization and technology leads only to an estrangement between them and human nature.

Industrialization

The mass housing project is, paradoxically enough, an out-dated method. Factory production is not, by any means in harmony with the concept of the housing project; on the contrary it is hampered by it. One of the many paradoxes of such project is that, although superficial technical uniformity is achieved, in fact, many disparate techniques, materials and details are used side by side. The technical concepts underlying mass housing are anything but uniform. It is true that many fac- tory made units are used, but the overall constructional ethos of, for example, high rise blocks, is not based on the idea of industrial production, neither it is the outcome of the preference, experience and imagery shared by architects and contractors over the last forty years.

Machines can produce uniform parts which, provided they lit into a coherent system, allow endless variations in form. The development project on the other hand by no means guarantees a coherent system of building by suppressing such variations. This need not surprise us, for its practice is based not on a structural concept but on a method of working. In 1918, the dawn of mass housing, the industrial production of components hardly existed, and it was possible to increase output only by efficiently organizing the method of working on the building site itself. Since repetition is undoubtedly faster than a series of continually changing operations, it was decided to seek for each project as many simple, over recurring operations as possible. This rationalization of preindustrial methods gave rise to the repetitive unit long before industrialization became a reality. *The housing project was the desperate effort of a machineless world to achieve the equivalent of machine production.* Unfortunately, this effort succeeded only by severing the natural relationship between man and the built environment because traditional building methodology was riddled with work patterns which made sense only in terms of the natural relationship. Industrialization cannot really come about as a result of introduction of as many industrial products as possible into this methodology; for to apply mass production successfully, it is necessary to find a method which is founded on the logic of production itself. As long as we refuse to do so, our attempts at 'rationalizing' house construction will remain as confused as those of the automobile industry would have been if they had persisted in their early efforts to mass produce what were effectively powered seventeenth-century coaches.

The dream of a dwelling made more or less in the same way as the modern motor car is already fairly old; but parallels drawn along these lines are too obvious and far too misleading. They tend to make us set out again in search of 'the dwelling' – a 'thing' to be discovered by the effort of 'redeeming design.' Mechanical production is not by any means synonymous with the principles of mass housing as they are understood today. It is still possible to make full use of mechanization *without* total uniformity of product. The use of the machine does not automatically bring about uniform dwellings and uniform ways of living.

The industrialization of housing which is so often discussed is nothing but mechanization of the mass housing project. If we wish to investigate conditions necessary for an industrialized *housing process*, we must bear in mind that this does not automatically imply industrialization of the mass *housing project*. The 'natural relationship' presupposes that the dwelling is independent and that it is possible to alter, improve or replace it, *independent of its surroundings*. Up to now this has been possible only with the detached one-story house, a fact which goes far to explain its popularity. To revise the housing process this flexibility must be made possible in the ease of high-rise dwellings as well. This stated briefly is a concrete problem which must be solved in order to derive contemporary housing-process.

The industrialization of housing which is so often discussed is nothing but mechanization of the mass housing project. If we wish to investigate conditions necessary for an industrialized *housing process* we must bear in mind that this does not automatically imply industrialization of the mass *housing project*. The 'natural relationship' presupposes that the dwelling is independent and that it is possible to alter, improve or replace it, *independent of its surroundings*. Up to now this has been possible only with the detached one-story house, a fact which goes far to explain its popularity. To revise the housing process this flexibility must be made possible in the ease of high-rise dwellings as well. This stated briefly is a concrete problem which must be solved in order to derive contemporary housing-process.

If we look at an urban structure as a conglomerate of building each building must be independent in the sense that. it can be built and demolished irrespective of other buildings. Rising land values and the consequent necessity to build high has caused buildings to become bigger – and this in its turn has caused an even greater departure from the concept of the dwelling as an independent unit. In the organism which is the town, we want to see something quite different: the independent dwelling as a cell leading its own life, rejuvenating and renewing itself in response to the stimuli emanating from social rather than eco- nomic or technical pressures. For a 'natural relationship' these cells must be small enough to correspond to the components of society itself.

The fact that urban expansion at present means a growth in the size of building units has caused a coarsening of town structure. The size increases enormously, but the number of component parts decreases. New areas of Amsterdam for instance have higher densities than the old central part, but they are arranged in a smaller number of structural units. If we visualize the town as an organism built up of independent living cells, it becomes clear that our modern cities have become, in evolutionary terms, increasingly primitive organisms with a coarse structure, little flexibility and little vitality despite their unprecedented and excessively large scale. A *truly* modern town should in fact have an infinitely complicated structure, built up of a much larger number of cells than an old town. It would then become 'natural' in the sense that in nature more complicated organisms develop a multiplicity of basic organs.

It would be interesting to investigate the social and cultural influence of this current inability to build big towns with complex structures. How is it that we always resort to enlargement of scale and structure? Such an investigation into the 'biology of towns' could give us a considerably better insight into the elusive phenomena with which our lives are inextricably interwoven. Unfortunately, we cannot wait for creation of such a science, and in anticipation we just try to create towns of the future which despite their size do not sacrifice the complexity of small cellular construction.

The bottleneck in the development of town planning is to be found in the field of housing. The coarsening of urban structure and the discrepancy between it and society are assuming increasingly insufferable proportions. The technical problem is therefore not that of prefabrication of the mass housing project, nor its industrialization, but development of the independent dwelling, and the reintroduction of the 'natural relationship' which goes with it. The town must assume a structure in which that which must be small is small and that which must be big is big. It must be possible to find a method of building which gives full scope both to man and machine, to the 'natural relationship' and mass production side by side, for the discrepancy between them is founded in the housing project, not in housing itself.

2001
WHAT USE THEORY?
Questions of purpose and practice

Editors' Note: *This essay was presented at the 19th EAAE International Conference: Re-Integrating Theory and Design in Architectural Education, May 23, 2001, Ankara, Turkey.*

What use theory?

Theory asks a question and seeks an answer. The question must be about some aspect of the real world around us. That link with the real world allows research to check the theory.

Without such a link, we have not theory but ideology. Theory, after all, is what captures the spirit as well as the mind when we contemplate the world around us. In principle, any question is a valid basis for theory.

Academic freedom should not allow restrictions on questions asked. Curiosity is the only motivation for true academic pursuit. Not all academic theory needs to be useful to practice.

But practice needs useful theory. Practice is what makes the world around us. Practice needs a theory about that world to give direction to its acts and to explain its experience.

Theory needs to contemplate the world for the world to make sense to practice.

To study the built environment

A few years ago, I wrote a book titled *"The Structure of the Ordinary."*

In this book I chose not to speak about architecture but to look at the built environment as an autonomous entity and to seek what general laws were governing it.

It is not my intention to dwell on the contents of that particular study, but I want to explain why I think it is important to study the built environment as such. Indeed, I believe this field of study should be the basis for any theory about architecture. That is the thesis of my talk today.

Built environment as subject for expertise

Every professional discipline needs a part of the real world to which to apply its expertise. For the medical profession, knowledge of the human body is the basis for its ability to heal the sick. The legal profession must know society's laws as it claims expertise to interpret them and to help them come about. For the engineering profession the behavior of physical bodies under the impact of forces is the basis for its expertise in making machines and erecting structures.

Similarly, the architectural profession must know built environment as the basis for its claim for designing good buildings.

The basis of a profession's expertise is not that profession's invention. The human body is not the invention of the medical profession. The law of the land is not determined by lawyers. The behavior of physical bodies in space under the impact of forces has not been decided upon by the engineers. Similarly, the built environment is not an invention of architects, or of any other profession, for that matter. To be sure, we are not the only ones for whom the study of the built environment is essential. Planners and geographers, for instance, have a similar interest. In the same way knowledge of the human body is also important for biologists and biochemists. Knowledge can be shared among disciplines, but each must draw from it a rationale for its own existence.

The basis of a profession's expertise is not that profession's invention. The human body is not the invention of the medical profession. The law of the land is not determined by lawyers. The behavior of physical bodies in space under the impact of forces has not been decided upon by the engineers. Similarly, the built environment is not an invention of architects, or of any other profession, for that matter.

To be sure, we are not the only ones for whom the study of the built environment is essential. Planners and geographers, for instance, have a similar interest. In the same way knowledge of the human body is also important for biologists and biochemists. Knowledge can be shared among disciplines, but each must draw from it a rationale for its own existence.

Our task, therefore, is to explain in what way architects contribute to that shared body. What, exactly, is the expertise, or the added value, if you wish, that we contribute to the whole? Here is one question we may theorize about.

Built environment's autonomy

As already said: built environment is not our invention, but our subject.

We know built environment as too large and too complex to be controlled by any single party or any single expertise.

Think of the large urban fields of the contemporary world cities. Think of the vast stretches of suburbia. Of the equally extensive areas of so-called informal building in many of the most populous cities of the world. Think also of the beautiful fabrics of historic towns and the complex and dense urban tissues that for have sheltered humankind for millennia.

Although very different in many ways, all built environments also share certain constant properties. That is why we can understand and recognize them and can appreciate them no matter where we come from. For that reason, we may say built environment has autonomy. It is subject to laws and principles that are not of our making.

Built environment has its own autonomy, just as the human body has its own autonomy.

For that reason, any theories about architecture, or about the role of the profession, must relate to a knowledge and understanding of the built environment as such. It is the source and the justification of all theorizing related to our profession.

Knowledge of the built environment links theory to practice.

Architecture is fully immersed in the everyday world

The bulk of the work we do becomes part of environment's inescapable everydayness. We may build large and important projects, but they are to provide places where ordinary people spend their lives, like office buildings, factories, schools, hospitals, apartment buildings and so on.

In our contribution to the built environment we are not alone; there are other players. The very fact of our immersion in everyday environment means that our expertise fits in with other forces.

Clients have always been important agents in environmental decision making. Today, they have become professionals too. They and their consultants determine a very large part of the entire process through which buildings come about. Increasingly, architects are found among the employees of institutional clients.

In addition to clients, local governments set standards and rules and enforce them. They too, employ people with an architectural background.

Manufacturers of materials, of components and of systems determine the kit of parts that architects design with. Their impact on everyday environment is very important.

With these other players we share technology and know-how. The industrial revolution of the early days is no longer revolutionary. To be sure, innovation will continue to take place in a significant way but the general systemics of building technology in steel, concrete, plastics and glass have now been established and everyone is familiar with them.

In a similar way, building typology – for high-rise and low-rise applied to various uses – has been settled. Here too is knowledge we share with the other players in the field. As always, typology allows for endless variation and interpretation, but by and large, a common language has been established that can only evolve gradually and by common consent of the players involved.

Indeed, to the extent that major innovations in technology or typology may occur in the future, we can be sure that they will not be the product of a single discipline but will emerge from the complex and evolutionary balance of forces that we are part of.

The increasing complexity of decision-making relative to the built environment also affects the way architects organize their work among themselves.

As projects get bigger and bigger, architectural firms also may become larger and larger. But within those firms, specific design responsibility becomes more fragmented. Most of the talented graduates from our schools will not design entire buildings but will find themselves assigned special tasks. They may work on a facade, on a site plan, or on the fit out of a particular floor or wing of a larger building.

The changing role of the architect

The few remarks made so far about the context that we work in, may suffice to show how the role of the architect has changed dramatically in the last half of the past century.

Those who still believe in the avant-gardist ideology complain that the profession is becoming marginalized.

But it seems the opposite is closer to the truth. Our profession is getting more intimately involved in all parts of the process through which built environment is maintained and improved. We are drawn into built environment in an increasing variety of roles.

Architects work for homebuilders. They work for regulatory agencies. They may soon work for manufacturers. They are employed by developers. They participate in design teams for large projects. They do a facade only. Or a fit-out job in a large office building. They renovate old buildings.

The problem we are wrestling with is not that architectural design is no longer in demand. But the roles we play and the tasks we are called upon can no longer be explained by the avant-gardist ideology we have grown up with and which we still cling to. It is not so much a problem of practice, but one of self-image and thus of ideology.

What is there to learn?

What, exactly, is there to learn from the built environment? I offer only a few examples.

When we look at any of the environments I have mentioned before – the big modern metropolis, the extensive suburban field, the vigorous informal sector, the still extant historic urban fabrics- we find certain constant qualities:

One: There is variety in coherence

Similar typologies and patterns are repeated; similar systemics are employed. They may vary from one environment to another, but within a particular fabric, they tend to be rather constant.

Two: There is a hierarchical structure – different levels of intervention are apparent

We are, for instance, roughly familiar with the distinction between urban structure, buildings, interior fit out, and interior design. These levels coincide with professional domains of expertise. Therefore, these levels are also domains of intervention.

Three: The different levels of intervention allow lower level change in the context of higher-level stability

Continuous change makes environments endure for centuries.

Four: There is a variety of values

Values and preferences differ from place to place and from culture to culture. People look for values they can identify with.

Fifth: Inhabitation is territorial

People tend to establish territorial boundaries all the time. We also constantly cross boundaries.

Architecture in denial

Put these five observations against the avant-garde tradition we come from. Compare them with our ideology of freedom of self-expression and of artistic autonomy.

We noted variety in coherence. It demands that we accept local extant typology and fit our work in accordingly. It expects us to repeat patterns peculiar to a location. It means we must share systemics with other designers.

In contrast, we prefer to do our own thing. We tend to judge buildings for the way they are different, not for the way they fit in.

We noted that built environment operates on different levels of control; each level contributing to the adaptability and flexibility of the whole. In contrast to this layering, the modernist ideal is to design the building all the way down to the furniture. We prefer vertical design control.

We noted that the various levels of control contribute to adaptability and flexibility of the environment. In contrast, we do not like change, but prefer our buildings to remain the same forever.

We noted a variety of values and an increasingly dynamic mix and exchange of values regarding local environment. In contrast, we come from a tradition that tried to impose a uniform architecture worldwide. We now operate in a tradition that puts self-expression of the architect above all. Both traditions ignore extant values and local preferences.

We noted that inhabitation imposes territorial boundaries; that inhabitants prefer to control their own. Throughout history, environment has known gates and boundaries as architectural expression of territorial reality. In contrast, we dream of free-flowing space, glass facades, and freely accessible buildings. Territorial boundaries do not find expression in the (post) modernist vocabulary.

Ideology or theory?

Each of the points mentioned may be debatable. But there is overwhelming evidence that our architectural ideology is in conflict with the reality of built environment.

Our ideology is individualistic and self-referential. Built environment is about common values, thematic qualities, shared spaces and boundaries.

We believe all constraints to be detrimental to good architecture. Built environment derives its quality from commonly accepted thematics.

That is not a good climate for theory.

An ideology imposes.

A theory proposes.

Practice already knows more

This obsolescence of our professional ideology does not help those in practice.

They have learned to operate in the real world. Intuitively they understand the autonomy of the built environment and have found ways to work in it.

But if they are asked to explain themselves, they become apologetic. They come back to the ideology they have been taught in school and by which we still organize architectural education and structure our criticism.

The problem is not with practice. For all we know, most practitioners have adapted pretty well. Architecture's problem is the lack of theories explaining the present reality. Without such theories we remain unable to explain our role and our expertise. We will also find it increasingly difficult to discuss the way we can contribute to the built environment and to develop the skills and knowledge that must enable us to do so more effectively.

How did we get into this conflict between practice and theory?

Our involvement with the built environment is a relatively recent phenomenon. Our ideology of the architect as a free and inventive agent emerged in Renaissance times. At that time, architecture had a limited focus. It had to do with special and monumental buildings: the palace, the place of worship, the castle, and the mansion for the rich. In architectural discourse everyday built environment was taken for granted,

But Modernism made traditional crafts and materials obsolete. It rendered traditional typology of houses and towns inadequate. Normal everyday environment became a problem. The architectural profession, along with builders and manufacturers, moved in to invent ordinary environment anew. From then on built environment was considered an architectural problem.

Indeed, the very revolution of Modem architecture was closely connected to the claim that ordinary environment was worth the architect's attention. Peter Behrens was the first to show us that factories could be architecture. Walter Gropius made an artistic statement by designing a school building. Le Corbusier turned the large apartment building into avant-garde architecture. Mies van der Rohe proposed monumental glass towers for bureaucrats to work in. Tony Garnier was the first to propose an entire contemporary city, down to the smallest dwelling, as an architectural design.

Modernism wanted to invent the environment of the future. Modernist architects believed this to be a sacred mission. They rejected history. The many beautiful historic environments, rich and full of vitality, that still could be visited and studied, were ignored. The idea that we could learn anything useful from the past did not occur.

Beginning to look at built environment

In the middle of the twentieth century, Modernism's limitations became visible.

Robert Venturi's "Complexity and Contradiction in Architecture," examined historic evidence to show that architecture could not feed on a uniform ideology alone. Aldo Rossi saw in historic urban fabric a source of artistic inspiration and space making. He looked at precedent and extant environmental fabric, turning away from a self-generated 'international style'.

Others moved beyond the search for inspiration. They believed environment has something to tell us. They sought a way of systematic study and, from what they learned, advocated a different kind of professionalism.

Muratori, in Italy, advocated a painstaking examination of the typology of everyday environment as the product of a culture rather than a profession.

John Turner, observing informal settlements of the poor in Peru, showed us that orderly urban fabric could emerge without professional involvement.

Three theories

In short, we became aware of built environment's autonomy. That it had always been there and always would be there regardless of the architect's involvement.

At least three other theories proposed in the second half of the last century already accepted built environment's autonomy. They consequently did not propose another architecture, but suggested ways in which the profession might adjust its methods in light of that autonomy.

In the sixties Christopher Alexander established the concept of Patterns and suggested that a pattern language could be found in healthy built environment and that architects needed to understand those patterns and work with them.

Robert Venturi and Denise Scott Brown suggested in "Learning from Las Vegas" that ordinary, contemporary 'vernacular' should be taken seriously by architects.

Finally, I myself proposed open ended 'support' buildings within which inhabitants could have their customized dwellings. I posited healthy built environments revealed a "natural relation" between environment and inhabitation that we had to respect and make possible again.

All three theories suggested that we could not just impose our preferences on built environment but had to respond to its autonomous reality.

Alexander saw that there was an innate quality in good environment that architects could not just invent but had to discover from extant and historic cases.

Venturi and Scott Brown noted that living environments reflected people's preferences and values and suggested that architects accept such values and work with them, rather than trying to impose their own.

I, myself, argued that inhabitation was a creative force needed to guarantee sustainable environment. And I drew attention to the hierarchical structure of complex environmental form that had to be recognized in the making of architecture.

Post-modern self-indulgence

However, although the profession was shying away from the Modernist claim for a uniform architecture, it did not come to see built environment as something we could learn from.

Post Modernism rejected the missionary zeal of the Modernist architect. Realizing built environment escaped the architects' dreams, it was better not to bother with it at all. Architects retreated into architecture for its own sake. The idea that our involvement with built environment was inevitable and that therefore we had better study it, did not gain currency.

The result was two sided.

On the one hand the newly claimed artistic freedom produced an increasing freedom of expression and an increasing sophistication in the making of architectural form. Indeed, the skills displayed by the present generation of architects are very much higher in comparison to what was done when I was a student of architecture. While we still admire the pioneering work of the giants of Modernism, there is no doubt that the profession at large now is much more sophisticated and skilled than it was in their days.

But the emphasis on form making as a goal in itself also led to an obsessive emphasis on self-expression and to a profound lack of interest in any shared context. Architectural thinking became increasingly self-referential.

Becoming more and more immersed in everyday built environment, we became less and less aware of its autonomous qualities. Consequently, we failed to study the subject of our expertise.

Much to be done

The points just listed already make for a full agenda of theoretical study. To be sure, many of us already study and theorize aspects of built environment. There are those who study housing and residential morphology. There are those who study typology. There are those who advocate adaptability and change. Alexander's pattern language continues to attract students and practitioners. There are those who study systems. And others who seek to adapt design methodology to the new roles the profession finds itself engaged in, in daily practice.

But in the prevailing ideology such patient studies are pushed to the margin. There is no desire to seek a new framework in which they may fit.

I am not proposing a mega theory that explains all. I am proposing that the built environment in its autonomy provides the framework for many theories and many research agenda's. It is where our theories relate to one another and where their validity can be examined. It is where a new awareness of our professional expertise must grow from.

Indeed, we must replace ideology with theory. Ideology imposes a view and refuses to learn.

I have spoken of theories that help explain and guide the way practice is done, that allow us to let go of an obsolete ideology.

The same theories will help us to structure education anew.

Where the built environment is the subject of both study and practice, there need not be a tension between the two. It is an outdated ideology that keeps the two apart.

There is much to be done.

INTERMEZZO BY THE EDITORS

SK/JD: What I'm fascinated by, at least as you recount it, is the extent to which you were rather isolated and singularly committed to exploring the implications of these ideas. And you didn't, apparently, have a lot of conversations with others until the SAR was formed. Then you began working with HANS VAN OLPHEN, THIJS BAX and FOKKE DE JONG, FRANS VAN DER WERF, and so on, and then you had a real working group so you could plant seeds that with their help actually blossomed, and you could all see where those ideas led.

JH: That was very helpful.

SK/JD: So, you were a real working group.

SK/JD: You know, forgive me, but for my own edification, could you talk a bit about the fact that in the post World War II period there was a lot of experimentation going on with housing on a very large scale and I wonder to what extent, the route that you chose was in part based on a cultural difference because I am thinking of, you know I want to go back to this thing, you know, you look at what the Smithsons were doing and other people like that, they were building large scale housing blocks, they were influenced by the CIAM principle of the need for light and air, and a kind of strict logic of town planning and laying out cities. And at the same time, you were looking at indigenous architecture; you were trying to humanize industrialization in a different way so I'm wondering how you struck out on your own? What were the forces? Were they cultural forces, was it something about the Dutch milieu that was more intimate, and more conversational, was there more of a self-help tradition?

JH: Yes, these are very good questions.

SK/JD: You must have been aware of what was happening in England and you were looking at that critically I suspect.

JH: Yes, I didn't like it. And the Smithsons I thought was just old air, which was not really true but that is what I thought at that time.

SK/JD: Well, that was part of TEAM TEN

JH: Yes, I think TEAM TEN was just mistaken.

SK/JD: That's provocative! TEAM TEN was anti-CIAM (Congres Internationaux d'Architecture Moderne)

JH: Yeah, well that's what they said. They wanted to be the new CIAM.

SK/JD: Bakema was part of that group.

JH: He was very much part of it. Aldo VAN EYCK was also. And I didn't go to those meetings because I didn't like what they were talking about. Both of you have to understand that in order for me to figure out things, the questions that I had, I decided not to get into discussions with other people. Not to criticize other people. I'm not going to spend my time to discuss with Smithson that he's wrong. Or that I don't agree.

SK/JD: Or have them critique your work. You didn't want that either . . . well, I don't think that was on your mind, really. You just wanted to focus on trying to sort out your own observations and thoughts.

JH: Exactly.

THE BUILT FIELD

1964
THE TISSUE OF THE TOWN
Some suggestions for further scrutiny

Editors' Note: *This early essay by the author, grounded in a careful reading of historical urban form, lays out some of the key lines of thinking that he continued to examine throughout his career: "Cultivating a tissue means influencing and stimulating a process; applying architectural techniques in such a way that living organisms come into being." It was published in Forum, Vol XVIII, No. 1, 1964, 22–37.*

When the generations preceding ours thought about architecture and town planning, they thought of the things marked on Nolli's map. The streets, squares, public buildings, palaces and villa's; i.e. all the things connected with public life and all the things relating to beauty expressed in form. Architecture and buildings are not synonymous, and architects and historians have only been interested in architecture, in the beautiful form as expressed in buildings.

In the recent past, an interest has developed for the building which is made to serve the humble and everyday functions. It was discovered that a factory and a humble dwelling could also be architecture. Architects and historians attacked academism and put architecture in the service of ordinary and everyday needs. In this way the scope of fine building was enlarged and the commonplace emancipated. The ordinary building was considered worthy of the attention which formerly was only given to churches and palaces. It therefore became important that a workshop should have an aesthetically justified aspect, and the way was cleared for making the housing of ordinary people an excuse for erecting monumental buildings.

But what is blackened on Nolli's map is fundamentally different from what is drawn in detail. It is not a collection of the less important buildings; it is an organic unity which must be considered as a whole. It is the tissue of the town. A totality of built up matter, in which the streets were left open and in which architectural monuments were scooped out. The tissue of the town was not produced by architects but by a building community. That is the reason that it was taken for granted, that it was never recognized, let alone studied, as a unity. The scope and creativeness of our everyday language is different from those of a literary production, even when an attempt is made to use the everyday

Figure 1 Map of Rome, detail (Nolli 1748)

DOI: 10.4324/9781003011385-6

expressions in literature. In the same way there is a distinct difference between the tissue of the town and the architectural production in it.

The tissue of the town is the result of a process; the process of communal building. And the community is always building, whether by its own wish or in spite of itself; this is unavoidably entailed in its existence. This process needs to be studied because, like so many processes in human life which originally were not recognized, it now needs to be consciously directed and stimulated.

The tissue of the town is the result of a process; the process of communal building. And the community is always building, whether by its own wish or in spite of itself; this is unavoidably entailed in its existence. This process needs to be studied because, like so many processes in human life which originally were not recognized, it now needs to be consciously directed and stimulated. Therefore, it is also necessary that the tissue of the town be studied. The tissue of the town is the clay out of which is the town is molded. One cannot begin to plan a town before its tissue is known; before it is known so well that the town-planner can play with it without damaging it. Town planning is primarily cultivating the town tissue.

The tissue of the town has its own structure. In that structure the entire process of communal building is comprised, in the same way as the entire tree is comprised in the texture of the wood. With the same tissue many designs in the planning of a town are possible. But they all lie within a certain sphere. Outside that sphere only other forms in town planning are possible, based on another kind of tissue. A true regeneration of our towns and the structure of our urban environment is only possible with a true regeneration of the tissue itself. When the tissue has not been studied, every town renovation is either a meaningless gesture or a refurbishing of old designs. By the same token, a change in the structure of the tissue is also bound to necessitate the planning of another kind of town.

By the structure of the tissue the structure of the community can be known. That is the reason why in our towns the dwelling can be known as a unit. But this unit cannot be removed without losing its identity. The dwelling in the tissue can only be known as part of a whole. It is characteristic for a tissue to be made up of identifiable parts which, however, can only be known as parts, because they are met within a collective body. This indivisibility of what can be known in parts on the one hand and is only found collectively on the other hand, is characteristic for all organic phenomena. This makes the tissue the distinctive mark of the town. Without tissue there is no town. A great number of stones do not make a building, neither. Do a great number of buildings make a town.

It is characteristic of an organic tissue that the parts which can be distinguished as parts are all of the same construction and of the same kind and yet have different forms. Sameness of construction and sameness of kind embracing an endless variety of forms; this is the feature which makes the tissues of the old towns organic.

An organic tissue has the distinctive feature that the whole has a much longer life than the parts constituting it. The characteristic that the parts are inseparable from the whole, are determined and influenced by the whole, and that this is the very reason that they can change and evolve, seems paradoxical.

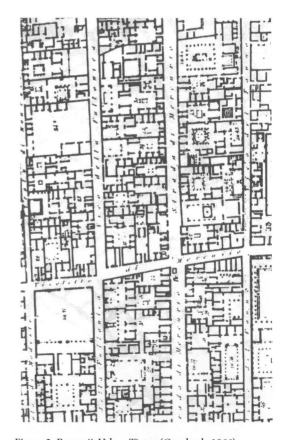

Figure 2 Pompeii, Urban Tissue (Overbeck, 1866)

The tissue of the town

Figure 3 UR, ca. 2000BC; (Sir Leonhard Wooley)

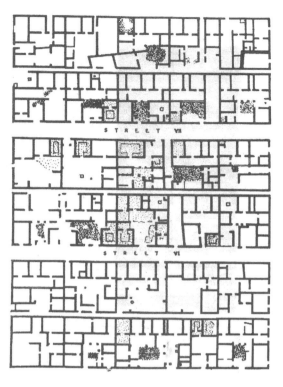

Figure 5 Olynthus, 5th century BC (Professor D.M. Robinson)

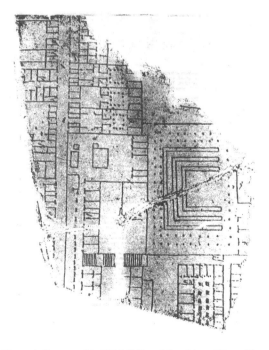

Figure 4 Forma urbis, 200 BC; (Laxel Boethius – The golden house of Nero – 1 and 2)

Figure 6 (detail) UR, ca. 2000BC. (Sir Leonhard Wooley)

The tissue-structure of a town is decided by a great number of factors. By the materials which are available, by the intelligence of the people using them, by the time during which the materials have already been used, by the social relations with which the forms which are built must be in agreement, by the climate and by the conditions of the soil. In the tissue a whole civilization is reflected. That is the reason that archeologists excavate the old towns.

The tissue-structure grows like an organism. The dwelling as a simple cell becomes a group of cells. Was the tissue of Ur, or Olynthus or Pompei built up out of dwellings or out of apartment cells? The apartment cells have grown into groups which we call dwellings. Sometimes these groups can be clearly identified and sometimes not.

The units of a Dutch Renaissance town can be clearly distinguished. The plan of any house on one of the canals is unmistakably influenced by the collective existence of the dwelling units. The narrow, elongated shape, made the most of in an inimitable fashion, is the outcome of the entire tissue structure. At the same time, however, independence and individuality were brought to their highest pitch.

The dwellings of the 'new' quarters of Olynthus can also be easily told apart from the old core of the town, which looks like that of Ur. But here it is a different kind of distinguishing. It is much more a matter of an 'introverted' individuality, noticeable in the ground-plan rather than in the outward form. The tissue of Olynthus is magnificent. Its structure is of the same order as that of Ur. The same grouping of cells around an inner courtyard with here and there a single cell facing the street. The same circumstances and the same social structure produce the same forms. Just as the gardener makes a wild plant into a cultivated one, Greek civilization has intelligently developed the organically grown structure. The geometric town plan and the geometric ground plan of the buildings do not impair the tissue but enrich it. With the Greeks the capacity for abstracting went hand-in-hand with a deep insight in the ties man is born with.

In the three big Amsterdam canals a similar example is found of how a tissue structure developed in the course of centuries has been cultivated. They do not represent the beginning of a new way of thinking as regards town planning but a consummation, the final triumph of a highly developed building process organized with great insight.

Only in the small and middle-sized towns did man succeed in the past in intelligently cultivating an organically grown tissue structure into the distinct theme for urban development. And even so, this was only the case with newly founded towns or towns which were considerably enlarged. Rome, Carthage and Athens were chaotic towns. We know too little of these towns to learn much from them in this respect. Of the old tissues, only fragments are left. Boëthius quite rightly pleads for a study of these last remnants left to us.

A town housing millions of people demands its own structure and planning, with arrangements all its own, to keep the tissue healthy. For such a metropolis also houses a community which has the individual person and the family as its component parts. Also, in such a town the dwelling is therefore the smallest unit composing the organism. But the larger the town the bigger and more complicated the arrangements necessary to make it possible for the dwelling to remain that definable unit which it is in a small town. Water-supply, sewerage, means of transport and communication demand ever more complicated infrastructures. If this demand is not met, the town will suffocate in its own tissue. Is this what happened in Rome?

As the town grows the tissue coarsens. It is no longer composed of houses but of tenement buildings and housing blocks. The cell of the tissue is no longer the dwelling but a bigger building, housing many families together. This happened in Rome and it also happened in Amsterdam.

This coarsening does not result from the free choice of the urban population. It results from a technical necessity; when a certain population density was exceeded, the tissue of Olynthus and the Amsterdam canals became inadequate.

Is it really coarsening of the tissue? The cell in the tissue is the smallest interchangeable unit. All at once this unit is no longer the dwelling but a random building, housing a random number of people. So the cell has grown bigger. The tissue has grown coarser.

Figure 7 Amsterdam (a view stretching from city center to suburban development to the south of the city)
Credit: Google Earth

Figure 8 Medieval center
Credit: 1967 aerial photo; Copyrights Dotka Data 2020

Figure 9 17th century working class residential area
Credit: 1967 aerial photo; Copyrights Dotka Data 2020

Figure 10 The three main canals of the 17th century
Credit: 1967 aerial photo; Copyrights Dotka Data 2020

Figure 11 Residential area in the second part of the 19th century
Credit: 1967 aerial photo; Copyrights Dotka Data 2020

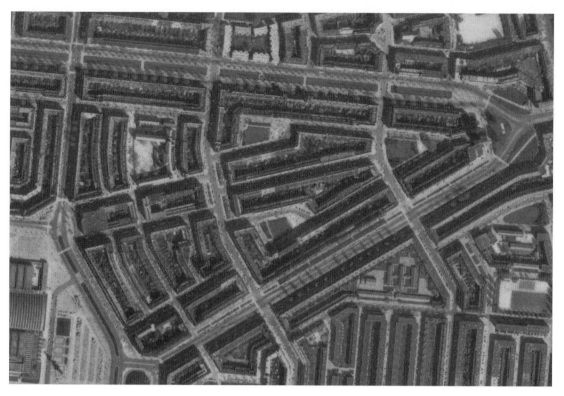

Figure 12 Part of Berlage's plan
Credit: 1967 Aerial photo; Copyrights Dotka Data 2020

Figure 13 Amsterdam's development after WWII
Credit: 1967 aerial photo; Copyrights Dotka Data 2020

The tissue of the town 37

Figure 14 Dokkum, the Netherlands
Credit: Google Earth

This coarsening of tissue implies a turning point in the relation between community and matter, which is reflected in the town. Whereas before this change the community molded matter after its own image, this is no longer so after it. A technical necessity dictates its own conditions for maintaining the compatibility between man and matter. Even when the tissue of the community is still composed of the small cell formed by the family, the tissue will yet become coarser.

Figure 15 Amsterdam extensions to the south in the mid-20th century
Credit: 1967 Aerial photo; Copyrights Dotka Data 2020

The tissue of the town

That was a technical necessity. Now it is possible to make structures in which the dwelling can be built to form the smallest independent unit; even elevated above the ground. We are technically able to make the arrangements to prevent the tissue of the densely built metropolis from becoming coarser than that of Olynthus. Yet we build as if the coarse tissue structure is inevitable. Once coarsening has set in, there is a tendency towards an ever-increasing coarsening. There are no natural limits to the size of the big cell formed by the tenement house. Once the first move has been made towards coarsening, there is nothing to restrain the growth of the cell. Engineering and economics show a tendency towards ever bigger units. He who traverses Amsterdam from its center to its periphery becomes aware of the constant coarsening which has taken place, and which still goes on.

Finally, the town will explode. There will no longer be any tissue. The units will become independent. The total estrangement between community and matter will have become a fact.

Criterion must be that as harmoniously as possible the structure of the community go hand-in-hand with that of the tissue of the town. The coarse tissue fits the totalitarian state, just like the fine-grained tissue fitted the Greek democracy. But if engineering does not permit a choice between a coarse or a fine tissue, matter may get a structure which can influence the community and even hamper it.

Is that what happened in Rome? Is it happening today? Haussmann, cutting the boulevards in the suffocating tissue of Paris, did something entirely different than the planners of the Amsterdam canals. He did not cultivate; he cut paths in the jungle. Anything done in the field of town planning which does not go and in hand with a conscious cultivation of the finest possible tissue, will never be anything but a well-meant emergency measure.

Berlage made an urban structure of grandeur, basing it on a tissue which was the inevitable result of the necessity caused by technical inadequacies. A coarse tissue which had only the street-walls in common with that of the old canals. Berlage accepted the wall; what else could he do? But we are expected to do more than only plan streets, squares and alignments. We must make a tissue for the contemporary town.

Figure 16 Rotterdam Center before the 1940 air raids
Credit: Wikipedia

Figure 17 Rotterdam Center, 1961
Credit: 1961 aerial photo; Copyrights Dotka Data 2020

Is a town a collection of buildings or is it more? We have expanded the skill and scope of engineering. We can build but we do not know what we are to build. We build harbors, factories, railways, roadways and independent buildings. Round about Schiedam the whole tragedy of our material environment is enacted. Going from Schiedam to Rotterdam one can see all the stages of disintegration. The parts make themselves independent. The roadways, the railways, the waterways, the harbors, the industries and the buildings all go their own way, in their own manner, on their own scale.

The traffic routes, of whatever type they be, are big continuous constructions. Must the tissue housing the people emulate it by becoming even coarser structured? By inflating its cells to a monstrous size? Or are we going to make continuous structures on a truly large scale, in which the independent cells can find their own size?

Our community cultivates the individual and also the community. The individual becomes ever freer in his choice of style of living and of the group he wants to belong to. Aided by the growing means of communication ever more groups get ever more intricately interwoven. The increase of individual possibilities is stimulated by a growing prosperity. The individual and the community must both grow. The combined development of the individual and the community is the hallmark of a vigorous civilization. This must be reflected in a clear urban structure and in a fine tissue structure. But if this is true, is what we build a reflection of our social evolution, or do we still live in emergency buildings, hurriedly constructed on entering a new era?

As regards architecture, an entirely new way of thinking is required to develop contemporary tissue for the contemporary town. It is in no way connected with building single projects or with the judicious arrangement of such projects. Cultivating a tissue means influencing and stimulating a process; applying architectural techniques in such a way that living organisms come into being. To do this, the attention must rather be directed toward the structure of what must come into being, than toward its shape.

The tissue of the town

Figure 18 Medieval center of Schiedam, enveloped by the outskirts of Rotterdam
Credit: 1961 aerial photo; Copyrights Dotka Data 2020

1971
YOU CAN'T DESIGN THE ORDINARY

Editors' Note: *This essay was published in <u>AD</u> /4/71. The essay had a note referring readers to a more detailed presentation of the authors' ideas in <u>AD</u> 1/70, pp. 32–38.*

We all know that when architects get together, it is fashionable to doubt. We feel free to doubt almost anything. We begin to think of this as a rotten world in which nothing is possible. The fact that we can afford to doubt is perhaps a token of our strength and confidence; because when people really think something impossible, nothing can be done about it. They do not talk about it. The fact that we question things is a sign that we think we can do something. We are very powerful. We must not be afraid to use that power.

"Environmental quality" is a much-used phrase. But one can only argue about such things as roads running through an urban tissue if we have some notion of what the tissue is. In this vital area, we know very little. The problems are not of the kind that can be tackled simply with money or organization; one has to know first whether one should do anything at all. We live in an age in which most things can be done. It might be worth determining what we should NOT do.

There are lots of beautiful cities and there are lots of people living all over the world living without the help of an architect or a specialist involved in environmental planning. Architecture might have little enough to do with the problems of housing. The profession evolved in an historical context; architects were trained, or trained themselves, to make architecture – that is, a special building, a church or palace. Most people housed themselves without architects.

Architects have always been inclined to make symbols, to make things that have certain implications about the society for which they are building. They have focused on special things. But one can only do that if there is something ordinary against which the special thing is to be seen.

During the twenties, or perhaps a little earlier, architects discovered that there was a total built environment. People lived in houses, and they used factories: architects decided that this was also their concern. However, they approached these things as if they were architectural problems. For them, everything that was ordinary became special. In architectural history books, you never see dwellings; you see Greek temples and Roman baths and medieval churches; it is very hard to find any documentation about housing alone. One of the reasons is that not much antique housing survives, but this is not the only reason. The most important reason is that people were just not interested. They have become preoccupied with the special thing. In books on modern architecture, however, you find houses and factories. They have become architecture. But the man in the street complains – "You cannot see whether a building is something important or not; they are all the same. There are no monuments." In fact, there are only monuments. The ordinary has been discarded because no one is willing to make the ordinary – they certainly cannot design it. The architect has become King Midas. Everything he touches becomes architecture; everything he touches becomes something special. King Midas died because he could not eat; when he touched bread, it became gold. That is what we are doing. We cannot nourish ourselves. We are making special things. There is no bread.

You can't design the ordinary

The ordinary has been discarded because no one is willing to make the ordinary – they certainly cannot design it. The architect has become King Midas. Everything he touches becomes architecture; everything he touches becomes something special. King Midas died because he could not eat; when he touched bread, it became gold. That is what we are doing. We cannot nourish ourselves. We are making special things. There is no bread.

What are we going to do if we cannot touch housing? The communal places, the communal buildings were once carved out of the tissue of old Amsterdam, but the building of the last 20 or 30 years is altogether different. All buildings are designed to assume importance. They are set like monuments. The space around them is of no consequence in the texture of the city; it is unimportant. The new city is the negative of the old city.

In Amsterdam, the canals were designed by one man, but he did not touch the original fabric; he used the complete system of relationships and coordinates which already existed in the typical dwellings; he did not touch them, he just organized them. He did not

Figure 1 Tissue of old Amsterdam

invent a new kind of housing (which is impossible); he used what was there and enriched it. He was not working as an architect, rather as a gardener. It was a matter of deciding where things would grow, and how much they should grow; feeding and cultivating them to turn them into something very beautiful.

The same kind of thing, it might be claimed, happened in Paris when Haussmann demolished the old city. He made all the boulevards run smack through the old tissue. But what was built along them was based on

Figure 2 Paris, Boulevard Montmarte

the same system that had already existed, organized in a more direct way. There are courtyards off the streets (controlled by a concierge) and from them people go upstairs to their rooms and flats. The center of Paris is a megastructure. The cross-section through the buildings on the Haussmann boulevards is exactly the same all over – a first floor, about three meters high, then a mezzanine, and above four or five dwelling floors. The street section is ubiquitous – the public area at ground level, an intermediate level with balconies overlooking the street and a private area above. The pattern is medieval.

Perhaps we could learn the lesson, and accept that we just cannot invent houses, cannot design a dwelling. We can design a floor plan, but that is not a dwelling. We **can**, however, design places in which dwellings can grow, in which dwellings can be serviced – that is our job. Our job is to make the communal services – like roads and structures. We could provide structures and spaces for people to live in. In doing this, we become dependent on the people who are going to live there. This is a feeling most of us do not much like. Architects do not like making things for someone, even if he is to live there, having it all his own way. There are some who imagine that people do not want to do anything about their living places. This is simply because, since the beginning of the 20th century, the individual has been disregarded in all housing projects. Nobody has bothered with him. You cannot, of course, produce ***finished architecture*** if everybody gets in on the act. That is why uniformity has crept in; not because it was a technical need, not because mass-production was involved, but because the individual was disregarded.

We can design Support structures, and we can design detachable units. And we can accept the designers' role that goes with that. Dwellings will be made by ordinary people doing ordinary things. We will work then at an urban fabric, a tissue that will be alive and healthy. We will then be as strong as we are.

1979
GENERAL PRINCIPLES ABOUT THE WAY BUILT ENVIRONMENTS EXIST

Editors' note: *This essay was published as part of the SAR Open House, Blue Cover Booklet series in March 1979. The author wrote in a brief introduction: "These notes have been put together during the last five years, in an attempt to organize my own thinking. They constitute an outline of a theory of the built environment. As such, they lack explanation and argumentation for which I apologize. I am grateful to the SAR for this informal publication. I would like it to be a contribution to the ongoing dialogue within the SAR network that has been so stimulating and helpful to me." Approximately 20 years later, The Structure of the Ordinary: Form and Control in the Built Environment was published by the MIT Press (1998), a book which had its roots in this essay.*

0. Beginning

0.1

A house that is not occupied will decay. A town, abandoned by its inhabitants, will return as dead matter into nature's cycle.

What has been built exists only by human effort. It will only continue to exist by such effort.

People live together by sharing space. They share space by dividing it. Space is divided by material; by the act of building. The division of space means reconciliation of conflicting interests. The management of spaces rests on agreements and laws. The use of space knows customs and rules.

To build is to act together. The use of material demands the division of resources. The distribution of material means the reconciliation of conflicting interests. The combination of materials in space follows agreements and laws. The manipulation of materials knows customs and rules.

The existence of the built environment rests on mutual understanding and action.

1. About the site

1.0 Space and material

1.1.1

The house is in the town. The room is in the house. In the room is a chair. In the chair sits a person who speaks.

The site of an act is that part of the total physical reality in which the act takes place. Every act has a site.

The site of an object is that part of the total physical reality in which the object finds itself.

Each object has a site.

1.1.2

There exists an infinity of sites because there is an infinity of objects that constitute the physical reality.

1.1.3

A site is space and material. Space and material are complementary. They cannot be thought of separately.

Space is formed by material. Material is formed for the sake of space. Material is formed in space.

1.1.4

The house has rooms. In the room is a chair. Material makes space and space contains material.

1.1 Identification and position

1.2.1

Everything has a name. Things exist because they have a name.

A space that has no name is a mystery; an unknown. Material that has no name cannot be discussed.

1.2.2

People give things names.

An object exists because people agree about a name. It exists when it can be identified.

The name of an object is valid for a specific group of people, for a specific territory, for a specific time,

Those who know the name make the object exist.

1.2.3

There are columns, walls, floors, roofs, stones, trees, mountains. There are rooms, corridors, halls, courtyards, streets, squares, gardens and valleys. Material objects have names and space objects have names.

1.2.4

Those who want to distinguish themselves as a group tend to give names to those things for which they share an interest. By giving an object a name, it is taken into possession.

An object takes part in human relations once there is agreement about the name of the object. ·

1.2.5

A site is shared by people when people have named the objects that make the site.

The common site exists only in so far as it is a combination of objects that have a name for those who share that site.

To give names to objects is the first step towards the control of a site.

1.2.6

Everything has a position. The position of an object is the description of its place in the site.

1.2 Change

1.3.1

The site is subject to continuous change.

Cities rise and fall. Street are broadened. Buildings are taken down and new ones are built. Rooms are decorated. Holes are knocked into walls. Porches are added. Doors are repainted. Windows are walled in. Trees are planted. Hedges are clipped. Sewers are buried, roads paved, ditches dug, monuments erected.

Space changes and material changes: spaces change because material changes. The site changes by movement of material. To build is to change the site.

1.3.2

The site changes only by movement of material:

To add material is growth.

If by growth a larger territory is occupied, there is expansion. If growth occurs in the same territory there is congestion.

To take away a matter is reduction or decay. Replacement is to take away and add.

1.3.3

The site is taken into possession by putting up a sign. The site is taken into possession by changing it.

Use of site is change for the site.

To change is the third step towards the control of the site.

2. About consensus

2.1 Consultation

2.1.1

Nobody builds alone. Those who build must reach agreement about the position of the stones. The neighbors must agree about the position of the fence.

The members of the household must agree about the position of the chair.

Change of the site demands consultation.

2.1.2

People share the site.

To share brings out equilibrium. The equilibrium makes movement possible. To change the site demands consultation.

If the site persists without a consensus there is oppression. If the site changes without consensus there is conflict.

If consensus is not sought, conflict is unavoidable. As long as a conflict persists consensus is impossible. Only the lack of consensus is experienced.

2.1.3

The consultation relative to the site is about the identification and the position of space and material. The consultations rests on proposals about the possible position of identified spaces and material.

The consultation ends if a consensus is reached about space and material.

2.2 The four major questions

2.2.1

What stone should be placed and where should it be placed?
What space is needed and where will it be?
There are four questions that must always be answered in the process of consultation.
Those are the four major questions.

2.2.2

The four major questions are about the identification and the positioning of space and material:

What space?
Where?
What material?
Where?

2.2.3

The different parties must find the answer on these questions to reach a consensus. Only when the answers are found the situation can change in harmony.

The four major questions are the only questions that always must be answered if there is consultation.

2.3 A thousand other questions

2.3.1

A thousand other questions precede the four major questions. For each case those thousand other questions will be different. They will be different for each person. They are the reflection of the human condition: desires, dreams, fears, ideals, hopes, memories.

2.3.2

The thousand other questions must lead to the answer on the four major questions. Otherwise, they may be important for the actors, but they will be of no importance of the site: The site will not change.

What happens in our minds and hearts will only influence the site if it finally answers the four major questions.

As long as our thinking does not answer the four major questions, our thinking is of no importance of the site.

2.3.3

Some will praise the tree because of its fruits. Others will praise it for its shadow. Each has different reasons, but the tree can be planted.

No consensus is needed about the reasons to reach a consensus about the change of the site.

2.3.4

The thousand other questions lead to reasonings that support an answer to the four major questions.

Different reasonings can support the same answer.

2.3.5

A reasoning represents a value: To agree with the site is to express a value judgement. There is no relation between a value system and the site as long as the values do not answer the four major questions.

2.3.6

In the consultations about the site different goals can be reconciled by consensus on the answer to the four major questions.

No consensus is necessary about the goals to arrive at a consensus about the change of the site.

2.4 *Agreements*

People share the site. Each contributes to the common site by changing it. The shared site must be acceptable to all. The individual act that changes the site must be acceptable to all. This can be warranted by general agreements.

2.4.1

The agreements are based on experience:

> Man is part of nature.
> His acts form cyclic patterns.
> Problems return.

Each problem demands consensus once more. Consequences can be arrived at beforehand. Agreements are formulated: An agreement is consensus beforehand.

2.4.2

People who share a site are different. In the same site, the same problem is handled differently. By different people. But people are never totally different. Therefore, the different solutions have similarity: They are variations on a theme. The theme can be recognized in the site. The theme that is recognized becomes a framework for action.

Once the theme is formulated there is a rule.

2.4.3

Conversely:

> If a rule is formulated there is a framework for action. Within the framework actions generate variations on a theme. The variations show that people are different. The theme shows that a rule has been formulated.

2.4.4

If the rule does not reflect what people have in common, then the rule is perceived as coercion.

If the rule does reflect what people have in common, then the rule is perceived as acceptable.

Agreements are rules that are the result of consensus: they are experienced as freedom.

Only consensus brings the constraints that are perceived as freedom.

3. About systems

3.1 *Morphological systems*

3.1.1

In Amsterdam the houses along the canals have stoops. In Manhattan the streets run perpendicular to the Avenues. In France gardens are surrounded by walls.

In each site systems can be recognized: A system is a set of elements related to one another according to rules.

3.1.2

A system in which all elements are volumes is a morphological system. The systems that can be observed in the site are morphological systems. Their elements are material volumes and space volumes.

Some systems have only space elements while other systems have only material elements. Again, others have both material and space elements.

3.1.3

The relations between the elements of a morphological system concern the relative positions of those elements. Within the system the elements have only a spatial relationship.

3.1.4

Some morphological systems can be imagined that cannot be observed in reality. If, however, a morphological system is observed in reality, then it is a real system.

3.2 *Elements*

3.2.1

Doors, windows, houses, rooms, halls, gardens, balconies, streets, squares, alleys, joists, columns, stones, trees, pipelines, roofs, chimneys, stairs.

An element exists once it has a name. To have a name is the only prerequisite for an element to exist. The name is a matter of agreement. Elements exist because people agree.

Many names of elements define sets of elements. The name is alright as long as it can be determined whether an element belongs to that set or not. The set can be well defined or loosely defined. As long as

General principles about the way built environments exist

those involved can agree that an element belongs to a particular set, the name suffices. The existence of elements in the site therefore is dependent on those who are involved with the site. For different groups of people, the same site can be composed of different elements.

3.2.2

An element in a morphological system always is a volume.

There are material elements and space elements. Those who are involved determine whether an element is a space element or a material element relative to the way they observe the site.

A building is material as an element in the site. But the building can be seen as a composition of rooms: spaces.

The building can also be seen as a composition of walls. The material element in one system can itself be described as a variant from a space system.

3.2.3

A garden is a space as an element in the site. But the garden can be seen as a composition of trees, plants and shrubs. The garden itself can be described as a variant from a material system.

Elements themselves can be described as variants of a system. Systems are described by defining elements and their relation.

Every variant can make a site. Every site can be an element in a system.

3.4 Structure

3.4.1

The formal description of a system is the structure of that system. The structure of a system must describe what elements belong to the system and what position these elements may take in relation to one another.

3.4.2

By means of the structure, it can be determined whether a variant that is observed belongs to the system in question or not.

The structure of a system must allow us to determine whether in a specific variant:

a) All elements belong to the set of elements of the system: identification.
b) The elements as a group are allowed for in the system: selection.
c) The elements take the position relative to one another that is allowed for in the system: distribution.

3.4.3

If the structure is known, variants can be added that belong to the same system.

The structure of a system is what all possible variants of the system have in common.

3.4.4

The variant out of a system can change into another variant of the system without change of the structure. The structure of a system cannot change without changing many variants.

The change of the structure is demonstrated in the simultaneous change of the variants.

The structure is more permanent than the variants:

The invisible is more durable than the visible.

3.4.5

A structure is a matter of agreement. It formulates how we see an aspect of the site. The structure does not exist in the physical reality, it is the product of our thinking and our agreement.

4. About power

4.1 *Power*

4.1.1

The ability to change physical reality is power. The ability to change the site is power.

4.1.2

The site transforms by addition of objects, by elimination of objects, or by the change of the position of objects.

Who will decide that the tree in the street shall be cut down? The authority to eliminate objects is power.

Who will decide how the furniture in the room will be placed? The authority to change the position of objects is power.

Who will decide whether the fence shall be constructed? The authority to add objects is power.

4.1.3

An object that is part of a system is an element. A real element is part of a site. The ability to eliminate, transport or add a real element is power.

4.1.4

A real variant changes when the position of one of its elements is changed; when elements are added or when elements are eliminated. The ability to change a real variant is power.

Every change of the site by human action is the exercise of power.

4.2 Variants and power

4.2.1

An element is subject to a power if this power can change the position of that element or can eliminate the element or can add the element to a site.

A variant is subject to a power if all elements of the variant are subject to the power and if that power an eliminate or add elements to the variant.

4.2.2

A variant is subject to a number of powers if different elements of the variant are subject to different powers.

4.2.3

A variant that is subject to one power is a 'living' variant.

A living variant is always a real variant.

A living variant is a unity of power and morphology

A living variant is a unit of change and transformation.

4.2.4

A site can show many variants of the same system. Each variant can be subject to a different power. A site can show many different living variants.

The facades of the buildings along the canals in Amsterdam stand in one line, They form a continuous wall. The stoops in front of these houses never extend more than five feet. The inhabitants of Lexington, Massachusetts have no fences around their gardens. They mow their lawns regularly. In the Greek hill towns all houses are painted white.

Those who control a variant conform to the structure of the system to which the variant belongs.

Parties that conform to a higher order when they exercise their power in a given site create a site in which we recognize the variants of a system. This recognition allows for the formulation of a structure.

To control a variant is to conform to a higher order.

4.3 Structure and power

4.3.1

A power controls a structure if that power can change the structure.

A change of structure is a change of the rules that govern the selection and distribution of elements to make variants. A change of structure means that variants change too.

4.3.2

Variation occurs when different powers act: It is in the nature of systems that their variants are controlled by many different powers.

4.3.3

If a power changes the structure, then it forces the powers that control the variants to change their variants. The control of structure is the enforcement of constraints: rules, laws or customs.

The control of structure is the subjection of many powers to a higher power:

Structure reduces freedom.

4.3.4

A power that creates structure creates space for subordinate powers that will control the variants.

The creation of structure is the delegation of power: Structure gives freedom.

4.3.5

Those who fear to delegate power avoid structure.

4.3.6

Those who seek freedom must determine what structures are acceptable. Those who do not find structure to act in will not know freedom.

4.4 Systems and power

4.4.1

A system is a unity of structure and variants.
A system is a balance of power

4.4.2

A system is movement: the transformation of variants within the structure: the transformation of structure within the balance of power.

4.4.3

Will dare to put up the first fence around his open lawn in suburbia?

Sometimes the powers that control the variants of a system obey a structure that is not formally described nor formally controlled. The structure is embedded in customs and its control is by social pressure. The structure can be extracted by observation of the distribution of elements and the observation of social behavior when change occurs.

Such informal systems tend to be strong and durable. Their structure can change gradually over time.

4.4.4

The citizens in the 17th century New England towns held town meetings to decide on the rules for each of them to obey.

Sometimes the powers that control the variants obey a structure that they control jointly as one power, in a formal manner.

Such formal systems exist as along as the formal relations between equal powers hold. Their structures can change by formal agreement.

4.4.5

The village elder decides on the dispute between neighbors. Sometimes the powers that control the variants obey a structure that is controlled by a power that acts on their demands.

Such formal systems exist as long as the power that controls the structure is accepted.

Their structure can change by decision of the controlling power and the consent of the subject powers.

4.4.6

The Spanish king laid down the rules for town design in 16th Century America in "The Law of the Indies." Sometimes powers that control the various variants obey a structure that is beyond their influence.

Such formal systems exist as long as the power that controls the structure can hold its own. They last as long as their structure is perceived as just by the powers that control the variants.

4.4.7

It is in the nature of systems that their variants are controlled by different powers.

Systems are movement. Their stability in movement depends on the consensus of the powers that control the variants.

5. About relations

5.1 Relations of variants

5.1.1

When the street is widened, the gardens that line the street must go.

When the municipality changes its sewage system, I have to adjust the sewage in my home accordingly.

When the partitions in the office are rearranged, the arrangement of furniture must change, too.

A relation between two variants exists when the transformations of one variant are restricted by the presence of the other variant.

5.1.2

Suppose there are two variants: Va and Vb. If a transformation of Va is possible (within the structure of system a) in such a way that an element of Va could take the position now occupied by an element of Vb, then the transformations of Va are restricted by Vb and hence, a relationship between Va and Vb exists.

5.1.3

Suppose there are two variants: Va and Vb. When the position of an element of Va is dependent on the position of an element of Vb (e.g. because the element of Va must be connected to the element of Vb), then the transformations of Va are restricted by Vb and hence, a relationship between Va and Vb exists.

5.1.4

We recognize a relationship between two variants by observing their possible transformations. Change reveals the relationship. The exercise of power reveals the relationship.

5.2 Levels

5.2.1

When a relationship between two variants exists it is possible that the transformations of one variant causes the transformation of the other.

This will be the case when the displacement, addition, or removal of an element of the first variant causes the displacement, addition or removal of an element of the second variant.

5.2.2

The relative influence of one variant on another suggests two possible relationships between variants:

First case:

> A transformation of Va is possible that causes a transformation of Vb, but no transformation of Vb is possible that causes a transformation of Va.

In this case, we say that Va is a variant of a higher level that Vb.

5.2.3

Second case:

> A transformation of Va is possible that causes a transformation of Vb, whereas, also a transformation of Vb is possible that causes a transformation of Va. In this case we say that Va and Vb are variants on the same level.

5.2.4

When the street is widened the gardens along the street must change. Elements in the garden will be removed. The distribution of the remaining elements may become different.

In a garden along a street, elements can be removed or added or distributed differently without changing the position or dimension of the street.

The street pattern is a variant of a higher level than the arrangement in the gardens that border the street.

5.2.5

The houses in the city stand in a row adjacent to each other. The width of each house is restricted by the position of the two adjacent houses. Two houses adjacent to each other have a relation on the same level.

5.3 Relations on the same level

5.3.1

The houses along the street stand adjacent to each other. The width of each house is restricted by two adjacent houses.

There must be rules for the relation between the houses; e.g. No element may penetrate a neighbors' wall. No rainwater may be shed on a neighbors' roof. No windows may be made in a wall adjacent to which a neighbor may build another wall.

All houses must conform to these rules. All houses must be variants of a system, the. Structure of which embodies these rules.

To avoid conflict between powers that control variants of the same level, these variants must belong to a system that controls their relations.

5.3.2

The houses stand free from each other; each house stands on its own lot. The lots are distributed according to a certain pattern. They are elements in a system. Their selection and distribution form a variant from that system.

The houses must stand free from the lot boundaries for a given distance. The houses must be less than a certain height. A relation is formulated between the houses and the lots.

The powers that control the houses accept a variant of a higher system to separate the variants that they control themselves.

Higher systems yield variants that serve to separate systems on a lower level.

5.3.3

Powers controlling variants on the same level must either conform to a system that controls their variants and their mutual relationship or must accept the constraints of a higher-level variant to avoid a mutual relationship.

5.3.4

In both cases restrictions are accepted.

Two living variants on the same level must either be separated or must be part of the same system to avoid conflict.

5.4 Relations on different levels

5.4.1

The partitioning in the office space creates spaces in which different occupants can distribute furniture of a different selection according to their own wishes.

The partitioning constitutes a variant of a higher level that separates the lower variants.

The freedom of powers to manipulate their variants is assured by the creation of a variant of a higher level.

5.4.2

The partitioning in the office space does not affect the building structure itself. Different variants of partitioning can take place in the same building. Each portioning variant can change freely in the building.

The building is a variant in a system. It is a variant of a higher level than the partitioning variants.

5.4.3

There is a hierarchy of variants on different levels. There is a vertical order in which variants on different levels relate.

5.4.4

The network of local streets can change within the space created by the network of main roads in the city. The network of circulation in the city is connected to the network of highways in the state.

5.4.5

There is a hierarchy of circulation networks on different levels. There is a vertical order in which variants on different levels relate.

5.4.6

The water distribution feeds into the separate houses. The distribution of water in the house can change freely but it must connect to the distribution in the streets.

The distribution networks in the local streets is connected to the main network of the city.

There is a vertical order of distribution of resources in which variants on different levels relate.

5.4.7

There are different vertical orders to be observed in the site.

5.4.8

In a vertical order the variant on the higher level serves many variants on the lower level.

There is a proliferation of variants towards the lower levels.

5.4.9

The power that controls a variant on a lower level must accept the constraints posed by the variant on the higher level.

The powers that control the variant on the higher level has – within the vertical order of variants – power over those that control the lower variants.

5.4.10

There is a power balance between the powers on different levels. This balance resembles the power balance between the power that controls the structure of a system and the powers that control the variants of that same system.

The higher power can be constituted by the sum of the lower powers. The higher power can be dependent on the lower powers.

The higher power can be foreign to the lower powers.

When the balance of power knows no rules there is chaos.

When the balance is harmonious there is stability. When the balance is hostile there is oppression and rebellion.

5.4.11

Each variant of a higher-level imposes constraints on the selection and distribution of the elements that make the variants on the lower level. These constraints are similar in nature to the rules formulated by the structure of a system to which variants belong.

Therefore, it can be said that a variant on a higher level has structural properties in relation to variants on a lower level.

It is often said that such a variant is a structure, or that it has structural properties towards variants on the lower levels.

6. About organisms

6.1 *Organisms*

6.1.1

When I move into a barn with the things I call my own, the barn becomes my dwelling.

A dwelling is a volume in which a power resides with its belongings. It is a unity of power, material and space.

Any unit of power, material and space is an organism.

An organism is always one volume; one territory.

It contains all the material elements that are part of the organism.

All of these elements are controlled by one power.

An organism is part of the total physical reality. It is in itself a total physical reality.

6.1.2

Because an organism is controlled by one power it is a living part of the total physical reality.

Because it is part of the total physical reality, it is more than a living variant or even more than the sum of any number of living variants.

Although it knows order, we cannot describe an organism as a system in itself; it is always more.

If an organism would be a system in itself, then there would be a structure that determines what elements may or may not be part of that system. Such a structure is impossible because the power in the organism is always free to accept or reject new elements as part of the organism.

A system is a reduction of total reality for the sake of clarity and understanding. An organism is a total reality itself within the unit of a territory controlled by our power.

6.1.3

When, in a number of organisms, we observe certain similar configurations of elements, we recognize a system. We may succeed in formulating the structure of that system. We then can say that these organisms contain variants of that system. The variant from a system that is part of an organism is – by definition – a living variant. The power in the organism can accept variants of a system. It can transform them or reject them as a part of an organism.

6.1.4

A building is no organism.

A building may be a physical part of an organism: the house that stands on its own lot.

A building may maintain several organisms: as in an apartment building.

An organism may find its volume as part of a building. The material of that building that forms the volume of the organism is not necessarily part of the organism. It may be beyond the control of the power of the organism.

The tenants are not allowed to knock down a wall in their dwelling: Elements within the volume of an organism may not be part of the organism because the power cannot reject or replace them.

The extent of the organism reveals itself through the movement and change of elements as the result of intervention by its power.

6.1.5

The dwelling is an organism because it is a unity of volume, material and power. The room that belongs to the child may be such an organism as it reveals such unity.

A neighborhood may be an organism as it reveals such unity.

There are organisms on different levels. Elements in the organism on one level can be organisms themselves on a lower level. Every organism can be an element in an organism on a higher level. Organisms as part of the total physical reality or part of the continuity of space and material.

6.1.6

Organisms do not lend themselves to full description.
Every description is a reduction of reality.
Organisms do exist, but we cannot describe them fully.
We must speak of organisms lest we forget that systems are means.
While the goal is understanding of total reality which is impossible.

6.2 The distribution of territory

6.2.1

In an organism one power controls a territory.
The apartment has its party walls, the garden is surrounded by a hedge, the city has its marked boundaries, the new land is staked out; the deed is registered in the public records. Where territories meet, boundaries must be understood. There are rules according to which territories are divided.
The division of territories denotes a system, the structure of which must be understood to allow for change without chaos.

6.2.2

The territories must be accessible. Movement of goods and people must be possible. Organisms share a network of circulation spaces: roads, streets, alleys.
The space network is the variant of a system. The nature of the system determines the distribution of territories or organisms that share the network.
The garden path leads from the street to the door. The corridor leads from the door to the rooms. Within the organism there is a circulation variant that is connected to the variant of circulation outside the organism. The two variants are on different levels.
The circulation variants within different organisms are connected with each other by a circulation variant on a higher level. Organisms share a space network outside their territories.

6.2.3

The child has its own room. There it finds its own toys. The child and its room and its toys are an organism.

The family lives in the house. It has its belongings in the house. There is a unity of power, space and material.
The town has its territory. It maintains its own infrastructure and it is governed by the city council. There is a unity of space, material and power.
The room is in the house which is in the town: Organisms can contain other organisms.
An organism can contain a circulation network. That network can be connected to a network of a higher level that is part of another organism of which also the first organism is a part.

6.2.4

The room inhabited by the child is the territory of an organism. Not all spaces in the house are organisms by themselves. There is a kitchen and a living room. There are spaces that are shared by all its inhabitants. Some spaces in the organism are territories of organisms, some are not. Of those that are not, some are communal spaces, some are circulation spaces, and some are both.

6.2.5

The citizens of the town have connected their territories by a network of circulation spaces. They also have joint activities. They assemble to trade, to play and to worship. There are spaces for common use: the marketplace, the village green, the town hall, the church. The town as an organism contains different spaces. Some are territories of other organisms, some are not.

6.2.6

An organism may contain three kinds of spaces:

1. Territories of other organisms
2. Networks to serve these territories
3. Spaces for common use of all inhabitants.

6.2.7

The distribution of space reveals some systems. But it serves organisms.

6.3 Distribution of material

6.3.1

In an organism one power controls material.
The power is free to admit or reject material into the territory of the organism: material goes in and out.

6.3.2

The house is part of the organism. It is part of the material that belongs to the organisms.

The house has similarities with the other houses in the neighborhood. These are similar materials and similar elements.

These are similar ways in which the elements are put together: in which the elements are distributed in space. People share resources: hence the use of similar elements.

People share values and habits: hence the similar distribution of elements in space.

Because people share resources and values and habits the houses reveal variants of systems the structures of which can be formulated.

Organisms contain variants of material systems because their power share resources and values.

6.3.3

Water comes through pipes.

In an organism there are networks to distribute material and energy. The network in the organism is the variant of a system.

6.3.4

The network in the organism connects to a network outside. There are two variants on different levels.

The network in the organism is part of a vertical order.

Organisms contain variants to link themselves to outside sources that are shared with other organisms.

6.3.5

Within an organism, variants of different systems are combined. Some of the variants are material, some are spatial. Some variants are networks, some are not.

It is characteristic for an organism that it contains a number of variants from quite different systems. The combination makes sense to the organism.

6.3.6

Within an organism, variants of different systems are combined.

Each variant is a link with the world outside the organism.

An organism contains variants in so far as it is connected with the world outside.

6.3.7

An organism can contain lesser organisms.

These organisms share the networks in the higher organisms.

An organism contains variants to serve lesser organisms.

6.3.8

Insofar as material is admitted in an organism to serve a relation with the outside world, insofar will the material reveal in its combination the variants of the systems.

Insofar as the material in an organism is admitted to serve the lesser organisms that are contained in the first, insofar will that material reveal the variety of systems.

The sum of all the material in an organism, however, is always more than the sum of its material variants.

6.4   Distribution of power

6.4.1

In an organism, one power controls a number of variants of different systems.

6.4.2

The variant within an organism belongs to a system. The structure of that system cannot be controlled by the power that controls the organism.

There is a balance of power that takes many forms.

6.4.3

The material that is accepted by an organism is produced by a power outside the organism.

There is a balance of power that can take many forms.

6.4.4

There is a balance of power between organisms.

The higher organism controls the variants that serve the lower organism.

The higher organism may control the structure of the system from which the lower organism uses variants.

Systems are the vehicle for the balance of power between organisms.

6.4.5

Some powers control organisms. Some powers control systems. There is a difference of interest. When the systems do not serve the organisms, the organisms will suffer.

6.4.6

The street in the neighborhood is controlled by the municipality that will control the repairs of the pavement or the cutting of trees. The owner-occupant of a historic house may not be allowed to alter its facade.

The heating in the apartment is controlled by the management.

The variant within the territory of an organism may be controlled by an outside power

Then the variant is no longer part of the organism.

When the variant that is controlled by an outside power exists in the territory of an organism there is reason for conflict. The outside power will find its control restricted because it does not control the site in which the variant is distributed.

Those who control the organism find a foreign body in its territory. When two powers dispute the control of a variant the variant becomes a dead variant.

6.4.7

When an outside power controls the structure of a system, the organism can control the variant of that system; then there is a balance of power based on agreement.

When an outside power controls the variant itself, the organism finds a foreign body in its territory. The organism becomes weaker.

6.4.8

It is the nature of systems that their variants are controlled by many different powers. When the powers that control these variants are powers that control organisms, the variants will be part of organisms.

When the power that controls the variants are powers that do not control the organisms in which the variants find themselves, then the variants will only exist for the sake of the system.

6.4.9

When an organism finds many variants in its territory that it cannot control, most of the material within the organism will be dead. An organism is a unity of material, space and power. If the material is dead, there can be no organism. There will only be a power in space surrounded by foreign material. The material will only exist for the sake of the power that produces it. Those who produce the material will determine the existence of the material. The selection of the material will be determined by its production.

Life will be separated from material.

0 End

0.1

The existence of the built environment rests on mutual understanding and action.

To build is to act together.

The use of material demands the division of resources. The distribution of material means reconciliation of conflicting interest. The combination of materials in space follows agreements and laws. The manipulation of material knows customs and rules.

People live together by sharing space. They share space by dividing it. Space is divided by material; by the act of building.

The division of space means reconciliation of conflicting interests. The management of space rests on agreements and laws. The use of space knows customs and rules.

A house that is not occupied will decay. A town, abandoned by its inhabitants, will return as dead matter into nature's cycle.

What has been built exists only by human effort. It will only continue to exist by such effort.

1984
THE GENERAL FROM THE LOCAL

Editors' Note: *This is an edited version of the author's keynote address for the 8th International Forum of the European Association for Architectural Education, Newcastle upon Tyne, England, April 13, 1983. The author had already been Head of the Department of Architecture at MIT from 1975–81 and remained teaching there, providing an international perspective on the education of architecture students from around the world. This essay was published in Places; volume 1, number 4, Spring 1984*

There used to be a time, not so long ago, when students from developing countries were admitted to western European and North American schools to learn things the western way. Both teachers and students were convinced that this was a good thing to do: developing countries could best develop by applying the western ways. There was no alternative.

We have lost that innocence. On both sides we know now that the issues are much more complex. It is not just a question of transfer of knowledge, skills, and technology from one place where there is plenty to another where more is needed.

In developing countries westernization is seen as a mixed blessing at best. Among the younger generations there is a renewed interest in their cultural heritage. They see how local customs and forms disappear rapidly to make place for an image of western affluence, wellbeing, and power that stands for the state of "being developed." Others in the western world share their concern. Is there a way, we have come to ask, to be developed and yet not westernized?

At the same time architects from developed countries have become involved. Professional expertise has gone international and much of it has to do with the Third World. Consultants of all kinds come with government aid programs, with commercial projects, and at the request of local authorities. In such contacts clarity and simplicity are sometimes lost. The dilemmas of the Third World architects who returned to their country after a western education are now shared by many of their colleagues in Europe and the United States.

It is, however, not only in Third World relationships that the western architects and architectural educators question their responsibilities and their roles. Within the context of the western European tradition itself questions are raised as well.

Indeed, one could, with a little effort, advance a plausible argument that we have no business to educate people from other cultures, that we had better first deal with our own problems. I am opposed to that idea of retrenchment for reasons that I will explain, but you may agree with me that we are far removed from the happy times when we felt that we had something indispensable to offer to those who had the misfortune to be born in another part of the world.

Of course, architectural education in the west cannot ignore the Third World. There are many good reasons of political, economic, ethical, and even philosophical nature to say this. Not in the least there is the practical expectation that a growing number of western students in architecture will, in the course of their careers, become involved with Third World questions either directly or indirectly. It will not hurt at all when they can study with Third World colleagues with whom they may work in the future.

But I believe that there are other reasons for connecting education to Third World problems. These are of a more intellectual nature and they have to do with the future of our profession as a whole.

I firmly believe that our profession will only have a future if it can deal with a profound and central question that comes from an interaction between architects from both sides of the world.

I am talking about the following question. What is generally valid and generally applicable in the field of architecture? A profession can only be a profession when it shares certain principles, theories, and methods that it holds as valid and useful in all circumstances and in all places. What are the shared principles, theories, and methods in architecture? If we cannot answer this with a reasonable degree of consensus, we will not have a profession and we will continue to lose credibility in a rapidly changing world.

I am talking about the following question. What is generally valid and generally applicable in the field of architecture? A profession can only be a profession when it shares certain principles, theories, and methods that it holds as valid and useful in all circumstances and in all places. What are the shared principles, theories, and methods in architecture? If we cannot answer this with a reasonable degree of consensus, we will not have a profession and we will continue to lose credibility in a rapidly changing world. This question, which I hold to be fundamental, can easily be ignored in a homogeneous culture where practice is in harmony with its context. It becomes unavoidable, however, when such practice is confronted with a different cultural context. The best reason that I can see for the education of Third World students in European schools is that such education forces us to sort out what is universally valid and applicable in architecture. It makes us define the field. It is good for architecture everywhere.

The making of buildings and settlements is, by definition, a local affair. Architecture is the making of the right building at the right moment in the right place. It is an act that can never repeat itself in the same way. It is intimately connected to local conditions, customs, climate, culture, and resources. We are interested in the enormous range of possible contexts, the variety of social, cultural, technical, and economic conditions within which architecture must come about. What can we bring to bear in all circumstances and all places that may be helpful and effective?

When this question comes up, as it inevitably does when one contemplates the state of architecture today, I often think of another discipline in which the tensions between the local and the general must be relevant too. I refer to agriculture. There is nothing more local than the raising of crops. To farm is to attach oneself to a piece of land. Certain plants only grow in certain places. To make them grow the farmer must know the place. Architecture, the art of settlement, is like that. It is not only that the building must serve local needs. This functional argument is much too limited. The building must be built by local workers, it must perform in a local climate, it may use local materials, and it must honor local codes. Therefore, it must be nursed into existence in harmony with all these factors.

A successful project is cultivated locally. But the act of building is also an instance in a continuous process of change and renewal by means of which built environments live and prosper. If this analogy with farming is acceptable, what then, we must ask, may the cultivation of the built environment share dispersed as they are across the far corners of the world?

Agriculture is a professional field. It studies the nature of plants, their properties, metabolism, and chemistry. It also concerns ways of cultivation and their relation to local conditions. It must also have to do with the exercise of appropriate judgment in time and place. It may be that other families always seem to be happier than one's own, but I tend to think that we have not come that far yet in architecture. We have not yet separated that clearly the local from the universal. Unlike the farmer, who, I suspect, knows what he is doing, the architect is often conf used about his role in the world. We like to debate a variety of images of what an architect is and what he does. We think of the architect as an artist, a reformer, an organizer, a mediator, an orchestrator. We borrow from many fields: science, sociology, psychology, technology, linguistics, economic and most recently, anthropology. But who and what are we ourselves?

Let me offer my simple conviction. I believe that the architects' business is built form. He must understand it and be capable of organizing it. To be sure, the built environment is a social artifact. Everybody understands it in an implicit way. It does not exist by the grace of architects but will exist as long as people inhabit the earth. Built form is not our exclusive product but it is the subject of our expertise. The architect may be more sensitive to built form than the layman and she may be very skillful in her manipulation, but these qualities are not enough to establish his expertise among the many other professionals who have an impact on the built environment. It is also necessary that an architect understands form in an explicit, codified way; understand the deployment of materials in space, the organization of space itself as a vehicle for behavior, for power, for territorial organization, for self-expression, and for collective coherence among people. In this way the general must emerge from local experience.

This professional understanding of form, it seems to me, must come to us in two major ways: we need, first of all, *theories* that formulate this shared understanding of form. These theories must explain to us the *behavior of form* under the pressures of habitation and social interaction in the context of technology, climate, and topography. Through the continuous shaping and reshaping of such theories the large amount of facts already available about built environments can become comprehensive and useful to the architectural profession. In time our theories may point toward new questions and help focus a search for new data. They may contribute to the general study of human settlements that we share with other disciplines.

Second, there are ways of working. *Methods of design* and *form manipulation* can be developed and studied. We can learn from a comparison of methods and can seek general principles as well. Methods are, of course, related to theory. Implicitly or explicitly they rest on theory. They link theory to practice as they shape the processes taking place. The application of a method tests its underlying theory. Shortcomings of methods lead to new theoretical work. Hence the international discourse that we seek must lead toward theory and methodology. I have argued that in the comparison of different local problems we will find what we share in our professions. I will try to make my point by applying it. Let us consider the educational needs of a Third World student in architecture with those of his fellow student from a western country.

To begin with there is what can be called the question of conflicting values. Our Third World, we all know, is torn between the values of the western world as these are reflected in products, styles, and criteria that he learns about, and the indigenous spaces, forms, and materials that represent his own tradition. Chances are, when he comes home to practice his profession, his position is not shared by those be must work with or wants to work for regardless of what that position may be. The ramifications are many. Background, religion, family, peer group, economic means, career expectations, and political motivations all contribute to the inescapable awareness that the world of architecture is not one of homogeneous value.

Our western student will not operate in a world of homogeneous values either. I do not mean to say that the West does not have different cultures and traditions, but even the architect who stays within his own country finds himself trying to operate in at least three separate value systems at the same time.

There is, first of all, the professional world: the peer group system. It manifests itself in magazines and other publications, at professional conferences, and especially in our teaching. It is a double-edged sword. On the one hand, it demands that our student becomes a "leader" in the eyes of his peers. There is only true prestige and glory in the eyes of the profession itself. He is expected to look down on bureaucrats, lawyers, and technicians who are believed to hamper quest for architectural excellence and is encouraged to treat clients and users with benevolent paternalism. On the other hand, he must obtain this professional glory by finding his own "voice." Above all, he must be original. To be good in architecture is to be different, or at least to be part of the latest development. The worst is to be accused of doing something already done by someone else.

When this student enters the world, he will find that his client is unaware of the values within the architects' profession. He has his own notions about good and bad. The client today, moreover, is seldom the user of the building. The users themselves may have their own value system that is different from that of client and architect. I do not have to elaborate further. The western student will never operate in a homogeneous value system either.

It is useless, obviously, when considering an educational program, to try to decide what is the right value system. It is also foolish, obviously, to try to create an artificially homogeneous value system in a school. Most of our educational system as well as our professional skills still stem from a distant past where a homogeneous value system shared by all parties involved could reasonably be expected. Because we refuse to see the discrepancy between this professional tradition and today's reality, we fall hopelessly short in professional and educational effectiveness. It takes a confrontation with the problems of the Third World to acknowledge this discrepancy.

Some may argue that technology is an even more important aspect of the relation between developing and developed nations. When we talk about development we think about technology. We believe that our culture need not be superior to another. We want to live in a world of different cultures. But what really separates nations is their control over technology. Western European technology has triggered the serious imbalance with which we now must deal in the world. We know the devastating impact that can come from a single-minded application of new technologies on the subtle but vulnerable ways in which traditional materials and building systems are integrated with house form, lifestyle, and climate. We know how people can suffer from well-intended attempts to modernize the built environment.

Some argue that inevitably modern technology will take over from traditional ways and that a price must be paid. Others argue that technology is basically neutral: that any form can be made in different ways and that performance has more than one solution. There is no reason, from that point of view, to condemn technology as long as one knows it well and contains it. Still others argue that technology consists not only of materials and engineering principles but of ways of working that are inevitably linked with forms of organization and, therefore, with social structure. Hence, import of technology is import of social structure that is inevitably disruptive.

There is, of course, truth in all these positions. We are only slowly beginning to understand the complex relationships between ways of making, social organization, and cultural value. One thing, however, is clear. The architect who operates in developing countries will not operate in a homogeneous building system. His abilities of form making cannot depend on just one way of building.

But his colleagues in the West have already wrestled with this problem for a long time. The age of industrialization brought a proliferation of materials and building techniques. The architect and the engineer parted long ago. I believe that there is a causal relation between the ideology of abstract form in modern architecture – the international style – and the proliferation of new materials and ways of building that took place in the beginning of this century. But this is not the moment to explore this interesting connection.

Because of that ideology, however, we have been able to avoid the problem in theoretical and methodical terms. The question of form making in a technically diverse world is dearly felt yet remains unexplored. There is no explicit, rational debate. Architectural education has not come to grips with the issue either. There is the design studio and there is the building technology workshop. They have no common theory of form making and remain in an uneasy relation to one another as do the architect and the engineer.

In the western world we have been able to circumvent the problem for much longer than we can rightly afford to. In the Third World we can no longer ignore it. To teach our student from the Third World we must come to grips with an issue that is equally important for his friend in Europe.

It is not uncommon that we come to see our own problems better when we first study those of our neighbors. The case of mass housing is another example. In Europe, particular socioeconomic conditions coupled with a rapid increase of the urban population and the devastation caused by World War II brought forth extensive deployments of repetitious blocks composed of uniform units. They were the result of the belief that the good environment for the modern citizen could be provided by massive infusions of capital, expertise, and centralized organization. The underlying ideology was that decent living for all was, first of all, a matter of professional responsibility: a gift from those who "knew' and 'could' bestowed on those who were 'unable' and 'ignorant.'

This was a powerful dream. However, it was a typically technocratic dream and when transported to developing countries its futility as a general solution became painfully clear. No government, no matter how rich, can provide ready-made dwellings to all its citizens. The only hope for decent shelter for all is to encourage people to develop their own. For some 20 years now in Latin America, the Middle East, and the Far East, and more recently in Africa, architects and other professionals have been involved in a slow and difficult learning process. They have come to share the basic understanding that a built environment must be cultivated first of all by those who inhabit. People have always built for themselves, but they need professional help. This worldwide experiment entailed a radical change of professional attitude vis-a-vis the built environment because the western European model, which was taught for so long in architectural schools, was diametrically opposed to the idea of gradual cultivation.

The case of mass housing is a good example of a problem in which the experience of many in very different locations around the world seems to lead to a consensus among experts about some general principles. The western student will benefit from study of what is done in some Third World countries and what is advocated by such international agencies as the World Bank. His Third World counterpart would learn from alternative approaches that are now tried out in the West.

We can now see the central issue with which the architecture profession must wrestle if it wants a future for itself. The question of conflicting values, the problem of a variety of ways of building, and the issue of housing for the masses are each part of a conflict of two professional models. The first model is the one that we have inherited from the western European architectural tradition. In this model the architect is seen primarily as the maker of the exceptional product, for an exceptional occasion, and for exceptional use. Even in residential construction it sees the architect as the maker of monuments: buildings that by their very existence must transcend time and must symbolize special values. In this traditional model the architect shared his client's values. The user was not known as a separate power, and skills and trades operated in a homogeneous technical system known by all. This professional image may have been appropriate in the past, but today it offers a hopelessly obsolete model.

The alternative model sees the architect engaged in the cultivation of the everyday environment that was taken for granted in the past. In this model the result is not static but must change and grow over time. It is not an exception to but reality itself. It is full of meaning but not a symbol for society. This alternative model of the professional role is based on the awareness that monuments will eventually grow in a healthy built environment, yet that a healthy built environment can never be made out of monuments. This simple truth has been revealed to many of us, but it is still not generally understood. European architects were the first to declare their concern for the quality of the everyday environment. The Chartre d'Athenes architects saw everything that was built – the dwelling, the factory, the railroad station – as important and worth their attention. However, the sad reality is that we never examined the attitude necessary to deal with the everyday environment. We continued to approach all these new and exciting problems as we approached the problem of building the exceptional. Classic symbolism was replaced by technological symbolism and is now traded for historic reference. Avant-gardism, form ideology, and, above all, peer group approval remained the yardsticks for professional esteem. They are still, when all is said and done, the formal criteria in education. We may have abolished the beaux arts way of working, but we have not abandoned the dream of professional achievement as it was enshrined in the academy. Our genuine concern for the built environment as a whole is not matched by our behavior, methods, or skills. The reasons for this ambivalent attitude are, of course, part of the broader dilemma of modern professionalism: when does expertise nourish the common good?

We must ask ourselves whether we ca n afford to be confused much longer. But I believe one thing is certain. The challenges of the Third World will bring forth a new practitioner more in tune with the intelligence, sensitivity, and under standing necessary to do a good job for the everyday environment. The new role model will come into its own. It will be equally valid for the architect in the developed countries as it is for his colleague in the Third World. The question of course is *how* it will come about.

Will the Third World eventually produce this new architect in spite of westernized education, or will it be the result of a joint effort to deal with the realities of the built environment rather than with the dreams of an obsolete profession? Who, indeed, will learn from whom?

1988
LIVES OF SYSTEMS

Editor's Note: *This is Chapter 3.2 in an informally published book Transformations of the Site (Awater Press, 1988), a book which later became the author's seminal The Structure of the Ordinary: Form and Control in the Built Environment. MIT Press, 1998).*

The great architectural traditions in the world all had their organizations of those who knew the secrets of the trade. There is a direct linkage between the structures of their physical systems and the social bodies that knew how to make them. Members were often sworn to secrecy and, once initiated, tied to their brotherhood for life. The knowledge that they shared was secured by a formal social bondage with its own rules and rituals. Yet, the Maestri Comacini and the masons who build the cathedrals may not only have been exceptional in the sophistication of their products but also in the nature of their associations. We may assume that the closed societies who guarded their knowledge so jealously were themselves formalizations of what originally existed in a more open and general way. Architecture as a high art always grows from the vernacular. What is interesting about truly vernacular systems is exactly that the interaction between the knowledge of the tradesman and the knowledge of the layman is still very open and fluid. There may be secrets, but they will be revealed to anyone who really wants to know. The way of building is still the fruit of common knowledge and experience, but its quality may depend on a smaller class of men who have devoted their lives to a thorough mastery of it. It is one of the characteristics of the vernacular that a distinction between expert and layman can be made, but that they can communicate and appreciate each other's role. The layman can admire, but also judge the expert's work, whereas the expert values that judgement and the guidance that it gives him in his quest for excellence.

Someday we must be better equipped to chart the mutations and variations of vernacular species throughout the history of human settlement, or at least be able to indicate a way to engage in such a task and to suggest a taxonomy of what can be discovered.

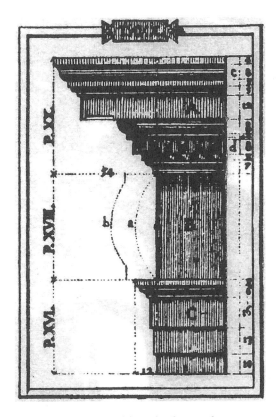

Figure 1 A column capital from the classic order

DOI: 10.4324/9781003011385-10

Whatever classification such a study may yield, however, it must recognize the two major technical ways: the one that builds in wood and the one that builds in stone. Of the wood building vernaculars that can be named the latest and perhaps the most dynamic is without any doubt the North American stick-building tradition that came into its own in the early nineteenth century and presently forms the shelter for the majority of the population in the United States and Canada.

It is a true vernacular, a way of building understood by all, but at the same time subject to constant change and perfection through application of the latest known technology. One only has to walk into one of the do-it-yourself shops run by numerous chains, or to look at their advertisements to realize the extent to which the construction of the whole house including its services and equipment is the result of one coherent implicit order complete with its systems in an established hierarchy, with a rich array of elements and parts, materials and components that can be combined in endless variety on each level.

The system has changed a great deal in the course of time, but there is also remarkable continuity. The sash window of a house built two hundred years ago, for example, is indeed different from the window sold today, but its details are still known, and the essential hardware needed to put it together is still available in the hardware store around the corner.

It is interesting to note that exactly this type of window, with similar details, although larger in size, is found in the seventeenth century facades along the canals in the towns of the Dutch republic, where it probably originated. Thus, the balloon frame system of the nineteenth century in North America employed elements that were developed earlier and has itself changed considerably in its life of about a century and a half.

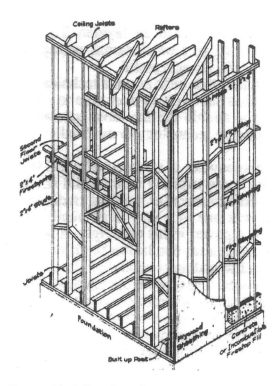

Figure 3 The balloon frame house construction in the US, which came into existence in the 1830's

Figure 2 Example of a catalogue from a home-project center

It is exactly those changes within continuity that are of interest. There are two major reasons to examine the rapid development of this young but fully developed vernacular. First, because its changes have been caused to a considerable degree by the development of industrial production that occurred roughly in the period of its existence. Second, because it offers us an opportunity to study the conditions apparently favorable for a vernacular in our own modern times.

Whatever the changes may have been to which it has been subjected in the course of time, the North American wood vernacular always had two things that are essential to it: the "two by four" and a dimensional module. The length of wood of a standardized cross section was by itself the result of industrial thinking. It lent itself to mass production and mass distribution. It was, as the basic component, small enough to be handled by one person, to be shipped easily and be cut out of any light timber available on the continent. This required it to be placed at close intervals into a light, space enclosing frame that derived its stiffness from the siding across its members. Today the "two by four" is less than two by four inches, and the module is now sixteen inches instead of the original two feet. Hence even standard dimensions have changed over time, but the principle has stayed the same.

The modest dimensions of the "two by four" and the sixteen-inch center to center placement must go together. They make a mode of construction with a module of measurement all in one. This combination of basic element and unit of measurement is also found in the brick as it was used in the Northern part of Europe. The size of the brick plus the mortar joint makes the module. For centuries the "header" of the brick was the module in which buildings were measured.

The module of the wood frame is manifest in the carpenter's square by means of which the craftsman can measure and size all the wood needed for the structure from basement to roof without any further knowledge of geometry. This method, as elegant in its simplicity as it is sophisticated, has been informally developed in the course of time. It is easy to learn by anyone with the ability to think in three dimensions and takes less time than any other way to figure the dimensions of the various parts.

Around these basic principles the elaborate system we know today has grown and, as new materials and new technologies developed in an industrialized world, many parts were subsequently added, and others were changed. What used to be lath and plaster is now a mass marketed product called "dry wall," a gypsum sheet that can be nailed or screwed on and needs little more finish than paint or wallpaper. Screws are now driven in with electric powered screwdrivers. They need no hole to be driven in as they cut themselves into the wood.

Plywood, a product that can only be produced in mechanized plants, is now used to cover the outside under the siding. It is attached to the two-by-fours by means of nails or staples that are driven in with a "gun." Within the wall aluminum foil and glass-wool 'batts' are placed for better insulation; both the fruits of industrial mass production and technology. Bathroom tiles are available in plastic as well as in earth-ware and they are placed by means of a two-component adhesive which is the product of industrial chemical processes. These tiles are placed on thin cementitious sheets that can be cut with an ordinary saw, like wood, and nailed or screwed in place. And so on. The system as it now exists would undoubtedly amaze the nineteenth century craftsmen, yet they would recognize it immediately as the one they used to work with.

There is no conflict between the most advanced industrial mass production of components and an implicit, vernacular system. The products of modern research and technology, based on costly and elaborate machinery and materials that were unknown one or two generations back are easily manipulated by craftsmen and laymen alike. This is no coincidence. The industrial and technical innovations, a few of which I described above, are the result of a concerted and sustained effort in the last two decades to drive prices down and quality up in two ways: industrial mass production in the factory, and reduction of labor on the site. As skilled labor was expensive, the new products not only had to make the building better but had to make it easier to be built. In fact, building had to be so easy that anyone who could drive in a nail or hold an electric drill could be hired. The result was that the system became more and more accessible to the layman. The do-it-yourself market was an unintended offspring of a professional attempt to produce good and cheap products that was only too successful.

We see now, in the stick-built house, a technical system that is shared by expert and layman, that has evolved over time to a high level of technical sophistication, making available the most specialized achievements in material science and building technology to the dweller homeowner as well as the craftsman.

This dweller homeowner is an essential agent in the development of the system, because the home building industry did not develop this implicit system out of interest in a vernacular building tradition. The market that it found for its products was one of a very large number of small, individual, buyers. Each of them is a power in their own right. It was a market for on-site construction of very many houses that had to be different from each other. This meant that only the smallest and most neutral of elements could have a chance to become part of all houses. These were the elements that the industrialist is interested in: elements that can be produced in very large numbers to serve a very large market. Hence the fragmentation of the market and the resulting variety of forms was perfectly compatible with industrial mass production of materials and elements. In fact, it was an incentive.

Moreover, the buildings that had to be produced on the site had to be adaptable. They would each be under control of a separate owner-user, who, more likely than not, would insist on his own interpretation, and also, because the system is manipulatable, would expect to improve on it in the future by gradual transformation. If you cannot control those who build, you cannot dictate their product. If you want them to use your product it should be so general that it allows them maximum freedom of composition.

When we consider this fruitful relationship between the dictates of industrial mass-production and the desire of many small user-builders to do their own we should not be confused by the evident uniformity of the suburban tract house. The distinction between industrial production, prefabrication and onsite assembly must be understood. Builder-developers, even when they have a very large project, produce by on-site assembly a series that is much too small to have any meaning for true industrial production. They must use an already available way of building. They will, however, try to repeat the same design as much as possible, because it is easier to control and plan the on-site assembly of a hundred of the same units than to have a hundred different ones. The vernacular system by itself is easily capable of producing a hundred different interpretations, but the developer, wanting to economize effort, will seek uniformity. The buyers, on the other hand, looks for the design that is closest to what they would put together themselves, if given a chance. The developer, in the face of this conflict of interest, finally produces a mixture of restricted variations with its "options" and "custom made additions." The tension is therefore not between the off-site manufacturer and the homeowner but between the on-site developer and the would-be user. True mass production by industrial means calls for such large numbers that no on-site series can ever be large enough to pay for the marketing of a component that takes years of research, innovation, testing and tooling.

Industrial production has therefore been successful in the realm of materials and small size components of so general a nature that every house builder can use them. The North American continent was large enough to stimulate a sustained effort of research and development. The implicit two-by-four system, generally known and used everywhere, offered the context in which industrial innovation could take place to be assured of a universal market. A market of resident homeowners, each insisting on their own separate interpretation, made the vernacular of interest to both developer and builder. Although builders sought uniformity the system always allowed them to compromise when the market required them to do so. They never had to invest in any large-scale manufacturing. Their job was one of specification and assembly in a generally known system, never to take the risk of developing one of their own.

Those producers who ignored the qualities of this extremely sophisticated and elaborate implicit system by trying to create their own-possibly guided by the myth that "systems" somehow have to be nontraditional-invariably paid the price of failure. In an age where a living tradition like a vernacular seemed to have no merit for an international technical elite, many of those who were smart enough to stay with it anyway felt that they had to apologize for it. Somehow this was not "industrial building." It took the monumental failure of a government-initiated competition for experimental "industrialized" systems called "Operation Breakthrough" to convince everyone in the United States that the traditional way of working, with its "small" improvements, is hard to beat. The lesson may have been learned but it is not yet really understood. The American vernacular is not recognized as a most interesting development of industrial production. Much less is it understood that this was possible not in spite of, but because of the existence of a generally accepted and applicable implicit system. The industrialization of the North American vernacular is one of the best kept secrets in the world of settlement studies.

Anyone who has had the opportunity to see from the air the vast surfaces covered with row upon row of wooden houses must conclude that the successful industrialization of a vernacular that allowed the rapid assembly of these houses did not enrich the quality of their large-scale deployment. The drive for a mass market led to a single-minded concentration on the nuclear family as the ideal unit to be recognized and served. The smallest client is the largest in number and therefore compatible to a mass market approach. This commercial motivation did not have much attention for the neighborhood as a whole. On that level no market for mass production of components can be identified. Whatever quality the neighborhood can have must come by way of territorial-local-development and attention.

If we go into the streets of suburbia itself, however, leaving aside deficiencies on the neighborhood level we will quickly discover that the houses on their lots are not only the result of one technical system but the articulation of a value system as well. This implicit system has its rules on selections and distribution of elements as clearly as any vernacular. It has to do with the house itself, with its position on the lot and the treatment of the space around it. The house stands in the middle of the lot, yielding a good deal of front yard for public scrutiny and dividing the space between neighbors equally. It has a lawn that should be kept with great care, and it has shrubs and bushes particularly placed so as to hide the foundations. The total effect is one of delightful contradictions; there is a strong suggestion of a building placed in a natural landscape: there are no fences nor formal flowerbeds or any geometric patterns. But there is also the discipline of the artificial; the clipped bushes around the house and the well-kept lawn. The position of the house in the middle of the lot with due emphasis on the front yard is typical for the suburban house of the modern Western European middle-class culture. The lack of any fence or garden wall either in front or to the side, the studious avoidance of any overt expression of territorial boundary is a typical American variant and a diversion of the otherwise worldwide rule that the territory be explicitly marked and protected.

Thus, the North American system suggests the wide open prairie in which the lone house stands. No matter that the neighbor in suburbia is only twenty yards way, one should not be fenced in nor offend outsiders by preventing them from looking in. Thus held up, the image of openness and vast expanses creates, of course, the opposite effect. The suburban environment without fences, once buildings get closer, becomes one of inevitable social interaction. Two territories of the same level don't want to mix with one another. Where there is no physical separation, continuous vigilance is needed to keep the elements belonging to each apart. Cats, dogs and children must stay within invisible boundaries. No random elements subject to purely private activities should lie around to mar the systemic interaction of a shared vernacular. Continuous signals by the way of greetings, gestures and little courtesies must be emitted to ascertain that all is well. Where distance decreases, tensions increase, and social control extends.

Such generalizations about the American suburban value system do no justice to the many differences in its forms that can be witnessed from region to region. A serious study would be justified to rescue it from the disdainful remarks of those of us who are happy to have escaped its limitations. What we see is remarkable. An implicit system of great strength that in a relatively short period of time covered a larger area than perhaps any other vernacular in history.

Like its technical counterpart, the suburban spatial system could develop by virtue of a culture of small powers in their own territories sharing similar values. What we see is not uniformity but conformity. We see variety within shared constraints where even the individual action of the house owner is possible. The suburban territorial powers choose to exercise their control within the confines of a strict rule system, never codified but understood by all. What is worth our attention is not that in many cases the developer puts down rows of exactly similar houses, but that variety appears when the inhabitants take over, exploiting the true potential of the vernacular.

Vigorously maintained over several generations, that vernacular is now changing, as all implicit systems do when conditions change. Change of implicit systems is always gradual and piecemeal. They never disappear overnight, nor do they jump into existence full-blown and new. They develop and grow with the social fabric that nurtures them and with the technical innovations that they are a context for. As they represent a kind of collective image of what building and environment are all about they are the visible token of human coordination and at the same time the framework shared by everyone.

Implicit systems representing people's values have been classified to a certain extent in the form of styles and fashions particularly when they gave birth to extraordinary aesthetic achievements. As the context for technical innovation and perfection, as the soil in which ideas grow, as the matrix in which ideas are tested, they have, to my knowledge, never been studied. Yet there seems to be evidence in abundance that it is in such frameworks of collective understanding, that technology in building is developed. In the typical fashion of living things, the implicit system is both the product and the context of technical innovation.

One cannot conceive of a concrete block without the image of "the wall" as part of "the building," and the same goes for a roof, a floor, a window and other parts of conceptual systems. The names that find their way in our language indicate where the constants of convention lie. As long as the wall can be made easily in the many variations that the image demands, the elements that makes it may change. The wall comes into being by distribution of the element called "brick" or "block." The brick is the result of production and distribution; commercial non-territorial activities. The wall is, however, the result of a unique decision on a unique place; a truly territorial act. To make the wall in one piece in the form of a prefabricated slab and present it as an element is no longer an interpretation of the image of "wall" but its violation because it changes the implied relations of human action. The prefab wall does not offer another way to play the game. It changes the game. It is a powerplay.

The distinction between the concrete block and the prefabricated concrete wall-as-an-element is subtle but fundamental. They both have their technical rationale but when we probe their difference in the systemic context that we explore here we must again look at their role as elements through which powers relate.

An element as part of a system relates to two parties: those who produce it and those who build with it. There is a separation of initiative. To produce concrete blocks and sell them to others means that the producer does not know the actual configuration of which the block will be part other than in general terms. The most successful element will be the one that least dictates the distributions that can be made by those who use it. Only when the element is sufficiently neutral can the producer expect successful continuous production. Moreover, it is the essence of industrial production that the producer can take the initiative of production. In this game the prefabricated concrete wall has no chance. It simply does not pass the test of leaving sufficient freedom to other powers who work with it. There is no basis for initiative here. One would end up with a stock of unsold walls.

If one would know that in a specific project in a specific place a wall is needed, however, one could indeed offer to make that wall all in one piece and put it there. The initiative then is not with the producer but with the local actor who decides on the variant. This is indeed prefabrication; the assembly of a local interpretation away from its locality to transport it from there to where it belongs. The prefabricated "element" is, by definition not an element in a system. It is the element in a specific configuration. The fundamental difference is one of initiative.

The element of a system is there before any finite position has been assigned to it. The prefab "element" must serve a predetermined configuration. Prefabrication is just another way to build a building: the assembly of a predetermined configuration of parts. The contractor/builder never takes the initiative. He is the producer who waits until the client has decided what should be made. The producer of elements in a system, on the contrary, must take initiative. He produces first, for the local actor to follow, by making a configuration. The industrialist, who must invest in his plant and his research and product development can only be the producer of elements in a system. The implicit system that is within the collective image allows the industrialist to produce just one element. He need not invent a whole system.

Thus, bricks have been produced industrially for centuries. So have tiles, roof tiles, floorboards, floor and roof timber. In the brick and stone vernacular we now have concrete blocks, sand cement blocks, and gypsum blocks. New kinds of mortars and plaster, prestressed concrete beams and planks have followed. All this is known in the trade as "traditional" building because "industrial" building has to do with cranes, clean assembly, and the immaculate and magical fitting of joints. Thus, mechanized on-site assembly and prefabrication are confused with industrial production. The source for this misunderstanding lies in the tendency to focus on the elements and the tools we use. We can only gain clarity when we look at the powers in play. Then it is obvious that "industrial building" is a contradictory term in itself. To build is to put together the configuration that is unique in its place. Parts of that configuration may be assembled off-site; they are prefabricated. Ultimately all is brought together from materials and products that have mostly been produced by industrial initiative.

The road of the industrially produced element from the plant where it is made to its final place in the site can be in several stages. Usually there are points of pre-assembly that can easily be indicated. The steel profile is cut and welded into a window or a frame in a specialized shop. This window, pre-hung, is then brought to the site and fitted in the wall. When the window facade is large, several pre-assembled pieces are brought together on the site and a larger window wall can be built. Sometimes this secondary assembly can be done off-site, or in a shed on the site, before the larger configuration is installed in the building. Costs, means of transportation, available skills and risks of damage as well as timing of the construction process are all factors that influence the decision of how and when the stages of pre-assembly will be.

Sometimes the same window is bought by so many local users in so many different variants so consistently over time that it justifies making them before any specific builder asks for them. Then we have the transition from pre-assembly to industrial production. A new element, like the brick and the concrete block is born in the implicit system. It happens less often than we think. To follow the example given, most steel windows are custom made. The window available in the catalogue is no more than a suggestion of a manufacturer who is equipped to make any window out of the mass-produced profiles he has in stock. He will make the window in the catalogue exactly the way he makes the others: after you order one. The catalogue is designed to make selection easier for those who build, and it saves time and coordination in the shop. Doors, of course are now pre-determined elements. Few in the Western hemisphere will make a single door anymore. But not so long ago a door was still an assembly of a system by itself. Everyone knew how a door was made. Details, joints and profiles were of a clearly defined set, which allowed for the creation of a rich variety within their limits.

Thus, the production of the environment is the result of an intricate series of coordinated stages of assembly. It allows for the making of endless combinations that never have to repeat themselves. The implicit system that is the result as well as the cause is infinitely rich. It is not technology that defines its limits. In any technology, industrialized or not, the movement from the material source to the finished, on-site position, a progress from one stage of refinement to another, can become extremely complex and varied.

The limitations are in the coordination between people and the willingness and patience to bestow love and care to the work at hand. Systems become simplified not by technical innovation but by our desire to cut costs and time, and above all to cut the number of decisions to be made as well as the stages that have to be coordinated. To standardize a door and make it an element in a catalogue cuts off a whole process for making that one unique door for that one unique place. The road from the industrial, unalterable, element via a sequence of variants within variants assembled in ever greater complexity and specificity is shortened considerably. The building begins where the industrial product stops. From there, the first assembly leads to the second, and so on. Every route in the building process, from assembly to assembly can be shortened by decreasing the number of decisions to be made and the number of manipulations to be done. A decision to cut intermediate stages of assembly inevitably reduces variety. **It is not industrial production but the elimination of decision-making stages between the factory and the site that produces uniformity.**

In the historical building, however, where the doors are all custom made, we may nevertheless find only two or three types in a set of twenty-five doors. Nor are all windows in a facade different. The small-scale developer today will build three similar houses if he happens to build them at the same time in a row. So, apparently did his colleague in ancient Rome. It is only human to try to simplify our lives, and by doing so, we choose our own, more modest system from the broad implicit one we all share. In those self-styled limitations we find our own and are recognized by others. Thus, can we distinguish the unique touch of the master builder as much as the particular vernacular of a locality.

The variety we see in our environment is directly related to the process involved in its assembly. Repetition and uniformity reveal the exercise of a single power manipulating larger numbers of elements. Neither the implicit system that people may share, nor the technology they may use, will lead to a decrease of variation by themselves. **The uniformity that may be evident in a given environment is not the result of technology or industrialization but comes from a specific imbalance in the exercise of power.**

Production will always become systemic when the producer cannot dictate the final product, but wants to take the initiative. The systemic is basically

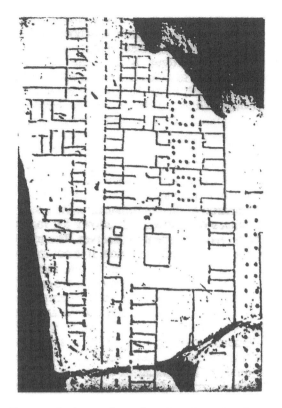

Figure 4 An image of an urban tissue in ancient Rome, showing the repetition of house types each varied from the other.

a delegation of decision making. It allows for the production of elements while leaving the decision about their local assembly to others. The systemic therefore goes with the distribution of power. Wherever we see the "powers of habitation" (to use the apt phrase introduced by Donlyn Lyndon) proliferate, we see a development towards the systemic mode and the wholesale production of materials and elements that sustain it.

But when the powers of habitation are weak or non-existent the producing powers want to take over. They will try to determine the final assemblies as much as possible, produce them in one location and distribute them like single elements to the places of use. It is this tendency to control the assemblies rather than the elements they are made of that leads to the typically contemporary mode of production known as prefabrication. Prefabrication is assembly off-site. As we have seen, it does not necessarily have to do with mass-production or with the development of systems. The so-called "prefab systems" are not systems but methods of centralizing the act of building.

The most important representatives of this method of production are the so-called large concrete panel prefab systems. These are basically the manufacturing of assemblies that must be known beforehand. One way or another the building that must be built is cut into large sections of walls, floors or roofs and roofs. These will be produced in a factory complete with doors, windows, electric wiring, pipes and wall finish to be shipped to the site for assembly by means of large cranes. It is important to understand the annihilating impact of this way of working. We must remember that the normal building is always an intricate combination of different technical systems. These same technical systems are now used in a very strange way. In the assembly hall a segment of a wall or floor is made, within it a window or a door with some wiring and some piping. The size and shape of these segments are solely determined for the sake of combining them quickly on the site. The process is much like baking triangular pieces of pie first and then putting them together in a whole, round pie.

In large panel fabrication each subsystem is fragmented, and the fragments are then poured in concrete never to be changed again. This is the opposite of industrialization where the objective is to produce elements that can be combined in many ways. This strange behavior cannot be explained from any technical or economic point of view. **We must observe the balance of power behind this phenomenon, rather than its morphology or technology, to understand it. This way of working will make sense to those who are only interested in large-scale production and not aware of any desires of future users or owners to modify what they own or the need of future users to adapt to their needs the building they inhabit.** The subsystems that together make the building normally tend to be "live" configurations, and their life is often shorter than the life of the whole. Their independent transformation is needed to assure the usefulness of the whole. We see here the single-minded exercise of technical and organizational interests unaware of any territorial activity related to the building's use. **It is the triumph of production for its own sake.**

In all this, one should not overlook the symbolic aspect of building activities. After all, those who transform the site want to express their own environmental values by the configurations they make. What is a better expression of clean, decisive and organized power than the instantaneous combination of simple large elements manipulated by large cranes and a few operators, creating part of a city out of thin air? It is understandable that this way of working is attractive among "decision makers."

As a study of contrasts, it may be interesting to look at another kind of system, born in the same age as the one discussed previously, that came into being because small scale territorial powers had to be served where they were not seen previously. This is the system of interior partitioning that developed with the rise of the skyscraper and the large office building to allow division of space independent of the structure that contains the total volume to be divided. We see in these large buildings the familiar division between public and private space, the latter to be leased to users who can control to a fair degree the spatial organization of their territory. Sometimes the landlord will adjust the accommodations available to the user. More often, simple unadorned floorspace is leased and the further subdivision and decoration is left to the tenants who are free to choose their own products and systems. The wall partitioning system is only one of several subsystems needed to create a satisfactory territory for the local power in the building. It is not unusual that the ceilings, including lighting, and even air-conditioning, are subject to the users' manipulation. In whatever way intervention is possible the principle clearly asks for the assembly of freely manipulable systems; and that is what the industry has provided.

We see in the large office building the familiar signs of small-scale exercise of power, like variety and individuality of configurations and the continuous change within a larger framework. The response to this market has been a proliferation of different infill systems in a wide price range, offering a variety of materials and finishes. There is the familiar tendency to keep the basic components small enough to allow freedom of distribution for the greatest possible number of interpretations feasible in the given price range.

When we examine these systems more closely, we will find that they can be described in different ways. First there is the conceptual WAY OF SEEING things in which we are shown that the system offers walls of different kinds (opaque and transparent, with or without sound insulation, electric outlets, etc.) available in different modular sizes. In this format the overall on-site distribution can be discussed. From a technical point of view, however, though we find that there are usually a limited number of basic elements; metal, plastic, or wood profiles, the components needed to join them and the panels to be enclosed by them. These are the materials and elements that are produced industrially and kept in stock. The rest is, again, a sequence of assemblies; on-site or off-site, depending on the system's properties. As with a set of Chinese dolls we find assembly within assembly. The technology in which this intricate hierarchy of assemblies is best balanced will be the most adaptable and will therefore have the best chance for survival.

When we look at the class of infill wall systems as a whole, we recognize another true vernacular: a system that exists in the collective image of those who use and produce it. The forms in which it can manifest itself are infinite in material, detailing and dimensioning. But it exists because there is a social agreement that brings together the powers of territory with the powers of production. It represents a balance of interests that is fertile ground for invention and innovation. The vernacular is where technical expertise and the layman's interest find a common ground.

In this particular case we also see the emergence of a new, separate systemic level in the order of enclosures. It is not often that the emergence of a new level in an old order of thing can be witnessed. The one we have briefly discussed here is, from its earliest emergence until today, somewhat more than a century in the making. It may have had its days of highest prestige. Other modes of spatial division are being explored now under the influence of new lifestyles and economics. The office landscape seeks a demarcation of separate places by means of elements that operate more on the level of furniture. Such solutions have, as we may expect by now, their own underlying power balances that make them exist.

In all developing countries a majority of the new urban dwellers live in houses that have been built by their own initiative; more often than not on land that is sold to them without formal registration in areas that were not approved for urban development by the municipal authorities. In a great many cases the land is simply occupied by means of a well prepared "coups" in which scores of squatters take an area which is the property of an absent owner overnight, forcing the hand of the authorities. All such acts of unapproved or illegal settlement are known by the bureaucratic establishment as the "informal sector." In places like Cairo, Ankara, Mexico City, Jakarta, Johannesburg and any other metropolis in the developing world the dwellings built by the informal sector outnumber those built by municipal permit.

This informal sector encompasses a broad variety of inhabitants ranging from the poor to the lower middle class. It includes miserable shanty towns without much hope for substantial improvement, but also to a very large degree, neighborhoods where people build solid and large houses up to four and sometimes five stories high that, once completed, cannot be distinguished as illegal. It may take twenty years to get to that point, but those who seek security for their children in real estate investment and a roof over their heads make the effort.

The houses thus built are often put together by the dwellers and their neighbors themselves, but in most cases, small, equally informal, contractors actually do the job. By its very nature the process is an implicit one. But those who put their trust and resources in these structures have every reason to build as solidly as they can. Many owners rent an extra room or a second floor as soon as it is completed to relatives or newcomers. With the money thus returning on their investment they can build more. There are others who do it purely for investment, own several buildings and probably make a good profit on their property. In short, this "informal" sector, so studiously ignored in the statistics of the bureaucracy, operates by and large as normal urban environments have operated for millennia in the past. In defiance of all the rules that formal organizational and political power can produce, these districts are in continuous transition, areas of seemingly endless development. Sometimes the results are surprisingly successful, sometimes less so; sometimes a dismal slum is the final result.

It is here that we find reinforced concrete construction technology firmly entrenched. The observer who, for instance in Cairo, ventures into these neighborhoods, will see building after building going up with concrete floors. In a surprisingly large number of cases the structure is a complete reinforced concrete skeleton with columns, beams and slabs.

Figures 5 and 6: Construction in a developing country built of concrete and masonry

For obvious reasons this widespread and extremely productive practice has scarcely been studied in any depth. Local governments, regarding anything not on record as dangerous slums, do not encourage inquiry. The inhabitants themselves have their own reasons not to advertise their modes of operation. We can only guess about the various kinds of expertise that operate. However, anyone can buy cement and steel rods as well as sand and gravel. Even if there is a formal distribution of cement and steel, a black market is available. Once the basic principles are understood a simple floor can be constructed by anyone. Many inhabitants in these sectors are sometime construction workers. They make some extra money in their spare time helping out a neighbor. Or they start a local contracting business on a shoestring themselves. Spans are seldom wider than 12 feet and simple rules of thumb are sufficient to make a safe floor. If a skeleton is planned the advice of someone more knowledgeable may be needed. One may know a student in engineering who can help out, or a supervisor at the construction site where one has a job is approached.

Thus, reinforced concrete technology has become vernacular in the true sense of the word. A knowledge which was the property of a small elite only a few generations ago has now permeated the very fabric of everyday building habits. It should not surprise us. In the same informal manner, our own children as well as those in Latin America and the Middle East have picked up the secrets of the combustion engine. Compared to that, the concrete slab spanning twelve feet poses a fairly simple problem.

Similarly, it is not so difficult to make a window out of extruded steel profiles. It is probably easier to weld a window correctly than to shoe a horse. It is definitely easier than making that same window out of wood in the traditional way. It takes a relatively small investment to buy the necessary equipment to set up shop. So here we see sections of facade for downtown shops and office buildings as well as windows for the villas of the well-to-do (windows are usually still too expensive for the informal sector) produced in simple workplaces.

Sometimes the welders are at work in an environment that is almost medieval in other respects. They produce on demand in small series or unique pieces. Once the basic component, in this case the steel profiles, is available, the stages of assembly are relatively easy to do. The steel shopfront is becoming commonplace for the hole-in-the-wall shop, replacing the wood facade that is so much more difficult and time-consuming to make. Steel may be expensive, but good wood is hard to come by in Latin America and the Middle East. Besides, the steel front has a definitely modem age flavor.

Many more examples can be found: the message is clear. Industrial products feed the informal and vernacular building processes around the world. Cement, reinforcement bars, steel window profiles, plastic pipes for water and sewage, concrete blocks, sand-lime bricks, red bricks, hollow extended bricks, electric wiring and electricity outlets, lightbulbs, nails and screws, water faucets, hinges and door-locks and so on and so on; all are mass produced industrial products that now are distributed into the far corners of the world to be assembled by skilled and semi-skilled workers and laymen alike in the small-scale processes that create the environments of the masses, at least two-thirds of which are not on record but nevertheless very real. There is no conflict between industrial production and small-scale ad hoc building processes. On the contrary, they thrive on each other.

In all this there is no trace of explicit systems. The elements themselves are explicit but the distribution patterns and the rules that govern them are part of the people's collective knowledge of the built environment; a knowledge, that has partly trickled downwards from centers of more formal technical expertise, and is partly the result of collective learning of the urban ways of life. If the elements are available, the intricate patterns of assemblies within assemblies, of variant within variant, seem to develop themselves as surely as social patterns do. That is, they will develop as living configurations multiply and diversify, revealing systems, the structures of which are never explained but are known by all involved.

2003
MAKING URBAN FABRIC FINE GRAINED – A RESEARCH AGENDA

Editors' note: *This essay was published in the Proceedings, CIB W104, Dense Living Urban Structures, Hong Kong, 2003. In a succinct way, it describes the Open Building approach and discusses the skills and knowledge embodied in this approach but so far not sought in conventional architecture. The author argues that acceptance of this approach opens the way to new design skills and methods as well as new environmental knowledge. This, in turn, implies a new research agenda specifically geared to architectural design.*

Introduction

The concept of Open Building implies the separation of the so-called 'Base Building' from the interior 'Fit-out.' This separation allows each dwelling unit to be designed individually and to change independent of other units in the same building. The result is a fine-grained organization of the large building. Kendall and Teicher[1] give a comprehensive overview of residential Open Building projects worldwide. Since that book was published in 2000, other projects have been completed.

To explain the concept, two projects are briefly shown. One is relatively recent and the other is one of the first to be executed.

The NEXT21 project in Osaka, Japan (Figure 1), built in 1994 but planned as a continuing experiment with new building technology, energy systems, and urban living, intended to suggest the apartment building of the future. It was experimental in many ways. It is also an Open Building project. Professor Yositika Utida, leader of the design team, called it a three-dimensional urban design. Consistent with that, thirteen different architects were initially invited to design the individual dwellings inside the Base Building.[2]

The Molenvliet project (Figure 2) was the first base building project in the Netherlands. Architect Frans van der Werf treated it as part of an urban fabric that could be continued on an urban scale, consisting of public and private courtyards formed by the base building and connected to one another and to the major streets, where cars could be parked. In this base building, tenants could design and change their individual dwelling units. This process has been supported to this day by the public housing corporation which owns the project.[3]

The Open Building approach can be considered a general model for fine-grained urban fabric in contemporary environment. As such, it is worthwhile to compare this new approach to the making of architecture in general and consider where professional ways of working need to be changed.

Open Building may sound revolutionary in its demand for adaptability, but in a more historic perspective it can be seen as a return to age-old qualities that got lost in Modern times. Densely packed urban fabric is often found in historic examples, but it was always fine-grained: such fabrics consisted of many small living cells that could change, adapt, disappear and appear on their own. When we look at air survey pictures of the city of Amsterdam, for instance, we see how the famous seventeenth century canals are truly monumental in size in their geometric layout, but this large scale urban structure is balanced by the many individual houses that front the urban spaces, making it a fine-grained living fabric. Step-by-step, as the city continued to grow from the late nineteenth century

Figure 1 NEXT21, Osaka, Japan

Figure 2 Molenvliet, Papendrecht, the Netherlands

until now, we see a coarsening of the fabric. Eventually, the smallest exchangeable unit – the living cell if you like – is not a single house but a large apartment building. This trend has been universal, and as a consequence, our contemporary cities are coarse grained and inflexible. In a culture where commercial, political and educational efforts are focused on the individual as a free agent, expected to act and choose for him/herself, the built environment is an anomaly, unable to respond to the variable and energetic small-scale life of the occupant.

The international Open Building network advocates giving large buildings and large projects a fine-grained quality responsive to the needs of the individual inhabitant. Where the historic dense fabric used to be a horizontal distribution of autonomous living cells, the contemporary high-density city fabric must distribute those cells also vertically.

Obviously, technical problems must be solved to achieve a vertical fine-grained fabric. Contemporary dwellings and workplaces are complex machines full of piping and wiring that provide energy, heating, ventilation and cooling, various means of communication and take away waste. But in our day and age, this need not be a barrier. In fact, progress is already made in this regard under the pressure of real-life demands. Large commercial office towers today are flexible structures. Owners lease entire floors and let the occupant companies bring in their own contractors to fit-out floor plans designed by specialized interior architects. In the same way, we find shopping malls to be virtual Open Building projects where retail space is fitted out individually. The Open Building movement has concentrated largely on residential buildings of which I have shown just two.

The real barriers to making the Open Building approach a common practice are not technical. They have to do with the fact that, as professionals, we lack familiarity with the properties of fine-grained high-density urban environments. Our tradition as professional architects, engineers and managers is with monumental buildings: castles, palaces, temples, churches and mosques and perhaps also the large mansions for rich clients. We have not learned to see our products as living entities subject to internal change over time. That static view is becoming increasingly counterproductive. We now begin to suspect that everyday environment is too complex, too dynamic, and too much rooted in social and cultural habits to be a mere professional invention or to be determined by static programming. Large contemporary buildings are not, in fact, buildings in the traditional sense, but are pieces of urban fabric to be cultivated. Our making and designing must be geared to that cultivation. A new professional attitude must be developed. Here lies the challenge Open Building is posing.

Three areas of conflict

To support this statement, I will mention three aspects where our traditional ideology is in conflict with the realities of everyday living environment.

Firstly, everyday environment is about change and transformation as much as about permanence. The 'base building' of a large building is relatively permanent precisely because the interior fit-out can change. For the same token, in an urban structure of streets and public spaces, buildings are the changeable parts and the street system is more permanent. Thus, environment exists by virtue of change organized in a hierarchical fashion. Time is the essential fourth dimension needed for environmental sustainability. But time is a traditional enemy of architecture. Architecture is meant to endure – it is the stone placed in the running stream. When we speak of environmental fabric, we speak of that stream.

Secondly, we have been taught to seek centralized design control. The great masters like Le Corbusier, Mies van der Rohe, Walter Gropius and Frank Lloyd Wright sought to design not just the building, but also the chair in it and everything in between as well as the city. They lived in a period of renewal and revolution in which it could be believed that good architecture demanded such total control. And because their works are so beautiful and seductive, we still feel that it should be our privilege to work that way. We resist distribution of design control. But in practice, expertise of environmental design IS distributed. We distinguish between furniture designers, interior designers or architects, architects, urban designers, and landscape architects, as well as, today, planners and industrial designers. This distinction of expertise reflects the distribution of design control that comes naturally with environmental form. The separation of Base Building from Fit-Out design as advocated by Open Building introduces a new layer in that hierarchy, already well understood in office building and shopping center design, in response to the increased size of contemporary buildings of all kinds.

Distribution of design control does not figure in architectural theory, it is not discussed as such in professional circles, nor taught in professional schools. But it is a fact of life. The issue of design distribution goes even further than the distinction between different kinds of expertise. Within the confines of a single expertise design tasks now demand groups of individuals subdividing among themselves the work for large jobs. Of the many bright and talented students that graduate from our schools, only very few will ever do an entire building in their life. They will do what we still feel to be 'partial design.' They work in larger teams, or manage such teams, or become consultants on specific aspects of design. In addition, consultants like the structural engineer, the experts in heating, ventilation, and air conditioning, and in various utility systems, as well as those specialized in acoustics and lighting, are also involved in making design decisions. Moreover, architecture has become more and more a matter of composition of industrial systems and these systems, in turn, are the products of industrial designers. The latter have an increasing influence on the look and feel of environmental form. In short, everyday environment thrives on a dynamic distribution of design control. Indeed, the concept of a 'building' is becoming outdated more and more. As designers, we operate in a continuum of environmental form in which we do our bit.

Finally, good everyday environment, as we still admire in historic examples, is coherent. Buildings adhere to a shared typology, we see the same patterns consistently applied, and we recognize a certain systemic way of working in all instances. In other words, to collectively produce a good environment, it is important to know what we have in common, and what values we share.

Sharing values is not what the architect is taught in school. We operate in an ideology of self- expression following the superficial idea that good architecture must always be original and different. Of course, to be different, there must be something that is normal. So, what is shared is as important as what is individual. Already in the seventies, Dean Lawrence Anderson of MIT's School of Architecture and Planning was heard to sigh: "Too bad no one wants to design a background building." We just do not know anymore how to talk about ·what we have in common. Here too, Open Building points in the right direction. To make a higher-level structure, ·we must consider what is shared on the lower level. Our design must contain and represent what many lower level designs will have in common.

A research agenda

The three issues of conflict between environmental reality and professional ideology have a direct impact on the way we design. There is a common aspect: All three demand that designers coordinate what they do with others.

Sharing values demands that we have ways to establish what our designs must have in common; this is the basis for all coordination.

The distribution of design responsibility clearly demands ways in which designers can define design tasks and in which they can handle the interface: setting clear boundaries within which they can carry their own responsibilities.

Change and permanence, relates to both sharing of values and the separation of tasks. Values must be embedded in specific forms with their own life span of longer or shorter duration. These forms, in turn, assume a distribution of design control compatible with them.

Coordination and methodology

In all cases, we have to do with questions of design coordination in one way or another. Design coordination, in turn, calls for design methodology. In a culture where design is only seen as an individual problem of self-expression and in which we assume each must handle form in his or her own way, design as a problem of coordination is seldom discussed and design methods are considered unnecessary constraints to the individual's creative freedom. Consequently, design methodology is unknown in our present culture. But this neglect is based on a misunderstanding. Good methods respect the creative act as inscrutable. When we design, we must have our own domain of control. But where what we do connects to the work of others, we want that exchange to be effective and efficient. That is where method comes in.

Capacity

When the separation of Base Building from Fit-Out was first proposed by SAR (the Foundation for Architect's Research in the Netherlands) a new interface between designers was called for and that is what our methodological research focused on. For instance, the designer of a base building cannot just show a few floor plans to justify their proposal. They must find out what range of possible plans – given certain requirements and values -might be possible in the proposed base building. This is now known as the problem of capacity. When ·we walk into an empty room, we may say: "this could be a bedroom, but it might also be a study, or perhaps a playroom for the children." By saying this we indicate the capacity of the room for holding lower level designs. In the same way an urban designer, who decides about house lots and street widths, will ask what kind of houses could be built if the lots have certain dimensions. Or they may consider what ways there are to park cars in a given street-width, and how trees might be planted in it. In all those cases the designer does not determine the lower level design decisions but must have a fair idea as to the range of solutions possible within what is proposed.

Positioning

The physical interface between the base building and the fit-out needs to be organized too. Modular grids are commonly used to locate the position of columns, walls, floors and other parts of buildings. Such locations can be subject to agreements and rules. SAR proposed the establishment of **position rules** for the placement of parts. To do so we suggested a grid of alternating narrow and wide bands. The advantage of such band grids is that they allow for easier and more varied position rules compared to single line grids. The position rules we suggested were such that elements of the fit-out system would always meet the base building in the narrow bands of the grid. This constrained the margin of interface to a technically feasible range while leaving each party free to dimension what is was responsible for.

Zones

Positioning objects in space is of prime importance for all environmental designing and it is once again surprising how little it is discussed in practice if at all, and how underdeveloped our ways of handling grids are in general. In our research we also made a link between positioning and the question of capacity. We found that variations of floor plans in a given context are seldom random, because culture is not Random. People seldom will choose, for instance, to make a bedroom without a window, while bathrooms and kitchens, on the other hand, are often placed in the middle of a building. This led us to the concept of zones, whereby zones behind facades and those internal could be distinguished. We also defined zones for public and private use as well as for inside or outside use. Zones allowed us to equate a base building floor with a particular 'zoning distribution' and this, in turn, indicated where certain functions of the dwelling might be located. We found that each dwelling type had its own characteristic 'zone distribution.' With the help of such zonings and assumptions for positioning of functions, it would be possible to quickly generate a series of possible 'basic variants' that gave a good idea of the capacity of the base building for holding a variety of dwellings within the assumed values. With zones mediating between the two levels of intervention, it was possible to efficiently evaluate the relation between floor plan values and base building capacity and to tinker with either the values or the base building to arrive at a desired solution. In a later stage we used the concept of zoning also in urban design. Here the zones indicated areas to be built or to be left open and capacity of an urban design to hold certain architectural solutions could be studied by varying either the urban design or the assumed building typology.

Methodology is not the only area of research, however, that will help us to deal with present environmental reality. Looking at historic evidence we already saw that the balance between change and permanence is central to the health and sustainability of environmental fabric. In all sciences, the key to an understanding of physical phenomena, including those of living things lies in their patterns of transformation. We discover intrinsic laws by looking at such transformations. Environmental form, in all its varied manifestations throughout history, follows certain constant laws and principles that can be discovered by looking carefully at patterns of transformation. I followed this approach in my recently published book *The Structure of the Ordinary*[4] in which I suggest three orders of control – morphological, territorial, and cultural – that each in a different way frame environmental form. The book is only a first attempt but may demonstrate that here too is an area of research and inquiry of great importance that has been hardly explored. Conventional environmental form is to the architectural profession what the human body is for the medical doctor. We need to study it to make our intervention beneficial and to render environment healthy.

Conclusions

Donald Schön[5] has argued that each profession, the medical doctor, as much as the engineer, the lawyer, and the architect, must have a certain artistry to be a good professional. The architect need not be reminded of that. Nonetheless, if creativity is an essential ingredient for all professional expertise, it is, by itself, not enough to define a profession's expertise. A profession needs to have a specific domain of knowledge by which to be identified. It also must have the specific skills needed to intervene successfully in that domain. For the contemporary architect that domain is everyday environment in its full complexity.

I have mentioned two large areas of inquiry that relate exactly to these two conditions for true professionalism: one having to do with design methodology, the other with our knowledge of environmental form. The study and development of methods pertains to the design skills we need to do our bit in a larger field of interventions. The study of environment as an autonomous and living organism, following its own laws, can provide us the knowledge base on which our design acts must rest. The two together suggest a domain of knowledge and skills particular to the architectural design profession.

I have tried to show that research along the lines of the Open Building approach is relevant for the architectural profession at large. With the appropriate skills and knowledge, our profession will be better equipped for the reality of large projects and the increasing distribution of design control in contemporary practice. More importantly, it can contribute greatly to the creation of urban fabric of a fine-grained quality which is compatible with large projects of all kinds, making it more resilient to change and more responsive to human life.

References

1. Kendall, S. and J. Teicher (2000). *Residential Open Building*. London and New York: Taylor and Francis.
2. Utida, Y., K. Tatsumi, S. Chicazumi, S. Fukao and M. Takada (1994). *Next21, Special Issue of SD (Space Design) No. 25*. Tokyo: Kajima Institute Publishing.
3. Van der Werf, F. and H. P. Froyen (1980). "Molenvliet Wilgendonk: Experimental Housing Project, Papendrecht, the Netherlands." In *Harvard Architectural Review*. Cambridge, MA: MIT Press, 161–169.
4. Habraken, N. J. (1998). *The Structure of the Ordinary: Form and Control in the Built Environment*. Cambridge, MA: MIT Press.
5. Schon, D. A. (1987). *Educating the Reflective Practitioner* San Francisco, CA: Jossey-Bass.

CONTROL

1968
SUPPORTS, RESPONSIBILITIES AND POSSIBILITIES

Editors' Note: *This essay was published in Architectural Association Quarterly, Winter 1968–69 (pp. 25–31)*

> "It is characteristic of many who speak most of individual freedom in such matters that they do not think well enough of it to imagine that it might also be efficient."
>
> **J. K. Galbraith,** The New Industrial Stat

The idea of building supports is a very simple one.

Why should we go on building all these identical dwellings in endless rows or piled one upon the other? Why not build some kind of superstructure in which people can have their own dwellings made in accordance with their own individual wishes? Let us call such a superstructure a **Support**. After all it is a new kind of building with a newly defined function and it deserves a special name to identify it. Let us further imagine a set of elements (wall-elements, facade- elements, cupboards, sanitary cells) to be used in a Support to make dwellings and call these a *set of detachable units*. Why should we not build supports in great quantity and let people choose their own detachable units in the same way that they choose their furniture, their household equipment or their cars? Why not indeed? The very simplicity of the idea arouses suspicion. Things just are not that simple. Practical and experienced people will have no trouble in pointing out a host of difficulties that will arise if one tries to realize it. Of course, the simplicity of an idea does not guarantee easy realization. On the other hand, many people like the idea. In fact, it sprang up in one variation or another, in many places, and in many minds all over the world. But an idea can be supported by the wrong reasons as much as it can be opposed for the wrong reasons.

Supports cannot be voted into existence. Even if everybody would be willing to have a try at them, the philosophy behind them should be quite clear to enable us to make the right decisions at the right time in the process of realization. If we know why we want something we shall be able to know *how* we shall get it. That is why I have spent my time trying to formulate why we should build Supports, working from there on a method for realization.

I have tried elsewhere to formulate the philosophy behind the Supports *(see note at end)*. We had the opportunity at Stichting Architecten Research (S.A.R.) to work out a method of design for the realization of Supports that we are trying out step by step in practice. But this is neither spectacular nor exciting. Discussing Supports almost daily with all kinds of people in all kinds of circumstances, a pattern of recurring questions and opinions emerges. I have often been tempted to assemble these questions and their answers to try to get hold of the pattern. Perhaps it would tell us a great deal about the society we live in and the fears and hopes that motivate it. But I am sure that is beyond my capacities. However, I will try to comment, more or less at random, on a few points that might be of interest to those willing to consider the desirability of building Supports.

Supports and detachable units

First of all, misunderstanding about Supports may arise when it is not understood from the beginning that the point of view taken is not a technical one, but one of human need. Man wants to be responsible for his material environment; people want to identify with it. To be able to identify with one's own environment one must be able to do something about it. An environment may be very beautiful and comfortable, but if it is not adaptable it cannot be a home. People living in it will not be dwellers but only guests. To dwell is to take action. Beauty and comfort cannot give identification. Only action can give that. Identification goes together with responsibility and responsibility presumes that there is a possibility to act. What can we do to build and produce in such a way that people again will be able to identify with their own material environment?

The production of Supports and detachable units can of course be argued from a technical point of view. If we are to build dwelling spaces in considerable quantity, Supports have the advantage that they can be standardized in design and construction and be built in great quantity without the builder having to decide about standard plans and all the details and specifications that go with finishing the dwellings. Building Supports gives great possibilities for the standardization of elements and also for prefabrication. It leads also to the rationalization of the building process. In a similar way, detachable units can be fabricated by industry in a continuous process. Detachable units should become new kinds of durable consumer goods, as it is in the creation of consumer goods that industrial production has been most successful. This is one reason why the idea of Supports should appeal to those who have until now been so continuously frustrated in their efforts to apply industrial production methods to housing. This frustration itself may be a proof of the fact that the problem is not one of production in the first place. If that were the case, we should have solved it long ago. Nowhere have we been more successful in this century than in the field of production.

The moment we say, 'Let us industrialize housing and make standard components out of which dwellings can be made', we are faced with one crucial question: how shall we define the components to be made? In other words, what parts of the building should be broken down to enable us to produce these parts as factory-made elements? All industrial housing systems can be classified by the way this question has been answered. The most naive approach is to slice up a given house or building in much the same way as a birthday cake is cut up into digestible pieces; the decision where to cut being made exclusively for reasons of production, transport or assembly.

More sophisticated systems recognize the fact that mass-production can only be realized if different kinds of dwellings and different plans can be made out of the same components. How does one find a series of components out of which a great variation of different dwellings can be made? Given a series of known and accepted types of floor plan this question also can be answered on grounds of production methods, transport and assembly. The result will always be the standard housing project as we have known it all along. The producer has to compete in a market where costs mean everything, with the disadvantage that he still may not be able to make what the client or local authorities may have in mind, and thus is not assured of the continuous production he needs to prove that industrial production is cheaper, better and more efficient.

Then again, some architects and builders recognize the fact that in a given superstructure a variation in floor plans can be made by means of the same finishing elements. Here once more the division is made exclusively on technical grounds. The result is again the kinds of buildings we already produce, the kind of housing and living we already know. Mass-production is not assured any more than by the traditional mass housing methods. No new market opens, no new needs are answered.

Industrial mass-production outside housing production has been such a tremendous success because it did answer new needs, opened new markets and surrounded us with products that were not known before. New things, new companions in our daily lives with whom we want to live for many reasons even if the process of living together raises its own problems.

It is my conviction that we can only introduce industrial mass-production in the process of housing if we start thinking about human needs. As soon as we pose the question, 'How shall we make dwellings?' we are on the wrong track. People do not need dwellings in this sense. A dwelling is not a thing people need. A dwelling is the result of people fulfilling the need to dwell. The goal of production should be to make it possible for people to do so.

Indeed, a dwelling is not a thing to be considered for production. We might as well say: 'People need freedom, so let us mass-produce freedom.' A dwelling is not a thing that can be specified and defined by a description of components, or, for that matter, functions or shapes. It can be a cave or an attic, a villa or a castle, a flat or a duplex. It just might be that we have in this era, in this generation, as little need for flats or houses as for castles and caves. Perhaps we cannot really apply our modern means of production efficiently and abundantly to the production of houses and flats any better than we could to the production of castles and caves. We should start trying to apply our production power to the production of things we really need for living and dwelling.

That is why I think we should build Supports and detachable units. A Support is a thing that can be specified and produced. A detachable unit is a thing that also can be produced and specified. Specification of these two items starts with a statement of human need. By definition a Support is a building that contains everything for which not one single occupant is responsible – everything in the sphere of communal responsibility. Detachable units are the things the individual dweller will be responsible for. Thus, the decision about where the Support ends and the detachable unit begins is not made on technical grounds and it is only then that we can expect our technical solution eventually to be the best technical solution possible.

Supports and 'flexibility'

Discussing supports easily leads to the topic of 'flexibility.' This term has by now been worn down to the point of having no meaning whatsoever. Many architects think of Supports as structures which offer large areas of floor with as few obstructions in the way (e.g. columns and ducts) as possible. Such a structure they argue, gives maximum flexibility. Others even leave out the floors and think about skeletons to be filled in. Such conceptions are also the outcome of a 'technical' point of view – in this case the technical point of view of the designer. Not however the designer of Supports but the designer of dwellings (those things that are not things). It is quite clear that if I, as a designer of dwellings, want maximum freedom, an unobstructed floor area is what I like to see. And if I prefer to think in three dimensions instead of two, I shall choose the skeleton. It will enable me to design any kind of dwelling I like.

The designer of Supports, on the other hand, is occupied with another problem. He does not want to design dwellings. He tries to conceive of a building in which other people, who are not designers, will be able to recognize possibilities to live by, through the means of detachable units. A Support therefore should not be neutral. Neutral things are hard to identify with. And to dwell is a process of identification even if it is not consciously recognized as such. The Support should incite and intensify this process. It should give real form, real spaces; spaces that are not rooms (yet) but nevertheless tempt the imagination, suggesting more possibilities for living than the occupant could have thought of before seeing them. A Support should, by its architecture, provoke use. It should offer places, dark or sunny, small or roomy, that could just be places to sit, to eat, to sleep. Places that suggest possibilities for kitchen, bedroom and living areas in unending variations and combinations. I think the designing of Supports calls for real architecture and real architects who compose shapes and spaces that eventually may have much more character than can be found in any other design for housing that we can think of today.

The same principle applies to the design of detachable units. Automatically most designers think of detachable (or 'flexible') wall-elements in the first place. We have at S.A.R. come to the point of trying to do away with wall-units as much as possible. Dwellers (who are not designers or technical people) do not easily identify a wall-unit. Much less will they identify themselves with such a unit. We try to think of things the occupant recognizes as useful. Things to put other things in, to do something with or to do something in. We think in terms of cells and cupboards that, arranged in patterns, define 'rooms' and serve them at the same time. We add screens, not walls, where only visual partition is necessary. It is in this field of designing detachable units, 'units for living' as we like to call them, that unknown possibilities await discovery.

The term 'flexibility' also comes up in discussions about the function of Supports as urban infrastructures. Why should Supports be seen as static and be allowed to stand there for much longer than the lifetime of a single dwelling? After all the urban shape changes too. How can we safely build those permanent infrastructures without them becoming a nuisance to later generations? Pushed to the extreme the argument runs like this: would it not be better to conceive of a technical solution which enables us to take apart the whole construction in say 20 years and then start all over again? Or re-assemble the elements into something new, better suited to the newest demands of urban design? Would it not be better to make supports themselves also 'flexible?'

The fact that urban design solutions are subject to change is undeniable. It can also be taken for granted that the rhythm of change is accelerating. When we consider the subject of change of the Supports themselves, we must again take human need as a guideline and not simply technical possibilities. Suppose building techniques and productivity would enable us to reconstruct our urban areas every 20 years, however unlikely this may seem at the moment, would such a possibility be desirable? It is no use doing things just because they are possible. Such a possibility would, I think, only appeal to designers and production people, not to those people we build for. Change in our material environment is the outcome of a social process, the process of man in continuous contact with his environment. This process takes place in two spheres, in the sphere of the individual family and the sphere of the larger group, the community. In both spheres the rhythm of change is dictated by two forces: the technical possibilities and the decisiveness of those who are responsible. These two forces of course influence each other. We are bound to take decisions only about what is known to be technically possible. On the other hand, new technical possibilities increase the field we can decide about. The greater the technical possibilities the more submissive our material environment will become. Increasing change will be dictated by our desire for change and our ability to decide about it. Technical freedom being equal in the communal sphere, the process of making decisions will always be slower than in the individual sphere. The greater the number of people involved, the more time and energy it takes to decide about change. The greater the area of the material environment we are thinking of, the greater the number of people involved will be and the slower the change will be. In the future our ability to change our material environment in the communal spheres in harmony with those involved will depend in an ever-increasing degree on the social, administrative and political forces at work.

Supports are part of the urban environment. The urban environment, being the outcome of communal needs, spans the generations. We want our material environment to be adaptable to our individual needs. We also want it to be a link with other generations. Indeed, we want to change what has been given us by former generations and we should do so with greater freedom; we do not want, however, to start all over again. Besides, it takes generations to complete a new urban area. It takes at least a generation to grow the trees. For a community to identify with an urban area takes longer than one generation. The process of communal identification is much more a process of 'adding to' or 'filling in' than a process of replacement. If replacement is asked for it will be piece-meal, bit by bit, a slow and continuous sequence of corrections towards greater harmony.

The division into a communal sphere and an individual sphere on which the concept of supports and detachable units is founded springs from the point of view that the individual dweller needs a greater sphere of responsibility than is left him in the housing project of today. It leaves the communal sphere only vaguely defined as 'not-individual.' Certainly, the involvement of the community – in the shape of any group of people bigger than a family, be it neighborhood, or inhabitants of a country or any discernible group in between – deserves further study. Here we touch the subject of relationship between man and material environment as a continuous and dynamic interaction. A subject which will be left unexplored as long as technical people stay just technical people and those skilled in the humanities see our material environment only as a scene in which the subjects of their study just happen to move about. It will, I am afraid, take generations before we reach the situation in which housing and urbanization will be seen and studied for what they are: the outcome of a process in which man and matter are no longer separate units but names for different sides of one phenomenon as inseparable as night and day. It certainly will take generations before we have developed the tools and methods to study and influence this phenomenon a little less haphazardly and ignorantly than we do today.

Freedom and creativity

This view must also be kept in mind where the ability of the dweller – who is neither technician nor a designer – to 'create' his own dwelling is questioned. Here two camps can be recognized. There are those who seriously doubt this ability. I have noticed that this doubtful mood can be found especially among the people who have spent much of their time and energy in furthering the cause of better housing for the masses. Public and semi-public officials who have for many years fought the battle for better housing conditions are likely to adopt a paternalistic view about the needs and abilities of the people whose well-being they have so close to their hearts. More than anyone else perhaps they know the hazards and pitfalls that beset the partisan for a better environment. Will people indeed be able to house themselves? Who will answer that question? But then, are people indeed able to raise their own children? We do not require an answer to that question before we decide that people have the responsibility and the right to raise their own children. Until now, no substitute has been found that does not make things even worse. We can organize education and information for parents. We cannot organize the raising of people's children. In much the same way we can organize education and information about housing and about dwelling, and this certainly has to be done. That will not be taking away responsibility. We can also, as specialists, try to produce and design in such a way that people will be as much sustained as possible in their act of dwelling without their responsibility being taken away from them either. We could try to do this by the design and production of Supports and detachable units, for example.

On the other side there are those who greet the idea of Supports as an opportunity at last for everybody to be 'free' and 'creative;' those who believe in the artist hidden in every man's soul waiting to be freed and given the opportunity to make beautiful things. It has to be seen how far creativity is the result of freedom. I am inclined to think that perhaps creation is a process of liberation, which makes freedom the result of creativity, vaporizing instantly when the creative action stops. We must, I think, refuse to see the housing process as anything other than a story of human bondage. It sounds a trifle too easy when one uses the words 'freedom,' 'creativity' and 'beauty.' I much prefer expressions like 'possibility to act,' 'involvement and identification' and 'integrity and honesty.'

Both the doubters as well as the defenders of the ability of people to 'create' their own dwellings think too much of the dweller as a would-be architect. They find it hard to imagine a situation in which dwellings come into being without actually having been designed by a specialist. The dweller, in the designer's eyes, becomes somebody who is going to do what until now specialists were doing. That leaves the specialist with something less to do and he asks for an answer to the question about the ability of the dwellers to 'create.'

It might be argued, however, that the specialists have not less to do than they are doing now. They simply have to do something different which, I am sure, asks as much of their professional skill, or, for that matter, of their 'creativity' as they can offer. I have already stressed the point that a Support should be far from a neutral kind of structure, but it can only be a good Support, provoking use as a good Support should, when it is an artistic creation in the fullest sense of the phrase. But even more to the point is perhaps the fact that to design a Support is to design possibilities, a set of suggestions and invitations, which can be translated into architectural form. The monologue that is, until now, given by the architect, becomes a dialogue. That does not mean that the architect has given part of his monologue to somebody else to recite. It is just another play he is in where to do his part well he has to say every word his role requires and he has to say it clearly in a well-articulated and inspiring way to be understood and to make it possible for the other fellow to act his part.

Hence, I do not think we have to speak of the dweller as somebody who overnight is becoming 'creative.' He is the person who gets the opportunity to choose from different possibilities and from different products. That is something he has been doing all along in selecting and buying furniture, clothes, cars, washing machines, camping equipment and everything that keeps the household going. On the way he is developing a definite feeling for quality. A sense of what is going well for him and what is not; keeping an eye on what the neighbors are doing and trying hard to please himself but not being too different from the crowd he feels he belongs to. It comes quite naturally. That is why I like to call the relation between man and his material environment the natural relation as opposed to the unnatural relation – which in fact is no relation at all – we have become so addicted to. As for beauty and architecture, that is something for the designers of supports and detachable units to worry about. That is our responsibility in the first place.

Note: In *Forum* (Holland), Vol. XX, No. 1, December 1966; *Forum*, Vol. XX, No. 4, November 1967; S.A.R. publications, Eindhoven; the author's book *The Supports and the People*, Amsterdam, 1961. See also article in *Interbuild/Arena*, October 1967, pp. 12–19. *Editor.*

1972
PLAYING GAMES

Editors' Note: *This essay was published in AD 4/72. In it, the author makes clear that the design of Supports is not one of design in the first place, but a change in the rules of the game, which suggests that those advocating this approach must enter politics.*

A book I wrote, *Supports and the People*,[1] provoked interest; stirred by this interest, a group of architects got together to do something about housing. We were fed up with the way things were going; we felt that the machinery of housing and technology did not produce the kind of hardware that people needed. We felt that architects had to play a role, and that they had no opportunity for doing so. So we created a small foundation and pooled some money to do housing research. When we started, we had a very clear idea of what we wanted to do, based on the idea of Support structures and detachable units. We wanted to prove that they could be made; we wanted to show that the individual could be a participant in the housing process.

Six years later, we still continue. No one quite knows how, because there is no finance, but SAR (Stichting Architecten Research) goes on, and a lot of work remains to be done. We realized that if you want to involve the householder in the housing process, and can do it by building Support structures (some kind of building in which he can do something himself, in which he can be responsible for his own dwelling), you do not have to design. The problem is not one of design in the first place; it is a problem of changing the role of the people involved in the housing process. The dwelling is not the result of an architect making a design; it is a result of many, many specialists, and many other people acting and making decisions; out of that comes the dwelling. And if you want to do away with the dwelling and you want to make Support structures and involve the householder himself, then you need some kind of common ground to act on, some kind of coordination. That is why we decided in the beginning to propose a set of rules that the architect could follow, to make it possible for the dweller to be a participant in the housing process.

These rules have been developed, and we have been working with them ourselves, and perhaps they have been developed into what you might call a methodology. This is a technique itself, and it is a tool. We need that tool if we want to change the process, but the danger is that people concentrate on the technique and the methodology and become so involved with it that they sometimes forget what is was developed for in the first place. So, before we talk about methodology, we have to get back to the basic idea of why we want to use these tools, and what it is all for.

When we started, we did not realize how difficult it is for people to change their roles, and the more we progress and the more pilot projects we embark on – builders are now interested in thinking in this way, investment people are starting to think in this way, industrialists are trying to work out proposals – the more we realize that people have to change their way of thinking. It is not a matter of technology. It is a matter of people knowing what they want to do and why. We did not realize in the beginning how much the whole process of coordination of all the parties involved would be affected. If we make proposals, plans and drawings, we say 'This is what it is going to look like' – and you need to do this to convince people, but what you actually do is something else.

Suppose you have a field, and in this field, soldiers are on parade. There are people moving on the field. There is an organized structure of decision-making – the general at the top, and a chain of command going on down to the soldiers. Everything is organized. People know how to make decisions, what language to use, what they can do, and what they cannot do. Now throw in a ball and let the soldiers play soccer. Change the whole thing. Throw in a ball so that the people in the field will move differently. For the general on the sidelines it represents chaos; even for somebody who does not know soccer it is chaos, because he only sees people running around kicking a ball, and he sees no organization or meaning in it.

But if you know the rules of the game you recognize the organization and it has meaning. To play the game you have to change the structure, you have to change everything from top to bottom. That is actually what we are going to do, evolve different kinds of movements, which we cannot control from the outside. I cannot control a soccer game from the outside. I can be a referee, or I can be a trainer; but once the ball is there and the people start playing, it goes on and one cannot predict in detail what will happen. That is what we want to do in housing.

How do you change the game? You can't just throw in a ball, because nobody knows the rules. You can talk about a different kind of game; you can talk to the people involved and say: "You should do it differently." They will ask: "What do you mean?" They want us to show them what to do; but the demonstration can only be made by other people acting, not by making a drawing of a soccer game. I can choreograph a parade, but not a soccer game.

Now we need two things. We have to know and use the rules of the new game, and we have to be ready so that when people start asking questions, we can answer them. This is very difficult, both for the people and for us, because we are conditioned by the decisions we make and the roles we play.

The basic dilemma of designers or architects, or whatever we call ourselves, is that we are frustrated because we discover that we don't want to operate in the game. Some of us would like to persuade people to play a new game. This means that we must go into the decision-making process, into politics. Others are more inclined to professionalism: how to design Support structures; how to design in such a way that the individual can be involved; how to design in such a way that industry can make things in which the individual can be involved with the builders, and build things in which the individual can be involved. The danger is that these two aspects do not unite. What we need is people who can operate in both fields, people who know how to do it, and people who know why.

At the SAR, we concentrated very much on the professional role; now we are concentrating hard on the other. We have made posters, and we are making more. We are approaching politicians. We are approaching all the decision-makers because now we are sure that we know what to do and how to do it. In Holland, persuasion is difficult. Everything is organized. You have neat houses whose tenants have each signed a contract undertaking that when the lease ends the house will be exactly as it was when he moved in. The organization that leases the houses even provides nameplates, because all the nameplates must be the same. They will even fix the color of the blinds. I know of one area where people have to take all the plants out of their gardens when they move, because their gardens had no plants when they moved in. Try to tell people who organize like this that individuals should be involved; or talk to a builder, or the investment people. Their reaction is the same.

Other people in other countries have worked hard to involve the people. In 1945, in Egypt, Hassan Fathy found that houses could be built of clay bricks in a traditional way, and that the houses were cheaper and better than any others. The people could build them by themselves. He managed to build a village, but he describes in a book the tremendous opposition it raised. He went no further, because the whole bureaucracy and the professionals were against him, not because he was building cheap houses, but because he was challenging their image of a new world. That is something you may not do; but you will have to do it.

Note

1 N. J. Habraken, *De Dragers en de Mensen* (Amsterdam: Scheltema and Holkema NV, 1961); N. J. Habraken, *Supports: An Alternative to Mass Housing* (; London: Architectural Press, 1972).

1972
INVOLVING PEOPLE IN THE HOUSING PROCESS

Editors' note: *This is an edited version of a talk given at the RIBA on 18 April 1972 and published in the* RIBA Journal, *1972.*

At SAR for about six or seven years, we have been trying to make a philosophy work. This philosophy is based on the idea that the housing process can develop further and be a good process only if the occupants are personally involved in that process. I am not going to try to argue this philosophy, but I would like to say that this involvement is, in my opinion, necessary not only because the occupant ought to be able to make decisions about his dwelling, its equipment and interior spaces, and, if you like, be able to identify with his direct environment (all this, of course, is most important), but for many other reasons.

The main reason, perhaps, is that the process simply does not work if the occupants are not involved, and the people who have specialists' parts in the process cannot act properly if the dweller does not also play his or her role. One aspect of this philosophy is that we believe that the technical solution – production – is not possible if the user is not involved. This seems a paradox, because the whole housing process as it works now is based on the simple assumption that you can work if you leave the occupant out of decision making. If you accept this, the whole process as we see it today is logical and it hangs together, but if you want to introduce the occupant, the whole thing has to be rethought and each part of it has to be reconsidered.

But it is not a paradox that you can use industry or technology properly only if you start by thinking about involving people. One might argue that if that were not so, we would already have adequate industrial production of housing (which at this moment is a problem) and so would have enough houses, because wherever industrial production really works, we have too much and not too little.

So, one argument for trying to start from the other side by thinking about the occupant himself is that we might be able to solve our problems better. This also applies to the architect. In fact, we started SAR because we believed that the architect should take the initiative. Whatever you may say about him or her – and a lot of criticism, of course, is possible – he or she is still the one person who tries to bridge the gap between human needs and technical possibilities. Architects are trained to think in these two worlds, and they try very hard to do so. So, if we believe that by starting with the involvement of the occupant we can find better solutions, it is natural that we also believe that the architect has a role to play.

If you want to follow your own beliefs and you are an architect, you have to start by trying to find a way of starting in your own work and your own way of thinking. SAR was set up by ten architects' offices, and, as I remember very well, when they started putting together money to do research on housing and support structures, one of the main reasons was that they had a strong feeling of not being able to do what they should do, a feeling that housing was developing in such a direction that the architect really could not play a part in the two worlds of technology and use. It was felt that the architect was reduced to being someone who had to doll up something that had already been decided upon by industry or, even worse, bureaucracy. This feeling of not being able to act as an architect was, I think, the main reason why these ten architects' offices decided to set up a foundation to investigate the possibility of making an impact on the housing process, industrial production, and urban development by taking the individual into account.

Of course, architects cannot act alone. If you want to change a process, all the parties involved have to participate, but you can start by defining the new role of the architect and try and follow it up. That is what we tried to do – to work out what you could do as a designer in this new role – and from that came what might be called a design methodology.

The problem was that you do not design the finished dwelling but things that will be put together by other people whom you do not know and who will come in later. A lot of decisions have to be made after the designer has finished working, and he or she does not know who is going to make them. That means that you need some kind of design methodology which is based on design as a decision-making process. This is a continuous process in which the architect comes in at a certain point and makes decisions with other people, leaves the job again, and then other people come in and make decisions.

Out of this vision came a methodology based on communication, because if you do part of a job and someone else then takes over, and later still another person takes over, you can work together or hand it over only if you can communicate about the problems.

This communication, of course, deals very much with values of use. If we say that the design process is a decision- making process, then decisions are made on the basis of the kind of value you give to certain solutions in terms of use. We tried to make communication about values in the design process clearer so that we could be explicit about what our decisions meant and about what one could do with those decisions, and out of that develop some kind of tool. This tool, like all tools, can also be used by people who are not interested in support structures, but just in design. In fact, this tool is used in that way, and I do not think it is bad because we have found that architects who do so can do the job better and can have better communication with the client. They have a more explicit way of showing the client different options. Moreover, structuring the decision-making process in such a way ensures that the decisions are made at the right time. We found that several architects who used this tool found that clients gradually became interested, and once they saw the possibilities, they started thinking about other kinds of housing in which they really could also give choice to the user.

All this is what we call today 'software,' and the hardware illustrated is the result of it. It can be judged only in the social and technical context of Holland at this moment. It is not an example of what support structures should be, but an example of how far we have progressed in trying to work together in a different way. I would like to stress this point. The illustrations are the results of a continuous dialogue. Of course, the dialogue itself is not only about projects and hardware: much of it is to do with ways of working and attitudes, arguing with people, and trying to convince people. Maybe this is the most important part, but I cannot show it to you. The simple fact is that now more than 30 architects' offices have joined SAR. People in other disciplines have also joined, and in different places – even places we do not know of ourselves – and are working in the same direction. A continuous dialogue about possibilities is going on and growing, and this is the most important part of the work. Some things have been done not by us but by others with whom we have not been directly involved.

The first illustrations are of a pilot project carried out by the municipality of Amsterdam. It was the initiative of two architects called Rijnboutt and Frieling who work for the department of housing. They got the backing of their superiors, and the federation of Amsterdam housing societies was willing to be the client. A team was put together in which a builder and some manufacturers also took part. The idea was to build a support structure and produce detachable units and see whether it all would work. The design had already been done by Rijnboutt and we acted as consultants to the group. They are now concerned with the working details, cost problems, and so on. I think there is a reasonable chance that the project will be built.

It is a small project of about 100 dwellings on a not very interesting site which was available outside Amsterdam. The building will be three stories high. There is a walkway around the ground floor level and stairs to reach the two other levels (Figure 1). This particular scheme is based on the idea of a column structure, with fixed stairs and fixed places for the ducts (Figure 2). It was developed on the basis of a very specific set of requirements by the municipality, and any dwelling possible in the support structure had to meet these.

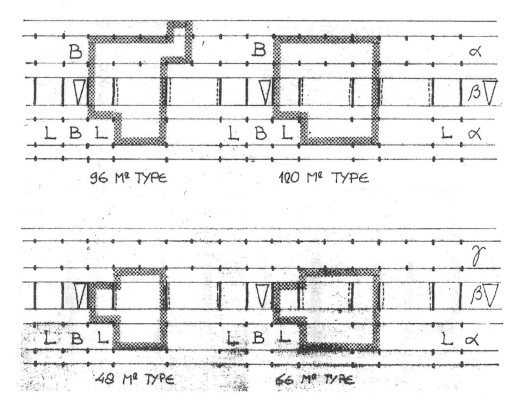

Figure 1 Principle of Amsterdam project. Lower part gives ground floor with sheltered pedestrian circulation γ leading to stairs that give access to dwellings on second and third floor. Upper part gives second and third floor Spans are 3m and 6m. Sectors marked B are for storage. Dotted lines in β zone give place for vertical ducts. Different possible sizes of dwellings are indicated.

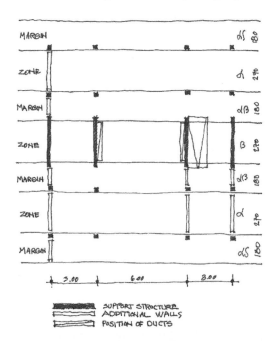

Figure 2 Principle of loadbearing system and zoning of the support. Ducts are near walls in the B Zone. The support itself will have additional (party) walls and façade elements. Detachable units will be interior partitions, sanitary cells, and kitchen equipment.

A report was made on an extensive study of the possibilities of this particular structure (Figure 3). It gives an analysis of all the space required by the client for the different functions, the positions these spaces can have in the support, and the combinations of space that are possible within the spans of the structure. Finally, for each possible dwelling size, all combinations of functions and spaces that give floorplans which meet the client's requirements are written out in codes: these we call 'basic variants.' Basic variants give the relations of functions in a given area of space in the structure. Each represents a set of floorplans that all have the same functional organization in common (Figure 4). By giving all the basic variants that fit the requirements of the client in terms of space standards, space relations, and location of equipment, you can make explicit the possibilities which a particular support gives within a set of requirements. It is a way of testing out a scheme against given criteria, so the client knows what he will get. Communication on the use value of the support is therefore possible, and decisions of a technical nature can be weighed in terms of use value and costs.

Involving people in the housing process

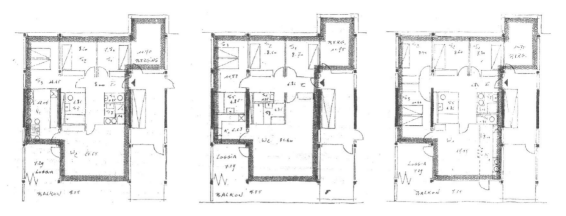

Figure 3 Three different floor plans in one of the possible areas of the support. Floor plans are part of a larger series worked out to test the support design to the criteria given by the client (e.g. municipality of Amsterdam) on room sizes, sanitary equipment and space relations.

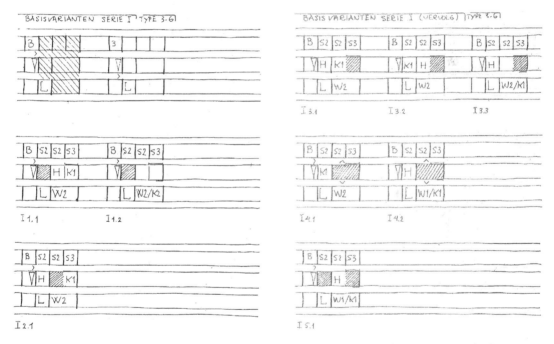

Figure 4 Notation of basic variants for one possible floor area according to a given set of requirements. Codes designate specific functions and their position in the zoning system without actually giving specific dimensions (maximum and minimum dimensions are given by the zoning). Each basic variant represents a set of possible floor plans having the same functional organization.

Once the support is built and the user can make decisions about positions of detachable units to organize the space available, there can be floor plans quite different from those given in the analysis. But this way of analyzing a support design enables the parties responsible for the design to be very explicit about the many decisions that have to be made before the user comes in. You can compare different designs in terms of possible use and can discuss the patterns of use that you think have to be offered to the user; that is, you can judge the constraints given by the support.

The illustrations show the result of about two years' work. It took that long simply because a whole team of people had to adjust to a new process. Because the parties involved had to learn a new way of dealing with problems – arguing about what should be changeable and what should not, what should be the values, what should be important, what costs would be involved, what would happen in the future, and so on – it was time well spent. They found new tools in the methodology proposed by SAR, and once they got through the initial difficulties, they became enthusiastic.

The next project illustrated is a completely different one which was developed about the same time. This came about when we were approached by a building company, who asked us to design a support structure system. The reason why they wanted one was not that they were so much interested in the occupant being able to move around walls or sanitary cells, but that they wanted to give a choice to their clients. Each time they were approached by a client, they were handed a design and they had to change and retool their production system. What they wanted was to continuously develop their production by means of a support structure which they could improve in the course of time, giving more possibilities and options to the client, so that they could have designs of different kinds of dwellings with different kinds of floorplans very quickly, and know exactly what they were getting.

At the same time, we were approached by the municipality of Rotterdam which, for its own reasons, proposed that we set up a pilot project to show what it would be like to have 'flexible housing.' We brought the municipality and the building company together, because we wanted to develop something in 'real time.' The two parties found a third one, an investor, who was interested, and the group asked us to develop a support structure principle which could lead to low and high-rise dwellings of different types: they would then build a pilot project in Rotterdam. The first one was to be a high-rise scheme, about eight stories high, and what is illustrated is a result of the research for the support system. It is not the high rise building that is going to be built but one of our sketches of a possibility. We put in an interior street because for this particular project it was considered a good experiment in a high rise building as an alternative to outside galleries.

This high-rise scheme is one particular interpretation of the support system principle which is completely different from the Amsterdam system. It is based on loadbearing walls parallel to the facade. The idea is very simple: the only restriction is that you can make openings in the walls only in standardized sizes. We worked out three different sizes for the outside walls and three for the inside walls. The spans between the walls can be chosen freely as long as they are on a module of 30cm and do not exceed 4.8m. One reason for this principle was that it gives great freedom in sizes of dwellings, which can be decided on independently of the loadbearing structure. The party walls are non-loadbearing. We wanted small openings in the facade, and, for reasons to be explained later, we thought that this would also be a very efficient way of building in concrete.

The principle of this particular interpretation of the system is explained in Figure 5. This is the size of dwelling, about 100 sq. m., which can accommodate about three bedrooms and a living room according to the standards for subsidized housing in Holland (Figure 6). What seems to be a random pattern of openings has certain regularities: those in the exterior wall have a relation to those in the interior wall. Each pair of openings in the exterior wall has one larger opening in the inside wall next to it, and in the center line of this opening is positioned the vertical shaft for ducts. Thus, two exterior openings, one interior opening, and a shaft form one group. The illustration shows two of these groups and the single openings in between. You will see that non-loadbearing walls run

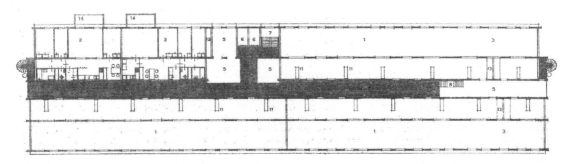

Figure 5 Study for a high-rise Support based on loadbearing walls parallel to the façade with standardized openings.

Involving people in the housing process

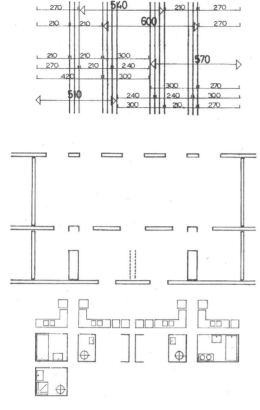

Figure 6 Diagram showing principle of the Support. Gives areas of approximately 100 m² with possible positions for interior partitions, sanitary cells and kitchen units.

perpendicular to the facade and always span two parts of the support structure. That is one reason for this scheme: detachable parts meet only the support structures, not each other, which makes installation fairly easy. The main reason for making it like this is that we tried to get the maximum possibilities of use with the minimum of detachable units and energy in placing them. There are four places where you can have either sanitary cells or kitchen elements (Figure 7).

The floorplans explain the possibilities of the scheme. Dwellings of different sizes can be made in a range from one room studios to dwellings with three or four bedrooms. For each possible dwelling size, an analysis can be made of the basic variants possible in it that are in accordance with the requirements for subsidized housing in Holland and, as I have explained, the basic variants show the range of use patterns. They do not give all possibilities the user has, but they do allow the validity of the support to be judged.

We made models to explain in another way what it is all about. The empty model gives the support structure as it will be when it is finished. At this stage, the first occupants can come into play and decide where they want to live and what size of dwelling they want. In fact, when we started, the client, an investment company, said that they wanted that because they knew that their investment would be obsolete in 15 years and that it took them 50 years to get out money, so if they invested in support structures and detachable units it would be possible to reactivate their property in 15 years. So again, the client's motive was not to give possibilities to the occupant but just to keep their property up to date. But when we had worked out this scheme, he said, 'Well, I didn't expect it to be that simple, but if it is really going to be like this, we could try to give a choice to the first occupants about what they really want to have.'

We at SAR did not design the actual pilot project. The design of the support that will be built in Rotterdam will be by the office of Maaskant Van Dommelen. This again is part of the role game: we have designed the system for the builder, then the client and their architect take over. The architect accepts the principle of the support structure but gives it their own interpretation. For example, they have designed a larger continuous outside space, and also what they call an 'outside detachable unit,' a wood and glass box that spans one or two openings and can be put in front of the support structure on the outside balcony where the occupant wants it, so that the occupant can decide whether he or she wants all the outside space or wants to add something to the inside space. This is one illustration of how someone else can take the principle and play around with it.

We found it necessary to make a full-scale model of part of this support structure because many professional people did not really recognize the possibilities of the space in the support structure as we thought it would be. At our school, we can hang wall elements on a grid ceiling so that you can change floor plans very quickly. It is possible to make a new floorplan in 20 or 25 minutes, and we used this to show how it worked in terms of space. We found, a bit to our surprise, that in Holland architects did not like our proposal: they like large glass facades. We argued that these smaller openings could work very well, and we found that this argument would be settled with a full scale-model: they said, 'It really looks nice . . . it works.' We also found that people who were not professionals immediately reacted very strongly to the model, saying, 'I could do

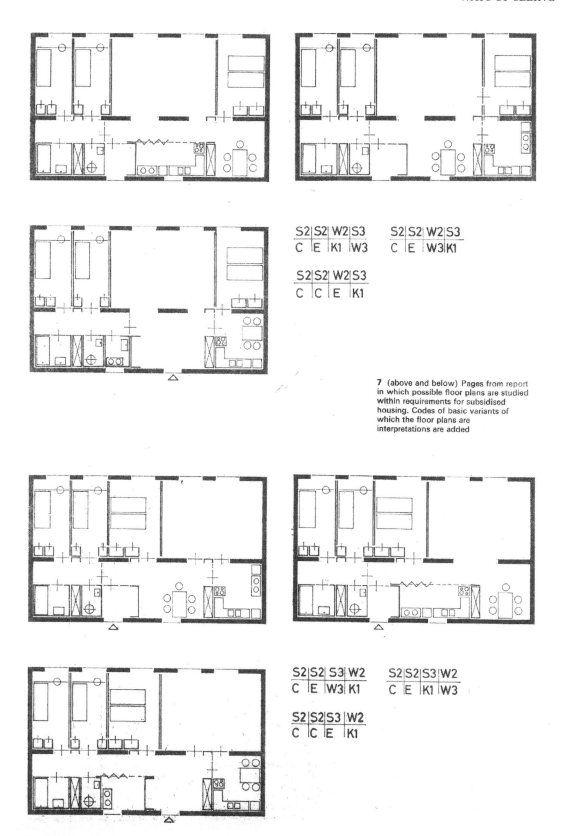

Figure 7 Pages from a report in which possible floor plans are studied within requirements for subsidized housing. Codes of basic variants of which the floor plans are interpretations are added.

Involving people in the housing process

this' and 'I could do that', or 'I would do it this way' and 'I would make the dwelling like this.' Their suggestions are always different from the kind of floorplans that we as architects make.

Also illustrated is another interpretation of the same support principle. We had to design it for this particular builder so that he could make high and low-rise projects, and also different kinds of dwellings.

Figures. 8, 9, and 10 show the type of gallery street, from which you can reach three different levels, with dwellings on each level. Again, the positions of the stairs and the ducts are fixed. You see a different pattern of openings, but the internal relation of the detachable units to the support structure is the same. The rather odd shape for the size of the dwellings comes naturally: that is the easiest way to do it (Figure 11).

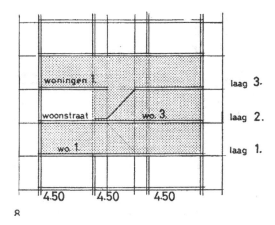

Figure 8 Cross section of the high-rise support based on the same system as in Figures. 5–7. A circulation area gives access to dwellings on three floor levels.

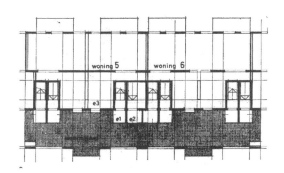

Figure 9 Floor of the support of Figure 8 on the floor of the circulation. Stairs lead to floors on upper and lower floors.

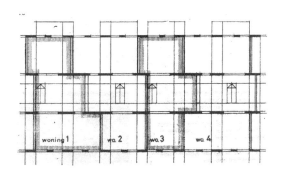

Figure 10 The floor of the support of Figure 8: Stairs and shafts are fixed but party walls are non-loadbearing.

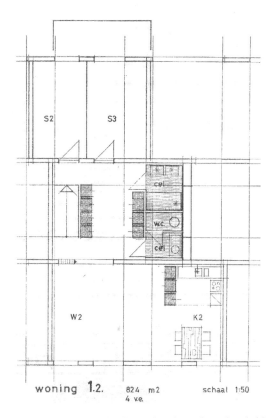

Figure 11 Example of a floor plan shows how detachable units can fit in to make dwellings in a given area of the support

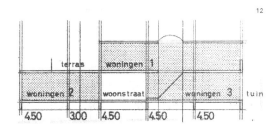

Figure 12 Cross section of a low-rise Support based on the principle of loadbearing walls parallel to the façade.

The next illustrations deal with a particular way of using the idea of design roles to facilitate decision making, the design stage, and communication among the parties involved. Architects De Jong Van Olphen

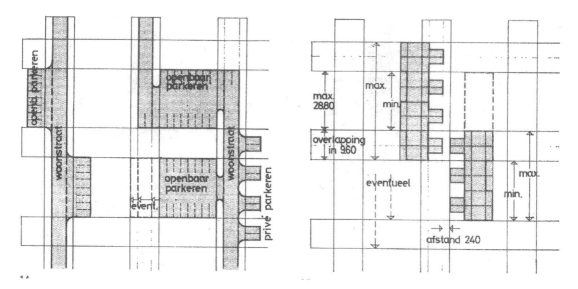

Figure 13 Two pages from the booklet with rules for positioning elements used by De Jong Van Olphen Bax in the design process for a housing scheme in Gouda.

and Bax are working on a scheme for about 900 dwellings in the city of Gouda. They tried to structure their work in such a way that other parties could be involved in the design process in a better way. The parties in this case are the clients (a developer and a building corporation) and various representatives of the municipality, of user groups, and of higher authorities to which the municipality has to submit new urban planning proposals. They decided not to start with a sketch plan or global scheme, but they submitted a booklet containing proposals for elements out of which different plans could be composed, as well as rules for positioning these elements in a grid system in such a way that they could not conflict with each other. The elements were roads, pedestrian circulation, parking spaces, open spaces for communal use, lots, and finally six different dwelling types, each being representative of a set of variations to discuss possible design solutions. Because the elements and rules formed a coherent whole and were understood by all involved in decision making, different approaches with their variations could be worked out very quickly and the different options could be studied and discussed freely (Figures 14 a, b, c). Costs of the elements were also known, so that cost estimates of the options could also be calculated without too much effort. The discussion involved, among others, such issues as orientation of dwellings, patterns of circulation, principles of parking, use of communal spaces, relationships between private and public spaces, degrees of density, and mixtures of dwelling types. A project that we are still working on is another example of how some people become interested in what we are doing and start working in the same direction. We were approached by a developer who also has a plant for prefabricated concrete elements. He pointed out that most systems that we have in Holland are for high rise and big projects in big cities. But 40 or 50 per cent, or even more, of what is built each year are small projects of 10, 20, or 50 houses in different areas of the country, and this has not been put into a system at all. It is still done traditionally which becomes more and more difficult because labor costs go up and the whole process involved becomes so cumbersome. So, he asked us, 'Can you design a system for terrace houses in which you can have different sizes of dwellings and, in each size of dwelling, different kinds of interior possibilities? And can you do it in such a way that 10 or 15 houses in a row can all be different and still make it possible to put them up very quickly? Is it possible to make one house in one week?' We said we would try.

In discussion we came upon a few strategies. One was that it would not be possible, we thought, to launch the whole system at once. So, we tried to cut it up into subsystems that could be developed independently, so that we could start, for example, with the system for the loadbearing elements, and then add a system for the roofs, and then a system for the infill,

Involving people in the housing process

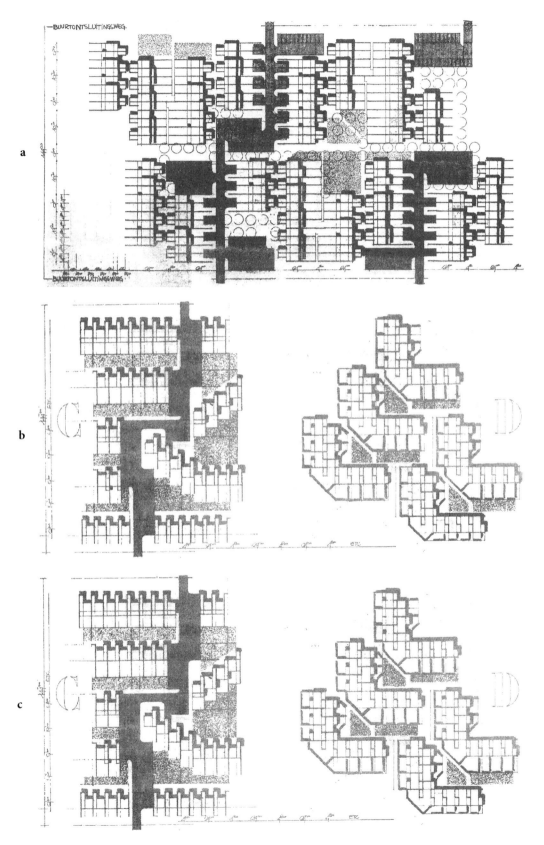

Figures 14 a, b, c: Examples of variations generated in the design process for the Gouda project.

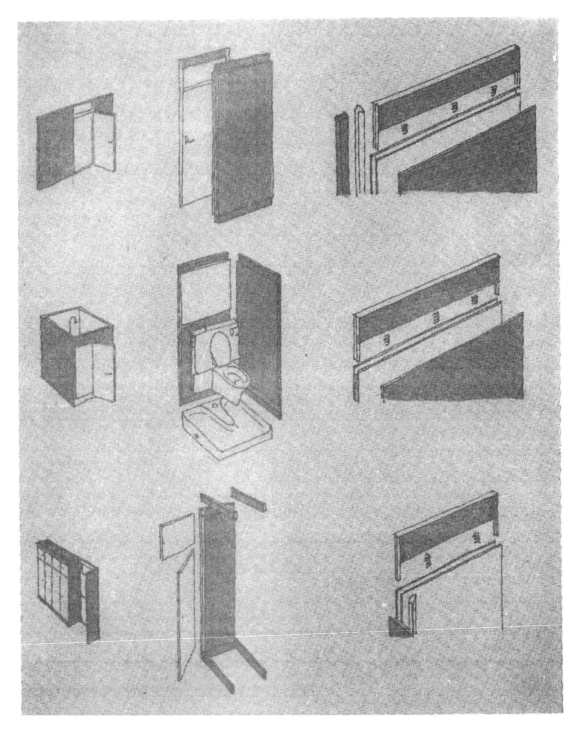

Figure 15 Principle of a Bruynzeel set of detachable units. Components (right) are combined into elements in the factory. Elements are combined in the dwelling space into functional groups.

and so on. Second, we tried to do it in such a way that all the piping and wiring could be reached after the dwelling was finished.

If you want a dwelling in which people can later change things, the piping is most important, and we wanted it to be as it is in an old fashioned house, in which you can tear away parts and find your piping and wiring and change or add something. Another problem was that if you want a lot of possibilities, you need small elements, but if you want to work very quickly on site in one or two weeks, you need large elements. So how do you get a really flexible system in which you can still work with large elements in the field?

The solution., we think, can be found by making a distinction between what happens in the factory and what happens on site. In the factory, small standardized components are assembled into large elements. This makes for a great variety of possible large elements, which are then transported to the site and put together to make the building as specified. The detachable units are then put in to finish the dwelling. A final solution on these principles has not been reached, but a preliminary catalogue has been put together and the general principles have been accepted so far.

Finally, something of the set of detachable units that has been developed by Bruynzeel Ltd. is illustrated. Bruynzeel is a Dutch company specializing is kitchens and other interior elements. They have been working for about three years on them: the first year was a failure because they tried to make a set of detachable units out of components they already produced – kitchens, doors, wall elements, and cupboards – and then fit them into a whole. After a year they decided that this would not work and that they had to start all over again. The decision was made to set up a research group that was given freedom to develop a whole set of detachable units independent of what the firm already made.

The principle is that first you have element groups that you can recognize by their function: walls, sanitary cells, kitchens, and cupboard walls. Then you have the elements that are transported to the site and put together to make an element group. Then there are the components out of which the elements are made in the assembly plant. Different elements are made out of a limited number of components, and out of the different elements the larger groups are made according to the specification of the user (Figure 15). The development team devoted such attention to the wall elements because everybody knows that it is not difficult to make a detachable wall element, but it is difficult to make one very cheaply, and they had to compete with traditional materials. They came up with a scheme which is interesting because there is a lot of choice in the finish. It has two panels attached to a core, so you can choose different thicknesses, different acoustical properties, and different finishes. A full-scale dwelling space based on the Amsterdam project has been built to try out the system.

1972
CONTROL HIERARCHIES IN COMPLEX ARTIFACTS

Editors' Note: *The original paper was published in Proceedings, Conference on Planning and Design Methods in Architecture. J.P. Protzen, Editor, Boston, 1987 (International Conference on Planning and Design Theory)*

Abstract

When we examine the composition of complex artifacts, we are likely to see a hierarchical structure. The kind of hierarchy we find depends on the criteria we apply for the decomposition of the configuration under scrutiny. One criterion can be to consider the whole composed of parts that lend themselves for control by separate agents in charge of the design or maintenance of it. We will seek for such control units in the complex artifact. Hierarchies composed of control units tell us about the ways we can partially transform the artifact and how different designers may best distribute, among themselves, their design joint efforts. Hierarchies composed of control units we will call control hierarchies.

Three kinds of control hierarchies are distinguished. The first, called **assembly hierarchies**, are commonly known and predominantly technical in nature. They tell us that a unit on a higher level of the hierarchy is composed of parts we find on the lower level. Control is one of assembly of smaller parts into a larger one and the process is a sequence of assemblies.

In the other two control hierarchies the entities we find on a lower level do not assemble to form a higher-level unit. The relation between the levels is not one of assembly but of 'dominance' where the transformations on the lower level are constrained by the higher level. Of these two, one has to do with the control of physical elements and is called a **dependency hierarchy**.

The other has to do with the control of spaces in which we distribute our physical parts and is called a **territorial hierarchy**.

The paper also discusses the relation between these different hierarchical structures. It particularly touches upon the relation between dependency hierarchies and territorial hierarchies and considers how the same physical configuration can have different territorial interpretations.

Introduction

Designing is a social activity in which various parties seek consensus about what to do: the professional designer, the client, and other consultants must work together in the design process.

Looking at the design process in this way, we must consider the interaction between, on the one hand, the parties who act and, on the other hand the configuration shaped under their action.

Studying this interaction, we see, in the configurations we make, the hierarchical structures that are the subject of this paper. When we look only at the forms and not the parties who act, we learn little about designing. When we look only at the people and not at the forms that result from their efforts, we may remain equally ignorant about designing; but when we study the interaction between the two, new perspectives emerge.

My paper is based on experiences and studies about the design of environmental forms: buildings, neighborhoods and other settlement forms, but I will try to formulate as generally as I can the principles I found because I believe they can be applied to the design of any kind of complex artifact.

What I have to say has nothing to do with functional or aesthetic objectives. The function we attach to the object we are designing and the purposes we attach to our designing make us a designer of a certain kind of artifact: e.g. architect, mechanical engineer, etc. When, therefore, we seek to discover what is of interest to designers of different disciplines, we must disregard specifics of function and purpose and focus on the interaction between the designer and the form as such.

1. Agents and configurations

1.1. I will call an agent P, any person, or group of persons acting as one, capable of transforming a configuration C. I will write PP for a combination of such agents, each transforming their own configuration, and P or Px for a single agent.

Suppose there is an agent P acting to transform a configuration called Ca.

For P to transform Ca there must be parts of Ca to be taken away, to be added, or to be displaced. (I do not consider the displacement of Ca as a whole to be a transformation of it, but such displacement can be the transformation of a larger ^{whole of which Ca is a part}.)

Thus, P may see Ca as composed of parts b.
We can write:

$$Ca \; \Delta \; b,b,b, \ldots \quad\quad\quad 1)$$

in which Δ may be read as 'composed of'. On each side of Δ we see the same whole described in a different way. On the left we see the whole as a single object. On the right we see it as a configuration of parts. We do not define Ca as a set of parts but as a configuration of parts. The same set of parts can yield a different configuration when b's are differently positioned in space relative to one another. Thus, there is implied in Δ a set of parts and a set of position relations among the parts.

1.2. There are many ways in which Ca can be seen as composed of parts. What parts an agent P decides to see is for it to decide and may have to do with convention, function, preference, or convenience. The important thing is that, to act at all, P must agree on what parts C is made of. We will therefore say that the expression 1) is correct for a particular P.

1.3. P can see each part b as a configuration in itself; ^{thus, a particular part **b1** becomes **Cb1** and}

$$Cb1 \; \Delta \; c,c,c, \ldots \ldots \quad\quad\quad 2)$$

and again, this WAY OF SEEING $Cb1$ is a matter of choice for P.

1.4. Looking at 1) and 2) together, we have a description of Ca as a part-whole hierarchy. We are accustomed to seeing complex things as part-whole hierarchies. We may see, for instance, a wall as composed of bricks, a window as composed of a frame and other parts that fit the frame, a door as a frame that holds a part that moves, etc.; and a house as composed of walls, windows, and doors, etc.

2. Moves

2.1 In this paper, however, we want to look at Ca not just as a composition of parts, but we are interested in P acting on Ca.

Whatever P does will be a combination of three basic acts:

Take a part away: elimination
Add a part: introduction
Put a part somewhere else: displacement or rearrangement

But P, we may assume, will act with purpose and seek to establish certain relations between parts b in a sequence of basic acts. Such purposeful combinations of basic acts are intended to 'arrange' parts and we may call them 'arrangement moves' or 'moves' for short. Connecting parts, putting parts on a distance from each other, stringing them along an imaginary line, or making them conform to certain geometric patterns, are all arrangement moves.

3. Control

3.1. Control is the ability to decide on moves. When agent P can decide to transform a configuration Ca, by moving (displacing, introducing, or eliminating) all and any of the parts Ca is composed of, we can say that P is in full control of Ca. When Ca is controlled by an agent we will write:

$$PCa$$

Because we do not know anything about **P** other than that it controls **Ca**, we really have identified **P** by **Ca** and, therefore **PCa** stands for an agent as well as for a configuration **Ca** under control.

3.2 We have seen that **Ca** can be composed of parts **b**. Thus, by way of demonstration we may have:

$$\text{Ca} \,\Delta\, b1,b2,b3 \qquad\qquad\qquad 3)$$

We have also seen that **b1** and **b2** and **b3** could be configurations by themselves composed of parts **c**. That means that **Cb1** and **Cb2** can be under control of their own agents **PCb1** and **PCb2**. And we can write:

$$\text{PCa} \,\Delta\, \text{PCb1, PCb2, PCb3} \qquad\qquad 3.1)$$

We can think of the house **Ca** which is composed of walls **Cb1** and windows **Cb2**, and doors **Cb3**. And there is an agent **PCb1** that assembles the windows out of smaller parts **c**, and another agent **PCb2** that assembles doors out of other smaller parts **c**, and an agent **PCa** that assembles doors, windows, and walls into a house.

3.3 To have a situation as given in 3.1, it is necessary that the four agents involved see the whole configuration **PCa** in the same way. These agents must agree on the way they will see the whole **Ca** and its parts. We begin to see the complex whole as the result of a social agreement. Thanks to this agreement the different agents can act meaningfully on their own.

4. Assembly hierarchies

4.1 Part of the agreement implied by 3.1 is that the configurations **PCb1**, **PCb2**, and **PCb3** can be independently composed of smaller parts **c** in different ways because otherwise no agent could exercise control over them. If that is the case, we can say that **b1**, **b2**, and **b3**, are control units. And if **Ca** can be transformed by combining **b1**, **b2**, and **b3**, it is also a control unit.

For instance, we may see the porches of different houses in a street as a configuration by itself, but that configuration of porches cannot be a control unit. The larger control unit a porch is part of is the house it belongs to.

In case of the porches along the street we can identify a configuration composed of other configurations:

$$\text{Ca} \,\Delta\, \text{Cb1, Cb2, Cb3} \ldots \qquad\qquad 4)$$

And we know that the porches are control units so we can write:

$$\text{Ca} \,\Delta\, \text{PCb1, PCb2, PCb3} \ldots \qquad\qquad 4.1)$$

But there is no agent **PCa**.

4.2 In this paper, while any spatial distribution of control units **Pb1**, **Pb2**, etc . . . can be seen as a configuration, we will be particularly interested in a configuration **Ca** which itself is a control unit as well, so that we can write:

$$\text{PCa} \,\Delta\, \text{PCb1, PCb2, PCb3} \ldots \qquad\qquad 4.2)$$

Which means that agent **PCa** can decide which configuration **Cb** will be part of it and where a configuration **Cb** will go in the configuration **Ca**; while each **PCb**, as a configuration by itself and as a control unit, will have similar control over its own parts.

4.3 In expression 4.2) we have, from among all the possible configurations we may see as part-whole hierarchies identified, one that is at the same time a control hierarchy. That is to say, a hierarchy in which all parts are control units. Control hierarchies are the hierarchies we normally tend to consider when designing and building complex artifacts.

4.4 In a control hierarchy each agent can assemble its own configuration from parts it can select and arrange. There are different kinds of control hierarchies that we will discuss later on. In the control hierarchy of expression 4.2) **PCa** is an assembly of several configurations **B**. And each configuration **PCb** is an assembly of configurations **PCc**. When this is the case, we will speak of an **Assembly Hierarchy**. An assembly hierarchy is a part-whole hierarchy in which the parts are control units. (The expression 4.1) we see a part-whole hierarchy as well, but it is not a control hierarchy and therefore not an assembly hierarchy.)

4.5 In these general expressions we are not interested in the identities of the agents involved. The individuals who control the parts **Cb** may be in joint control of **Ca**, forming together a **PCa**. Or a different individual, or group of different individuals forming one agent, may be **PCa**. In the latter case this agent **PCa** may or may not, be mandated by the **Pb**'s to take care of **Ca**. Regardless of identities, **PCa** will always be an agent distinct from those on the lower level of the assembly hierarchy because it has a different control responsibility. **PCb**'s only control part; **PCa** controls the combination of these parts.

Control hierarchies in complex artifacts

5. Dominance

5.1 Now let us consider two parts b that together make a configuration Ca

$$Ca \triangle b1, b2 \qquad (6)$$

Suppose we do not know what control situation is at hand but that we can observe, over time, transformations of **Ca**; that is to say, we can observe the results of control exercised on **Ca**.

Let us use an abstract example and take two rectangles of the same shape marked **b1** and **b2** respectively in a field **F**. Let the field **F** with the two rectangles in it be the configuration **Ca** (see Figure 1).

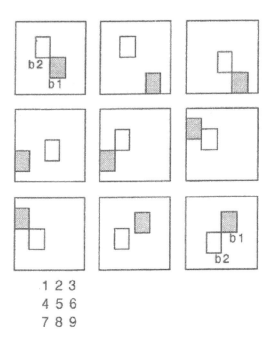

Figure 1 (1–9)

5.2. Suppose we now observe a sequence of transformations as, for instance, given in Figure 1 (1–9). The configuration **Ca** consist of two rectangles located in a square field. **Ca** transforms because the rectangles **b1** and **b2** change their location within the square they inhabit. The transformations should be read from 1 to 9 in Figure 1. We see that each time, when **b1** moves, **b2** moves to connect itself with one corner to a corner of **b1**. Apparently, **b2** wants to maintain a relation to **b1**, while **b1** is free to disturb that relation by displacing itself.

When we see a pattern like that, we can conclude that **b1** dominates **b2**.

5.2 Dominance is defined as follows

If there are, in a configuration, two parts **b1** and **b2** and we find that, when **b2** is displaced or transformed, it does not force displacement or transformation of **b1** but, when **b1** is displaced or transformed, it may force displacement or transformation of **b2**, the **b1** dominates **b2**.

5.4 Because our example consists of abstract rectangles, we cannot see why dominance takes place. We will see later on that reasons for dominance can vary. Perhaps **b2** needs to connect to **b1** for functional reasons (say for instance that **b2** must plug into **b1** to function) in which case the configurations determine dominance independent of the agent in control. It may be that agent **P** in control of the configuration just likes **b2** to be in a diagonal relation to **b1**, and that another agent controlling this configuration would not follow the same pattern. The dominance situations we find in real life are of both kinds. Sometimes function demands it, and sometimes it results from human preference or habit. Often, the distinction is not so clear. Our interest is in the behavior of forms under the control of agents, not the motivation of agents. We are looking at dominance relations among configurations and parts rather than dominance relations among agents.

5.5 Figure 2 suggests that **b1** is, in turn, dominated by a part outside **Ca**: **b1** seeks to place itself adjacent to that third, outside part. In that case, we find a chain of dominance among three parts. It is not difficult to see that complex situations can result from such chains of dominance.

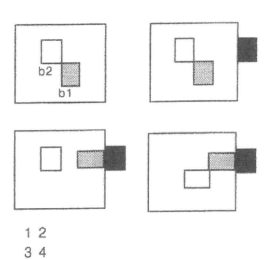

Figure 2 (1–4)

6. Dependency hierarchies

6.1 Hierarchical structures based on dominance among control units can be seen in many artifacts. We will call them dependency hierarchies

For an example that is rather similar to that given in Figure 2, but less abstract, think of a chair relative to a desk and of the desk relative to a wall against which we want to place it. When, in our design, we move the desk, we want the chair to come with it and when the wall is shifted, we will also adjust the table to stay with it.

Once we know dominance, many examples can be found in real life.

For another example a wall may contain a window. The designer can give the window different positions in the wall while the wall stays in place, but when the wall is displaced, we expect the window to come with it. Buildings may line up along a street. The buildings can be taken down, altered, or newly built while the street remains the same. But when the street must be widened, or even shifted in its course, buildings must adjust. We take it for self-evident that the street pattern dominates the positioning of buildings. Similar examples will be discussed in more depth later on.

6.2 If we take the symbol $\neg$ to mean 'dominates' we can write, when two parts **b1** and **b2** of a configuration have a relation of dominance:

b1 $\neg$ **b2**   7)

and it may also be that **b1** and **b2** are control units: **PCb1** $\neg$ **PCb2**   7.1)

6.3 As we can see from the examples given and from the Figures 1 and 2, lower level entities such as **b2** in expression 7) in a dependency hierarchy cannot combine to make the higher-level entity (**b1**). A combination of chairs does not make a table. A configuration of buildings does not make a street. Even when we would have, in the situation of Figure 1, two parts **b2a** and **b2b** wanting to connect to corners of **b1**, these two lower level parts could not combine to make a **b1**. Unlike with assembly hierarchies, in a dependency hierarchy, configurations on the lower level are not parts of a higher-level configuration.

We therefore <u>cannot</u> write:

b1 $\triangle$ **b2**   8)

because there is no way to make a desk out of a number of chairs, or a wall out of windows.

But we can write:

Ca $\triangle$ **b1, b2**

For instance: my workstation (**Ca**) consists of a desk (**b1**) and a chair (**b2**); or the facade (**Ca**) consists of a wall (b1) and a window (b2).

So, where **b1** and **b2** are on the same level in an assembly hierarchy, they are on different levels in terms of dominance.

7. Shape and dependence

In the example of Figure 1, **b1** and **b2** are exactly the same shape and inhabit a free field; nothing in the shapes of Figure 1 makes dominance likely; we recognize it only in the sequence of moves.

In many cases, however, we find the forms themselves of such shapes and composition as to suggest the distribution of control we call 'dominance'.

7.1 Consider the series of Figure 3. We see a configuration **Ca**. In it we can distinguish two configurations that are themselves composed of smaller parts: on the highest level of assembly we have: **Ca** $\triangle$ **Cb1, Cb2**. Here **Cb1** is made of 'pegs' (**p**) and forms a cluster of enclosures: **Cb1** $\triangle$ **p1. p2, p3** . . ., while **Cb2** is a distribution of squares (s): **Cb2** $\triangle$ **s1, s2, s3** . . . .

We can see, therefore, an assembly hierarchy of three levels: the lowest level parts are pegs and squares (**p** and **s**), the middle level parts are **Cb1** and **Cb2**, and the highest level is **Ca**, the combination of these two.

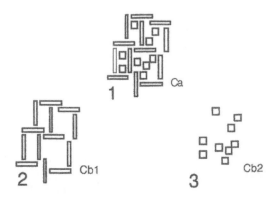

Figure 3 (1–3)

Control hierarchies in complex artifacts

7.2 Let us assume that **Cb1** and **Cb2** are control units so that we can write **PCb1** and **PCb2**. Let us further assume that, by agreement among agents **PCb1** and **PCb2**, the relation between **Cb1** and **Cb2** is such that the squares must be located in an enclosure formed by pegs. No square may be found outside such an enclosure.

Figure 4 gives an example of a sequence of moves under the assumed circumstances. In Figure 4, squares move in #2 and #4. In the same Figure 4, pegs are moved in #3 and #4. We find that the agent in control of squares can take out and bring in and displace parts without forcing transformation of the configuration of pegs. On the other hand, we find that transformation of **Cb1** (the pegs) easily disturbs the configuration of squares (**Cb1**). To open an enclosure or to shift the boundaries of an enclosure, it may be necessary for **PCb1** first to 'evict' the squares inhabiting it: that is to say it must force **PCb2** to move its squares a certain way.

Of course, when **PCb2** refuses and gets away with it, **PCb1** is no longer in control of **Cb1**; it must dominate to exercise control. Thus, the systemic and morphological conditions are such that whoever controls **Cb1** will dominate **Cb2** or, to put it differently, the condition for control of **Cb1** is to dominate **Cb2**.

Configuration **Ca**, behaving under transformation as it does in Figure 4, makes us see a two-level dependency hierarchy. We can, from there, begin to construct a dependency hierarchy of greater depth.

7.3 Once we have seen configurations like those given in Figure 4, we may guess, next time when see a similar configuration, that there will be a dependency hierarchy there. It is so familiar that we have a name for it: dominance by forms of enclosure. Of course, we can only be sure when we watch such a configuration transform, because it need not follow the assumption of enclosure Figure 4 is based on.

When we deal with complex artifacts, we often 'see' dominance in this way. We do not need to watch the transformations of the artifact to predict its 'behavior' under transformation, because we are familiar with it and recognize it in the shapes of the configurations at hand.

But while it seems that morphology determines dominance, we may find, on closer scrutiny, that convention also plays a role. It is 'natural' that the chairs 'follow' the table because their use is habitual. It is 'self-evident' that the street dominates the buildings, but one can imagine a case where the distribution of buildings determines where the streets go. Thus, dominance is closely related for form, but that relation may be conventional as well as formal.

7.4 Common vocabulary tells us that we have an innate sense for dominance relations in complex forms. When a higher-level form transforms and lower level forms must yield, we speak of a 'structural' problem. What we call 'frameworks' or 'infrastructures' are usually higher-level forms in a dependency hierarchy. The framework allows us to attach a diversity of objects to it. We can change and rearrange these objects without disturbing the framework, but, when we redesign the framework, the distribution of lower level objects is disturbed and must follow the new arrangement.

7.5 Be it convention or morphology, there are shapes that we easily recognize in terms of dominance relation. Among them, different shape-families can be identified, suggesting different kinds of dominance relations between levels. Three are suggested here:

- 7.5.1 The relation of enclosure gives us one family of dependency hierarchies. Figure 3 is of that family and the relation was established in the case of 7.2.
- 7.5.2 A relation of supply usually yields tree-like higher forms by means of which lower level configurations are served. In Figure 5 #2 we see an example of two tree-forms together. In Figure 5 #3 the levels of the parts are shaded differently.

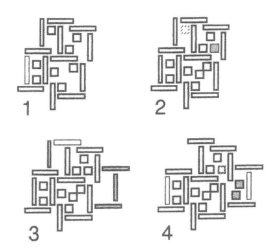

Figure 4 (1–4)

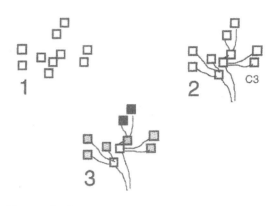

Figure 5 (1–3)

The configuration of squares in this example (Figure 5) is taken from Figure 4. By means of the connections, squares are placed in dependence relations among themselves. This example shows how, in a dependency hierarchy, the same physical entity (square) can appear on different levels. Because we are looking at a configuration of parts, not a diagram, the connections are parts of the configuration as well. The connection parts, by themselves, do not constitute a configuration of another level. They belong, like the squares, to a single configuration.

Please note that in the same configuration the supply can move two ways. If it is a water supply system, the water is distributed from a central point to the various branches. If it is a waste collecting system, the flow goes from the branches towards the center. But the dominance situation remains the same. The center always dominates the branches. Branches can shift freely, but when centers shift, branches must adapt.

7.5.3 A third family of relations, relations of gravity, are those where one configuration 'carries' or 'supports' another. When, for instance, a lintel is placed on columns, the lintel must be displaced if the configuration of columns is to transform, but the lintel can be displaced without disturbing the configuration of columns. Thus, if one agent controls the columns and another the lintel, the column agent dominates.

6.6 Of these three families only the third is fully determined by physical constraints. As already pointed out earlier, in most cases morphological constraints (e.g. enclosure) may suggest, but do not always force, dominance. Usually there are, in addition, agreements among the agents in control of the parts, having to do with the purpose and function of the artifact we are designing. Or simply having to do with preferences shared by the agents.

Very often we are so familiar with the dependency hierarchy at hand that we find the relation of dominance quite natural. Yet this may be the result of habit and convention and not of natural laws. It is because we are familiar with the forms we make – know how things transform and are manipulated by various actors – that they strike us as self-evident.

8. Control distribution

8.1 As noted when discussing Figure 1, we can determine a dominance situation by observing the transformations of a configuration without knowing exactly who controls what. In the hierarchy of Figure 3, we defined the configuration of squares (**Cb2**) as a single control unit of a level lower than the configuration of pegs (**Cb1**). But it is easy to see a large number of control units in **Cb2**. Indeed, every square could be one, so could every group of squares in a single enclosure. It follows that we can think of many separate agents controlling one or more parts, instead of a single agent controlling all squares. Thus, different patterns of control distribution are easily possible relative to **Cb2**.

In the same example, the configuration of pegs (**Cb1**) does not so easily suggest a distribution of control. Its parts must act together to form the enclosures, leaving less freedom for independent moves.

In other words, the configuration of Figure 3 is most naturally understood as a single configuration of pegs, enclosing many configurations of squares. This difference between the higher and the lower level in terms of control distribution is typical for dependency hierarchies. We imagine them quite naturally as a single agent in control of the higher level confronting a number of lower level agents all in the same vertical relation with it. Think of the street with many houses along it, the table with many chairs around it, the wall with many windows in it. Indeed, the tree branch with many leaves growing from it.

8.2 When we return to the squares (**Cb2**) in Figure 3, we see how an agent could control any number of squares distributed over any number of enclosures. Yet, so suggestive is the form, that we feel that control over squares in more than one enclosure is almost like playing the same role twice. The dominance relation between squares and their enclosure is evident and

Control hierarchies in complex artifacts

powerful, while the relation among squares, short of sharing the same enclosure, is not evident in Figure 3.

The same can be said of the example of Figure 5. One agent could control different squares of the same shade, but the relation we recognize is the one of dominance, not the interaction between parts of the same level.

The very nature of the hierarchical structure is to isolate entities on the same level and to establish vertical relations. For that reason, the distribution of control over the lower level configuration is freer and more variable.

8.3 We can also imagine a single agent in control of a higher-level configuration and, at the same time, having control over some of the lower level parts. But it is clear that this agent must play two different roles. Being a higher-level power makes it dominate a number of lower level agents and being a lower level agent at the same time may cause a conflict of interest. A same agent may exercise control on different levels, but that does not make the parts it controls into a single configuration. The form makes the same individual act as two different agents.

8.4 Thus, we can see, in the Figures 4 and 6, a great variety of possible control distributions over the same form. But this variety does not diminish the autonomy of the physical situation and the relational agreements we attach to it. In order to change the dependency hierarchy, those in control must get together and decide to change the relational conditions they have agreed upon so far.

9. Territorial hierarchies

9.1 Control over a physical configuration means that we can transform the configuration. Transformations must take place somewhere and, unless we also have control over a space to work in, we may not be able to move. Yet, control over physical parts is not the same as control over space. In complex physical organizations we can distinguish a separate hierarchy based on the control of space. This **territorial hierarchy** has its own autonomy which, like the physical hierarchies discussed so far, is based on agreement among parties.

9.2 We define here control of space as the ability to determine what goes into the space. A territory **T** is a space under control of a party **P**. Each territory has boundaries and **P** controls **T** when **P** can decide what may cross the boundary to enter **T**.

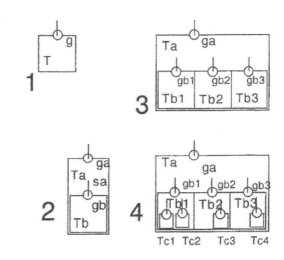

Figure 6 (1-4)

9.3 Suppose a single territory **T** is entered through a gate **g**. (Figure 6 #1). Outside that gate we must expect another space **s** under control of another party. (If there is no other party to be kept out **g** is meaningless and there is no **T**)

This means that **s** must have guarded boundaries too and hence its own gate. If **ga** in Figure 6 #2 is the only gate through which **gb** can be reached, we find that whoever controls **ga** must dominate whoever controls **gb** because **Tb** can only admit what enters **Ta** first. It follows that **ga** is access not only to **sa** but also to **Tb**. It is therefore correct to say that there is a larger territory **Ta** which encompasses all space accessed through **ga**. In other words, **Tb** is included in **Ta**.

This relationship is easily understood when we read for **Ta** the state of Massachusetts, and for **Tb** the city of Boston.

9.4 Because the total space of **Ta** encompasses both **Tb** and **sa**, we can say that, in **Ta**, **sa** is the <u>public space</u> while **Tb** is the <u>private space</u> of **Ta**.

There are many cities in Massachusetts. We can think of a situation, more common than our example so far, where several **Tb** are included in one **Ta** as in Figure 6 #3. When we control any included territory **Tb**, we can freely step out in the public space **sa** of **Ta**. But we can close off our territory from whatever comes from **sa**.

Hence the boundary relation is asymmetric. Agent **PTa** may not close our door **gb2** and imprison us. Thus, all inhabitants of a **Tb** have free access to **sa**, they are also inhabitants of **Ta**, and **sa** is the space they share: their public space.

These definitions of public and private space are in accord with the normal usage of the terms. We must not speak of public and private territory, but of public and private space, because we are talking about spaces that are parts of a territory, and sa is not a territory by itself but only the public part of a territory.

9.5 Consider a deeper territorial structure as in Figure 6 #4, where each **Tb** in turn contains one or more territories **Tc**, Inhabitants of **Tc**, stepping outside their gate, will enter a common, public space **sb**.

This time, a territory **Tb** is the sum of **sb** and all included territories **Tc**, and **sb** is public space to all those so included. However, to a visitor from territory **Tb2**, who goes out into **sa** and approaches the gate of **Tb1**, **Tb1** as a whole is private space she cannot enter freely. Once admitted she will find herself in **sb** which, to those coming from **Tc**, was public space.

We see that the concepts of public and private space are relative and depend on which way we move. Going outward, moving into ever more encompassing territories, we move always into public space. Returning and going inward into ever deeper territories, we move always into private space.

Understanding the hierarchical structure of territory frees architects and urban designers from confusion, often encountered, about 'private,' 'semi-private,' 'semi-public' and 'public' spaces. Any space we may find ourselves in can be seen as public or private depending on which other space we see it related to.

10. Territorial interpretations of configurations

10.1 Territorial boundaries are determined by control, and although it is convenient to mark them with walls, fences, or corner posts, this need not be the case. Territorial boundaries are often invisible, although clearly defined, like those between nations. When we observe bathers on a beach or campers at a campground, we also see territorial divisions without readily visible boundaries. The wall and the gate, on the other hand, may not mark a territorial boundary at all: for a house in its surrounding garden, the doorway is not a territorial gate- the boundary is between the garden and the street. There is no one-to-one relation between physical forms and territorial organization.

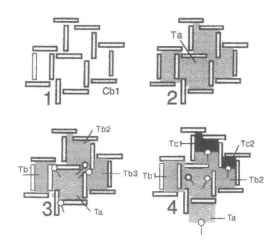

Figure 7 (1–4)

10.2 Any given configuration of physical parts can be interpreted territorially in different ways. Figure 7 #1 shows the higher-level configuration **Cb1** of the earlier example of Figure 4 #4. If we read in this picture a constellation of walls, we may first see it as one territory bounded by the outer walls of the configuration, as is shown in Figure 7 #2.

In Figure 7 #3, Ta is still bounded by **Cb1**. We see inside **Ta** a hierarchy of three included territories **Tb**, the boundaries of which still follow closely the wall configuration. To read a territorial hierarchy in this figure, gates have been places and it is assumed the boundaries, indicated by **Cb1**, are otherwise closed.

In Figure 7 #4, the territorial organization departs from the spatial organization suggested by **Cb1**. First, **Ta** has expanded outwards and its gate is now located away from **Cb1**. Second, we find that **Tb2** and **Tb3** have merged into one territory **Tb2**. Third, we find that the boundaries between the public space of **Ta** and included territories **Tb** no longer follow the walls locating **gb1** and **gb2** free in physical space. Fourth, we find new territories included in **Tb2**, making a deeper hierarchy. Their boundaries and gates are placed within the spaces formed by **Cb1**.

10.3 Another variation of territorial interpretation of **Cb1** assumes that it is fully occupied by territories of the same depth, all with their gates at the periphery of **Cb1**. (Figure 8 #1) This implies a larger territory containing **Cb1**. This situation is analogous to an urban block surrounded by public streets.

Control hierarchies in complex artifacts

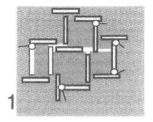

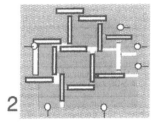

Figure 8 (1–2)

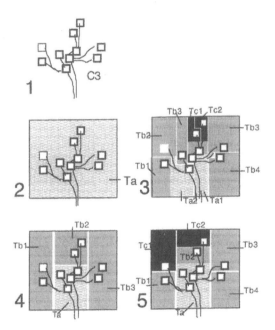

Figure 9 (1–5)

The final interpretation of **Cb1** follows the same organization but here the outer boundaries of the territories are found well outside of **Cb1**. (Figure 8 #2) We can think of front yards, and five territorial gates are no longer within **Cb1**.

10.4 In addition to this exercise with a form of enclosure we can look again at **C3** of Figure 5 #2 repeated in Figure 9 #1. This time in relation with territorial control. **C3**, obviously, can be under control of one party and therefore be inside a single territory **Ta**.

The 'gate' of **Ta** is here indicated by the crossing of the boundary by the supply lines. (Figure 9 #2)

The territorial hierarchy of Figure 9 #3 follows exactly the dependency levels of the supply configuration **C3**.

In Figure 9 #4 we find several levels of the dependency hierarchy of **C3** within the public space of a single territory (**Ta**) while in **Tb1**, **Tb2** and **Tb3** each time two control entities (squares) of the same level of the Figure 9 dependency hierarchy of **C3** inhabit the same territory.

Figure 9 #5 completes these variations of the ways in which a dependency hierarchy can be located territorially. The gates of the territories are where the supply lines shown in **C3** cross boundaries. This gate location produces a territorial hierarchy of three levels, with **Tc1** included in **Tb1** and **Tc2** included in **Tb2**. The squares of **C3** are placed in the territorial hierarchy in such a way that there is no correspondence between the levels of the two hierarchies. For instance, the two squares in **Tb2** and **Tc2** are on the same level in the dependency hierarchies, but the territory in which one is located is included in the territory in which the other is located.

10.5 Figures 9 and 10 refer to **Cb2** of Figures 3 and 4 #4. When we interpret the squares as buildings brought together in common lots surrounded by a public street network, we get something like Figure 10 #2. In Figure 10 #3 all territories in the 'block' are still directly related to the outer public space. There is no difference of territorial depth compared with Figure 10 #2, but there are more territories; most squares being located in their own territory.

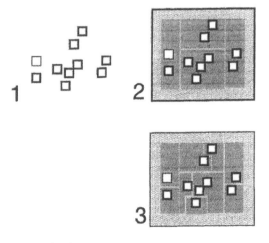

Figure 10 (1–3)

11. Relations between territorial control and dependency control

11.1 We have discussed the relation between two kinds of control hierarchies

a. The physical configurations revealing dependency relations among their arts, and
b. The territorial organization revealing relations of inclusion.

So far, we have done so only in terms of location of the one relative to the other. But each combination of a territorial situation with a physical configuration can be interpreted in different ways as a control situation.

If, for instance, a party controls a territory, and in that territory, we find two physical control units, (e.g. the two squares in **Tb1** in Figure 9 #4) then different control distributions may occur. We may have one agent controlling both the territory and the two squares, but we may also have one agent controlling the territory and another controlling the squares. This simple example may show how complex control situations may easily result in any given combination of a configuration and a territorial organization.

11.2 In many artifacts we have more than one dependency hierarchy. In Figure 11 we see again squares on different levels of the dependency hierarchy in the supply form we examined earlier. But now, all the squares together are also part of a lower level in relation to the configuration of pegs in which they are located. When we imagine, added to that combination, a territorial organization where gates for the supply form may be located differently from the gates for other uses of the territories that are found in it, we see a whole which only begins to suggest the complex control situations we may find in a single house.

Figure 11

Final comments

Knowledge of hierarchical properties of environmental forms and other complex artifacts is of value to designers.

Control hierarchies help us understand how the artifact predetermines the relation between those who act upon it and how, in turn, the way agents relate to one another shapes the artifact.

The hierarchies we see in our artifacts are the result of explicit or tacit agreements among those who act upon them. Conventions about WAYS OF SEEING the world, about our relations towards things and among agents determine, to a large extent, the artifacts we make and the ways in which they transform over time by the acts of agents.

This paper seeks to formalize the general principles according to which complex artifacts 'behave' when subject to agent's control. Apart from a few examples, it does not describe particular cases observable in real life but aims at making such description possible. By means of control hierarchies presented here, we can begin to examine the ways artifacts shape the behavior of designers, the relations among designers, and the way those relations shape artifacts. Understanding the hierarchical structure of our artifacts and the control distributions exercised upon them will help us to organize ourselves when making complex artifacts, how to work in teams and delegate responsibilities and, above all, how to understand the capacity of artifacts to transform and remain useful over time.

1987
CONTROL RELATIONS IN THE BUILT ENVIRONMENT

Editors' note: *This is an unpublished working paper written in August 1987, continuing the authors use of notation and diagrams to explain control hierarchies*

We want to observe the built environment as a changing and living entity and understand its 'behavior.' To do so, we look at it as a complex configuration of physical parts that change over time. That is to say, we do not look at it first as a functional artifact responding to human needs. We know that the changes we observe in the built environment are the result of human action – of control.

Any complex configuration can be seen as composed of sub-configurations. We are particularly interested in those sub-configurations that 'behave' individually; those that lend themselves to control. Those configurations we may call 'control units.' A decomposition of an environment in control units is a particular way of decomposing a larger whole. When we do so we will find asymmetric relationships between the control units – so-called 'dependency relationships.'

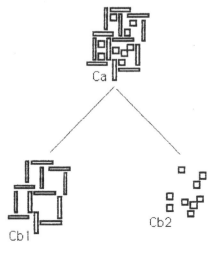

PART-WHOLE

Figure 1 suggests an 'environmental form' **Ca** of two different basic parts. Like all configurations, it can be decomposed in many ways. Figure 1 gives one way that can be seen as a theory of its assembly. Such an assembly hierarchy is a particular kind of part-whole hierarchy.

Figure 2 gives another decomposition of **Ca**, this time in two sub-configurations **Cb1** and **Cb2**.

DOI: 10.4324/9781003011385-16

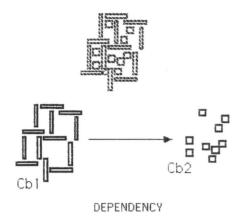

DEPENDENCY

In Figure 3 in observing the movement within **Ca**, we may conclude that **Cb1** dominates **Cb2** and that the two are in a 'vertical' relation: they make a dependency hierarchy.

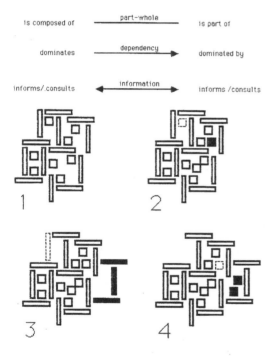

DEPENDENCY: FOUR MOVES

Figure 4 gives us an example of movement of parts that suggests the dependency relation between **Cb1** and **Cb2**.

The general definition of dependency among configurations is: **if there are two configurations C1 and C2, and we find that movement of Cb2 does not disturb Cb1, but movement of Cb1 tends to disturb Cb2, we conclude that Cb1 'dominates' Cb2 and that Cbc2 is 'dependent' on Cb1.**

We have now found two possible relations between configurations: one of **assembly** resulting in a part-whole hierarchy, and one of **dependency** resulting in a dependency hierarchy. The first relation is indicted by a single line, and the second by an arrow (see diagram below).

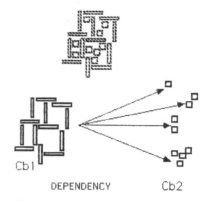

DEPENDENCY

In Figure 5 **Cb2** can be seen as composed of a large number of smaller sub-configurations that each have a dependency relation with **Cb1**. This is normally the case. (Note that the diagram **Figure 5**, although also a tree structure, is not a part-whole hierarchy because the parts of the lower level **Cb2** do not make the higher level **Cb1**).

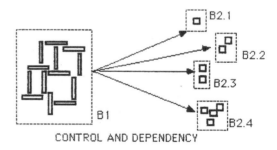

CONTROL AND DEPENDENCY

In Figure 6, We can now consider the relationships between the parties in control of the various configurations. As far as the exercise of control is concerned, their relationships are of dependency, exactly like the relations of the configurations they control.

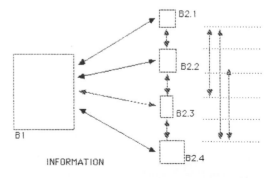

INFORMATION

In Figure 7, When we consider a third relation between parties as one of exchange of information (indicated by a two-way arrow in **Figure 7**), we find that the same configuration offers many more relations; there is no dependency.

Control relations in the built environment

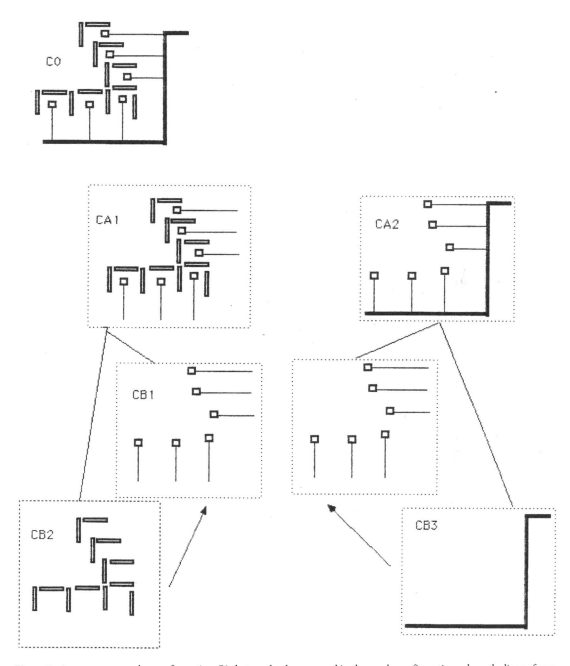

Figure 8 gives a more complex configuration **C0** that can be decomposed in three sub-configurations along the lines of control: **CB1, CB2** and **CB3**. We find that **CB1** is dependent on both **CB2** and **CB3**.

We can therefore see, in **C0**, two configurations **CA1** and **CA2** that each can be decomposed like **Cb1** in **Figure 2** (above). But **CA1** and **CA2** do not, together, make **C0**. There is no part-whole hierarchy here. Rather, **CA1** and **CA2** are partial interpretations of **C0**.

Environmental forms are usually of this structure, be it with many more control units on both levels, when considered from the point of view of control.

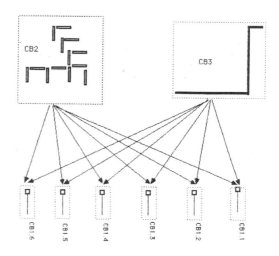

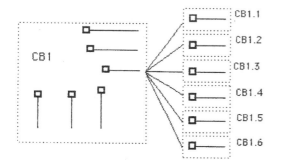

Figure 10 gives the dependency relations of **C0**. The diagram begins to approach a tower-like form, but there are no horizontal relations between the parts **CB1** on the lower level (**CB1.1** – **CB1.6**).

Once more, in **Figure 9**, we can see **CB1** as composed of many smaller control units.

2004
CHANGE AND THE DISTRIBUTION OF DESIGN

Editors' Note: *This essay was published in the Proceedings of the 10th International Conference of the CIB W104 Open Building Implementation network, Paris, CSTB, France, September 2004*

A Two-level environment

In January 1699, Jules Hardouin Mansart, Superintendent of Buildings and "Premier Architect to Louis le Grand, King of France, put his signature to the design for what we now know as the Place Vendome. (Figure 1). His design included a monumental façade wall of exquisite proportions in the neo-classical manner. The square, including the façade wall, was subsequently built by the city of Paris on the request of the King. But no buildings were behind the façade. The land behind was for sale. In the next two decades, noblemen, bankers and other prominent and wealthy citizens who served the King in various administrative and financial functions built their houses there with their own architects. These buildings kept changing and adapting over time. But the façade as Mansart built it is still what we see today.

Mansart's scheme was a remarkable interpretation of what we may call a "two-level organization", by which we mean that one designer provides the spatial framework within which other designers subsequently can do their own thing. We have here an instance of time-based building in a very straightforward way. Mansart built what was to perform for a long time and to serve many. He thereby provided a context for what might change more frequently and serve individual clients. In general, such a distinction of levels of intervention separates what is relatively permanent from what

Figure 1 Place Vendome, Paris. Behind the uniform façade are different houses

is relatively changeable. But the way Mansart applied this principle challenged conventional notions. The façade of a building is normally seen as the expression of that particular building. Here it became part of the level of the urban design.

We are more familiar with a level distinction in which the façade of the building is part of the lower level architectural design. When, for instance, H.P. Berlage designed the new extension of Amsterdam in the first half of the 19th century, he designed public spaces like boulevards, streets and squares. He also determined the height of the buildings along these spaces, but architects designed them and produced the facades that made those spaces become real.

Another example

The Place Vendome was not a unique intervention. Earlier in the 17th century, King Henry IV initiated the building of the Place Royale (today known as Place des Vosges). (Figure 2) Citizens could buy lots around it

DOI: 10.4324/9781003011385-17

Figure 2 Place des Vosges, Paris. Different interventions but (nearly) identical facades

on the condition that the facades of their houses would be built according to a preconceived design, including an arcade on the ground floor. The Place des Vosges is larger than the Place Vendome and makes a more domestic space with its trees and flower beds and its more home-grown architecture. But the square's façade wall is clearly the result of a unified design, although in practice it was built one lot at a time.

Although both squares have uniform facades all around, the distribution of ownership is different. In the case of the Place Vendome, the facades were actually part of the urban infrastructure, like the pavement of the square or the statue in its center. But in Henry IV's Place des Vosges, the facades ere owned and erected by the private citizens.

Taken as examples of two-level thinking, the difference is significant, however. In case of the Place Vendome, designers only decided on their own level of control behind the already erected façade. In the case of the Place des Vosges, the higher-level designer put down rules to constrain lower-level design. He basically told the lower-level designer: 'do whatever you want, but make sure you do the façade my way.'

The latter case is more complicated but also more flexible because laying down rules for lower-level design can be done in many different ways. The setback rule, for instance, telling architects to keep houses at a certain distance from the street, belongs to that mode of interaction. By the same token, an urban designer may impose a building height restriction, or stipulate that facades be done in a given material or that certain patterns should be followed for the sake of a consistent and well-conceived public space.

This way of working makes the urban designer reach across the level distinction to constrain lower-level design. It introduces a certain coherence in the lower level where normally variety is the inevitable result of different designers each doing their own thing.

A Natural phenomenon

In history, such coherence in variety came about in a less formal manner. The 17th century facades along the canals of Amsterdam are all of a kind but no two of them are alike. That did not happen because a higher-level designer had laid down rules, but because the house type was familiar to both inhabitants and builders. Coherence resulted from the culture at work. Yet the level distinction was very clear. Each house could change, or be replaced, without disturbing the higher-level urban organization.[1, 2]

Distribution of design responsibility along different levels of intervention comes naturally with complex form-making. We may shift the boundaries a bit, but life itself imposes the level distinction. When ignored, it will re-establish itself in the course of time.

The famous 'Crescents' in 18th century Bath, by father and son Wood, were originally designed as identical houses behind a common monumental façade. But since home ownership was dispersed, individual houses changed in time: expansions were made, and interior spaces were altered. But the facades remained unaltered by common consent.

The result, eventually, was similar to the Place Vendome distinction: variation behind an urban screen. Eventually, similar projects with unified facades came about in English domestic architecture. Most of them were built for speculation. Variations in the house plan might be made already when a house was sold before building started, but otherwise would surely come later.

The disappearance of levels

In Amsterdam, Berlage was the last to heed the level distinction in urban design. Cornelis van Eesteren's internationally renowned post-war extension of the city was not structured by urban space. Following CIAM ideology, he arranged building volumes within free-flowing space. Urban space was no longer structuring lower level design. As a result urban designer and architect both used the same medium, and it was no longer clear where urban design stopped and architecture began. This confusion still plagues the profession.

The disappearance of levels of intervention was not restricted to the distinction between urban design and architecture. It also took place within the building itself. Modernist architectural ideology claimed top down design control. The masters of the avant-garde like Corbusier, Mies von der Rohe and also Frank Lloyd Wright taught us by example that full vertical control, including even the design of furniture, was necessary to achieve good architecture. They lived in a time of fundamental change in which all design conventions and building habits were rendered obsolete. In such uncertainty it is understandable that those responsible for large projects insisted on full vertical control.

However, the upheavals of modernity only reinforced an attitude that already prevailed in the time when architects only did special buildings like churches, palaces, and grand houses. It goes back to Palladio whose marvelous villas we tend to understand as firmly controlled by a single hand. In that sense, Le Corbusier's Unité d'Habitation, fully controlled too and conceived as standing in a park, is very Palladian.

We have been educated in a tradition that was ignorant of the uses of levels in urban form. Mass housing in which inhabitants cannot influence the layout of their dwelling is part of that ignorance. Our present interest in time-based building seeks a remedy to the rigidity and uniformity that comes from excessive vertical control.

Learning from the past

As I have shown, level distinctions in complex environment may be achieved in different ways. Those we have noted so far: The Place Vendome, The Place des Vosges, Berlage's Amsterdam extension, and the Amsterdam canals, are architectural expressions of a primarily territorial level distinction. Yet a hierarchy of levels may result from technical conditions as well. In climates where protection from the cold, wind, or rain is important, the first act of building usually was to create a large envelope later to be subdivided. Medieval European architecture was based on a single large volume, defined by stone walls and a timber roof, erected as quickly as possible to provide sheltered space within which further subdivision could take place in a more protected environment. The English custom to refer to large buildings as "Hall" still comes from that practice.

So does the "grange", or barn, used in Medieval French agriculture: A timber frame held up a large roof that extended outward to low but heavy stone walls. This model was followed in buildings for a wide variety of purposes as we can learn from the 9th century document St. Gall design for a monastery.2

This way of building produced a large volume of interior space that was subsequently subdivided in response to practical needs. The same custom could still be witnessed a few generations ago in the New England tradition of "barn raising" where the agricultural barn's timber structure was prefabricated by the local carpenter to be erected in a single day with the help of many neighbors in a kind of festive ritual.

In China, about a decade ago, I saw a house just built in a country village. After materials had been amassed over a period of time, a solid brick masonry shell, some six by ten meters in surface area and two stories high with symmetrical façade had been built in a few weekends with the help of neighbors. Inside, the roof was supported by two timber posts, and the entire space was temporarily partitioned by a few bamboo screens just two meters high. The subdivision within the house had yet to be done in more solid materials once resources would allow (Figure 3). Similar examples are found in many other vernacular architectures.

Figure 3 Near Xi-an, China. Farmhouse shell just built

Once technically feasible, internal adaptability can achieve its own architectural expression. Most vernacular residential architecture has a dominant space in relation to which smaller scale change can take place.

The houses of Pompeii, preserved by volcanic ashes for almost two millennia, show us, for instance, that each house had an atrium: this large space with an inward sloping roof open in the center to let rainwater fall in a basin on the floor, was where guests were received and business was done. It was formed by walls two stories high behind which rooms were located. The ground floor rooms were open to the atrium and those on the upper floor had light coming in from above the atrium roof.

Pompeii's excavations show us irregular distributions of these surrounding spaces suggesting change and adaptation over time. In fact, we sometimes find that rooms have been turned around from one house to the neighboring house. The upper floors under a timber roof must have been even easier to subdivide. There is also evidence that these spaces could form suites for relatives within the extended family or could be rented out as separate apartments.

We see the atrium function the way a public space functions in a city: allowing change and adaptation behind surrounding walls. In this way atria were stable islands in the dense Pompeiian field, around which second order design decisions were made over time. (Figure 4). These were buildings without an exterior. The spatial sequence from street to atrium, with possible extension to a second courtyard behind, identified the house, while actual boundaries to neighboring houses behind the surrounding rooms remained invisible while the street front was occupied with shops and workplaces.

The Venetian Gothic palace is another example. It had on its main floor a large hall running from canal front to backyard, with open facades so that air could move through the house. On both sides of that central space were rows of rooms the arrangement of which allowed not only different uses but also change in size and decoration. Here again we find a two-level spatial organization securing permanence of the major space while allowing adaptation to inhabitation's second order preferences. (Figure 5)

Figure 5 Venice, Central hall on the main floor of Gothic houses (Drawn over a detail from Moretto, L'edilizia Gotica Venziana, 1978, Filippi)

From these two examples of major spaces in vernacular houses, it is only one step towards the courtyard house. The open courtyard too, is the 'public' space within the residential unit around which rooms are formed like houses around a square.

The Mediterranean courtyard house is also found in a variety of interpretations along the North African coast and all the way East across the Arabian peninsula, and it traveled West from Spain to Latin America. Indeed, its influence extends as far North as Paris, (Figure 6) where gates give access from the street to courtyards surrounded by apartments. India and China have their own traditions of courtyard dominated urban fabric in many variations going back for millennia.

The Medina of historic Tunis (Figure 7) may serve as a case-in-point for many others. The rooms around the courtyards show a clear typology by themselves: they have a niche in the back wall facing the double courtyard door and two other niches to each side. This pattern is executed in endless variation of size and shape: even in one house no two of such rooms may be the same.

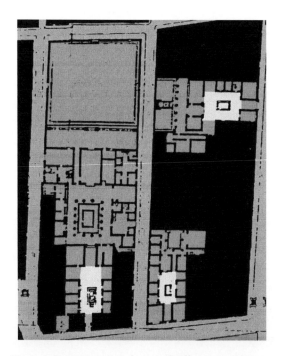

Figure 4 Pompeii, Atria in houses of different sizes. (Drawn over detail of the Overbeck Plan der Stadt Pompeii, 1866)

These few examples may show how vernacular architecture usually provides a dominant space that is

Change and the distribution of design

Figure 6 Left bank, Paris courtyard

Figure 7 Tunis medina, courtyards and dead-end streets (Drawn over a base map by the Association Sauvegarde de la Medina, Tunis)

stable relative to second order variety and change in response to day-to-day uses.

New ways of time-based building

As a counterpoint to these many historic examples we may note how large contemporary buildings tend to change their skin. The high-rise office building in the Hague, for instance, for which Michael Graves designed a new envelope is in many ways the opposite of Mansart's Place Vendome. Here the building, to prolong its life, sheds its skin when the urban environment changes. The curtain wall facade almost acquires autonomy; it may be part of the building, but it may also help shape urban fabric.

We begin to understand how the large contemporary building will, eventually, establish its own hierarchy of changeable subsystems. The very size and permanence of such extensive frameworks make their façade a relatively short-term garb. At the same time, interior flexibility must respond to a large and varied population. By their sheer bulk the high-rise and other large projects de facto become three-dimensional extensions of urban fabric. Inside, public space becomes increasingly important as a permanent framework around which day to day use, either residential or commercial or administrative, may settle. Seen in this way, we become aware of the latent architectural potential of such new environments without historic precedent.

A debilitating heritage

Modernist ideology did not know architecture in relation to levels, neither upward in urban design nor downwards in interior organization. Indeed, Modernist environment, for all its novelty, can be understood to a large extent as the reduction of complex urban fabric to a coarse single level product – hence its inability to make large things without imposing uniform repetition on inhabitation. In this respect the avant-garde movement was a regressive movement. It is truly ironic that our time, which calls itself dynamic and full of change and individuality, has produced an architecture more rigid in its articulation and less capable of dealing with the dimension of time than any period before in human history.

We still suffer the consequences of a functionalist tradition. We proudly rejected the Modernist's dogma of 'form follows function', but still expect each project we engage in to respond to a 'program' listing in some detail expected functions to be taken care of. A time-based architecture must assume functions to be largely unpredictable except in the most general of terms. Where architecture cannot follow function anymore it must take over by itself to establish a context for change and variety by inhabitation. This new initiative will lead to an articulation of levels of form-making. But that also implies distribution of design responsibility and we have not yet abandoned the modernist opinion that such distribution is a dilution of the architect's role. The dilemma renders academia clueless. Change and the distribution of design tasks are not yet subjects for architectural theory, nor do they feature in school's curricula.

A new architecture?

But practice already knows better and real life runs ahead of theory and teaching. Commercial office buildings offer empty floors for lease, to be filled in by specialized fit-out contractors executing designs by specialized fit out designers. Shopping malls leave retail space open for leaseholders to employ their own designers.

Residential architecture slowly follows suit. In the Netherlands the work of Frans van der Werf, spanning over some thirty years, has been the most extensive and the most advanced so far. His Molenvliet project in Papendrecht (Figure 8), done in 1974, was the first project ever to explore the architectural and urbanist potential of a distinction between a 'base building' designed by the architect and the subsequent 'fit-out' done by the user. Frans van der Werf developed an 'urban tissue' in which public courtyards giving entry to the dwellings alternate with garden courtyards to be cultivated by the users. Within this fabric, users chose the location and size of their units and designed their own floor plans. Van der Werf's most recent project in Zevenaar follows the same basic principles and received a prize for sustainable building. An international network for Open Building meets yearly somewhere in the world and in several other countries, most notably Japan and Finland, similar open residential projects have been executed.[3]

Figure 8 Molenvliet project, Papendrecht, the Netherlands. Frans van der Werf, 1978.

It is now clear that in commercial architecture, workplace architecture, and residential architecture level distinctions serve the need for change and adaptation by day-to-day inhabitation. The dynamics of time-based building are already a fact of life and come naturally to the built environment, but as long as that reality is not fully embraced by the architectural profession as inspiring and challenging, a truly new time-based architecture will not take wings.

Notes

1 Actually, there were at least two types along the three major canals of Amsterdam. The type with a gabled façade similar to what had already been done in the medieval core of the city, and the broader façade with a cornice that was introduced in the 17th century.
2 See: Walter Horn and Ernests Born, *The Plan for St. Gall*, 3 vols. (Berkeley: California Press, 1979). One volume brief version by Lorna Price, University of California Press, 1982.
3 See also: S. H. Kendall and J. Teicher, *Residential Open Building* (London: Spon Press, 2000), which gives an overview of more than a hundred projects executed by that time.

SHARING FORMS

1997
FORMS OF UNDERSTANDING
Thematic knowledge and the modernist legacy

Editors' Note: *This essay was published as a chapter in* Historiography, Urbanism and the Growth of Architectural Knowledge: Essays Presented to Stanford Anderson *(ed. Martha Pollak). Cambridge, MA. MIT Press, 1997. It appeared a year before the authors' seminal book of theory* The Structure of the Ordinary: Form and Control in the Built Environment *(MIT Press, 1998) in which the author posited three 'orders': The Orders of Form, Place and Understanding.*

The loss of common ground

The practitioner's knowledge, as Schön has taught us,[1] is a knowing-in-practice that is learned by doing and that must, necessarily, be largely implicit. All good practitioners have what he calls an "artistry" that allows them to operate in complex and unclear situations where values and interests are conflicting and each case is, to an important extent, unique.

Knowing-in-practice is to be contrasted with the formal and codified knowledge by which a professional is usually identified. The latter I will call the "knowledge base;" it is the domain of expertise claimed by a profession. The ability to operate from that base is what the professional is hired for in the first place. Schön argues convincingly that the knowledge base is not enough by itself. Knowing-by-doing is gained by going beyond it. The medical doctor, for instance, must know the human body, but she or he needs to know more to be able to diagnose an illness and cure the patient. The lawyer must know the law but needs to know more to apply it successfully in real-life cases. The building engineer must know physics, materials and building construction, but needs to know more to design the best possible structure.

Of all the professional fields, architecture is where the virtue of a knowing-by-doing is most readily accepted by its practitioners. Schön rightly chooses the design studio in the architectural school a place where the age-old master-apprentice model is still preserved – as a subject for study. Without doubt, knowing-by-doing is also more deliberately cultivated in the architects' office as compared to the situation of the lawyer or the medical doctor. In engineering, medicine, and the law it seems easier to forget that the knowledge base as such is not enough. In architecture, on the other hand, we may ask what, exactly, the knowledge base is beyond which the architect must reach to be a good professional? This is the question I want to explore in this chapter.

While the lawyer has the law and the medical doctor has the human body, the architect has the building as his domain of expertise. This he shares with the builder, the developer, and other consultants working on real estate. The architect, we may assume, knows the building in an architectural way – a way that is different from the way the builder and real estate agent know it. If we try to substantiate this reasonable assumption, however, we find that it is not at all clear what such an "architectural knowing' entails.

Many within the profession seem to agree that, if there is such a thing as architectural knowledge, it is there in an implicit way. Quite a few architects will argue that any attempt to make it more explicit will destroy it. But the problem is not necessarily that architecture does not codify its knowledge base as formally as other professions do. Granted implicitness, however, there should be some evidence that knowledge is shared among architects at all, because it is only by sharing that a professional knowledge base can be claimed.

Can any signs be found that tell us that there is, among architects, a common way of knowing built form, however implicit this knowing may be? Because, without such signs, how can we be sure that there are not as many ways to know the built environment as there are architects?

A common knowledge should be reflected in the language used within the profession. To share knowledge, a minimal vocabulary is needed. At the very least, we may expect that architectural elements in the built environment – as distinct from technical elements for instance – have their proper names. This would not yet imply any codification or formalization, but only a shared recognition. It would not, by itself, mean that we can describe the built environment as an architectural system – as an ordered and predictable phenomenon in the way the medical doctor can describe the human body and the builder can describe the technical behavior of the building. It would only indicate that the built form is known to us as we know a face, and it would support the idea that we all know it in the same way. A vocabulary of names of typically architectural elements would render the built environment discussable in terms of architecture, without need to redefine it over and over again.

Today, this modest requirement is not met. When we discuss architecture among ourselves, in teaching or otherwise, we have an alarming tendency to coin a personal vocabulary and to give things new names every time. Much effort is spent explaining to one another how a particular environment "could be seen" and comparing such ways if seeing. Moreover, we often do not address the building as an architectural form as such but tend to describe the way we experience it – how it can be used, how it behaves in its setting, what impressions it evokes. This way of discussing architecture is more a way of speaking about it in social and poetic terms. It encourages a personal language. As a way of speaking it is not authentic, but largely borrowed from the critic whose task is to explain to laypeople the "meaning" of the building and to dwell on the impression it makes on the beholder.

A professional language for architects cannot be impressionistic but must provide a stable base for discussion of the form, among peers, with reasonable clarity and precision. Here we must admit incoherence. Schön's reference, a verbatim report on the interaction between teachers and students in the design studio, only supports the impression we already have: that there is very little in terms of a shared vocabulary allowing a lucid description of architectural form as distinct from the technical form or the poetic form.[2] There is, among architects, no common language of general significance, and apparently no desire to have one; each of us struggles in a personal way to describe what he sees.

It has not always been like that. Palladio was trained as a mason and knew how to build a building as well as any master builder. But his careful studies of the way the ancients used to build provided a base for designing, more linked with the general classical education of his patron and clients than with the trade of building. In other words, he found in classicism a truly architectural way to describe the form to be built. Rediscovered from antiquity and offering a precise terminology describing parts and their relations, the classicist architectural system, as interpreted by the Renaissance architects, held for a long time. It was, for all practical purposes, a knowledge base for seventeenth- and eighteenth-century architects: it allowed them to describe the subject of their skills.

This unifying knowledge was swept away by the modernist movement. In the late nineteen fifties, when modernism was triumphant, Summerson already pointed out that it had no form language. He suggested that the "program" has taken the place of the classicist system as architecture's unifying force, replacing, as he put it, the formal with the social. Summerson notes that this leaves a dark void between the program and the final form, requiring the designer to move from one to the other by a leap of faith. He quotes both Gropius and Gideon admitting, in so many words, to the lack of a common form-knowing (this is my term) by which this void could be bridged.

Avant-garde: a means of survival

Our failure to claim the built form as a common knowledge base makes architecture an individual adventure. What cannot be shared among professionals cannot be shared between the professional and the layperson either. In the past, overlap of professional knowledge with the layperson's experience allowed the latter to appreciate professional competence and, to a certain extent, to judge it. A general classicist education allowed the professional architect, like Christopher Wren, to be a gentleman and made it possible for the gentleman, like Thomas Jefferson, to be an architect. Today, all professionalism is far removed from daily experience. Most professions have come to define their knowledge base in such a technical ay that its codification does not connect to the layperson's view anymore. Architecture has lost its connection with the layperson, too, but achieved this by not defining a knowledge base at all, disallowing the sharing of any judgement with laypeople as effectively as by default as other professions do by excessive formalization. Given this divide, we reserve on our side the right to pass judgement. We tend to claim that we are hired, not just to make good buildings, but to decide what is good and bad, expecting that, at the same time, our clients will suspend their own opinion on this score. The client is necessarily reduced to arguments about cost and functionality.

A well-known anecdote renders early evidence of the making of this claim, showing how the professional and the layperson had already lost their common base by the end of the nineteenth century. When Louis Sullivan submitted his plan for the Auditorium Building in Chicago, Professor Ware of Boston was invited by Mr. Peck, the chairman of the client committee, to give his opinion. Sullivan reported the meeting to his brother in a letter, from which I quote:

"Mr. Peck:... assuming that you yourself, instead of Messrs. Adler and Sullivan, had from the inception of this project been engaged to design this building, would you, in your opinion, have arrived at a result substantially similar to theirs, or do you believe that you would have produced a result somewhat or a great deal better?

Professor: Had I been entrusted with the designing of this building I do not believe I should have reached the same result. But had I reached such a result I should consider it the inspiration of my life."

After a few more paragraphs reporting on the interview, Sullivan ends his letter:

"The atmosphere is considerably cleared, and I am considered an artist, it seems. Poor fools!"[3, 4]

There are good reasons for the tacit assumption, apparently made on both sides, that the client could not know anymore from the building itself what was appropriate. A building like the Auditorium had no precedent. The classicist system of designing, although still present in some stylistic aspects could not account for it.[5] Here was a building the size of a city block, multi-functional, built in a new technology, producing a spatial organization that could not easily be typified. In that situation, the work could only be based on the legitimization of the architect, and that legitimization depended on trust.

The anecdote helps us to understand the modern professional's situation. In a world where there is no longer a commonly shared orientation as to what the good building is about, recognition must come from the personal reputation of the architect. This calls for a bootstrap operation to produce the heroic ascendency of the individual who is different. This form of heroism is now the accepted mode and one cannot consider oneself a good architect anymore unless one has distanced oneself, by one's work, from what is more broadly normative. Frank Lloyd Wright, Sullivan's apprentice and himself a powerful role model for subsequent generations, understood this very well and played to perfection the role of outsider. This placed him in a typical modernist dilemma because, on the one hand, he preached a new 'organic' architecture while, on the other hand, he could not associate himself with those embracing what he advocated without weakening his outsider's image. His second paper in the special issue of Wendingen, for instance, is a long diatribe against those who corrupt and prostitute organic architecture by emulating it. He also takes distance from his pupils and followers. Although he was admired in his lifetime by many, he could not risk to teach and lead.[6]

This attitude we recognize as the now generally accepted avant-garde position. It excuses the architect and the artist from explaining themselves. But a role, to be sustained over time, needs an approving audience. We have reason to suspect that the architect's audience wants him to play the outsider's role, seeing it as proof of authority and artistry. In Sullivan's day, the Western world was full of energy and new beginnings, driven by an almost innocent power of invention. But it was also rapidly becoming incomprehensible within the framework of values and meanings of the past. The architect as avant-gardist makes the incomprehensibleness of the environment acceptable to the layperson, but thereby also perpetuates it. In modernism, it was probably the best way to sustain professional self-respect and assure recognition by the public.

The attitude is still with us today. Although we can understand why it emerged and how it served a profession in a period of turbulent transition, we now also see that it does not allow the cultivation of a body of knowledge. It encourages the mystification of the trade, and must, necessarily, fall back on creativity and originality as goals by themselves. But these qualities, indispensable as they are, cannot be claimed by a profession for its foundation. It is, after all, difficult to believe that the advancement of other professional fields could happen without them. Yet, in the course of time the amazing architectural innovations of the 20th century and the previous one came increasingly to be explained in terms of personal artistic achievement and originality. Now these qualities have become basic criteria in contemporary architectural historiography.[7, 8]

The romantic image of the artist who is different persists among professional and laypeople today. It is based, not on shared knowledge, but on a shared belief; a joint identification with ideological overtones. As for peer group comparison, prestige is no longer achieved by becoming a first among equals, but by remaining different; by being, literally, incomparable. To the avant-garde ideology, the common ground is an obstacle to success.

The quality of the ordinary

Where Individual achievement and originality are the dominant objectives, precedent and context become a problem: their presence and inevitability must be explained. Up until Palladio's time, the built environment as a context for architecture, like daily bread, remained unquestioned. It was tacitly understood that architecture, the art of the special building, took place in a living tradition. Architecture appeared amid the everyday environment the way flowers bloom among the leaves of a healthy plant. It is a matter of debate to what extent Palladian space and form were rooted in local as opposed to classical precedent, but we can be certain that the craftsmanship used for his architecture was basically the same by which the whole environment was built: masons, bricklayers, plasterers, and carpenters plied the age-old trades. Within that familiar field of action and habitual form, an architect could operate to a specific purpose. His innovation was not the result of alienation but could grow from confidence in a stable context. There was certainty that the built environment as a whole would sustain itself. This may not have made innovation easier, compared to today, but it gave context. Where the vernacular act was like "water in water" to borrow from Bataille,[9] architecture was the fish in the water, recognizable in its transparent environment, but impossible without it.

Only much later, when this stable context, which so far had been taken for granted, slowly crumbled under the weight of modernity, the everyday environment, by default, attracted the attention of architects in two ways. In terms of theory, the ordinary came to be seen as a source of inspiration: the recognition of something that has become precious. In terms of action, the ordinary was to be replaced by architecture: a territory to be invaded. Both ways deserve our attention.

As for the first, there always was a kinship between the common house and the church, the temple or the mosque. Early evidence of it is found in the remarkable ninth-century St. Gall model of a monastery (Figure 1 and Figure 2). It shows plans for the whole range of buildings of a monastery, which range can be ordered, without difficulty, as a continuous transformation within a single architectural theme, from one building to another; from the hen house, via the workplace, the guest house, and the abbots house, to the church as its final apotheosis.[10]

This continuum between architecture and the ordinary had ceased to work when Sullivan and Mr. Peck asked Professor Ware to solve their dilemma. A few decades later, the everyday environment had become sufficiently foreign to be deliberately borrowed from or to be inspired by. I should mention here young Le Corbusier's studies of the Mediterranean vernacular and his later fascination, shared with others, with the steamship and the motorcar, grain silos and cooling towers. Four decades later, we find Venturi and Scott-Brown studying Las Vegas.[11]

Le Corbusier, Venturi, and Scott-Brown, each in his or her own way, the first in search of plasticity, the others in search of symbolism, had the courage to suggest architecture could find inspiration in the ordinary. By doing so, they effectively invented the notion of the ordinary by giving it recognition. But this served only to underline the distinction between it and architecture. Le Corbusier saw the ordinary as a foreign species: a source of artifacts to borrow from in the way the

Forms of understanding

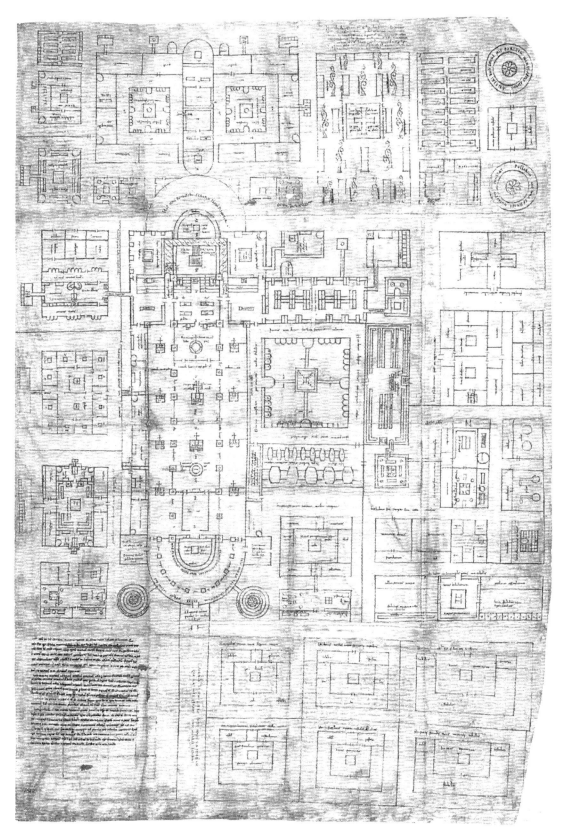

Figure 1 Plan of St. Gall. In the lower left-hand corner, the House for Distinguished Guests of Figure 2. (From a facsimile print of the 92 Neujahrsblatt, historischen Veriens des Kanton St. Gallen (St. Gall: Fehr'schen Buchhandlung, 1952.)

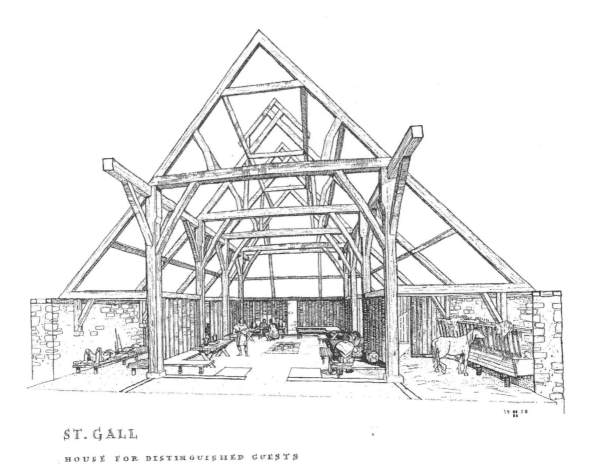

Figure 2 Plan of St. Gall. House for Distinguished Guests. (Reconstruction by Walter Horn and Ernest Born, from Lorna Price, The Plan of St. Gall in Brief (Berkeley, University of California Press, 1979.)

artist always had borrowed from nature. But Learning from Las Vegas made a link: the title could make one think that architecture might relate to the ordinary as man relates to the ape. The resulting commotion among the profession only showed the extent to which it had allowed itself to believe that architecture was a self-generating enterprise.[12] But in the end, the profession declined to learn and decided to see the book only as a justification for taking freely from precedent: the beginning of postmodernism. No one seriously questioned the idea that architecture was independent of the ordinary. In any case, the Palladian model remained intact: at best, Venturi and Scott-Brown's advocacy of the mundane as something worth studying is comparable to Palladio's measuring of Roman ruins. In both cases, there was a scrutiny of precedent in support of a new definition of architecture. But where Palladio sought a lost perfection – indeed a discipline – Venturi and Scott-Brown looked for something fresh and innocent: a liberation from modernist constraints.

The most determined attempt to rediscover the everyday environment in terms of architecture was made by Christopher Alexander in his pattern language studies.[13] By describing patterns as timeless forms not invented by architects, but of importance for their work, Alexander showed a way that could lead us to see how architecture depends on the everyday environment. But he did not follow that route to its final conclusion. His desire to also establish the objective truth of patterns made him present them as "solutions" to "problems," which put him in a functionalist mode. This prevented him from presenting patterns as primarily sustained by social convention as opposed to professional research.

It seems to me that the power of patterns is exactly that people know them and agree to apply them and by doing so make the built environment a collective endeavor in which architects would benefit by participating. Without this conventional dimension, the pattern is at risk of becoming a catalog item for the architect to pick and choose from. Alexander's proposal remains ambiguous. We are not sure whether he wants the pattern to be just another architectural inspiration or to be used as a vehicle for agreement with others.

This ambiguity is at the core of our professional condition and leads us to the fundamental and unsolved problem with which modernism has left us: that is, the invasion of the ordinary under the now generally accepted assumption that everything to be built can be architecture. This assumption is radical, universal, and virtually unnoticed, but nevertheless acted upon with deliberation.

The idea that everything that is built should be included within the architect's domain was not posed abruptly but emerged gradually over a long period of time. In the middle of the seventeenth century, Le Muet[14] already designed a series of houses in which, for the first time, the humble urban house was seen as an object of architectural attention, equal, in this respect, to the mansion of the seigneur. There is reason to believe that he formalized a typology already in place. This led him much further along toward the ordinary than Serlio, who, a century earlier, in his book on "domestic architecture,"[15] was mainly concerned with palaces and large mansions. In the few designs for humble houses included in his book, Serlio demonstrates his ignorance of the state of the art of his time. This much we may conclude from the studies on mundane houses in historic Venice by Tricanato[16] (Figure 3 and Figure 4).

In modern times, the architecture of the ordinary dwelling acquired moralistic overtones, beginning with Victorian designs for the "cottage for the worker" and culminating in massive public housing programs. Among the early probings into the territory of the ordinary we may count also the bold demonstrations of Behrens and Gropius showing that places for work and manufacture could be architecture. But is particularly domestic form that is made to serve new visions for architecture and urbanism, as first, and most arrogantly, demonstrated by Le Corbusier and his Plan Voisin.

Soon all this is serious business and well before the Second World War, in Europe, professional design of domestic, utilitarian and commercial space is no longer an exception.

The professionalization of the ordinary reversed its relation to the special: for the first time in history, the special no longer grew from the mundane. It used to be that the mosque and the church grew from the ordinary house by invention and elaboration. Now, the daring skyscraper is there first and is used as the model for the standard high-rise apartment building. In the past, the monumental masonry dome evolved from the mud brick version. Now, the daring prestressed concrete bridge eventually leads to the mass-produced concrete slab applied to housing construction. Where in the past the special was the product of everyday practice honed to perfection, now daily practice is a domesticated version of innovative engineering and design. Where first the special grew from the ordinary as a plant grows from fertile soil, now the ordinary is a reduction on a massive scale of what is achieved in the special building.

Although this reversal of the direction of influence and parentage seems so far to have escaped the attention of the historian, it seems worth a study and an assessment of its consequences. The phenomenon may well be just modernist and therefore transitory, but today, for the first time in history, domestic space is no longer the soil from which architecture grows. The modernist mass housing projects, in their reductionist monumentality, abased the ordinary and rendered it powerless. Being products of architects, and discussed and published as architecture, these projects have led some of the younger generation, who mistakenly see in their banality a lack of design, to strive for something "exceptional" when engaging the next housing project, thus only exacerbating the problem.

It is now generally assumed, within the profession and among its teachers, that all parts of the built environment are within the professional domain.[17] The fact is irreversible, but the astounding aspect of this change is that its impact and meaning have remained largely unexamined. In fact, the profession has gone about it as if it made no real difference for the role of the architect or, for that matter, for the environment. Consequently, the new task was engaged upon without a reexamination of the professional role, maintaining the Palladian preeminence of the special building as well as the avant-gardist disdain for shared values, leaving unrecognized the problem of the ordinary.

Yet it seems legitimate to ask how today's making of the ordinary must be understood and how it relates to the traditional WAY OF SEEING architecture. So far, our teaching and our theorizing have not addressed the remarkable fact that everything is special now.

Figure 3 Detail of Venice from the map by Jacopo de'Barbari, showing the house type of Figure 4 in the urban fabric near the arsenal, as identified by Tricanato.

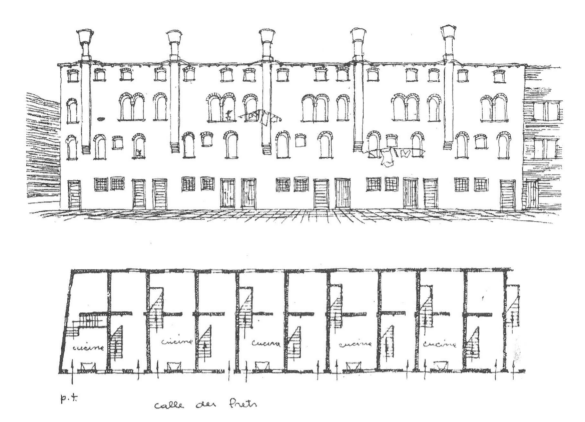

Figure 4 Collective housing in Venice, quattrocento. (From Egle Renata Trincanato, Venetia Minore (Venice: Filippi Editore, 1948). One of a very large number of examples of diverse types of low-income residential construction from the duecento to the settecento. The one shown here, of two duplex units on top of one another, each with its own ground-floor entrance, has been reinvented in modern times.

Thematic knowledge

It has become customary to bemoan a lack of coherence in the modern built environment. I once assisted at a formal gathering of corporate managers where a well-known architect was invited to speak. As his audience without doubt expected him to do, he spoke of the apparent randomness of the present-day cityscape and its lack of overall quality in spite of the fact that individual buildings might have merit. He expressed the wish that a latter-day John Nash would appear who could, by a grand gesture, bring order to the apparent chaos. We have all heard similar wishes expressed: would it not be desirable that somehow our incoherent modern environment would be shaped by an ordering hand?

Unfortunately, apart from the question as to what extent the incoherence is real, this remedy is not available to us today, precisely because, in contrast to the nineteenth century, there is no longer a generally excepted environmental fabric out of which the grand gesture can be made. John Nash lived at the end of a long period in which a strong typology for both building and urban form had been developed. The British terraced house as used by Nash and his colleagues – with its typical sunken area between sidewalk and façade and its vertical development between party walls – first emerged in the late seventeenth century[18] and had generally been employed for over a century already before it appeared in Regent's Park.[19] The uniform façade, shared by a row of houses, had been applied by Adam, Wood and others. The shaping of urban spaces with the help of such facades had already been done in Bath and in the well-known London squares, particularly of the Bedford estate. It is not a belittlement of Nash's achievement to conclude that his monumental vision was accepted and acted upon because there was a good deal of precedent available. Nash's proposal, not less brilliant for it, was easily understood in the context of time and place and therefore could be implemented in a relatively short time with the cooperation of a host of collaborators, designers, tradesmen, builders,[20] and also clients willing to invest in his scheme. Regent's Park and Regent's Street were not the result of something revolutionary, but the apotheosis of something familiar. Nash's intervention was the end of an era, and one of the last occasions when a shared knowledge of the built environment could inspire collective invention, still admired today, summarizing all that had been done before.

A similar consensus as to what the built environment was about can be seen in Haussmann's restructuring of Paris by a network of boulevards (Figure 5). There are of course good reasons to label this enterprise not only ambitious but also innovative. However, Haussmann's genius operated particularly in the realm of management and financing. This made possible the monumental interventions on the level of the urban structure. On the level of the urban fabric itself, however, conventional form was relied upon to absorb the resulting reverberations. The boulevards gave new life to an extant living urban fabric which was adapted to the new scale by the thematic development of the familiar Parisian urban courtyard building – a type that originally appeared as the feudal Parisian hotel to be adapted, eventually, for bourgeois society.

Figure 5 Aerial photograph of central Paris showing Haussmann's boulevards

Here is Marcel Proust describing one of these earlier examples:

> It was one of those old town houses, a few of which for all I know may still be found, in which the main courtyard was flanked-alluvial deposits washed there by the rising tide of democracy, perhaps, or a legacy from a more primitive time when the different trades were clustered round the overlord-by little shops and workrooms, a shoemaker's, for instance, or a tailor's, such as we see nestling between the buttresses of those cathedrals which the aesthetic zeal of the restorer has not swept clear of such accretions, and a porter who also did cobbling, kept hens, grew flowers- and, at the far end, in the main house, a "countess" who, when she drove out in her old carriage and pair, flaunting on her hat a few nasturtiums which seemed to have escaped from the plot by the lodge . . . dispensed smiles and little waves of the hand impartially to the porter's children and to any bourgeois tenants who might happen to be passing and whom, in her disdainful affability and her egalitarian arrogance, she found indistinguishable from one another.[21]

Haussmann's planners and architects did not only use this building type, while adapting and standardizing it for wholesale application. They also maintained, as a characteristic pattern, the typical Parisian *entresol* (Figure 6 A&B, and Figure 7 A&B). This low floor just above the ground floor, usually serving the shops or workplaces below, is previously seen in eighteenth- and seventeenth-century Paris. Its consistent application along the boulevards determined to a large extent the scale experienced by the pedestrian on the sidewalk; the combined height of ground floor and entresol could be used to enhance the shop's facades and to create high gateways leading into the courtyards. This made for a flexible facade zone at street level almost independent of the five or six residential floors above, with their standardized windows and cast-iron balconies.[22]

In Haussmann's Paris, as in Nash's London, the continuation of available patterns and types synergized the work of all parties involved, making it possible for them to cooperate without undue discussion as to what the built environment should be like. The ingredients of the new were familiar enough to channel all energies toward achieving it. To appreciate the efficiency and power of a shared image *we* must think of the inevitable proliferation of radically different proposals that would appear, indeed would be solicited, if an urban intervention of such scope were to be considered today. Different designers would come with totally different images of what the city should be about. That there is little evidence of such debates in the times of Haussmann and Nash cannot be explained by heavy-handed top-down decision-making only, which, of course, did apply in both situations. The possibility of alternative worlds to be chosen from simply did not arise.

Nineteenth-century London and Paris fit into a long tradition of built environments in which a shared typology was a unifying force. Of course, we are familiar with the many older examples available to us: Venice, Amsterdam, Imperial Beijing, Medieval Cairo, Imperial Kyoto, and a host of other cities of consistent and well-knit urban fabrics come to mind. Indeed, we are familiar with whole families of environments each member of which shares similar characteristics: the porticoes of the north Italian medieval and Renaissance cities (such as Bologna and Padua), the Greek colonial towns, and the Middle Eastern urban fabric based on a variety of courtyard house forms, are obvious examples. In discussions about urban quality these environments have become standard references. But the point still to be made is that their worth as models of environmental quality lies not primarily in the public spaces and monuments we have so diligently studied, but in the more anonymous urban fields that surround them and make them possible. These environments all show types and patterns by which we recognize them, in the same way we recognize the tree, first of all, and most certainly, by the shape of its leaves.

Classicism served for a long time as a unifying architectural system shared by architects and their clients. Types and patterns are also shared forms, but they are rooted more deeply and are more durable than architectural style. They evolve slowly over time, tending to persist while styles are applied to them. The Amsterdam canal houses of the Baroque and the classicist periods for example, in spite of their different facades, have a strong kinship in spatial organization. The same can be said, to give another example, of the Venetian "palaces" of the Gothic and Renaissance periods.[23]

Figure 6 *(A&B)*: Entresol, Paris. Historic examples from the Left Bank. (Photos by the author)

Forms of understanding

Figure 6 *(A&B)*: (Continued)

Figure 7 (A&B): Entresol, Paris, along Haussmann's boulevards. (Photos by the author)

Figure 7 (A&B): (Continued)

This leads us back to the topic of knowledge. These constant forms – stylistic systems, types, and patterns – represent a deeply rooted, but largely implicit, knowledge of space and built form, shared by clients, builders, and architects, by which built environments always have lived. I will call this shared knowing of form "thematic knowledge," meaning knowledge of the built form to the extent that it reflects the agreements, tacit or otherwise, honored by those who act on it. Thematic knowledge is the knowledge of what is not to be different, what is to remain constant. It is "thematic" in the sense that it is recorded by the act of building itself: each instance built is an affirmation of the shared theme by which the actors identify themselves in contributing their personal interpretation of it.[24]

Now that we assume that our built environment, in its ordinary wholeness, is a professional product, thematic knowledge can no longer be taken for granted. We have lost the innocence that comes from the self-evident. The implicit way in which thematic knowledge presented itself in the past is no longer sufficient. It now must be understood and cultivated with deliberation to be effective again. We therefore would do well to study the impact its application, or lack thereof, can have on the health and quality of the environment. The purposeful study of what has so far been known only by doing, and subsequently has been rendered powerless by default, may well be the key to a renewal of the professional role.

Forms of understanding

By way of arguing its role and importance, I conclude this chapter with a few more words about thematic knowledge.

First of all, the difference between thematic knowledge and scientific knowledge should be appreciated. In nature, we also find regularities like systems, types and patterns, which we employ to explain what we are looking at, and with which we develop theories that must allow us to predict what happens when we intervene by experiment. If it turns out that nature's behavior cannot be accurately predicted, we have only one course to take: we must change our theories. The built environment, on the other hand, although it resembles in many ways a complex living organism, is, ultimately, an artifact. Any regularities, systems, patterns, and types we find in it are therefore not reversible but are subject to human agreement as expressed by our acts. Therefore, if discrepancies occur between the theory we hold of the built environment and the realities we observe, more than one way is open to us. We may change our theory, but we also may seek to change what happens. In fact, if something irregular is found, it may well be the beginning of a new pattern. Whether this will be the case is to be decided among participants and cannot be the result of objective investigation.

For this reason, thematic knowledge lives in a social body from which it cannot be separated. Our understanding of it must be gained by a study of the built environment, not just as a form, but as a form representing agreement among the agents making it. When we seek its cultivation we want to understand, among other things, what social and physical conditions are beneficial to it, and what mechanisms can be most effectively be employed in support of it.

Indeed, thematic knowledge does not depend on function, meaning or techniques; it is a knowledge of built form to the extent that it is a shared form, and to that extent only. This becomes clear when we consider how agreement is reached in the built environment. For instance, people may agree to plant a tree. One of them will go along with that decision because he wants to sit in the tree's shadow. Another may value the fruits it will bear. Yet another expects to enjoy looking at it from her window. The form is what unites people, not necessarily its meaning or usefulness. Therefore, seeking agreement about meaning or function is not the way toward agreement about the form. The same function can always be met in another way and a given form can always convey different meanings to different people. Individual actors follow certain themes of form-making for their own, usually complex, reasons. These themes are joined, changed, or abandoned over time but, as we recognize them, we feel we 'understand' the built environment. It is the form, and the form alone, that unites us as inhabitants.

Hence, when we speak of types, patterns, systems and styles, we describe various ways in which a social body can share form. These can be called "forms of understanding" because it is by their acceptance that mutual understandings are reached among actors and all manners of agreements, rules, habits, conventions – tacit or explicit, formal or informal – are followed. The study of the occurrence of forms of understanding therefore entails the study of what is common and similar in contrast to the study of what is special and different to which we are now so much accustomed.

The forms of understanding we see in the built environment are closely linked to the names we give them. As already mentioned, the vocabulary we use to describe the forms we see indicates the extent to which we share knowledge of the built environment. Its name makes a form real. When observers recognize a type it is always, to a certain degree, their creation. With the best of intentions, they can only assume that what they see is what the people who built the observed form saw as well. A pattern, likewise, is always, to a certain degree, a post-hoc interpretation observers agree on. But when we find that there is already a name for what we observe, we know we are on firm ground. The name used is an irrefutable indication of understanding among those using it. Names forms support and legitimate thematic intervention. We may, for instance, have different opinions as to what exactly the Pompeiian house type is all about, but we do know, among other things that a space called "atrium" was part of it. When we use that word, we partake in thematic knowledge and a world of its own is evoked by it.

Let me describe how I think a Pompeiian citizen might "know" an atrium:

A space, partly exposed to the sky, but shaped like a large room with a roof coming down to an opening in the center, below which is a basin to receive the rainwater. The rays of sun diagonally penetrate the shaded space so that a spot of light travels across the floor, scanning tiles and mosaic pebbles. The walls of that space, standing back in the shade, have painted decorations and are pierced with dark holes for windows and doors to adjacent rooms and for passages to other parts of the house; and at some places there are recesses offering a place to sit in. Beyond, a dark portal is the gate to the outside, and when it opens, the sun-drenched street is visible. On the other side, in the axis, is found the ancestor's shrine.

The description of a place is inevitably personal, but its name legitimates it in a society. Each culture had its particular names for architectural forms. There is the *iwan* in the traditional Arabian house, the *serambi* of the Malayan house, and the *zaguan* in the Latin-American tradition, to name only a few that come to mind.[25] We already discussed the entresol as another example. Closer to home, and more modestly, we know of the attic, the basement, and the porch. These are all architectural forms in that they have clear identity but at the same time are technically and functionally indeterminate and open to interpretation. Typically, such names are known by laypeople and builders alike.

The last century or two, as we have seen, have yielded little in terms of new names by which we may discuss an environment so dramatically different from those in the past. The "strip" and the "mall" come to mind as characteristic of the latter-day North American environment. These examples are more urban than architectural. Le Corbusier, who with his unerring instinct for the built form's autonomy, proposed names for what he believed to be new generic forms: the *pilotis*, for example, and the *brise soleil*. Although these names do not denote space as much as shape and have functional origins, they evoke architectural images. But the invention of a single architect does not alone make an environmental understanding and modernist individualism did not encourage the use of words introduced by a colleague, even if the forms themselves were emulated.

While thematic knowledge – as found in systems, styles, patterns and types – resides within a social body, this body may or may not be located in one place. The thematic coherence we find in historic cities represents a knowledge congruent with a location. But, as with the neoclassicist way of building, thematic knowledge may reside within a social network as well, operating internationally and independently of any particular locale. The modernist idea of an "International Style" was not new; neoclassicism was there before. Modernism as a style, however, belongs to an artistic and intellectual elite recently denounced by its own children, while neoclassicism, by and large, tended to go with power and a certain education. Both were architectural systems residing in a network society.

The international acceptance of the skyscraper, to give another example, can also be seen as evidence of thematic knowledge, this time not stylistic but typological and loaded with symbolic significance, residing in a worldwide, predominantly commercial and bureaucratic network society. In the 20th century, the network mode has become increasingly dominant for a number of reasons, not the least of which is the increase in professionalism, itself essentially a network culture.

Thus, there are at least two modes by which a social body can harbor thematic knowledge: by network and by location. There is evidence in abundance that local societies are not stagnant in developing their own environmental knowledge. Large parts of the fast-growing cities in the Third World and, in fact, much of the suburban culture of the first one, have yielded new patterns, systems, and types, revealing local coherences in ways not found elsewhere. This knowledge, however, is rarely valued by professional designers. Even when they happen to be involved in it, they tend to be apologetic about it and to dismiss the forms as "vernacular" or "informal" or even worse, "suburban," because their involvement does not give them peer group recognition. But in extent and variety these newly emerged environments undoubtedly exceed the thematic knowledge accepted in the profession.[26]

They are just not on record as being architecturally significant.

One of the most interesting aspects of environmental knowledge, once we bring ourselves to study it, will lie in the comparisons to be made along the two distinctions mentioned above: the one between the network and the local, and the other between the formal and the informal.

I have argued that thematic knowledge was always the source of architecture, that it is the soil in which architecture grows. If the whole of the built environment is to be architecture, this soil can only be our product, and must be cultivated intentionally. To that purpose we must now learn to appreciate the dialectic relation between the cultivation of "forms of understanding" on the one hand, and their transformation toward more specific architectural articulation on the other.

It is easy to see, however, that our present architectural culture, obsessed with originality and self-expression, will find no merit in an epistemology of the thematic, and that it cannot be expected to engage in its exploration. If such knowledge were made available, it would be reluctant to accept its findings, and much more so to openly use them.

On the other hand, as we all know, the architectural profession is already fully immersed in the everyday built environment, making every kind of building in it. This reality is a strong argument for the recognition of thematic knowledge, and the deliberate cultivation of it.

The difficulties we encounter when trying to reconcile the new reality with professional self-esteem come mainly from an outdated architectural ideology. Although postmodernism rejected correctly, albeit for the wrong reasons,[27] the modernist quest for a unifying style, it perpetuates, with a vengeance the avantgardist tradition. We now suffer the consequences of this outdated position, useful as a means of professional survival in a time of transition, but a liability now that an architecture of the special is no longer of essence. Therefore, postmodernism cannot be a harbinger of the future, but must remain, as its name indicates, an extension of the past. Our WAY OF SEEING ourselves as professionals is increasingly out of tune with our daily practice, creating problems of identity for both the practitioner and the student. As long as this discrepancy persists, we will remain a profession without a knowledge base.

An attempt to cultivate thematic knowledge could be supported by a historiography in which we look at the emergence of common forms – as opposed to just new forms – taking into account those who are sharing them. The main objective should be to understand our present environments, so radically different from those in the past, as the result of a collective search for new thematic knowledge. We should look at what, in an age of invention and revolution, eventually became commonly accepted and is now already taken for granted in practice. We should study modern architectural history as the slow but certain emergence of a new body of patterns and types. In doing so, we may find a rich sediment of already common forms and spaces – perhaps even the beginning of a new vocabulary – deposited over time by experiment and innovation. We should advance theories about the nature of such "forms of understanding" and their role in society, because it is by these forms that environments prosper and professional competence must be measured.

Notes

1. Donald A. Schön, *Educating the Reflective Practitioner* (San Francisco: Jossey-Bass, 1987).
2. Schön's reference: the protocols recorded by Roger Simmonds and others of a study on architectural education directed by William Porter of MIT and Maurice Kilbridge of Harvard in the late 1970's.
3. John N. Summerson, "The Case for a Theory of Modern Architecture," in *The Unromantic Castle* (New York: Thames and Hudson, 1990).

4   Willard Connely, *Louis Sullivan as He Lived: The Shaping of American Architecture* (New York: Horizon Press, 1960).
5   According to Connely, Professor Ware suggested some changes in the facade and in the tower that were readily accepted by Sullivan and Adler.
6   Frank Lloyd Wright, *In the Cause of Architecture*, second paper, May 1914, as printed in the Wendingen book on Frank Lloyd Wright's work, consisting of seven issues of the magazine, edited by Wijdeveld, published by Mees, Santpoort, the Netherlands, 1925.
7   Take, as an extreme example, the popularity of Ayn Rand's *The Fountainhead*. But we all are familiar with more daily evidence of the tacit acceptance of the avant-garde position of the artist (including the architect) by the general public.
8   In spite of a good deal of responsible studies done to place innovative architecture in the context it grew out of, the emphasis is always on the individual oeuvre, or the attempt to identify a distinct 'school.' We still must wait for a more comprehensive attempt to explain the architecture of the last two centuries as a search for a new common ground to replace the older one, the search for a new vocabulary, and the emergence of new types of spatial organization among designers who consider themselves cultivating very different architectures; in short, stressing what was new and shared rather than what was new and different. This kind of study might explain the rise and fall of modernism against the background of the gradual emergence of new contemporary vernaculars. But we are probably still too close to it ourselves to be able to do that.
9   Georges Bataille, *Theory of Religion*, trans. Robert Hurley (New York: Zone Books, 1992).
10 Walter Horn and Ernest Born, *The Plan of St. Gall* (Berkeley: University of California Press, 1997), as well as Lorna Price, *The Plan of St. Gall in Brief* (Berkeley: University of California Press, 1982). The authors, moreover, trace the development of the type back to the Germanic culture of the Iron Age.
11 Robert Venturi, Denise Scott Brown and Steven Izenour, *Learning from Las Vegas* (Cambridge, MA: The MIT Press, 1972).
12 The original introduction to the studio task as quoted from in the preface of the first edition of *Learning from Las Vegas* suggests a desire to really come to grips with the reality of the new environment: "Such a study will help to define a new type of urban form emerging in America and Europe, radically different from what we have known; one that we have been ill equipped to deal with and that, from ignorance, we define today as urban sprawl. An aim of this studio will be . . . to come to understand this new form and to begin to evolve new techniques for its handling." The emphasis on "the forgotten Symbolism of Architectural Form" given in the preface of the revised edition points in another direction.
13 Christopher Alexander et al., *A Pattern Language* (New York: Oxford University Press, 1977).
14 Pierre Le Muet (1591–1669), *Maniere de bien batir* (1664; reprint, Farnborough, England: Gregg International, 1972).
15 A. Placzek, S. Ackerman and M. N. Rosenfeld, *Sebastino Serlio on Domestic Architecture: The Sixteenth Century Manuscript of Book VI in the Avery Library of Columbia University* (New York: Architectural History Foundation; Cambridge, MA: The MIT Press, 1978).
16 Egle Renata Trincanato, *Venezia Minore* (Venice: Filippi Editore, 1948). Trincanato's research on urban domestic residential forms for the ordinary people of Venice of between the twelfth and sixteenth centuries shows a variety of buildings holding small apartments of an amazing sophistication in arrangement.
17 This assumption may hold true for parts of Europe, but in the world at large the actual role of the architect is severely limited. Most residential construction is done without architectural design, and of that only a small part is done by professional builders and developers as we know them in formal processes. All the rest, now called 'informal construction,' is the result of a much older process, based on the involvement of craftsmen and small contractors as much as dwellers and their neighbors and relatives. However, my topic here is how architecture sees itself, and in that perspective, the everyday world is its product.
18 John Summerson, *Georgian London* (London: Peregrine Books, 1978). See, particularly, Chapter 5, "The London House and Its Builders."
19 Stephan Muthesius, *The English Terraced House* (New Haven, CT: Yale University Press, 1982). "As the level of the ground floor was usually that of the street or footpath, the front part of the basement was normally situated completely below ground. To make a separate front access possible for the basement, and also to give it a proper window, a space was created in front of it, about 1.50 m to 3 m wide, which was called 'the area.' Thus, the front of the house was separated from the ground floor by a bridge. The door to the basement was usually fitted underneath the bridge, and a small, steep flight of stairs in the area led up to a footpath."
Nash deviates from this pattern in some places where he places the entrance of the house at the back side to keep the uniformity of the façade. This allowed him (e.g. Carlton house terraces) to keep the basement area above ground, forming a full-size base for the giant columns.
20 Summerson, op. cit., Chapter 13.
21 Marcel Proust, *The Guennantes Way*, trans. C. K. Scott-Montcrieff (New York: Random House, 1934).
22 Ordinances given out during Hausmann's time and before only regulated building, street width, building height, and access to air. Neither type nor pattern were subject to formal regulation. I rely on a study by Sabate Bell on the development of regulation in urbanism in

Paris and Barcelona: Joaquin Sabate Bell, *El Proyecto de la Calle Sin Nombre: Los Reglamentos Urbanos de la Edificacion* (doctoral thesis, Universitat Polytechnica de Catalunya, Barcelona).

23 John McAndrew, *Venetian Architecture of the Early Renaissance* (Cambridge, MA: The MIT Press, 1980), 195. "Renaissance palaces are no bigger or showier than the preceding late Gothic ones that are equally proclamations of the glory and wealth of a family. They look different mainly because their owners wanted them to look different, and the difference is only skin deep."

24 I use the term for both the knowledge shared and for its epistemology: our understanding of how it works, how it can be discussed, and how it can be cultivated.

25 The i*wan* is a vaulted niche facing a courtyard with a platform where one can sit. The *serambi* a porch-like form in front of the wood and bamboo framed house raised a few feet above the grade level on whitewashed piers, originally with its palm leaf roof, but now under corrugated cement sheets: the *zaguan* is a passage from the street to the courtyard, usually closed on the street side with doors with glass panels. It is comparable in age to the Roman *facues*.

26 It is the exceptional merit of the Aga Khan Foundation, by its publications and prizes, that it focuses on the link between professional architecture and thematic knowledge, however tentative and pragmatic its intellectual foundation may be. This reinforces my belief that the development of a truly thematic architecture, liberating us from modernism's obsession with the special and the individual, may occur more easily outside the Western tradition.

27 The wrong reason being that it hampered "self-expression" and was, itself, the expression of a former generation. This is too selfish a reason and of interest only to a professional body. A better reason would be that a single system of understanding is not sufficient in a world as large and complex as ours. There are different social bodies and social bodies tend to have their own forms of understanding, perhaps akin to one another, but not the same.

1998
THE POWER OF THE CONVENTIONAL

Editors' Note: *This essay was published in Rethinking the XIXth Century City, Attilio Petruccioli (ed), Agha Khan Program for Islamic Architecture at MIT, 1998.*

Nineteenth-century urban renewals and extensions reveal the impressive energies and creative forces of that time. We marvel at the apparent ease and conviction with which massive projects were undertaken and brought to a successful conclusion. We tend to look at interventions like those of Nash in London and Haussmann in Paris as the beginning of modern times. No doubt, to a large extent they do belong to our own times perhaps more than to those preceding them, if not for their architectural and urban properties, then certainly for the processes which made them possible. Haussmann's innovations relative to the financing of large projects have been commented on already by Julian Beinart. Nash's entrepreneurship in his daring Regent Street and Regent Park proposal is still a model for contemporary ambitions.

I would like to point to the other side of the coin and argue that these projects, like others of the same period, could be successful because they were carried out in a context where consensus on urban and architectural form was still strong and coherent. Many subjects concerning urban space, building typology, and architectural patterns, which we now have very different opinions about and which today may give rise to a wide variety of possible solutions for any large project at hand, were in those days still taken for granted and hence not subject to discussion or a search for alternatives. I would also suggest that this implicit understanding among the actors involved was very efficient, precisely because it made discussion unnecessary and allowed all available energies to be pointed in the same direction.

Nash in London

The design of Regents Park and Regent Street in London demonstrates the power of conventional form. John Nash's scheme gave structure to central London. He introduced the idea of the wide urban park bound by monumental crescents, applying it with admirable ease and grandeur at the end of a long and productive life.

Most elements marshaled in Nash's grand scheme were borrowed; they had first been developed elsewhere by others. The Georgian terraced house first emerged in the late seventeenth century and its use had been widespread for over a century prior to Regents Park. Wood, Adams, and others had already employed the unified façade shared by a row of houses to shape new urban spaces. Similar facades appear around the squares of the Bedford estate in London. Neoclassicism was quite familiar to professionals and laymen alike, although Nash's interpretation of it was decidedly new.

Nash's achievement is neither diminished nor denied by observing his borrowings. He employed the familiar device of the monumental façade across a number of terraced houses to create giant screens. It was a given that state-of-the-art screens could be built to receive houses following a familiar typology. Employing them allowed him to focus on urban space and the facades that formed it.

Familiarity of style and typology made it possible for citizens to invest with confidence in the scheme, knowing that their houses, shops and offices could be properly and functionally built behind the monumental facades. The same familiarity allowed contemporaries to appreciate the qualities of his particular vision and also to criticize occasionally hasty or haphazard detailing.

Nash's design of sweeping grandeur and dexterous structuring of the urban environment created a form not seen before. This was achieved, not in spite of the home-grown typology and heavily systematized form, but because of it. This was no avant-garde invention rejecting the past and blazing a new path to the future, but an apotheosis of the familiar, utilizing potential developed over a long timer, within forms and types well known to the citizens of London, albeit not in so grand a manner.

Nash's work achieved the ultimate expression of the customary. In both cases, the monumental and explicit act of design was made possible by the powerful presence of the traditional and the implicit.

Nash owed his opportunity to personal status and reputation and favorable circumstances. Wealth, power, and traditional craftsmanship conjoined with royal patronage allowed a single individual to lift an established architectural system to the level of urban infrastructure, then play with it. An old man by the time he was given this opportunity, Nash did not produce more than the principal sketches, confident that they could be developed, detailed and coordinated within the state-of-the-art understanding by others with more energy, patience and remaining time. A general can marshal thousands of troops and machines because training and discipline imprint the rules of the game on every player. Just so could this seasoned, talented, and well-placed designer marshal the skill and industry of a city, transforming it almost overnight. Such is the power that type, style and pattern lend the professional designer who is able to harness them. We also cannot fail to appreciate the architectural profession's ultimate dependence on the conventional, how society's collective environmental knowledge establishes both context and limits of design.

Haussmann in Paris

In Paris, urban mansions for nobles featured *cours d'honneur* accessible from the street. The main house sat between that court and the formal garden. Its wings housed quarters for servants, staff, artisans, stables and storage. Eventually, this form was adopted to a more democratic society, providing apartments around a common courtyard. The transition is described by Marcel Proust:

> "It was one of those old town houses, a few of which for all I knew may still be found, in which the main courtyard was flanked – alluvial deposits washed there by the rising tide of democracy, perhaps, or a legacy from a more primitive time when the different trades were clustered round the overlord – by little shops and workrooms, a shoemaker's, for instance, or a tailor's, such as we see nestling between the buttresses of those cathedrals which the aesthetic zeal of the restorer has not swept clear of such accretions, and a porter who also did cobbling, kept hens, grew flowers – and at the far end, in the main house, a 'countess' who, when she drove out in her old carriage and pair, flaunting on her hat a few nasturtiums which seemed to have escaped from the plot by the lodge . . . dispensed smiles and little waves of the hand impartially to the porter's children and to any bourgeois tenants who might happen to be passing and whom, in her disdainful affability and her egalitarian arrogance, she found indistinguishable from one another. Remnants of this earlier type can still be seen on the Left Bank and in the Marais, in older parts of the urban tissue."[1]

Eventually, buildings around a courtyard accessible from the street were specifically build as apartments. They frequently retained workplaces and shops on the ground floor, surmounted by five or six floors of residential space. The vigilant concierge stationed at the entrance to the courtyard henceforth became a Parisian institution.

The model is extremely efficient in terms of public/private land use. The mass of built space behind the street facades is dense enough to support continuous ground floor commercial activity along the streets. Pedestrian traffic turns the boulevards into social spaces, rather than massive traffic arteries. Such communal living was already a highly compatible part of French urban culture.

Integral to the type was the entresol, a narrow floor suspended between ground floor and the first residential floor above. The entresol forms a vertical margin between the two zones. It is used as an extension for shop and workspace below, often providing a place for offices or storage. But it can also be connected to the apartment above. Or it can even constitute a separate apartment floor. The combined height of ground floor and entresol provides a continuous one-and-a-half story façade independent of the floors above. This effectively relates to the pedestrian space and scale of the street (and hence of the urban fabric). The pedestrian space is reinforced by sidewalk trees, the lower branches of which are at about the entresol height.

Behind the façade, shop height is sometimes increased by pulling the entresol back from the street to become a mezzanine balcony with full-height space. Courtyard entry gates are often executed in full combined height, even when the entresol floor remains visible inside the gate.

Continuous use of this pattern on the building level contributed substantially to urban structure. The courtyard building and associated patterns were firmly in place when, under the prefecture of Baron Haussmann, the monumental restructuring of central Paris began. The recent cutting of Regent Street into London's urban fabric had been a modest enterprise in comparison. Haussmann's urban intervention on a grand scale effected profound and radical changes in the historical urban structure, innovative both in form and in financing.

Yet the urban fabric level was allowed to retain continuity of types, patterns and materials. Haussmann's engineers and architects did not try to invent, but rather to build from the collective image; use of the courtyard building, including the entresol pattern, continued. Optimized for speed and efficiency, its construction was institutionalized and standardized. Floor heights became standardized, almost uniform. Windows with their wrought iron balconies were mass-produced. Interplay of the ground-flo0or façade with the entresol injected variety and life into the zone of pedestrian experience, saving the boulevards from utter monotony.

Haussmann's use of levels was both rational and successful. It was easiest to experiment or innovate on one level only. To rebuild a city by changing the configuration of the urban structure, while simultaneously reinventing urban fabric on the level of the building would have been too difficult and disruptive. Limiting innovation to the urban structure and systematically adapting from precedent whatever had to be done on the building level made the transformation of central Paris possible. Of course, these choices were not made consciously. We can safely assume that the possibility of an alternative never occurred to him.

The success of Haussmann's ambitious scheme was therefore due to the marriage of innovation (financial and managerial) with tradition (typological). Forms built to shape the new boulevards were, to a large extent, based upon a shared image. Exactly what was to be built was known by all the players, from construction worker to developer and bureaucrat. Many discussions, explanations and deliberations which we would now consider essential to implementation of a project on that scale were simply dispensed with. Self-evident forms evincing shared values required little planning and allowed immediate action. The design process, on the level of the building, was accordingly short and simple. Common understanding greatly facilitated coordination between all parties involved in its execution.

The transformation of Paris demonstrates the tremendous power of the shared image to an extent which cannot be fully appreciated unless we consider what the process would be if it were undertaken today. Throughout all of the stages of feasibility studies; traffic, environmental impact and engineering studies, pre-programming, programming, and then again at each successive phase of design, different proposals by a variety of design teams would have to be solicited, then evaluated. Each might well articulate a vastly different conception; to stand out in a crowded field, the winning design scheme would certainly not just expand on the existing typology. Nor would it merely reinvent at the urban scale. It would also intervene on other levels of the form in innovative ways, reinterpreting or reinventing, seeking to engage the existing fabric in a memorable dialectic at every opportunity.

By comparison, Haussmann virtually designed Paris by imperial decree. Not that the absence of alternative proposals was not a result of heavy-handed top-down decision-making; the idea that radically different proposals for the urban environment can be entertained, that the urban form appropriate to a people can be debated, or that environment constitutes a commodity to be selected from among variable options or styles is a (post) modern one. In nineteenth-century Europe, it was unthinkable.

Haussmann's interventions for renewing the city of Paris were immune neither to architectural nor to social criticism; both were at times quite fierce. But from our current perspective, we must marvel at the degree to which questions were not even raised. Conventions and consensus were harnessed to glorious effect, ultimately recreating Paris in one mighty (and efficient) intervention.

Closing comments

In a time when the original and the new dominate all thinking, it may be worth considering the power of the conventional. Shared typology and patterns as well as shared systemics bring efficiency and speed to complex projects because what is already shared need not be discussed nor specified in great detail. Shared forms also result in coherent environments. There is no reason to assume that a context of commonly accepted principles of form inhibits creativity or innovation. On the contrary, it can be argued that the one needs the other and that the truly creative is best measured against qualities already achieved and proved, while the exceptional needs an established coherence to be appreciated at all. Study of historic precedent shows that shared forms can result in environments of undisputedly high quality. A discourse on the quality of the common- what its constituent parts are and how it came about – may be more beneficial to environmental quality today than a sustained focus on the new and the exceptional.

Note

1 Marcel Proust, *The Guermantes Way*, trans. Moncrief and Kilmartin, 1st ed. (New York: Random House, 1920), 22.

INTERMEZZO BY THE EDITORS

SK/JD: When you moved to MIT in 1985 to become Head of the Department of Architecture, why do you think they hired you? They didn't hire you because of the SAR philosophy, did they?

JH: Partly, because they liked the idea of being a research university. They liked the idea of some of my research. In those days, nobody did research in our field. I think I was the first to research formally in architecture. History of architecture was something else. Well, the reason that they asked me was that, first of all, they knew me because two years earlier, I was invited to do a tour in America. I had, maybe, 10 universities that I visited. We ended up in Boston and Cambridge and I gave a talk to both Harvard and MIT together. I was told that that was the first time that Harvard and MIT had the same room listening to one person.

SK/JD: Did they do it at MIT or at the GSD [Graduate School of Design at Harvard]

JH: At that time, the present GSD was not built. The next day, MIT asked me to come back, talk some more. And I got in a very big room with a very big table and people were sitting on the floor and sitting on the table. And I had no idea who was a professor and who was a student. Julian Beinhart was sitting on the floor. And they all had very peppy questions and I liked that very much. So, I had a very good impression of MIT. And then they got in trouble because Donlyn Lyndon decided to leave as Head. They got tired of him and spent a lot of time finding a replacement. And they couldn't find one. And then Stan Anderson, who had visited me in Eindhoven earlier proposed that I be asked to apply. So, I got a phone call from them, would I come and be a candidate? At least that's what he meant, but I did not understand. I said I would come if I can refuse to become the department head. I cannot say yes or no yet. Of course, it is very self-evident that I didn't notice the system at work. So, I came over and they were all there; they had a committee of maybe 10 or 15 people. Everybody was involved. And they talked to me. It went pretty well. The reason it went pretty well, I found out afterwards, it was sort of funny that, if you were a candidate and they asked you to say something, you tried to convince them how good you are. And when they gave me the floor, I said, "What is your problem? Tell me about your problems." And everybody started talking. And I got a very good sense of what those problems were. And they said, "This is perfect. He's actually talking to us. He's actually asking us questions." So that was the reason they asked me. And another thing, there was one question Leon Groisser asked. At that time, I didn't know Leon yet. Leon said, "If you would be invited to become just a professor at MIT, would you come?" I said, "No. You make me department head or not."

SK/JD: That's good.

JH: I meant it because I thought if I become dependent on unknown professors in America, I'd better stay in Holland.

SK/JD: One thing you wrote while you were at MIT was "Notes of a Traveller."

JH: Yes.

SK/JD: Do you remember that one?

JH: I do. I like that.

SK/JD: I still like that. It's one of your best ones. You wrote that your belief, or ideology, leads to research.

JH: Yes, that's so.

SK/JD: That's very interesting. If you believe something, then you've got to do research. I think that would be strange to most people. You say, "Ultimately we act on faith. We assume our ideology is right. If not, we would find out." You wrote, "Our research task was to do such and such." You wrote this when you were nearing the end of your term at MIT as head. It was 1980.

JH: Okay.

SK/JD: What did other people think about that paper at MIT? You probably spoke to people about it and how did people respond to your way of thinking about the origins of research?

JH: I can't remember any discussion about it. It's the usual thing, you know. MIT is basically a group of individual people who run their own programs. Have their own agenda. And they keep themselves informed about what everybody else is doing. But there is no desire or feeling that we all should agree about the same thing.

SK/JD: Not agree necessarily, but at least engage in argumentation with each other.

JH: It didn't happen.

SK/JD: The same as lack of discussion about your other paper "Around the Black Hole."

JH: Yeah. That one. Right. The students got excited about it. They were organizing the meeting with the professors to explain what they thought about it. And everybody was hemming and hawing, of course.

SK/JD: Do you remember that paper was a critique of the studio as the dominant mode of education and that's why it was the black hole. Everything just falls in and disappears! That must have put you at odds with Maurice Smith.

JH: Okay, yeah.

SK/JD: Did you ever, did you see eye-to-eye at all?

JH: Yes, we did. I think so. I appreciated what Maurice tried to do. I listened to what he said. And I liked him, and his instincts. His feeling is fascinating with complexity. With the way forms work can change. So, I understood that. I'd never heard of him before I came to MIT. I came to listen to him. And he, somehow, appreciated what I was doing. Partly because he knew – he understood – that I understood what he tried to do.

ROLE OF THE ARCHITECT

1975
THE LIMITS OF PROFESSIONALISM

Editors Note: *This article is an edited version of the first John Dennys Memorial Lecture, presented by the author at the Architectural Association, in London, in 1975 and published in the Architectural Association Quarterly, 1976. A version of this article also appeared as "The Built Environment and the Limits of Professional Practice," in Plunz, Richard (editor) Housing Form and Public Policy in the United States. Praeger, New York, 1980. (pp. 19–32)*

1. Powers and built environments

For quite some time I have been concerned with the manmade environment as a dynamic, ever changing phenomenon. One can view the built environment as a phenomenon composed of space volumes and material volumes of every sort, form and dimension which presents itself in an endless diversity of combinations. Through observation we realize that this built environment is subject to continuing change. These are changes which take place gradually and, therefore, the casual observer would not directly perceive the built environment as a dynamic phenomenon. But yet when one would study, for instance, a representation of a solitary piece of an urban tissue throughout time at regular intervals, one would observe that the successive representations are not completely alike. A process of change is evident. The built environment is in a continuing condition of transformation. These transformations are the result of human attitude. Man caused the built environment to exist and he allows it to do so through continuing changes. Thus, we are talking about a process in which man continually intervenes. By studying the transformations of the built environment, we can learn something about this process. For the changes are naturally not arbitrary. Patterns crop up; we can identify variations on particular themes. In short, the transformations of the built environment betray certain laws of the process whereof this environment is the tangible manifestation.

Therefore, we can distinguish systems in the morphology of the built environment. Because we are dealing with the result of human actions, and because our actions are not arbitrary, we recognize a 'system' as the result. Thus, the relationship between human actions and their outgrowth, the material phenomenon, can, in principle, be formalized. We can talk about 'powers' which change the morphology. A power is, then, every person, or group of persons, who clearly has the capacity to change the built reality. The concept of power – thus used – says nothing about the power as being good or bad. At first glance, it is not even important who exercises power. A power in this approach is not more and not less than: 'that which modifies the built environment.' In this sense the concept of 'power' is used analogous to the concept of 'force' in mechanics. This concept is also used without its being important who exercises the force, and the question is even less significant whether the force is good or bad.

The use of such an approach is that one can better understand how things work. Thanks to mechanics, we can now predict what will happen when we let a force work on a construction. In the same manner, it is interesting to know what happens to the built environment when a 'power' appears.

Can we uncover laws with which we have to deal regardless of the meaning of our exercise of power? Is it, after we have formulated such laws, then also not easier to predict what would happen to the built environment when a definite exercise of power takes place? Can't we then also consider power relations that are significant for the existence of built environments? In short: to what extent are we free and to what extent are we restrained in the exercise of power? If there are laws to be formed of a general nature, regardless of the question who exercises power and why, then these laws should tell us something about man's lack of freedom. And insight into man's lack of freedom is ultimately the beginning of all wisdom.

It is about man's lack of freedom that I would like to speak. To do so there are two matters which must be mentioned to begin with.

In the first place, it is apparent from what I just talked about, that the concept of 'change' is of essential importance. It is through change that we recognize 'power.' Power is precisely, as related to the built environment, 'that which changes that environment.' It is the transformations that we can observe which enable us to make a connection between power and morphology – between our effort and the shape of the built environment. That is an important fact because with the concept of 'change' the concept of 'time' is introduced, and this concept has never really played a role in the thinking of those who have been concerned through the centuries with the shape of the built environment. It means we should view the built environment as a phenomenon of four dimensions wherein, not only space, but also time is to be considered if we want to understand something about human actions in relation to the built environment. Through the introduction of the fourth dimension via the concept of 'transformation,' an entire field of problems comes into focus with which we must deal almost literally in an entirely new perspective. It is my firm conviction that the thinking of architects, urban designers and planners only has a future if these disciplines succeed in choosing the aspect of 'change' as the foundation for their theoretical speculation. This means, indeed, a fundamental reorganization of thought in these disciplines, which will bring some tension to the professional world.

Of a less fundamental nature, but perhaps of more importance for what I want to say today is another aspect of the theoretical approach I am interested in and of which I gave you a very quick sketch. I am talking about the fact that this approach appears to be possible through a precise division between 'power' as I have defined it and the built environment. On one hand, there are the morphological systems that describe the relations of physical elements in space. They clarify, if you like, 'themes,' the variations of which we observe in reality. On the other hand, there are the 'powers' which change this physical reality. The one reveals itself through the other.

The one is an image of the other. The laws we would like to find are laws which apply to all powers and all morphologies which they influence. This means – as I said – that it is of no importance who the powers are. It is of no consequence for such laws whether architects, urban designers, town planners, bureaucrats, bankers, politicians or laymen exercise power. The laws, if they exist at all, should apply to all of these parties in their exercise of power, regardless of their intentions, ideals, desires or ambitions.

2. Professionals and others

This is a way of dealing with a problem which may be regarded by those interested in such formal approaches as significant and necessary. But the significance of such an approach has not been generally understood with regard to the phenomenon of the built environment. If one keeps track of the matters which have been brought up in our architectural world concerning the built environment, then it is readily apparent that we are mostly concerned with objectifying our own role regarding this phenomenon. That is understandable, because we are all actors in the process which brings the built environment to its fruition. And so, the architect sees above all an architectonic phenomenon, the structural engineer sees an engineering problem, the banker sees an object of financing, the occupant sees an environment in which he must live, and the member of a housing management corporation sees an object to supervise. In short, each one sees in the built environment a terrain for the exercise of his power. It is difficult to view objectively something in which one plays so much a part and from which one borrows one's social and professional identification. Therefore, the built environment did not readily emerge as a phenomenon in its own right.

At the same time, as professionals of one kind or another, we are all in agreement that the quality of the built environment is at stake. That all of our work and all of our striving is particularly based on that. We do not grow tired of emphasizing that regularly. But if that is so, there are, in my opinion, two suppositions which underlie our professional existence in relation to the built environment, regardless of the disciplines in which each one flies his own colors. Two suppositions, moreover, consequently justify the existence of this branch of architecture. The first supposition is that the built environment does not exist for us, but that we, as professionals, exist for the built environment. The second supposition is that we, as professionals, can present a significant contribution to the origin and existence of this same built environment. These suppositions have engaged me for quite a while. If there is a built environment, what is my position as a trained professional with regard to this manifold and all-embracing phenomenon? Is this position a necessary one? Are we indispensable? Or would it be better without us?

It behooves my own discipline to be somewhat modest. Doxiades calculated, for example, that the percentage of existing buildings in the world brought about through the efforts of an architect was not more than five per cent of the total. It is an interesting figure. I am unable to ascertain if it is exact, but from simple observation, it becomes clear that the efforts of architects are limited in their scope. Therefore, we should realize that the so-called 'primitive' cultures which have awakened the interest of architects so much in the last years are not the only areas in which architects have not played a role.

These 'primitive' cultures are cultures which otherwise often display very complex built environments which are the result of an exceptional harmony between the people and their self- formed environment. We also know that in the so-called developing countries 40 to 60 per cent of the urban population live in dwellings which are built by the inhabitants with their own hands and on their own initiative. By this I mean what is generally referred to as 'squatter housing.' It is what the French call a 'bidonville', what in Brazil is called 'barriadas,' what in Turkey is called a 'geoncondu' and in Chile is indicated as 'pobladores.' The phenomenon is so universal that countless names exist for it and also many forms can be differentiated.

Regarding this, I think Turner was the first to point out a good ten years ago that something other than a 'slum' was being discussed. It is now recognized in ever-widening professional circles that what is being considered is an age-old process from which the beginning of an urban environment appears. We know how such processes, when they can persist, have proven to be the cause for the existence of city districts which are just as complete as any other environment with which we are familiar, districts in which the casual observer would never recognize the primitive beginnings.

It was to Turner's credit that he has shown as well how the attitude of professionals such as us, in this spontaneous process, were, more often than not, causing harm. Thus, there apparently exist built environments in which we (and I mean not only the architects) with our professional training and our manner of working, can better be done without.

Those who will face facts can only determine one thing. The person who is not a professional, such as you and I, is not only the object, but also in many cases the direct cause of the existence of the built environment. What comes to mind, then, is an interaction between man and matter which I characterized as long ago as 1962 with the term 'natural relationship.' I did this based on observations in the prosperous Netherlands about the same time that Turner made his observations in Peru and came to identical conclusions.

Now it goes without saying, that you – after what I've just contended – would insert a marginal note. All is well and good you'll say, but we live in a complex and highly technically developed society. What may be true of the past, and what still may apply to developing countries and primitive cultures need not be the foundation for the building process in our own rich West European situation. It must be recognized also that in our countries the omission of the professional, the architect, the structural engineer, the city planner, the bureaucrat, housing experts in general, and so many others would constitute a total disaster. We cannot go back. The knowledge, the experience and the understanding which we have gathered through generations of labor and research and which are administered and applied by us professionals are indispensable power for the existence of the environment, and that many cases are indicated in which the user, the dweller himself, is the only power known to the process. Beside that we have – in the Netherlands for example – the process of housing the people which is correctly characterized by the dweller who, by definition, has no power, and by the process which is totally controlled by the professional elite of which you and I take part.

Thus, there are clearly two demonstrable extremes. In the one process it is a disaster if the dweller is eliminated and in the other it is a disaster if the professional is eliminated. The difference between these two extreme examples lies in the exercise of power. But if we want to look at that difference more closely, it must be determined that it has not to do with the fact that at one time the power enjoyed a professional training while that is not the case in the other example. We must not look at who exercises the power but at the way in which the power is exercised. And then an important difference becomes clear. The dweller operates (by definition) as a power in a dwelling, the dwelling which he himself will occupy. Here we have the dwelling as a material-spatial phenomenon, a unity of the exercise of power. A built environment which develops in this manner, through the action of dwellers themselves, is consequently the result of a fine-grained power structure. There are many powers at work which reflect each other in a directly demonstrable piece of the morphology: the dwelling. This is the distinguishing characteristic of this kind of process. It also has its limitation, because it is clear that a pressing need will develop for greater, more encompassing powers as soon as the process acquires some magnitude. The greater powers are consequently demonstrable more often than not. Sometimes they are composed of a collection of smaller powers. In processes of very limited proportions, however, we find sometimes only the fine-grained power structure of individuals who operate in their own direct environment. The more extensive examples exhibit, consequently, those other powers which cover and bind, powers which work structurally and organizationally in relation to the many smaller, limited powers.

Now the professional expert – the architect, the planner, the administrator, and the bureaucrat – by the nature of his faculties is always representative of this organizing and structuring power. It is not true that the organizing power is always professionally exercised (we have already seen that, for example, a group of dwellers banded together is able to form such an organizing power) but the reverse is hardly the case: Our capacities and our proficiencies, no more than our ambitions, only allow us to be part of the organizing and structuring powers in the complex processes from which the built environment arises. The character of this power exercise is consequently one operating from the outside in the broader context, in contrast with the other power which operates, as it were, from inside the boundary of the private dwelling outwards.

Thus, the issue is two forms of the exercise of power which stand out from the rest by the direction in which the power works. And since they operate in opposite directions, they allow the possibility of a balance.

Our lack of freedom as a trained elite is evident here. It is in the nature of our profession that we can only be one of these two powers. We have no choice on that point. And it is interesting that the so-called mass housing process only allows entrance to professionals as you and I. This process in its one-sided manner of exercising power is a counterpart to the squatter-housing which defines its limitations by the fact that the organizing power is not present.

3. **Three inclinations**

Now I have proposed earlier that the shape of the built environment is a reflection of the exercise of power. If that is true, and we have the extreme case of Dutch public mass housing, then it must be possible to point out aspects which can only occur when such one-sided exercise of power is involved. That is indeed the case, and I will give you some examples.

One such aspect which appears only when the user has no power over his own dwelling, is uniformity. The repetition of the same doors of the same color in the line of facades on a street. The repetition of the same identical floor plans in a block. The duplication of identical blocks in a quarter of a town. It has astonished many people that it must be this way which is apparent from the general reaction over the 'dullness' and the 'monotony' of our public housing about which everyone complains currently in an almost monotonous manner.

There appears now such a relation between power and morphology, for we see that everywhere when the fine-grained power does not work through the dwelling itself, uniformity develops. This occurs regardless of the affluence of the country in which this process is enacted and regardless of the question as to which people or disciplines make decisions. Conversely, **one never encounters uniformity where the user is directly a power himself**. In well-to-do owner-occupied suburban environments, there are no complaints about uniformity. Nor is that the case in the campongs in Indonesia to name just another example. Accordingly, it can be observed that the phenomenon of uniformity is affected (in so far as I can use that word) as soon as the power is again introduced through the deficiency from which it developed. When the same uniform dwellings are partly rented under the management of a housing association and the other part is sold to dwellers, it can be seen within a few years that the purchased dwellings exhibit differences. That is quite visible from the outside. Doors are painted different colors, dormers are installed, sheds and other additions are built on, windows are poked out or walled in, garden fences are eliminated or introduced, and so forth. We can safely assume that within the dwelling, encroachments on the uniformity take place much sooner. The difference which can be perceived -in the one case uniformity and in the other not – has nothing to do (and I repeat this with emphasis) with the question of what kind of people now exercise power. It has nothing to do with knowledge, proficiency, religious conviction or the interests of the political establishment. The difference is only the result of the position which the power takes with regard to the built environment. It has to do, as is said, with the scope and the direction of every exercise of power. From the outside to the inside or from the inside out. From the large to the small or from the small to the large.

Let me try to clarify this: I believe that we can suppose that every power, regardless of its kind – professional or not, planner, housing manager or dweller – always has three characteristics which determine its appearance. I'll mention these three characteristics for you in brief:

In the first place, there is the striving toward as large as possible a territory for the exercise of power. Each power will try to make as many decisions as possible for as large a part of the built environment as possible. This first characteristic I would like to call **the inclination towards expansion**.

In the second place, each power strives to devote as little labor or effort as possible while exercising its power. Each seeks the easiest way to make itself felt, if only because it would benefit the first-named expansion inclination. This second characteristic I would like to call **the inclination towards the economization of labor**.

Finally, **each power strives through its influence to express its own personal value system**. In other words: if power is characterized here by change of the environment, then these wrought changes will better reflect that which the relative power thinks is 'good' than would the situation which previously existed.

I would like to define this as inclination towards quality whereby naturally, then, quality is an absolutely relative concept. Now the phenomenon of uniformity is especially made clear through the inclination towards the economization of labor. It is undeniable that it is simpler for an architect to design 100 conforming dwellings than it is to present 100 different dwellings in his plan. It is certainly also simpler for a party to build 100 similar dwellings than 100 different ones, even when there is no talk of industrialization. It is also easier to manage 100 identical dwellings than to keep 100 different dwellings under control. Derived from the exercise of power of the architect, builder and housing manager, uniformity is, consequently, the obvious physical characteristic which is in keeping with the nature of their exercise of power. Also, the dweller, who owns his own residence and is, therefore, responsible, will follow the three inclinations in the exercise of power. He will strive to adapt his dwelling with as little difficulty as possible to what in his own value judgement makes a 'good' dwelling. In doing so, it is not significant to attempt to copy his neighbor exactly. Nevertheless, he will borrow a good idea from his neighbor and apply it in his own way as he sees fit. The chance of uniformity is consequently nil in this case but there is a chance of conformity and variety, for neighbors are usually not totally different.

I cannot refrain from adding yet one example: a typical working-class neighborhood built in the 1920's. In this established neighborhood in Eindhoven the whole body of dwellers, solidly organized, banded together as one power. They wanted among other things at one time to add exactly the same dormer to each residence. However, the municipality commissioned three different architectural offices to concertedly spruce up the neighborhood. The result was naturally that there are three different types of dormers to be seen. The division of the three types in this particular neighborhood coincides with the division of labor in the three offices. From this example it appears again that it is not important who exercises power – professional or layman – but that the relative position of the exercise of power is determined.

It also becomes clear that such concepts as 'efficient' and 'good' in regard to the built environment are absolutely relative. What is efficient and good in the one power pattern is a waste which leads to poor results in the other.

That is also illustrated if we were to look again at the two rows of houses which I talked about a moment ago, in which the one is managed as a whole through one and the same housing association and in the other each dwelling is managed by a private resident. The one solution is efficient and good for central control. The other solution is efficient and good for the individual resident. If one has a preference for one of the two manifestations, then one does not only choose a form but a process as well: a relative power.

4. Public and private territory

But enough about uniformity. There is another point to mention. Why are some streets straight and others crooked? For the seventeenth century canal belt around Amsterdam's center, everything is straight as an arrow the length of hundreds of meters. Not only are the canals straight but the walls of facades stand precisely in a line and the trees are planted again in a line of uniform distances along the water. If one must plan such a large territory, that is unquestionably the manner of working which originates from the inclination towards the economization of labor. The older medieval canals, though, are crooked by the same inclination, just as the streets and alleys that link them. These urban spaces have been developed from paths over which people walk on an irregular terrain. If one walks down a dike, for example, one walks obliquely to the bottom in a crooked line. That is the easiest way of descending. Consequently, it is easiest to follow these lines as, bit by bit, one builds one house after another along these routes. In towns which have grown slowly in a process in which each house came into being through a separate power, streets are never straight. Our image of the small, medieval town which developed from such a slow, fragmented process administrated by many small powers has been characterized accordingly by crooked streets. But from the middle ages we are also acquainted with the bastides which were established in the thirteenth century by the English king and his vassals. The street patterns were designed for these bastides and, therefore, all the streets there are straight without exception. Such is

Figure 1 The medieval center of Amsterdam

also the case in the Dutch town of Elburg, where in the fourteenth century, the citizens established a new town, planned by one man.

Along the straight canals of Amsterdam and the straight streets of Elburg, however, stand houses which are all different with an endless variety of stoops and facades. I don't have to tell you why that is so. This variation is in harmonious contrast with the straight line of facades along the street. However, a student who would today try to present in his design such a straight line of varied facades, 200 meters long, for example, would be sent home with an insufficient grade because his professor rightly assumes that a uniform facade of the same length can be built there. This professor is correct, for his value system suggests to him that a wall of facades may not be dull. How does one prevent such dullness and still expect uniform buildings? Answer; by not only bending but also 'breaking' the facade wall. That is what is now consequently happening. Every architect knows that you must now 'stagger' the facades in a housing project. The alternative – totally different dwellings with different facades which can then stand in a line – runs counter to the first law; the inclination towards expansion of their own influence of power. It is inevitable. When dullness must be avoided under pressure from public criticism, then staggering facades is the easiest solution, even though we know that it costs more in money and labor. The expansion-inclination prevails in the exercise of power over the inclination towards the economization of labor. And in a wealthy country we can permit ourselves to spend more money to support the existing process which is finally managed by us.

There has been found, in addition, a remedy to combat dullness without causing whole building masses to be staggered. And we see this remedy consequently employed in the most recent building plans. By this I mean the placing of outside storage, sheds and garages in front of dwellings on the public street. When one does this, the real building mass can remain intact as one block and yet the rectilinear quality is broken. The latter is a more efficient remedy which, consequently, has developed swiftly as a general trend in the Netherlands. But because the power pattern doesn't change, uniformity occurs nevertheless; repetition of the same colored doors, repetition of identical facades, repetition of identical outside storage units, sheds and carports, repetition of identical blocks. This only suggests a more complex form of repetition of identical parts with which the effect of dullness is combated.

I believe that I'm nearing the point at which people will blame me for cheap criticism of the most recent developments in public housing architecture. I would regret it if that were to happen, for I only want to demonstrate that there are – literally – forces at work which exceed the influence of individual professionals. The development sketched by me is a necessary one as long as we remain working in a system in which the shape of one dwelling is no longer determined by the efforts of one power. There is, for example, no outcome known to me from processes wherein the fine-grained exercise of power is in order, and wherein, consequently, sheds and outside storage are still placed between the dwelling and the public street. When we trace through the medium of old maps the way in which the relation between dwelling and such additions were solved earlier, we see that these elements are continually to be found behind the dwelling. This also happens when there is enough land to place the dwelling farther back. It is a pattern which is independent of the amount of available land. One always observes the same; small streets and canals with relatively deep lots on which the house itself is always directly situated on the boundary between public and private land. We can

guess at the reasons for such a universal solution; private land in this manner is best used for private purposes: growing vegetables, planting trees, constructing sheds and buildings and workshops without its being influenced by the public sphere or without the private goings-on damaging the public space. The aspect of safety probably also plays an important role. And earlier the towns were often unsafe too. Consequently, we see that where a yard directly borders public land (with broad lots, for example, or corner houses) practically without exception a stone wall is encountered. All of this is in agreement with the expansion-inclination of the exercise of power, complete over every square meter of private territory.

It is consequently interesting in another respect to observe in the old towns as well, how much this first law of the exercise of power came into play. Namely, there is always a tendency to minimize the public area. The streets are invariably small in comparison with the depth of the lots. Not to speak of the alleys. The buildings push their way as much as possible to the front. Whenever possible people encroach on the public land for their own benefit. It is consequently not surprising to learn from research that the famous Amsterdam stoops are built on public land. The official line of landed property lay even with the facade from the beginning. The stoops, cellar stairs, hoists, and cellar-shops are an appropriation of public land. A form of 'squatting' or what the Dutch call 'kraken' which in the course of time has grown to a common law. But yet the municipality has the right to demand demolition in the public interest such as is evident from jurisprudence.

Minimal public space is consequently the unassailable phenomenon as long as urban fabrics develop in a process in which the dwelling's owner has the upper hand. However, the architect has seen the public domain – the square, the church, the street, the public building – as his work ground. So has the bureaucracy. And it is these last two forces which in the course of this century have acquired ever more power. Accordingly, plans are developed in which the public space receives increasingly greater attention. This culminates in the 1920's with Le Corbusier's proposals to place the dwelling on 'pilotis' in the open field. Every square meter is then public. The extreme is reached.

Thus, one pays attention to similar phenomena. I remember that I once stood on the highest balcony of a housing block with the functionary who was responsible for the management of the site at which we looked. One neighborhood consisted of one-family row houses. It struck me that the backyards of the houses were all divided by low wire so that the effect developed of a continuing green strip which lay behind the houses and which was to be viewed in one glance. 'Why don't you permit the people to put up fences?' I asked. 'Isn't it a pity to leave so much valuable land open so that they have no privacy there?' The answer was: 'We can't start on that! It would be a mess in a very short time!'

It is true. There, where the new dwellings are in the possession of the residents, one already consequently encounters an inconveniently arranged situation of fences, sheds, and hedges. Yes, even chicken coops and pigeon houses. We again see the laws of the exercise of power. Is there a central administration? Then wire between the yards is already a concession. Expansion- inclination, efficiency and value judgement of this power would be served best by a public backyard, a solution which is often proposed by architects and students. Are there residents who exercise individual control? Then the three same inclinations ask for special delimitations of as large a piece of private territory as is possible to develop all kinds of private things.

5. Values, national and international

In the Netherlands in the last half century, the growing attention to the public space has likewise been increasingly combined with a reduction of housing density and therefore also a reduction of the number of people who live on a hectare (2.471 acres). This has again contributed to the objectionable dullness. More public space, less public. One doesn't run into many people anymore. Restriction of public territory with simultaneously constant housing density would thus not only produce more private property, but what's more the extant public territory would be more thickly populated. This remedy for dullness, although it would perhaps lower costs, is however still untested, for it is in conflict with the first law of the exercise of power in the currently working process: the inclination towards expansion of the efforts of the working powers. Moreover, it is, in this process, much less simple to develop a close and fine-grained territory than an open coarse-grained territory with the same housing density. This has to do again with the inclination towards economizing labor. There is no escaping: in the given process the inclinations of power lead of their own accord to the manifestations which have dominated mass housing since the beginning of this century. I have already pointed out, that, hence, the efforts which are being undertaken to imitate the forms of the fine-scaled exercise of power, are concessions of the currently established form of exercising power. They will probably still take place because they are the only means of maintaining the current process. Thus, it is predictable that public housing in the Netherlands for instance, will evolve further toward being of small scale. Therefore, costs will climb, and increasingly more professional work will be necessary. For this fineness of scale is now costly in the current process. In the other process – in which the division of power is fine-scaled, that is an open question. In as much as we understand from given examples, such fine – grained examples, from history have been developed from the same three laws of the exercise of power, of which certainly the inclination towards the economization of labor and materials does not fall in last place.

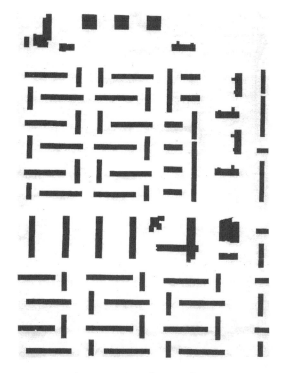

Figure 2 1950's era extension of Amsterdam

But we are a prosperous civilization in the western countries, and we shall probably be able to take the liberty to keep seeing the problem as a problem of planning and execution which can be solved by examining 'new dwelling types.' The process, in which, however, there is no place for the fine-scaled division of power, leads of its own nature to the enlargement of scale, uniformity and expansion of the public space. This can be observed over the entire world. Everywhere, whereby the state's central authority with the help of professionals such as you and me, the housing need is wrestled with, these phenomena are observable. So much is this the case that the results from country to country are hardly to be differentiated. Regardless of the differences in geography, climate and culture, regardless of the prevailing political system, liberal, socialist, communist, or whatever hybrid, the above characteristics still develop. The immunity from political ideologies of these phenomena is especially striking. I have yet to succeed in demonstrating the morphological differences between the public housing products of capitalism and those of Marxism as long as the process in both cases is not the process of the fine-grained division of power.

If each land thus becomes gradually acquainted with its professional process which denies the fine-grained exercise of power, it also becomes acquainted with the other along with it. I am again pointing to the squatter housing in the Third World. But there are less-extreme forms. In each class, and within everyone's income, there are people, such as those who exercise 'self-building.' When they hire an architect and a contractor, they also use that term. Moonlighting building laborers in the Netherlands make a living from it; for many English the 'cottage' is still the ideal, as is la petite maison-en-compagne for the Frenchman. In Yugoslavia, I saw great numbers of private buildings – large, heavily constructed houses which took many years to build. But it was worth it, for the house is an investment for generations. My guide in Zagreb estimated that seventy per cent of the housing in the city came about in this manner. But the skyline of Zagreb is dominated by tall apartment blocks, designed by architects who apparently have studied the international magazines well. Thus, each country has along with the official housing its own fine-grained process, a process which, nevertheless, exists, is certainly not encouraged, and is even less studied. It happens, however, legal or illegal. It may be scornfully called kitsch by some or 'anonymous' architecture by others, but it points least of all to anonymous residents and it presents in its manifestations substantial differences which correspond with the climate, geography, culture and economy of the respective countries. All of this is in contrast with the results of the official process, such as I have previously touched on.

For in the official housing as well, the morphology is representative of those who make decisions as in the third inclination of power, the one towards expressing one's own values, has been suggested. Here, it is the intellectual, professional elite which expresses the value judgement and in so doing is only answerable to its own circle. The dialogue about what is good and bad takes place among professionals and they only need to convince each other. The rules are developed by the same circle which also executes the rules. An architect who advocates that a new form is 'better,' does not familiarize himself with its future users but with the authorities. The authorities listen to professionals and experts. Results are also compared internationally: via publications, conventions, exhibitions and excursions: the dialogue among professionals continues. However much inspired each one is with the best intentions, being captured in the laws of the process drives one increasingly farther away from the point of departure: the expression of what is good or bad in the opinion of the user is not to be recovered in the results. What is 'good' in the opinion of the decisionmakers is what the environment exhibits. It is a process of the self-fulfilling prophecy controlled by the inclination toward valuation of the prevailing powers.

6. Adaptability and participation

The examples which I have cited until now as an illustration of the relationship between the morphology and the manner of exercising power from which this arises, were examples in which the built environment can be seen as a static form. But I have emphasized in the beginning of my argument, that it is exactly from the aspect of change that we can best learn to understand our built environment. For power shows itself by its hold on the environment. Therefore, I want to give a few examples of a more dynamic nature.

A power by itself strives toward stability. When a power has established its value-judgement in the built environment, it wants to maintain it. Therefore, changes arise from relationships of powers. Through outside influences, a power reacts. When there is, therefore, talk of a one-sided exercise of power, it can be expected that the morphology grows rigid. This is especially the case when it is exactly the organizing, structuring power which dominates. The continual change which we can observe in the historical cities – where within the framework of a given structure a continual process of fine-grained adaptation and change took place – was consequently the outcome of the fine-grained exercise of power from the ground up.

It is this small-scaled dynamism which makes a town a living organism, a dynamism which we consequently miss in the built environment in which the fine-grained exercise of power is not present. The unchangeability of the small-scale, the rigidity of the new towns is the outcome. Because in the current process, the exercise of power only works in one direction, action is only to be noted when there is growth and expansion. Then there is space for the initiative of the encompassing exercise of power. This explains why we feel so much more at home in urban expansion but are powerless when a new life appears necessary in the existing old districts. In the problem areas of urban renewal, the limitations of the one-sided, professional exercise of power become inevitably clear.

The existing, one-sided exercise of power does not want change from the fine-grained exercise of power. Neither the inclination toward expansion, nor the inclination toward their own economization of labor, nor the inclination toward establishing their own quality judgement allows change of what has only recently been achieved. That's why there is money and attention for more complicated dwelling types which must counteract dullness, but there is no need felt to spend money for adaptability within the dwelling itself. For these small scaled adaptations in and around the individual dwelling can only be the outcome of the exercise of power from the inside out which is not present in the functioning status quo. Therefore, when we talk of change in existing urban districts, we mean only the change as a result of the encompassing exercise of power: the breaking through of roads and subways and the cutting down of trees to create room for a new, one-sided, exercise of power.

I have limited my examples to the morphology, the shape of the built environment and the change thereof as the result of a specific form of exercising power. That the one-sidedness of the current exercise of power is felt increasingly in European countries as a problem is, however, especially expressed in the cry over participation which has been heard in recent years. It is good breeding to explain that one is for participation and that participation procedures – however complicated and time-consuming – are worthwhile in principle.

The impression exists that the solution lies in such procedures and that the great attention paid to participation would be a sign of a fundamental improvement of the state of things. However, it seems to me that this is a sign that something isn't right. **For true participation can only be founded on a power-relationship.** A power on a lower level asks for participation in the exercise of power on a higher level. To ask for participation is an acknowledgement of not having power in another party's area. That is of itself a healthy thing. For each power is restricted and, therefore, has reason to demand a voice when another power appears which will determine its restrictions. But in this image, there is talk of a relationship of two powers which are in some state of equilibrium to each other, powers which each work in a different direction and which must seek a balance. If the participation is to count, then this must be effective and signify two powers that seek a balance. Both powers must be identifiable and acknowledged in the process. But in the process in which we are involved, the one power, which works expansively from the inside out, is currently not present and the only form of power operating is that which pushes from the outside to the inside. As long as this is the case there can be no discussion of a balance of power and true participation is not possible.

Therefore, the participation procedures run aground and degenerate into a sham. They are only annoying and troublesome in the existing status quo. Only in a true balance of power can similar procedures work positively. As long as this balance is not present what one calls participation procedures are only an expression of the problem instead of the solution.

7. Bread or cake?

I have been talking about our lack of freedom to do what we want because we do what our position makes us do. I am discussing the situation in which we exercise our profession. I am not talking about the exercise itself, and certainly not about the competence of those who carry out the exercise. We work in a defined power structure and it defines the boundaries of what can be reached. Let me summon one last image:

The territory of the Technical University in Eindhoven, The Netherlands, is approximately similar in area and proportions to the town of Delft, circumscribed by the old town walls. In Delft one confronts

The limits of professionalism

an entire town with diverse canals, squares, churches, countless houses and even a number of university buildings as well as at least three students' clubs. If one has a preference for variety in the morphology, a mixture of working and living places, integration of urban functions and yet more of such matters which are characteristic of old Delft, then it is good to know that we cannot make something like that because such a built environment is the result of a fine-grained power structure.

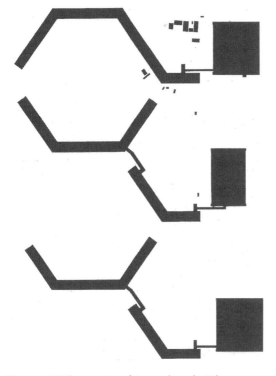

Figure 3 1970's extension of Amsterdam: the Biljmermeer

How is one to be compared to the other? How can one say that one is better than the other? They are two worlds which have not been divided by three centuries time, but by two different processes. Versailles differs from seventeenth century Paris. Louis XIV could not make Paris any more than his subjects could live in Versailles. The French kings were the prisoners of their power. Marie Antoinette asked herself why the mutinous, hungry multitude was given no cake when the bread was gone, for cake was the only thing which could exist in her world. In the world which we as professionals can bring into existence, bread hasn't been offered for many years. You and I are also the prisoners of our power.

In the beginning of my story, I sketched two extreme ways in which a built environment develops. On the one hand, the squatter district in the Third World in which only residents exercise power. On the other hand, the Dutch public housing in which only professionals exercise power. Both are extreme. Both are, therefore, misshapen built environments in the literal meaning of that word. What the strength of the one process is, is exactly the weakness of the other. Consequently, it is not a question of choice. If we keep track of the examples of urban environments which occur as successful and harmonious – the architectural high points from the past – we see, consequently, a process in which both forms of the exercise of power occur together and hold each other in balance. I am pointing once again to Amsterdam which, therefore, is currently viewed, in general, as one of the most striking examples of West-European planning. The canal-belt and the Jordan still form a framework of sometimes almost monumental allure and of great clarity and simplicity. In this framework a fine-grained process has been going on for ages. Although this process is slowly but surely dying, it can still be observed.

But there are, of course, many more examples to name of the complementary functions of both forms of the exercise of power. I need not go into that further. It is, thus, not a question of choice. The tragedy of our century is exactly that a choice has been made. In the overrating of the professional ability, perhaps driven too much by ostensible helplessness and ignorance of how to house the masses, the professional exercise of power has been acknowledged in an almost casual way as the only correct one.

Looking back to the past we can identify moments in which the choice had been made, unconsciously, but as a result of extremely self-evident matters. In the same manner, the housing act in the Netherlands in the beginning of this century made money available to house the working classes. This law is still one of the best examples of national social policy. But those who have the money determine what is good, and so the exercise of power never fell into the hands of those who were yet to have a house. It is useless to ask if it could have been otherwise.

In the 1920s Corbusier praised Louis XIV as a great town planner and he proposed besides that a large part of Paris be demolished – which was indeed in a miserable state of affairs – and that a number of apartment buildings of gigantic proportions be erected. This incident acquires in retrospect an almost symbolic meaning for the unconscious choice which had been made about that time in professional circles. The balance had already been tipped by the Industrial Revolution and now the consolidation took place. From this time on, the professionals were sent inevitably to an increasingly extensive and increasingly more detailed exercise of power in order to fill the created vacuum.

I have talked about human lack of freedom and have attempted to sketch for you how we presently work in a situation which limits our results. The signs point out that our actions can give less and less of an answer to the questions which are put to us. If we listen to the criticism which is expressed on all sides regarding the built environment and to the problems which crop up concerning it – in the new districts as well as in the old – do we really believe, then, that we can provide an answer within the presently operative, one-sided power structure? If we believe that, we can proceed with the order of the day. But if we don't believe that, if we have our doubts at that point, then there is much to do. Then it no longer makes sense to look for new dwelling types to provide the answer, but one then must look for new process forms, new management forms, new financing forms and new production methods. But above all, it is then time to speak soundly and openly about the possibilities of the complementary, relative power. About the introduction of the fine-grained exercise of power which is necessary for that.

1980
NOTES OF A TRAVELER

Editors' note: *This essay was published in the Journal of Architectural Education, 1980 (pp 4–7). The author was nearing the end of his 5-year appointment as Head of the Department of Architecture at MIT. In it, the author explains his personal journey in the field of architectural research.*

Research is an attempt to explore new territories and to add them to the map of knowledge that we maintain and revise constantly. The researcher is the traveler. After numerous adventures and hardships, doubts, anxieties and excitements, he returns to explain to the people back home what he has seen and how it fits into what everybody already knows. Those who welcome him back want to know what he can add to the picture of the world with which they are familiar. He is expected to fill in a blank spot. Sometimes it does not fit and the map must be revised, a cause for controversy and debate. The shared view of the world is at stake!

The social connotations are obvious. A body of knowledge is something to be shared among the natives of a culture. It is to a large extent what makes them a tribe. The interpretation of the accumulated facts in a theory is what makes that culture. The map of their world holds them together, while at the same time it makes individual movement possible, as well as easy communication.

Communication (1)

In architecture today there is no map we share. We may or may not share certain skills, beliefs and attitudes-perhaps even some ideologies and languages, but there is certainly no map of the world that we share. In fact, we are not even sure that we share the same world. A commonly understood and accepted map may never be possible.

For those of us who have decided to travel anyway and try to venture beyond the compounds of friendly neighboring villages, this primitive state has its disadvantages. When we survive and come back to report, it is hard to connect. The tales of our experiences sound out of place and cannot be verified. We speak of animals no one has seen before and are at a loss to describe them. The words we choose cause confusion, while we stretch their meanings. This unavoidable breakdown of communication brings a sense of isolation. Even the exchange with other travelers is difficult at best. We are not even sure we have explored the same continent. It may be impossible to piece together the data each of us brought home. Even in the best of circumstances one's research will have accumulated a very modest structure of knowledge that is shared by relatively few individuals. Its purpose, its methods and its achievements will only be understood by a few.

Isolation

The isolation of those who do operate in what could be called a research mode in architecture must not be confused with the isolation of individuals in the sciences who may be so specialized that they can only talk to a few others. For them, there is indeed a map to point out where they are. They can be reached. Their isolation exists because the body of knowledge is so vast that no one can encompass it all. Their problem is a technical one. Our problem is the opposite: it is existential. We do not know where we are. We report about different worlds. To reach each other takes an act of faith-one may never return to where one came from.

Communication (2)

These problems of communication are disconcerting. I like to believe that two researchers in different places within the physical sciences who meet on a social occasion need no more than a few minutes to connect their respective standpoints. Although it may be more difficult for them to describe what is within their specific territory of investigation, they have no problem identifying where the territory is. The rest of their conversation can be the exchange of mutually useful information.

Location

I often find myself avoiding an attempt to establish location, because I know there will be no time to work it out satisfactorily: explaining words that have several meanings and avoiding misunderstandings that only bring disorientation. What is the territory I have traveled? I am exploring design. And here I find myself explaining what I mean by it. For me, design is the formulation of decisions about what has to be made, in such a way that someone else can make it. Yes, it has to do with creation – but a creation is not a design, and a designer is not just someone who creates, but a person who documents something that did not exist before in order to allow others to act. Therefore, design is a social activity that has to do with explicit communication. Design only makes sense when we work with others or when we project our own activities. I am sure that these few sentences are not sufficient to establish rapport with others. Design, for many of my colleagues, is first of all a creative adventure. So it is to me when I design; but I can study creativity, the road to synthesis, the issues of problem-solving and originality, without ever studying design or even mentioning it. The research of design, to me, must deal with the communication and formulation of a coherent set of decisions. It must tell me something about people interacting in decision making and execution.

But that is not obvious to all in "my" field. There are those who see "a design" as a product in itself, a work of art, never really meant to be executed or to trigger action by others. For some, a design is a statement about buildings, that should be appreciated-and bought-as an object of contemplation. There are those for whom "a design" is an expression of the designer's feelings and no more than that. I have no problem with that kind of preoccupation at all, but I have reached this point and have not yet fully indicated where I am when I "do research in design." We are still trying to establish location. It may take me a bit longer before I can begin to tell you what I learned in that research.

Communication (3)

I would like to compare notes with other travelers, but the very nature of our problem-the lack of a shared map of our world-must make me very careful to avoid generalizations. What may be true for the kind of expeditions that I was involved in may not be at all valid for those who move in different directions. Any advice I can give to would-be explorers can only be personal in nature. I have to talk about my own experiences and I will do so. But then those experiences may be difficult to place in a context that makes sense to others, for the reasons mentioned before.

Social support

Stanley was sent by the New York Herald. Columbus had the backing of a Spanish royal couple. In research, one needs supporters as well.

No research is totally separated from the "real world." Because it takes time, space and money and never produces these things itself, research is dependent on those who nourish it materially. Research, therefore, is ultimately the fruit of a social and political world that shares enough beliefs and values with those who do the research to allow them to do so, to accept the risk of their failures and claim some credit for their successes.

If this is true for all research, no matter how far removed from day-to-day concerns, no matter how "pure," it is inescapably true for research in the design of our physical environment. Design is a form of human interaction. The ultimate test for the "success" of any research results lies in the question of whether those results will be accepted or rejected by the social body to whom they are supposed to make sense. In design, moreover, any attempt by the researchers to test what it does, how it goes, or how it could be changed, has to be done in conjunction with those who design. Any formulation of a design theory is an attempt to describe the behavior of designers. Any introduction of a design method is, finally, an attempt to change the behavior of people who design. Research in design is therefore doubly connected to the social fabric.

Conditions (1)

In the social context, we have several conditions that must be met to make research go. One is the condition of support, the willingness of those who do not do the research to believe in the researcher's objectives enough to fund the work to be done. The second is the condition of interaction, the willingness of those who are supposed to benefit from the research to try out and use the results. It is self-evident that the willingness to interact is at the same time a form of support. It is hard to respond or even to criticize unless one is willing to believe that the attempt itself is worthwhile.

A third condition is one that protects the research done. One cannot expect everybody to be enthusiastic about untested new ideas. There is always a hostile environment. There is always fear of new ideas. There is always competition ready to denounce another party's efforts. It may not be enough to have only support- there must also be people who actively protect the work and leave the researcher enough time to do the research.

Conditions (2)

I was very lucky as far as my working conditions were concerned. The research was paid for by a group of professional architects who were ready to interact with any results we found. At the same time, they were willing-first by their prestige, and later through their active engagement in the debate-to protect what was going on. The ideal condition is to have support, interaction and protection from the same group. We came very close to this.

Conditions (3)

Time is another, very important, condition. Research takes time. Those who support and protect must have patience. It is here where the interaction becomes crucial. In cases where the results come slowly and failures are apparent, it is only the confidence developed through interaction that gives grounds for continued support. If someone says, "Hey! These people are onto something!", and that someone carries some weight because they know what they are talking about, it can make all the difference. The judgment as to how long is long enough is the most difficult one to make in any research setting. It is here where the chemistry between the individuals involved is most important.

Design research

Clearly the odds are against those who do design research. The field is unknown. There is no commonly accepted ideology to bind supporters, protectors and interactors together. There is no commonly shared body of knowledge to explain what the research is all about and where it can bring us. There is no track record for the profession as such, to give confidence to those who are able to offer support. For the same reason, those from the profession who could interact with the researchers often find it difficult to do so (and they are usually operating in small scale organizations that don't allow them to spend much time on interactions with no immediate pay-off). In short, those who can interact have no tradition to support. Those who create research agendas offer widely different theories, are often removed from the social context to which their work must contribute, and are often not even knowledgeable about each other's work.

Ideology

The interesting issue is, of course, that protection, support and interaction can only come if there is a common understanding about what the issues are that should be pursued. In other words, it is exactly the shared ideology that sets the intellectual, political and social context that is missing. To create better conditions for research in design is not a matter of research management alone. It has to do with stating a belief, embracing a speculative theory that is broad and convincing enough to make people then concentrate resources and energy on the narrower issue of design.

There must be an outline that allows us to distinguish relevant from irrelevant directions. The ideology allows us to draw the first contours of the world. We put our research in. There is no research without an ideology, just as there is no science without it. We must distinguish between the two and feel free to discuss both. To stay with an ideology without applying it in our own area of knowledge and expertise is ineffective. To stay within our fields without exposing ourselves in the larger context of human concerns, where no one is an authority, is dangerous. Not to know the distinction is perhaps the most objectionable of all. All of this, of course, is not new, but it has to be repeated again and again.

My ideology

The belief on which we started our research was that the dweller should make decisions about the physical environment in which he or she lived. If the user was to make decisions, while at the same time there seemed to be a role for professionals to play, the question became "who is deciding" on division of the physical world into two realms: the elements about which the user personally makes decisions and those about which they do not. From there flowed a whole series of questions: what constitutes a design decision? how do the decisions of different parties relate to each other?

It was clear that the ideology challenged vested interests and their modes of operation in the professional worlds of government, finance and technology, in that it assumed different human relations and territorial claims.

It would be a contradiction to expect that the first objective of research must be to test and possibly refute the ideology that supports it. Ultimately, we act on faith. For better or for worse, we assumed that our ideology was right. If it was not, we would find out. Our research task was to be executed within the boundaries of a narrow professional field by those who were knowledgeable in that field. But this task was defined from a much wider context that gave it a goal to pursue. This context was a belief to be accepted without proof. Even now, when it seems that the methods finally developed in the research do indeed "work," this does not mean that that philosophy was "right," although success may make it more acceptable, more likely to be "right."

Method

Our problem was the following: all right, if the users must be able to change their own physical environment, how must professional designers operate to make that possible? If the 'support' is that part of the building that the user cannot individually change, how do I, as a designer, design a support? We found that the design process that we were familiar with was based on the assumption that everything was subject to professional design decisions. That is how we got into design methods, and decided to develop the methodological tools that would allow professionals to operate effectively in the world that the ideology demanded.

Expertise

The decision to focus specifically and exclusively on method was a decision to stay very close to where our own skills and expertise were. We were designers and design was what we were interested in. At a time when we tend to think in terms of global problems, where experts of many fields have to cooperate to deal with the issues, it is necessary to repeat that one can only cooperate from the strength of one's own expertise. And ours was design. We decided to stay with it. If others in their own fields would do the same-but within a shared ideology-cooperation would come. We were often told that our research group should have sociologists, financiers, engineers, lawyers and others in it. Financial constraints, as much as an instinctive sense of its prematurity, saved us from making that mistake.

Vehicle

On the level of ideology, we are all amateurs. If that is what gives us direction as to where to go, our specific expertise – this case design – is the vehicle that must bring us there. Here, we cannot accept any but the most rigid standards of clarity and logical consistency. The captain of the ship will allow the socio-political context to influence his decision as to where to sail, but he will darn well make sure that his ship is run in a strictly professional way. His life depends on it. Any amateurism, any rhetoric or public relations gimmickry, anything less than just plain skilled craftsmanship, will make the expedition vulnerable as it charts its course. The researcher who cannot distinguish social from professional responsibility is in trouble.

Architects, like other professionals, operate in the real world. Their research is constantly in danger of confusion between the two issues mentioned here. As long as we are unable to clarify the vehicle we operate –

our territory of expertise, as distinct from other fields – our voyages will be difficult to plan.

Companions

The crew has to be chosen to come aboard. What kind of designer do we need? Here the choice is clearly the result of the stated objectives. The remarks I can offer are therefore very much to be seen in the context of the particular research in which I was involved. Anyone in a design research operation must, of course, be a skilled designer in the narrow sense of the word. That is, someone who is visually literate, can think in three dimensions, and feels at ease with manipulating built form at a reasonable level of complexity. But, assuming that there are enough people who have the training and the talents to fulfill these minimal requirements, what else is important?

I have learned to distinguish a number of abilities that I like to think every architect should possess, but that I know every researcher in design must have. The two most essential are the ability to understand other peoples' values and the ability to understand time and change.

Value

First and foremost, there is the question of values and value judgment in design. Any investigation about design should distinguish between the kinds of decisions to be made and the kinds of information to be formulated and communicated, on the one hand, and the values of these decisions and communications, on the other. In research, we want to understand design as an activity that deals with value judgments, but which therefore should be distinguished from them. The objective of research in design is not to express our own values as designers, but to understand issues of form and decision-making as they relate to different criteria, representing different values.

The subculture of architects, and the education that produces them, puts stress on the quest for the good, as distinct from the bad. We feel we are the protectors of quality, however that may be defined. Our education is largely directed by two things: that the student learns how to establish his or her own value system and to express it in built forms-architecture as a form of self-expression, a way to set a standard, to safeguard the quality of the environment and to educate the layman; and that they are initiated into a peer group that knows what is good or bad, and is aware of those elusive and secret do's and don'ts that make one a "good" architect – the hidden agenda that makes one fit ones own value system within that of the colleagues he or she admires.

These two educational goals may be mostly implicit, but they are strong. They can also be in conflict with each other. The ensuing stresses are enough to make a problem of any curriculum. There is precious little in all his to prepare a person for a detached approach toward understanding how issues of form and quality interact. We do not train ourselves to understand issues of value in the built environment without immediately deciding whether or not we agree with them. Those who have never learned to observe and understand, but only to pass judgment, may or may not make good architects, they will never make good researchers.

Change

As housing and residential settlement was the subject of our explorations, and adaptability to users through their intervention over time our goal, change became a crucial factor. It takes some training to be able to see the built environment as something that is in constant flux, and to discern patterns of movement and the various rhythms of change of different methods to take account of the possible variations that may be made by others after we are done.

Yet these transformations have been with us for a long time. Urban designers know that their work should create framework within which architects work over rime. We know that buildings tend to come and go while streets remain. We know that buildings can stand for long time while their interiors are done over by each succeeding generation. Yet we have never absorbed this knowledge into our attitudes and methods. We tend be defensive about issues of change. We don't want to have others change what we have done. But what is done today could be seen as an incentive for action by others who follow. As others will act anyway, recognition of that inevitable fact may lead us into a solution that allows for more continuity than could be arrived at in ignorance of the dimension of time. At any rate, the game becomes more interesting and less uptight if one feels at ease with change.

Time (1)

Time, and the changes it brings with it been the architect's enemy. The architectural creation was always a statement that had to defy rime. Its function was a symbol of truths and powers that had to reach beyond the generations. The movements of the everyday environment could be ignored. Architecture was a stone in the waters of time.

Time (2)

The rejection of possible future change is one way to fight change. Rejection of the past is another. Understanding what might happen after our intervention is only half of the picture. The other half is the acceptance of what has been done before, the recognition of what exists: the power and meaning of the site. It is no coincidence that the "modern architecture" generations hardly ever put other buildings in their presentations. They did not like the past. Is it a coincidence that restoration was invented in the same period by others in the field? It is yet another way to stop time.

Values (2)

The site and the past are constraints. Rules and regulations and constraints as well. They are invisible sites. At the same time, they are expressions of values, creating a certain value system. Architects have a hard time seeing norms and standards as anything but hostile harassment. But those who move into housing often have to live with the results of such rule systems, and the study of design cannot ignore them. No method can succeed if it does not involve the formulation of norms and the evaluation of their impacts.

Companions (2)

If you ask me what it takes to be a member of a party exploring the continent called design, you will get a description of the strange creatures one encounters on the way and the strange geographies one has to feel at home in: a story about the hostile regions of regulatory processes, the frightening herds of other people's values, the shifting sands of time, the weird animal called change, and, finally, the unknown tribes of users. It is enough to decide that architecture should leave housing alone, as it generally has done in the past.

Mapping

An expedition is not mounted to enjoy the scenery, but to map new territory. Research wants to build theory: the mapping of a body of knowledge. When the narrow goal of my involvement in research was to develop methods as design tools, a good part of the attraction was the opportunity to understand design better. Over the years, we built up a set of formally defined elements by trial and error, arriving at a description of their relations and the operations that allowed their manipulation. Slowly, an underlying logic revealed itself. The construct that eventually emerged could be gradually recognized for what it was – or rather, for what it stood for: a theory that needed explicit formulation.

In retrospect, it is almost self-evident that a preoccupation with method would lead to theory. To map our world, we first of all need the means to describe its elements and their relations. Because we were interested in design as a way to convey information, the formal means of description of the built environment became a primary occupation. But any formal way of describing implicitly contains a theory of what one wants to describe. A method of description needs a classification of elements, which must be put in their (spatial) relationships. How we choose to classify them depends again on how we see the world. The interaction is both inescapable and fascinating. To develop the means, a theory is implicit. To explicate a theory, a formal way of describing its elements is needed.

Experimentation

As theory and description relate to one another like Yin and Yang, there are two other elements of interaction as well, that seem to be common to all research: experimentation and observation. As we observe the world, the need to explain what is seen leads to theory. Its communication leads to description. Theory and the means to describe lead us to keener and renewed observation, and so on. The one balances the other. But the force chat drives it all is experimentation. In design research, experimentation is done through design, the exploration of which is possible within given constraints – the observation of the impact of specific values on form, the evaluation of a given space for its capacity to hold change – all this to test the methods of design as tools for intervention.

Observation

Experiments deal with intervention into what is explored. Observation leaves the world as we find it, and is the beginning of all research. It is not just seeing: it is seeing with detachment – the suspension of knowledge and certainty. It is curiosity, before the question is asked. The answer is the end of observation and the beginning of theory. The theory leads to understanding, and understanding makes us see the world as we could not see it before. It allows us to see more, which may lead again to observation.

Observation leads to a record – a sketch, a photograph. But the record is not "an observation," but rather the beginning of an answer. The use of media can get in the way of observation. The eye that can observe is the eye that discovers.

Discoveries

The most exciting part is the act of discovery – the recognition that the concept of position is central to everything that design stands for, the role of values as the messages conveyed while we design (expressed in terms of elements and position), the concept of levels, that brings order in the vastness of the design subjects to which we turn, or the concept of function as a relationship of action on different levels. Discoveries are the result of theory applied to reality. They are the building blocks of new theory. The concepts we "discovered" often found their way in our operations – and proved useful – long before we could adequately define them. They emerged by observation and experimentation. The best discoveries make us recognize the self-evident as part of a theoretical construct.

Communication (4)

These notes must sound like the incoherent ramblings of a weary traveller, clutching his soiled collection of papers brought back from faraway places. I am in the midst of shuffling and ordering my notes to construct the map that has to explain it all. But to whom? First of all, to oneself. But one travels to expand the world one shares with others. As our world of design is one of confusion, not much factual information can be conveyed in a short message. Lacking a shared body of knowledge, we feel that a brief exchange can perhaps only serve to convey the excitement, enthusiasm and discovery that true exploration brings as its rewards. It may still be an out-of-place kind of activity, but it surely is worthwhile once you have tried it.

Research

Does all this really have to go under the term research? While I use the term daily out of convenience, I am not sure. How does one define the term? If research is an activity that helps us understand the world by developing maps that allow others to follow the route and verify what we have seen, the answer may be yes, we do research in architecture. If research is an activity that takes place in a structured system of discourse, accepted by all participants, an activity that allows us to add knowledge and understanding like building blocks to a structure we all understand, the answer must be no. We are not there yet. We are still wandering about, comparing notes, when our paths happen to cross. But we may get there. Sometimes I am sure we will.

1980
AROUND THE BLACK HOLE

Editors' Note: *This essay, published in MIT's PLAN in 1980, was written near the end of the authors' term as Head of the Department of Architecture at MIT. In it, the author frames his critique of architectural education which was to continue through his career, with suggestions of what needs to be done to bring the profession, and the education of architects, more in touch with the realities of everyday built environment.*

> "Much as I admire the exuberance of Queen Anne or the fantasy of Art Nouveau, I need to find a new language for myself." (student)
> "We were asked to do a 'dream house.'" (student)
> "His 'de Stijl' tennis club was interesting." (teacher)
> (Quotations from applications for the M. Arch degree program at MIT.)

I. Teaching design

If we try to formulate the components out of which a design curriculum can be built, we must begin by making a distinction between creative action and design. The two are mutually reinforcing but they are not the same. To paint a painting is not to design one, and many buildings have been built, sometimes revealing admirable architectural quality, without any "design" in the sense that we understand it. To design is, in its narrowest definition. to notate explicitly and unambiguously what has to be built in the future, most likely by someone else. In its broader definition, the design is the solution of a problem stated by the question: What should be built? Whatever else we may want to project into the activity called "design," there are always these two components: that design is an act of communication, and that design is a problem-solving activity.

Both are issues with a clear intellectual dimension and open the door for rational and reasoned enquiry and method. In fact, one could go so far as to state that design is the rational component of action, if not of creation. We say that something is "done by design" to indicate that action was taken with pre- meditated goals in mind and by rationally selected means.

It is not fashionable in architectural circles to connect the activity called "design" with intellectual endeavor and clearly exposed rational constructs. A good number of my colleagues will dismiss such attempts as irrelevant and having nothing to do with the essence and true nature of design as such. Some feel it to be positively dangerous to try to capture the activity they call "design" within the boundaries of a theoretical enquiry. There is great reluctance about the exposition of rules, principles, or methods in the teaching of design. The idea that such rules and principles could ever gain universal acceptance by all designers is almost unheard of.

It is often argued that architectural design, by its very nature, poses so complex a problem, in which so many aspects must be related, that every attempt to unravel it must inevitably reduce it to the point of meaninglessness. The art of synthesis cannot benefit from analysis or even sharp intellectual scrutiny. But to accept such arguments at face value is to avoid the issue altogether. The very complexity of the design activity can be seen as a challenge for a more orderly application of our rational faculties. One does not have to argue that such an application must rule out the uses of intuition, experience, or even rule-of-thumb, and the notion that one's creative force is endangered by reasonable questions is too silly to take seriously.

All this is not to say that intelligence is not applied in architectural design. In a way, it even seems to judge from the writings and verbal expositions now fashionable in the field that there is no lack of it. But even a cursory reading of the more prestigious magazines that attempt to theorize about design suggests that we tend to indulge in attempts to shroud the problems rather than to pin them down. The postmodern verbalism appears to be just another way of continuing the myths of architectural creation as an impenetrable secret known only to a chosen few.

A discussion of design education must be based on some understanding of what it is that must be taught. What are the skills, methods, habits, tricks, and canons that teaching must bring to the ignorant and clumsy? In so far as there is method in design education, it is method of teaching rather than method of design. But how can one judge the teaching if every attempt to clarify what must be taught is countered either by silence or by the excessive use of words? Perhaps the methods that govern the teaching activity can offer a clue.

The teaching of design as it occurs today can only be understood as a social event. It is first of all a form of human interaction. It is the process in which those who "are" engage in a complex ritual with those who "are not," in order to bring them to the point where they also "will be." It is not the transmission of knowledge or of specific skills that is the major objective-although undoubtedly a transference of knowledge and skills takes place but rather the introduction to an existential mode.

The model, of course, is that of the master-apprentice relationship, where the master, in possession of great secrets, initiates the young, ignorant, and perhaps talented novices. This model in one way or another pervades perhaps all education. But the special twist we have developed in architectural design education is that the secrets to be revealed are not to be known outside the person of the master, there is no body of knowledge or skills to be made explicit, even to the most favored student. Nor is there much explicitly shared among the masters themselves. Julian Beinart has pointed out emphatically that architecture differs from two other prestigious professions medicine and law in that it does not have its own codified body of knowledge. Hence, the substance of the masterapprentice relationship is not what is to be conveyed; rather, it is the relationship itself. The medium is indeed the message. That is not to say that nothing is transmitted, but what is transmitted cannot exist nor be recognized outside the persons involved. Clearly this is something different from the sciences; but it is also different from the arts. as their secrets used to be guarded by guilds or other societies. Artists and artisans used to know very explicit skills, not only codifiable but more importantly shared among groups of masters, so that what was transmitted was to a degree autonomous of the individuals who guarded it.

Teaching by implication, which is the inevitable result of the social format that dominates architectural education, would not necessarily be bad if we could only have some assurance that what is transmitted has relevance to the problems that lie at the heart of our times. However, there is no such solace. Design is primarily seen as a creative effort and unfortunately, creation is equated with "freedom" from restraints and rules (other than those imposed by peer group pressure of course).

The key phrase is "self-expression." This creates inevitably a painful and ambivalent situation in the teaching relationship itself. Whose self-expression are we talking about? The official word is that it is the students who must be encouraged to "find themselves" and to "express their own values." We applaud their "ideas" and put high marks on "originality" and "creativity," while we take pains to shield them from false "outside values and perceptions"; we make it, known that we deplore the reductions and limitations imposed by the "real world's" undeserving lawyers, politicians, and technicians, who make work of real quality impossible. All of this may even be true, from a certain perspective, but such preoccupations do not by themselves make skilled and confident designers. Nor do they constitute a basis for design education, although an exploration of them may have some therapeutic value in a liberal arts setting.

The situation becomes even more difficult When we see the inevitable contradiction between cultivating the student's creative freedom and instructing that same student in our own architectural value system. The tensions evoked by such oppositions in both the student and the teacher are too well known to need elaboration here. They may be the inevitable ingredients of any design education, but if there is not much else outside the teacher's own codes and canons, the situation becomes obsessive in its contradictions.

The social basis for design education begs the question of the school as an institution. We need not be surprised to find that what drives education is what is happening in practice, outside the schools. It is a matter of near-total consensus that it is experience in practice that qualifies a person to teach design. That is why those in the schools are encouraged to practice, and why almost universally schools seek to have those in practice to do the teaching in the schools. After all, that which is to be transmitted is in the person and his/her works. The personal ingredient that cannot be shared or codified is "experience." The tokens of that experience are in the designs made and – hopefully – executed. Direct interaction with the bearer of that experience is presumed to impart whatever is needed in order to be "one of them." Lacking codified skills, or knowledge, or even rules of design, the schools – insofar as they teach design-are dependent on practice. In fact, they can only be houses where space is provided for the desired interaction to take place. It is only fair to say that as this interaction nourishes the student, it also rein-forces the architect/ teacher by means of a social contact that, for all we know. is the essence of what is called "design."

Hence, the successful school teaches design much as the successful hostess stages a dinner party: by careful arrangement of the personalities involved. It is not achieved by explicit exposition of commonly accepted principles, nor by demonstration of shared methods. nor even by a methodical analysis of cases. The school therefore has nothing to store or expand as a teachable commodity. If there is an accumulation of such a thing as "design aptitude," it is to be found in those who practice it and in their products, not in the schools.

In such conditions, the question as to whether the field is good because those who practice had good teachers. or whether the schools are good because those who teach are good practitioners, is a moot one. The term "school" in architecture, not surprisingly, more often indicates a group of architects than an institute of learning. It is the social form again that gains the upper hand. The "field," if there is one, is outside, and the school like the hostess – may have a role to play relative to it, but, by absence of any substance of its own, it cannot be expected to drive it.

This century has witnessed profound changes in the cultural, political, social, and technical contexts in which architectural design must be exercised. It seems legitimate to ask whether these changes have prompted in the design ability some new ways of working, new under- standings of design as a tool, or new skills to deal with new problems.

Now that we are in the era of postmodernism, we are allowed to look back to see what modernism has yield- ed. If we put aside for a moment the rhetoric of an artistic ideology, and the styles and forms that were its results, what is it that the period of modern architecture has left us in design abilities that allows us to cope with the design challenges of today?

Although the question is relevant to our own need to understand where we are, it is unfair to the generations that made modern architecture. We should not judge them by the body of skills and tools that they left us; here again, we can only understand what happened if we look at it in social terms. The onslaught of social, technical and political upheavals in the Western world swept away the two pillars on which the profession had rested until the First World War. One was the power base that had supported architecture: the period of modernism was one Tn which architectural support was replaced by corporate and bureaucratic power. The other was the disappearance of craftsmanship and vernacular consciousness that had always provided the skills and accumulated technical knowledge needed for sound performance.

Modern architecture may be seen as revolutionary in its own terms, but as part of a larger cultural history, it was perhaps first of all the result of a desperate and agile attempt by a profession to survive and find new ground on which to stand. It had in a few generations to shift its power base as well as its technical base. We should there- fore not mock or criticize the former generations too much. They held the banners of architecture high in those days. They produced good architecture against severe odds.

More importantly for our purposes here, they adopted the one-to-one mode of implicit design education, which we have now expanded into an end unto itself.

In retrospect, it was inevitable. To develop a body of knowledge, codified skills, and shared methods, an institutional basis is needed as well as a context of some stability. It both the power base and the technical base fall away, we should expect a nomadic tribal situation to be the one with the best chances for success. Teaching by implication is presently a survival mechanism, a behavior adopted to protect the species in a time of uprooted existence. The "avant garde" was the network of scattered and displaced individuals trying to continue a tradition of architectural excellence in a fragmented world. It may be of interest to note, in passing, that the Beaux Arts tradition of teaching – so violently denounced by that avant garde – was the most institutionalized form of transmitting design abilities since the cathedrals were built. As such, they became a liability for the profession's survival when times changed.

II. Values, space and materials

Apart from some stylistic preferences that now can be safely denounced while we indulge in the newly – gained security of the postmodern age, what is it that the past generations have left us? The best way to assess the strengths we have inherited is to identify the problems that are specific to design in our own times. What are the situations we have to cope with that were unknown before the period' of modernism? What are the design tools developed since that allow us to overcome them? Even a superficial attempt at an assessment gives astonishing results. For none of the design challenges typical to our times is it possible to point out a well-developed answer. In fact, not only is there no parallel development of the design ability to deal with these challenges, but in most cases the challenge is not even recognized as something worth serious consideration.

The preoccupation with design as a form of (self) expression makes the values of the designer the central subject of design. They are the values to be expressed. If there is any overt discussion about values. it is about those held within a peer group! Yet it is exactly the conflict of values in any form of environmental interaction that is so typical of our times. Before the industrial revolution, design and architecture were practiced in a relatively homogeneous value situation. The client's values were those of the designer, and their interaction was direct enough to solve whatever distinction might emerge. Secondly, the client was not yet distinguished from the user, either because they were similar in their preferences, or because the user was so unimportant as to be not supposed to hold values of his own.

It was only with the advent of modern times, and with the subsequent delocalization of the designer and his emergence as an agent not necessarily part of the culture he designs for I that the value problem became a problem. It is no longer self-evident that architects and clients share the same values. Mismatches occur frequently, and mutual suspicion and defense mechanisms have developed rapidly. The consequent complexities and frustrations in the client-architect relationship have escaped serious social and psychological, inquiry so far, but they are only too well known among the groups involved. In a way, this problem is the easiest one relative to values. It is basically a problem of conscience for the designer difficult enough, but not of profound social relevance.

The issue changes when we consider the other value conflict that was born in the age of modernism: the one between the designer and the user. Here we open the whole Pandora's box of conflicts between one class and another, between rich and poor, between power and powerlessness, between concentration and decentralization of decision making. The designer's personal dilemma – his instinctive alliance with those who have the power is insignificant in comparison with the social and economic results of the institutionalized use of design as a means to impose values on those who have no power.

This is difficult indeed! It is further aggravated by the international scope of architectural practice today. We have not only the conflict between classes and powers, but also the contradictions between cultures. The Third World is the place where these come together. The local professional, who after considerable sacrifices has ac- quired a "good" education in the United States or Europe, returns to his country to impose values that were not his own upon others with whom he never shared values.

When he finds out his mistake, he discovers that there is no such thing left as an indigenous value system, and that those he wants to redeem often desire the very elements that he has recently rejected as alien to his culture.

The problems of value are clearly beyond the powers of the designer to solve. But he will inevitably be confronted by them. In an educational culture where the onetoone relation between teacher and student is paramount, one might at least expect such problems to be topics of discussion. Alas, it cuts too close to the bone. The explicit exploration of other peoples' values, and the admission of the fact that a designer ought to be capable of working with values that are not his own (quite apart from the question of when and where he must reject them) are far beyond the scope of the cult of self-expression. Hence, by his sheer inability even to conceive of other peoples' values as worth consideration, the student moves into the "real" world severely handicapped.

Apart from this attitudinal barrier, by itself enough to wreck a career, if not a user's environment, there are some interesting capabilities involved. Even the designer who is willing to take alien values seriously will find himself unable to cope with them, unless he has consciously trained himself in the skills to project such extraneous vocabularies into possible forms. It takes great skills of a very special nature to do it. Previous generations did not need to deal with the issue of value, because only one system was known to them. We have to because values are too important not to be distinguished from the designer. What are the skills needed here? What methods and theories support them? What exercises allow for their efficient acquisition? As long as the battle is between the values of the teacher and those of the student, we will never know such skills, nor will we have the tools to advise our clients wisely or to protect our users. Worse, not knowing our own values from those of others except in superficial terms of "style" and "preference" among peers we may never share any, in the true sense of the word.

One aspect of architectural design that developed in the period behind us is what could be called the "programmatic approach" to architectural form: the sometimes-exaggerated preoccupation with the summation of functions and activities, translated in square footage and relational charts. Although on first encounter a perfectly rational and useful approach, this particular activity is more than a response to "the Increasing complexity of the environment and the diversity of the demand." Functionalism was the ideology of the modern architecture. It began, perhaps, as a metaphor in Corbusier's infatuation with airplanes, steamships, and other feats of engineering, or, even earlier, with Sullivan's appeal to integrity in his much abused "form follows function." But from there, it was picked up by the more practical minded as the justification if ever one was needed to state clearly the problem.

So far, so good. However, when we look again at the problem of "deciding what to build," we see how function acquired alarmingly ideological overtones. It was believed that certain programmatic entities ought to have their own identifiable form: the factory, the school, the hospital, the dwelling, etc., etc. The building type became functionally defined. Thinking in functions has become so much the overriding habit that many among us may have a hard time discerning how it could be otherwise. Yet, whether followed or precluded by it, forms relate only partially to function, and it is form first of all that the designer must have knowledge of. The manipulation of spaces – their arrangement and their distinctions – is the designer's expertise. It is only by separating form from function that we can study and understand the relationship between the two. This being so, our vocabulary of space forms, which allows us to distinguish and classify spaces by their morphology and relative position – much as the botanist distinguishes plants by their leaves and flowers, and thus can describe them – would be expected to be at least as rich as our functional terminology. Yet, ask a student to describe his design without describing its function, and he will have a hard time doing it.

When we take away all indications of spaces, and forms that have functional connotations, we are left almost speechless. There is very little in our language that allows us to distinguish a hierarchy of spaces, their relations, their morphologies, and their positions in a larger whole. Would that we could distinguish twenty different kinds of space, in the way the proverbial Eskimo knows twenty words for snow!

A society's language reveals its preoccupation; and ours ls functional. We know schools, factories, churches, and dwellings, but we have no language to classify buildings in terms of relational organization or spatial hierarchies. We know living rooms, bedrooms, kitchens, dining rooms, etc., etc., but we have no words to distinguish a room with a certain way of admitting daylight from another one. Those that we do know mezzanine, alcove, entresol, bel 'etage, basement, attic – are invariably remnants from a premodern time. We distinguish between a parking lot and a playground, but we have no special words to denote the spatial quality of various urban spaces.

Shared knowledge and understanding within a profession are embedded in the vocabulary that it uses. The poverty of the designer's vocabulary is not only the result of functional thinking but is confounded by the cult of self-expression that does not know a need for communication about the design except somehow, magically through the design. Whenever new terms are coined, they are usually expected to distinguish one group from another. They serve the local cult but deny communication to the profession at large. There is a certain attitude that encourages using words in one's own way: after all, they must first express one's self, not communicate. There is a sloppiness in the use of terms that makes many almost indistinguishable.

Although not surprising, the situation is the opposite of what one might expect. In a society where there is more variety than ever in the subjects of design, and where the designers pride themselves on the variety of form and expressions at their disposal, one finds a lack of means for intelligent articulation, an inability to convey precise thinking about forms and space that is alarming.

Although we have formally taken leave of the decades of functionalism, the habit of thinking from the use towards the form is still very much with us. Somehow, it is still believed – I suspect by many – that the program, if only described in great enough detail, will reveal the form needed. Certainly everybody knows that embarrassing and uncertain jump into the form which must be taken eventually; yet the notion that one first states the problem and then proceeds towards the solution has never been replaced by another model. Even the new interest in rehabilitation, where one starts from the form to find a function that matches it, has not yielded an alternative. Yet, it is only when we feel at ease with the built environment as such and can discuss and describe it as freely as the botanist can describe his flora, that we can expect to think about procedures of design in a free and creative way. The relation of form to use, as much as the relation of form to perceived value, gives us the mechanisms to talk about design processes. Only the ideology of self-expression has no need of process. But design as an exploration of a possible environment, and its potential for use and meaning must begin with the autonomy of form to proceed towards its possible meanings and possible uses, given certain conditions.

The easy and free movement back and forth between form, function, and value calls for a specific design ability that can be discussed, exercised, and cultivated. Unless this is possible, design procedures cannot be discussed, because the steps from which they are composed are not known.

When we look back at the period of modern architecture, it is easy to identify another preoccupation of those days that proved to be a design challenge that was never properly explored. I am referring to the emergence of new materials, like concrete and steel, and the development of mechanical systems that serve the building's environment. We all know that the building, generally speaking, has developed into in increasingly complex combination of systems and subsystems in the last fifty years. The emphasis in relation to that phenomenon has been – quite understandably – largely of a technical and engineering nature. The architectural designer's response has run the spectrum from glorification of technology (resulting in a disastrous infatuation with prefabrication and "systems building" through an interest in aesthetic expression of its "meaning," recently re-emerging in the slogan of "high tech") to a studious indifference, a playful Catholicism, or a self-imposed limitation to certain personally preferred materials like steel, wood, concrete, or brick and finally to a negation of it all in an arrogant abstraction of immaterial form. Most of these attitudes can be explained as responses of a profession that was primarily occupied with the question of what was "good" architecture and what was "bad" a question, as we have seen, mainly posed in the context of personal or professional values. This may be the reason that we have once more missed the opportunity to address squarely this contemporary and unique problem in terms of design skills and methods, which ought to serve any architect, in whatever context, expressing whatever values. If one accepts the view of the building as a combination of a number of very different systems, each with their own elements and structure, forming configurations in space that join and separate, support or complement each other, and sometimes have quite different life spans and "modes of existence," then one accepts a sophisticated (and I would say Intellectually interesting) model that poses very intriguing design questions.

A building consists always of a number of physical systems that, taken separately, have their independent deployment in space, but which, moving in unison, make a whole, much like a piece of music that has several voices or instruments, the melodies of which can be traced independently but which in unison make harmony. This is nothing new.

Architecture history shows us abundant examples. The design skills to orchestrate and harmonize such spatial voices, however, seem not to have developed with the increasing number of possible instruments at hand. To the contrary, there seems to be a distinct atrophying of this particular architectural competence. Here again, we have a typical design capability that one would expect to be most useful as a powerful tool for dealing with the complexities of today's architectural problems, a tool that would allow designers to organize and orchestrate the engineers, rather than be organized by them. Yet this particular ability is not discussed commonly as one of the cornerstones of the architectural design capacity. We do not really have the vocabulary to deal with it, nor the design methods to handle it, nor the explicit exercises to train our skills relative to it. Where we could operate from considerable strength, we have failed even to raise the issue, and we now operate from a position of weakness, "System" is a bad word in architecture, but no other term has emerged to identify the separate voices that make a building. If we think of the rich methodology that music has accumulated in the course of time, with its concomitant vocabulary and notation systems, our art is one of extreme poverty where it ought to have its greatest strength.

It is fair to say that many of the recent masters of architecture e.g., Wright and Aalto, to name only two – delighted in the interplay of physical patterns within the building. Yet, perhaps distracted again by the function of technical systems, which is the engineer's interest, architectural design education never picked up the issue of harmony of physical systems lo general. We know less about it and have limited language to discuss it, let alone the knowledge to exercise and teach the skills that go with it.

III. Abandoned territories

As I have tried to argue, the era of modern architecture was one in which the profession's social and technical foundations were swept away and a new basis had to be found. The mechanism of survival was the retreat into the mysticism of architectural expression, reflected in a mode of education by implication. The shifting of the power base that supports architecture produced, among other things, the issue of conflicting values an issue so far denied explicit discussion in professional circles and not explored in education. The loss of traditional craftsmanship and vernacular produced, among other things, the proliferation of technical means – the systems that make buildings. This is another issue that calls for explicit design skills never formally explored in education or practice. The preoccupation with function as the only entity that seemed to be universal and "scientific" enough to become valid currency in a modern age deflected attention away from the architectural designers' natural grounds: the vocabularies of space and form as legitimate subjects for knowledge and method. This has created a vacuum – where the core of professional expertise ought to be. The result is a crippling inability to reach out from there towards issues like "use" and "value," Their relation with form cannot be discussed, because form is not known by itself. The mistaken belief that architecture must rest on the self-expression of the designer, who is asked to find his own "use" or "language," has rendered us not only ineffective to those who work with us but virtually incoherent among ourselves.

This less than satisfactory state of affairs has made the profession too weak, intellectually speaking, to address a number of issues that are typical for this age, and that pose interesting design questions. By lack of vision or ability, we have failed to move into new territories that seemed to be ready for design exploration and have even abandoned some that were already ours in the past. In the context of this article, I can only briefly indicate the most important among them:

1. **Regulations**. Codes., norms, and standards are the designers' enemies. They're seen as unavoidable constraints at best. Indeed, they restrict our freedoms of self-expression and force us into valves that are not our own, or even worse that we must share with colleagues. But any regulation poses the problem of value and form and their relative dependence, as well as their autonomy. No other profession can be expected to clarify that relation, let alone to predict to even a limited extent the impact of a norm or rule upon the environment that receives it. One cannot blame the lawyer, the bureaucrat, the engineer, or the politician for failing to understand this relationship. It is not their field. Yet each code is a design decision by nature and is a value judgment as well. Only a profession that controls a body of knowledge and skills about form-and understands its transformations and its movements under the impact of rules can be expected to contribute in new ways to the study of regulation.
2. **The large number**. The deadening repetition of uniform units in housing, as well as the multiplication of bays in the large building without any relief, are the features of architecture most

despised by the public. The issue of power (who manipulates what, on what level, and in what detail) lies at the root of uniformity as it emerged this century; this is an issue that I do not want to go into here, although it poses very interesting design challenges. But on a more mundane level, there is perhaps a question of skill in how to handle the large number. We do not seem to have made much progress since the Chicago school produced designers who could bring a building the size of a block into human scale without losing the urban scale in the process. The way they did it was by the formal juxtaposition of systems of a different scale within a facade, for instance. Or, to use a metaphor I suggested before, by making harmony with different voices, an art long lost. In terms of technology, there does not seem to be a reason to let uniformity take over, even within one project. The modern architect's claim that the repetition of a thousand similar units is what industrial production demands is superficial and false. There is much more symbolism in repetition than we are ready to admit. The elaboration of various voices improvising on a single theme is architecturally and technically possible today, but we don't discuss it, nor is It a subject for inquiry, experimental research, or education.

3. **The large size**. It is not uncommon today to have buildings built large enough to shelter several thousand people, or approximately the size of the classical Greek town. While in urban design there exists a traditional knowledge of a hierarchy of spaces to structure such an environment (square, street, main street, alley, etc.), no such hierarchy of spaces has developed regarding the large building. Large buildings are just more of the same basic elements multiplied. Because the function is declared to be the same, the need for a hierarchy in spatial terms is not seen. Certainly, individual architects have explored the issue to some extent. But the issue itself is beyond the single contribution. It is waiting for a concerted effort toward the exploration of available means, and the development of a spatial language to deal with it.

4. **Levels of intervention.** Size and number raise a question about the extent to which a single designer's intervention can be valid. The dream of self-expression knows no boundaries. The masters of modern architecture dealt with everything; they considered the design of teacups as well as cities. But the realities of life, including technical feasibility, suggest a vertical order in the environment as well as in the profession. One designer's work creates the setting for another. The urban design holds the building which holds the interior unit. In terms of design skills, the calibration of such interfaces poses very interesting questions of method and design articulation. Unfortunately, the issue – as one of educational and methodological interest – is studiously ignored. It is, of course, an issue of interplay between designers that is, of communication and the sharing of certain rules that allow us to work independently, yet in concert. It is certainly done in practice, but in a "seatofthepants" way. Explicit exposition of what it takes, and the development of skills to handle it better, cannot flourish within the implicit mode of teaching.

5. **Site.** The levels of intervention overlap with the issue of site. But to recognize the potential and qualities of a site is to recognize those who operated on the same level previously. The period of modernism hated the old cities and therefore dismissed them as legitimate site constraints.

The cult of self-expression hates the architect who was there before; hence, the site is non context, beyond what is legally required. It is another interesting design challenge missed an opportunity to have a dialogue with the other designer, rather than delivering a monologue. The sharing of Patterns because they happen to be there has only very recently been seen by some as a virtue. We have not yet explored – it becomes a tedious repetition – the interesting methods and skills needed to do it well. Nor is there a strategy in education to teach it.

6. **Change.** Finally, and perhaps most importantly, there is the issue of change-the manifestation of the dimension of time in the built environment. This dimension has traditionally been ignored by the architect because architecture has had to do with monuments that is, those buildings that must rep- resent a society's claims beyond the present. Architecture has had to defy time. But today we profess concern for the everyday environment, and it is indeed this environment that is at stake.

Continuous change of form, of use, and of meaning is the essence of the everyday environment. There is, however, little debate about the dimension of time in our work. Architectural thinking is still basically static, and as long as this is the case, we cannot expect to be adequately equipped to deal with the everyday environment and its dynamic qualities. Site, levels of intervention, regulations, size, and the large number as well as value, form, and function all come together in a different perspective when the dimension of time is considered.

IV. Final apologies

Before we declare a crisis in education, as well as in the field, it is good to remember that architecture, from a particular point of view, is doing nicely. There is, these days, a remarkable freedom of expression and considerable sophistication in the manipulation of forms, spaces, and their "meanings."

The reader who has had the patience to follow me through the previous pages will understand that, to my mind, this exciting display of virtuosity is not based on solid ground. It is the result of self-indulgence rather than the breaking of really new ground. The very lack of a tradition of explicit sharing of design skills and methods and their mutual development does not allow a professional anything to add to. There is no accumulation of understanding or ability that can be transmitted, tested, and improved.

The mode of implicit interaction, and the reinforcement of self-expression as a goal in and of itself, leaves the ambitious designer no other way to make his mark than by being "original." The emphasis is on innovation, which is the source of fashion, rather than on the patient cultivation of shared values and methods, which are the source of style.

More importantly, it seems to me that we have left large territories of professional interest shallow. We have abandoned places where we ought to operate with strength. If preservation of the species is our concern, then there is surely cause for alarm. The implicit mode of survival does not hold anymore. As a discipline, we must define the center of our interest as it rests in shared methods and a shared description of its elements; we must articulate a vocabulary that allows for the formulation of procedures and the identification of problems to solve. To the extent that there is such a discipline, there can be institutions of education that protect and cultivate the common ground.

The architectural designer is – perhaps more than any other professional in continuous contact with people who have their expertise in other disciplines. No true interdisciplinary contact can be expected unless each discipline has its own field of expertise, codified and explained with sufficient clarity to be recognized from the outside. There was a period a decade ago, when architects believed that sociology would provide the answer to the programmatic question. More recently, there have been those who advocated borrowing from linguistics to lend structure to what was seen as "meaning" in built form. With a growing awareness of cultural differentiation and the scarcity of resources, anthropologists and economists may be sought after in the near future. As we all live in the same age and intellectual climate, it can be expected that methods and theories in different disciplines will show similarities of direction and may share philosophical points of departure. But to discuss these, sufficient identification for both sides is a prerequisite.

The hope to find one's own image reflected in another discipline is, inevitably, vain. There is no substitute for building one's own house first, if that metaphor can be used here.

By now the reader must be convinced that I am trying to save the profession, if not the world. Unfortunately, I must confess that my aims are much more selfish. I find the situation simply to be intellectually less than stimulating. It seems that there is so much in the art of design today, even in the narrowest terms, that we do not even touch. The age of self-expression and originality is not only damaging to a profession that is fast becoming a luxury, but worse, it is rather boring.

1999
NOTES ON A NETWORK PROFESSION

Editors' Note: *This essay was originally published in Places, Volume 12, No. 3, 1999*

> I saw that there is no Nature,
> That Nature doesn't exist,
> That there are hills, valleys and plains,
> That there are trees, flowers and grass,
> That there are rivers and stones,
> But that there is no whole to which all this belongs,
> That a true and real ensemble
> Is a disease of our own ideas.
> – Alberto Caeiro

One: How holding fixed values no longer works with global practice

Visitors. Teachers in architecture schools take students out to observe everyday environments. Environments are read to extract meaning from them, which is expected to guide intervention sympathetic to what is already there. Inevitably, this act assumes we are visitors, coming in to acquaint ourselves with something unfamiliar. Even when we take students to an environment they already know, we do so to help them see it afresh. While the purpose is to penetrate and understand, the act itself implies detachment. We are divorced from the natural affinity that renders intervention self-evident and is the source of true vernacular.

This divorce comes with the professional condition. We expect to work in places we have never been before, and to judge work from places we have not visited. We belong to a network organization, which is itself part of a broader and thoroughly networked culture. The knowledge and skills we share are applied all over the world. With them go our preferences in lifestyle and taste. Those sensitive to the dilemma our condition brings turn to reading environment as a means to connect.

Network institutions and local architectures. As a network profession we serve network institutions as much as local forces. The relation between ard1itecture and network instructions is far from straightforward.

In history, for instance, commerce and religion formed network organizations but did not necessarily bring their own architecture. Storehouses, hostels and roads were most easily produced by local builders for local money following local style. When commerce bore arms however, the network brought its own architecture, which was distinct from local vernacular and often influenced it. Warehouses and bastions of the crusaders are still standing in Acre and those of the seventeenth-century Dutch trading companies can still be found as far as Taiwan, South America and Ceylon.

While Islam's practice and teaching were uniform to all subjects, the architecture was not. Think only of the Indonesian, tin-roofed barn mosques, the mud brick, castle-like structures in mid-Africa, the monumental gates of Samarkand's courtyard mosques or Sinan's domed spaces.

Within the larger Christian realm, the Roman Catholic Church was a networking institution if there ever were one. It had to be because, without territorial power of its own, it needed to maintain its hierarchic organization across a politically fragmented Western world. It imposed doctrine but not an architecture.

The Gothic cathedral has little in common with the Italian basilica and, for that matter, Bernini's exuberance is not Bohemian baroque.

Art and technology traveling. When power and lifestyle combine, art and architecture travel with them. Roman political and military dominance brought extended roadway infrastructure and codified town building to far-flung cultures, demonstrating an entire way of life including its architectural and artistic taste. Tying into the empire's network, local elite often preferred Greco-Roman styles when building and decorating their houses.

Classicism, from Palladio on, spanned a politically and territorially diverse world. It was a true network architecture, producing similar appearances wherever applied in whatever materials available, including eighteenth-century Neoclassicism, then continuing into the nineteenth. Thanks to printing, architecture could now be known without actually visiting a site; it was passed on to the far corners of a Western European culture by a steady stream of pattern books. But it was part of a broader network culture maintained by an international elite that shared an education in Latin and Greek and a view of history, and which wielded economic and political clout. Architects were part of this network, as were scholars and lawyers, but nobility, commerce and politics were at the center.

Amsterdam's seventeenth-century town hall, designed by Jacob van Campen in the classicist Baroque maimed, is a case in point. Compared to his competitors, van Campen was not only more talented but also better educated and better traveled. Selected by a council formed by members of the city's most powerful trader families, his design fits in an international culture. The town hall was placed in the middle of an urban fabric with which it had little in common. The same town council that commissioned the building extended this centuries-old fabric, with three monumental concentric canals without altering its basic properties. Today, the town hall still stands as a masterpiece; the fabric still is a marvel of urban culture. One is a network product, the other is rooted in local typology.

Professionalism takes off. With Modernism we see professionalism acquire power. Not only engineers and architects, but also lawyers, administrators, medical doctors and educators came into positions of influence and dreamed of a world that could be re-made by imposing their ideals. The International Style reflected the aspirations of that professional culture as much as did global accounting principles, medical practice, science and agricultural methods.

The neat distinction between the monumental building and everyday urban fabric was still possible in seventeenth-century Amsterdam but soon faded. Buildings spawned by network institutions came to serve everyday life: schools, hospitals, hotels, airports, railroad stations, office buildings and convention centers represented not only new functions (often supported by network organizations of their own), but also a more general professional culture.

Designers struggling to define new typologies for new functions applied what they invented globally. Their ambition to reinvent the world was not limited to the single building. Urban fabric too became a global product. Modernist mass housing, developed by a confident bureaucratic and technocratic class, proliferated independently of political or economic context. Communist and capitalist governments, in rich as well as poor countries, relied on the counsel of their experts who brought them the same solutions under the banner of progress, often sharing with them the ambition to shape a new world.

Retreat. The Post-modern generation took the network nature of the profession for granted, but the search for a collective signature was abandoned. A desire for self-expression and artistic autonomy replaced the quest for a shining new world. The rejection of the International Style, usually argued on artistic grounds, was also an admission that the world is simply too large and too diverse to be captured by a single convention.

The result for the profession, however, was an increased self-centeredness. Status, no longer measured by the norms of a broader culture, is now an internal affair. We want to be recognized by our peers: they are the network. The site of intervention is primarily context for a job that must earn such recognition.

One would expect that the transition from Palladian internationalism, restricted to a handful of building types executed in a codified style, to a practice dealing with all aspects of the built environment at any place of the globe, would have triggered a thorough and explicit examination of the knowledge, tools and methods needed for the new and so much more ambitious and complex task. It did not. The profession's self-centered attitude perhaps explains the remarkable fact that neither architectural theory nor architectural education so far has asked what the extended claim of operation means for the role of the profession, the tools it applies and the knowledge it needs. Both the Modernist ambition to shape a new world and Postmodernism's fixation with individual expression avoided issues of method and epistemology. Consequently, we still explain ourselves in terms of a threadbare Palladian professional image.

Two: How in everyday practice architecture will have less and less to do with discreet buildings.

Systems, traveling and locally applied. In contrast to design professionals, who are still wrestling with an exclusive ideology, manufacturers and suppliers are not compelled to condition their involvement as a matter of self-image. Materials and utility systems already penetrate into the far corners of the world. In the barriadas, electric wiring, plastic piping, corrugated roofing, plywood, dement and steel reinforcing rods are commonly applied. Sophisticated manufacturing, which requires large investments in money and research, feeds informal environments everywhere.

The affluent parts of the world now enter the next stage: more comprehensive subsystems are emerging. Steel and concrete skeletons are fleshed out to form internally flexible base buildings. They combine with interior fit-out systems, roof systems and facade systems to make a building. These new subsystems not only are technically defined but also perform a particular environmental service. Traditional utility systems like electricity and plumbing as well as security and control systems are broken down to be part of them.

In the building economy, the percentage of value added by system manufacturers has been increasing steadily in the last two decades. Value added by the local contractor is steadily decreasing. Architecture has already become the judicious composition of available hardware systems.

It is now recognized that self-stable subsystems, that is, systems minimally dependent on other systems, speed construction and boost variety and adaptability. "Open building" is now an emerging international network of researchers and systems designers seeking to improve conditions for self-stable systems. Interfaces must be simplified and codified, hierarchical relations must be better understood. Big as well as small projects will increasingly combine such progressively autonomous subsystems, purposefully designed for adaptation to local preferences of look and feel.

Disappearance of the building. Systems travel easily because they do not predetermine type or pattern. Yet, self-stable subsystems eventually will change architecture. Martin Pawley recently pointed out how in the City of London buildings retain their historic facades behind which a new fabric is built, a phenomenon that is heralding "the end of the single building as the basic unit of the urban environment, and the beginning of the rule of general-purpose serviced floor space."

Just as facades in historic environments are conserved while the buildings behind them change, in other parts of the world big buildings will receive new facades as well as new interior fit-outs while their base structure remains. Over time, thanks to the practice of independently applying subsystems, the building as an integral unit of function and identity will disappear. Parts of the building, like the London facades, may jointly form an infrastructure of urban scale. Other parts, like the fit-out system applied for a specific inhabitant, will be much smaller and more transient than the building's frame.

The fine-grained large project. One consequence of this new "open building" hardware is that it will no longer be necessary or advantageous for large projects to be repetitive and similar. The large project will become truly fine-grained, containing smaller, independent acts of inhabitation.

In a traditional neighborhood, a hundred houses may all be variations within a chosen theme, responding to inhabitants' preferences. Already, in upscale apartment building and in most office buildings, individual units of occupancy are similarly varied. The large building becomes a three-dimensional neighborhood, providing a new urban fabric.

This fine-grained approach to the large project will eventually be commonplace. Environmental intervention will no longer be measured by discreet buildings identified by their unified design. We will see large fields of base buildings to be filled in after completion as inhabitation demands and cladded with a collage of different facades mediating between inside and outside, public and private. More and more functions that we now think of as requiring a special architecture will be accommodated within the continuum of the large project, their identity no longer expressed by an entire building but a partial facade, an entrance or only an inside public space. The multi-functional building, as it is now called, is merely a transition stage towards a true continuum of three-dimensional fabric, accommodating inhabitation that need not be predetermined.

The design net dispensed. The large, fine- grained intervention, produced by partial systemic acts, each with their distinct cycles of renewal and change, spells the end of the Palladian tradition. In everyday practice, architectural design will have less and less to do with discreet buildings.

The large project, so far, reveals the controlling hand of a single designer, and hence shows repetition. But architectural intervention will increasingly coincide with self-stable, systemic levels to serve ongoing inhabitation.

Already, for the majority of very talented designers who leave the world's schools to work in large firms, tasks are inevitably partial. But with the newly emerging systems, the partial act will acquire new autonomy, as design becomes less centrally dominated and more immersed in environmental fabric itself.

Eventually this more sophisticated reality will sink in, and schools may begin to ad- dress the needs of the new breed of designers to enable variety within user's preferred conventions. In short, the task of architects will be to help cultivate an environmental fabric.

Three: How inhabitation takes care of its own

The majority of the world. Our network is our cage. We visit the same universities to study, the same hotels and conference halls to meet, the same office buildings to negotiate, the same architect's offices to work. The environments we observe and make pictures of are those designed by co-professionals.

I once remarked, at a seminar on typology among Asian architects in Korea, that the Seoul middle class seemed to have spawned a new residential type: applying traditional elements like the compound wall, the gate and the blue-tiled roof while accommodating the nuclear family with, the car, the modern equipped kitchen and air conditioning. "Where could this be seen?" some asked. From a window in our high-rise conference site I pointed to what I had found at a pre-breakfast walk: a compact, low-rise fabric below.

"Oh," was the response, "but that's not architecture!" Precisely.

That present practice lays claim to every possible aspect and function of the environment as worthy of architectural attention does not mean we design all that is built. The amount of new environment untouched by the architectural network far exceeds what is designed by it. From the profession's perspective, it is called "informal" or "vernacular." And it is very prolific. Ranging from the *barriadas* in Latin America and other expanding economies in the world to well-to-do neighborhoods with expensive villas in those same countries, new typologies emerge in response to new circumstances and inhabitants' aspirations.

Do architects operate there? They do. But those who work for the rich feel embarrassed to admit following their preferences. And those working for the poor are ignored and their reports not read. Well informed on what aspires in the professional world, these colleagues, for reasons of their own, help cultivate new environmental species.

(And may well be a role model for coming generations.)

Autonomous environment. Environment has an autonomy of its own, meaning that it is too extensive, too complex and too much tied into human existence to be controlled by any one profession or power. This autonomy is manifest in historic fabric as well as in latter-day informal or vernacular environments.

Those who study vernacular and historic fabric so far have been operating at the margin, partly because many of them have turned away from a practice they find destructive, partly because the profession at large cannot see what their research has to do with the new and large projects it covets, partly because other fields, like geography, have engaged in these studies. But their work can help us escape the professional cage and may well contribute to a general codification of environmental form.

In the past, architects often have drawn inspiration from autonomous environment, observing it and transforming it by artistic selection and discipline. But the Modernist tradition rejected the historic and the vernacular as possible sources, and after Le Corbusier the industrial landscape no longer promised a better world.

Indeed, the autonomy of the environment is not divorced from professional intervention. No one will claim we are in full control of what we are involved with ourselves. By now, professionally produced environments across the world – urban, suburban, industrial – are subject to such raw and calculated proliferation that they can no longer nourish us. Yet we are drawn into them more and more.

Repetition. Sameness and repetition can be observed in most of formal architecture regardless of place and circumstances. It is, after all, the result of implicit assumptions nurtured by the professions – architects, builders and developers – who, for good reasons, prefer proven ways to reduce risk.

Designing, as well, is drawn into this self-protective convergence. The architect's compulsive desire to do things differently from other architects seldom challenges the network's limited typology or its state-of the-art procedures and technology. Doing so might well prove suicidal. Moreover, architecture, like all human institutions, tends to seek variety within the framework of its own conventions. Hence the architectural canon just underneath the Postmodern, pluralist skin remains surprisingly limited compared to the rich variety of actually present environmental species.

Cultivation. Indeed, human nature seeks variety within a framework of conventions. A truly global profession must be capable of respecting conventions other than their own and stimulating the variety they imply. This calls for cultivating environmental form, rather than producing or inventing.

If we must operate everywhere all the time, having undergone the same kind of education, reading the same magazines and visiting the same web sites, what of the knowledge and skills we share among our fellow professionals is generally applicable to nurture the peculiar?

The agriculturist and the botanist may offer useful models. Professionals in these fields seem to have figured out how to marry general knowledge with local cultivation. The former allows them to be effective with the latter. We must likewise be able to compare environmental form effectively and to determine a new species when we see one, to be able to decide what varieties may best perform in what circumstances, to be able to make them bloom.

This requires thorough knowledge of environmental form – its morphology, its mutations, its behavior. This knowledge must utilize general concepts of environmental structure, such as types, patterns, systems and territorial and morphological hierarchy.

The local and the network. The world we must study may already be very different from what we think. The distinction between formal and informal, for instance, is one drawn from our peculiar perspective. Reality is less clear cut, partly because society is becoming more informed, partly because ways of building are becoming more sophisticated.

We tend to assume, for instance, that geographic location equates with environmental type. That notion may be outdated. The same networked form may appear in different locales; consider the "California style" suburbs that are preferred by well-to-do middle class in far corners of the world. Different network institutions may spawn their own architectures (businessmen living in California-style suburbs prefer Hilton-style opulence when they travel.)

Local environment must accommodate buildings that are nodes in worldwide networks, like hotels, banks, convention centers, airports, fact0ries, schools and hospitals. Conglomerates of such nodes raise new questions of environmental coherence. The local is becoming more pluralistic and less homegrown.

On the other hand, network institutions may blend in with local fabric, like they have in the past. One of the most attractive international hotels in Amsterdam is located in a handful of interconnected seventeenth-century canal houses newly fitted out inside. To the chain's advantage, Amsterdam by- laws did not allow it to tear down the old buildings to build their standard type. A preference for local ambiance is often found among vacationers seeking sunshine at the Mediterranean, spawning instant vernacular environments of which Port Grimaux was noted with embarrassment in architectural circles but many others, less architecturally ambitious perhaps, remain unnoticed as is their purpose. Environmental coherence need not be pseudo-vernacular, but these examples show that architecture serving network society, including banks, hotels and sports facilities, will go with what is local if that is found advantageous.

Network Inhabitants. Inhabitants of the local – and all inhabitation is local – function in networks, too. A single person may constitute a node in more than one active network (religion, hobby, work, relatives). This may not only reduce the time that person actually spends at home, but also divert her attention from local affairs when there (if she is reading books, surfing the web or telecommuting). Does such partial presence in body and mind make for a different environment? The situation was already very familiar to us before the Internet, but in past millennia, a few saints, scholars and warriors excepted, local time was devoted to local affairs.

Moreover, my neighbor and I may find no overlap comparing the networks into which we are locked.

We may share neither religion, nor race, nor work, nor hobbies. If sociocultural coherence is low, what does that mean for the environnlent we share? Must our homes express such differences as true nodes in different networks?

Perhaps, on the contrary, formal coherence may be even more important because environmental preference is what brings us together. Just because we can easily relocate, sharing environmental coherence may be more important than ever. But then again, such coherence does not signify shared experience and need not be rooted in local formal tradition. Our common preference may be for an imported or recently (designer) invented environment.

2002
MEMORIES OF A LOST FUTURE

Editors' Note: *This essay was published in BACK FROM UTOPIA, the Challenge of the Modern Movement. Hubert-Jan Henket & Hilde Heynen (editors), Rotterdam, 010 Publishers, 2002.*

For the Alchemists, not knowing that they'd never be able to transmute matter into gold was not their misfortune, but their reason for being.

Orphan Pamuk[1]

Images

Pilotis separate a pristine box from an immaculate lawn.
White slabs float in space.
A balcony with a steel railing takes flight from a façade.

A curved wall elegantly negotiates a floor of regimented columns.
Chair of bent chrome tubes and dark leather occupy a linoleum floor.
A glass vase on a glass table holds clear water and a flower.

Shadows stretch under a 'brise soleil.'
The Mediterranean sun minutely exposes the imprint of rough boards in a concrete wall.
Plastered surfaces mostly while, sometimes painted, chrome yellow, Prussian blue and red ochre.

Steel window frames like spider webs in a white wall.
Vertical black profiles frame a façade.
Screens of glass rise up and up, towards a thin edge.

But always forms in light: sharp and clear. No hesitation, no apologies.

Who can forget that stark poetry, never known before? It's part of us.

And yes, the temptations from size and number, too:
Window after window, row above row and block upon bloc.
An irresistible discipline: horizontally across the field and upwards into the sky.
No one before could project so much power so anonymously.

Ah, great expectations, ambitions, hope!
Can our cities survive?
(We must act now! The fate of environment is in our hands.)

Black and white photograph of men and women posing on the steps of La Sarraz[2]. Pieces of balsa wood, cut to identical length, pasted on cardboard, arranged in rows.
(Let me show you! The future can be designed.)

CIAM, ship of passage towards a professional identity, tried to align architectural ideology with the powers that shape environment.
It sought justification for that alignment.
(We must know the shape of cities of the future.)
Pamphlets extol upon the supremacy of collective power.
Or, in the same vein, call for entrepreneurial initiative.
(In any case, design must be centralized of course to assure the future.)

The result was always the same: the large project, buildings in free space, all land for public use.

DOI: 10.4324/9781003011385-24

The blocks still stand all over Europe, and to the East far into the Slavic plains, and to the West across the ocean.
(Let there be an international style.)

Figure 1 International style house

Yet, we remember most vividly the work on the domestic scale:
We carry with us that villa Poissy, a silent ship in space, and other houses done by Jeanneret.
We know by hear the pavilion of stainless steel pillars, polished marble and reflecting water, and earlier, Tugendhat, and later white Farnsworth hidden in the woods.

We love Mrs. Schröder's house of colorful parts and movable carpentry in which she lived so frugally into very old age.
We remember, too, of course, Schindler's vulnerable but confident poetry and Neutra's sensitive craftsmanship on the slopes of California; and Mallet Steven's mansion overlooking the Mediterranean Sea.
There are Van der Vlugt's bold white houses that survived the burning of Rotterdam, and Oud's whitewashed neighborhood.
And so much more: Johnson's patio house in Cambridge, Mass., Eames's industrial collage among the trees. Gropius's balloon framed suburban habitat, and so on . . .

From that century of uncontrolled forces and megalomaniac interventions we remember houses best of all.

Palladio, venerable godfather, stay with us.
Your scale of work we feel at home with.
Architecture still lives by the villa.
Without theory or political distraction and without teamwork or commerce:
Spaces of human scale, studied more carefully, produced more leisurely.
Nothing else so happily shaped.

1. In Orphan Pamuk, *The Black Book, the Letters in Mount Kaf*, trans. Güneli Gün (London and Boston: Faber and Faber, 1994).
2. Figure 1 Photograph in Eric Mumford, *The CIAM Discourse on Urbanism, 1928–1960* (Cambridge, MA: MIT Press, 2000), 16.

The carpenter's lament

We abandoned the monument for another mission:
Workplaces, factories, schools, shopping malls, and dwellings; dwellings for the many who could not find shelter on their own.

Can you design one house? Can you design ten? Can you design a hundred?

We want to give them the house of the future: something better than they ever had. We must determine what they really need.
Build what is best for them.

We want to give them light and air. Make the green lawn below the building accessible to all.
Free space to play and relax.

We want pervasive beauty. We must design it all: the town, the building, and the chair.
One cannot trust others to continue what one begins.

• • •

Ours is a time of industrialization. Efficiency demands we make the same things many times repeated.
We have much to do . . .
Creativity must be honored. Think of something different, something new, something they will remember us by. Each designer must find his own expression.

• • •

They say, however,
That shopkeepers have their own designers and we are asked to leave off where they begin.

They say the office occupant will bring his own designer and we are asked to leave the building empty.
They even say people want their own fenced-in yards.
But don't you think people like communal space?

They say people want to control their own . . .
But we have a responsibility. We have to show the way.

They say industrial systems allow endless variety in configuration.
But only one or two solutions are really good, of course.

The users do not understand architecture.
Yes, they understand their equipment, their computers and their cars.
That's something else.

The developers do not understand architecture.
They just know what sells.

The bureaucrats do not understand architecture.
But makes rules on behalf of society.

The politicians do not understand architecture.
They want to please the voters.

It is said that function is dead.
But how can one design without a program? What other way is there to justify what we do?

•••

Vitruvius, teacher of beauty and order.
Alberti, liberator of architects!
What went wrong?
After centuries your words cannot help us anymore:
(While we, today's teachers, coin new words in vain.)
You told us environment is a matter of architecture
(Instead of architecture being a matter of environment.)
And this we honestly believed and tried to live by.

•••

"We must plant towns," King Louis said when they were building Cathedrals.
And the citizens, freed from bondage, built the Bastides granted them.

Flora, goddess of spring and summer, patroness of gardeners!
Teach us how we may farm habitat and workplace and make them bloom!

How to trust systems, rules, habits and customs,
How to improve them.
How to work with them, and
How with all else that arises from sharing and from which healthy environments grow?

Figure 2 Life in multi-family housing

The river

Environment knows form, space, color, light and shadow.
It extends in space and time without interruption.
Architecture is an attitude first of all.

We are an avant-garde, slashing a path through the habitual, clearing new space.
Then we brought a single style to the entire world.
Then we declared ourselves born to create:
Paper flowers from an invisible tree, all different in shape and color.

Architects were exceptions in the continuity of environmental production.
Then they became a profession, with its own education.
Their numbers grew; students and teachers multiplied, and now all that's built could be architecture.
Don't you think so too?

But how can it be special any longer?
What attitude answers the new ubiquity of architecture?
Modernism never told us.

•••

Look:

The small building only makes sense as part of a larger field.

The large building only makes sense as a container of small places.
The pedestrian finds refuge in the mall, the atrium, the passage and the corridor.

Inside, life goes on: a new shop, a new office, a new home, another kitchen or bathroom, a different place to work, to sit or to rest.

Outside, life goes on: facades redone, volumes added to, volumes connected, windows and entrances displaced, streets and squares transformed.

Consider:

We work in teams and hierarchies. Consultants do their share. We are consultants, too. Design responsibility is dispersed, delegated, separated and managed.

Of the many bright and talented graduates of our schools – so much more sophisticated than their teachers – few will ever do an entire building in their life.
They will do partial designs: an infill, a façade, an extension or an alternation. They will be in a team or may coordinate a team.

Say it:

We work on any scale and for any program, doing our part all the time.
There is nothing wrong with that.
Each intervention a contribution to the whole:
The large frames the small, and the small enhances the large.
We are everywhere, neither ignorant nor ignored.

Nevertheless:

Modernism left only images.
(the pilotis, the cantilevered slab, the glass façade, etc.)
But no direction: what will guide us now?
Why can't we just do our own thing?

Flowers from an invisible tree.

•••

Move with the built field, steadily.
The land has become man-made, and the man-made has become a landscape.
Because change is constant environment endures.

What is built up later comes down. Gravity goes only one way.
The river goes only one way, steadily. Currents, ripples and eddies.
Water in water?[3]

The beautiful flower tossed into the flow,
drifts across patches of light and shadow,
believes itself at rest, dreams of the invisible tree
and
when water-logged, descends towards the deeper tow.

But the fish swims in all directions.

Figure 3 Reflections

Note

3 Georges Bataille, *Theory of Religion*: 'every animal is in the world like water in water', Zone VBooks, New York, 1992.

2006
QUESTIONS THAT WILL NOT GO AWAY
Some remarks on long-term trends in architecture and their impact on architectural education

Editors' Note: *This essay was published in Open House International, Vol 31, No. 2, June 2006. The text is based on the transcript, edited by Maria Voyatzaki, of a talk given for the 6th EAAE/ ENHSA meeting of Heads of European Schools of Architecture, June 2003, Hania, Crete, Greece. The same subject of this article is dealt with in some depth in Palladio's Children, Seven Essays on Everyday Environment and the Architect, published by Taylor and Francis in 2005.*

The emergence of the architect

In the past, the architect's job was about special buildings: the palace, the castle, the mansion for the rich and above all, the place of worship: the temple, the church and the mosque. You may add a few categories to this list, but it remains exclusive. Consequently, everyday environment was never considered architecture. For thousands of years it came about through a process so deeply rooted in social patterns and material skills that it was taken for granted, much like we take our breathing for granted. We still make that distinction. When we travel to see architecture, we walk through the streets and squares of a foreign town toward our destination: then we stop and look.

At the same time, we know every-day environments can be amazingly rich and beautiful. Think of Venice, Cairo, Damascus, Kyoto, old Beijing and Pompeii, and so many others. As long as human shelter was produced, environments of high quality have come about. Master builders are known to have contributed to their beauty, but the concept of the architect we identify with is rather recent. It is the product of the Renaissance. Alberti first formulated the new professional role that emerged in those days:

> Him I consider the architect, who by sure and wonderful reason and method, knows both how to devise through his own mind and energy, and to realize by construction, whatever can be most beautifully fitted out for the noble needs of man.[1]

For Alberti, the subject is not architecture, but the architect. In his passage and many others, he defines a new kind of person, one who knows how to design. This new professional wanted to be free from everyday environment and its traditions, constraints and limitations. From now on, focus was on innovations and a new way of building. The common fabric or rural fabric was not what Alberti had in mind. For instance, he explicitly recommended to build outside the city in free space unencumbered by adjoining buildings. In that sense, too, he preceded Modernism.

Figure 1 Rotonda. Detail of the Villa Rotonda, Vicenza, Andrea Palladio, architect

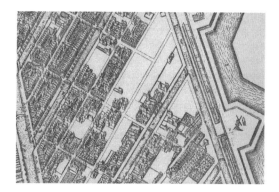

Figure 2 Jordaan, Amsterdam. Detail of 17th century map, Balthasar Gerards.

Figure 3 Amsterdam stoops. Detail of entryways along a 17th century canal

Figure 4 Palladian façade of a courthouse in New Fane, Vermont, USA

The new language of architecture resulting from that emancipation spread across the Western hemisphere independent of whatever traditional environments were already there. The rural villages in the Russian plains, for instance, had their onion-domed churches, but outside stood the Palladian villa of the landowner. In the New England villages on the American continent, that villa was transformed into a courthouse or a townhall. In those days, already, architects formed a brotherhood that transcended national boundaries, making architecture in what we now call the network mode. Architectural history is the story of what they did.

The co-existence of architecture and everyday environment has yet to be studied in detail. No doubt there was interaction, interdependency, and mutual borrowing, but for all we know, it was a happy coexistence. Architecture as an international culture, found its place in the common fabric which took care of itself, had always been there, and was what those who made architecture could depend on.

Everyday environment becomes a problem

In Modern times, all this changed. Traditional ways of building became obsolete as new materials and new techniques emerged. Age-old building typologies could no longer serve the needs of a rapidly changing society. New ways of transportation and communication disturbed familiar local processes. For the first time in history, everyday environment was not to be taken for granted. It became a problem to be solved. Responding to that challenge, architects assumed invention and design could provide the answer.

The Modernist architect set out to deal with this new task with great ambition and the best of intentions. Indeed, Modernist architecture as we know it, was thoroughly occupied with the idea of a new everyday environment. Think of the many architectural icons we still admire: Rietveld's Schröder house, the laboratory for much that is still part of our architectural sensibility, was the modest residence of an elderly lady pursuing a Spartan lifestyle. The famous Weissenhofsiedlung in Stuttgart which brought together the most advent-garde architects of the time was all about residential buildings. Ludwig Mies van der Rohe's vision of office towers with undulating glass facades was a proposal for a place to work. Duiker's pristine concrete and glass sanatorium was built for working-class people and paid for by the socialist party. Walter Gropius' Bauhaur was intended to be an example of what daily working environment could be. Le Corbusier's radical Plan Voisin was a proposal for a new everyday environment. His Unite d'Habitation, supposed to stand free, like a Palladian villa, on a well-manicured lawn, was only a next stage in his pursuit of that elusive vision. The most elaborate vision of all was Tony Garnier's proposal for a "Cite Industrielle," by which he set out to convince himself, his peers, and his clients, that in the machine age everyday environment could be humane and pleasant if designed properly. The architectural preoccupation with a new everyday environment was not always benign. European mass housing schemes as built before and after the Second World War were also considered experiments in a new architecture and urbanism. Still today, many millions of people live in the relentlessly uniform apartment buildings that came to cover urban fields from the Atlantic all the way into the far plains of Russia.

Contradictions

All these examples – the famous Modernist icons and the infamous housing blocks – were done by architects who shared the belief that making good architecture, as they understood it, was not in conflict with everyday environment.

But if we examine the properties peculiar to everyday environment and compare them with what architects actually did, we find important contractions. Most obviously, there is the simple fact that one cannot claim at the same time that the entire built environment is to be architecture and that architecture is special and different. How can everything be special? This question by itself should give us pause to ask what we actually are doing. Already in the 1970's, Lawrence Anderson, Dean of the School of Architecture at MIT, summed up the dilemma for me when I heard him sigh: "Too bad nobody wants to do a background building."

Sharing values

What is common cannot be special, but it can be of high quality. Famous urban environments from the past teach us it is quite possible that an entire environment is beautiful, functions well, and is well executed. That kind of quality first of all requires that those who work in the same location share values to a significant extent. Alas, such a sharing is not part of our tradition. As already pointed out, the Neo Classicists did not heed local custom. Driven by their own vision, Modernist architects as well aspired to an international style among themselves independent of local thematics. But all that is history. Post Modernism liberated us from professional conformity as well. As a result, because everybody wants to be different from everyone else, we just want no comparison at all. Nevertheless, today as in the past, sharing of qualities in a same locality is what makes a good environment.

Figure 5 Houses in Venice along a canal

Figure 6 Detail, interior of the Sonneveld House, Brinkman and van der Vugt, architect, 1933

Figure 7 Detail, exterior of the Sonneveld House, Brinkman and van der Vugt, architect, 1933

Figure 8 Façade detail, Bergpolder flats, W. van Tijen, architect, 1934

Figure 9 Alexandria, Egypt. Public housing built in solid natural stone, financed by Saudia Arabia

Figure 10 View of high-rise flats in Hong Kong, 20th century

Change and transformation

Another issue where our architectural instincts are at loggerheads with the common environment has to do with change over time. In our tradition, time is the enemy and must be held at bay. Good architecture, we instinctively believe, is the stone in the midst of running water. The common environment, however, is the running water and change by way of adaptation over time is essential for its continued existence.

Change goes hand-in-hand with permanence. Houses may come and go, for instance, but the streets remain. The balance between what will change and what will remain long-term is becoming increasingly important when projects become larger and larger. A housing project of several hundred uniform units cannot just stay rigid when time goes by but must adapt to life's variety. A skyscraper in which a few thousand people work is not a building but a vertical environment the size of a classical Greek town. Nevertheless, we tend to treat it as just another big building. The large project is with us to stay, but it must become increasingly fine-grained and adaptable. Practice already moves in that direction. Today's commercial office building offers tenants empty floor space to be fitted out by specialized fit-out teams according to a design done by an architect of the tenant's choice. In the shopping mall too, retail space is left empty for the retailer to take care of. A world-wide 'open building' network of researchers and architects promotes a similar adaptability in residential buildings. And in a few countries, like Japan, Finland and the Netherlands, governments support research in flexible building. In spite of this reality, so far, architects do not see small-scale adaptability as an invitation for a new kind of architecture. On the contrary, we regard such trends as encroachments on our autonomy. Here again, we find a conflict between our traditional instincts and the real world we must operate in.

Distribution of design responsibility

The issue of change is closely related to matters of design responsibility. The old masters of Modernity, Gropius, Le Corbusier, Mies van der Rohe and Frank Lloyd Wright designed their buildings down to the furniture in them. We still feel the ideal commission is one that allows us to do the chair as well as the urban context. In practice, of course, such full vertical design is seldom possible. To be sure, there is nothing wrong with someone who can design a building as well as a chair or a neighborhood. The issue here is not design ability, but design control. For everyday environment to be alive and healthy, such control must be dispersed, allowing different parties to take care of things on different levels in the environmental hierarchy.

Distribution of design control is not only related to change and adaptability. For today's complex projects, partial tasks must be distributed among members of design teams. This also involves many consultants on building structure, utility systems, lighting and acoustics and so on, who, of course, are heavily involved in design decisions as well. Parallel to that, architectural design has become more and more a matter of composition of hardware systems available on the market. Kitchen systems, bathroom equipment, curtain wall systems, or systems for windows or doors of different sizes and shapes, have also been designed. Industrial designers invent the kit of parts with which we play and as such have an increasing impact on environmental quality. Here too, we can speak of distribution of design control.

As we work, we therefore are part of numerous and disparate networks of skills and knowledge and what is built is placed in an intricate environmental fabric as well, tied to networks of utility systems, using products and materials shared with many other projects, and adhering to valued prevalent in local or extraneous culture. The very idea of 'architecture' as a self-contained and single centered act does not apply to work in everyday environment. In reality, as architects, we operate in a continuum of design where we do our bit.

Reality and ideology

In the mismatch between ideology and environmental reality, the former inevitably must give way. It is often said that the architects' role is diminishing, and his influence is gradually diluted. From the point of view of our outdated self-image that may seem so. In reality, architects have not been marginalized at all. In the new distributed way of operation, increasingly aware of local contextual issues in often rapidly changing environments, architects are fully immersed in everyday environment. They are involved in almost every aspect of environmental form. Their numbers are steadily increasing.

Architectural firms of course manage to live with the conflict between ideology and reality. They could not be in business otherwise. But while they do, they often are apologetic for compromising the ideals learned in their student days and often repeated in professional discussions and by critics of architecture. Caught in the tension between self-image and reality, they lack an intellectual support system that only schools can provide.

As educators, we suffer from the same dichotomy. The role model which hampers the practitioner in the field shapes our teaching and thereby separates us from the real world, making it less and less inspiring. How to come to grips with the new reality? The necessary adaptation will be slow, difficult and painful. Allow me to conclude with a few broad remarks about that uncertain task ahead of us. They are quite personal, based on my own experience.

Creativity

First, a disclaimer. In the traditional role model, it is axiomatic that the creative impulse is suffocated by everyday environment's constraints. But truly creative talent is stimulated by constraints. What else makes creativity important? There is no reason to assume that design for everyday environment is less demanding than what our forebears did. On the contrary, sharing values, designing for change and permanence, and coordinating distributed design responsibilities, demands not only great sophistication in designing but promises an architecture that will be more lively and dynamic and complex than has been seen in the past. It will be an architecture in which the permanent is truly structural and meaningful and the short-lived full of energy and surprises; where form is thematic in unending variation and renewal, and where the act of designing is significant and respected on all levels of intervention. This new architecture demands both invention and talent to come into its own.

Nevertheless, creativity cannot define a profession. Creative people are found in all walks of life. They shape medicine, law, science, and engineering. It is not enough to call ourselves a creative profession and claim privilege for it. Donald Schön, in his reflections on the practitioner's role in society, has pointed out that the skilled and knowledgeable professional must possess what he calls 'an artistry' to be a good practitioner. That goes not only for architects, but also for engineers, lawyers and medical doctors. But a profession's identity is defined in terms of knowledge and skills. It will be asked: What is it your profession knows that others do not? Do you have the skills and methods to apply that knowledge successfully?

Skills and methods

The new skills we need all have to do with cooperation. Sharing environmental qualities makes us listen to others. Change must honor what was done earlier by others and permanence must offer space for who will come later. Distribution of design control calls for ways to parse design tasks so that they support one another.

The tool of cooperation is method; it comes to the fore wherever we seek to work together.; Method is no more or less than a generally accepted way of working. A good method allows each of us to do our own work with a minimum of fuss. But method does not dictate results. It facilitates interaction between designers, leaving judgement to the individual, allowing her to experiment and explore. Indeed, in architectural design as in music, method allows coordination, but thereby also stimulates improvisation. In music, we play together because we accept methods of scales and tonalities and harmony. Given an accepted theme, each can improvise as part of a larger whole. The skills that come from using method creatively we may call "thematic skills."

In architecture, such skills include, for instance, making variations on accepted typology, or using agreed upon patterns, or setting up a system of parts and relations for the creation of different forms in the same style. All this helps to share values. In terms of change, too, the abilities to explore variations allow us to anticipate possible changes in programs, or in context, without abandoning form principles already set into play. In terms of distribution of design control, thematic development of possible lower-level variations helps us to assess the capacity of the higher-level form we are working at. Just as we assess the capacity of a room to hold different uses by imagining how it might be fitted-out as a bedroom, or a study, or a playroom.

New teaching formats

If you try to organize your design teaching that way, you will find the traditional studio format does not help. Learning a skill demands exercise, and exercise demands failure and time to try again. The jury invited to a design studio does not ask what the student learned, but only looks at what is produced at the end. The studio format is the sacred cow of architectural education. I hesitate to question it and do not argue its demise. But in studio it is impossible to exercise distribution of design responsibility, or to deal with the sharing of values and qualities among designers, or to handle issues of change. Studio fan no longer be the only format for teaching design. Other ways must be invented.

Research and knowledge

Finally, we need to teach knowledge about everyday environment. How it is structured, what we can learn from historic and contemporary evidence, how different examples compare, how it behaves over time and responds to change of inhabitation or other circumstances. Teaching architectural design without teaching how everyday environment works is like teaching medical students the art of healing without telling them how the human body functions. You would not trust a medical doctor who does not know the human body. Knowledge of everyday environment must legitimize our profession.

Recently, schools of architecture promote research, if only to establish their academic credentials. But we do not have a clear research agenda of our own. Architectural research is mostly attached to other fields, like building technology, management and economics, or the social sciences, to all of which we add a certain architectural perspective.

In contrast, the three questions about everyday environment I have mentioned earlier – how values are shared in environmental design, how change and permanence make environment live, and how the distribution of design responsibilities can make it bloom – are questions architects are best equipped to investigate because they have to do with the making of form and the ways in which it is done. In other words, only by a return into everyday environment can our profession establish a research agenda of is own.

I have already spoken too long. Yet, my exposition remains rough and incomplete, for which I apologize. But I have spoken with a sense of urgency. We have been in a state of denial for too long, as a result of which we suffer a lack of direction and confidence. To restore our self-worth we must say out loud what we have suspected for some time: that we are part of everyday environment and depend on it, and that the everyday environment shapes us before we can help shape it, . . . and that we must find ways to contribute to it to the best of our abilities.

Note

1 Leon Battista Alberti, "On the Art of Building," in Joseph Rykwert, Neil Leach and Robert Tavernor, trans. *Ten Books* (Cambridge, MA and London: The MIT Press, 6th printing, 1996).

2013
METHODOLOGY AND IDEOLOGY IN ARCHITECTURE

Editors' Note: *This essay was published in Umbau 26, in 2013.*

A distinction to be made

Methodology is the study and knowledge of ways of working. Questions about how we do things and how we improve the way we do things are essential for all professions and deserve close study in professional theory and education. It is therefore remarkable that we architects seldom discuss the way we work.

This lack of interest is caused by a failure to distinguish bet ween design ability and creativity. The creative act is essential in all professions, and perhaps more so in architecture. Creation is a mystery that escapes rational explanation. It does not necessarily need design: paintings and sculptures are usually created in direct interaction with the material that is shaped. Designing in architecture includes the creative act, but also entails conveying what is created to other parties who must approve or execute it. It also involves cooperation among designers working in the same location or in the same team. Most importantly, the distribution of discrete design tasks in large projects is a typical contemporary aspect of designing itself. These varied interactions demand shared ways and means of working, which is where method comes to the fore. In short, where creation is a lonely act, designing is a social one, and while creation is immediate and personal, designing involves working with others.

Of course, in real world practice architects do interact with others in many ways. But what needs to be shared and how that is best done is neither studied nor taught. When asked what architecture is about, we tend to refer to the creative act and are inclined to consider that necessary interaction an unwelcome constraint to our individual adventure. This not only makes for an ineffective profession, but also denies its practitioners a source of inspiration. It is in interaction with the world around us that creativity is sparked, and ideas are born.

A methodical evolution

In the early nineteen sixties, I suggested another way of working on housing projects. I proposed that architects make a distinction bet ween the design of the individual floor plan of a single apartment and the design of the collective structure shared by all apartments. This was, in fact, a methodological proposal. There were varied reasons for it: one could point out that in a sophisticated modern society in which households and individuals had come to expect the freedom to decide what they needed residents should be granted control over their own dwellings. One can also argue that distinguishing the long lifetime of the collective building from the short lifetime of the individual 'infill' is an important condition for environmental sustainability. Another motivation, this time from the point of view of technology and production, is that kitchen systems, bathroom systems, partitioning systems, and all kinds of piping and wiring systems are best developed in direct exchange with a market of users, just like all other durable consumer goods. Last but not least, our recent inclination to retrofit outdated buildings implicitly embraces the proposed two-level design approach.

Whether they be social, technical, or political, these reasons are now all recognized and support one another, but the proposal itself, for those of us who design, was a methodological one. Instead of considering an apartment building a single design object, we should proceed in a two-level manner: first design the collective part, and then have others design the individual units.

This way of working is not new in itself. A similar distinction is made between urban design, which shapes a collective framework, and architectural design, which takes care of the buildings in it. More recently, developers of commercial real estate routinely build large high-rise buildings within which individual companies can hire empty floors to be fitted out in response to their own needs by architects commissioned for that particular job and executed by specialized "fit-out" divisions that are owned by large general contractors. This approach is also followed in the design of institutional buildings. The large shopping center likewise offers a collective environment with- in which retail shops will have their own interior fit-out, taken care of by specialized companies who do both the design and the execution.

The increasing size of buildings reinforces the need for a two-step approach. With the help of contemporary technology, we now routinely create buildings that contain more people than lived in the average classical Greek town. Such projects can properly be considered three-dimensional urban design. But any collectively inhabited building always needs the same separation to have a healthy life.

Examples

The general examples cited above may show how hierarchical distribution of design tasks is increasingly a reality in contemporary practice. But the profession has failed so far to consider its potential for a new architecture. The large office building that allows lessees to construct their own interiors is still treated as an "empty building" rather than as a long-term, three-dimensional built environment with well-defined public spaces and well-conceived zones for private settlement. The large shopping mall – the icon of collective retail environment – never could decide if it should be a very large warehouse, a kind of extended hotel lobby, or an interior urban environment. In our profession, the architectural interaction between the individual and the collective is not the subject of theory or research. In the apartment building, likewise, the distinction between the two levels of design intervention is not yet generally recognized as a new paradigm. In most cases architects resist it and insist on their "right" to design the floor plan as an integral part of the whole.

Of course, the real world will prevail. The demand for sustainability, for response to user preferences, and for technical efficiency will eventually cause us to accept the two-level distribution of design control. Under the heading Open Building, a growing and dedicated group of designers, academics, and managers has been active on this front for decades[1], and hundreds of experimental projects are on record.[2] This is not the place to dwell on this development in any detail, but a few of the major stages are worth mentioning.

In the late eighties, Osaka Gas Company asked a prestigious team of designers to help it build the apartment building of the future[3]. In addition to numerous advanced technical innovations related to the use of energy and the management of waste, a clear distinction between the level of the collective environment and that of the individual inhabitation became the leading concept. Professor Utida, the leader of the design team, declared that he wanted to make a "three-dimensional urban design". True to that idea he invited thirteen different architects to design the eighteen residential units in the collective framework. A dedicated facade system was made available for them to use in the design of individual units. NEXT21, as the project was known, was by no means the first of its kind in terms of separation of design responsibility,

Figure 1 The NEXT21 project in Osaka, Japan

but it stood out for its attempt to architecturally think through the distinction between the individual and the collective and, most importantly, for its impact as a prestigious research effort initiated and conducted by a large institution known for its dedication to research in building technology.

From then on, the government in Japan took notice, and the concept gradually established a foothold in political circles. In 2008 the Japanese legislature enacted a law that provides a significant tax reduction to owners of durable dwellings. To earn the tax advantage, extensive technical requirements must be met. These basically demand that each subsystem can be replaced in due time, depending on wear and tear as much as on user preferences and changing lifestyles. Cast in technical terms, the law ensures the long-term maintenance of the collective environment, as well as the adaptability of the individual unit for inhabitation.[4] This is the first time this approach has attracted formal governmental support.

In the sixties and seventies, when the idea of separation of design responsibility was new and untested, many architects pursued the tenets of Open Building; some of them did pathbreaking work.[5] More recently, however, the initiative for the two-level approach has come predominantly from the client – not only from developers involved with commercial offices and shopping centers as already mentioned, but also from some government institutions and public housing corporations, the leadership of which decided that the separation of levels of intervention makes managerial and economic sense.

The City of Helsinki, for instance, in cooperation with the national building research institute, held a competition for the Arabianranta housing neighborhood for designs done in the Open Building mode. It turned out that the result yielded a profit for the developer of the project, who subsequently offered the winning architect additional similar projects.[6]

Professionals in hospital development and management in the United States and Europe are studying the approach's potential to speed up hospital projects and to facilitate alterations to the building over time. The most advanced result to date is the new intensive-care hospital in Bern. Here the cantonal Office of Properties and Buildings that served as client called for a strict separation of a "primary structure" that could last a century and a "secondary system" that could change in a matter of decades. A first competition was held for the design of the primary system and, once construction had begun, a second for the interior layout.[7]

A Dutch development company renovates industrial and commercial buildings to make them accommodate a variety of private users. It also erected what it called a "Multifunk" building, which can hold separate residential and commercial fit-out territories in any proportion the market wants.

It demonstrated that the extra investment for that approach was acceptable to owners who saw the advantage of adaptability over time.[8]

Also in the Netherlands, a large not-for-profit housing corporation took the initiative to build several buildings, the empty floors of which were offered for hire in a public auction for any use, commercial or residential, with the inhabitants taking care of their own interior fit-out. The corporation's director, who initiated these projects, calls them "Solids", argues that a true Solid can live a long time, and that it can therefore bear a higher initial investment that will return a profit in the long run.[9] He mentions two major conditions that must be met to make a long-life building feasible: it must be internally adaptable and it must be loved by the inhabitants. The second requirement is an interesting new architectural criterion. He points to the survival of nineteenth century loft buildings with cast-iron facades in SoHo, New York City as evidence of its impact.

The fine-grained large project

These are just a few examples of a worldwide trend towards buildings that are made adaptable to small-scale occupation. While projects tend to be bigger and bigger and need to live longer, we are entering

Figure 2 The Molenvliet project, Papendrecht, The Netherlands. Architect: Frans van der Werf, 1976. The first Open Building project in the Netherlands

the era of the fine-grained large project. This trend will fundamentally alter the complex interactions among the many professionals involved in the creation and maintenance of the built environment. It will be a slow process, but one that is eminently compatible with a society that is increasingly becoming fine-grained itself: individual responsibility and the freedom to choose are already considered birthrights and are actively promoted by industrial manufacturers and, more recently, by new modes of communication.

The trend is slow, because changing a familiar way of working is painful and risk y, and professionals therefore tend to avoid it as long as possible. Where the commercial and technical worlds can be expected to voluntarily reject habit when the opportunity for gain is clear, the architectural profession, locked in an ideological self-image, will remain unprepared until clients insist on the new way of working.

Of course, as architects we depend on client initiative and cannot single-handedly dictate change. But we claim to understand built environment and could therefore be expected to promote a vision for its long-term improvement and to educate clients and politicians. Most importantly for the profession itself, we should make sure to have the competence to operate successfully in the fine-grained built environment that we will be asked to design for.

Capacity, not function

The distribution of design control in increasingly large projects is in direct conflict with the idea that good design demands full top-down control. I remember being given a tour in downtown Chicago by a partner of a leading architectural firm who showed me the various high-rise buildings they had done. As evening descended upon the city, a variety of interior lighting fixtures on the ceilings became visible behind the geometric patterns of the curtain walls. My guide regretted the fact that he had not been allowed to control the arrangement of those fixtures and apologized for "the messy result." In those days, a powerful example of the architect's ideal of full top-down control was found in the Chicago Lake Shore Drive apartments by Mies van der Rohe. Here the architect's chairs graced the lobby, and the sunshades behind the windows were moved up and down in uniformity so as not to spoil the facade design.

The anecdote may seem incidental and outmoded, and it surely represents a degree of design control that is seldom granted, but we still consider a building's inside and outside an indivisible whole. For reasons that merit closer investigation than is possible here, architects implicitly adhere to the idea that the program, translated in a detailed layout, is mirrored in the building's exterior. Interior layout is often used to make interesting exterior shape or, even worse, is forced to follow exterior shape. In Hong Kong's high-rise urban fabric, a tendency can be noted to make a specific floor plan justify its more expressive exterior, thereby seriously limiting interior adaptability.

Figure 3 Example of the Parisian courtyard type building along the Haussmannian boulevards. A loose fit between the exterior and interior occupancy.

The idea that interior program must shape the exterior is clearly a remnant of modernist functionalism. The same mistaken ideolog y makes us think that without that match, a neutral architecture is called for. This is refuted by historical evidence. The Venetian Gothic palace, the Amsterdam canal house, and the Parisian courtyard building flanking the boulevards – to name just three examples – are far from neutral architectures; both their interior and exterior shapes are part of a typology that is always functionally open-ended. For that reason, these examples have endured for centuries.

Although functionalism has been rejected already by a previous generation, a new paradigm is still needed to replace the idea that architectural expression is driven by program and function. The overriding question to be answered addresses the variety of uses that can inhabit a single building. This is known as the question of capacity. Capacity assessment, a methodological tool, makes architecture balance a building's interior and exterior in the same open-ended way that we witness in historical examples.

Relations between designers on different levels demand attention in two directions. By necessity we have learned to accept a given 'site' as an inevitable constraint from above, but we continue to balk at the thought of releasing downward control. How the "site" we are making today may help or inspire designers who will work in it tomorrow is a new question that must be taken seriously.

This includes attention to the degree of control to be delegated. For instance, should a facade be the result of lower-level design or belong entirely to the collective building? Or how can the transition between interior collective spaces and interior private territories be given shape?

Interaction among designers

The vertical relation we have discussed so far is not the only feature of the contemporary built environment entrusted to us. Horizontal relations among designers operating in the same street or neighborhood are equally important today – another topic that has yet to receive serious attention in architecture. We tend to omit neighboring buildings in the pictures we show of our work. Historically, vernacular typology took care of local coherence. It was self-evident and unquestioned. Today, a more sophisticated way of working is needed to make an urban field in which the whole is more than the sum of the parts. The question as to what is to be shared is now a professional one.

There are familiar words for it: pattern, type and system are different means for sharing architectural values and can be the subject of negotiation and agreement among designers operating in a common urban fabric. These concepts offer thematic clues to be shared among designers. So far, the profession has shown little inclination to use them as professional tools.[10]

Thematic aspects need not be a limitation to self-expression. To express ourselves meaningfully we must employ a shared language. How you work with a given type will be significantly different from what another designer may do with it. In music as well, individual performers identify themselves by the variations they make on a shared theme. Architects have an innate ability to pick up thematic forms in a built environment. Without it no environmental coherence would be possible. But we do not talk about that ability nor is its use taught in schools. A fixation on originality and self-expression has put the subject out of bounds.

The idea that total freedom makes good architecture has perhaps been the most damaging force to the coherence of urban environments. There is no such thing as a blank slate. We always add to and change what has been done earlier. For a good designer, local constraints are a source of inspiration.

We tend to consider it a bureaucrat's task to regulate what needs to be shared. Something architects should not deal with. But regulations are powerless when designers are not willing to share form, and much less needed when they are. In absence of architectural cooperation, formal rules are the symptom of a pathology rather than its solution.

Our ideological heritage as makers of the exceptional monumental building, eschewing local thematics, seeking top-down control and idolizing self-expression is entirely outdated. It stems from the time when the Renaissance architect escaped the common field to create a new architectural tradition based not on local customs and habits but on general networks of style: from Palladianism of the sixteenth century onwards to the International Style in early modern times. For many generations it was a glorious liberation of creative powers in what became a global culture. But with the advent of modernity we were called upon to shape everyday environment for a new future, thereby returning to what we came from, five centuries ago – this time not to be subject to it, but to invent it anew. Unfortunately, we did so without realizing that this new task posed a formidable new methodological challenge, and that as builders of monuments we were not able to take it on.

Once we acknowledge this fateful misalignment, we understand why methodology remained outside the realm of architectural theory and education. Method comes to the fore when designers want to interact and cooperate. As long as we think of architectural design as an act of self-expression only, and believe that creativity is diminished rather than stimulated by interaction among designers, our profession will be stranded with an outdated self-image that keeps us poorly equipped for the cultivation of everyday environment.

Sources

1 The Open Building network was formed in 1996 as W104 under the umbrella of the CIB (International

Council for Research and Innovation in Building and Construction).
2. For an overview of 132 projects, see Stephen Kendall and Jonathan Teicher, *Residential Open Building* (London: Spon, 2000). For a more recent record of projects, see the overview prepared by Professor Jia Beisi of the University of Hong Kong (http://open-building.org/archives/booklet2_small.pdf.)
3. NEXT21, an experimental project initiated by the Osaka Gas company. Design team: Professor Yositika Utida, Meiji University; Professor Kazuo Tatsumi, Fukuyama University; Associate Professor Seiichi Fukao, Tokyo Metropolitan University; Associate Professor Mitsuo Takada, Kyoto University; Shinichi Chikazumi, Shukoh-Sha Architectural and Urban Design Studio.
4. Professor Kazunobu Minami, Shibaura Institute of Technology, Tokyo: "The New Japanese Housing Policy and Research and Development to Promote the Longer Life Housing," paper delivered at the CIB W104 Conference in Bilbao, Spain, 2010.
5. Among many others: Architect Frans van der Werf, Molenvliet project, Papendrecht, the Netherlands, 1974; Professor Kazuo Tatsumi's promotion of "two-step housing" in Osaka, Japan; Professor Ottokar Uhl, Dwelling of Tomorrow project, Hollabrunn, Austria, 1976; Georges Maurios, Les Marelles project, France 1975; Lucien Kroll, La Mémé student housing, Brussels, Belgium 1974; Arch. Nabeel Hamdi and Nicholas Wilkinson, PSSHAK, Adelaide Road project, London, UK, 1979.
6. Arabianranta compeptition project, won by Esko Kahri Architects in close cooperation with Tokoman Data Co. Sato development company, investors, pilot project completed 2004, 78 units custom-designed for sale.
7. INO Intensive Care facility, Inspelspital Hospital, Bern, Switzerland, 45,000 m². Client: Canton Bern Office of Properties and Buildins, Giorgio Macchi, director. Primar y system: Kamm Architekten; Secondary System: Itten + Brechbuehl; f irst half completed 2011. The two-system approach is now the standard at the Canton Bern Office of Properties and Buildings.
8. Multifunk Building, Ijburg, Amsterdam. ANA Architecten; developer: Lingotto Vastgoed; 2006.
9. Frank Bijdendijk, director of Het Oosten, a non-profit housing corporation in Amsterdam. The first phase of the Solids project in IJburg, Amsterdam, designed by Baumschlager & Eberle, was completed in 2011. Another Solid in Amsterdam West, designed by Tony Fretton, was built in 2011.
10. Despite its popularity with students, Christopher Alexander's Pattern Language did not lead to a methodical application of the concept in support of professional cooperation, but has mainly been used as a catalogue to pick and choose from in individual design.

PART II

WAYS OF DOING

INTRODUCTION TO WAYS OF DOING

In a recent conversation with the editors, John Habraken reflected on his focus on methodology.

> I got into methodology without knowing I was. SAR from the beginning was trying to find an answer to the question raised by the separation of infill and base building: If you have two base-building designs, which one is the better one if you do not have any floor plans by which to evaluate them? Moreover, since two design parties – for the individual layout and for the base building – had to know what the other would do, how could they avoid technical and dimensional mismatch? The first question was particularly relevant since the Dutch government at that time had strict rules for floor plans for subsidized housing.
>
> As you know, after the first year we proposed rules that would answer these questions. We introduced design rules. Only later I was visited by two French architects who wanted to know about SAR and when I explained to them what we tried to do, one said: "Ah, so you are working on a methodology!" That was the first time the concept was named for me. Later on, Thijs Bax, a colleague at SAR, traveled to England and explained to me what the methodologists were doing there. I remember Christopher Jones was the dominant person, it seemed. My reaction to what Thijs told me was: They try to find design rules that assure 'good' architecture; that is not methodology; what they are doing is proposing recipes. And I was no longer interested in what was going on there at the time. I still think SAR was the first to introduce Architectural Design Methodology as a subject for research and the invention of design tools.

The articles that follow in this section of the book reflect on the methods he was developing to put his observations and theories into practice. **WAYS OF DOING** – as with the previous section, starts during Habraken's early professional years in the 1960s and spans almost six decades of research, practice and teaching up to 2021. These articles emphasize Habraken as a researcher and methodologist and tend to be more focused on an achievable, pragmatic approach to creating the varied, organic and fine-grained environment he is advocating.

As with **WAYS OF SEEING**, the articles in **WAYS OF DOING** are grouped according to specific themes and within each theme are organized chronologically. The themes of Part Two are as follows:

Examples of WAYS OF DOING
The Open Building approach
Tools
Cultivating built environment
Summing up

DOI: 10.4324/9781003011385-28

The following examples touch on these themes and provide a sense of the depth and breadth of Habraken's analytic and methodological approach. As in the previous section, these articles exhibit a variety of voices, ranging from that of the detached scientist, painstakingly exploring, step by step, how to work to any keen observer, inspired by what he sees around him. As Habraken himself has reflected, when he is at his most analytical, he is "talking to himself" – exploring, reflecting, trying to figure things out on his own terms.

Basic Principles for the Building of Supports and the Production of Support Dwellings Study (Dragers), written in 1963, represents one of his earliest, most comprehensive outlines of a methodology for the creation of multiple dwelling structures which distinguish between a permanent, even standardized but also capacious framework within which varied, individual dwellings can be independently shaped using a 'Fit Out' or 'Infill' system (called 'detachable units' at this early stage). This anticipates but predates the formalization of the conceptual approach which is now referred to as open building. The narrative explaining the definitions and methods for creating support dwellings is illustrated with a series of simple but elegant, hand-drawn diagrams representing both two dimensional and three-dimensional relationships. He admitted later that some sketches were almost done 'tongue-in-cheek' and were not meant to be taken literally, for example the image of the 'caravans' or 'trailers' inserted into the open framework.

The Leaves and the Flowers, published in VIA, the Architectural Journal of the Graduate School of Fine Arts, University of Pennsylvania, 1980 is a retrospective reflection on a design competition for the Amsterdam City Hall from a decade earlier and constitutes a record of how his methodology can be used to create a highly contextual but open-ended design. He concludes that he. " . . should give structure so that there is a point where one must stop, to leave the process open to those who come next – the smaller groups of occupants and their consultants who will inhabit this new place. To inhabit is to build. The process never ends."

Concept Design Games. (with Gross), *Design Studies*, No. 3, 1988. While the editors were still studying with Habraken at MIT, he won a National Science Foundation Grant under the auspices of the Engineering Directorate, Design Methodology Program, to develop Concept Design Games. By the time a team of students and faculty had been assembled for the task, Habraken had already begun to 'play' design games on his own. The light-filled room in N52 above the MIT Museum was spare but functional. A basket of everyday objects – clothespins, pegs, nails, washers and stickers – were the early tools for exploring methodology and the rules of play. Out of the very ordinariness of mass -produced objects emerged intricate assemblies which suggested strategies, moves, concepts and constraints. This article provides a helpful overview to the applied research and the subsequent workshops that grew out of it.

The Control of Complexity. *Places*, Vol. 4, No. 2, 1987. This paper addresses the issue of how large projects can be designed without relentless uniformity and rigid control allowing for variety and adaptability over time. Starting with the analysis of complex and varied but coherent vernacular neighborhoods and building on the idea of thematic design, the article records the work arising from a design methods and theory course in the M.S. Architecture Studies program at MIT.

Open Building as a Condition for Industrial Construction. This paper was published in *The Future Site – Proceedings, 20th International Symposium on Automation and Robotics in Construction*, ISARC, Delft. Editors: Ger Maas and Frans van Gassel, 2003. In the abstract to the paper, the author writes: "Open Building advocates the direct relation between industrial manufacturing and the user/inhabitant. To make the industry-consumer relationship possible, base-buildings must offer space available for user-controlled fit-out. To date, a fairly large number of experimental projects have been executed on a global scale. They demonstrate the potential of the approach. A redistribution of design control involving all professional parties in the building industry is implied. To open this market, economic, legal, political, and bureaucratic policies must adapt."

Change and Distribution of Design, 2004 is a wonderful example about how Habraken applies his theories to the analysis of historic precedents, describing well known spaces and places with new insight – clarifying spatial organizations and architectural assemblages through the lens of territorial control and different levels of design.

More recently, **Cultivating Complexity-The Need for a Shift in Cognition**, published in 2016 as a chapter in *Complexity, Cognition, Planning and Design* is a helpful synthesis of his research and definitions for both Open

Introduction to WAYS OF DOING

Building and Thematic Design. The focus is on control fields and the continued ability of inhabitants to shape and adjust their own environments over time. This article also touches on the potential of a Fit-Out Industry to support the fine tuning of individual dwellings in large projects. Understanding the relationship between fine grained field control and territorial definition is a critical theme which is then illustrated with a series of concrete examples – seminal projects from around the world – that are proof of the efficacy and validity of Habraken's thinking.

Tackling issues of architecture and urban design as a scientist, through patient, consistent investigations into theory (how things work), experimentation, research and refinement, the articles represented in **WAYS OF DOING** stand out as a remarkable chronicle of design methodology in sharp contrast to the popular avenues of architectural self-expression that paralleled Habraken's exemplary career.

EXAMPLES OF WAYS OF DOING

1963
"GRONDSLAGEN" – BASIC PRINCIPLES FOR THE BUILDING OF SUPPORTS AND THE PRODUCTION OF SUPPORT DWELLINGS

Editors' note: *This document, produced in October 1963, is the first time that the author put into drawings his ideas about Supports and Detachable Units for housing, something that he had refused to do in his book Supports: An Alternative to Mass Housing, published a few years earlier. These drawings are also the basis for what emerged as SAR 65.*

Introduction

In my book, "*Supports and the People*" I advocated a new way of housing. By definition, supports are structures within which two or more dwelling units can be installed, reorganized or removed. In my narrative, I argue that the contemporary housing problem is not a technical problem in the first place. Once we would know what we really want we would surely be capable to technically implement it. The reasons to build Supports were not technical reasons.

Supports are necessary because they make the dwelling unit independent; that is to say, it no longer is an inseparable and integrated part of a larger building project. In turn, the independent dwelling unit enables the user to take the initiative and thereby returns to him the responsibility for the immediate environment he lives in. In this context, the concept of initiative does not suggest a do-it-yourself system but refers to a person who seeks what is advantageous and who tries to spend his money in the best way and who, by doing so, influences the industry that seeks to serve him. The user, therefore, must be involved with the emergence and the appearance of his dwelling. At the same time, this would provide a relation between the user and the housing industry which would be direct in contrast to the present mass housing situation. This relation, that is to say a continuous interaction between user and producer, is the foundation of the Support industry which I propose.

In this context, I have advocated that the contemporary production technologies, including conveyor belt production, are not in contradiction to the independent dwelling unit and that the production of large numbers of dwellings, all different from one another, are not in conflict with the principles of industrial production. The uniformity of dwelling units in mass housing is not the result of these ways of production but the result of the absence of the individual human being. That is to say, the absence of the direct relation between user and producer.

If we want to discuss the application of industrial production in housing, we must, first of all, recognize the fact that the act of building does not happen in a factory but on-site. By nature, building is a location-bound activity. Place bound activity is what makes a building, something else than an industrial product left on an empty lot and for that matter makes a neighborhood more than an open-air arrangement of such products. This is a good thing because a building is always part of a man-made landscape which we call a town. A town is a sustained and complicated organism that is independent of any particular way of making things.

This place-bound quality makes real estate investment something long-term and relatively expensive. It is not in the nature of industrial production, which typically aims at the individual consumer, to make expensive and durable goods. The use-life of its products depends on the relation between user and producer

DOI: 10.4324/9781003011385-29

and their price is also dependent on the consideration that replacement must be possible. To make the best use of industrial production it is important to take into consideration the site-bound character of the building act as part of the man-made landscape. It makes no sense to try and make building a fully industrial process. It does make sense to distinguish site-bound action from the entire process before deciding what the possibilities are of a user-related housing industry.

Load-bearing structures in buildings are naturally heavy – they need to be strong and durable. Their sustainability makes their mode of production a secondary issue. Whether they should be entirely composed of industrial parts or only partially or not at all depends on considerations of time, place, and costs. For that reason, Support structures will be recognized by their shape and purpose rather than their mode of production.

This is different for the dwelling unit in the Support structure. Making this unit entails a way of working that largely can be classified as "finishing" or "fit-out." This way of working encompasses the subdivision of spaces, their finishing by many details and the use of a variety of materials which makes it labor-intensive, vulnerable to weather conditions and subject to mechanical damage; a way of working which becomes increasingly difficult to be done on-site.

The result of this fit-out process determines to a large extent the appearance and the character of the dwelling unit; qualities that are much more time-dependent than place dependent. In which part of a town the fit-out of a dwelling is done is not important. But how it is done depends to a large extent on the vision of the generation who occupies the unit.

Hence the time-bound part of a building – the part that largely depends on taste, fashion, lifestyle, and individual priorities – is most compatible with the labor conditions and technical conditions of industrial manufacturing. In turn, the industrial manufacturing process is well suited to a product the replacement of which is influenced by subjective user-dependent issues: The user-dependent production process demands a time-related final product.

In this way, the idea of Support building fits the industrial production process very well. The Support is place-bound. In the event that it is composed of industrial components, these are intermediate parts that are combined on-site into an integrated and unified whole for long term use. A place-bound construction is not more than that it allows industrial production the largest possible range where it prefers to be, that is in direct relation with the user in a play of continuous reciprocal influence.

Because the design of Supports has to do with ways of working, a study of their basic principles is a first requirement. The following pages are no more than the result of such a study but are by no means a final result of it.

It is self-evident that a Support must be a different kind of structure than, for instance, the framework for an office building. Because it must contain dwellings, we may expect that function to influence its shape. A dwelling unit consists of a number of spaces that vary greatly in size and purpose. Together they make a unit that must be entirely separate from other units. In addition, such a unit must be connected to various kinds of utility systems. In addition to supporting them, feeding and separating the units are functions that will directly influence the shape of a Support.

We have to do with structures that must satisfy very specific functions and can be expected to have equally specific forms. But this form must allow for a great variety of dwelling shapes and, in addition, must adapt itself in many variations to the site-bound requirements of urbanism, traffic flow, and other higher-level infrastructures. Being site-bound the Support must present itself in a range of ways; after all, it is the skeleton of a town. The specific shape of the Support dictated by its purpose, therefore, cannot be more than a basic one. In turn, this basic shape must be the theme on which urban variations can be made.

The elemental spatial figure that is developed in the following pages is such a kind of basic form. Without a doubt, others will be possible, but the given example will suffice to illustrate the way of thinking presented here. And it is more than that: it offers the foundation for a rational methodology of the design of Supports and for the industrial manufacturing of dwelling units in them.

Dwellings can be formed in great variety in any Support, but on the other hand, a Support dwelling has its own architectural characteristics. A Support dwelling industry will be most successful if those characteristics find a response in the selected way of working. It is important that this way of working allows for the user's preferences regarding the distribution of spaces and functions and the level of detailing and finishing. But also, that it defines a clear theme on which the variations are made.

"Grondslagen" – basic principles for the building of supports

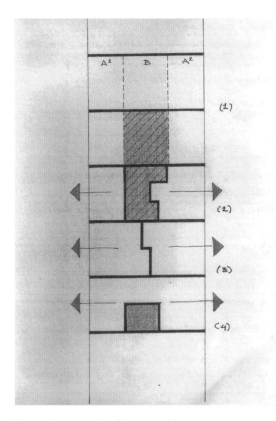

Figure 1 accompanies the text on this page

The usual support dwelling will generally be composed between four other dwelling units. One on its left side, one to the right, one above and one below. Only two sides will be open to the exterior.

The floor plan for the usual support dwelling must be composed between two party walls. These walls need not be straight. (1)

The space between those two walls will always be subdivided into 3 zones: Two zones related to the outside and one in the middle. By definition, we can say that the two outside oriented zones are formed by rooms that border directly on the facades. The middle zone will be formed (by definition) by the spaces it falls between. (2)

At any place in the support building, the dimensions of the zones can be different.

The middle zone in the dwelling can disappear fully or partly in which case the exterior zones merge or remain separated by a wall. (3), (4). The two peripheral zones will always be there.

Let's call the zones A1, B, A2.

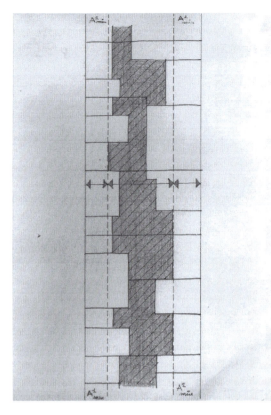

Figure 2 accompanies the text on this page

If we would draw the floor plans of a number of sequentially located dwellings, we can indicate the actual zones.

Because in a Support the floor plans of the dwelling units can all be different, we can assume that a schematic rendering of the floor plans will reveal the zones as arbitrarily shaped without any apparent regularity.

Nevertheless, a pattern can be indicated.

By definition, the zones A will have only walls that run from the facades to the inner boundary of the zone. If we discard the possibility of angled, interrupted or curved walls it can be said that only walls running perpendicular to the facades will be found in the zones A.

After all, as soon as a wall in zone A is placed parallel to the façade, the space on the inside of it automatically classifies it as zone B.

In a zone A found in a particular Support fragment we can always identify a part with a minimum depth (or width). But it will be difficult to determine a general minimum depth – A-min. – for a zone A in a particular Support without any given floor plans. But we may assume that the actual A-min in any part of an inhabited Support will vary within a particular margin.

"Grondslagen" – basic principles for the building of supports

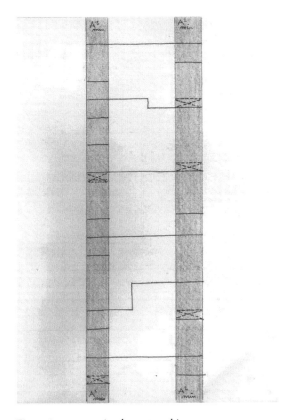

Figure 3 accompanies the text on this page

In any case, we can decide that two zones can be found in any support that run parallel with a façade, within which only interior walls will be found that run perpendicular to the facade.

A particular pattern emerges in the randomness of floor plans of a support: bands can be found behind the facades within which only interior walls are seen that run perpendicular to the facades. In case such walls are parts of a party wall two of them will be connected across the support building.

In the drawing, this pattern has been shown schematically.

This pattern can help us to find the best location for vertical load-bearing elements and vertical chases that have to be made in any support structure whatever shape it may have.

We now can say that the pattern found tells us that vertical elements have the least impact on the floor plan when they are placed in bands behind the facades and when they run perpendicular to the facades just like the walls in zones A.

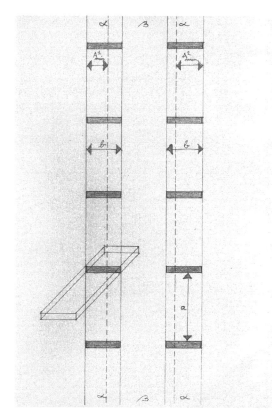

Figure 4 accompanies the text on this page

Apparently, it is possible to reserve bands in a planned floor space to locate vertical elements in such a way that the freedom to make floor plans is maximized.

The following considerations may help a further specification of these bands:

> Structural considerations, as well as design considerations, make it desirable to keep the dimensions of the vertical elements uniform and make their distances regular.

The distance (a) between two vertical elements in the same band, will be determined to a large extent by structural considerations, but also by the size of an average dwelling unit because (a) will always influence the subdivision of the available floor space.

The bandwidth (b) indicates the maximum dimension of a material element in the band. It need not be the same as A-min. In fact, it may be reasonable to make it significantly larger. The spaces behind the facades are usually relatively large and deep and therefore can accommodate load-bearing elements that relate to them, while A-min. can be the result of a few exceptionally short stretches of wall in an otherwise generously dimensioned design. An optimal bandwidth (b) can be expected to be close to A-average.

"Grondslagen" – basic principles for the building of supports

Figure 5 accompanies the text on this page

Keeping in mind the considerations mentioned in Figure #4, it is possible to reserve vertical volumes within the total volume of the yet-to-be-designed Support for the placement of vertical load-bearing elements and utility shafts. These volumes, being related to the facades of the Support-to-be run in two parallel rows. We do not know anything yet about the dimension between the two rows or the dimensional relations between the volumes in a row. But the pattern that appears mirrors the A1, B, A2 figure. Therefore, let us indicate, for the time being, the width of the rows and the distance between the two with alpha1, beta, and alpha2 ($\alpha1, \beta, \alpha2$).

The entire figure, although intended to be thematic, already suggests the building of load-bearing utility shafts. We will see later that there is much to say about that.

It is particularly important that the volumes can be interpreted as closed, as walls for instance. Here we find a possible form that relates to dwelling units, one that is a typical 'support,' in contrast to the usual skeleton of, for instance, an office building which also allows free distribution of interior partitioning.

We now have allocated volumes for the vertical elements of the Support. Now, what can be said about the horizontal parts?

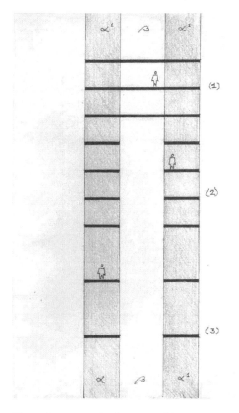

Figure 6 accompanies the text on this page

Of course, it is possible to construct a Support floor at normal single floor heights. This will limit the maximum height of a dwelling unit to a single floor. (1)

This can produce a useful support.

However, it makes sense to look for what at least must be done to connect the already decided-upon vertical elements to make a single spatial whole of vertical and horizontal parts.

In that case, horizontal planes must be penetrated to allow for dwelling units of more than one floor. Which of the horizontal floors can best be removed? We will select zone Beta (β) because zones alpha (α) are most suited for rooms. This means that for the time being only horizontal volumes will be found in zones alpha (α) (2)

When looking for a minimal necessary structure we can decide that floor elements in the alpha (α) zone at every other floor height are sufficient to construct a stable whole.

In this way, we will have a pattern of horizontal structural volumes at every other floor height only in the zones alpha (α)

"Grondslagen" – basic principles for the building of supports

Figure 7 accompanies the text on this page

This produces a spatial figure, or rather two identical spatial figures that run parallel to one another, composed of horizontal and vertical volumes of similar width at regular distances from one another.

For the time being these figures remain schematic, not yet materialized. However, their form shows that each can be statically stable when we materialize them.

The combined figure we now have is the elementary figure for an entire set of possible Supports. It is the minimal, self-stable form that can be individually materialized to design a large number of different Supports of the same family. This elemental figure makes for a theme for further play.

That does not mean that the elementary figure in its pure form will ever be built by itself. Maybe it will be, but first of all, it is a design figure – a minimum point of departure from which a final design can grow.

Nevertheless, we will see that the elementary figure can still be distinguished in many Supports of this type after they have been individually designed, detailed and constructed.

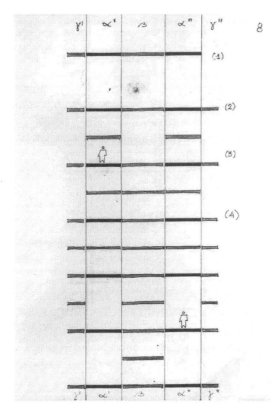

Figure 8 accompanies the text on this page

In this drawing, a number of possible Support schemes based on the elementary figure are indicated.

When we can say that the depth of a dwelling unit is

alpha1 + beta + alpha2 (α1, β, α2)

A few extra bands outside the alpha bands must accommodate exterior public access and private balconies. This makes for the scheme

gamma1, alpha1, beta, alpha2, gamma2. (χ1, α1, β, α2, χ2)

Starting from a vertically alternating floor system where every second floor repeats the previous one, a Support building can have very different floors by adding alpha (α) beta (β) and gamma (χ) floors in various combinations. For instance, the following four combinations of two floors are:

for (1): *(χ1, α1, β, α2, 0) with (0,0,0,0,0) in which (0) is no floor.*
for (2): *(. gamma1.alpha1.beta.alpha2.gamma2.) with (.0.0.0.0.0.) (χ1, α1, β, α2, χ2) with (0,0,0,0,0)*
for (3): *(χ1, α1, β, α2, χ2) with (0, α1,0, α2, 0)*
and for (4): *(χ1, α1, β, α2, χ2) with (0, α1, 0, α2, 0) with (0, α1, β, α2, 0) and so on . . .*

Where the combination of the two elementary figures is noted:

(.0.alpha1.0.alpha 2.0) with (.0.0.0.0.0.)

"Grondslagen" – basic principles for the building of supports

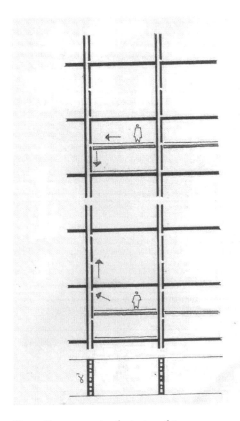

Figure 9 accompanies the text on this page

As for ventilation ducts and sewage drains, much is to be said to install them as part of the Support structure so that hollow Supports elements or load-bearing channels are made.

There is no need, then, to have a separate ventilation channel system or a separate sewage drain system. To make sure the Support will function well a surplus of connecting points is needed. This is assured when each load-bearing element performs a double function; particularly when the load-bearing parts are walls as in the previously suggested scheme.

The production of this kind of load-bearing elements is expensive to make in traditional building technology, but we speak of elements that can be applied in many Support structures and therefore can be the result of continuous industrial production, just like today's sewage pipes.

The load-bearing elements proposed here allow a stable structural system with relatively little material.

A good separation between two dwelling units is assured when the vertical elements of the elementary figure are hollow walls. This separation needs mass. For that reason, an optimum width of alpha is to be found.

The possibility of all this demands closer study.

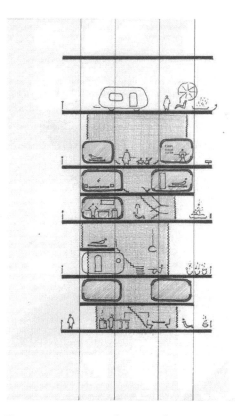

Figure 10 accompanies the text on this page

Assume a Support made as one of the many possibilities developed from the elementary figure.

It naturally will be possible to build a traditionally finished dwelling unit in it.

But how can a true industry be conceived with which we can install units in such a Support in endless variety?

What would be the most characteristic way to make this industrial dwelling?

This drawing is intended to be a caricature. Would it not be easy if the unit could be placed in the Support as if it was a caravan? This would require a minimum of local labor. (1)

Could a dwelling unit be composed as a number of "caravans" parked around a central living space? (2), (3), (4), (5).

A dwelling unit composed by means of "boxes" or "cells" that are entirely finished spaces; that can be arranged in many different ways; while the entire volume of the unit can add to the whole?

What are the advantages of this idea?

"Grondslagen" – basic principles for the building of supports

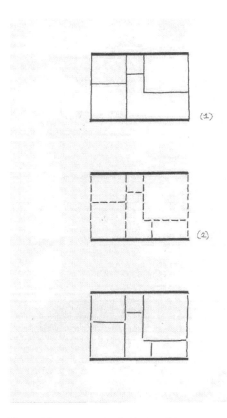

Figure 11 accompanies the text on this page

The question raised by the idea of prefabrication is:

In what parts can the unit be subdivided that are easy to produce, and can be put in place with a minimum of work to offer a maximum number of variations?

Because in the past dwellings were built by masonry walls making a monolithic structure, prefabrication became a matter of making walls, but in parts. The unit becomes a combination of prefabricated wall elements. This has big disadvantages:

1) to be able to make many variations the elements must be small. This means many complex joints to be made on-site, rigorous dimensioning, ducts to be added later. One must make a 'Meccano system' (a model construction system created in 1898 by Frank Hornby). (2)
2) When one makes large elements, one must abandon the possibility of making many variations.
3) The use of wall elements must be followed by the installation of various ducts and separately installing ceilings and floor finish.
4) The biggest problem is that a partition wall is not an organic part of the dwelling. A wall element always serves two spaces that each need a different finish. Each joint in a wall system is a problem of isolation between two spaces.

A dwelling does not consist of walls but of spaces, therefore it makes sense to prefabricate spaces, not walls.

The smallest spatial unit in which a dwelling can be divided is the room.

Combinations of more than one room can be larger units, with the entire dwelling prefabricated and inserted into the Support as the largest possible option. (1)

This last option does not allow for variation when in the Support unless the entire unit has been made of wall units in the factory with all the difficulties of that way of fabrication. Moreover, transportation will be difficult.

Transportation difficulties can be avoided by separating the entire dwelling in two or three parts. (2)

True variation and change are only possible when single rooms are prefabricated; that is to say when boxes can be placed in the Support in a variety of combinations. (3)

In that case, one makes parts that are finished wholes by themselves, including heating, electricity, finishing and even furniture, that can be connected to the main utilities in the Support. A maximum of variety with a minimum of labor.

Fitting out such boxes in a conveyor system is a known technology.

Between two rooms there are no joints that can cause sound problems. Insulation can be decided separately for each box, as the finishing of surfaces are for automobiles. Contact sound is minimized.

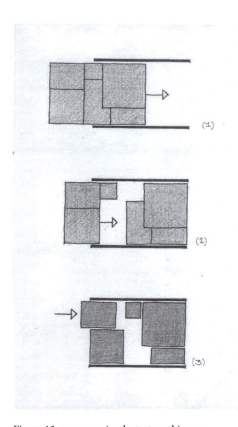

Figure 12 accompanies the text on this page

"Grondslagen" – basic principles for the building of supports

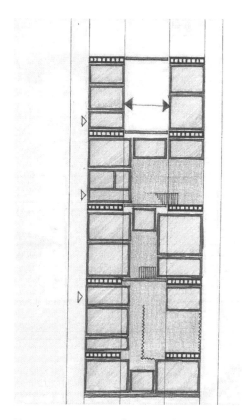

Figure 13 accompanies the text on this page

A dwelling unit's full space in a Support is obtained by erecting two facades and two-party walls in zone beta (β). This space need not be filled with boxes in its entirety but can also be used by itself.

If, for instance, boxes are placed in alpha (α) zones a free space in beta (β) is the result, which needs only limited finishing. Depending on the size of beta a bigger or smaller remaining space is obtained; with the same boxes, a bigger or smaller remaining overall space is obtained.

Roughly speaking a dwelling has two different kinds of spaces: First of all, spaces with a specific function like kitchen, bathroom, wet cell, bedroom, study, etc. Secondly, the living space that has no single particular function but which we want to be large and communal, while the other spaces generally tend to have limited dimensions.

The spaces of the first kind lend themselves to be produced as "boxes". They often demand more intensive detailing.

It may well be characteristic for the Support dwelling that for relatively little extra money (for the beta (β) zone) a more generous dwelling can be obtained with the same dimension for the boxes (alpha (α) zone). This extra space is most to the benefit of the general living space.

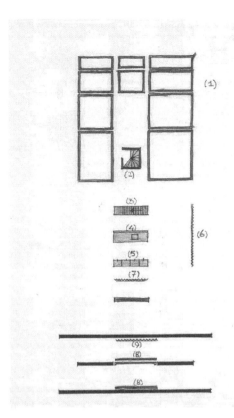

Figure 14 accompanies the text on this page

This also means that two dwelling units of the same overall value can differ significantly in price because this difference is mostly determined by the construction of the boxes.

Volume remains the highly valued property and becomes less expensive in relation to the total cost of the dwelling unit.

A basic production program for a Support dwelling factory could consist of:

(1) Boxes
(2 and 3) Some types of stairs, for instance, open and enclosed
(4) A free-standing kitchen unit, not in a box
(5) Storage closets that can serve as visual separation in the general living space
(6) Facade elements
(7) Interior partition elements in the general living space
(8) Floor finish for the general space
(9) Ceiling units for the general space.

With, for instance, 8 boxes of different sizes and the six functions mentioned earlier, 48 different rooms are possible. If the same function in the same box can be designed in three different ways, we already have 144 different rooms. The boxes themselves can be combined in different ways making for X different floor plans.

By normalization and standardization of the elements that make the boxes and their interiors, this program of 144 rooms can be executed efficiently.

"Grondslagen" – basic principles for the building of supports

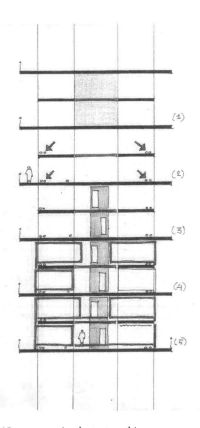

Figure 15 accompanies the text on this page

A schematic rendering of the stages of execution for a Support dwelling of the type:

$(\chi 1, \alpha 1, \beta, \alpha 2, \chi 2)$ with $(0, \alpha 1, 0, \alpha 2, 0)$

(1) masonry for party walls and placement of floor elements in zone beta. (β)
(2) installation of utility lines for electric power, gas, water, and sewage drain connected to the vertical Support channels.
(3) placement of a stairway.
(4) the positioning of the boxes and connecting them to the Support channels.
(5) installation of additional elements in the general space.

1967
THE LEAVES AND THE FLOWERS

Editors' Note: *This essay was published in VIA, Culture and the Social Vision, Architecture Journal of the Graduate School of Fine Arts, University of Pennsylvania, MIT Press, 1980. It explains the authors competition entry to the competition for the design of a new Amsterdam Town Hall. The competition entry was undertaken shortly after the author took on the job of organizing a new Department of Architecture at the Technical University, Eindhoven (1967). The editors have deleted several images of typical Amsterdam canal houses and the entresol's of Paris.*

I take this opportunity to write about a few things that are very dear to me: architecture, first of all; secondly, the beautiful city of Amsterdam that I love so much: and lastly, a design exercise I did, the drawings of which I have not seen myself for many years. They are for a project I did almost ten years ago, a competition to design the new Amsterdam Town Hall. I had just taken on the organization of a new Department of Architecture in Eindhoven and, although I had not time for this competition, for some reason or other I was so intrigued with the problems it posed that I spent several nights pondering them.

It has suddenly dawned on me now that the problem I saw in the competition was indeed representative of so much I have always been thinking and writing about that it was quite understandable why it had intrigued me at the time. And now, ten years later, I can perhaps explain what it was I tried to do then.

I also realize, looking at the drawings I made at the time, that the problem is still worth some attention. In fact, it is perhaps even more pertinent now than it was ten years ago, in the sense that perhaps there will be an opportunity now for dialogue.

What was the exercise about? A big building, mostly housing administrative offices, but accessible to the citizenry as well – a place where the community could feel at home, as well as conduct business. It had to be done on a site that was part of the fine-grained historical tissue of one of the most beautiful and characteristic cities of Western culture. It could not be a palace; it could not be an office building. It could not be a high-rise; it had to be accessible to everyone. It had to function for many, many years in an uncertain future. If it had to be a symbol, what powers should it represent? If it had to become a functioning place, what values would people attach to it? These were the obvious questions posed by the competition.

First there was the city of Amsterdam. The rich urban tissue, so distinct in scale, monumental in its tree-lined canals, ever human in its abundant variety of individual buildings, a generous organism full of vitality, capable of growth and self-renewal for many centuries. Would it be possible to cultivate the organism, to have it sprout yet another part? Could something grow there in an almost natural way, or did something have to be imposed, alien and artificial- a dead stone in living vegetation? Here you can see the themes that have fascinated me for so long: growth and change, the continuation of patterns as results of human action; the way living urban tissues are developed out of many small, individual entities; and, above all, the · underlying structure, the relatively constant holding the relatively ephemeral; the unity and diversity; the beauty of the extraordinary that compliments the beauty of the ordinary-the leaves and the flowers that speak of the same tree.

DOI: 10.4324/9781003011 3c

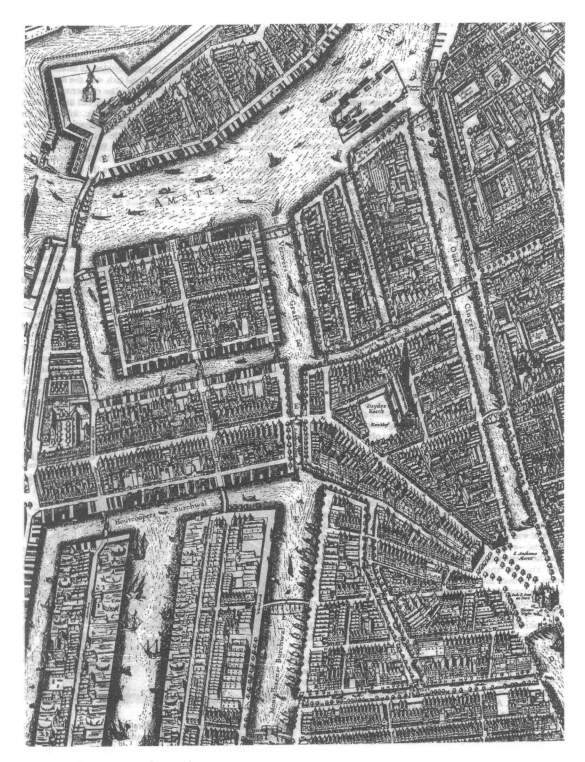

Figure 1 17th century map of Amsterdam

Let me show you part of a seventeenth-century map of Amsterdam that gives you the site of the project (Figure l). It is the rectangular island neatly divided into four blocks by two streets. It faces the River Amstel at the point where it flows into the city. As it bends at that point, there is a beautiful view down the river from the site we are interested in. At the time that this map was made the city was engaged in its most ambitious extension plan ever. Three major new canals were to circle the existing town. When these were completed the city had more than doubled its building area (Figure 2). Ambitious and bold in scale as it was, the new extension was a continuation of the old. The elements were the same: a hierarchy of canals and streets were laid out in an orderly pattern, along which buildings were built, following the same patterns as those that the citizens already knew.

Certainly, there was development in style, in materials, in the treatment of facades and floor plans. But it was development, not innovation. No revolution.

No alienation either, apparently. What is most remarkable is the consistency in the dimensions that are the most structural of all: the size of the lots, the width of buildings. Six meters is the dimension that perhaps denotes the scale best of all. It is the space you can span with a wooden beam from one brick wall to another.

Around 20 or 21 Amsterdam feet (28.3 cm) seems to be the dimension that was used from earlier times. On the new canals, where the rich merchants built when the city was at the peak of its prosperity, we find 30 – foot lots, and sometimes a person bought two lots to build one monumental house in stone. The

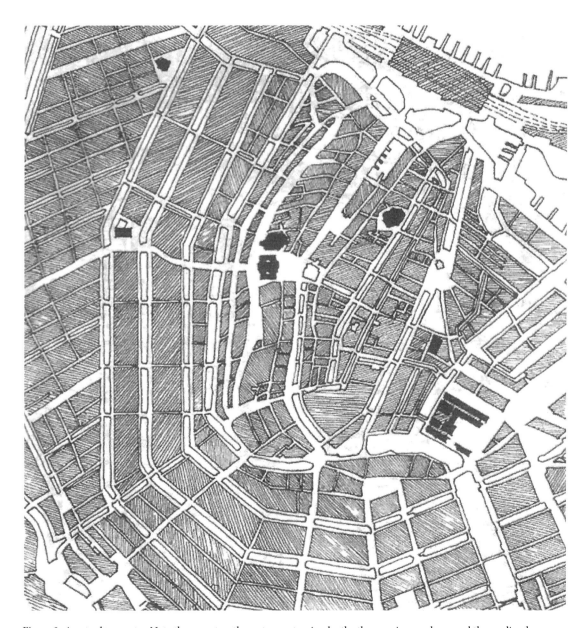

Figure 2 Amsterdam center. Note the seventeenth-century extension by the three major canals around the medieval core.

Figure 3 Aerial view of the center of Amsterdam. In circle: site of the new town hall.

working class and lower middle class, the bulk of the population, built in brick on 20 – foot lots, sometimes less, sometimes a bit more. Six to seven meters seems to be the dimension that most reveals the underlying system.

And the system of the town is really walls perpendicular to the streets – brick walls, one next to the other, each holding its own floors. Since the time of the early fires in the fifteenth century that devastated the city, party walls have had to be brick. And they held the building together. The facades were really non-structural "curtain-walls" that literally were hung on the structure behind. That is why they could be mostly glass in large wood frames with brick filling up the spaces in between.

The site today is still surrounded by many of the same buildings that you can see in Figure 3 (Figure 3). I felt that the new use of the site should have a structure akin to what the town was about: walls perpendicular to streets at distances around 20 feet. some less, some more. That structure had to be established first. It should be a continuous thing that could cover the entire site – a structure that had to be the essence of the urban tissue I had tried to understand. It is another characteristic of the Amsterdam tissue that building facades line the streets in straight lines. They press themselves forward, possessive of the public space they make together. Straight lines are consistent with the digging of canals in flat land. Curves are only found in the medieval part. where dikes and cow paths followed the flow of the Amstel River. The flat facades display color, texture, and sharp profiles against the sky, but no plasticity. The skies are often gray and cloudy. Shadows do not work in that atmosphere. The facades are cut out against that sky and the steeples of the churches, whether they are medieval or renaissance are open webs, drawing their inky lines against gray clouds.

The tightly packed buildings that jealously hide the often-generous gardens behind them suggest a dense tissue in which streets and squares are carved out. The new structure had to have that same quality. I tried to develop it in such a way that I had a choice of streets and alleys and squares to work with. The continuous structure had to represent a tissue in which public spaces could be carved out. The actual organizational decisions made in this exercise meant less to me than the general principle. Should the program change. should the dialogue develop through which the real thing had come into being. then there would

The leaves and the flowers

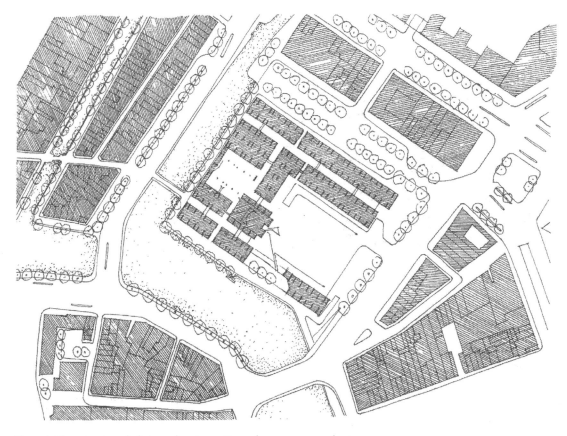

Figure 4 The extension of a living urban tissue. New urban spaces carved out.

be an overall structure that could easily be understood by everyone involved. Then we would see how to proceed in developing this neighborhood called a "town hall" (Figure 4).

Because that is what it wanted to be: a piece of urban fabric. If you look at the site and see what was there, virtually until the bulldozers cleared it, you will understand why I felt we did not need a big building, but an urban tissue that would house the various activities anticipated in the elaborate and detailed program (Figure 2). I have been told that Rietveld once said, when asked about the way he would go about designing a new extension of a town: "I think I first would fill the site with houses and then take some away where streets were needed." I cannot vouch for the veracity of this quote, but it is something I have remembered ever since I heard it. Its' naive poetry gives the essence of what urban space is all about.

So I wanted to carve out streets and places. You will understand that this poses some problems in the design of a structure. Somehow its parts and dimensions must allow for such choice. Well, if you measure the dimensions used in this structural grid you will be surprised not to find any real 6-meter dimension. What you find is two dimensions that together are 2 times 6. One is 7.20 meters and the other 4.80 meters, or roughly 24 and 16 feet (Figure 5).

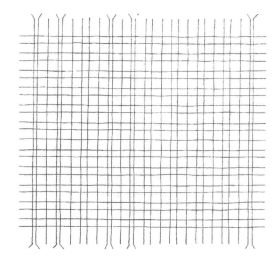

Figure 5 The grid applied to the site

These two dimensions are repeated differently in the two horizontal directions. In one direction it repeats simply on a straight a,b,a,b rhythm. Material is 6 feet and space in between is 24 feet. In that direction, then, I can make "streets" 24 feet wide, and they can repeat on a 40-foot grid. In the other direction there is a more subtle rhythm. It basically runs a,a,b,a,a,b; the a is 24 feet. But you will notice some 10-foot dimensions thrown in. They come in at places where I wanted to make "alleys" that run perpendicular to the rectangular 24-foot "streets." So it is not as neutral as it seems, and that is no coincidence. A good structure must be interrupted from time to time if you have reason to do it. And you can only do it convincingly, I think, when the basic principle is really well formulated and clear. In the other direction there is also an interruption: an a,a axis in the a,b rhythm.

There you have the first articulation of the new territory: lines crossing in space. Now imagine walls 16 feet deep, 2 feet thick and 4 floors high set on the distances described above and you have the first spatial formulation of the structural principle. With these decisions the scale is set. We have established a material-space relationship in dimensional terms that from now on will govern all the decisions we make, whether they are about urban space or buildings, inside space or outside, communal or individual. There are two additional rules: first, larger spaces are made by taking away material; second, you can take away the upper part of a structural wall if you like, but not the lower part. In other words, in cross-section you may see less structural material as we build higher (Figure 6).

Figure 6 The primary structural elements as distributed on the site after carving out the urban spaces.

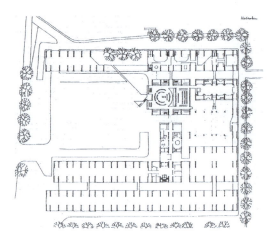

Figure 7 The main floor plan of the City Hall

As you can see on the plan I took away most material at the southwest quarter of the site to get a large urban space with the help of some of the old buildings – that relates to the river (Figure 7). The bridges in Amsterdam have a strong pitch (you can even see that on an old map, where they are wooden constructions), to allow ships to pass under them. This means that a bridge that connects two streets at the same time separates them because it is raised to eye level or higher. The new town hall square rises toward the northeast until it attains about the same height as the bridge over the Amstel River. At that point, the river becomes visible. As one moves toward it, one can look down the river's axis into the distance, where a sequence of bridges links the two parts of the city that are separated by the water (Figure 8a, b). The new square we will call Amstel Place (Amstelveld in Dutch), which is the name of the place that was there before the site was cleared. It is a place with a long tradition, and it seems proper to keep the name.

Next I took away material in the middle of the structure on the northeast side. That is the square inside the structure. It must have a glass roof like the streets and alleys that connect through it. I will tell you more about these spaces later on but let me first give you an overall view (Figure 9). There are two major 'streets' running southeast-northwest or, if you like, running parallel to the river side. They must have names. In the age-old tradition that names streets for what the people do there, we should call one the street of weddings and the other the street of the bureaucrats, because the one closest to the river feeds into the houses where people get married, whereas the

The leaves and the flowers

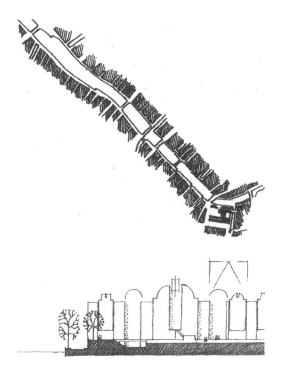

Figure 8 a, b: Looking back up the river as it flows toward the city center.

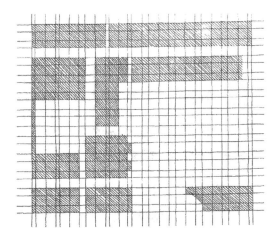

Figure 9 The public spaces in relation to the grid

other brings you too all the places where you can get passports, pay your local taxes, register your newborn infant – in short, the places you go for the profusion of permits and forms that local administration feeds to those it serves.

Again, more about that later. These two streets simply are where the structure permits them. There are secondary streets and alleys that connect them. The one between Bureaucrat Street and Citizen Square is the same width of 23 feet. Another continues in the same direction but is 15 feet wide, and then there are a number of alleys no more than 9 feet wide that you will have no problem finding (Figure 9).

There is one more place where material was taken away: the 'building' that is on your left when you enter the structure from Amstel Place. This is the town hall proper. It is where the city council meets. It is the real center of the government, the 'special' building nested in the tissue of 'ordinary' buildings and streets formed by the structure.

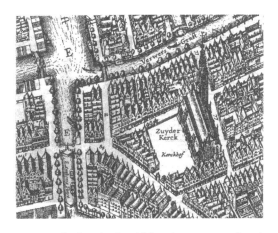

Figure 10 The "South Church" (1616) as it appeared in the 1625 map.

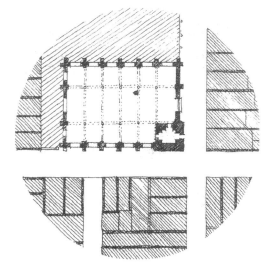

Figure 11 The "South Church." Like the medieval churches embedded in the urban fabric, it creates a covered public space

I would like you to have a look at the way the 'special' buildings – the large churches in which the citizens of Amsterdam have congregated throughout history, are planted in the tissue of Amsterdam. There are two large medieval churches and at least three major ones that were built in the Renaissance. The church that you can see in Figure 10 is the Zuiderkerk (South Church), built by Hendrik de Keyzer between 1603 and 1611. As I was writing this, I took out an old history book on the architecture of the Netherlands and found a plan of that church (Figure 11). It is the first time I have really seen the plan, but I have been in the church itself several times. The structure of the building, both its spatial organization and dimensional structure, astonishes and delights me. I had always thought that the large interior system looked like a town square lined by houses, and the image is strengthened by the way the building is placed in the urban tissue. It is not a freestanding building in an open space. The church itself is as jealous of the public space as the houses. It lines up right at the street edges. There is no way in which you can perceive the whole building from any one vantage point. The view is always partly obscured by houses (Figure 12a,b,c). The building does not stand apart, but it is intimately integrated with the city fabric. The cemetery is walled off from the streets. It is not the mass of the building that its builders were interested in; its interior space was what mattered most. That space is in fact a public space like any other town square. The only difference is that it has a roof. The middle space in the Zuiderkerk is about 40 feet wide. Its bays are half of that: 20 feet, the width of the townhouses around it.

What more is there to say? The same pattern is revealed by the medieval churches. The Ouderkerk (the 'Old Church'), although more complicated in its structure – the result of enlargements in history – is built on the same structural principle: a large public square covered by a roof and lined by secondary streets, the dimensions of which, again, equal those of the houses and streets in the town. It is not the horizontal dimensions that make the structure different from the fabric of the town, but the vertical. As you walk through the maze of streets, canals, and alleys of the urban environment you see the high roof and steeple from afar. As you come closer, the streets do not open up to make a place for a large building, but they lead you to the interior, where you find a large space. It is an architecture of space, first of all.

Now let me take you into that urban tissue that I hoped to be the result of my exercise in structure and dimension. Perhaps you are troubled by the long, narrow Bureaucrat Street. I think I already indicated that all the "streets" and "alleys" should be open spaces right

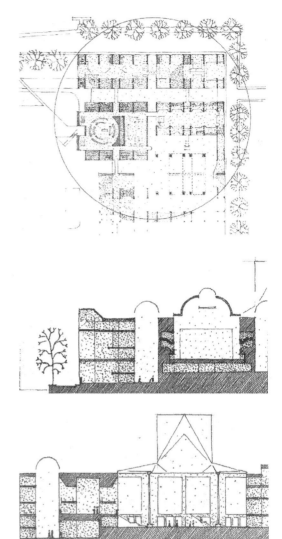

Figures 12a, b, c The 'town hall in a town hall;' The council chamber building surrounded by 'Citizen Square,' 'Amstel Square'... and 'Wedding Street'

from the ground floor to the glass roof. The length of this street does not bother me at all. To begin with, it is typical in its size and dimensions for the tissue around it. You will note that the street in the old town that you find perpendicular to it, to the northeast of the site, has the same width and is even longer. This will only work on one condition: that the facades that make the street have individuality and are not endless repetitions of the same design. As we are conditioned to think of massive repetition of uniform elements, we assume almost automatically that any long, straight facade must have such a uniform repetition. But what I would like it to be is a series of individual 'houses.' After all, the people who work there, and their activities, are different from

The leaves and the flowers

each other. They surely arrange their furniture differently. Why should they work behind uniform facades?

But uniformity, as we all know, is the result of centralized decision-making. It is not the result of industrialized building. On the contrary. We can produce systems of industrially made elements that allow themselves to be combined in endless variation. There is no reason why our streets should not have a variation similar to the older streets. This should not be an aesthetic exercise, however. When we want the result to be a living thing that in its long lifetime will reflect the changes and idiosyncrasies of its population, then we must conceive it as the result of that life within. Consequently, the issue is decentralization of decision making and recognition of the individuality of the smaller units in the organization of the inhabitants.

Along Bureaucrat Street the public will find all the offices that serve as the meeting places of the municipal administration and its citizens. These offices, where bureaucrats and public meet, should be on the ground floor. The activities that back them up should be above them. In other words, the smaller office units in the larger bureaucracy should be housed vertically. They should have their own stairs and elevators. The idea is not new. Again, we can observe it in reality. Along the canals of Amsterdam many of the historic houses are now occupied by a variety of commercial enterprises. The public enters these from the street. Sometimes such organizations occupy several buildings connected by opening cut in the party walls. The result can be awkward where the floors are not on the same level, but the principle is clear.

The Administrative units that will occupy the houses in our new structure are the units that must serve as the clients to the architects who made the building (Figure 13). Yes, indeed, I am talking about architects, not one architect. When we take decentralization of decision-making seriously, we should start with ourselves. Who wants to make all the decisions in such a large enterprise as the one we are discussing now? The very concept of structure means delegation of decision making. Variety within a framework. What I would like to do is to work out a system of rules regulating the choice of elements and their combination in space in such a way that many of us could work with the project and create parts within the larger framework. This is not new either. The American shopping mall is conceived on a similar principle. There, the occupants deal with their own interior designers,

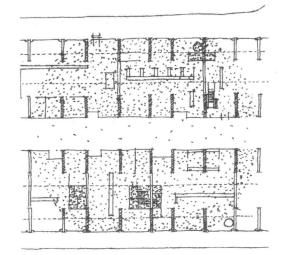

Figure 13 Bureaucrat street

building their shops in the larger framework. It would be worthwhile to develop this principle. I am convinced that there is a younger generation of architects in the Netherlands who would be happy to play this game: the result could of course be much better than any precedents we can point to now. It certainly would be much more interesting than anything that even the most talented architect could design alone.

Here we touch the heart of what I am used to calling the 'support' concept. I use the term 'support' because the framework in which the individual interpretations of different architects who are serving different administrative units of the municipality are developed should be much more than only a number of loadbearing walls or columns. It must – in itself – be a true piece of architecture, strong enough to hold the variety of forms that will be expressed within it, complete enough to be good art, satisfactory even when empty. If you want another example, take the Rue de Rivoli in Paris – a true Support of a strong and dominating architecture. But within it you find a rich population of shops, restaurants, cafes, and even hotels. True, the Rue de Rivoli is perhaps an extreme case in the sense that it does not allow any expression of its interior variety toward the street. From within its arcade, however, things are different. The late nineteenth century shopping arcades in London (not to mention Milan) are another case in point. The Rue de Rivoli, by the way, is interesting because its structure is a faithful reflection of the Parisian urban fabric. Here, too, its dimensions and spatial organization can be recognized in the ordinary streets of Paris, the dominating feature of which is the *entresol*, a low floor above the ground floor that sometimes falls back as a mezzanine, sometimes even disappears, to allow for a much higher space or a monumental entrance. But that is another subject. Let's go back to the Amsterdam environment and the lessons it teaches us.

Although I have not mentioned it explicitly, you will have understood that, of course, the outside facades of our support should be governed by the same principle. Don't ask me to give you details of that aspect. I am not prepared to go that far. Something must be left for your imagination. I can, however, point out some aspects of the historic facades of Amsterdam that in my opinion could very well be incorporated in the rules of the game that we want to play here. I mentioned earlier the fact that these facades are true 'curtain walls.' The traditional Dutch townhouse has its own version of the *entresol*. The ground floor is usually very high. The tall windows let the light penetrate deep into the interior space. This height allows for a mezzanine that often can be reached by a separate stair. The interesting proportions that are the result of that solution do not need to be stressed. Such a mezzanine, together with the high ground-floor windows, could serve very well in our administration building, it seems to me.

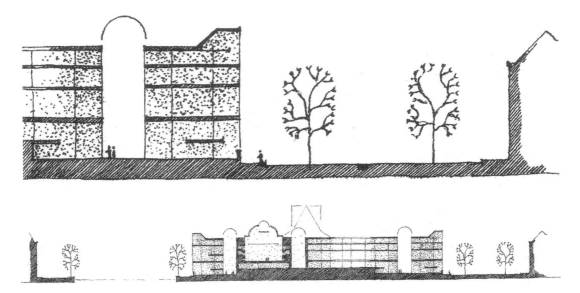

Figure 14 a, b: Cross section perpendicular to the river, across the council chamber and bureaucrat street

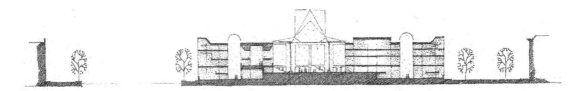

Figure 14c: Cross section perpendicular to the river across "Citizens Square"

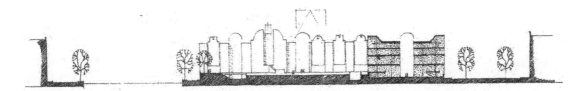

Figure 14d: Cross section perpendicular to the river across "Amstel Square"

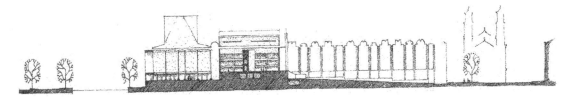

Figure 14e: Cross section parallel to the river

And then of course there is the top – the silhouette against the sky that marks the roof. The structure should have roofs; they make the top floor that much more interesting, or they can serve as lofts to house whatever additional functions may be needed by the clients – a storage space to put old files in, a place to relax and drink coffee. In our vertical organization concept, it is the bosses of the administrative units who, perhaps, want to be in the top spaces with their high-pitched ceilings.

To conceive of a physical system for the variety of facades would be an exciting design challenge. I must concede that I keep thinking of this in metal. They should not be all glass, although glass should be dominant. They certainly must be flat. Metal in a flat surface with glass in it, hovering over an almost total glass first floor would be nice. It would lend itself to the kind of cut-out profile that the sky needs.

But let's go to the Wedding street, leading to the eight houses facing the Amstel in which weddings take place. (Figure 15). The cars come around the lower part of the Amstel Place to unload the wedding party at the entrance to that street. They then disappear in the underground garage under the Amstel-place to

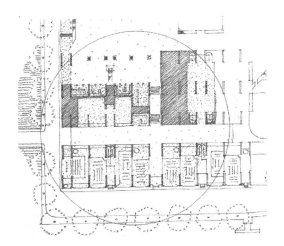

Figure 15 "Wedding Street" and the spaces for the wedding ceremonies overlooking the Amstel River

wait. Finally, they pick up their party on the river side, where relatives can make pictures of the young couple as they descend the steps to the outside street, lined by trees.

The spaces in which the ceremony takes place are again those high spaces with tall windows looking over the river and the houses on the other side. The water of the river sometimes reflects against the ceiling as the sun comes through. The mezzanine gives some of the guests the opportunity for a good view from above.

As even Dutch society has its class structure, some weddings are more important social affairs than others. A party can use the main entrance and proceed through the Citizen Square inside. This, of course, will also be the route taken by all those other groups to be received by municipal dignitaries – foreign visitors, local groups, demonstrators, petitioners, and the like. Citizen Square should have a light glass and metal roof. Its slender columns follow the rhythm of the structure. Have you ever seen those old Byzantine churches in which the builders used columns found in even more ancient Roman ruins? Some are better than others, some are fat, others are slender. What I would like to do is to invite some artist to make a few columns. Public buildings in Holland are allowed some 2% of building costs to be spent on art objects. This would be one way to use that money. The structure that covers the roof on the Citizen Square should be light and transparent, web-like, the metal frames painted in bright colors.

A stair climbs from this Square into the building on the river side. On its second floor we find the large, formal banquet and reception hall. (Figure 12a). This hall looks out onto Citizen Square. Its space extends horizontally across the wedding street into other reception rooms that look out over the river. A bridge spans the interior street.

The Assembly Hall is on this same level. It is connected by three bridges to the adjoining buildings. One comes from the Banquet Hall to make a more formal entrance. The other two bridges lead from the reading and committee rooms of the council members at the river side and from the building facing Amstel Place, where the mayor and the aldermen have their offices. There are internal stairs and entrances in each of these buildings. The Assembly Hall is, in fact, two spaces. One, facing Amstel Place, is the real city council chamber; the other is for special committee meetings of a less formal nature. Both spaces will have balconies between the structural walls for public and press, accessible by stairs and elevators from the ground floor of this building.

Light for this space will penetrate from the top and reflect toward both sides of the structure above the balconies. On the Amstel Place side, a wall stands apart as a façade, identifying this town hall within a town hall as a separate entity. A balcony protrudes into the public space outside, from which the Queen can wave at crowds when she visits the city, and where the mayor can preside at other celebrations.

As we have taken our tour through this little town within a city, I have tried to explain the objective of this exercise: the design of a structural concept in which structure means much more than just physical elements that bear loads. It concerns the concept of a Support, in fact, this time not applied to residential use but to the operations of a municipal administration. It concerns the development of an architectural theme that in its spatial variations and dimensional rhythm picks up the themes that reverberate from a past that is still alive. The exercise illustrated the continuation of some values as they are expressed in the composition of physical elements in space.

At the same time, it is an exercise in the dispersion of decision making. There are no big buildings. There are only big organizations that want to centralize decisions, and the message that I would like to put across is that there should be a hierarchy of decision making in design, that one decision will give structure to those that follow. As I accept the structural concepts imbedded in the city of Amsterdam that tell me how to deal with this fascinating site at the Amstel River, I find myself in a situation in which decision making is delegated to me by that physical fabric that is already there, and I have to listen very carefully. But the corollary is that I should give structure so that there is a point where one must stop, to leave the process open to those who come next – the smaller groups of occupants and their consultants who will inhabit this new place. And to inhabit is to build. The process never ends.

1987
SHELL-INFILL HOUSE

Editors' Note: *This study on the application of the systems approach in housing design was prepared at a time when the author was in close contact with several leading Japanese architects and academic researchers, as well as people in the Japanese building industry. Part of the involvement had to do with discussions about the licensing in Japan of the Matura Infill System that the author was heavily involved with in the Netherlands as co-inventor.*

There are 22 sheets, starting with the introductory page.

SHELL INFILL HOUSE

A STUDY ON THE
APPLICATION
OF THE
OPEN
SYSTEMS
APPROACH
IN
HOUSING DESIGN
SUBMITTED TO
MY
COLLEAGUES
AND FRIENDS
IN
JAPAN
MAY/JUNE
1987
N. JOHN
HABRAKEN.

SHELL INFILL HOUSE

Shell-infill house

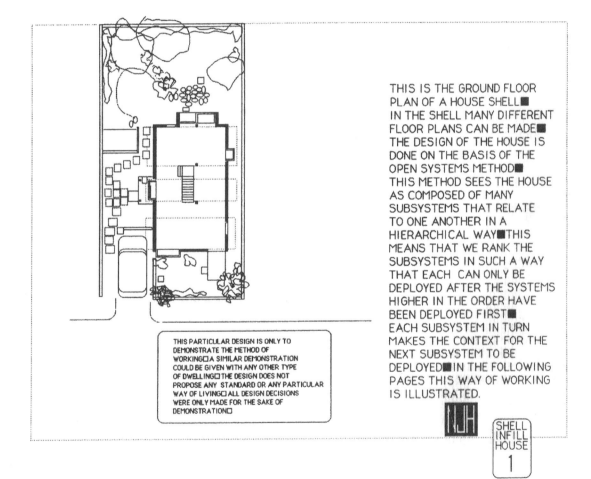

THIS IS THE GROUND FLOOR PLAN OF A HOUSE SHELL. IN THE SHELL MANY DIFFERENT FLOOR PLANS CAN BE MADE. THE DESIGN OF THE HOUSE IS DONE ON THE BASIS OF THE OPEN SYSTEMS METHOD. THIS METHOD SEES THE HOUSE AS COMPOSED OF MANY SUBSYSTEMS THAT RELATE TO ONE ANOTHER IN A HIERARCHICAL WAY. THIS MEANS THAT WE RANK THE SUBSYSTEMS IN SUCH A WAY THAT EACH CAN ONLY BE DEPLOYED AFTER THE SYSTEMS HIGHER IN THE ORDER HAVE BEEN DEPLOYED FIRST. EACH SUBSYSTEM IN TURN MAKES THE CONTEXT FOR THE NEXT SUBSYSTEM TO BE DEPLOYED. IN THE FOLLOWING PAGES THIS WAY OF WORKING IS ILLUSTRATED.

THIS PARTICULAR DESIGN IS ONLY TO DEMONSTRATE THE METHOD OF WORKING. A SIMILAR DEMONSTRATION COULD BE GIVEN WITH ANY OTHER TYPE OF DWELLING. THE DESIGN DOES NOT PROPOSE ANY STANDARD OR ANY PARTICULAR WAY OF LIVING. ALL DESIGN DECISIONS WERE ONLY MADE FOR THE SAKE OF DEMONSTRATION.

SHELL INFILL HOUSE 1

OVERVIEW OF THE MAJOR SUBSYSTEMS THAT MAKE THE HOUSE DESIGN■ A. THE SHELL OF THE HOUSE■ B. THE STAIRS■ C. THE WINDOWS AND OTHER FACADE ELEMENTS■ D. THE INFILL WALL SYSTEM■ E. THE KITCHEN AND BATHROOM EQUIPMENT■ F. THE FURNITURE■ THE RESOURCE SYSTEMS LIKE PLUMBING AND ELECTRICITY ARE NOT SHOWN HERE, THEY MAKE A SEPARATE ORGANISATION DISCUSSED LATER■

SHELL INFILL HOUSE 2

Shell-infill house

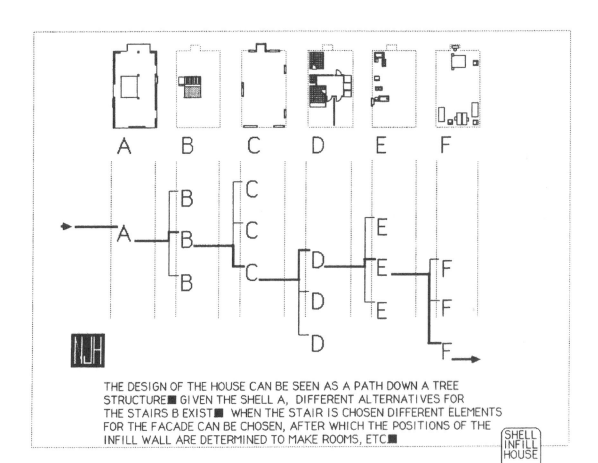

THE DESIGN OF THE HOUSE CAN BE SEEN AS A PATH DOWN A TREE STRUCTURE■ GIVEN THE SHELL A, DIFFERENT ALTERNATIVES FOR THE STAIRS B EXIST■ WHEN THE STAIR IS CHOSEN DIFFERENT ELEMENTS FOR THE FACADE CAN BE CHOSEN, AFTER WHICH THE POSITIONS OF THE INFILL WALL ARE DETERMINED TO MAKE ROOMS, ETC.■

SHELL INFILL HOUSE 3

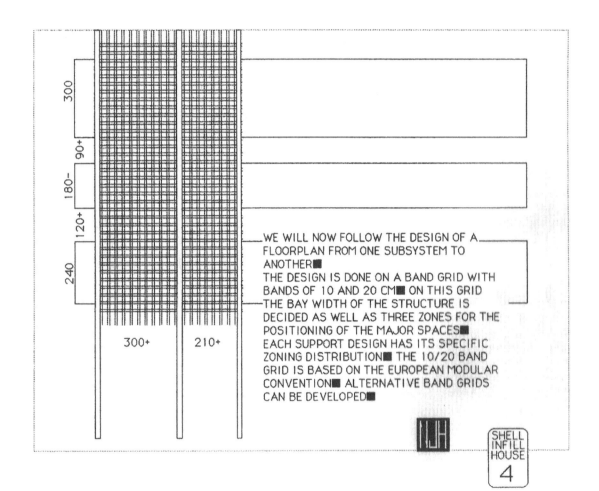

Shell-infill house

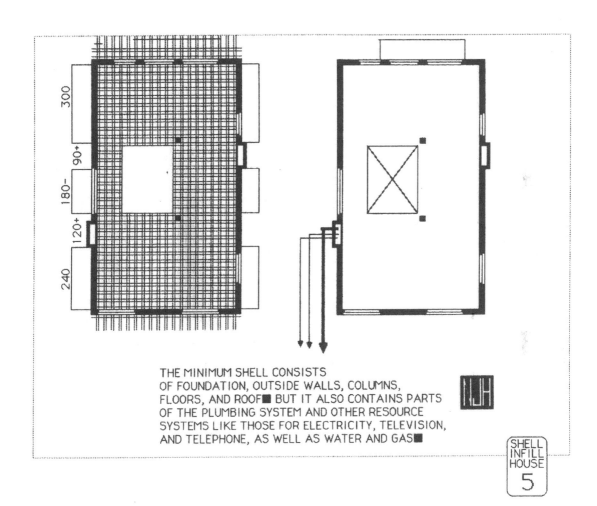

THE MINIMUM SHELL CONSISTS
OF FOUNDATION, OUTSIDE WALLS, COLUMNS,
FLOORS, AND ROOF■ BUT IT ALSO CONTAINS PARTS
OF THE PLUMBING SYSTEM AND OTHER RESOURCE
SYSTEMS LIKE THOSE FOR ELECTRICITY, TELEVISION,
AND TELEPHONE, AS WELL AS WATER AND GAS■

SHELL INFILL HOUSE 5

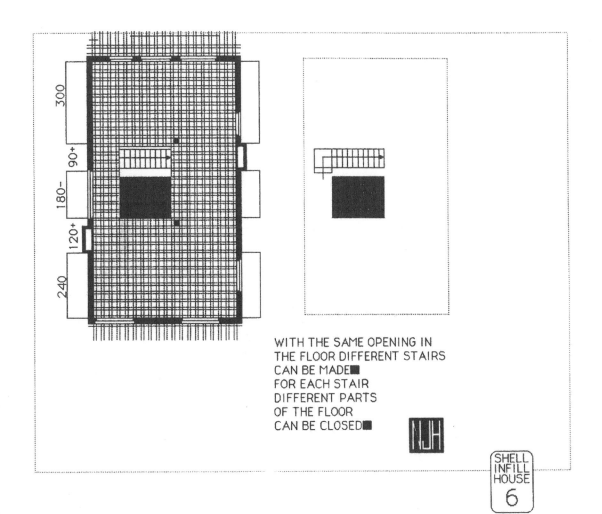

WITH THE SAME OPENING IN THE FLOOR DIFFERENT STAIRS CAN BE MADE■
FOR EACH STAIR DIFFERENT PARTS OF THE FLOOR CAN BE CLOSED■

SHELL INFILL HOUSE 6

Shell-infill house

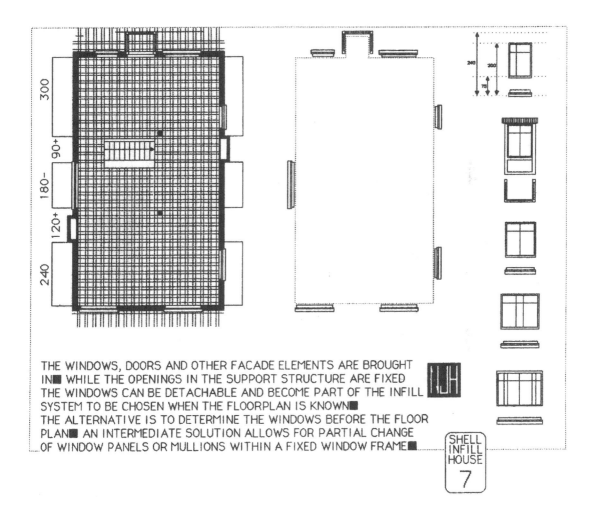

THE WINDOWS, DOORS AND OTHER FACADE ELEMENTS ARE BROUGHT IN■ WHILE THE OPENINGS IN THE SUPPORT STRUCTURE ARE FIXED THE WINDOWS CAN BE DETACHABLE AND BECOME PART OF THE INFILL SYSTEM TO BE CHOSEN WHEN THE FLOORPLAN IS KNOWN■ THE ALTERNATIVE IS TO DETERMINE THE WINDOWS BEFORE THE FLOOR PLAN■ AN INTERMEDIATE SOLUTION ALLOWS FOR PARTIAL CHANGE OF WINDOW PANELS OR MULLIONS WITHIN A FIXED WINDOW FRAME■

SHELL INFILL HOUSE 7

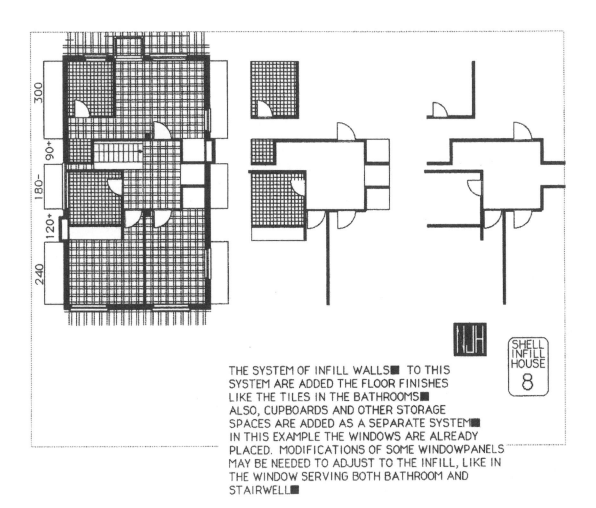

THE SYSTEM OF INFILL WALLS■ TO THIS
SYSTEM ARE ADDED THE FLOOR FINISHES
LIKE THE TILES IN THE BATHROOMS■
ALSO, CUPBOARDS AND OTHER STORAGE
SPACES ARE ADDED AS A SEPARATE SYSTEM■
IN THIS EXAMPLE THE WINDOWS ARE ALREADY
PLACED. MODIFICATIONS OF SOME WINDOWPANELS
MAY BE NEEDED TO ADJUST TO THE INFILL, LIKE IN
THE WINDOW SERVING BOTH BATHROOM AND
STAIRWELL■

SHELL INFILL HOUSE 8

Shell-infill house

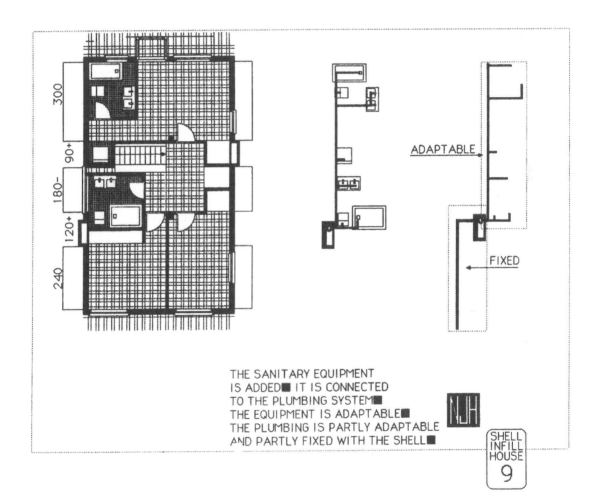

THE SANITARY EQUIPMENT
IS ADDED■ IT IS CONNECTED
TO THE PLUMBING SYSTEM■
THE EQUIPMENT IS ADAPTABLE■
THE PLUMBING IS PARTLY ADAPTABLE
AND PARTLY FIXED WITH THE SHELL■

SHELL INFILL HOUSE 9

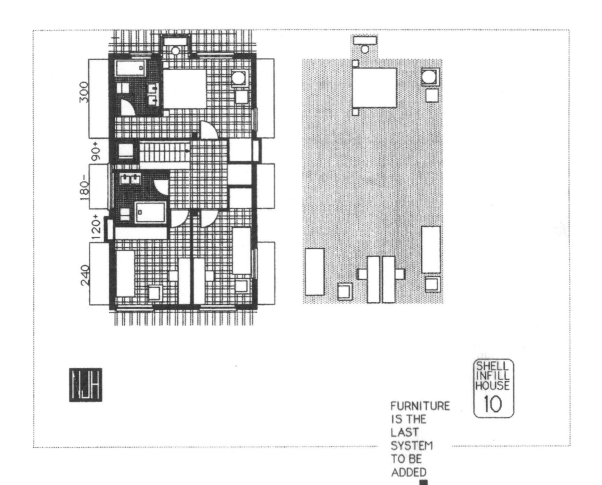

FURNITURE IS THE LAST SYSTEM TO BE ADDED

Shell-infill house

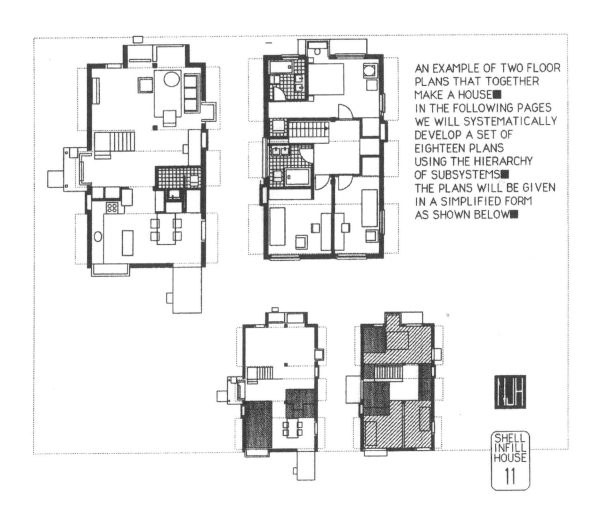

AN EXAMPLE OF TWO FLOOR PLANS THAT TOGETHER MAKE A HOUSE■
IN THE FOLLOWING PAGES WE WILL SYSTEMATICALLY DEVELOP A SET OF EIGHTEEN PLANS USING THE HIERARCHY OF SUBSYSTEMS■
THE PLANS WILL BE GIVEN IN A SIMPLIFIED FORM AS SHOWN BELOW■

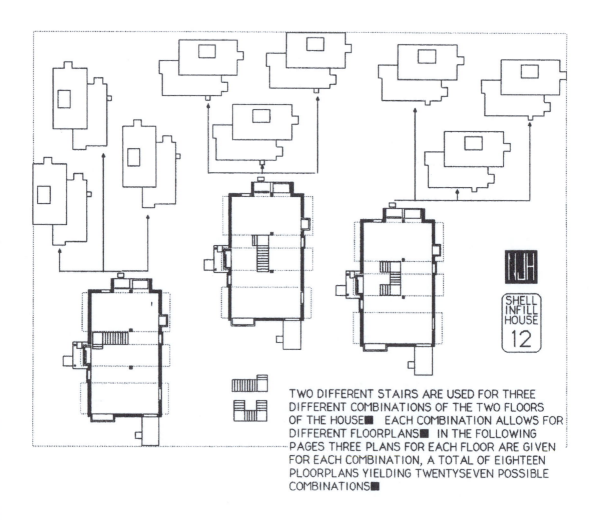

TWO DIFFERENT STAIRS ARE USED FOR THREE DIFFERENT COMBINATIONS OF THE TWO FLOORS OF THE HOUSE■ EACH COMBINATION ALLOWS FOR DIFFERENT FLOORPLANS■ IN THE FOLLOWING PAGES THREE PLANS FOR EACH FLOOR ARE GIVEN FOR EACH COMBINATION, A TOTAL OF EIGHTEEN PLOORPLANS YIELDING TWENTYSEVEN POSSIBLE COMBINATIONS■

Shell-infill house

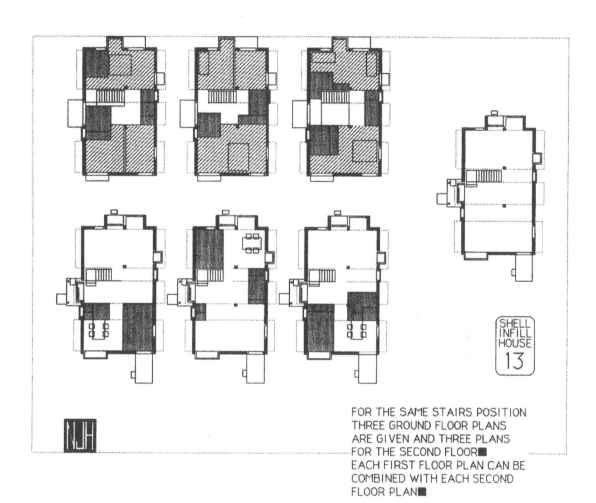

FOR THE SAME STAIRS POSITION THREE GROUND FLOOR PLANS ARE GIVEN AND THREE PLANS FOR THE SECOND FLOOR■
EACH FIRST FLOOR PLAN CAN BE COMBINED WITH EACH SECOND FLOOR PLAN■

SHELL INFILL HOUSE 13

ANOTHER STAIRS POSITION YIELDS SIX MORE PLANS; THREE ON EACH FLOOR ■

SHELL INFILL HOUSE 14

Shell-infill house

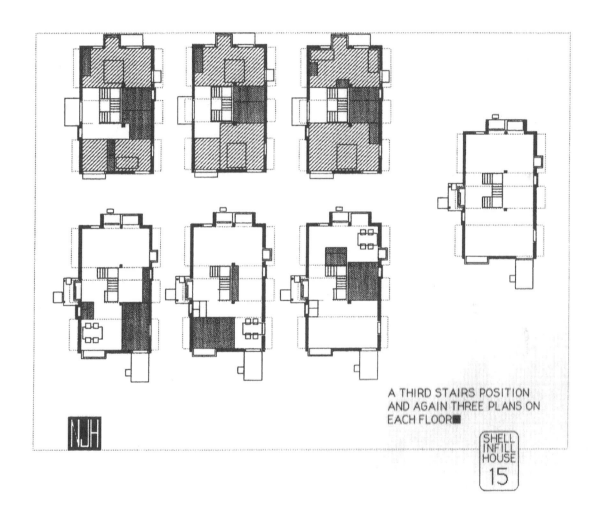

A THIRD STAIRS POSITION AND AGAIN THREE PLANS ON EACH FLOOR■

SHELL INFILL HOUSE 15

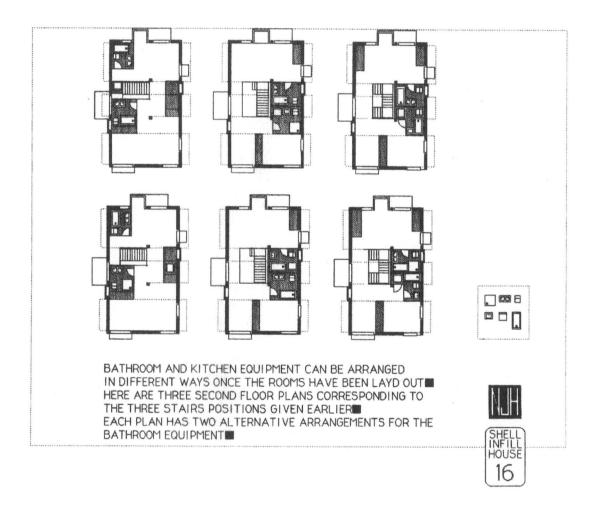

BATHROOM AND KITCHEN EQUIPMENT CAN BE ARRANGED IN DIFFERENT WAYS ONCE THE ROOMS HAVE BEEN LAYD OUT■
HERE ARE THREE SECOND FLOOR PLANS CORRESPONDING TO THE THREE STAIRS POSITIONS GIVEN EARLIER■
EACH PLAN HAS TWO ALTERNATIVE ARRANGEMENTS FOR THE BATHROOM EQUIPMENT■

NJH

SHELL INFILL HOUSE 16

Shell-infill house

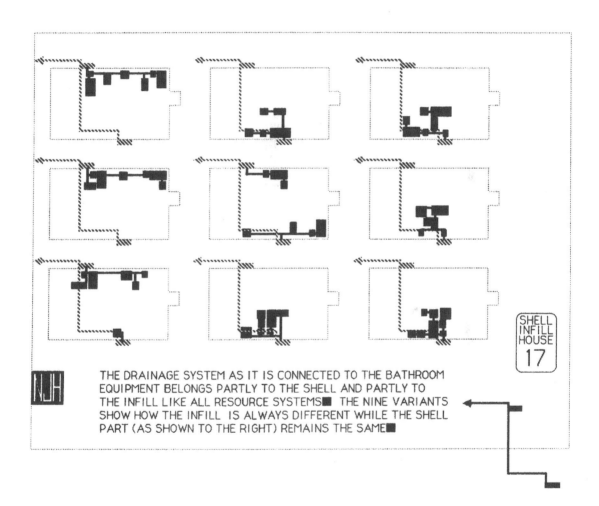

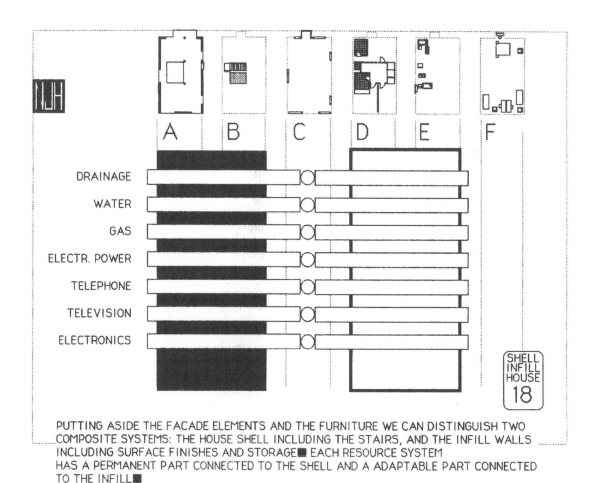

PUTTING ASIDE THE FACADE ELEMENTS AND THE FURNITURE WE CAN DISTINGUISH TWO COMPOSITE SYSTEMS: THE HOUSE SHELL INCLUDING THE STAIRS, AND THE INFILL WALLS INCLUDING SURFACE FINISHES AND STORAGE■ EACH RESOURCE SYSTEM HAS A PERMANENT PART CONNECTED TO THE SHELL AND A ADAPTABLE PART CONNECTED TO THE INFILL■

Shell-infill house

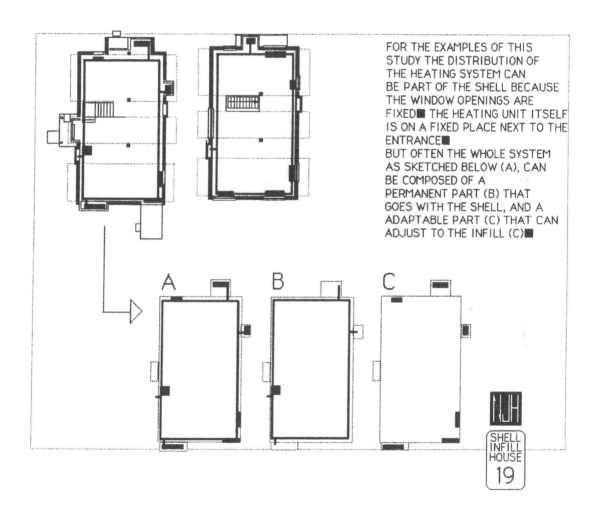

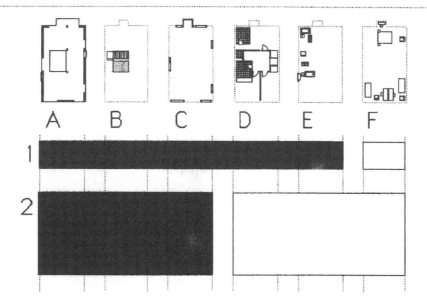

THE SUBSYSTEMS WE HAVE DISCUSSED SO FAR MAKE FOR A VARIETY
OF PLANS THAT CAN BE PRODUCED AND DESIGNED EFFICIENTLY ■
BUT THIS SYSTEMATIC WAY OF WORKING ALSO MAKES
FUTURE ADAPTATION TO USER PREFERENCES EASIER TO ACHIEVE ■

IN TODAY'S TECHNOLOGY IT IS ONLY THE FURNITURE THAT IS EASILY
ADAPTABLE TO USER NEEDS ■ ALL OTHER SUBSYSTEMS,
ONCE INSTALLED, ARE DIFFICULT TO CHANGE OR TO SEPARATE. (1) ■
THE SHELL-INFILL APPROACH SEEKS TO MAKE THE SUBSYSTEMS D AND
E MUCH MORE ADAPTABLE INCLUDING THE RESOURCE SYSTEMS THAT
ARE CONNECTED TO IT ■ THIS INFILL CAN BE DISTINGUISHED FROM THE
SYSTEMS A, B, AND C THAT MAKE THE MORE PERMANENT SHELL (2) ■

Shell-infill house

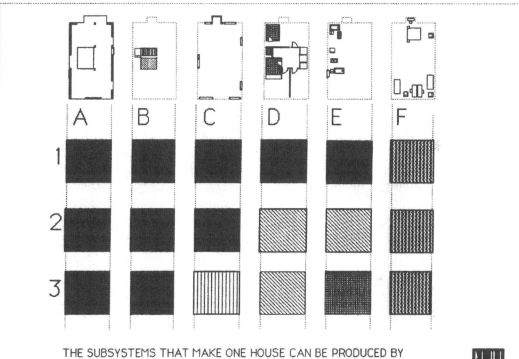

THE SUBSYSTEMS THAT MAKE ONE HOUSE CAN BE PRODUCED BY DIFFERENT COMPANIES■ DIAGRAM 1 GIVES THE NORMAL SITUATION WHERE ONE COMPANY OFFERS THE WHOLE HOUSE TO THE CUSTOMER EXCEPT FOR THE FURNITURE■ NO.2 SUGGESTS HOW THE BUYER CAN FIND A SHELL WITH ONE COMPANY AND A INFILL SYSTEM WITH ANOTHER■ CASE NO.3 GIVES A SITUATION WHERE A LOCAL BUILDER PUTS TOGETHER A HOUSE WITH PRODUCTS FROM DIFFERENT COMPANIES■

1994
THE SAMARKAND COMPETITION SUBMISSION

1994

The Samarkand Design was a submission for a competition initiated by the AGA KHAN PROGRAM at HARVARD and MIT that aimed to improve the quality of architecture in Muslim Countries in various ways. These included, for instance, a prize for the best building executed every year in one of these countries, salaries for professors at Harvard and MIT, collecting a library and paying PhD students.

I was studying Urban Fabrics at the time, and saw in the competition an opportunity to demonstrate a particular approach to urban design. The competition gave an extensive functional program for two complementary neighbourhoods; a FESTIVAL COMPLEX and a CULTURAL COMPLEX.

The FESTIVAL complex asked for a large open space for people to celebrate and meet, a conference hall, a chamber music hall, an open-air performance space, a hotel, various exhibition spaces and all kinds of shops.

The CULTURAL complex should a least have a Mosque, an Astronomy observation building, a Library, an Art Exhibition space and an Art School.

The site is on both sides of a dry river valley that was never built upon although it is close to the three monumental mosques from the times that Samarkand was an important city on the Silk Road.

I assumed that most submissions to the competition would show lots of free standing buildings in a campus like arrangement and decided to do the opposite. I decided to follow historic urban fields without free standing buildings but with well defined public spaces.

In such a plan the various buildings could not be recognised by their external shape and would have facades and particularly gates to identify themselves as well as the spaces that they formed together.

I explained in my submission that a spatial structure had been proposed by the responsible urban designer (myself) and that the many specified functions and their buildings would be designed by as many separate architects. Residential construction and shopping spaces would flesh out the final fabric, with their own architects. The latter would not necessarily be built or used by the festival or cultural organizations.

Unfortunately, the process of distribution of the many individual design tasks could not be shown in the competition. I did explain in my entry that if such an approach would be implemented, the distribution of design tasks can only be done efficiently when the designers are familiar with the qualities of everyday built environment that Open Building designs for. I did not expect the jury to understand this, but simply wanted to see what the result of my approach could be.

The following narrative story gives the experience of a couple visiting friends who live in the new housing built as part of the Festival Center, and moving about with them within the Festival and Cultural Complexes.

"We came to the Festival Center to visit friends who lived there. We entered the Festival Center by car through the main gate (1), and came upon a long space at the end of which we could see the main Festival Entry Court Gate (8). As we drove around the fore-court, on the way to parking under our friend's apartment, we saw many shops on our right (3), and, turning around, we passed beside a stretch of housing (4) in which our friends had their apartment. We had their permission to park in the underground garage, which occupied space below the housing. After parking, we came up into the Festival plaza and walked across to the main gated entry to the shopping street, located between the shopping center (11) with its parking (10) and the Chamber Music hall (12). From there, we could see down an incline to the skylights of the Exhibition Hall (13) and beyond it to the Festival Garden in the Valley (16). We met our friends for lunch in a cafe close to the end of the long 6-meter wide shopping street (2), located inside the Concert Hall (14) where we would attend a concert later in the evening. From the cafe, we could look out into the Main Festival Entry Court (7) and glimpse the administrative offices (9). Our friends told us that there was a hotel (5 and 6) nearby.

After lunch, we went around the corner of the Concert Hall and walked down an incline to what our friends informed us was the roof of the exhibition hall, where we could once again see its skylights (13). From there we could easily look down on the Festival Garden, as well as up to the bridge (18) linking the Festival and Culture Centers. Instead of continuing down another incline into the Garden (16), our friends recommended we take a look at the Open Air Theater (15), a semi-circular building where tiered seating looked out to the stage. We walked through the theater and back up to the shopping street, turned left and left again to enter the bridge (18) to cross over into the Cultural Center.

Halfway across the bridge, we came to a pavilion-like structure which, our friends told us, was the place where dignitaries could sit to watch events that took place from time to time in the Festival Garden in the Valley. The bridge continued on, crossing the road (19) some twenty feet below, passed through a new housing development to emerge into the Culture Center Square. We could immediately see three major gates, and to our immediate right, the minerette of the Mosque (23 and 25). To the right we could see the gate into the new Mosque. To the left, we could see the gate to the Observatory (24), and straight ahead, we could see the gate leading into a small Court (26). This was the entry Court to the Culture Center's Art School (27), Art Museum (28) and Library (29). Entering the Court, we could see in the distance, between the Art Museum and Library, the ancient Mosques (30) which had been such an important stopping point on the Silk Road.

After seeing the Culture Center, we returned via an inclined pedestrian way (21) between blocks of housing, to the Valley Floor, across the road (19) and the Garden in the Valley (16), to the Exposition Center where we spent the rest of the afternoon, before having dinner in the shopping street (2) and returning to the Concert Hall (14) for the evening performance."

The Samarkand competition submission

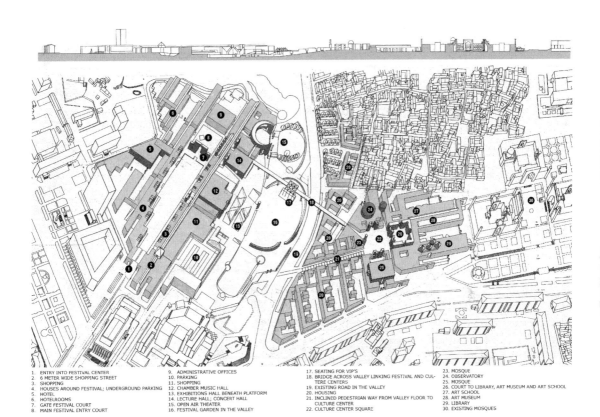

1. ENTRY INTO FESTIVAL CENTER
2. 6 METER WIDE SHOPPING STREET
3. SHOPPING
4. HOUSES AROUND FESTIVAL; UNDERGROUND PARKING
5. HOTEL
6. HOTELROOMS
7. GATE FESTIVAL COURT
8. MAIN FESTIVAL ENTRY COURT
9. ADMINISTRATIVE OFFICES
10. PARKING
11. SHOPPING
12. CHAMBER MUSIC HALL
13. EXHIBITIONS HALL BENEATH PLATFORM
14. LECTURE HALL; CONCERT HALL
15. OPEN AIR THEATER
16. FESTIVAL GARDEN IN THE VALLEY
17. SEATING FOR VIP'S
18. BRIDGE ACROSS VALLEY LINKING FESTIVAL AND CULTERE CENTERS
19. EXISTING ROAD IN THE VALLEY
20. HOUSING
21. INCLINED PEDESTRIAN WAY FROM VALLEY FLOOR TO CULTURE CENTER
22. CULTURE CENTER SQUARE
23. MOSQUE
24. OBSERVATORY
25. MOSQUE
26. COURT TO LIBRARY, ART MUSEUM AND ART SCHOOL
27. ART SCHOOL
28. ART MUSEUM
29. LIBRARY
30. EXISTING MOSQUES

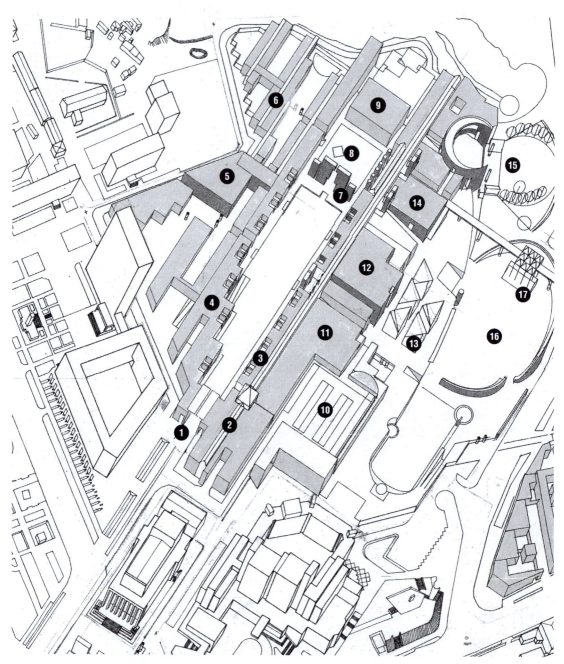

1. ENTRY INTO FESTIVAL CENTER
2. 6 METER WIDE SHOPPING STREET
3. SHOPPING
4. HOUSES AROUND FESTIVAL; UNDERGROUND PARKING
5. HOTEL
6. HOTELROOMS
7. GATE FESTIVAL COURT
8. MAIN FESTIVAL ENTRY COURT
9. ADMINISTRATIVE OFFICES
10. PARKING
11. SHOPPING
12. CHAMBER MUSIC HALL
13. EXHIBITIONS HALL BENEATH PLATFORM
14. LECTURE HALL; CONCERT HALL
15. OPEN AIR THEATER
16. FESTIVAL GARDEN IN THE VALLEY
17. SEATING FOR VIP'S

The Samarkand competition submission

18. BRIDGE ACROSS VALLEY LINKING FESTIVAL AND CULTERE CENTERS
19. EXISTING ROAD IN THE VALLEY
20. HOUSING
21. INCLINED PEDESTRIAN WAY FROM VALLEY FLOOR TO CULTURE CENTER
22. CULTURE CENTER SQUARE
23. MOSQUE
24. OBSERVATORY
25. MOSQUE
26. COURT TO LIBRARY, ART MUSEUM AND ART SCHOOL
27. ART SCHOOL
28. ART MUSEUM
29. LIBRARY
30. EXISTING MOSQUES

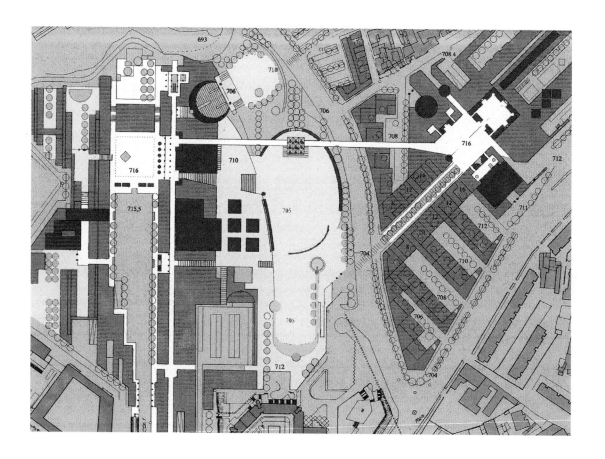

The Samarkand competition submission

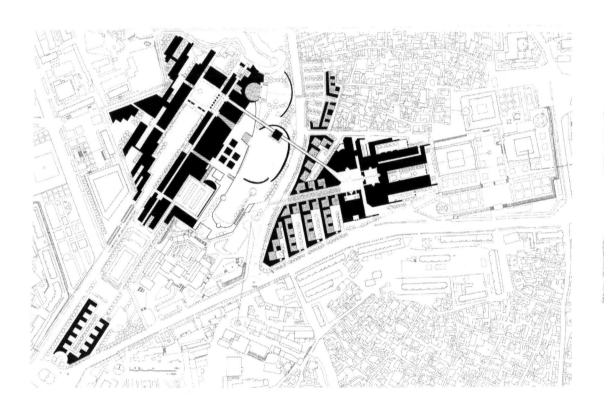

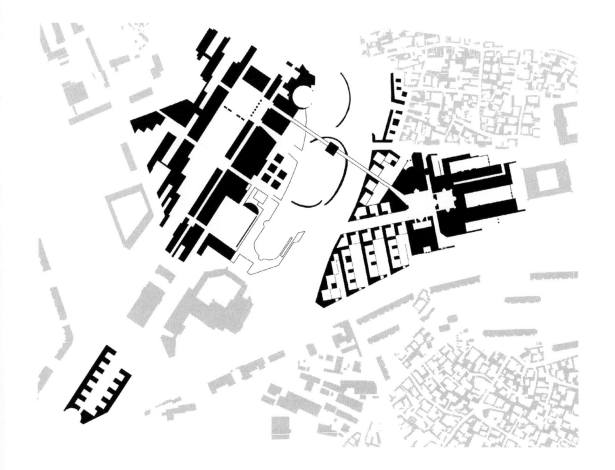

INTERMEZZO BY THE EDITORS

SK/JD: *Early on you wrote an article called, "Quality and Quantity, the Industrialization of Housing." The ideas there had been first formulated in Supports.*

JH: *Yes.*

SK/JD: *So, that essay was just an expansion, an elaboration of it. That was just before SAR 65 was published. What I'm really curious about is how you saw the industrial production of everyday objects: refrigerators, cars, parts for buildings. And you understood that your proposition was that only if the users could make decisions would the power of industrial production really come into full effect.*

JH: *Yes.*

SK/JD: *That's an amazing idea. Because now we see it in IKEA and other consumer-oriented items. But to imagine that in the building industry; well, I'm continually amazed at how that came up in your thinking. This is just for clarity, I'm not questioning per se, but I'm curious, why didn't you end up simply finding a way of continuing the traditions of those cities you admired? You know, they were self-built within a known fabric. Maybe you could tweak that idea and carry it forward. What led you to embrace industrialization of housing as part of what you called 'the natural relationship?'*

JH: *Well, the answer is that in those days, everybody talked about industrialization. What that meant was that you have the same floor plan repeated in a kind of conveyor belt system turned around. That was people's idea of industrialization, which I think was a stupid idea.*

SK/JD: *You were trying to reform industrialization or make it become something that would be useful or amendable rather than negative in the housing process.*

JH: *Yes; I became convinced that the way people talked about industrialization was only standardization. Had nothing to do with the potential of the industry. And so I wrote articles that tried to understand myself, what I was talking about.*

SK/JD: *Who else were you talking to at that time, and arguing with about these ideas? I am sure you were having exchanges with other people.*

JH: *Not really very much, no. When you know enough in our profession, when somebody has a crazy idea, you invite them to teach something or to give a lecture. That's what happens. The people listen to you. They think it's interesting because they've never heard of it. But they don't take it seriously; it's just a guy with an odd idea.*

SK/JD: *But you didn't give up.*

JH: *No, because if you read my stuff, I'm trying to understand myself what was going on. So, every article I wrote was an attempt to develop my own understanding.*

SK/JD: And you use writing in that way.

JH: Talking to myself.

SK/JD: Talking to yourself. . . . That's very interesting. This is one of my recurrent questions; I think I've read everything you've written.

JH: More than many have done.

SK/JD: And I'm fascinated by the consistency of the questions throughout 60 years.

JH: Okay.

THE OPEN BUILDING APPROACH

1964
QUALITY AND QUANTITY
The industrialization of housing

Editors' Note: *This essay was published in Forum XVIII, Nr. 2, 1964, when the author was the editor of the journal. The essay reiterates the proposal put forward in SUPPORTS: An Alternative to Mass Housing but focuses on the question of the role of the building industry per-se in realizing the concept of the separation of SUPPORT and INFILL.*

Owing to various events, public attention in Holland has more than ever before been focused on the housing problem. In 1962, the Economic Institute for the Building Industry published a building-note containing a great amount of data concerning building and housing. It appeared from this that, before that time, Holland had had a building policy without being possessed of the most elementary data. In the note, an attempt was made to determine what the dwelling requirements would be for the next decade. In doing so, it was assumed that a population increase was to be expected and that the average family would become smaller. To many, the extrapolation was a great surprise. The true arrears in housing with regard to the need proved to be much greater than was generally assumed and the capacity of the building industry was so slight and showed so little tendency towards a sound expansion that it took a great deal of optimism to expect an early end of the housing shortage.

At about the same time, the millionth postwar dwelling was finished and handed over to the occupants with the usual formalities. It seemed the right moment to look back on what had been achieved. This retrospective was disappointing. Not only too little had been built, but the quality of what had been build was bad. The desiderata as to the dwelling and the views on housing and dwelling had changed so rapidly that in too many cases the floor plan, the details, and the urban design situation of the dwelling of some ten years earlier made a hopelessly outdated impression. Of course, there were some favorable exceptions, but nobody could console himself with the thought that the only thing we had to do was to proceed with greater speed on the path thus far followed. Since 1945, not a single aspect of housing, neither the technical nor the architectural nor the financial and the administrative aspect had developed in a direction which held out any hope for truly new possibilities in the future. What made the retrospection most disheartening was indeed that it offered so few attractive prospects. Little else was offered than a reproduction in enormous numbers of what even now was hallmarked as inadequate.

Possibly as a reaction to all this, a new Minister for Housing and Building came into office. With great energy and equal self-reliance, he set himself to find a way out of the deadlock, with as his first and foremost object an increase in production. All this gave rise to a widespread feeling of discomfort and a suspicion that the whole trend in housing was rather towards lowering rather than raising the standard of the dwelling. This feeling of uneasiness was not allayed by the new drive for stepping up the rate of production by making use of all available means. The thought that combatting the housing shortage should imply that the endless rows of building blocks in the polders are to be multiplied in the shortest possible time is gradually becoming unbearable. Especially among architects, it is feared that in an atmosphere in which the thought of productivity is so predominant, there will be neither money nor interest for research to find out what the prerequisites are for a fundamental improvement in dwelling and housing conditions, and that, in the long run, the housing industry will be restrained rather than stimulated. These facts have made it clear to anyone, if it had not been clear before, that building in Holland is wanting in quantity and in quality. Everybody is now convinced that this time, we are faced with a problem which does not solve itself as time progresses and which is not merely caused by negligence, obstinacy or ignorance. This does not imply that the general prospects have become less hopeless. The fact that people have become aware of the emergency as such, has, alas, not yet given a clearer insight into the problem. Remedies, if ventured at all, get bogged down in mere formulas such as organization, normalization, industrialization, better financial control, planning, etc. But on the whole, the insight is lacking that because it is a problem embracing so many factors, the core of the problem must lie in a faulty interplay of all these factors or rather in a lack of interplay, which makes all work done ineffective.

This must be taken to mean that there is no will to coordinate, to cooperate, but that all attempts in that direction are fruitless. If this is so, it becomes necessary to give thought to what the laws are on which the complicated process which we call building is founded or should be founded.

A choice which is not necessary

I think that the most important aspect of our housing problem is to be found in the fact that we are faced with a deficiency in quality and quantity at the same time. We not only have too little but what we have is also not good enough. It would be a mistake to think that we are faced with two problems, each of which can be solved separately. The deficiency in quality and the deficiency in quantity are both aspects of the same problem. There is, therefore, no sense in urging the solution of one of the aspects. No. It is of the greatest importance that the correlation between these two deficiencies be investigated.

As long as this correlation is not clear, a minister must inevitably think that he can give priority to the quantitative aspect. Under these conditions, he may be able to step up production a little by makeshifts, probably at the cost of other aspects of the country's political economy, but his endeavor must of necessity result in the wrong kind of dwellings and consequently in establishing the wrong kind of machinery for producing housing.

On the other hand, a drive for the improvement of the quality of the dwellings to be built cannot be effective if it is done on the lines of a warning that in this materialistic world there are things of greater importance than mere number and quality. And the architects cannot be exonerated from this moralistic attitude. In the altercation about production and efficiency, the architect is inclined to champion 'more' and 'higher' so-called quality, though he is often at a loss to explain what may be understood by it.

Something thrown in free, in the manner of the 2-percent for the monumental arts can only yet further obscure the problem. It is indeed necessary to give attention to quality, because too many people only think in terms of quantity and only take quantitative measures. But if so, there is only one way of discussing it. From the start it must be clear that it is impossible to build a sufficient number of dwellings as long as the ones that are built are not considerably better. We have a housing shortage because we build the wrong kind of houses and because they are of the wrong kind, they are bad in all respects.

A subjective concept as quality of course requires some elucidation. But I shall refrain from trying to give a definition or even a description. Such an attempt seems rather fruitless and can only lead to discussions which are not to the point. If the correlation between quality and quantity is under discussion here, it will be wise to get an insight into this concept of quality by studying the above-mentioned relation, for we cannot we also learn to understand a person by studying his way of dealing with others? When we consider the relation between quality and quantity, the most striking thing we notice is that when people think of building, they evidently take the two concepts to be in contrast to each other. It is almost taken for granted that a better quality has an adverse influence on the quantity and the other way around. This almost proves the proposition that the building trades still live in the past. For formerly it was indeed necessary to choose between these two. In the past it was usually impossible to make large quantities of anything of good quality; quality was something unique and never found in things produced in large quantities.

That was before the advent of the machine, before the industrial productive process had been established by which human making is now governed to such a large extent. Wherever the influence of industrial production is noticeable, it is possible to step up quantity and quality simultaneously and to the same extent. Now it is possible to manufacture things of a very high technical perfection and a very high use-value in large quantities and in a very short time. In daily life the motorcar, the refrigerator, the washing machine and the wireless set are some of the but too well-known examples of this remarkable phenomenon. Is it not after all a fact that wherever industrial production is in full operation, we sooner have overproduction than shortage?

This is one more argument proving that there is no question of industrialization in housing. The method now adopted for mass-producing dwellings is based on a repetitive performance of certain actions on the building site and takes the necessity to choose between quality and quantity for granted. It is a way of producing which owes its existence and standards to the relations which existed before the industrial revolution. Mass-housing chooses quantity.

There is a sense in all the measures which go with mass-housing as long as the only aim is stepping up production on the building site. That is to say, if factory production is only thought of in the second place. The industrial methods of producing in factories are only applied in so far as they support a traditional method of building, producing a traditional form of dwelling. There is, however, no attempt whatever to create a method of building and a form of dwelling which fits in with the industrial machinery. This outdated method, therefore, automatically leads to the maxim that a choice must be made between much and good.

But outside his home, modern man is used to having great quantities of good things offered to him and he instinctively rebels against this choice. We may perhaps rightly say that this resistance is based on the dream of prosperity of our modern times. But this does not make this resistance less real, for if we do not succeed in giving our dwelling a form which is taken for granted, it will be wanting in quality even when the workmanship is perfect.

The thought in itself that a choice should be necessary between quality and quantity is outdated and static. It is based on the idea that somewhere there is some total which the sum of quality and quantity cannot exceed. Proceeding on the assumption that there is a certain amount of productivity with which we must content ourselves, we come to the conclusion that we have to choose between much and bad or little and good. But after all, the most important characteristic of the machine is that it can continually raise our productivity. Since a long-time production has not depended any more on the number of people available for labor, industrial production is expansive and bent on making ever more of what is good.

Seen in this light, the outcry that the builders should work with more efficiency to help us put an end to the housing shortage, sometimes even accompanied by an appeal to the patriotic feelings of these laborers, is a pitiable show of romanticism. In former days, there may have been some sense in pushing the laborers because their numbers and the pleasure with which they worked determined how much was produced. Now there is only sense in giving more thought to the actual potentialities of the industrial machinery.

The primary standard of quality

This leads directly to the overfamiliar fact too often stressed, that it is imperative that our housing should be industrialized. It evidently is the only way in which quantity and quality can be made to go hand-in-hand. But if this is the case, those who think in terms of quantity are evidently right, for they have been the first and most obstinate advocates of the industrialization of housing. That is indeed true, but thoughts which only go into the direction of quantity evidently erect at the same time an unsurmountable barrier to the realization of this so eagerly sought for industrialization. For the very reason that industrialization is primarily seen as a means to achieve a quantitative improvement in the housing situation, all endeavors in that direction fail. For if the only object is making a great number of dwellings it means that we aim at making the dwelling as we know it now, which is the form of dwelling of the mass-housing projects, along industrial lines, in factories.

But the form of dwelling we know now is a nonindustrial form in which all aspects of it are determined by this fact, and therefore totally unsuitable for industrial production. We are not concerned with the dwellings we know now, and which are subject to so much criticism. Why would we produce them along industrial lines? We expect much more of the industrial machinery. We expect it to give us a form of dwelling which is much richer and has more possibilities, a form of dwelling in short, which is of a much higher quality and we moreover expect that this form of dwelling shall be produced in abundance. Let us assume that a manufacturer puts himself to manufacturing 19th century coaches on the assembly belt. Let us assume that he succeeds in producing large quantities of handsome little coaches, complete with spoked wheels and brass lanterns. It can even be imagined that this factory should succeed in producing more coaches of better quality than could ever have been thought possible in the 19th century. Yet anybody would agree that as a means of transport the vehicle would be unacceptable. The means of transport belonging to the industrial machinery is the motorcar. The primary qualitative justification of the car is that it is inconceivable without the industrial machinery. Therefore, the car of average quality ranks higher than a perfect coach. One can disagree about the relative quality of the various car makers, but there is no doubt as to the fact that the first quality car is preeminently the means of transport of our contemporary industrial apparatus and that for that reason it is an integral part of our time.

The first thing we may demand of our present-day dwelling is that it is inconceivable without industrial machinery. This is a demand as to quality and not as to a certain technical constructional perfection. It is based on the assumption that the machinery of production which we have at our command implies a form of dwelling which is in keeping with it. This demand as to quality is the link between the form of dwelling and the way in which it is made. It is also the link between the way in which we live and the way in which we create our material environment. Every machinery of production creates its own product to satisfy a certain human want. This want may be basically unchanging, but the way in which it is satisfied depends entirely on the method of producing which is available.

Our sense of quality is also formed by the means which we have at our command. We may expect that in a given era with a given technical skill, under given economic conditions, the highest achievable is achieved. If this expectation is fulfilled, our sense of quality is, in principle, satisfied. This sense is linked with an intuitive feeling of what is the highest standard which can be reached. There is, therefore, no sense in measuring our material conditions by the standards of the past. Of course we have more than in the past. But with material wealth all around we can truly say there is a deficiency as long as more seems possible.

In this connection the real improvement in housing in the recent past is therefore irrelevant; we have failed to keep pace with the possibilities.

So, industrialization of housing is not only necessary because there are too few dwellings, but also because only the industrial machinery can produce the form of dwelling that is in agreement with our present-day sense of quality. This quality is of an entirely different order than the quality which can be ascertained by measuring and counting. This latter quality, the banal technical quality, can only be taken in consideration when a form of dwelling that is taken for granted is looked upon as of this era, is within everybody's reach. Therefore, there is no sense in listing dwelling requirements and desiderata, hoping to contribute something to the solution of this problem. Such a list could only be based on the present conditions and it is this very basis which is wanting in quality. It is not so difficult to keep apart the two kinds of quality which must be recognized. The one is decided by the way in which a certain procedure that is taken to be right is applied. The other depends on the crucial question whether the right procedure is followed. We could call them a secondary and a primary standard of quality. The primary standard of quality as formulated demands a form of dwelling that can only be realized by taking full advantage of the modern industrial machinery.

What is this form of dwelling? When can we say that full advantage is taken of the industrial machinery? How are we to find this form of dwelling? To ensure quality and quantity in our future housing, we must find the answer to these questions.

A matter of relation

This 'new form of dwelling' is, of course, not meant to be a 'form' or 'shape.' No object is meant by it. Today it is possible to find thousands of new 'forms.' If this were the problem, there would not be any problem. We must therefore not set ourselves to designing dwellings in order to find the new form of dwelling. But what must we do? The 'new form of dwelling' is used as a term to indicate that there must be a way of living and making which is sure to make man live in harmony with the time he lives in and with the environment which results from it. Of course, the danger of such a formulation is that the whole problem may be drowned in generalities which nobody can understand. Yet it must be stated that the primary standard of quality depends that man live in harmony with his environment and era. And this statement offers more hold than may appear at first sight. Did not it first become clear that the primary standard of quality demands that our housing can only be conceived as a product of the technical skill and the means of production of the time we live in? This only means that quality and quantity depend on the relation between dwelling (the product) and the way of making (the productive resources). So the standard of quality required is based on a relation between two quantities. There is also an indication of relations in the demand that man live in harmony with his material environment and his era, viz. the relations between man and his dwelling and man and his productive resources. So, our attention is drawn to the interaction of three quantities in all: **man, object and method**. If we succeed in bringing about the right kind of interrelation, the result will be the contemporary form of dwelling.

Seeking this form of dwelling means investigating into the interrelationship of these three quantities.

When in this three-polar relation one of the poles changes, the balance can only be restored by adapting the two poles to the new situation. If we have true industrialization, the introduction of the industrial production machinery into the method of building means a fundamental change in this method. But in order to keep the three poles – method, object and man harmoniously in equilibrium – the way of dwelling (man) and the shape of the dwelling (object) must also change.

Finding new contemporary methods for satisfying the unchanging daily wants of man is one of the most difficult tasks man has set himself. Perhaps because in trying to do so, we must always visualize forms and constructions (visualizing them in relation to man) which no one has ever yet beheld.

Yet this is the task continually set to us. Man is the only being on earth to whom the task has been set to find ever new forms in ever changing circumstances in order to safeguard his being and well-being. In order to stay alive, he must be constantly creative.

Man can adapt himself to each new situation because every time again he can change and rebalance the triangular relation under discussion. His primary sense of quality is a kind of safety-signal which gives warning when he fails in his task. This signal is in no way connected with property or comfort in the materialistic sense. The sense of primary quality is a standard of value telling us when we fail in our task to make today what is wanted today. That is the law underlying our housing and building problem. The engineer who does not think beyond reproducing a form of building which he happens to see about him, in large numbers, will never solve the problem.

He will get entangled in constructing traditional housing blocks, using ever bigger industrially produced units. Or, if he wants to be progressive, he cannot design anything but a dwelling which is manufactured on a conveyer belt like an enormous refrigerator. The architect who can only think in vague terms of 'more' and 'human' and 'better' and 'different' cannot solve the problem either. The only thing he does is plead for a dwelling which is only more expensive, or he loses himself in fantasies which are only interesting as material for publication. It is, therefore, not very surprising that the problem has not yet been solved.

This coherence between our sense of quality and the relations existing between man, his material environment and the way he gives shape to this environment also explains why technical skill, material prosperity or resources at our command are quite irrelevant to the essence of the primary standard of quality. It is not the magnitude of the quantities which matters but their position in the interrelationship with man. Seen in this light, there certainly have been higher dwelling-qualities in the past than we have now, even if we could not feel at home in these forms of dwelling if they were offered to us now. The recent interest in 'primitive' forms of dwelling from the past is an indication that we have a feeling that are the result of a well-balanced relation between man, material environment and method of production, the lack of which is so sorely felt in our own time. The primary standard of quality is better reflected in the wholeness and finish of the towns of the middle ages and in the settlements of the Dogon and the Pueblo Indians than in what we ourselves have built. If then it must be said, we can say that the pattern formed by the above-mentioned interrelation reflects the essence of human culture; for the very reason that this pattern of relations is the decisive factor, irrespective of the standard of knowledge, of resources and of technical skill.

Way of building and industrial product

If the primary standard of quality demands that the present-day industrial technique of producing is fully applied in housing, it does not imply that the dwelling of the form of dwelling must be industrially produced in all details. It would be over-simplifying the problem if we should say that, as quality and quantity go hand in hand in the industrial product, all we have to do is to put the dwelling on a line with any other industrial product. The dream of the 'machine a habiter,' sometimes interpreted in this sense, belongs irrevocably to the romantic past of our modern era. The 'only' prerequisite is that the new form of dwelling be inconceivable without the industrial production machinery. This raises the question as to what part the industrial production machinery must play in the attempt to house man as befits him. How does the modern industrial machinery of production fit in with the pattern formed by the relations of man, method and matter in our era?

Building is an essential and irreplaceable human activity for which mechanical factory-production cannot be substituted. What is 'built' can never be the final result of an industrial process. It is possible to think of the industrial product as being a component part or if desired an element in the building activity. As such there is no difference between it and the non-mechanical but factory-made brick. It is evident that the principle of using structural parts which are manufactured elsewhere as building stones is very old. As long as the manufacturing industry confines itself to manufacturing such parts for building purposes, we cannot speak of a new relation at all.

Building itself is always making a new environment, i.e. making at a given moment, in a given place, for a given situation. Place and environment always influence the decision as to what shape is to be given to what is built. For this reason, building is always a unique act, which can never be exactly repeated in another place at another time. In building, something is recorded in the same sense as something is recorded in writing.

It is not an absolute act, if such an act is possible, but an attempt at formulating, leaving a track, confirming our existence. Indeed, building is an irreplaceable human activity. No reflection on mechanical industry and production can be fruitful if this is not realized.

Let us on the other hand consider the industrial product which is not meant to be a building component but an independent finished article, finished and complete in itself, as we come across in so many forms. No greater contrast can be imagined than that between the built form and this industrial finished product.

This latter product is not bound to any particular spot; it has come off the conveyor belt and remains movable – it is movable property. It never betrays any direct marks of having been made by man, because by definition the accidental imprint of human hands is foreign to it, as it is always made by man by means of the machine. So as regards the methods of production, it is only indirectly related to man and therefore the industrial finished product can only in the most general way be called a symbol of human activity.

The built form and the industrially produced object also differ in their relations to time. The way in which an industrial product is used determines its life. The durability of the materials used, and the soundness of the construction employed are chosen to fit the time that the object is expected to be used. It is made to be replaced. This possibility of quick replacement, so typical of the industrial product, creates an entirely new relation between man and this product. It is the relation between man and the object; made by him, which largely determines what picture man has of the industrial product. The dream of the industrial machinery producing in abundance, putting on the market ever more goods which are all intended to enrich our daily life; a machinery moreover which permits us to consume the goods at whatever rate and in whatever quantities we like, nay, continually tries to entice us to use ever more and to consume ever faster, is the dream of modern man, living in an industrial abundance. In so far as this dream is true – and even perhaps to a large extend in so far as it is believed in, even if it is not true – the relation between man and his material environment is very special and entirely new. It is, moreover, very largely a relationship between man as an Individual and his Individual material environment. The industrial finished product by which the dream is best symbolized is the product designed for man as an individual. The automobile, the wireless set, the refrigerator, the television set, the washing machine are all products which appeal directly to the consumer. It is therefore understandable that many compare the dwelling itself, which is after all also produced for individual use, with these products.

But the built structure, as we know it, has its own relation to man. Even when something is built for a special person, to meet very individual requirements, it is an action which concerns the community. There is no getting away from the fact that building is always adding to the landscape made by man, to

Figure 1 There is no specialized craftsmanship – the individual man builds his own dwelling

Figure 2 The specialized craftsman works at collective projects only. Two different patterns of interrelation exist side-by-side

the communal environment. Therefore, the relation between building and time is always attuned to the community. Even if we should become so rich and so clever that we could replace our cities as quickly as we can replace our motorcars, we would not do so because the relation between man and the building is a different one. That which is built has a longer life span than man. It links the generations rather than belong to one single generation. What is built is a continuum. Every building activity is only adding to or altering the continuity. Building is essentially continuing to build on what is there; it is an activity in an endless chain of building activities, not a single link of which can be considered by itself. What is built is always a legacy handed down to posterity.

This legacy, however, is not handed down only to be preserved. In the face of all attempts of the Society for Preserving Ancient Monuments, we must state that altering and adding to what exists is inextricably linked up with building.

Altering and adding to what already exists are the means by which we become reconciled to what previous generations have handed down to us and by which the legacy becomes acceptable and valuable. This shows another difference with the finished industrial product, which cannot be altered, which can only be replaced. With the machine, an entirely new kind of thing has therefore come into man's environment. Before that time, everything, from the building to the smallest utensil, was man-made in the same sense. Everything was of the same order. The machine has put an end to this. Building is still the same: a form of making which requires man to act from place to place and from moment to moment. By its side, the industrial product has appeared, or rather, by its side there is now the manufacturing machine, the industrial machinery which, once put in motion without any apparent effort, turns out an endless flow of products.

When we contrast the industrial product with the building, we can only take the finished product into consideration, the product as offered to man in his everyday life. Of course, our industrial machinery manufacturers innumerable objects which serve as semi-manufactured articles with which other articles are in their turn manufactured. Building is largely based on judiciously assembling such industrial manufactures. Yet the result of this work is unmistakably 'built' and its relation to man is quite different from that of the independent finished industrial product.

This contrast is of the same order as that between the motorcar and the traffic bridge or road. There is indeed a great contrast between these two kinds of products. When we try to specify it, we discover that this contrast can be recognized in the entirely different relations which exist between man and these two kinds of products.

If therefore an attempt should be made to classify the things surrounding us by the standard of the relation between these things and man, at least two classes could be distinguished: the class of what has been built and the class of what has been industrially manufactured. Everything belonging to the first is also adapted to the community; the things belonging to the second class are most effective when they are brought to bear on the individual person. The first kind of things spans more than a generation; the second never spans more than but a part of one man's life. The one is continually altered and added on to; the second can be discarded and replaced. The one is of relatively simple construction; the other is a complicated and relatively fragile piece of work. The one forms man's environment, is man's environment; the other constitutes the things with which man surrounds himself, which he chooses to have about him.

The dwelling: a dual unity

Man will always build, as he has always built, making cities, streets, squares, churches, halls, stations, shops and also his dwellings. But this does not imply that what we do, for our housing today, after the advent of the machine, must exclusively be the result of the human activities as described here. Studying our relation to our dwellings we recognize more and more elements in that relation which are characteristic of the relation between man and the finished industrial product. All the modern appliances and conveniences which can be found in a dwelling belong, in our opinion exclusively to the sphere of industrial product. Kitchen, bath, heating, ventilation and numerous items like doors, windows, lighting, ornament, and finishing materials area so evidently products of the industrial machinery that we have the feeling that a large part of the dwelling must be judged by the same standard as any other industrially produced article of utility which we have at our command in daily life. It is by that standard that we make our demands, and we demand the replaceability, the finish and above all the free choice in buying which is offered by the industrial article. Another important factor is that the entire interior of the dwelling, the arrangement of the rooms and their finish, are so much part of our individual life that today it seems unacceptable to us that all this should not adapt itself in appearance and life span to the rhythm of our lives in the same way as so many other industrial products all about us adapt themselves to us and enrich our lives.

So, there are many things in our modern dwelling which could be made to have the same relation to man as the finished industrial product, so much so even that people are sometimes inclined to feel the superficial wish that it be possible to manufacture dwellings in the same way as motorcars. On the other hand, little observation is required to come to the conclusion that our entire method of building is adjusted to the fact that the dwelling is exclusively seen as something built and is offered to the occupant as a product of building. In other words, all our work aims at making the relation between man and his dwelling quite similar to that existing between man and building. The dwelling is still in all respects a building. This has not yet been changed by any industrial machinery. Moreover, because of the ever-increasing number of semi-manufacturers used in the dwelling, it has become an increasingly more complicated building. If we only think of all the ducts and conduits for gas, electricity, water, heating and all of the industrially manufactured articles like doors and windows and finishing materials which are carried to the building site in bits and pieces, there to be integrated in the indivisible whole of the dwelling as a product of building, we shall no longer be surprised about that fact that that work is not very productive.

To this must be added another important factor. Today's dwelling in all its complexity is offered to the people as something built. The relation man-building as mentioned earlier has therefore been declared to be the only one possible for the relation between man and his dwelling. But the rigidity and uniformity in housing, and the complexity of the structural building today render it impossible for the individual to make structural or other alterations in his dwelling. In the past, change in the relation building-individual was the chief means by which the individual could reconcile himself to the building left to him by previous generations. We hardly have the possibility anymore of keeping the man-product relation harmonious in spite of changing times, while, on the other hand, the present-day rapid evolution of usage and custom convinces us of the necessity that this possibility of adapting the material environment to the individual be greater than ever.

Both because the people persist in seeing the dwelling purely as a built structure, and because at the same time building becomes more and more complicated, considerable violence has been done to the relation between man and dwelling. Does not everybody know that as regards housing, the individual is absolutely helpless? It is clearly a matter of a strained or severed relation.

The primary quality has by no means come up to its standard yet. But is it so strange to see the dwelling as something built? It cannot be denied that the dwelling has always been a structure that was built. We may even say that the concept of building is derived from the making of dwellings. Before the development of the industrial machinery of production it would, moreover, have been difficult to imagine the dwelling to be anything but a built structure. If the dwelling may not be a built structure and it can neither by an industrial product like the motorcar, what strange and ambiguous thing must it then become?

Yet, in terms of relations, the dwelling has always been characterized by some sort of dualism. The dwelling has always been the everyday environment of the individual and has always been meant for individual use, but on the other hand it has always been part of the environment, too, a cell in the permanent tissue of the city. The dwelling was turned inward towards the individual and outwards toward the community. In this way, it partook in the two rhythms, the life rhythm of the individual and that of the community, of the home and the city. It was adapted to the fashion and taste of the living generation, but being part of the built environment, it bridged the gap between past and future.

The dwelling has always been present in two worlds. It marked the boundary between these two worlds or rather was a margin between them, a playground in which the world of the individual and that of the community built up a relationship.

Two relations become independent

So, the two relations we observed, that between industrial products and the individual and that between building and community, have in principle always been present in the relationship between on the one hand the dwelling and the individual and on the other hand the dwelling and the community.

The relation between the individual and the finished industrial article, which has evolved in our modern times, is so to say a relation – which has already existed in the relationship individual-dwelling – become independent. The built structure, now standing over against it, has therefore become the other aspect of the dwelling, become independent. In so far as the dwelling is part of the total built environment of man; in so far too as the individual meets the community in or via his dwelling and joins in the communal life; in so far as the dwelling is still a built structure, also for the individual. The development of the industrial product machinery has made it possible for relations between man and matter which have always existed to make themselves more manifest. But

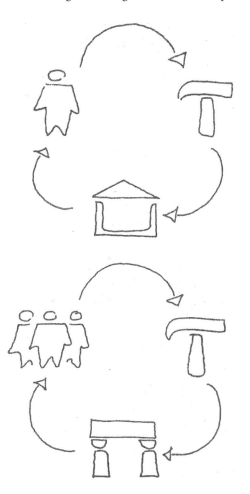

Figure 3 The craftsman works also for the individual. There are still two different patterns of interrelation

if we wish to profit from this, we shall have to make the relations between the individual and the industrial product and between man and building also grow as independent as possible. But if this is the case there is no sense in trying to look on the dwelling as merely a built structure, neither is there any sense in declaring it to be an industrial product.

The dwelling as a single, non-ambiguous object which can be produced as a self-contained form has lost its sense with the development of the methods of industrial production. The main problem is verbal. We always say 'to build houses' which automatically suggests that it is a matter of making 'things.' Things which are self-contained and recognizable, and which can be offered quite finished to the consumer. But if we would not speak of building dwellings but of 'producing for the sake of man's housing' it would make it a little easier to say that today there is a dual production for housing: industrial production and building activity. It would then be easier to understand that the product of the building activity has its own relation to man, entirely different from that of the finished industrial product and that thereto the distinct relations determine in what way industrial product and built product must be made to fit in with each other.

So, in our housing it is a matter of how to combine judiciously that which we build and that which we produce industrially. If formulated this way it may become clear that the two kinds of products both remain independent. For the primary standard of quality demands that the relations of man, method and object be as harmonious as possible. Now there are two distinct methods of production and it is our task to try and make both methods establish their own relations to man and to the products. How that will have to be done is still to be found out, but it is clear, however, that in itself it is not a sound principle to incorporate ever more industrially produced parts in a built structure. In so far as these parts and fixtures are in any way connected with the relation between the individual and his dwelling, it is wise to try and make the industrial product as self-contained as possible. It goes without saying that building, regardless of what is built, will always benefit by the use of industrially manufactured products, apparatuses, and building units. But this does not imply that everything our factories can produce to enhance man's comfort and to improve man's environment must be used as a building unit and incorporated in the structure. Seen in this light, we can say that we must endeavor to make the industrial product self-contained, which at the same time implies making the part that is built self-contained. Thinking further on these lines we must indeed characterize the contemporary dwelling as an arrangement of industrial products in a built environment. How will it in actual building be possible to make what is built and what is industrially manufactured independent of each other?

Making what is built independent

In principle, the practical consequences of this theory are not new. We must begin by making structures, indeed completely built structures in which it will be possible to make dwellings by combining and joining industrial products. This principle has come to be recognized by many. Some time ago I myself stated that divorcing the supporting structure from what constitutes the dwelling proper is essential to the construction of a dwelling which befits man and is therefore of an acceptable quality. For the supporting structure I chose the name SUPPORT. By definition a SUPPORT is a structure in which one or more dwellings can quite independently be built, rebuilt and demolished. The independence of the dwelling was necessary because only thus the relation between man and his dwelling could be made to function naturally. That 'natural relation' between man and his dwelling is necessary because it is an essential component of any housing process. The independent dwelling which we desire can of course be fitted in various ways in the support structure. It can also be made of brickwork. But it will be clear that the becoming independent of the industrial product as discussed runs fairly parallel with it, and for this reason too the SUPPORT becomes the built structure made independent. I am still convinced that making the dwelling independent is the main thing we must do as to our housing. But it now becomes clear that thinking in terms of available means is synonymous with making the dwelling independent. Building SUPPORTS is no luxury but a necessity, seen from the productive angle as well as from the point of view of man. For that matter, the primary standard of quality does not differentiate between the two but shows that the relations are always basically the same.

The structure that may be called a SUPPORT needed a name of its own because, after all, it is a structure with its own typical function. This structure is a self-contained and finished object and therefore needs a name of its own to distinguish it from other kinds of structures. Consequently, a SUPPORT is a different thing from a skeleton of a (tenement) building because a skeleton is always an integral part of a bigger thing and can only be measured by the standard of that object. One can imagine some builder building SUPPORTS without needing to bother about what later will be added in or onto them by others, just as some roadbuilder can build roads. It is also possible to imagine an urban designer designing SUPPORTS in the same way as now he lays out streets, squares and canals. On the other hand, it is hardly possible to imagine someone only building skeletons. The SUPPORT is the built environment made to be a self-contained unit, in which it is possible to arrange an industrial product. In order, however, to attain this independence, it will be profitable to speak of constructing skeleton-like structures. For if today, at this moment, under the present circumstances, we wish to achieve a differentiation between the built structure and the industrially manufactured product, the most practical thing we can do is begin with the skeleton.

If in today's housing we could bring ourselves to make the skeletons of the housing projects into self-contained units, if in other words we could bring ourselves to building supporting structures fit for universal use, so, standard skeletons which are independent of floor plans for dwellings, the first, all important step towards the development of a truly contemporary dwelling would have been taken. In the first place, it would then be possible to make the dwelling independent. Without using new techniques and industrial products yet, it would become possible to build dwellings which ben be built, rebuilt and demolished independently. The relations of man, method and dwelling would then at least be restored in principle.

This relation can then be improved by increasingly using self-contained, industrially produced parts for the making of dwellings, and by making the standard skeletons grow more and more into complete and independent support-structures. All this can come about gradually; it is a matter of evolution. But in order to set this evolution in motion, it is necessary that the first fundamental step be taken. That step must be giving independence to the minimum that can be made independent in a built structure, and that is the skeleton. We can begin doing so now. Suh a standard skeleton gives considerable scope to the floor plan of the dwelling which is made in it. For this reason it is possible to apply all now existing and known methods of building in (and against the outside of) the skeleton. The skeleton itself can easily be constructed in large numbers. No new calculations and detail drawings are required for each separate skeleton before it can be constructed. Measurements and the production of parts and formwork can be normalized. The initiative for building and carrying out the plans can

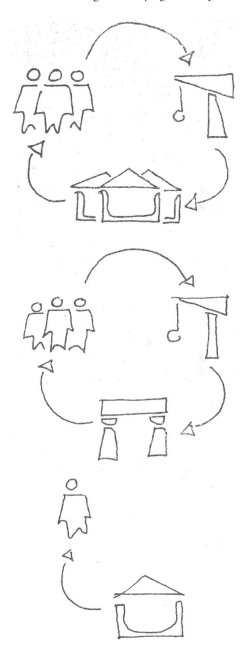

Figure 4 An organized building trade becomes more and more unable to serve the individual directly. In reality, only one pattern of interrelation remains, in which there is no place for the individual.

be taken by any by group, or person, in any way concerned with housing. The authorities, architects, urban designers and manufacturers will all benefit by it if a beginning should be made with the building of standard skeletons.

The architect gets something on which he can base his plans and which at the same time gives him free scope for his architectural and urban design activities. The standard skeleton releases him simultaneously from the necessity of starting, for each project again, with designing the basic structure, of making the detailed drawings of it, and of submitting the plans for approval to ever so many official bodies. With the standard skeleton he sets out from a generally accepted basis. The authorities get in the standard skeletons a means of setting new standards which offer more scope for future development of the notorious labor-saving methods of building. Because the realization of standard skeletons will automatically stimulate the industrial production (as it will be shown later) it will be the foundation for truly effective saving of labor in the building industry and on the building site. The skeleton is the basis for normalization and standardization. Not the normalization of dwellings nor the standardization of floor plans, but normalization of control, financing standards and organization. The urban designer gets in the standard skeletons a fundamental datum on which he can base his work. By reckoning with the standards and the requirements as to the construction of the standard skeletons, it becomes possible for him to decide the urban structure without trespassing on the field of the architect. The standard skeleton is automatically the meeting place for the activities of the architect and the urban designer.

And last of all, the manufacturing industry profits most from the standardization of skeletons. It can easily be understood that, once normalized structures are built, it becomes attractive for the manufacturing industry to build elements which can be used in and on these structures. For the manufacturer it is important that he can produce without knowing beforehand what exactly will be the architectural form that is built with his product. He will always try to find a universally applicable product. The introduction of standard skeletons will enable him to supply much larger numbers of such products. It will then even be possible to compose complete dwellings out of such industrially manufactured products in the skeletons.

Making the industrial product independent

In order, however, to learn how a skeleton can become a SUPPORT, and what the main difference is between these two structures, we must go back to the industrial product and first put the question of what exactly must be understood by making the industrial product independent; in asking how far this idea can be made concrete. A beginning in this direction has already been made in the various attempts which have been made during the last few years, to construct units in which the parts of a dwelling which require much labor – bath, toilet and kitchen equipment – are combined in one aggregate to be completely finished in the factory and afterwards put, as it is, in the dwelling. The bath-cell produced as a complete unit is well known.

Such units have never been used on a large scale in our present-day housing projects, in which they were foreign elements. They were too far removed from building-stone and although from the point of view of industrialization they seemed to be very rational and attractive, there was no room for them in the existing way of building. They were too much self-contained. But this is the very reason why they give us an indication of what may be possible, as placing self-contained industrially produced units in a built structure is just what we aim at. The units will then make up that part of the dwelling which is complicated and requires much labor and time when constructed on the building site, where the conditions are unfavorable. As cost of labor rises it is therefore very sensible to remove such activities from the sphere of building to the sphere of industrial production. But such a change can only be successful if it is made as part of a well-defined program for industrial production, in order that an uninterrupted production and a universal applicability may be ensured. In the method of building followed up to now, there is no room for such a program. The making of standard structures, however, would supply the framework it so badly needs.

So, from the point of view of industrial production, it would be sensible to make all those things in the dwelling which are complicated and require a lot of time and technical machine-work, into units or cells, which are offered for sale like any product. And making a built structure that is not subdivided for a wide range of uses would make the use of such products possible. But thinking on these lines we proceed from the assumption that the dwelling (which here is the dwelling to be

Quality and quantity

constructed in the skeleton or structure) can be taken apart in units which can be manufactured separately.

That of course is the consequence of making the industrially manufactured product self-contained, but it is worthwhile to investigate in what way this taking apart can be done. In what parts can a dwelling be divided? Setting out from the premise that in a Support a dwelling must be made by combining and joining industrially manufactured objects, we find ourselves confronted with the question what these objects may be. This question makes us think almost automatically of wall-elements. Since Corbusier found out the difference between supporting skeleton and the wall to be placed free and non-supporting in the skeleton, constructors and architects have been busy designing industrially manufactured wall-units, out of which walls can be made at will in a given space. In office buildings, such movable walls have already been generally accepted. It is Konrad Wachsmann who has most thoroughly investigated this idea with regard to building housing.

Yet it may be asked if a wall unit is the most appropriate element for assembling a dwelling in the built structure. I have the feeling that accepting this premise shows a kind of automatism in thinking. Of course, throughout all ages, dwellings have always been made by making walls. Making an enclosed space has always been identical with making walls and therefore it is not surprising that, when we are concerned with applying the industrial way of producing, our first thought is for making industrially manufactured wall-elements. But this thought has its drawbacks.

In the first place, there are numerous technical drawbacks, because a wall-element which is fit for universal use tends to become extremely complicated apart from the fact that it is difficult to get sufficient sound insulation, and last but not least, because the principle of separate elements implies seams in the walls. There are technical objections and we may assume that in our present age they can be eliminated. But there is more. A wall belongs by nature to two separate spaces. This implies that by erecting a wall or wall-element, two spaces are determined. Either the finish must be the same in the two spaces or the finishes must be different on the two sides of the wall. If we need the latter kind of wall, we cannot speak of a universal wall element; there will soon be a large number of kinds. Moreover, making a dwelling or a space for living is more than just making walls. Apart from ceilings and floors which may also differ from room to room, there are also technical fittings for lighting, electric power, water supply, and drainage. All these must be laid on separately and if necessary, fastened to or on these walls, ceilings and floors. And it is the construction of these wires, pipes and conduits that requires so much laborious and costly work on the building site. It is not possible to think out a universal wall element with all these things worked into it. Wall elements which can be interjoined offer only a partial solution of the problem for the very reason that a dwelling is made up of much more than only walls.

So, with a view to this, it should be realized that a dwelling is not made up of walls; a dwelling is made up of enclosed spaces. Such a space is an independent part of a dwelling. It is, moreover, an organic part of it. In its finish and details, and in the way the services such as electricity, water heating and ventilation are grouped, it is a self-contained unit. A division of spaces for living purposes is the only division which is feasible without at the same time demolishing the dwelling.

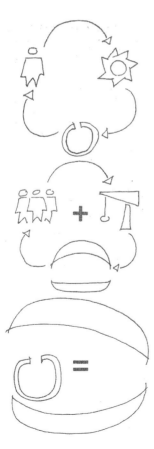

Figure 5 True industrialization gives again two new patterns of inter-relation. Together they ensure the individual housing of modern man

Would it, therefore, not be sensible to try and produce completely finished self-contained rooms if we aim at industrially producing independent parts of a dwelling? Why do we not make room-cells completely finished with all conduits, wiring, finished floors, ceilings and walls, which can be placed in a built environment in more or less the same way as a caravan is placed in a garage? In this way a dwelling could be made by combining a number of such units in a built structure.

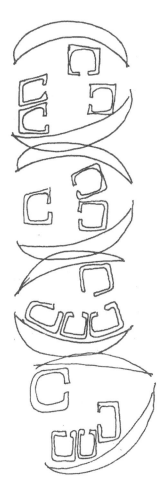

Figure 6 A built environment offering space for variable arrangements of industrially produced cells.

Such units contain the greater part of what requires much labor and time. They can be produced quite independently and can be industrially manufactured, which means that the first requisite for applying the industrial machinery efficiently has been fulfilled. Moreover, in the dwelling as a while, they are logical self-contained units.

Between two poles

Yet the production of "cells" forming self-contained finished compartments out of which a dwelling can be built-up need not imply that the dwelling must consist entirely out of a combination of such cells. For apart from these industrial products, there are the built structures. These give the industrial product a built environment. This environment can vary from a naked skeleton to an entirely closed architecturally finished space, with all the variants which can be imagined between these two. So this built environment can indeed take the part of the garage mentioned earlier, while it would not be wise to fill this built space entirely up again with industrially produced rooms. This is a field in which the merits of various possibilities can be balanced against each other. After having investigated the principle of making the built structure and the industrial product independent of each other we can give our attention to the composition of the dwellings themselves. It was stated that these would be made up by judiciously combining the industrial products in a built environment. A general rule as to how this is to be done cannot be given but we can give some indications which will always be of value in the future, when the industrially produced room-units must be 'placed judiciously' in the built structures. So, it is possible to imagine that after the industrially manufactured cells have been placed, some room in the built environment is left. And this is very desirable for if all rooms in a dwelling would have to be made like boxes, it would considerably limit the possibilities. We cannot get away from the fact that, with a view to the manufacturing and transport possibilities, the measurements of such boxes would be subject to certain restrictions. Indeed, our manufacturing industry is not interested in manufacturing transportable rooms. Its interest is directed towards what is complicated and requires a great deal of time if manufactured on the site. So, the units which are to be industrially made cannot be too voluminous but must at the same time contain as many of the technically complicated fittings of the dwelling which it to be built as possible. This is an indication that it would be sensible to manufacture those rooms of the dwelling which have a clearly defined typical function and which inherently require a great deal of labor, as factory-produced units which are to be placed in the built environment. In this respect we can think

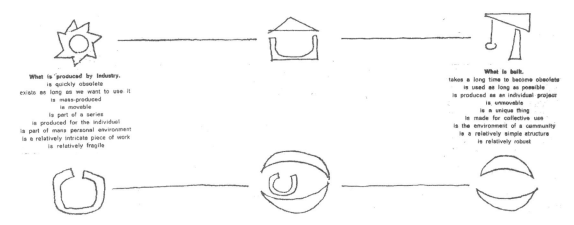

Figure 7 What is produced by industry; what is built

of toilet and bathrooms, kitchens, cubicles for technical equipment, storerooms and also smaller bedrooms and studies or workrooms. If these last three are made as industrial products they can be given a better sound insulation than would otherwise be possible.

By the side of these spaces we have the living space proper, which, because it is indeed space to live in, has no specific function but whose primary requirement is that it be spacious and capable of all uses which may be required by our way of living. This space will almost automatically come into being when the built cells are placed in the built environment, when the caravan has been put in the garage. In this way, the contemporary dwelling can be visualized as a built environment in which are placed a number of cells which are industrially produced to meet specific functional requirements. Pondering on this setup, some characteristic qualities and possibilities present themselves.

In order to prevent this talking of forms and rooms, without illustrating them in any way, from becoming complicated, it may be advisable to stick to the figure of the caravan in the garage. It proved to be desirable to place the caravan in the garage in such a way that only part of the floor space was occupied by it, because the remaining space could be living space proper. Let us assume that such a caravan contains a kitchen, bathroom and toilet and some smaller bedrooms. These cells are connected with the main conduits for electricity, heating water and drainage which are present in the built environment or are laid on in it. The remaining living space still offers all sorts of possibilities. It may, for instance, be divided into two living rooms by means of wall elements (which here,

because it is indeed only a matter of partitioning, are in their right place) or by means of a wall of cupboards. The space can likewise be divided into living room and a large bedroom, as is already done to some extent in present day housing. It is also possible to visualize the remaining space of the garage as becoming open-air space. It would also be possible not to use a kitchen-cell but to place a kitchen unit, made up of a sink with everything pertaining to it, in the large living space. This unit too could be a self-contained industrial product. Of course, the remaining living space can be finished in all sorts of ways, from traditional, plastered walls and boarded floors and ceilings to the most complicated mounted panels.

The theme of a built environment in which space-cells are placed and which for the rest is completed by adding whatever is offered by the entire range of known finishing materials, fronts, walls, cupboards, etc. allows endless variation, both in the shape of the built environment and in the choice of cells.

It would not be so difficult to design a series of room-cells which can be manufactured in a factory. For instance, we start from eight variously sized cells, each of which is capable of six kinds of uses (for instance, kitchen, bathroom with toilet, or shower room with toilet, bedroom, storeroom, study or workroom, and entrance hall with cloakroom or toilet and storage) we get a choice of forty-eight cells. If, moreover each cell of a certain size meant for a certain use has three possibilities as to arrangement, we get a choice of one hundred and forty-four cells. The industry producing such a series could have eight basic frameworks which could be covered and finished with parts of standardized measurements in such a way that the one hundred and forty-four units would in their turn be built up out of a certain number of parts – more or less in the style of a box of bricks with which various objects can be made. The frames could be fully finished on a production line. The cells made in this way could be supplied complete with lighting fixtures, built-in cupboards, all conduits, finished floors, walls and ceilings, sanitary conveniences and whatever else could be thought of.

Because the cells contain the greater part of what makes the construction of housing costly and slow, the built environment, with or without the fronts, finishes and other furnishings would be relatively cheap. This would result in a new relation between cost and space. In the building industry it is customary to base the cost of a building on the price per cubic meter. Although the relation is of course never a direct one it is customary to stick to the rule that the dwelling becomes more expensive as it grows bigger. In the abovementioned system this relation would become a bit different. It would be possible to adopt a certain basic cost-price per cubic meter of the built environment. The price of the dwelling which would come over and above it would depend entirely on the kind, quality and number of cells placed in it. In this way it would be possible for dwellings of the same size to show considerable differences in price. The most important thing would be that the consumer himself, by his choice of cells, could largely influence the price. This would offer a better possibility for everybody, rich or poor, to get the same space. Such a possibility is quite in keeping with the relations in our society. After all, as to quality in housing, it cannot be denied that the most important and highest quality a dwelling an have is to be found in its space. We must build big, cheap spaces which are to be filled by the occupants, according to their own needs and tastes, with industrial products which can be unrestrictedly bought. By giving the manufacturing industries the possibility of making self-contained 'dwelling products' it becomes possible to restrict the building activities to merely supplying architectural spaces of liberal dimensions.

It is possible for a young couple to begin with having this space finished and with placing a single bath and toilet cell in it, with a simple kitchen unit in the living space. For the rest, they may divide this space by means of cupboard walls. As the family grows, and, as we may assume, the income becomes higher, or something has been laid by, more cells can be added. The single illustration of a relation which can be easily pictured between the individual and his dwelling shows what can be achieved if the relation between man and industrial product on the one hand, and the relation between man and the built environment on the other hand, are separately studied and stimulated. It need hardly be said that in this way quality and quantity can go hand in hand. With such a general and great demand it will not be difficult for industrial factories to build up a manufacturing machinery which can produce in enormous varieties as to arrangement and finish as many cells as can be sold, The work required for constructing the built environment in which the cells can be placed is simple and can be conveniently organized. Full use can be made of every conceivable means for normalization and standardization. Prefabricated parts can be used. The measurements and constructions of the spaces, or if desired, structures can be completely standardized and normalized. In spite of this standardization the variations in ground plan and style of living in the eventual dwellings are in no way restricted. The building activities on the site can be considerably speeded up.

The time relation between man and his material environment is also clarified. The industrial product, and with it the arrangement of the dwelling, will be used as long as it fills an everyday requirement. The replacement depends on the relation of individual method and product. The built environment will be used as long as the community wishes to do so. It can be altered. It can be partly demolished, and something can be added to it. The entire continuous process of the evolution of mans' built- environment can be accomplished in harmony with the relation community-method-product. The life rhythm of the community and that of the individual are given their full value in their relation to the material environment.

If the above described dwelling is defined by saying that the dwelling is an arrangement of industrially produced units in a built environment, I think the definition states very accurately what the essence of the two relations is. But it is only fair to state that this arrangement is no down a form of building, too. Taking the word in that sense, we could say that, all considered, this dwelling too is entirely built. Of course, that is so. After all building is making a material environment. To prevent confusion, it is therefore wise to give a name of its own to 'the built environment' as we called it earlier, but which strictly speaking is an environment built by the community. Because of the advent of the machine and the growing of two different relations between man and matter, we now have two different kinds of buildings.

The term SUPPORT is justified because it indicates the one way of building. In it the dwelling is built, and the industrial production enables us to speak of arranging industrial products. This las form of building may, in a strictly architectural sense, not be building at all but from the point of view of man who in this way creates his own environment, it is building in its purest form. What restricts the term SUPPORT is that it suggests living above ground level. The concept, however, of an industrial arrangement in a built environment can be applied to all kinds of dwellings. It refers to a method of making. Therefore, also with respect to a detached house, it is conceivable and sensible to differentiate between spade built (the garage mentioned earlier) and what can be placed in it by choosing industrial products. One of the chief stumbling blocks in developing new concepts which must become common property is the finding of new terms and names. When here we use the term 'room-cells' and 'supports,' they denote the objects representing the two poles of the trend of thought evolved above. They correspond with the differences between the relation individual-individual environment and the relation community-material environment, with the difference between industrial product and building activity. It is a matter of two poles and therefore these concepts derive their main importance from the fact that they cause a whole field of forces to lie between them, which allows of a great variety of possibilities. It is what happens between the poles which is of the greatest importance. For there the potentialities and variations are endless. The main purpose the two poles serve is to define the field within which we must work. The two poles must be named to find between them a common field of action for all who are concerned in the housing of man. I am convinced that if this is our approach to our housing problem, we shall sooner come to a balanced combination of built structures and industrially produced dwelling than is now held possible.

Seen in this light the space which is left in the built environment after the cells have been placed in it, and which proved to be the living space proper, represents so-to-say the field between the two poles. In it everything happens, also from the point of view of planning, everything is still possible in it. It is the nucleus of the whole system. What we cannot define but get to know by defining other things is always what is most important. In this margin, which itself is not an industrial product, nor an independently built environment, nor a cell, nor a SUPPORT, lies the true quality of the above described way of dwelling and building. By the same token as the space within the vase is the most important thing, as the dwelling is not composed of walls but of rooms, we are not concerned with the industrial product or the built structure but with the playground which is formed between the two. The completely built dwelling is but too familiar to us; it has proved itself to be deficient in quality and quantity. The dwelling which is in all respects an industrial product reduces the environment to an article of utility such as a motorcar or refrigerator. Only by combining what is built with what is industrially produced, keeping the full identity of both intact, we get that which is in between, which cannot be made as a thing and which can still become whatever is required and which is therefore fully habitable. Returning to our starting point it becomes clear that no name can be given to true quality but that it can be found between things which can be named. Quality is found in a relation of two or more definable things and is in itself only definable because of the relation.

1992
AN EFFICIENT RESPONSE TO USERS' PREFERENCES

Editors' Note: *This paper was presented at the Housing Design 2000 Conference, Singapore, in September 1992. It discusses the author's experience with the development of an Infill System and a business venture that produced more than 100 infill packages between 1990 and 1995, before closing. The Infill system mentioned – MATURA – was technically far ahead of its time yet failed to secure continuing financial investments needed to bring it to market as what is essentially a new business model. This is an important lesson: no matter how logical a technical innovation is, if there is not a demand for it in the 'industrial ecology' or means of doing business, it will be unlikely to take root, especially without the sustained investments available in other industries such as computers, building products or in the automobile industry, and completely lacking in the construction industry. A Matura brochure asked these questions: 1. Who will step up to help create this new market? 2. Will entirely new kinds of companies be formed to provide integrated design, manufacturing, logistics and installation of factory-produced fit-out systems? 3. Can existing companies add this to their current market lines for market creation, not market sharing. It should be noted that in 2016, a company (www.Henenghome.com) in PR China introduced into the Chinese market an Infill System that answered these questions to the positive. It is now a profitable enterprise, saving money for the clients, reducing waste and delivering faster and at higher quality than the traditional way of working. Competitive companies are entering the market there.*

Introduction

In this paper I present a new way of outfitting residential units by means of a so called 'infill system.' An infill system allows the rapid installation of partitioning walls, central heating, kitchen and bathroom equipment with all piping and wiring related to such equipment. Installation is done per unit according to the floor plan chosen for that particular unit.

The infill system approach is not only of interest because it offers an individualized approach to large residential construction projects involving apartment buildings and townhouses. Its major attraction is that it is also economically competitive compared to existing modes of outfitting dwelling units. It therefore constitutes a breakthrough combining increased adaptability with more efficient production.

I will first discuss how infill systems offer an efficient and user-friendly approach to the renovation of existing housing stock. Next I will discuss briefly about the commercial advantages of infill systems in new residential construction. I will then say more about the specific infill system from which I derive the information given in this paper with the development of which I am personally involved. Finally, I will also briefly sketch the development of this new approach as it evolved in the past twenty years in the Netherlands.

An efficient response to users' preferences

Renovation, social dimensions of the infill approach

The following scenarios are what actually happened recently with two units installed by the way of a pilot project in the Netherlands. They illustrate how the use of infill systems can change the traditional ways of dealing with the problem of renovation of existing residential property in large projects.

First scenario

A unit in a public housing estate is vacated by users who move to another town. The housing authority in charge of the estate contacts new users from a waiting list. They are informed that the authority wishes to renovate the unit before they move in.

The prospective users, a young couple who both work, are given a number of alternative floor plans for their unit as worked out by an architect commissioned by the authority. They meet with the architect. As a result, they decide that a variation on one of the initial alternatives answers their needs (Figure 2).

The new floorplan is very different from that of the unit which is now vacant. The original apartment (Figure 1.1) was designed in the early 1960's for a family with two to four children. It had three bedrooms, a very small bathroom with only a sink and no shower or bath, and a narrow kitchen. There was no central heating. All rooms were around a small hallway. The new apartment (Figure 3.1) has a single large bedroom with an adjacent bathroom with shower and laundry machine. The kitchen is in a new location in open relation to the living room. There is also a small guest room.

The new floorplan is approved by the housing authority and new monthly rent is agreed upon. The authority sends the floorplan to a company that specializes in installing infill systems for residential construction and requests a price. Agreement is quickly reached because this job is part of an ongoing contract between housing authority and infill systems company for the renovation of the entire housing estate over a period of time. As part of the same overall contract a small local contractor is called in to clear the existing apartment and prepare it for new infill, a job that takes about a week.

Beginning the second week a container is delivered in front of the apartment building. A small conveyor of the type as is also used by furniture movers is installed to hoist parts from the container towards the unit's balcony on the fourth floor.

A crew of three people now installs the infill system. Within ten workdays they deliver the finished apartment to the users. The next few days the users have curtains and floor covering of their choice

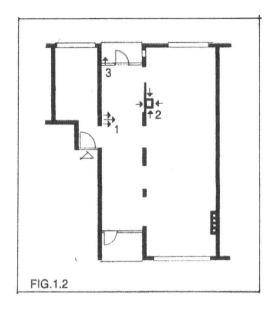

Figure 1.2 The support prepared for Infill, indicating 1) connecting points for gas, electricity and water – part of the support; 2) sewage main and ventilation shaft – part of the support; and 3) exhaust for the gas heater – part of the infill.

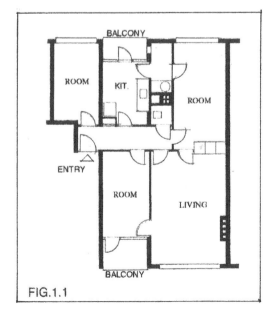

Figure 1.1 The original floor plan from the 1960's

installed by a local interior decorator and their furniture is brought in.

Second scenario

A couple in their late fifties, users of an apartment in the same rental public housing estate as mentioned in the first scenario, decides that their apartment no longer fits their needs. However, they are reluctant to relocate to another, newer housing estate because they have lived in the present apartment for a long time.

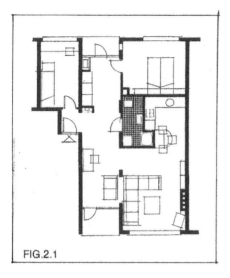

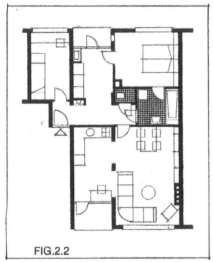

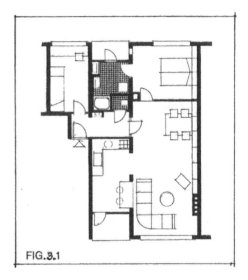

Figure 3.1 The floor plan of scenario one, as executed, compared with Figure 2.3

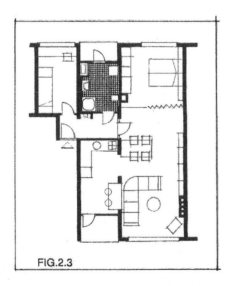

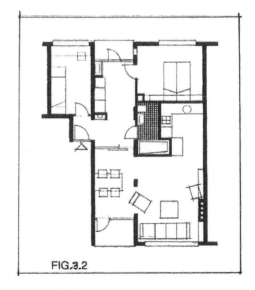

Figure 2 Three alternative floor plans presented to the users

Figure 3.2 The floor plan of scenario two, as executed, compared with Figure 2.1

They like the neighborhood where they have friends and relatives and are familiar with shops and other public facilities. They decide they prefer to have their old apartment renovated and ask for the cooperation of the housing authority. (Figure 3.2)

This is the start of a procedure similar to the one described above, but in this case the couple moves out of their apartment to stay with their daughter and son in law for three weeks. Their furniture is put in storage. In the first week the apartment is prepared for infill. In the next two weeks the infill package is installed.

Within a month they live in a completely new apartment fitted out exactly according to their wishes.

Voluntary expenses

As part of the normal procedure for renovation the users are asked to select the bathroom equipment and kitchen equipment to be installed in the new floorplan. The elder couple can afford to spend more compared to the young couple who are just starting. They select a very well-equipped kitchen. Also, the bathroom equipment they want is of high quality. The representative of the housing authority informs them that with their selection the costs of the infill package far exceeds the estimated costs on which the rent for the new unit was calculated. The couple responds that they are well aware of this and are prepared to cover the difference[1]. Accordingly, they pay the authority a lump sum and the equipment they selected is installed in their rental unit[2].

Advantages for the user

Seen from the perspective of the users the procedure described in the scenarios is the course attractive. It gives them an opportunity to select their own floor plan and they are free to decide on the quality level of the equipment to be installed. Moreover, the process is quick. Within several weeks after the rental contract is agreed upon the units are ready.

Advantage for the owner

It can be expected that the owner of rental property will appreciate the procedure as sketched above for social reasons. Tenants who have selected their own interior accommodations can be expected to complain less and will treat their environment with respect.

Moreover, serving their tenants on a one on one basis makes it possible to take into consideration the differences of income among them. Those who can spend more, and are indeed willing to do so, can have more. It is no longer necessary for the owner to expect all users, regardless of their differences in lifestyle and income, to accept the same single floor plan equipped on a level that is just affordable to those with the lowest income.

Economically attractive

Less obvious is that the owner of rental property also will find this way of working economically attractive compared to the alternatives available to him.

First of all, custom floor plans by means of infill systems as sketched in the two scenarios are not more expensive in direct costs. The price of the single infill unit to be installed independently, including cleaning out of the building shell and preparing it for the infill system, is competitive with the price paid to contractors for a comparable job in traditional renovation processes.

If here things are equal, economic advantages for the owner follow because the whole process becomes much easier to control and can be done in a more gradual fashion. To illustrate this we may first consider the alternatives against which the new infill system approach should be compared.

Traditional alternatives

Without the infill systems option the owner of an apartment building has basically two alternatives where renovation was concerned:

- In a first alternative the building will be vacated and gutted completely to be refitted, after which new tenants are admitted, or former tenants may return. This procedure is inevitably socially destructive. It also takes extensive planning and a good deal of social engineering before the building is empty. Even if the owner tries to help tenants to find new places to live there will be those who find it difficult to leave but equally difficult to stay in a gradually emptying building.
- In a second alternative the building is renovated while the tenants stay in place, in which case they are submitted to a longer period of discomfort and noise when workers go in and out to redo

bathrooms and kitchens and electric circuitry, taking apart most of the house before they put it back together again. This procedure asks much patience and endurance of all parties involved and also a good deal of cooperation between owner and contractor. It is not uncommon that a full-time social worker is occupied with helping tenants to cope. Inevitably there are older people and those who are ill or already under stress for other reasons who now have to live through all this for months on end.

Compared to these traditional ways for renovation we now may consider from the owner's point of view the advantages of the new alternative offered by infill systems.

User friendly adaptation as a result

In both traditional cases the contractor insists on some economy of scale where the same parts can be installed in the same way in all units. Uniform floor plans are required. For the owner it is difficult and very time consuming to come to a single proposal acceptable to all tenants.

Usually the emphasis is on equipment. The original plan is maintained as much as possible while better bathrooms and kitchens somehow are installed. Differences in lifestyle, occupancy, and income cannot be taken into consideration. In the end no one is satisfied. The lowest income tenants feel they cannot afford the new rents. Those with a higher income feel they do not get what they want.

In case of infill renewal, on the other hand, variety of floor plans is the natural outcome of the process and not more expensive than uniform floor plans. This is because the infill process treats each unit separately. All subsystems are installed by the same crew in a single procedure.

Making two or more identical plans does not offer any advantages in terms of installation time or costs. Neither does it matter if several units must be renovated at the same time or in the same building. At all times the infill system for each unit is delivered in its own container and installed by a separate crew.

No gradual deterioration

Whereas the infill system does not care if floor plans are uniform or different, the benefits of personal adaptation are considerable for both tenants and owner. Tenants get what they want within the limits of what they can afford. Having been involved in choosing the environment they live in, they will be more responsible users. Demand for repair and maintenance will decrease. For the owner of the property this means that overall quality remains good with less effort.

Most important, however, is that in the one-on-one infill renovation process overall deterioration of the property is avoided. Renewal is now a continuous process of gradual adaptation to tenants' needs. Each time when a tenant leaves renewal and adaptation is possible. Because infill time is short, vacated units can be renovated and rented again within a month. As we have seen in the second scenario, renovation of a unit can happen while a tenant takes a three-week vacation. In this way renovation and adaptation become a form of continuous maintenance and violent swings in the condition of a rental property, from massive renewal after years of overall stagnation can be avoided.

Separation of 'support' and 'infill'

To renovate a housing estate not only the interior of the units must be renewed. The customized infill of single units must be complemented by improvement of the facilities shared by users like stairs, elevators, entry ways, parking facilities and landscaping.

Essential to the infill approach is that a clear distinction is made between the infill proper which is done in response to individual user's needs on the one hand, and the so called 'support' building that holds the individual units on the other hand. For the latter the owner must take initiative. In the case of the two scenarios sketched earlier for instance, the housing authority has planned complete replacement of the existing stairwells and the addition of elevators for the four-story apartment block. (Figure 4.1 and 4.2). It also plans for the replacement of some garage and storage space on the ground floor with new dwelling units. These works will be done in consultation with the group of tenants involved, but the work itself remains outside the units and is done at its own pace. In the same way the facades are cleaned and treated against moisture penetration and window frames are repaired at the outside.

These more general activities concerning the building as a whole for the benefit of all tenants no longer relate to the renovation of the units themselves. Bids can be put out independently and contractors know much better what is expected and find it easier to determine prices.

An efficient response to users' preferences

Figure 4.1 The building as it was before renovation began, with storage rooms on the ground floor.

Figure 4.2 The building after renovation, including new glazed-stairs, balconies and windows, and ground level apartments for the elderly.

New construction: commercial dimensions of the infill approach

What has been said so far shows that the infill approach is not only a technical innovation but has important social implications. However, these go hand in hand with commercial aspects. This becomes particularly clear when we consider the use of this approach as applied in new construction in the up-scale market.

Differences of supply and demand

Developers know that prospective buyers always demand changes in the floor plan of the units offered to them. Even when they like the floorplan they may want a door to be displaced to accommodate a beloved piece of furniture which otherwise will not fit in. Or they may want a wall replaced or taken out. Usually they like to choose their own bathroom and kitchen equipment as well as the colors of tiles and other surface finishes.

The response of developers to such demands for change and adaptation varies with the market situation. If competition is strong, they may have to give in more readily than when there is a great deal of demand.

But, if they had their way, developers would prefer not to offer any choice to buyers at all for the simple reason that it will cost them money. It is not at all certain that the costs of customization can be passed on to the buyer. The contractor's price is based on fixed predetermined floorplans and specifications. Any change will disrupt his planning, will cost more money and take more time. Contractors are well aware that the developer demands a change because otherwise the unit will not sell. This puts them in an advantageous position to negotiate the price of the adaptation. But it is also true that it is difficult for the contractor to manage such changes and to determine their exact costs. Prices will be established accordingly.

This situation which is familiar enough to all of us, basically puts developers, buyers and builders, on a collision course.

Reconciliation of conflict

The infill approach reconciles this conflict. The developer now asks for bids on the support building only and will be supplied with a finished building complete with facade, and all such facilities as are offered to all users: entrance lobbies, elevators, public stairs and corridors, parking facilities and landscaping. In short, the building as finished will clearly establish the kind of lifestyle and quality of services that the buyer needs to know before he can decide if the location is of interest to him. But the inside of the apartments will remain empty and ready to be filled in. Floors are smooth and ceilings finished and painted. At a fixed place in each unit there is access to electricity, water, gas, and sewage for the infill system to connect to for further distribution in the unit.

Building this 'support building' should not offer any surprises to the builder. He will be in control of logistics for a well-defined job. The builder is in fact freed from the part of the construction process that usually constitutes the greater risk to him and takes most of the overhead for on-site management and for coordination of subcontractors. It is well known that money is easily lost on finishing the interiors of dwelling units where it is gained in setting up the larger structure holding them. The builder, in short, now can do more with less overhead costs.

The developer from his part, now knows precisely what he can expect from the builder in terms of product and timing. For the infill he contracts the infill systems company. He is now in a position to offer the buyers exactly what they want and can structure his prices accordingly.

We can conclude that the infill approach sets free all parties involved: the buyer, the developer and the builder. It may also show how the system is not only a technical innovation but has very interesting commercial implications, putting developer and builder in a mode of operation that offers superior service to the buyer in a way that can be logistically and financially well controlled. This, of course, gives them a decidedly competitive advantage over those who operate in a traditional mode.

Open systems: technological dimensions of the Infill approach

In this context it is important to mention that the infill system providing this commercial breakthrough is a so-called open system. Open systems in building technology utilize as much as possible materials and components that are already on the market. For the infill system this means that partition walls and wall finishes, door frames and doors, kitchen and bathroom equipment, all are taken from the open market. This is radically different from what many people have in mind when they think of an industrialized system. The infill system we are talking about here is not so much hardware oriented as software oriented. It is based on a few important principles:

Separation of support and infill

The first and foremost principle on which the approach is based is that the infill system is clearly distinguished from the rest of the building in which it is installed. What is not infill is by definition 'support'. This comprises not only the shell of the building, including facade and roof, but also all load bearing parts as well as the major conduits that feed the individual dwelling units: those for gas, electricity, water and sewage. These conduits run to a specific point in each unit from where further deployment is done by means of the infill system.

Once the infill system is separated from the support it can be studied on its own. As far as the particular system is concerned on which I report here, we established the following principles for its development:

An efficient response to users' preferences 303

Re-ordering of the deployment of conduits

We found that the bulk of the costs of an infill package is in the technical equipment needed for the unit, including all the piping and wiring that go with it. This comprises at least the following technical subsystems: heating, ventilation, sewage, hot and cold-water supply, electricity, telephone, television, and various safety and control systems.

We found that a significant part of the costs of these systems is not their hardware but their installation. Installation demands multiple visits by different crews for different subsystems. It is a very difficult task for the job manager to orchestrate these visits successfully. We also know that very often one crew's work interferes with that of another and that the earlier crew must return to repair what got damaged later on.

The key to a successful infill system is therefore to find a new way to distribute all the conduits of the technical systems assuring that interfaces are eliminated as much as possible. In other words: we want to make sure that conduits can run through the unit without getting in the way of each other. Moreover, we want to make sure that conduits could be installed without workers having to cut open walls or having to leave walls partly finished, waiting for conduits to be installed.

Our search for disentanglement of subsystems resulted in the invention of two new hardware components: the 'matrix tile' and the 'base profile'. The two together serve as context for almost all other subsystems. In other words, they are the embodiment of the chosen ordering principle. (Figures 5, 5a and Figure 6).

Dimensions and positions

Having re-ordered the distribution of the conduits and, by doing so having minimized the interference of subsystems among each other, we now had to codify this ordering principle in exact positional and dimensional terms. Once a certain subsystem is deployed, we want to know precisely where all its parts are and what dimensions they have. This is achieved by the use of a so called 'band grid' as has been applied already for many years by those interested in open building systematization. A band grid allows for positioning rules for each subsystem thus formalizing the ordering principle that is chosen.

Contrary to modernist ideas of systematization our approach does not demand a dimensional standardization of parts but is based on positioning rules relating each subsystem, and each part in it, to the grid. Some parts, like door frames, have a range of fixed dimensions as determined by the manufacturer. Other parts, like a pipe or a stretch of wall, have variable dimensions. Variable dimensions result from a part's position in a larger configuration. They may also depend on the position of parts from other systems that it must connect to, the latter also being deployed according to their own rules in the overall ordering concept.

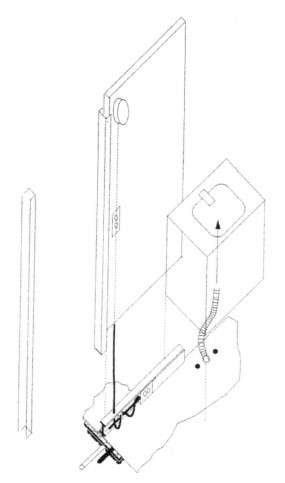

Figure 5 Organization of the Matura ® infill system. The so-called 'lower system' is structured by two new components: 1) a matrix tile holds conduits for water, sewage and central heating, and is laid on the load-bearing floor, and then covered by a floor board; 2) A 'base profile' holds all electricity and electronics. Elements of the 'upper system' such as plumbing fixtures, cabinets and walls, are from the open market, and connect to the conduits in the 'lower system.'

Figure 5a: The "lower system" in place (matrix tile + base profile)

SUB-SYSTEMS	SUPPORT	INFIILL
Concrete structure (walls, floors, etc)	▬	
facade system (windows, panels, etc)	▬	
roof system	▬	
stairs + elevators	▬	
interior partitioning (doorframes, panels,etc)		▬
kitchen equipment		▬
bathroom equipent		▬
heating		▬
gas supply	▬	
electric supply	▬	
electronics	▬	
water supply	▬	▬
sewage lines	▬	▬

FIG.6

Figure 6 Major subsystems in a building and their relation to support and infill levels. Some subsystems are exclusively in one or the other, while some appear in both. In all cases, interfaces are critical and must be worked out in detail.

Variable dimensions are not random, however. When the positions of all parts in the grid are known, dimensions can be calculated from the position information available and, consequently, each particular part with its own particular dimensions can be individually known and therefore produced.

This way of working also makes it possible to apply the infill system in buildings that follow their own dimensioning system or have no clear dimensioning system at all. In other words: the application of the infill system does not require that the building in which it is applied be designed in any systematic way. All that is needed is that eventually the positions of the building's parts are determined in the infill grid. These positions may not be subject to any rules but nevertheless can be determined. Once this is done the dimension of infill parts connecting to them can be calculated.

Although knowledge about the use of positioning rules in a band grid is already in the public domain for many years, the specific method of calculating actual dimensions of parts from given deployment rules is not. It has been developed for the benefit of the particular infill system I am reporting on here.

Production and installation

Given an exact dimensional drawing of the desired floor plan, our method allows for its translation in a technical design based on the positioning rules as discussed above. This translation is done with the help of a specially developed computer program. It is a kind of dedicated CAD program which understands deployment rules and can calculate dimensions in the way explained earlier. The result is not only a set of technical drawings, but a specification list of all parts needed for the particular infill package at hand. This information is fed into the production phase of the infill package itself. Parts are subsequently selected from stock, cut to size if needed and/or otherwise worked upon, sometimes combined with other parts, and finally packaged to be stored in a container.

This process, beginning with the technical translation of a submitted floorplan and ending with the container ready for shipping, is what is called the **production phase**. It is a phase that requires a highly sophisticated production process where each single product is a unique combination of a large number (about twenty) of well-defined subsystems.

But the product is not assembled. Its parts are transported to be put together in the building for which the floor plan was designed in the first place.

This second phase is the **installation phase**. It is basically a building job in which a fully prefabricated kit of parts is put together.

The separation between a production phase and an installation phase is important because each phase represents a very different way of working and organizing.

The net result, however, is that the installation phase becomes relatively easy and can be done within a very short time, reducing labor costs dramatically.

Saving on-site labor costs

It should be noted that the savings in labor costs on the site are not the result of repetition of tasks as is the case in the traditional building technology but of principles already discussed that may be summarized as follows:

1. The minimization of the interface between subsystems. This facilitates installation. Each subsystem can be laid out in one act and need not be dealt with again.
2. The prefabrication of all parts so that on-site cutting and adjusting of dimensions is almost eliminated.
3. The elimination of on-site measuring. Because of the use of the matrix tile no measuring is needed for the installation of any parts after the first few matrix tiles have been put in place.
4. The elimination of on-site mistakes. Because deployment of subsystems is done following clear positioning rules in the base grid, workers can easily read drawings and understand how things go together, thus reducing the risk for mistakes.
5. The elimination of the need for ad-hoc problem solving. Workers need not solve detail problems on the spot. The way things come together is fully predetermined.

Balance of costs

The gain from reduced labor costs in the installation phase pays for the production phase, resulting in a total for direct costs which is not more than what is needed with the traditional way of outfitting a dwelling unit. But at the same time the important social and logistical advantages explained earlier are gained, giving those who adopt the infill approach a competitive advantage in the market.

This shift from on-site labor costs to costs of industrial production also allows the utilization of subsystems that are deemed too expensive in the traditional mode of residential construction. For example, throughout our infill system we use electric cables and connectors that were originally designed for application in office furniture. The higher costs of these superior parts are easily compensated for by the fact that laying out these cables – in the appropriate channels without interference with other systems – can be done so fast that much more is saved in labor time than is paid in additional costs in hardware.

Past developments

A breakthrough as is represented by the infill systems approach does not come overnight. It should be expected that it is the result of a long period of gestation and development. The original idea of the distinction between support and infill was suggested in the early sixties[3]. The basic methods used in our system for the distribution of all parts by means of positioning rules related to a modular grid have been pioneered by the SAR research group[4], in the late 1960's and early 1970's, with financial support of architects offices and building manufacturers. In the early eighties modular positioning as advocated by SAR became formally recognized in the Dutch standards for modular coordination. The most important aspect of this development was, in my opinion, that it resulted from a concerted effort of a small number of dedicated individuals who succeeded in making positional coordination the topic of a broad-based debate involving representatives of all parts of the building industry[5]. This was the beginning of an industry-wide debate on first principles of residential construction.

Meanwhile other architects had implemented the support/infill distinction in a number of housing projects in the Netherlands. Their work demonstrated that the application of the distinction, with its advantages for users and owners, even without a sophisticated infill technology could be done within the constraints of costs and regulations of public housing[6].

One important result of the pilot support/infill projects was that they triggered the interest of some builders who began to see the potential for cost efficiency in this approach. The topic became particularly relevant when in the late 1970's, a severe recession in the Netherlands triggered by the international oil crisis forced the government to reduce substantially its financial support of housing construction. This, for the first time after the Second World War, forced competition among builders in the lucrative field of public housing. As usually happens in times re-examination, different directions were taken by different parties. Where some sought to achieve a better competitive position by drastic cost cutting in management and materials combined with more economic design, others recognized that Dutch housing was already among the cheapest in Europe and decided that only a new approach could open a promising future.

They organized themselves in a not-for-profit foundation called Open Bouwen (Open Building) to push for an alternative way. Open Bouwen advocates the distinction of different levels of intervention in the built environment, the general concept on which the support/infill separation is based. It also promotes the clear distinction of independent subsystems and their coordination by means of positioning rules in a common grid. The Open Bouwen movement has members from all branches of the building industry, from architects to developers, builders, and manufacturers, to managers of public housing estates. It operates on the assumption that the basic principles are sufficiently clear, but that now practical implementation needs to be encouraged.

Among the more notable results of the Open Bouwen initiative was the organization of a center for technical and design studies, by the name of OBOM, at the Technical University of Delft, financed by that university and the government[7]. In a separate development a number of studies about the economics and management of open building projects were done under the supervision of committees formed by representatives from the building industry and their consultants and financed by the ministry of economic affairs[8].

It eventually became clear that a more sophisticated infill system was needed to replace the ad hoc systems that had been applied in the support/infill projects done so far. In the course of time technical developments in the Netherlands had already produced a number of more advanced subsystems for residential construction. Among those can be mentioned a number of partition wall systems, industrially produced door frames that can be installed in a few minutes, and hot water heating systems that serve a single unit and fit in a closet. In brief, the time was there for a more comprehensive approach utilizing recent technological innovations as well as the methodological knowledge developed so far.

The Matura infill system about which I have reported here was a response to this need for a 'second generation' infill system. Its development took about five years and it is presently licensed for commercial production in the Netherlands[8].

However, this is not the only infill system presently under scrutiny in the Netherlands. In another initiative, a combined effort by a number of manufacturers

An efficient response to users' preferences 307

is under way under the name 'Esprit'[6]. Esprit advocates a 'plug-in' solution maximizing flexibility for the user. It aims for more advanced subsystems and new designs for integrated equipment in bathrooms and kitchen. Pilot projects have been implemented. Commercial production on a continuous basis is expected within a few years.

Another, much more pragmatic system has been applied in a few small office buildings and will be demonstrated for residential use in a project that presently is under way. Under the name of 'Interlevel' this system offers a very affordable raised floor of minimum height (about 10cm) under which conduits can run freely and on top of which partitioning systems and kitchen and sanitary equipment from the open market can be installed[6].

This brief sketch may suffice to show that the approach I have spoken of comes from a broad-based development that was under way in the Netherlands for several decades. It is against the background of this steady development that I hope my paper may now inform a larger audience of what is afoot.

Notes

1 In this particular case the lump sum paid by the tenants exceeded 20 per cent of the costs of the infill package as delivered. Some observers believe that rental users as an average would be prepared to contribute 15 per cent of the infill package price out of pocket. This extra money is not needed to make the infill package competitive with the traditional way of outfitting renovation units, but it is an indication of the willingness of users to invest in their dwelling environment if they get what they really want.

2 First suggested in the Dutch publication: N. J. Habraken, *De Dragers en de Mensen* (Amsterdam: Scheltema & Holkema, 1962). First English edition under the title *Supports: An Alternative for Mass Housing* (London: The Architectural Press; New York: Praeger, 1972).

3 SAR, Stichiting Architecten Research. (Architects Research Foundation), Eindhoven 1965–91, of which the author was director from 1965–75.

4 Major players were, among others, Ir. John Carp, at the time director of SAR, Prof. Age van Randen at the Technical University Delft, and architect Frans van der Werf, Rotterdam.

5 Most advanced among the many attempts to implement the support/infill idea were the projects by architect Frans van der Werf. Particularly the Molenvliet project in Papendrecht, the Lunetten project in Utrecht and the Keyenburg project in Rotterdam all influenced by the Open Building approach.

6 OBOM ('Open Bouwen Ontwikkelings Model 'or 'Open Building Development Model'). Founded 1985. Prof. Age van Randen director until 1992, subsequently led by Prof. R. Brouwer.

7 Among many others a major role was played by Karel Dekker, finance and management consultant, who authored a number of pathbreaking studies on new ways for financing and budgeting housing projects based on the support infill distinction.

8 The Matura system is licensed by Matura International bv, Delft, The Netherlands. It was developed by Infill Systems by a partnership of N. J. Habraken, Prof. Age van Randen, Mr. Ir. Frans. de Vries, and Jan van Vonderen.

1994
NEXT21 IN THE OPEN BUILDING PERSPECTIVE

Editors' note: *NEXT21, built in 1994 in a dense urban neighborhood in Osaka, Japan by the Osaka Gas Company, was designed to never be finished: it serves as a continuing research project into new ways of providing energy for buildings; as a place to try out new fit-out systems suited to changing inhabitant life-styles; and a place to study ways of bringing nature into the city. It is always fully occupied and continues to receive visitors from around the world. This essay was published in the: NEXT21: All About the NEXT21 Project (2005), Osaka Gas Company, LTD.*

Introduction

The NEXT21 project is rightly considered an extraordinary project of international reputation. To appreciate its role, it must be seen in the larger context of experimentation and innovation within which it emerged. Truly important innovations not only reflect the conditions they appear in, but, by their very presence, change them and point toward further development.

The context within which we can best understand the NEXT21 building is what is usually called the Open Building approach. I will try to explain how that approach shaped NEXT21 and how, in turn, NEXT21 influenced the Open Building movement.

The NEXT21 project was broadly conceived and important parts of it – like for instance the innovative heating and cooling generating system, the waste-water management system, and the green environments developments – can be considered innovations independent from the Open Building context.

But even these subjects profited from the Open Building environment within which they were conducted and in turn they contribute to a better understanding of that environment.

The project is also a remarkable demonstration of the Japanese ability for teamwork and cooperation among professionals. This not only allowed the successful execution of an extremely complex project in a rather short time span, but also its continuation as a vehicle for experimentation over more than a decade.

Moreover, the project is exceptional in that it was managed and financed by a large for-profit corporation as a long-term commitment of research and experimentation, the scope of which went far beyond its immediate commercial interests. This alone set a standard in the building industry that has yet to be matched.

The open building movement

What is open building?

The term Open Building can be understood in a variety of interrelated ways. On the one hand, it sees a building as a composition of a large number of subsystems. Agents who design and produce them make these subsystems available. Other agents may take care of their installation in a specific project. To assure a good fit with inhabitation, and to avoid waste, the Open Building approach demands that these subsystems remain relatively independent from one another and that interface conditions be simplified so that competing systems can replace one another with minimal disturbance to other systems. This could be called the 'flexibility' aspect of the Open Building agenda. It is related to manufacturing and installation.

On the other hand, the Open Building approach notes that ultimately, the 'control' of hardware in the built environment is a social phenomenon, subject to political realities and cultural preferences. Good environmental quality demands that such control allows direct response to the needs and preferences of the inhabitants.

The Open Building approach sees these different perspectives as complementary. A truly healthy and living environment must have a good match between the subsystems that are produced and installed, and the control patterns that suit the best human harmony and well-being.

In this way, we begin to see the built environment as a dynamic entity which is in constant change in response to the needs and preferences of inhabitants, using numerous hardware systems that allow such change to happen in an organized way.

In history, initiative for building mainly came from the smallest social unit which was the extended family – often composed of several generations. Available technology was always systematic but based on manpower and ad-hoc production. This way of working could lead to extremely complex and fine-grained environments easily adaptable over time to the needs of the inhabitants.

Today building systems are the product of high-tech manufacturing, making available many different systems providing a large variety of services. Moreover, building projects have very much increased in size. Open Building wants to make these large and complex projects responsive to initiative on the level of the individual household. It wants the large project to become fine-grained as well.

For that reason, the Open Building approach advocates the distinction between "skeleton and infill" (S/I) as it is known in Japan, or "base building and fit-out" as it is named in the U.S., or "support and infill" familiar in Europe. This basic distinction allows for the fine-grained control by inhabitants within the context of the large building. At the same time, it stimulates a systematic approach in building construction and manufacturing.

In the past century, many people have become concerned about the anonymity and uniformity of contemporary environments. The idea to separate the more permanent building envelope from the more adaptable interior occurred to different people in different places independently. It was first studied formally at the Foundation for Architects Research – SAR – in the Netherlands from 1965 onwards. The book by Kendall and Teicher traces the history of residential Open Building (Kendall and Teicher 2000)

It lists some 131 projects done before 1999 of which the NEXT21 project, completed in 1994, is number 123. In the decade between 1970 and 1980, some 25 projects are listed in countries as diverse as Germany, Sweden, Austria, Belgium, Netherlands, France and the United Kingdom. In that period, some early projects have proven to be seminal, such as: the MEME student housing building of the Louvain University in Brussels by Lucien Kroll; the Mareilles project in Paris by Georges Maurios; the PSSHAK project in Stamford Hill, London by Hamdi and Wilkinson; and the Molenvliet project in Papendrecht, Rotterdam by Frans van der Werf. These early examples contributed to a growing awareness of the Open Building alternative.

The first Japanesef project is listed in 1980 as the KEP Maenocho project in Tokyo, to be followed in 1982 by two more KEP projects in Tama New Town and also the Senboku Momoyamadai project in Sakai City, Osaka in that same year. In fact, the decade between 1980 and 1990 is dominated by 21 projects in Japan from a total of 31 worldwide. In that same decade also China and Switzerland introduced themselves to the Open Building stage.

In the course of time, an informal network formed itself. The term Open Building as the name of an organization first appeared when a group of individuals in the Netherlands got together to promote the implementation of the principles and methods developed by the SAR. Their work centered at the Technical University of Delft under the direction of Professor Age van Randen. They saw themselves as doers rather than researchers, advocating the wholesale adoption of the Open Building approach in the Netherlands. Later on, an international Open Building network developed with Dr. Seiji Sawada and Prof. Seiichi Fukao and others as active members from Japan. This network eventually was formalized at a meeting in Tokyo in 1996 as a task group of the International Council for Research and Innovation in Building and Construction (CIB). With Professor Stephen Kendall as chief coordinator, this CIB Commission now has 30 members in 14 countries. Dr. Kazunobu Minami from Japan served as one of the Joint Coordinators. (As of this writing, the international CIB W104 Open Building Implementation network has more than 300 in its contact list from 30 countries, and has two joint coordinators: Professor Jia Beisi, University of Hong Kong and Professor Amira Osman, Tshwane University in Pretoria, South Africa. It holds annual meetings in a different country each year and publishes peer reviewed papers in its conference proceedings).

The team that assembled for the Osaka Gas Company project for experimental housing was very well informed about international Open Building history, and its members had been personally involved in OB (S/I) projects in Japan. Early on, in Tokyo University, Professor Yositika Utida had a leadership role in the Kodan Experimental Project (KEP) housing construction initiative by the Japan Housing and Urban Development Corporation (HUDC). He also led the project committee of the Ministry of Construction (MOC) for the Century Housing System (CHS) which distinguished six categories of component systems, based on their durable years, and a modular system for the coordination in space. Professor Kazuo Tatsumi together with Professor Mitsuo Takada had been researching the "Two Step Housing Supply System" at Kyoto University, first applied in 1982 in Senboku New Town, Osaka, and later with the 1989 Senri Inokodani Housing Estate project. Early in the planning of NEXT21, the team of Japanese designers together with delegates of the Osaka Gas management group made a trip to the Netherlands to see the Molenvliet project and other experimental projects in that country. The result was that the NEXT21 building could become a culmination of much of the experience of Open Building available at the time.

NEXT21 as an open building project

Within the context of Open Building, the NEXT21 project introduced a number of innovations, some of which still have not been equaled by later initiatives.

Three-dimensional urban design

Professor Utida once described the project as 'three-dimensional urban design." This concept is indeed a logical result of the separation of base building and fit-out (S/I). The large building is no longer a building but becomes part of an "urban tissue." Just like a city is extended by the design of streets and squares complete with trees and sidewalks and the utility lines under the surface, the NEXT21 base building provides public space of bridges, elevators, stairs and corridors connecting a public garden on the ground floor with another one on the roof. The public circulation provided in three dimensions from the street level to roof garden connects individual dwellings to the urban street network, and just as in urban design, these individual dwellings can be built, changed, removed and replaced like buildings along a street.

Although the NEXT21 project fills no more than half a block, it is easy to imagine its concept applied on a larger scale accommodating a very large number of individual dwellings in a three-dimensional urban fabric. The transformation of the large building into a neighborhood, offering internal public spaces that give access to dwellings that can be shaped individually, is perhaps the greatest potential of the Open Building approach. NEXT21 shows how this can lead to a new architecture and urbanism that is different from just 'flexible buildings.'

Professional cooperation on two levels

A design team in collaboration with architect Shin-ichi Chikazumi guided the entire project. Thirteen different architects were initially invited to design the 18 individual houses contained within the NEXT21 framework. This was a logical step once this vision of a three-dimensional urban fabric had been adopted. But it also represents an innovation that has not yet been repeated elsewhere.

In all Open Building projects, design decisions are made on two levels: the lower level of the interior fit-out is to accommodate the user, while the higher level contains all that the users have in common: the load-bearing structure, the main utility systems and the public spaces. Given this distinction, design decisions on the lower level can be made in different ways. In some cases, the architect of the base building has designed the individual layouts in a direct one-on-one exchange with individual inhabitants. Sometimes, the project architect offered a number of alternative layout plans for the users to choose from, with the possibility of alterations on the user's behalf. In a few cases, such as with most of van der Werf's projects in

NEXT21 in the Open Building perspective

Figure 1 A view of NEXT21

the Netherlands, users were encouraged to design the interior of their units themselves, with minimal help of the base buildings' architect. In brief, a variety of procedures has come about to enable the user to influence the design of the dwelling, but it was usually assumed that just one architect would be involved for the entire project.

Yet, to have separate architects do the lower level design is consistent with ongoing practice in urbanism, office and shopping center construction. The traditional urban designer expects other architects to do the buildings along the streets and squares she proposes. In the case of office buildings and shopping centers, large areas of empty floor space are made available and leaseholders are expected to hire their own architect to design interior layout and finishes. The same might work in residential Open Building as well.

To be sure, in the case of NEXT21, only a few of the dwellings were designed in direct response to the demands of the inhabitants. In most cases, Osaka Gas submitted "user scenarios" as "guidance documents" for the architects to follow. This was done to obtain a wide range of different lifestyles that could demonstrate the buildings' capacity to accommodate a variety of dwelling solutions. It also secured a broad base for future research. Having the individual dwellings designed by different architects could stimulate variety even more. At the same time, this way of delegating design responsibility suggested a new model of professional cooperation among designers to better serve an emerging, consumer oriented real estate market.

Private gardens

Another innovation consistent with the idea of a "three-dimensional urban structure" was to provide individual units with their own exterior green space distinct from the common gardens on the ground level and on the roof of the building. Several of the units had small outside spaces for plantings as part of the private residential domain. Of course, the size and number of such little "gardens" depended on the individual unit design. But the addition of green outside spaces was encouraged as part of the overall experiment and the high space available for ducts under the floors made it easier to grow shrubs.

Such attention for green spaces goes beyond current practice in residential open building construction but may well be followed in future projects.

The façade system

A façade system was designed specifically for the NEXT21 lower level design. Using the system, each architect could design a façade expressing the interior layout. Keeping in mind future changes, the façade system was designed in such a way that it could be taken apart and installed again "from the inside," without need for exterior scaffolding built up from the ground level.

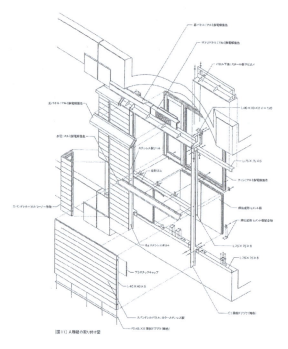

Figure 2 The NEXT21 Façade system

Figure 3 A view NEXT21 emphasizing its façade system as used by several different architects

In the open building experience, the role of the façade has been a difficult but important issue. A range of solutions has been considered over time.

Proposals have been made that each unit should be entirely free to publicly express its own interior as well as its owner's personal stylistic preference. Le Corbusier's famous Algiers proposal already suggested this possibility more than 70 years ago, and among the ill-fated "Operation Breakthrough" ideas for innovative housing solutions in the early 1970's in the U.S. was a proposal for a minimal loadbearing framework containing a variety of house designs.

At the other end of the spectrum are the many OB projects that limit themselves to interior variety behind a fixed façade designed for the entire building.

Frans van der Werf's seminal Molenvliet project struck a middle course. Large subdivided window frames were part of a fixed design, but within each frame, users could fit a variety of components and decide which parts should be transparent and what not, and where movable parts like doors and windows would go. Moreover, for each dwelling unit two colors could be chosen from a total of six, to paint the various façade parts. This way of working gave identity to the individual units by color and design and served their functional requirements. At the same time, it assured an overall harmonious architectural result. It was also technically simple and inexpensive.

Making façade parts demountable and replaceable requires sophisticated detailing. If, moreover, the façade's position must be flexible as well, parts of the floor and ceiling that first were interior may become exterior or the other way around, posing a number of difficult technical problems. For practical reasons alone, a strong case can be made for a fixed façade design behind which interior variety is possible.

In many countries in history, facades always sought to express individual dwellings within a given typology, resulting in a rich and thematic variety along an entire street wall. In contrast, the Parisian boulevards show how uniform and monumental facades can shape urban space without expressing interior variety. The same can be observed around the Bloomsbury squares in London and the public spaces of St. Petersburg. Different cultures seem to have different preferences in different times. The question whether the façade – or parts of it – should follow higher-level design or lower level design is not just technical but has important cultural aspects.

The NEXT21 project offered a new possibility: its façade system is part of the higher-level concept intended for overall application. But the actual use of the system is part of the lower level design. This combines lower level variety and change over time with higher-level harmony on an urban scale. Here, too, NEXT21 set a most interesting new precedent.

An open building research laboratory

In the ten years after its initial completion, the NEXT21 building has served as a laboratory for a large number of experiments. This was consistent with Osaka Gas' solid reputation for innovative research in building technology and environmental control systems in buildings. The experiments conducted in the past decade have been fully reported in the present publication. There is no precedent in the open building experience of a similar long-term commitment to research by a single company and here again the NEXT21 project sets an example.

As already noted, not all research projects done in the NEXT21 context are specific Open Building issues. Development of new heating/cooling sources and waste management systems can be labeled stand-alone subjects. But the distribution of new utility lines, including cabling, ducts, and piping of all kinds to each unit is very much an open building issue. For future "three-dimensional urban frameworks" to serve future generations, service lines must coincide with public spaces in the frameworks to allow their renewal, maintenance or replacement as new technology develops. Moreover, the testing of a "computerized energy providing service," for instance, could be done because users actually participated in it, contributing valuable feedback information.

Many other parts of the extensive research agenda as executed in the past ten years have direct bearing on the open building approach. All were related to the re-design and change of a few dwelling units, a process that led to a re-examination of many issues.

There are, of course, the experiments dealing with the technical issues of changeable or flexible infill, and also the displacement of parts of the façade system as examples of new product development and evaluation.

There are also the life-style oriented social studies where the small-scale interaction between user and equipment and space is considered. And there are also design oriented research items on the agenda, like the scenario-based technique of housing planning, and also the study of the capacity of a given floor plan in which an entire range of possible use scenarios could be accommodated by shifting the position of the kitchen unit combined with a few minor alterations of doors and partitions.

It is important to note that for all of these experiments and studies, the NEXT21 infrastructure already was available and in use. Similar research issues have been conducted in the past, but because no real-life experimental environment was available, they necessarily had to be done in a more abstract manner. It seems that the availability of the real-life adaptable environment offered a new and very different context for study and experiment, the potential of which we have yet to fully understand.

If we look at the NEXT21 project as a permanent environment for experimentation, we begin to appreciate its almost total "openness" as compared to most other open building projects on record. To successfully realize an open building project in real life within the budgets normally available and for the sake of users with average needs and preferences, the question as to what can be fixed for all the inhabitants and what must be adaptable for the individual is crucial. We have learned that "maximum" flexibility is not only impractical, but also undesirable. What is fixed and common has real meaning and the balance with what is adaptable and individual must be studied each time with great care. The answer to that question will be different from project to project depending on the agents involved and the culture we try to serve. The question, indeed, must remain on the table until enough experience has been gained. Only when open building has

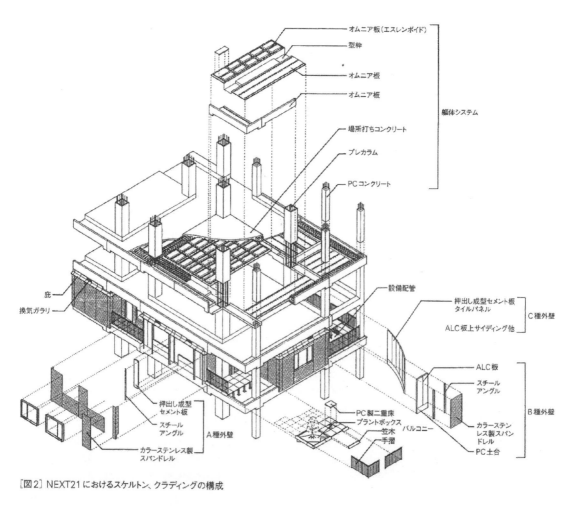

Figure 4 A 'systems" view of the NEXT21 project

become a general and normal approach will we understand more fully how that balance must work out and will we be able to make predictions. And even then, we can safely assume, there will be more than one answer.

However, for an open building project to serve as a laboratory as in the case with NEXT21, an extremely "open" technical solution is the right answer. Only then experiments can be done without pre-determined constraints. The NEXT21 environment is indeed a large systemic composition within which the balance between truly collective and permanent on the one hand and truly individual and adaptable on the other hand can be experimented with.

The present and future context for NEXT21

The completion of NEXT21 in 1993 implied a long-term commitment by Osaka Gas Company toward open building experimentation. This too was a precedent. Many earlier projects of an experimental character had been the result of extraordinary efforts by architects, clients and government agencies, but so far, they had been one-at-a-time events. It is in the nature of the building industry to experiment on an ad-hoc basis just as the entire industry operates on a project-by-project basis.

Ad-hoc experimentation allows the demonstration of the separation of two levels of design control. This, of course, NEXT21 also did in a rigorous and convincing way. But the development of new and more flexible sub-systems is another matter. This cannot be done as easily as on an ad-hoc basis and here NEXT21 could do something entirely new. It offered a stable context for installation and comparison of new sub-systems that might become available over time. The desire for easier installation and better service already had moved the market in the direction of the open building approach. For instance, in the last quarter century we have witnessed the introduction of flexible and "home-run" water lines, snap-together drainage piping, smaller and more efficient hot water units capable of heating a single dwelling and small

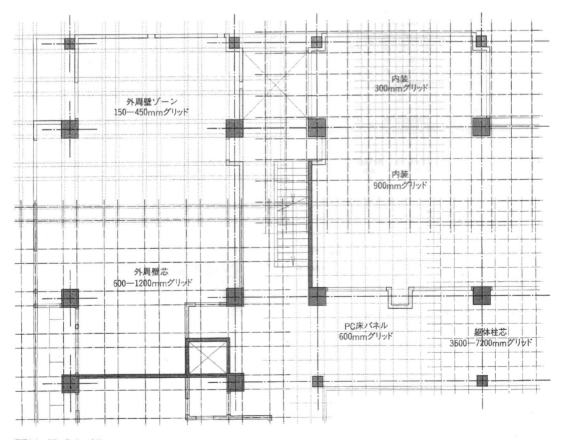

Figure 5 Dimensional coordinating grids used to manage the separated design tasks

enough to fit in a closet, electric cabling by means of click-together connections, easier to be installed partition systems, and many other improvements.

On the contrary, to organize all these pipes and cables without conflict, in combination with the deployment of internal partitioning and the equipment of bathrooms and kitchens, posed a very difficult methodological problem. The NEXT21 design team has confronted this problem in a sophisticated way. By doing so they have expanded our knowledge about the use of coordinating grids and zoning. Based on the careful studies of Professor Seiichi Fukao, in close cooperation with Shinichi Chikazumi of Shukoh-sha Design Studio, coordinating grids on several levels, closely interrelated, organize the design of all the subsystems. I believe this methodological aspect of the NEXT21 project should be studied carefully by all who want to follow this way of working. (see Figure 5: Dimensional coordinating grids)

As the open building approach makes progress, it becomes increasingly desirable for new products and sub-systems to be tested in an open building context. Here the example of the Osaka Gas Company may lead to emulation. We may eventually witness, elsewhere, the emergence of similar experimental sites where new sub-systems can be demonstrated and tested in a context of real-life inhabitation and management. Such permanent experimental sites might be run either by the manufacturing industry or government bodies.

Whereas Osaka Gas Company was the first commercial institution to make a long-term investment toward open building, recent cases point towards a more general trend in that direction. We may begin to see a shift toward long-term commitments to the two-level approach of open building for purely practical and commercial reasons. In Finland, a development company, after completion of a successful open building project of for-sale units, has decided to continue building several similar projects per year for the foreseeable future (Sato plus Koti 2004). In Bern, Switzerland, the local Canton supervises the completion of a new intensive care hospital built in the open building way and considers adoption of that approach as a general policy (Geiser 2004).

In Japan, Sekisui Chemical Company is about to launch a commercially available infill system, under development for several years, targeted for the renovation of the existing residential building stock. Finally, in the Netherlands, a major housing corporation has started the development of an entire urban block of nine-story buildings, renting out free space for residential and commercial purposes (The SOLIDS). If this suggests a shift in the open building history from ad-hoc experimentation towards long-term commitments for economic reasons, the NEXT21 project once again has been a pioneering effort.

References

Kendall, Stephen and Jonathan Teicher (2000). *Residential Open Building*. London and New York: E&F Spon.

Geiser, Stephan (2004). *The INO Hospital at the Inselspetal, Bern*. Proceedings of the 10th International Conference of the CIB W104, Paris.

Sato plus Koti, presentation by Esko Kahri, Architect (2004). *Sato plus Koti*. Proceedings of the 10th International Conference of the CIB W104, Paris.

SOLIDS Project (2011). Ijburg, Amsterdam. Developer: Het Oosten. Architect: Baumschlager – Eberle.

2003
OPEN BUILDING AS A CONDITION FOR INDUSTRIAL CONSTRUCTION

Editors' Note: *This paper was published in The Future Site – Proceedings, 20th International Symposium on Automation and Robotics in Construction, ISARC, Delft. Editors: Ger Maas and Frans van Gassel, 2003. In the abstract to the paper, the author writes: "Open Building advocates the direct relation between industrial manufacturing and the user/inhabitant. To make the industry-consumer relationship possible, base-buildings must offer space available for user-controlled fit-out. To date, a fairly large number of experimental projects have been executed on a global scale. They demonstrate the potential of the approach. A redistribution of design control involving all professional parties in the building industry is implied. To open this market, economic, legal, political, and bureaucratic policies must adapt."*

1. Introduction

Open Building implies a two-fisted strategy. In a social perspective it seeks to respond to user's preferences by offering flexibility needed for adaptation of individual units of occupancy over time. In a technical perspective it seeks ways of building where sub-systems can be installed or changed or removed with a minimum of interface problems. These two goals clearly complement one another and cover a wide spectrum of expertise. Open Building is supported by designers, managers, builders, and manufacturers, who each see advantages in it for their own professional role. In the 1960's, research at the SAR (Foundation for Architects Research) in the Netherlands proposed the separation of a 'base-building' and its interior 'fit-out' – the so called 'support/infill' approach – in pursuit of the same goals. True to its name, SAR focused on methods for designing such projects. The present open building network seeks a broader interpretation of the same principles, also to other use-types such as schools and health care facilities.

Open building as an organization is now formalized as CIB workgroup W104 which has a global membership and meets every year in another part of the world. To illustrate what the Open building approach stands for, I will show some examples of what could be termed open building projects. Next we will consider more specifically how open building provides a context for the development and improvement of industrial construction.

2. Examples and observations

2.1 NEXT21 project, Osaka, Japan

An experimental building, known as NEXT21, was completed for Osaka Gas Company in 1994 in the city of Osaka. Prof. Yositika Utida, Japan's premier authority on industrial residential construction, was asked to design the apartment building of the future. Not surprisingly, it contains the most advanced technology for the use of energy. Natural gas is chemically decomposed following principles first implemented for space craft. Solar panels are found on the building's roof garden. Waste from inhabitation is entirely processed for re-cycling.

Figure 1 NEXT21, partial view

2.1.1 Open building principles

Utida decided NEXT21 should also follow open building principles and assembled a team of designers to do just that. Prof. Kazuo Tatsumi and his younger colleague Prof. Mitsuo Takada at Kyoto University already had done several open building projects in the Osaka region. The office of Shu-Ko-Sha led by architect Shinichi Chikazumi joined to do actual design work and Prof. Seiichi Fukao of Tokyo Metropolitan University developed principles of modular coordination. This team, accompanied by experts representing the client, made a study visit to the Netherlands to see already implemented Open Building projects. [NEXT21].

2.1.2 Three-dimensional urban design

The NEXT21 building demonstrates a clear distinction between 'base-building' and 'fit-out' following the SAR definition: the base-building serves as a collective facility, and the fit-out is different for each unit. The NEXT21 base building includes parking, pedestrian circulation both horizontally and vertically, and two public gardens, one on ground level and one on the roof. Utida declared the base building to be 'three-dimensional urban design.' Drawing the full consequences of this analogy, he invited thirteen different architects to design the individual units, in the way individual architects design buildings in an urban scheme done previously by another firm.

Open Building as a condition for industrial construction **319**

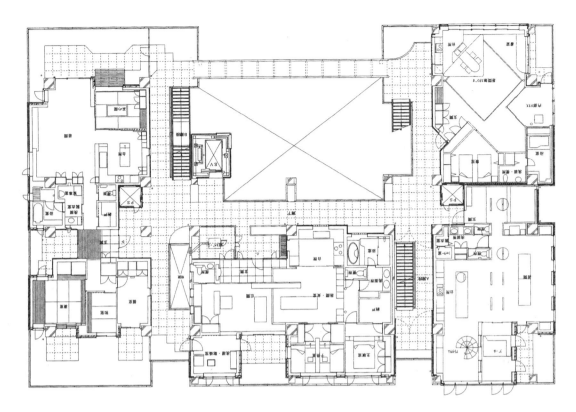

Figure 1a NEXT21: Dwellings on level 4; shows a bridge that crosses the garden on the ground level

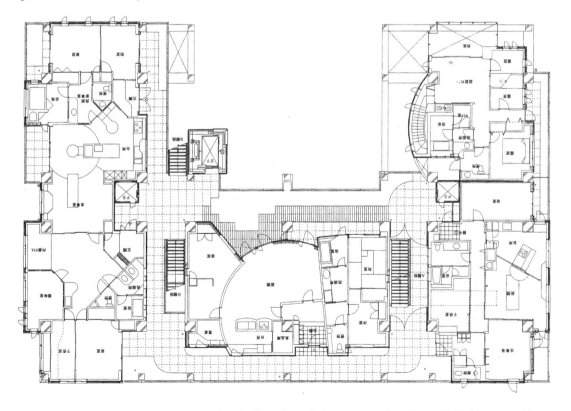

Figure 1b Dwellings on level 5: Floor plans of four dwellings (later the large unit on the right was divided into two with corresponding changes to the façade; similar adjustments were made elsewhere in the building)

2.1.3   State of the art technology

The thirteen architects applied available sub-systems to fit out individual units. But they followed clear rules for separation of base building and fit-out to enable the new distribution of design responsibilities. Subsequently, other architects were invited to redesign individual dwellings.

To facilitate this separation the base building offers not only empty spaces for inhabitation, but also a raised floor that can be reached by removable floor panels and under which the infrastructure of utilities like gas, water, and energy as well as waste drainage can be reached. Fit-out can use the double floor space to connect to these utilities and extend them throughout the individual dwelling, and to their companion infrastructure under the common 'streets' in the base building. Like in urban design, the spatial hierarchy is matched by a hierarchy in the utility systems.

2.1.3   Façade system

The NEXT21 façade system was newly invented and considered part of the fit-out system. Providing insulated aluminum panels and a variety of windows and doors, facades can be installed and taken apart without need for outside scaffolding, thus enabling easy adaptation from the inside later on. When dwelling floor plans change, the façade can also be rearranged to match, as has already been done on several units.

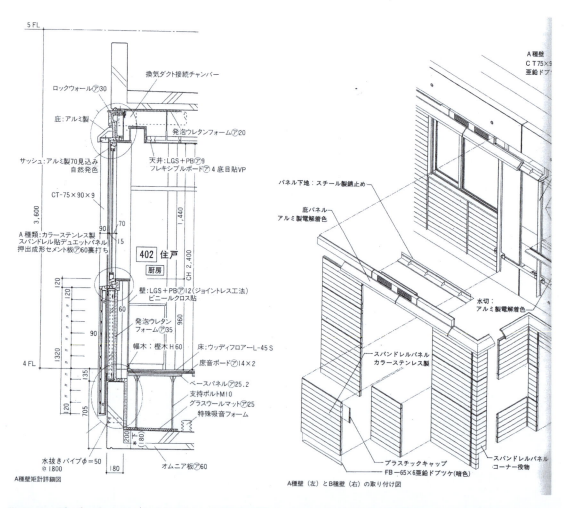

Figure 1c: The façade system for NEXT21. It is designed to be mounted and dismounted/altered from inside the building, eliminating the need for scaffolding, a key issue in super-high-rise buildings.

Open Building as a condition for industrial construction

Figure 2a Molenvliet; birds eye view

2.2 Molenvliet project, the Netherlands

The project in which Utida's team was most interested when visiting Holland was in the town of Papendrecht, near Rotterdam. Designed by architect Frans van der Werf, the Molenvliet Project is considered the first true implementation of the SAR approach. Built in the early 1970's, the project had to follow the strict rules for public housing of the time. But by making the base building/fit-out separation very clear in both technical and architectural terms, van der Werf successfully enabled the users to design their own spaces. Here too, the technology was state of the art.

2.2.1 An urban fabric

The Molenvliet project also can be called three-dimensional urban design. We do not see separate buildings but a continuous 'urban framework' which forms courtyards interconnected by pedestrian alleys and accessible from the public street where cars are parked. Some courtyards are public and give direct access to the units on the ground floor while open public galleries lead to units on the upper floors. Other courtyards contain garden space: both individual gardens for ground floor units, as well as collective gardens.

2.2.2 Users designing

Van der Werf allowed only two interviews with each of the user households to help them with their design. This proved sufficient. Because the units were for rent, cooperation of the owner of the estate, a non-profit corporation, was essential. Still, today, the management works in close cooperation with the users, and helps them adapt their unit's interior layout and equipment. [v.d.Werf]

2.3 A World-wide trend

Architect Frans van der Werf has recently completed his seventh open building residential project and is busy with the next. His open building projects are still much advanced in today's practice, but no longer experimental. Nor is he the only one working this way in the Netherlands. The NEXT21 project has triggered a spate of open building initiatives in Japan, most of which are supported by the government. Some are truly experimental, others already commercially viable.

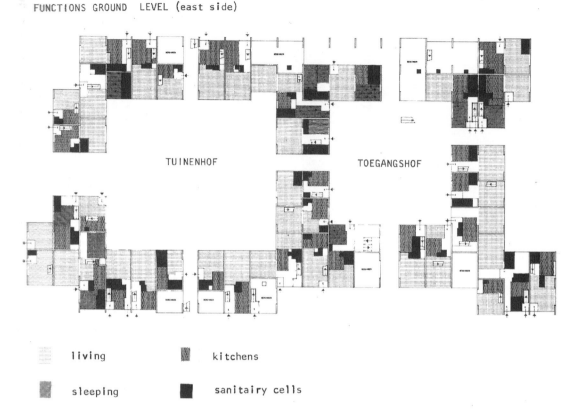

Figure 2b Part of the Molenvliet project showing the variety of fit-out in a uniform base building structure.

Finland also has government supported policies promoting open building in practice and in research. The CIB workgroup W104 on open building has members in these countries as well as from the United States, Mexico, Canada, Taiwan, China, Hong Kong, Singapore, Germany, and other countries.

A world-wide overview of residential open building projects up to 1999 can be found in a book by Kendall and Teicher [Kendall] They list 131 projects, some twenty of which are shown in some detail. The book gives an overview of technical, economical, and management issues related to this approach.

2.4 Commercial open building

The practice of Open Building is already quite familiar in commercial construction. Office buildings are routinely built as base buildings in which entire floors are leased to the occupant and fitted out by dedicated fit-out contracting firms according to the design of dedicated fit-out designers. Shopping malls shows this distinction as well. The mall's architect creates the public space in all its details, but leaves empty the retail floor space to be fitted out by specialized contractors serving occupant-controlled design.

2.4.1 Residential open building lagging behind

In that sense residential open building is only doing what already is familiar in other building types. The reasons for this lag are several. Commercial residential projects, in contrast to the commercial office building, usually operate in a sellers-market which leaves no incentive for innovation because the product is sure to sell anyway. Non-profit housing organizations also have little incentive to delegate design responsibility to occupants. Moreover, the fit-out of residential units is more complex compared to retail or office space. Kitchen and bathroom equipment in combination with general heating, ventilation, communication and power supply systems must be integrated in a small volume. Finally, we can note that in the practice of office buildings and shopping malls, the separation of base building and fit-out remains a very pragmatic affair, without much study or professional debate. There is reason to think that here too, performance is much lower than potential would allow.

2.5 A direct relationship

The examples given may illustrate that open building projects, both residential and commercial, combine two aspects. One has to do with hardware and entails the distinction of separate physical and spatial configurations – base-building and fit-out – and the potential for their systematization and industrial production. The other is the distribution of design control: where traditionally the large project was under unified design control, now part of it is under control of a large number of individual occupants.

Open building sees the distribution of design control as a condition for systematization in the building industry: A clear base-building typology enhances systemic development. Most importantly, it opens a market for fit-out systems serving individual households, retail units and business entities. Conversely, further systematization of fit-out makes individual adaptation easier and therefore is an incentive for further distribution of design control. Open building's strength, ultimately, is that it brings industrial construction in contact with the individual inhabitant in a direct relationship without mediation.

2.5.1 Infrastructure and consumer product

This direct relationship is characteristic for contemporary industrialized society. The cell phone, television, the computer, our clothes and most other things we use daily are the product of it. The most prominent example is the automobile. Here too, a complex product is directly available to the user and its systematized production is now capable of making each car customized on demand.

Surely, the lack of user control where residential construction is concerned is out of tune with contemporary society's values.

More to the point, an industry serving the user often demands an infrastructure: The manufacturing of cars requires a network of roads. Similarly, use of the mobile phone demands many thin masts and satellites orbiting the earth. By the same token, when we think of the individual dwelling as an industrial product under control of the user, a shared infrastructure must provide the space for that relationship to be productive in.

With the free-standing house this infrastructure may be the land on which we build with the roads that make it accessible and the utility systems that serve it. In higher density conditions it must be the base-building.

3. The systematization of building

The systematization of building is accelerating. It is generally agreed that in the past two or three decades, value added to the building by the manufacturer has been steadily increasing while value added by the general contractor has decreased proportionally. Designing a building has become an orchestration of available systems. Windows, doors, exterior wall panels and entire curtain walls, interior partitioning, floor slabs, elevators and stairs, balconies and banisters etc. etc. are all offered in manufacturer's catalogues. Not to forget the various utility systems bringing power, gas, water and information in our homes and getting waste out.

Do-it-yourself home project centers show us how many of these systems already have entered in direct relation with the lay person. In the North American continent, almost the entire free-standing house can be self-built. In Europe, do-it-yourself retail provides all sub-systems needed for apartment fit-out. Initially, systematization was not intended to serve the self-help user. The employment of unskilled labor on site pushed the production of intricate parts to the factory. But what makes it easy for on-site labor, makes it easy for the user, and a new retail industry was born.

The most advanced example of environmental hardware as a consumer product is found in the kitchen systems that have come to permeate residential environment, particularly in Europe and Japan. You can select your kitchen parts in IKEA outlets and put them together all by yourself. Those reluctant or unable to do so find dealers who are happy to assist their clients in designing their own and send a specialized crew to install the chosen combination. Not so long ago, the kitchen used to be an integral part of the building. Today, in the Netherlands, no developer will any longer install kitchens in houses put up for sale: he expects the buyer to order her kitchen directly from a dealer.

3.1 An open system

The Kitchen system itself is an open system because it is a composite of autonomous sub-systems. In addition to cabinets it also includes a countertop with a sink, a cooking range, an oven, a dishwasher, a refrigerator and a freezer. It may include a hot water boiler and an exhaust ventilator. Furthermore, we find in it lighting fixtures and outlets for electric power and data. The cooking range may be fed by a gas line and the sink needs to be connected to hot and cold water as well as a drainage system. The kitchen system designer may have designed the sub-system of cabinets, but all other parts have been designed and produced by other manufacturers who are not beholden to the kitchen system.

This openness has the advantage that a better subsystem can easily replace an older version, keeping the composite offering up to date. At the same time, the manufacturer and designer of, say, a faucet or dishwasher can compete for incorporation of their product in a wide range of kitchen systems.

3.2 Coordination of parts

The coordination of so many products into a larger composite system is based on the simple principle that standardization must only deal with interface conditions. Where products of two producers meet, conventions of details and dimensions must be established. Beyond that, each designer is free to do their own thing.

This successful openness was not the result of top down regulation or a single invention but the slow gain of practice. Over the years, the concept of a kitchen system became familiar to users and producers alike. Conventions of use and assembly became sufficiently stable for industry to formalize them. Social habit and consensus produced the sophisticated coordination we now take for granted.

3.3 Social conventions

This is a lesson worth remembering: The systematization in building occurs when habits are formed, and a way of working becomes generally accepted. Once a generally accepted routine appears, the door to industrial production of dedicated systems is open. It is often thought that industrialization shapes society, and of course that is true as well, but certainly in building practice, that is only part of the story. In the last century, countless inventions and proposals for building systems of all kinds have come to grief because they were not accepted by everyday practice. They demanded new ways of working but could not compete with already settled habits and customs.

What eventually became successfully produced by the manufacturer was more often than not already done in the field, and industry seized the opportunity to do it better and more efficiently.

Today, after the upheavals and revolutions of Modernism, our ways of building and living increasingly show stable conventional patterns, often on a global scale. These patterns breed systematization and this, in turn, makes true industrial production possible. The result is the increasing industrialization we have noted.

When I talk about conventions and habits, I do not mean only professional ways of working, but also the patterns of living of inhabitants. It is in the latter that industry can establish the direct relationship with the user that already has been so successful in many other aspects of our lives. Thus, we can distinguish two modes of industrialization in environmental production. The one which is most familiar serves the actual process of building. Here industry connects to the professional world to maintain a dialectical relationship with ongoing ways of design and management and on-site construction. The other, which is new, serves the user-inhabitant directly via dealers and specialized fit-out installers. Here, part of what used to be real estate becomes a consumer product, following a model already known in other aspects of daily life but not, so far, in environmental production.

The kitchen system is the most advanced example of that new trend. Bathroom systems may well be next. Eventually they will be combined in comprehensive fit-out systems as advocated by Open Building.

4. Re-distribution of design control

If fit-out systems would indeed be available like cars are today, we would have a new consumer market that rivals that of private automobiles. Before we rejoice in this seductive vision, we must ask ourselves how the base buildings will come about that must hold the countless fit-out units industry will make available to individual users. One answer is that the product will trigger the infrastructure. When the car first appeared, the freeways were not there: they came later. As with the kitchen system, fit-out systems will eventually establish themselves and base-buildings will result.

This answer is attractive to those of us who like to design and invent systems and believe in the potential of industrial production. But others will point out that we inherited from Modernism a centralized design decision process that is well established among professionals who see no merit in changing it. In conventional residential building practice, the first thing to be designed is the floor plan of the unit. Once that is known, all parties can get to work. The structural engineer can design the load bearing structure, the consultants for utility systems can design the distribution of all manner of conduits through the building. Bankers can assess loans, developers can calculate expenses and profits, bureaucrats can give permits. When we design a base building there is no floor plan. A new methodology of design and decision making is in order. But professionals, like normal people, prefer not to change their ways of working.

4.1 Systems design and instance design

Re-distribution of design control is part and parcel of industrial systematization. To make the kitchen system work two kinds of design are in order. There is the design of the system as such, and there is the design of the many instances of it. The two together make the kitchens appear in our homes. Hence, we find a distribution of design control. Details, dimensions of parts, connections of parts, materials, textures, and colors of the parts, all must be decided by the system designer. Her design decisions are general: they determine what all instances that can be made by combining the parts will share. In contrast, the design decisions pertaining to a single instance are unique because the user and the location are unique. This distribution of design responsibility allows industry to serve countless individual users.

4.2 A matter of policy

It is good to bear in mind that the examples of open building that I showed you, as well as all others that are on record, have been implemented in a state-of-the-art technology, without the benefit of any dedicated fit-out systems offered by the industry. In other words, these first experimental projects were demonstrations of re-distribution of design control first of all. They illustrate the power of the new game to be played. They also made clear how much easier it would be if dedicated fit-out systems would be available. It could not be otherwise: we have just seen how successful systematization follows already settled practice. If that is true, the issue of re-distribution of design in practice must be addressed head on to open the way for truly industrial fit-out systems.

Frank Bijdendijk, who runs one of the largest non-profit housing corporations in the Netherlands will tell you he does not think open building is a technical problem but a matter of re-distribution of responsibility first of all. He invested years of study and development to establish a policy where his tenants would be offered ownership – and hence full responsibility – for everything behind their front door. The housing corporation would be responsible for the building as a shared property of all inhabitants. Banks agreed to give mortgages to these new fit-out owners, the costs of which would be tax deductible like they are for owners of private homes.

Implemented on a national scale in the Netherlands, where the majority of households rent their homes, this would make a very large part of existing housing stock eligible for unit-by-unit renewal and renovation, creating a tremendous incentive for industrial innovation.

However, Dutch tax law was overhauled recently and no longer allows deduction of mortgage costs on fit-out ownership while maintaining the privilege for 'real' homeowners. We may assume this sad case of discrimination was not the result of ill will, but of ignorance. Economists, lawyers, politicians, bankers, industrialists and other policy makers need to know what open building policy is about. In a few countries, governments have begun to subscribe to this approach and support research and experimentation. Japan and Finland are among them. The Netherlands is one too, as you will hear from another speaker on this conference. But the need for re-distribution of design responsibility is not yet generally understood. Issues of open building policy are not yet topics of debate and study among professionals and policy makers.

But then again, as those who believe in the power of invention will say, once the car was known, the roads got built.

5. References

- see: NEXT21, *GA Japan Environmental Design*, January–February 1994, and *DOMUS*, no. 819, October 1999.
- van der Werf, Frans and Hubert Paul Froyen (1980). "Molenvliet-Wilgendonk: Experimental Housing Project." *Beyond the Modern Movement, The Harvard Architecture Review*, vol. 1, Spring.
- Kendall, Stephen and Jonathan Teicher (2000). *Residential Open Building*. London and New York: E & FN Spon.

INTERMEZZO BY THE EDITORS

SK/JD: At MIT, you partnered with Aaron Fleisher, I remember.
JH: Ah, yes.
SK/JD: To try to understand complexity; he was a computer guy, right? And I remember you trying to do something, trying to understand the form language of Amsterdam Canal houses, which led into other things.
JH: Well, yes, we were interested in each other because he was interested in creativity. And design. And I was interested in systematic things. And then, I suggested that it would be possible to write the rules for the design of an Amsterdam Canal house. Which I did. I still have it. And he put it into a computer program. So, you gave the dimension, the width, and you got the facade of an Amsterdam townhouse. And the second one was different, given different dimensions. It all worked.
SK/JD: Hmmmm . . .
JH: I liked it very much and he was doing a very serious job on it. And I did not understand all of his theoretical arguments for it, but he managed to do it. And I managed to write it down so that the rules worked. I tried to convince him to make it into a screensaver. I thought it would be fun for everybody to have all these facades that change all the time.
SK/JD: Yeah, I'd like that.
JH: He was not interested in doing that. It's too bad.
SK/JD: Well, what you just said was interesting. He was interested in creativity and you always thought that all professions have creativity involved in their work. Architects don't have a special claim on it. You are interested in the systematic, the methods, the tools. And then the book, Variations: The Systematic Design of Support. I think most people think of the words "systematic" and "variation" as contradictory.
JH: Okay.
SK/JD: And your efforts all through your career have been to let people understand that variations and systematic thinking, or systems, completely belong together.
JH: Yeah. Absolutely.

TOOLS

1965
SAR
Rules for design: a summary

Editors' Note: *This is one of the two fundamental reports on the work of the SAR (the other being "Brief Outline of the SAR Principles and Methodology"), both produced within the first year of the founding of the SAR in 1964.*

Figure 1 SAR logo

Introduction

The SAR design methodology has been drawn up as a means to effectuate a distinction between two spheres of production in the housing process. The methodology deals with the design of support structures and detachable units.

The format is similar to the brief outline beginning with general terminology and then dealing with rules for dimensioning and positioning of material and finally rules for dimensioning and positioning of space.

Modular co-ordination must ensure that the separate production of supports and detachable units remain coordinated. The zones and margins are the necessary tools for the design of the support structure. Set out below is a summary to this methodology.

Rules series 0. general terminology

Rule 0.1

The support structure belongs legally speaking to the immovables. It is for habitation and is designed in such a way that within it the occupant can decide independently about the layout and the equipment of his dwelling.

The detachable units are a set of elements belonging legally speaking to the movables, designed in such a way that by means of those elements the occupant can decide independently about the lay-out and the equipment of his dwelling within the support structure.

Motivation

The concept of support structure and detachable units has been introduced into the housing process in order to translate the right-of-say of the occupant into material terms.

The support structure contains all that does not fall within the competence of the individual dweller and about which he has no responsibility.

The detachable units contain all about which the individual dweller does have competence and about which he therefore holds responsibility.

Observation

The distinction between support structure and detachable unit is a distinction in right-of-say. The question of what belongs to the support structure and what belongs to the detachable units can therefore not only be answered on technical grounds but on the opinion that society has of the role of the individual i.e. on the amount of freedom the occupant can exercise. In each design this division must be explicitly stated.

The distinction between coarse building and finishing building is made entirely on technical grounds. Those terms refer to two phases of the production process. A support structure is a certain kind of structure.

A support structure can be a finished product within itself.

In the production of a support structure a distinction can be made between a coarse building phase and a finishing building phase.

Recommendation

Make the boundary between support structure and detachable units quite clear in the design process.

Rule 0.2

Support structure material is all material belonging to the support structure.

Detachable units' material is all material belonging to the set of detachable units.

Motivation

This terminology follows directly from 0.1.

Observation

The consequence of rule 0.1 is that in principle every material and every element can belong either to the support structure or to the detachable units depending on the division of responsibilities.

Therefore, the detachable units do not necessarily have to be industrial products. Even a masonry wall can belong to the detachable units if the occupant has right of say. (e.g. to remove it.)

Recommendation

Use the terms support structure and detachable units only in the sense as put forward in 0.2 and 0.1. Wherever a distinction in a technical sense is wanted, use the words coarse building and finishing building.

Rule series 1. size and position of material

Rule 1.1

Floor plans must be designed on the basis of a 10/20 tartan grid.

Motivation

The 10–20 cm grid enables the formulation of rules about the position of material. The 10–20 tartan grid is based on the conventions for international modular co-ordination; i.e. the basic module of 10 cm and a preferential module of 30 cm.

Observation

The 10/20 grid is derived from the basic grid of 10cms. The 10cm bands are 30cms center to center. The 20cm bands are also 30cms center to center. Therefore, 30cms is the module of the 10/20 grid. This is in accordance with the preferential agreement of international modular co-ordination.

The distance between two grid lines can be $n.30 + 10$, $n.30$ and $n.30-10$.

Recommendation

Use the 10/20 tartan grid for all your housing projects and also when you are not in a position to make a design for a true support structure. At any rate, communication during the design process will be facilitated and the development of detachable units will be stimulated.

Thus, should the occupant be permitted at a later stage to exercise his right-of-say about the layout and the equipment of his dwelling, the dimensions of the support structure will permit the introduction of a set of detachable units.

Rule 1.2

Vertical cross sections must be drawn on a grid of 10/20 bands vertically and 20cm bands horizontally.

Motivation

This rule conforms to the preferential agreement of international co-ordination that floor heights will be a multiple of 20cms.

Observation

The distance between finished floors is therefore always a multiple of 20cms.

Recommendation

The same as for rule 1.1.

Rule 1.3

In the horizontal cross section, material ends in the 10cm band of the 10/20 tartan grid.

Motivation

This rule applies to the Support structure material as well as the detachable unit material. The resulting dimensions of material prove to be quite useful in housing. This rule determines that the 10cm band shall accommodate all connections between support structure material and detachable unit material.

Observation

From this rule a series of dimensions are available for accommodating material.

Recommendation

Observe this rule whenever you consider communication within, and co-ordination of, the design process and the production process of importance. Disregard this rule only for sound reasons and after ascertaining that communication and co-ordination will not needlessly be impaired.

Do not disregard this rule wherever Support structure material and detachable unit material may be expected to meet.

Rule 1.4

The fitting dimension is the distance between material and the next grid line.

The tolerance field of the material is kept outside the fitting dimension.

Motivation

The concept "fitting dimension" has been introduced to lay down the position of material in a modular grid. The fitting dimension enables the following:

a. the use of non-modular material in a modular grid;
b. non-modular positioning of material in a modular grid;
c. the use of sub-modular measurements in dimensioning of material

The fitting dimension enables the exact positioning of material.

Observation

As follows from the rule, the fitting dimension always indicates free space.

As follows from rule 1.3, the fitting dimension in the horizontal cross section will always be between 0 and 10cm: 0 p 10.

As follows from rule 1.2, the fitting dimension in the vertical cross section will always be between 0 and 20cm.

Recommendation

A series of fitting dimensions of 0, 2½, 5, 7½ and 10cm proves useful for many of the traditional construction methods for the support structure.

If possible, use one fitting dimension throughout a project, especially where connections between supports structure material and detachable unit material may be expected.

The guaranteed free space is n. 30–10cm (i.e. for p=0 cm).

Rule series 2 – size and position of space

Rule 2.1

- An α (alpha) zone is an area that is inside, that is for private use and has the possibility of direct relation with the outside.
- A β (betta) zone is an area that is inside, that is for private use and has no possibility of direct relation with the outside.
- A γ (gamma) zone is an area that can be either inside or outside and that is for public use.
- A δ (delta) zone is an area that is outside and that is for private use.

Motivation

Zones give situations. (i.e. inside or outside, relation or no relation with the exterior, public or private).

Also, the fact that an area can be either for public or private use is a situational characteristic. Therefore, zones are a tool to lay down situations. The designer is free to establish which functions may or may not be desired or expected in a given situation. By means of zones, situational aspects can be linked to functional aspects and vice versa.

Observation

Each dwelling type is characterized by its specific arrangement of the four zones which it have been defined.

Two zones will always be separated by a margin (see rule 2.3).

A zone has only one dimension. The second dimension is introduced by the concept: "Sector" (see rule 2.6).

A zone does not necessarily have to be straight.

Recommendation

Indicate in your design what functions you designate to a given zone. This may be done by giving a zone-analysis. A zone-analysis indicates the decision for the sizes of the zones which have been chosen. Therefore, a zone-analysis represents the standards which have been set for the design.

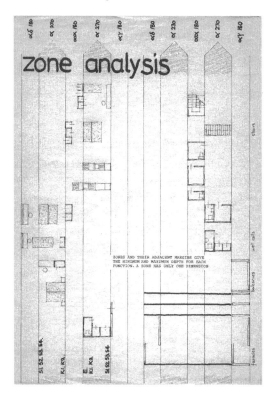

Figure 2 Zone Analysis

Rule 2.2

A margin is an area between two zones. It has the properties of two adjacent zones and therefore it derives its name from these zones.

Motivation

Margins enable decision making at a later stage about the position of the material and the dimensions of the spaces. (See also rule 2.4.)

Observation

An alpha delta (α δ) margin, an alpha gamma (α γ) margin and a beta gamma (β γ) margin always contain a facade.

A margin between a gamma (γ) zone and any other zone always represents the boundary between public and private territories.

Recommendation

In a zone-analysis the adjacent margins are always taken into consideration. If necessary, however, a separate margin analysis can be made in order to decide on the size of the margin by demonstrating what specific elements are related to the margin in the given design.

Rule 2.3

Specific living spaces are spaces designated to accommodate one main function of which the dimensions can be determined beforehand on the basis of an analysis of this function.

General living spaces are spaces designated to accommodate more than one main function. Therefore, the dimensions of the general living spaces cannot be determined beforehand but most follow from the lay-out variants.

Utility spaces are spaces designed not for living purposes but have a utilitarian character. The dimensions can be determined beforehand on the basis of analysis of the utility functions.

Motivation

The distinction between the three categories of spaces makes available to the design process groups of elements each having certain characteristics. The distinction between the space categories has been made in such a way that it is possible to determine beforehand the specific living spaces and the utility spaces on the basis of certain standards.

This enables an evaluation of a support structure by giving as many possible lay-out variants which are all based on the same space elements and therefore are all based on the same set of standards.

Observation

In principle one can establish separately from each design process the set of specific living spaces with which the lay-out variants in the support structure can be designed.

Reference is also made to rule 2.4 where a link is made between specific living spaces and zones.

Recommendation

When deciding upon the specific living spaces draw up a "Summary-sheet specific living spaces."

Rule 2.4

A specific living space ends in two successive margins.

Motivation

This rule links the dimensions of the zones to the dimensions of the specific living spaces. Because the dimensions of specific living spaces follow from functional analysis and the standards which can be derived thereof, this relates the dimensions of the zones to the possibilities for lay-out of the support structures.

Observation

On the basis of the zones and margins, the designer is free to formulate further rules designating certain types of specific living spaces to certain zones.

The width of an α (alpha) zone or a β (betta) zone represents the minimum depth of specific living spaces which can be positioned in this zone. The adjacent margins represent the extra depth available to specific living spaces, according to rule 2.4.

The size of an α (alpha) zone or a β (betta) zone together with the adjacent margins represents the maximum depth which the specific living spaces can have that are positioned in these zones.

If the total size of a zone plus margin is kept constant the designer is still free to choose between a small margin plus a large zone or a large margin plus a small zone. The first example demonstrates little variability but high minimum standard. The second example demonstrates much variability but a minimum standard which is relatively low.

Therefore, standards regarding the dimensions of specific living spaces are laid down by the dimensions of zones and margins.

Recommendation

Relate the chosen specific living spaces and the zones to one another in the "Summary-sheet specific living spaces." This makes the desired relation between zones and specific living spaces clear to other people.

Rule 2.5

The dimension of zones is always n. 30–10.
The dimension of margins is always n. 30 + 10.

Motivation

Because the width of an α (alpha) zone or a β (betta) zone represents the minimum depth of the specific living spaces which can be positioned in those zones (see 2.4) the zone is a guaranteed free space. A guaranteed free space always measures n.30–10 (see 1.4). Therefore, separation walls of specific living spaces which run parallel to the zones will always be positioned in the margins. Because material always ends in the 10cm band of the 10/20 tartan grid (see rule 1.3) the margins always have the dimension n.30 + 10.

Observation

The minimum margin therefore is 10 cm. There is always a margin between two zones.

Separation walls of specific living spaces which run perpendicular to a zone can lie in the zone.

Separation walls of specific living spaces which run parallel to the zone will always lie in the margin.

Rule 2.6

A sector is a part of a zone with the adjacent margins within which the arrangement of spaces can be freely chosen.

Motivation

A zone has only one dimension. The concept of sector introduces the second dimension. Therefore, a sector represents a specific area which has the properties of the zone.

Observation

There are alpha (α), beta (β), gamma (γ), and delta (δ) sectors.

Sectors are defined by the positioning of Support structure material in the zones and/or the margins.

Therefore, the Support structure can be considered to be an arrangement of sectors. A dwelling within a Support structure can be considered to be a sector group. A sector can be analyzed on its lay-out possibilities. This analysis takes into account all which has already been previously established in the zone-analysis.

Recommendation

Make a sector analysis of every Support structure. This will give information about the lay-out possibilities of the Support structure. But most of all it will facilitate the location and dimensioning of load bearing elements.

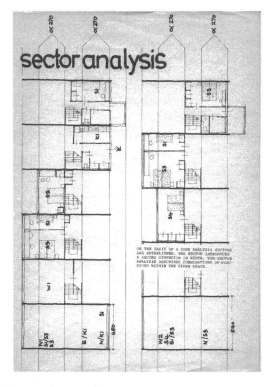

Figure 3 Sector analysis

Rule 2.7

A basic variant gives the position of the dwelling functions which together constitute a dwelling program within a given sector group. A sub-variant of a basic variant is a worked-out plan of which the dwelling functions and their positions conform to those of the basic variant.

Motivation

In a given floor space which can be arranged into a dwelling more often than not the number of possible lay-out variants remains quite obscure. e.g. by altering the position of a door one can already create a new variant. The concept "basic variant" enables one to note down specific functional organizations of a dwelling.

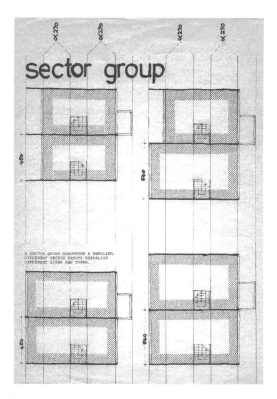

Figure 4 Sector group

By noting down all possible basic variants of a given sector group one gains insight into the spatial and functional possibilities of part of a support structure.

Observations

The basic variant is a code and therefore does not give the dimensions of spaces but only the position of the living functions. (The specific living spaces as well as the general living spaces.)

Because the relation between the sizes of specific living spaces and the size of zones, margins and sectors is known by previous analysis, the notation of a basic variant gives quick insight into the lay-out possibilities of a given sector group.

A new basic variant occurs whenever:

a. A function is exchanged for another function;
b. A function changes position.

Therefore, each basic variant really is the notation of a collection of sub-variants. Therefore, each floor plan may be seen as a sub-variant of a basic variant.

SAR

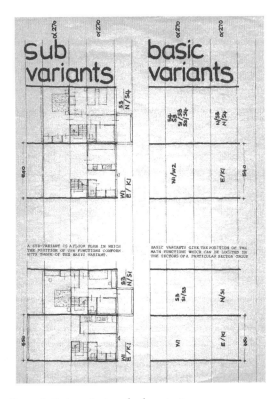

Figure 5 Basic variants and sub-variants

Recommendation

Note down the basic variants schematically. Under each lay-out plan note down the basic variant which belongs to that plan.

Always check if a basic variant is possible by drawing at least one matching sub-variant. In designing a Support structure note down only those basic variants which have been checked.

1988
TYPE AS A SOCIAL AGREEMENT

Editors' Note: *This paper was presented at the Asian Congress of Architects, Seoul, Korea, in 1988. The author dedicated it to his students in the Science Masters in Architecture Studies Program, Department of Architecture at the Massachusetts Institute of Technology, whose work is used in the paper to discuss the concept of Type. In this paper, the author also returns to his discussion of the role of the architect.*

Introduction

Figure 0 Lamayuri Monastery, Ladakh, India, by Solomon Benjamin

The post modem period in architecture allows us once more to be inspired by the past. Architects always have learned from precedent. Among architects there is a renewed interest in local traditional architecture. This reflects a desire to connect again to the roots of one's culture; a desire shared alike, it seems, by professionals and lay people. But making a connection between tradition and the demands of modem times is not an easy task. Sometimes attempts to do so lead to superficial borrowing. We may see the application of decorative and iconographic elements to buildings that have otherwise very little in common with any traditional example.

When we want to connect to our cultural traditions, we must study in depth the building types these traditions maintained for many centuries. We must study them, not in the way historians would do, but from a designer's point of view. We want to understand the design principles behind the building types to decide how we can use them today. Or goal is not to copy but to transform what was done in the past into something compatible with the values we hold today. We want to learn from our cultural heritages, not to deny present day realities, but to establish a continuity between tradition and renewal.

House type

While there are different kinds of buildings we can choose from – the place of worship, the palace, the castle, or the house – we should first of all study the house type. Because it is from the common houses that the more special buildings are derived. The temple, the palace and the castle usually offer enriched, enlarged, and embellished variations on the spatial and structural principles already found in the house type.

In the house type we find architectural values people share. The house is the place where we spend most of our time, where we are born, marry, raise children, and grow old. The house type is perhaps the most widely shared experience in a culture. Because we are

DOI: 10.4324/9781003011385-38

Type as a social agreement

so familiar with it, we may even forget to notice it at all. In their implicit way house types have always offered a stable physical environment fitting social life as the glove fits the hand. Amos Rapoport was, I believe, the first to seriously study house typology on a cross cultural, comparative basis. He argues in his book, "House Form and Culture"[1], that the house type cannot be explained by purely functional or technical reasoning. In other words: neither climate, available materials, family structure, nor use, tell us why a particular house type is shaped the way it is. Of course, we understand why, for instance, the Malay house was built from bamboo and that it stands off the ground for good technical and environmental reasons. But within technical and functional constraints there always remains room for further choice. Here the culture, the social patterns, and shared preference of a people are expressed in the house form itself. The particular shape of the Malayan house with its expressive roof together with the particular organization of its spaces inside express a people's identity and are closely linked to other cultural expressions like clothing, and customs of social behavior. This makes the house a cultural artifact: the collective product of what a people is all about.

Over the years at MIT I have had the opportunity to study house types with students who came from very different parts of the world. Many brought with them keen interest in the houses their parents and grandparents had lived in. They sensed that these 'old fashioned,' traditional, and local buildings represented important cultural values. I encouraged them to explore what they liked in those buildings and to learn from the experience invested in them. My interest as a methodologist was to learn more about the general principles of house typology: to find a method for the analysis and comparison of house types. This article offers a brief summary of some of the things we learned. I will also discuss ways in which designers can work from the traditional patterns to arrive at new solutions. In the context of a single paper my overview can only be superficial and incomplete, but I hope it will show the validity of the study of vernacular house types as a source for present day design.

Different WAYS OF SEEING the type

Each house type can be described in a number of different ways. Each way suggests a different systemic organization. Three WAYS OF SEEING the same type can be distinguished in all cases:

First of all, we can see the type as a **spatial organization**. Here we observe the kinds of spaces the house type offers and the ways in which these spaces relate to one another. The example of the Qa'a houses of Medina, Saudi Arabia, studied by Sameer A. Khasjugjee (Figures 1.1–1.3)[2] shows us a relatively narrow courtyard to which the most important spatial elements relate: there is the Diwan, a raised floor under a vault in open connection to the courtyard; and there is the Qa'a proper, itself having a center space with a skylight from the roof, and two diwan-like spaces connected to it opposite to one another. Then there are the stairs as well as the entrance. The latter is always angled to assure privacy from the street. There is, of course, much more to the spatial organization of this house type but what has been said may suffice to make the point that spatial organization is very much part of typology.

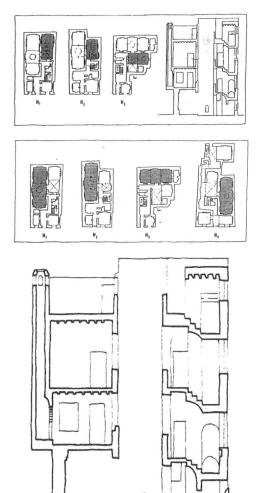

Figure 1.1–1.3 An example of the Qa'a houses of Madina

Secondly, we can see the house type as a **physical system**. In the Medina example we find heavy stone walls that change to brick walls on the second floor. The walls form rectangles to stabilize a building that can have four to five stories. The ceilings are high to assure sufficient ventilation in the hot climate.

Finally, we can see the house in a **stylistic way**. Here we look, for instance, at the way the windows are placed in the facade, the kind of windows and doors used, and the decorations applied around edges and surfaces both inside and outside.

We can, of course, choose other ways to see the type. The power of a type is indeed that it is a whole and we can always find another way to describe it. Each description is necessarily only partial. Descriptions need not be in conflict with each other; indeed, the type is always more than the sum of all possible descriptions given. For our purpose in this paper, however, the three WAYS OF SEEING suggested above may suffice. They touch the most important and general aspects of the type.

Relative independence of the systems

When we study the interrelation between these three systems – the spatial, the physical, and the stylistic – we find that they are relatively independent of one another. Using exactly the same construction principles as applied in the Medina house, for example, we could build a house with a very different spatial organization. Conversely, we could use a different technology to arrive at a spatial organization very similar to the one we find in the Medina example. Finally, we know from recent attempts to connect to traditional values that one can use stylistic elements from a traditional house type and apply them to a building that has no spatial or technical similarity to this type at all. Hence there seems to be a 'loose fit' between the three systems.

One can argue that any attempt to separate the three systems is a violation of the integrity of the type. This is true but as explained earlier, we do not want to copy but to transform in order to respond to new conditions. In that case we want to understand the relatively independent ways in which the type can be adapted.

It seems to me that from the three systems the most fundamental and the most stable one is the spatial organization. It seems most intimately related to our behavior. We see indeed how technology can change and new materials are adopted while the same space organization is maintained. An interesting example is offered by Jamel Akbar who describes in his doctoral thesis how a new settlement built by the people themselves, using concrete walls and roofs, nevertheless acquires the same spatial urban organization we find in the traditional mud brick towns of Saudi Arabia. Akbar is making the argument that as long as the social structure of mutual responsibilities is maintained, the same spatial organizations will occur.[3]

When I suggest that materials can be changed without affecting too much the type itself this does not mean the physical system is less important. We must distinguish the systemic properties of the physical organization from actual materials and construction methods. The latter are changeable to a large degree as long as the former is maintained. The thorough analysis of the Malayan house done by Wan Abidin (Figures 2.1 and 2.2)[4] suggests one could replace the wood columns and beams by similar ones of steel or concrete; or that one could replace the screens of bamboo matting, that let through air without admitting too much light, by screens produced from plastics or metals performing the same functions. If we would do so we would still recognize the house type, with its 'Serambi' – a porch where family activities occur under the shelter of the roof.

Figure 2.1 A Malayan house

Thus it appears that our recognition of the types physical organization does not depend very much on the kind of material used, nor is it particularly important how the joints are worked out This organization is primarily understood as a choice of kinds of physical

Type as a social agreement 339

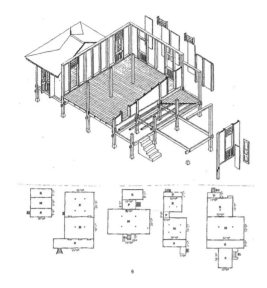

Figure 2.2 Rethinking the technical systems making a Malayan house

parts – that is to say: beams, columns, screens, etc., of a particular shape and size and the specific way they are related to one another when distributed in space. What the parts are made of and how they are joined is not a negligible matter, but still seems to be of a second order.

Nevertheless, we may prefer to keep the physical system while transforming the spatial. An example of the permanence of the physical system in a particular culture is found in the way houses are built in Japan today. In spite of what we hear about housing factories offering revolutionary technologies, the vast majority of the Japanese houses are still built in a wood post and beam system that stems directly from the centuries old Japanese house building tradition. The carpenter still knows the various parts and the way they are distributed in space to make a whole. He connects the parts by means of traditional joints, slightly altered sometimes to adapt to modem milling machinery. There are presently factories in Japan that mill house frames designed in this traditional system by means of a computer steering a fully automated array of machines. In this example we find continuation of the physical system without much continuity in the spatial system. The houses built so efficiently in this traditional physical system are mostly westernized in their space layout. On the other hand, stylistic elements may remain. The example also shows that the computer and production technology are very flexible tools. This allows the culture to define the system (the shape and size of parts and their relations) whereas technology offers ways to produce it.

A different choice was made by Khasjugjee, who decided to stay with the spatial arrangement of the Medina House but to modify the physical system (Figure 3.0). Where the traditional system has masonry walls running in both directions perpendicular to one another, structural walls in concrete now run in just one direction while those in the other direction are brick Infill. We see here how the type's spatial organization has been maintained but is built in a radically different way.

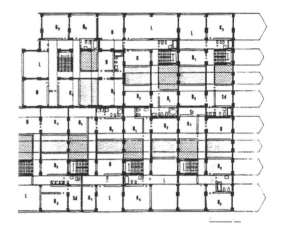

Figure 3.0 The Madina house reinterpreted with a new physical system

Hence there is freedom to vary or keep constant the one system or the other depending on what we judge to be most meaningful in the traditional type.

A third example of the partial modification of a house type is given in Jamel Akbar's master thesis on the modern use of the courtyard house in Saudi Arabia (Figure 3.1 and 3.2).[5] Here some adaptations are made in the spatial organization, among other things, to accommodate the car, but basically spatial relations remain in the traditional way. The physical system is a concrete structure with variable infill. The floorplans show how each house is different in size and layout within the rules of the type.

Variations within the type

A type allows for many different interpretations. No two examples are ever alike. As we have seen, typology is basically systemic. Within any system many variations of interpretation are always possible. Indeed, one can define a system as what is constant – in terms of parts and relations – among a large number of different expressions. We can once more look at the examples given so far to see their variations within the type. The examples of the Qa'a

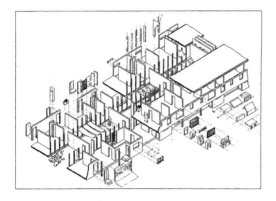

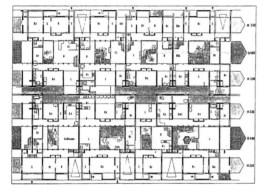

Figures 3.1 and 3.2 A proposal for a physical structure and its' infill; plan variations in a continuous urban tissue in Saudi Arabia

Usually houses of very different sizes are found within the same type. In spite of the contrary evidence in the Malayan house we find in most cases that the large house and the small house have rooms of about the same size. The larger house, however, has many more rooms and often it is more typologically complete. When the house has to be small, sometimes certain kinds of spaces belonging to the type are omitted, while others are maintained. We see an example of this kind of reduction in the sections of the traditional house of Ahmedabad, India, as studied by Arjun Nagarkatti. (Figures 4.1–4.3).[6] The three examples each have a 'front house' and a 'back house' separated by a narrow courtyard. We see how in the small house the front part is reduced to a single room. In his thesis, Nagark^{at}ti proposed a 20th century architecture with new structural systems, and an urban tissue based on the traditional house type. (Figure 4.4)

house illustrated here are from a much larger number, all different from each other. But in each example, we find the same spaces related in the same way (Figures 1.1–1.3). In the Malayan case we also find constant spatial relations in the floor plans, but very different sizes and proportions of the individual rooms (Figure 2.2). In Akbar's courtyard houses the sizes of the courtyards vary considerably (Figure 3.2). In a strongly ordered framework of parallel zones and spatial relations each house nevertheless shows a different spatial arrangement.

In all cases the result is that the houses are perceived as individuals, each having their own identity – but of a same family. Once we are familiar with one example, we can easily find our way in any other houses of the same type.

Now we see how the type serves a dual purpose. Each house within a type was built for a specific client with specific preferences and means, and on a specific site; but each was built following the same typological rules. The type makes us share its particular values and therefore share a culture, while at the same time it allows us to express ourselves as individuals within that culture.

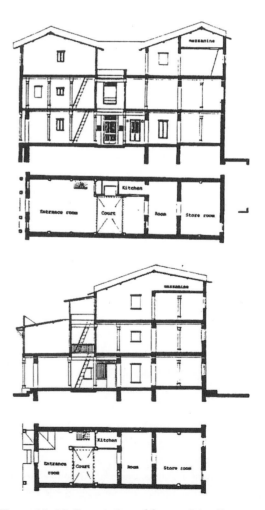

Figures 4.1–4.3 Cross sections of three traditional houses in Ahmedabad, India

Type as a social agreement

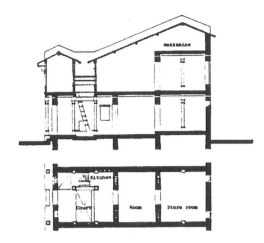

Figures 4.1–4.3 (Continued)

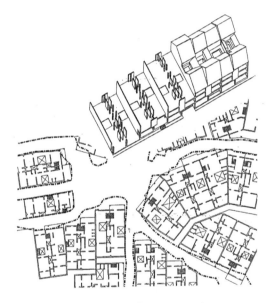

Figure 4.4 Revisioning a 20th century architecture using new structural systems, and an urban tissue based on the traditional house types of Ahmedabad

A study of the Pompeian house type, of classical Roman times, shows that the type has three open, courtyard like spaces: the Atrium, a space with a roof opened to the sky in the center; followed by a court surrounded by colonnaded galleries, called Peristyle; followed by a back yard. In the smaller houses the back yard may disappear first. Next the Peristyle may go, but the Atrium will always be there. We may thus find typological spatial arrangement in a 'degenerated' form, like the front part of the smaller example of the Ahmedabad type is 'degenerated'. Apparently, there is a hierarchy: some parts must be omitted before others and some may never be omitted. In the same way we would expect the poor version of the Medina House not to have a diwan and perhaps only a primitive Qa'a composed of two parts instead of three. We need to learn much more about the dynamics of variation within types, but the hierarchical principle of spatial organization may well be a universal quality of the house type.

Function and space

In the modernist tradition we are used to name the spaces of the house after the functions they hold. In the traditional house type the relation between space and function is more sophisticated. If a space has a specific name – like the Roman 'Atrium' the Arabian 'Qa'a', or the Malaysian porch called 'Seram-bi' – we may seek to describe the kinds of functions that usually take place in it. Usually we find there is not one specific function. The Atrium, for instance, was a place where many things might occur. It is best understood as the most 'public' space of the Roman house. Among other things it was the space where visitors were received or kept waiting before being invited into more private spaces of the house. The 'Serambi' is where we can expect the usual activities taking place on a porch; sitting and watching the street, meeting with friends and neighbors. But a better way to describe the Serambi is to point out that it is a link between inside and outside space, also connecting the more public street side and the front yard with the more private realm of the house itself. The identity of such typological spaces is not derived from the activities that take place in them, but from the position they take in the system; the place they have in the transition between public and private and, most of all, by their particular architectural quality and shape. Hence an Atrium can simply be described by the particular roof it has with an opening in the middle through which the rainwater flows into a basin in the floor. A Qa'a can be described by its physical organization of three parts; the floor of the middle part about two feet lower than the floors of the adjacent parts of which the ceilings are one story high while the middle space reaches to the skylight in the roof. A Serambi is a roofed floor without walls in front of the house and connected to the ground by a flight of stairs.

In this way, traditional house types always have certain rooms of a very specific architectural quality. These typological spaces can be described along the three axes suggested above: Their particular shape and architecture, their position relative to 'inside' and 'outside', and their role in the definition of public and private realms in the house. The names of these typological spaces are not functional. They evoke architectural qualities. Indeed, it is the function that derives its importance and meaning from the space it takes place in, rather than the other way around. It makes a difference whether the guest is received in the atrium or in another, more private space. Sleeping, eating, working, and doing business may happen in a variety of places, sometimes depending on the season. Cooking, for obvious reasons, usually takes place in a designated space and for formal reasons there may be a banqueting hall, but the norm is that there is no one-on-one relation between function and space.

House types, therefore, defying functional explanation, can best be described in architectural terms. This is not only true for the spaces but also for the physical organization. Here we also have typological parts like beams, columns, lintels, walls, etc., with their own identity but not necessarily defined in terms of materials and technologies. The Greek column is the well-known example of a physical architectural entity by itself. We know it originally as a marble column – itself believed to be the interpretation of wooden posts – but Palladio's classical columns are often made of brick and plaster, and later we see beautiful examples in wood built by carpenters on the North American continent. The analysis of a house type, therefore, is primarily an exercise in architectural distinctions, both spatial and physical.

Design rules

Once we understand house typology in this way there need not be any doubt that we can learn from it for modern design practice. The systemic rules recognized in the type are in fact design rules. They have a formal character. This insight is the basis for the study Doo-Ho Sohn did on a number of traditional houses in the village of Hawhoe, Korea (Figures 5.1–5.3).[7] The strong architectural quality of the houses is evident. At the same time, one only has to look at three of them to recognize a powerful typological base. There is variation within clear similarity. Sohn has appropriately decided to translate the systemic structure of the type in a formal way directly linked to the design activity. He has described the house type in terms of a series of design rules: rules reflecting decisions a designer must take to arrive at an instance of the type. He divides the design rules in two kinds: the truly 'typological' design rules that have to do with the ordering of the whole and the shapes particular to the type and, in addition, the 'technological' design rules, that have more to do with the making of the house rather than the shaping of it.

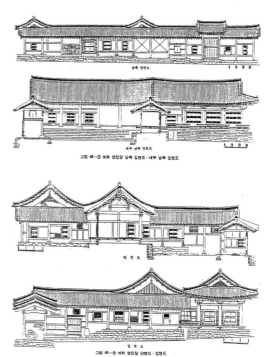

Figures 5.1–5.2 Elevations of a Yang-jin Dang house in Korea

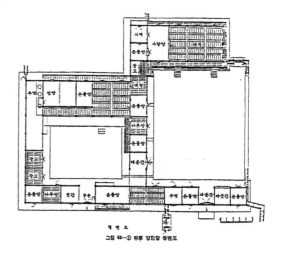

Figures 5.3 Plan of the Yang-jin Dang house

In the thesis study in which he describes his analysis, Sohn takes one more logical step to test the validity of his rules. He builds a 'design game' in which the design rules are used. The game consists of a site plan

Type as a social agreement 343

and a set of simple wooden rectangles of different sizes standing for commonly known spatial parts called 'Kan' from which these houses were composed. Players are invited to design a 'Hawhoe House' by arranging the pieces on the site following the given design rules. In Sohn's thesis, therefore, the type is seen to suggest a design method, placing it firmly in the architectural realm (Figure 5.4).

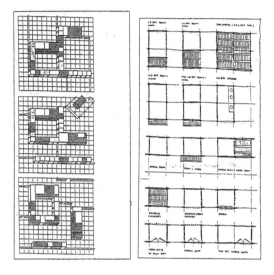

Figure 5.4 A design game based on an analysis of the Korean Kan house type and variations of Kan types.

Large scale application

The recognition that a house type is architecturally determined but not functionally, and that this is done in such a systemic way that variations of interpretation come easily, suggests a powerful new approach in residential design. We should focus on the formal architectural qualities of the type. Once these are established, we can always deal with programmatic requirements, making variations within the framework of rules. Because the type gives general principles, we no longer need to design a single example, fully defined in form and function, to be repeated endlessly across a site. Uniformity can be replaced by similarity. When many units are needed, we can just deploy the typological elements all units must have in common, leaving more detailed functional decisions to a later stage. The result of such an approach can be very rich and varied, and yet systematic and efficient to build.

This approach is chosen by Solomon Benjamin in a study inspired by the houses of Ladakh in the Himalayas of Northern India (Figures 6.1–6.3).[8] He found how the existing type derives much of its particular spatial arrangement from the sloping site on which it is built. The houses partly overlap, connected by partially covered walkways between them. This principle is used by Benjamin to formalize an urban tissue by continuous deployment of roofed spaces and courtyards, but without any firm delineation of the boundaries of the houses. The particular territories occupied by each unit are defined later. However, each unit will always have its courtyard, an entry and surrounding rooms on different levels, always thematically connected to the courtyard. Once more we see how relations are kept constant while dimensions may change. No house need be exactly like another. Yet the number of parts to be manipulated is limited and easy to understand.

Working in this way, different 'layers of deployment' are distinguished, each demanding a separate design stage. Thus, a series of overlapping 'deployments' are made. First the site is cut and filled to accommodate public and private zones. Next primary walls are deployed. After that the roofs determine the shape and position of the courtyards, and so on. Layers are not strictly repetitive in their deployment. Distances between walls may vary as we go, so do sizes of courtyards and positions of entrances. But relations are always as dictated by the type.

It may be evident that this 'layering' approach is only possible when a type is clearly understood and analyzed in its formal organization. Indeed, the hierarchical organization of the house equates with the hierarchical organization of the urban tissue. Both follow from the same typological source.

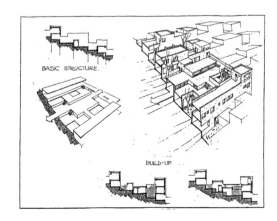

Figure 6.1 Basic structure and first stage in the design 'layering' of the tissue based on the Ladakh house type

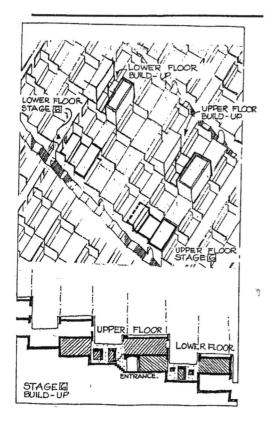

Figure 6.2 Built-up interpretation and principle sections;

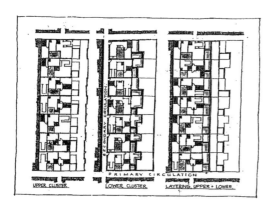

Figure 6.3 Plan examples

Following a similar approach Christina Gryboyjanni takes an additional step (Figures 7.1–7.3).[9] Her urban tissue is formally derived from the existing typological conditions in Kaisariani, a suburb of Athens. She transforms the existing neighborhood, not by elimination of its typological qualities but by adding to them, making the whole more intensive and richer. Accepting the tendency to build higher in what was originally a low-rise neighborhood Gryboyjanni introduces multi story apartment houses with narrow courtyards. In addition, she maintains the one-story house type originally found in the area. She accepts the existing street organization as an array of major and minor streets with communal courtyards behind the houses. The larger buildings are made to relate to the streets and the smaller houses remain related to the internal squares. The latter are raised to accommodate parking below and offer a crossing of the major roads by pedestrian walkways.

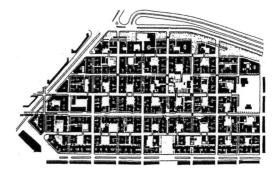

Figure 7.1 An urban tissue derived from the existing typology of a neighborhood in Kaisariani in Athens.

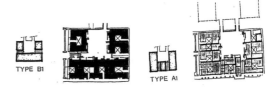

Figure 7.2 Two block types

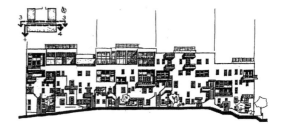

Figure 7.3 Elevation of the inside of block type B

Gryboyjanni's study is a good example of systemic elaboration where the traditional hierarchies of spaces and forms are not reduced by modernization but strengthened in their architectural expression. Once more the study of the typological systems leads to a natural variation: no courtyard or plaza is similar to another, no two houses need be the same. Yet there is a strong unity and a remarkable efficiency of expression.

The architect's role

When an architect connects in his work to a traditional type he does not borrow from another architect's work. Using existing typology is not a matter of professional originality or lack thereof. When we use a type, we connect to values we share with other people: clients and users as well as colleagues. From this common base the architect must deal with the specific problems at hand – the site, the program, the car and other modern amenities – to find a synthesis. In this way we make something new by transformation of What is familiar. In the type professionals and lay people share common ground. Here we can achieve a true architecture of the community.

When we transform the traditional type, we must decide what to retain and what to discard. Because the type reflects common values the choice as to what to keep cannot be a personal one but must reflect the shared values of the society we work for. The type is not an invitation just to pick and choose what we fancy but offers a frame of reference by means of which we can best discuss with our clients where to start and in what way to transform. A great advantage of the typological method is that the architect is liberated from the too narrow constraints of a peer group value system and invited to operate in a larger cultural framework.

In a world inundated by new things it is not a bad strategy for the architect to seek maximum continuity with the past without rejection of what is of our own times. Let the circumstances and practical needs be added to the spatial tradition and enrich it rather than replace what is still valued. The originality of the architect should lie in the ways he finds to assure this continuity in a particular way. The challenge to our profession is no longer to be avant-garde and to refuse the past, but to connect to it and transform it, in a continuous and sophisticated process to suit todays culture.

1988
THE USES OF LEVELS

Editors' Note: *This paper was delivered as the Keynote Address UNESCO Regional Seminar on Shelter for The Homeless, Seoul, Korea, 1988 and published in Open House International, Vol. 27 No. 2, 2002. It is an important paper because it clearly describes the concept of levels of intervention that was and continued to be a central theme of the authors' thinking and writing.*

Introduction

An international meeting of professionals offers a good opportunity to ask ourselves where we stand in relation to the complex problem called housing. One can have different opinions about the question when housing as we understand it today – as a professional occupation – really began. Some may argue that it was with the passing of the first housing laws in Europe at the turn of the 20th century. Others feel that the system only came into its own in the 1930's or even only after the Second World War. But it is safe to say that we can look back at least a half-century of professional effort on behalf of those in need of better shelter.

Against that background I would like to pose two questions:

First: what have we learned, in that period, about human settlement; what knowledge have we gained by research and experience that we did not have fifty years ago?

Second: How did we adapt our ways of working, our methods, to the new knowledge acquired?

If you ask me to answer these questions in a few words, my response to question one would be: "very much; we now know much more about all aspects of human settlement. Compared to what we know now, the generations before the Second World War seem ignorant."

But my response to question two would be: "poorly; our ways of working have responded inadequately to the new knowledge we gained. Our methods are still based on those first applied half a century ago."

Our major problem today as professionals – architects and planners, developers and engineers, involved in housing – is exactly this serious discrepancy between what we know and what we can actually handle. Like all other professions, we must develop new skills and methods to meet the challenges of our times.

In my talk today I would like to discuss this gap between knowledge and capability in some depth. I also want to present to you a way of looking at the built environment, a model if you like, that may help us to bridge it.

Today we need a fresh look at what we are doing. In conferences on housing, like the one we are having here, it is customary to point out how complex the problem of housing is: how many actors are involved and how many aspects are of importance to it. We also tend to remind ourselves of the magnitude of the problem: how many millions of people are in need of better shelter. It is easy to believe the task is really too large and too complex and that therefore the results will always fall short of our expectations. We try hard, but the problem is very difficult. We all would like to contribute to the well-being of mankind. We dream of a better world. But our work falls short of our expectations: there is so much more to be desired.

In a situation like that it is often useful to step back a while and reconsider the premises from which we operate. I want to argue that our vision of the built environment is outdated and show you a new model which is presently emerging among us: a model that fits better the more sophisticated knowledge we have gained over time. This new model is the major subject of my talk.

Things we have learned

I have composed a short list of things we have learned about the built environment and human settlement. Things that our view of the built environment must respond to if we want to act effectively. Things that today are important to keep in mind.

My list is not complete, and I am sure you can add to it. You may also feel that some things are less important than others. However, I am confident that most of us will agree that the items in my list should belong to our housing agenda and that we must be able to incorporate them in our ways of working. Here we go:

1. Housing is only partially a matter of production of buildings. We have learned that in housing the issue is not just to provide a roof over people's heads, but to create conditions that will, eventually, give everybody a decent house. In other words: the issue is not production of houses but the cultivation of a process. As you know, the World Bank has gone so far as not to give money any more for building projects, but only for training and organization to improve the housing process itself. *(The old model said: The primary goal is to give shelter; build as many units as you can, there is no time to waste; the need is so large. Mass production and industrialization of housing are most important)*

2. The job is not just professional. To produce cars it is best to hire the best engineers, managers, and marketing people: a professional crew. In housing, this is not enough. Professionals are important and, indeed, indispensable, but they must work together with users, user groups, and those who represent them: the politicians and other elected officials. I leave aside here the very important role of bureaucracy which probably must be seen as a class apart, neither professional nor user. *(In the old model, housing was seen as a professional job: the experts had to make all the decisions. The engineers and designers had to provide shelter for the masses in the most efficient and scientific way possible. User needs had to be studied but users could not be involved in the process)*

3. Change over time is important. The recognition that things change over time and must improve over time is perhaps the single most important new aspect introduced in our thinking about housing. Housing projects and neighborhoods must grow and develop over time. There is no such thing as an instant environment. What is good today is insufficient tomorrow. Many housing projects that were built in Europe in the 1950's, and were considered examples for other countries to follow, are now obsolete. They lack the amenities – central heating, kitchen and bathroom equipment – that people now expect but were not available twenty-five years ago. Being built in concrete these projects are extremely expensive to be renovated or to be demolished. *(In the old model, the dimensions of time were not considered: "We must design the best possible houses for the people. We must design the house for the future, for the better world of tomorrow . . . now!")*

4. Uniformity is not efficient. Uniform floor plans and uniform buildings do not guarantee industrialized building methods. On the other hand, truly industrialized methods make different solutions possible. Hence there need not be a contradiction between variety and industrial production. Indeed, we have now learned that the emphasis on uniform floor plans has slowed down the development of truly industrialized systems. *(In the traditional model, it was believed that uniformity ensured efficiency and industrialization. This is perhaps the most tenacious misunderstanding in housing, and I suspect some of you may challenge my denial of this principle. I will say more about it later on.)*

5. Users have different values and different needs. It is impossible to find a solution that fits everybody. A house is a personal thing and must adapt to the user. People like to share the same type of dwellings and to conform to certain lifestyles. But within that common context they want to identify themselves as different from their neighbors. The functional needs of households differ, too. Individual preferences are very important and can only be taken care of on an individual basis. *(The traditional mass housing model needs the*

uniform floor plan and therefore cannot recognize individual differences. It seeks the ideal prototype to be designed on the basis of scientific user needs surveys).

6. Local lifestyles and typology are important. Cultural values for each country and each region are important. People want to connect to their heritage. Of course, they also want modern amenities and they want to be respected in an international perspective. But these two demands must both be met. *(The old model believed in an international style and never considered different cultural values in the world).*
7. Housing projects must fit into their urban context and connect to existing urban fabrics. Context is important and can no longer be ignored. *(The generation of the modernist movement hated the existing cities and did not believe anything could be learned from them. The example was Le Corbusier's Plan Voisin).*

The new model

I do not believe anything on my list is really new to you. We are all familiar with the issues raised. But to most of us the list will look unrealistic as an agenda for action. How can all these things be achieved efficiently and effectively? Of course, we know that many parties, including users, are involved in the housing process. But how to organize it? Of course, variety would be better than uniformity but how can you control a process with so much variety? Of course, it would be good if individual user needs could be met, but how can this be achieved? And so on, and so on . . .

These are understandable doubts, but I suggest that they illustrate exactly the dilemma we are in. As long as we follow the ways of thinking and working we have inherited from the past, we will only see problems: things remain problematic.

Therefore, we need a new model in which the new agenda will fit more easily. I would like to describe to you a WAY OF SEEING the built environment in which the new issues fall into place more naturally. This new model relates to the work of many among us who have seriously tried to renew the housing process. It is currently the subject of discussion and study of a small but growing group of practitioners. It is based on a single, central concept: The idea of "LEVELS" in the built environment. This concept I would like to explain first.

Of course, having a new model will not solve instantly all the problems we may have. But I believe it gives us a direction we must follow to be more successful.

I will first talk about the concept of levels and the model based on it. Next, I will refer to work already done in practice to illustrate the new approach described by the model.

Levels

The concept of 'levels' is not really new. We already say, for instance, that the urban designer 'operates on another level' than the architect (Figure 1). What does this mean? Apparently, we understand the built environment to be divided in two groups of things: those that are decided about by the urban designer and those that are the concern of the architect.

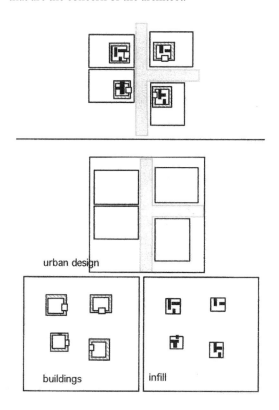

Figure 1 Three levels in the built environment

To understand the distinction better we must ask ourselves what happens when things change on one level or another. The architect designs a building within the context designed by the urban designer. He must respect, for instance, the layout of streets and the division of lots in the block. But within that context, he is free to act. He can change the design of his building in many ways. Indeed, different architects can build different buildings in different places but will share the street network designed by the urban designer. Although the urban design constrains their work, they are free within those constraints to do their own thing.

However, when the street network must be changed the design of the buildings has to be adjusted. The urban designer cannot act without effecting the designs of the architect. The relation, therefore, is asymmetrical. Change on the level of the building does not affect the higher level of the urban design but change in the urban design affects the lower level of the buildings.

All this is in accordance with our everyday experience. People who own houses know they can change their houses, even tear them down to replace them with new buildings, without effecting the street layout of the neighborhood they live in. But when the street layout would be changed, and the municipality would decide to cut a new street or to widen an existing one, or to rearrange a street's location, inevitably adjustments must be made on the lower level.

Apparently, the distinction that is made here is independent of the parties involved. We may talk about architects designing buildings and urban designers designing street patterns, or we may talk about home owners owning buildings and the municipality maintaining the public streets; in both cases we make the same distinction in the physical world between those parts that belong to one level (the streets) and other parts belonging to a lower level (the buildings). This distinction is so natural that its implications are understood by everybody.

Thus, it seems that the built environment is organized in levels and if we look further, we will find more of them. For instance, we talk about urban infrastructures like highways and railroads, and we understand them to be of a higher level than the streets of the neighborhood. Here again the same relationship holds. When a major traffic artery has to be cut in an existing neighborhood network the lower level of local streets must adjust. But within the given structure of highways, we can change the pattern of local streets without effecting the higher-level traffic pattern.

This hierarchical organization of the built environment also extends downward. We find in many buildings how the inner partitioning can be changed without effecting the basic building structure or its shape. This we see in office buildings but also in many residential building types. Apparently, we can distinguish 'infill elements' – like partition walls, but also kitchen and bathroom equipment – operating on a lower level in the built environment relative to the building (Figure 2). The same relationship as we found between buildings and local streets is found here. We can remodel the building and change the distribution of partitioning and equipment without changing the larger building structure or its external shape. But when we begin to change parts of the building and tear down loadbearing walls or extend a façade to get more room inside, we expect adjustments in the infill.

Figure 2 Two level organization: building with infill variations

A matter of terminology comes up here. It can be argued that what we call a 'building' includes the infill as much as the loadbearing structure, façades and roof. Therefore, a new term must be coined for what is left when the infill is taken out. This is called 'support' (or base building). In this way, we can say that a building is comprised of two levels: the 'support' level and the 'infill' level. In this paper, I will use both the terms 'building' and 'support' for the same level.

Once we see the concept of levels operating in the built environment, we discover the same hierarchical relation in many places. So far, we have been looking at environmental forms but within their technical systems we find the same subdivision in levels. Take, for instance, the window in the façade. We can replace it with another window of a different make or design but use the same opening in the façade made for the original window. In that case we do not have to change the façade wall. When we decide to change the façade wall, however, and make a different window opening, the window itself, obviously, must adjust.

In all conduit systems we find similar hierarchical organizations. (Figure 3) In the example of buildings and streets given above, the sewage system follows levels, too: there, is the system in the house and there is the sewage main running in the public street. On a still higher level, there will be the collector system of the city.

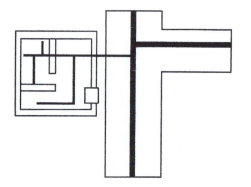

Figure 3 Two level conduit organization

Model

We have here a general principle of spatial organization that is actually operating in the built environment and we all understand it intuitively. Those who study this phenomenon believe that we can learn from it how to create and maintain complex environmental systems. I want to show you how the concept can describe things we do in practice. But to do so, we must first make a more formal representation. Figure 4 shows a very simple model of five levels. The terminology may be familiar with the exception, perhaps, of the word 'tissue.' The so-called 'urban tissue' is the level of the streets and related urban elements on the scale of the neighborhood, most directly related to the building.

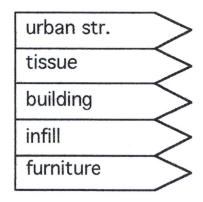

Figure 4 A simple five level model

The term is introduced to make a distinction with the 'urban structure of major roads and other infrastructures of the city. Of course, alternative terminology can be proposed, but the example of five levels will suffice to illustrate the use of the concept.

The five levels identified here are actual physical systems. We talk about walls, roads and other physical parts. These physical systems are what we put in place when we build. They must be distinguished from the more territorial concepts we also use in design, concepts like: 'room,' 'dwelling,' and 'neighborhood.'

The relationship between these two hierarchies is given in Figure 5. What we call a 'dwelling' can be seen as the juxtaposition of building and infill, whereas the neighborhood becomes a combination of the physical level of buildings and tissue. The territorial structure is an important subject in our modeling of the built environment but will not be discussed further here. We will use the five levels of physical systems to look at various examples of real-life projects to see how the different parties involved in these projects relate to the levels.

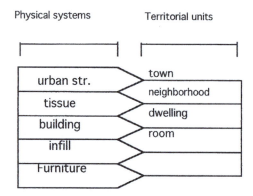

Figure 5 The five-level model of physical systems related to a territorial hierarchy

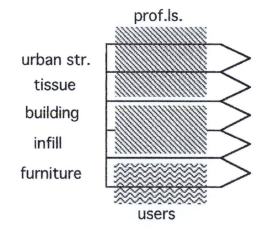

Figure 6 Control distribution

In our little model we can identify who is in control of a certain level by means of a screen pattern. Figure 6 shows the most common distribution of control in present day housing projects. Professional responsibility encompasses all levels except the furniture that is brought in by the user.

But among the professionals, further distinctions can be made, of course; for instance, between those responsible for the design of the buildings and their infill on the one hand and those responsible for the urban design on the other.

When we make such a control pattern in the levels model, we must make a distinction between design control and actual control during use. If Figure 6 gives us design control, we can still have different control patterns for the uses of this environment.

For instance, after completion, the single user still may control the furniture level only, but the apartment building may be under the control of either a collective of users, or an extraneous housing management. For the development of housing projects, both forms of control are important, and they will require separate diagrams.

Uses of the model

Sites and services

In the last decade, the so-called 'sites and services' approach has been applied in many parts of the world to provide shelter to people who cannot afford to rent or buy a completed dwelling. This way of working has been supported by the World Bank and other authorities as a way to make limited resources help the largest number of people. The sites and services idea makes a distinction between what should be done by professionals and what people can do themselves. The professional operates mainly on the level of tissue and urban structure. The users are made responsible from the level of the dwelling downwards. (Figure 7)

The distribution of responsibilities is different from the 'normal' case given in Figure 6. Of course, the model does not tell us what strategy is the better one. But that is exactly the point. Today there is not a single good strategy, but it depends on the circumstances of a case what control distribution can best be applied.

Comparing models in a systematic way is the first step toward a more sophisticated methodology in housing.

Core houses

It has often been pointed out that the sites and services approach makes it too difficult for people to acquire shelter. Critics say it takes a long time and too

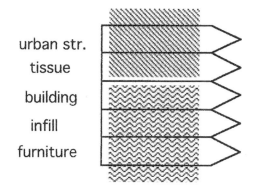

Figure 7 Sites and services

much effort before dwellers have a decent roof over their heads. Therefore, other projects offer some form of primitive shelter and let people fill in the rest over time. I am sure you are familiar with the idea of the 'core house.' With the core house approach, the building level is actually distributed among two parties.

The professional makes the core house, while the user, later on, will expand the building. Thus, in the sites and services scheme the whole of the building level is under the responsibility of the user, while in the core house the building level is only partly given to the user. (Figure 8)

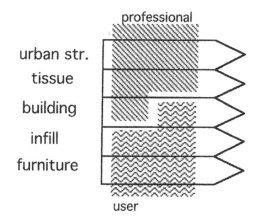

Figure 8 Core house

A particular interpretation of the latter form of control distribution was proposed in a scheme I was involved with in Egypt (Figure 9). Here, we designed only the surrounding walls for the dwellings, proposing that the users make the roof and fill in the volume. The rationale behind this solution was to protect people in the beginning as much as possible from the harsh desert winds. The walls also gave a more 'finished' look and a clear expression of the territorial organization.

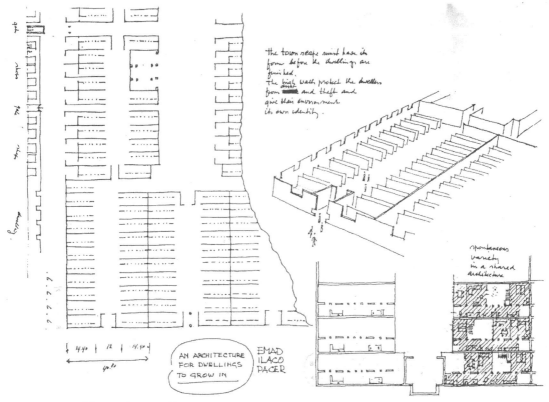

Figure 9 Proposal for a settlement in Egypt

Let me stress again, at this point, that I do not advocate any particular solution, but want to give you examples of different strategies that can be explained and compared by means of the concept of levels. In this way one can study alternative approaches to find the best possible solution in each case.

Systems and levels

The last example is also interesting from a methodological point of view for another reason. We see that walls are also designed to protect and define the separate compounds in the neighborhood and that, finally, the whole neighborhood had its own wall with gates. Thus, in the first stage, walls were designed on three levels. Use-control will be distributed among two parties: the individual users will bear responsibility for walls on the building and infill levels, but the building walls they share with neighbors as well as the walls delineating the compounds are a collective responsibility. (Figure 10)

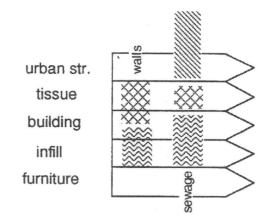

Figure 10 Walls and sewage in the case of Figure 9

Here we see how a specific technical system – in this case the configuration of walls – can be operating across different levels and be controlled by different parties on each level. We already saw the distribution of a single technical system across levels in Figure 3. In Figure 10, we also find the distribution of the sewage system as it could be in the example of the Egyptian compound project.

The uses of levels

Again, we see control by, respectively, the individual users, the collective of users, and the municipality. This distribution is not the same as with the walls. Each system can have its own control distribution. It is of course possible to have different ways of assigning control to a system across levels, using the same design. For instance, in Figure 10, the collective control of the sewage on the tissue level can be replaced by control from the municipality.

Support/infill approach

So far, we have looked at examples of control distribution for projects for the lowest income groups. A very different case is taken from the European housing situation. As some of you may know, I have advocated for many years the distinction between 'support' and 'infill.' This idea came from the necessity to build large apartment buildings for relatively high-density situations. The 'support' is what I have so far called 'building level' in the model. As observed before, we have here a question of terminology. Some people argue that infill is also part of 'building.' In that case the higher level needs a new name: hence 'support.' Infill comprises partitioning walls, kitchen and bathroom equipment and all the conduits for electricity, heating, water, drainage and gas needed to operate the equipment.

A clear distinction between support and infill was proposed to offer the users of the housing units the freedom to determine their own floor plan. The support could be built in rigorous repetition as a single project. But on the level of the infill each unit can be different. And the responsibility lies mainly with the user.

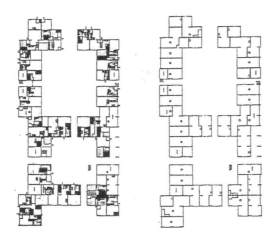

Figure 11 Molenvliet project/Papendrecht, the Netherlands

Figure 11 gives an example of a floor plan of a support project that was built already 10 years ago (1978) in the Netherlands. It was designed by architect Frans van der Werf. It is easy to see that this way of working is given in Figure 12. We see that the support level is under professional responsibility but that the user decides about the infill.

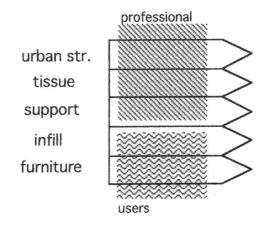

Figure 12 "Support/infill" approach

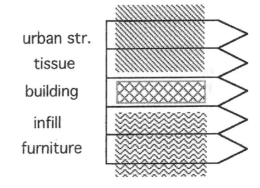

Figure 13 Support under collective control

I mentioned earlier that the control pattern can be about design control or about use control. If we switch to the latter in Figure 12, we can see the management of the housing estate controlling the tissue and support levels, while the users remain in control of their infill level, being able at any time to change and improve it. But we can also think of a scenario where the collective of users manage the building as may be the case when it would be a condominium. In that situation, Figure 13 would apply.

Efficiency

For a long time, it was argued that the support/infill distinction might perhaps be very desirable but that it was not efficient. You may be interested to know that at this moment the opinion among many professionals in the Netherlands has changed. It was found that, if one studies the technology seriously, the separation of the infill level offers better efficiency. There is no time to go into this question in great detail, but the major arguments are as follows:

- Clear separation of the infill level makes it possible to design and produce infill systems that are independent from individual projects. Their components can be produced industrially in large numbers;
- Installation of separate infill systems saves time and labor on the site, therefore reducing not only on-site labor but also overhead costs;
- Because the infill system is a separate industrial product, it can be improved over time;
- Where several infill systems are available, clients can choose and competition will produce a variety in styles and price levels;
- Because infill systems are not dependent on a single project they can be applied in a wide area. This is particularly interesting with a more united Europe in 1992.
- Because the installation of an infill system goes per-unit, it is not important that floor plans are the same; they can all be different;
- Individual units can be changed and improved over time to meet individual user needs.

You can see that in this case the initial motivation is technical and economical but that, at the same time, we can respond to several of the 'idealistic' points on the wish list I gave earlier.

At this moment in the Netherlands, there is an organization called 'Open Building.' It has more than a hundred members among whom we find not only architects and engineers but also contractors, manufacturers and experts in public housing management. They are convinced that the clear distinction of levels in housing production and design is the way of the future. Thy are not necessarily all that interested in the freedom of the user to change his own infill systems, but they regard the support/infill distinction as a good base for improved industrialization leading to a better product for less money.

It would be a mistake to believe that the support/infill distinction is only for rich countries like the Netherlands. The distinction of levels allows us to organize our work better and offers greater flexibility and efficiency independent of the available material resources. Professor Bao Jia Sheng from Nanjing University, who is present at this conference, has successfully applied the support/infill distinction in a housing project in Wuxi, China, with a very different budget compared to that available to his colleagues in the Netherlands. I assume he will report on that project himself. A few weeks before this meeting, I was informed that the support/infill approach is also applied in Egypt by the Ministry of Reconstruction. There, Professors Nasamat Abdelkader and Sayed Ettouney have developed a standard support system that can be applied in different sites around the country. The infill of the units will be left to the users who apply traditional materials.

Final remarks

To end my talk, I would like to make a few final remarks.

I set out to propose a model that allows us to describe different control situations in different projects. But by now you will have discovered that this model actually implies a methodological principle. The distinction of levels, as they operate in the real world, allows us to organize our work in a more sophisticated way. We no longer need to seek a similar solution for all purposes, but we can find the best approach in each case. In each project we can ask ourselves how responsibility will be distributed across the various levels to get the best results in the most efficient way.

The concept of levels therefore provides a planning tool that we can use to deal with the growing complexity of our task.

When we organize our work in this more sophisticated way, important methodological questions arise. For instance, how will the distinction between the levels be made clear? How do we decide exactly what belongs to one level and what to another? How do we define the subsystems to be found on a single level?

How do parties, operating on different levels, coordinate their work? You will agree that such questions are not particularly new. Issues of control distribution and coordination between parties always have been very important in planning and design and engineering. In the course of time, we have researched and developed numerous additional tools to help us organize the division of design control better.

Examples of such tools are, for instance, a better understanding of modular coordination: not for the standardization of components, but for the coordination of design among different parties. In the same way, we have experience with the uses of formal zoning systems as design tools to coordinate work on different levels.

When we operate on a particular level, we must, in this new way of working, be able to judge what freedom we offer to the party on the lower level. When, for instance, an urban designer makes streets and house lots, as we discussed in an earlier example, he wants to make sure that the house lots can contain the kinds of houses he has in mind will fit. This kind of investigation to check what can be done on a lower level can be formalized in what we call a 'capacity analysis.' Such an analysis can be done on all levels of the built environment. For instance, when we design a support system, we want to understand its capacity to hold the right kind of infill plans. Or when we make a core house, we want to find out in what ways the user can expand and improve it.

I mention these few examples of more formal operations to show that a specific methodology is involved that cannot be explained here. Much remains to be done but we know enough to be confident that the levels approach for open building is very promising. To use this new approach, therefore, new skills and methods must be applied.

Let me return briefly to a topic we discussed earlier: the issue of variety vs. uniformity. You may have noticed that I stressed method and the distribution of responsibility in a scientific and flexible way. In each example, we found, however, that the result is greater variety and flexibility. In the sites and services example, we can be sure that each house will be different and that houses will adapt over time to the needs of their users. The same is true in the support/infill examples. Here again the result can be that each unit is different and adaptable over time.

But you will also have noticed that this variety was not the goal but the result of a more efficient and sophisticated approach. The idea that variety can be the result of efficiency is hard to accept for many among us. Even among members of the Open Building organization in the Netherlands, I found that people said: I know now that variety and efficiency are not in conflict with each other, but I still find it difficult to believe. This is understandable because we have been trained for generations with the idea that rigid standardization of floor plans is necessary to be efficient. In the next decade, this old-fashioned idea will disappear.

I assumed, in my models, that the user can be regarded as a responsible party as much as the professional. Some of you may have their doubts about this assumption. But you will also have noted that the models of control distribution are different from what is usually called 'participatory design.' I firmly believe that those who want to participate must be willing to carry responsibility. Moreover, responsibility must be clearly defined. Only when these conditions are met, the users' role can be helpful.

I do not share the concern of some of my colleagues who fear that when the user participates, the professional role is somehow discounted or degraded. I believe the opposite is true. To organize and steer the process we have seen in the various models, professional skills are more needed than ever. As experts, we are responsible for the management of the process and our expertise must lie in our understanding of the control distribution patterns and the skillful organization of the different parties involved.

This new expertise must be developed. As I have said before, I believe much can be done here. A new level of sophistication can be reached. When the concept of levels is not properly understood, or when the control distribution is not properly studied and when the coordination between parties on different levels is not skillfully organized, problems will arise, no matter how much or how little money is available for your project. Those who want to take full advantage of the understanding of levels and control distribution must study it carefully and be aware of the methodological requirements to be met. To deal with the more complex world we live in, and to replace our outmoded methods with better ones will take much effort. In the field of architecture, we tend to look at the quick fix – another style, a new type to copy. This will not work when we are serious about the housing problem. To change our methods is hard work.

To end this paper, we now may come back to the seven points I brought up in the beginning of my talk. Let us see what levels means to them.

1. The levels concept allows us to choose the right process: we consider the different parties involved and can decide what their responsibilities must be. We also see how different projects can be structured differently with their own control distribution patterns. As such it is a planning tool.
2. In this model, both professionals and non-professionals can have a place. The need to arrive at the most effective solution with the best possible use of resources will determine the control distribution. In some cases, users can do a better job; in others, professionals must do it. The most important point is that on each level, for each subsystem, the responsible party is identified.
3. Change over time can be related to levels. Change on a lower level is easier and can have a faster frequency than change on a higher level. Clearly defined levels with systems assigned to each make change over time easier to organize.
4. Uniformity can be efficient when one party has to do many things. To build a support, for instance, repetition of the same bays is more efficient. But when systems operate on their own levels, different parties can use the same system simultaneously and work in parallel. We see this with the infill systems in the support project or with building individual houses in the sites and services project. In those case, variety is not the purpose but the result.
5. Separation of the lower level systems from the higher level allows for their change without disturbing the higher level. If that condition is fulfilled, adaptation to individual needs on the lower level is easy and efficient.
6. The building level can be designed to respond to local lifestyles and cultural values. This is what determines the quality of the urban environment. This level can also respond to specific housing types that people prefer. The lower infill level provides the modern amenities that have become international preferences: good bathrooms and kitchens, electricity, telephone and television. Adaptation to a higher standard is possible over time.
7. To fit a housing project into the local urban context is always the responsibility of the professional urban designers and architects. Their expertise should particularly be occupied with this question, leaving the lower level decisions to those who live in the projects.

Some further reading

For a theory of the built environment based on physical levels and territorial hierarchies see: Habraken, N. J. (1998). *The Structure of the Ordinary: Form and Control in the Built Environment.* Cambridge, MA: MIT Press.

For the application of the levels concept in general design education, see: N. John Habraken (1987). "The Control of Complexity." *Places*, vol. 4, no. 2. MIT Press.

And

Habraken, N. J. (1986). "Towards a New Professional Role." *Design Studies*, vol. 7, no. 3. London: Butterworth.

Habraken, N. J. (1987). *Control Hierarchies in Complex Artifacts*, ed. J. P. Protzen. Proceedings, Conference on Planning and Design Methods in Architecture, Boston (International Conference on Planning and Design Theory).

1988
CONCEPT DESIGN GAMES

Editors' Note: *This paper (co-authored by Mark D. Gross, a PhD candidate working with the author) describes the work of a group of researchers conducted under a grant from the National Science Foundation, at the School of Architecture and Planning, Massachusetts Institute of Technology, using games as a tool for research in design theory and methods. Games offer a means of isolating certain aspects, or concepts, of designing for purposes of scrutiny. A game provides an environment for a group of players, acting with individual goals and a shared program, to make and transform complex configurations, free of functional requirements. Adjusting game parameters emphasizes different concepts. They developed nine games that explore a variety of concepts of general interest to those concerned with organizing physical configurations. Beyond these particular concepts, they argued that games are a useful way to couch studies in design theory and methods. The paper was published in* Design Studies, *Vol. 9, No. 3, July 1988*

This report describes our work on using games as a tool for research in design theory and methods. Using games as research tools follows naturally from our previous work in design methodology and theory as applied to the design of built environments.[1-3] By way of introducing our current efforts, therefore, we review a few key aspects of this earlier work.

Human settlements are complex artifacts. They are often large and may extend over vast areas. They differ considerably from one culture to another. They also are used over long periods of time, during which they can be subject to dramatic transformations. Today even a single building is a fairly complex thing. It embodies an array of subsystems: the structure, various systems of partitioning, envelopes to shield it from the elements, and systems for heating, ventilation, electricity, water, gas and communications. The building must house many interrelated human activities that may vary considerably over its lifetime.

In studying the designing of buildings and urban environments we decided not to limit our attention to what a single designer does to a static artifact. In our investigations we observed two important principles.

- There are always many designers. The artifact to be made is designed in a process of cooperation and negotiation among many actors. The participating designers have different expertise and their responsibilities in the larger design task can be distributed in many ways.

- The artifact changes all the time. Human settlements are never finished, and we keep designing them. Though each designer can finish his individual task, urban environments and also individual buildings continue to be designed upon throughout their lifetime. Most design work in architecture and urban design relates to artifacts already in place that must be added to or changed. Even a new building usually adds to an existing urban environment; hence the design of the building alters a larger object – the environment of which it becomes a part.

Corresponding to these two principles, we introduced two new issues in our thinking about design theory and methods.

- Designing is a social activity that takes place among people who negotiate, make proposals, set rules for their conduct and for the work to be done, and follow such rules. In short, to a large extent, designing involves agreement-making and rulemaking.
- Designing is about morphological change. Designers must understand the transformations of complex physical organizations. We believe that complex physical organizations have certain transformational properties in common, regardless of their function.

These two issues must be seen in relation to each other. The interaction between designers and the configurations they organize and shape is at the core of designing. This brings us to study how designers manipulate and transform complex configurations, while making agreements and rules as to how to go about their work. Much of our work results from this enlarged perspective. The methods we have developed in the past seek to improve the performance of design communities working on buildings and urban environments that change and adapt.

Concept Design Games

When designing involves the interaction of many actors, all involved with transforming an artifact, we see similarities with board games. In the games we describe, several players work with a configuration on a board. As when designing, players must fit pieces into an existing field; rules, conventions and principles limit how they may move; and they make flexible, negotiable arrangements about what conventions and rules to use in a given situation. Last but not least, players make projections for configurations to be constructed. In these ways our games resemble real-life design situations. Yet, in contrast to real-life experience, the games enable us to study design actions by providing an environment that is manipulable and well bounded.

One of the most difficult aspects of understanding designing has always been that too many divergent acts occur simultaneously, defying simple description. We found it useful to develop a set of games that each isolates and focuses on a single aspect, each giving a clearer picture of what just some of designing is about. Seen this way, our games may appear remarkably one-dimensional, stressing one aspect while suppressing, or even leaving out entirely, other aspects of designing. However, our games always preserve the basic unity of the design experience in that a variety of actors work together in transforming an artifact. Thus, our games incorporate the two issues of designing mentioned above.

We found that in a game we can bring forward aspects that represent concepts guiding our designing. When we communicate as designers, we share certain concepts that cause us to act in certain ways; through these same concepts we also 'understand' each other's actions. Developing and playing games, we learn about the concepts we hold. That is why we call our games 'Concept Design Games'.

Figure 1 shows a simple example of using a game to illustrate a concept. Here we recognize the concept of 'dominance' by observing the players' moves. (Player A is said to dominate player B if A's moving a piece requires B to respond, but not vice versa. See Appendix II.) This is not a design game, obviously, but it may be the beginning of one. Rules creating a situation of dominance between players can provide a context for a game that also involves designing a configuration on the board to meet certain programmatic demands.

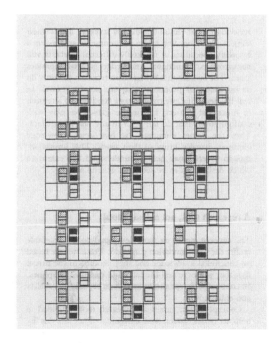

Figure 1 Use of a game to illustrate a concept

Understanding form, not function

The action-oriented approach we find in games stresses the role of the physical artifact. The configurations we engage with 'behave' in certain ways, and this behavior shapes to a significant extent the way we organize ourselves as designers. When we use the term 'behavior' in relation to the thing being designed, we mean the way the artifact allows or resists manipulation and transformation. Through studying change in the built environment, we have become aware of how such form behavior influences our actions as designers.

As with all investigations of physical phenomena, observing change is the key to understanding inner structure. Because our subject – the artifact designed – is of our own making, the changes we observe are the result of design decisions. We find a dialectic situation: we shape the artifact, but in turn the artifact shapes the way we organize our design processes. These dynamics reveal hierarchical structure in the artifact and territorial structure in the organization of design responsibilities. The concepts of hierarchy and territory drive several of our games. These concepts are relevant to all parts and at all sizes of the built environment; to the room as well as the city, and to the construction detail as well as to the larger built framework. We do not know whether these principles also apply to other complex artifacts outside our domain, but other investigations may well find interesting similarities.

What we can learn in this way about physical configurations differs from the functionally oriented knowledge that designers usually express about their subject. Buildings and urban environments are designed by many specialists of markedly different interests and backgrounds. Functional knowledge is what separates them. The artifact that brings them together can only do so by means of properties that are not functional. In real-life designing, we rightly pay a good deal of attention to functional matters, but in our games, we play with configurations that do not refer to any real-life artifact. Thus, the games eliminate the functional knowledge designers usually bring to their work. This limitation, though severe, may help us understand the extent to which designing can be seen as a general activity.

A research tool, not a design tool

The concept design games we have developed do not resemble reality the way simulation games do. The latter are based on functional knowledge and they succeed to the extent that they preserve real-life facts and real-life disciplines. In contrast, concept design games extract an aspect from reality and enlarge it.

Concept design games are research tools intended to help us better understand designing. They do this by opening to scrutiny the concepts we use as designers, as well as the structures of the complex artifacts we manipulate. They are not meant to be tools for designing, nor are they made to help teach designing.

A game box

One product of our work is a 'game box' that will allow readers to develop their own games, shaped around concepts that interest them. The game box is our way of making operational the idea of design games as a research tool.

The game box contains:

- A basic terminology for discussing the structure of games.
- An explanation about how to create a 'technical universe' to play with, for each game, from a larger set of pieces. We also present a set of pieces of different kinds, out of which many technical universes can be composed.
- An account of what we learned about game development, including a discussion of five strategic questions that game developers must address.
- A computer-based method to record game play.
- Nine games to serve as examples, dealing with a variety of concepts in which we were interested.

We found, not surprisingly, that by developing a game based on a particular design concept, we can learn much about the concept. Game development in itself is a powerful form of research. In our work, game development went hand-in-hand with game playing. As we developed each game, we played it, modified the rules, and played it again. The most interesting games may never be finished, because we keep changing them, probing new ways to see the subject, finding new ways to deal with it. The nine games we submit are therefore open-ended. We present a playable version of each game but also suggest variations on the game structure that might prove interesting. We found that each game opens a whole field of possible inquiry that we had no time to enter into. In this way, the game box is a research tool.

While game development is a form of research, a finished game can serve as a research tool as well. The game is a stage for exploring design behavior; it establishes a certain context. By playing the game we dan learn more about what we can do in that explicitly constrained context. We can use games this way to study how designers negotiate, come to agreements and follow conventions. We may learn about how design teams approach problems, or we may study alternative design processes. We can compare different ways designers can organize themselves relative to a design context set up by the game.

The scope of our project, however, did not enable us to study the extent to which concept games can serve these uses. Nor did we submit the games to players outside our development team in order to gauge the games' accessibility. Much less could we explore the development of research programs in which the game would serve as a tool. However, from our experience with playing the games, we feel confident that they can be used as vehicles in researching design behavior. Thus, the idea of the finished game as a tool remains untested although we believe it to be most promising.

The game box is a tool for demonstrating and testing concepts about designing. Based on our previous experience in design theory and methods, we selected concepts that we knew to be of particular interest. The reader need not share our interest in these particular concepts to find the games useful. We hope indeed that others will use the same game box in quest of very different ideas. But to follow our work, the reader must become acquainted with the concepts we chose to work with. Not all these concepts are generally familiar among designers. The next part of this paper presents several concepts in our games in summary form.

Properties of concept design games

The nine games we developed are very different both because the concepts that drive them are different and because we sought to make as wide a range of game forms as possible. It will not do to give a single game as an example because to understand that common properties of the games one must see several different games. However, rather than presenting detailed descriptions of several games, it seemed better, by way of introduction, to discuss a few aspects characteristic of all of them.

Variable physical organizations

All our games are board games and thus are played with pieces on a board. We played with the parts that wooden clothes pins are made from (we call them 'pegs'), nails of different sizes, and washers. We also used self-sticking labels bought in a stationary store. These pieces offered the variety of size, shape, material and color that we needed, and they have the advantage that they are readily available. Although we also made a more sophisticated set of pieces in acrylic, all our games can be played with the simple versions.

Each game uses only a selection of these available pieces and they are used differently in each game. An important part of developing a game is therefore making an appropriate 'Technical Universe' for it. The Technical Universe is the physical system out of which we design something. It is the sum of the constraints embodied by the pieces themselves and the allowed deployment relations, independent of the board they may be deployed on.

Not only can Technical Universes differ from game to game, several very different Technical Universes can serve the same game. This is because most games rest primarily on certain relational properties of the Technical Universe posing constraints on the players. Though we may play with configurations of different shapes, we may observe similar constraints.

Playing a game in different physical circumstances can clarify the concept under scrutiny. Figure 2 shows configurations from different Technical Universes. Each can be interpreted as having two systems (black and white). Seen in the context of transformation rules, the systems operate on different levels in a 'dependency hierarchy' where the higher-level system (black) dominates the lower level (white). It is possible to make the same hierarchical structure in each of the Technical Universes. In the first, the relation between the levels is connection; in the second, the relation is enclosure. To the extent that the hierarchical structure drives the playing, these two alternatives are equivalent.

Control distribution

The control of the players over a certain configuration on the board can usually be distributed in many ways. This contrasts with board games we are familiar with, such as Chess and Go, where the control distribution is inflexible; one part plays White and the other plays Black. Figure 3 shows alternative control distributions for the lower level of a configuration.

Control patterns over a given Technical Universe are an important variable in design games because they reflect the way we organize ourselves to work on a complex configuration. Depending on the purpose of the game, they may be set by the game developer or left open for the players to determine.

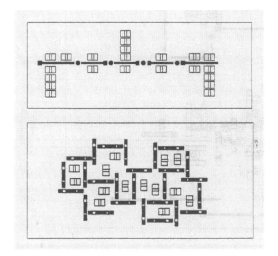

Figure 2 Two configurations from different Technical Universes

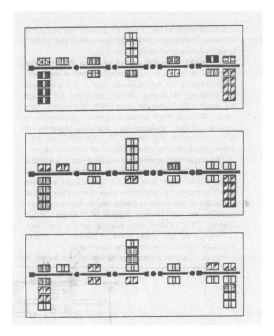

Figure 3 Alternative control distributions for the lower level of a configuration

Territorial organization

For a player to manipulate part of the configuration, be it a local part of a subsystem distributed across the whole board, he must have space to work in. Parties operating simultaneously within a restricted space operate within a territorial organization. There are 'private' spaces a party can work in without interference from others, and 'public' spaces where parties must share space.

As distinct from the control of *pieces*, the territorial organization has to do with control of parts of the board. Understanding the territorial distribution in a given field for purposes of design can be important for design efficiency. Multi-leveled territorial hierarchies may occur. We can learn about territorial organization in complex design situations by observing processes of urban settlement and change. We translated two basic urban organizational patterns into two territory games.

The territorial organization adopted for a particular instance of play cannot be fully fixed because usually we do not know exactly how much space we need to do our job. The territorial boundaries must shift within a given hierarchy of territorial organization. In territorial organization we find another variable of Concept Design Games. This variable, too, may be set by the game developer, or left open, allowing players to choose alternative patterns of territorial distribution.

Figure 4 shows a fragment of one of the games in which territorial organization is part of the Technical Universe. The boundaries formed by nails have gates and enclosure clusters of pegs. The territorial hierarchy is indicated by the letters at the gates, A being a higher-level territory than B. Note that the physical organization is not one-to-one with the territorial organization: the same kinds of clusters can occur on levels B and C, depending on the number of gate crossings needed to reach them. In Figure 4, the clusters with gates B are in 'public' space relative to the 'private' space containing clusters C. In this example, territory is formalized as part of the game by the use of nails to mark boundaries. In most games, territorial organization occurs informally, and boundaries are invisible; nevertheless, territorial organization can be used to subdivide and coordinate work on the board.

Program

Control over pieces and over parts of the board is common to all board games. As we have seen, in our design games, these variables become active, subject to change in development and play. The idea of a 'program,' however, is particular to design games. It is distinct from the 'goals' that individual players have in all board games, our design games included. The program describes certain board conditions that must be

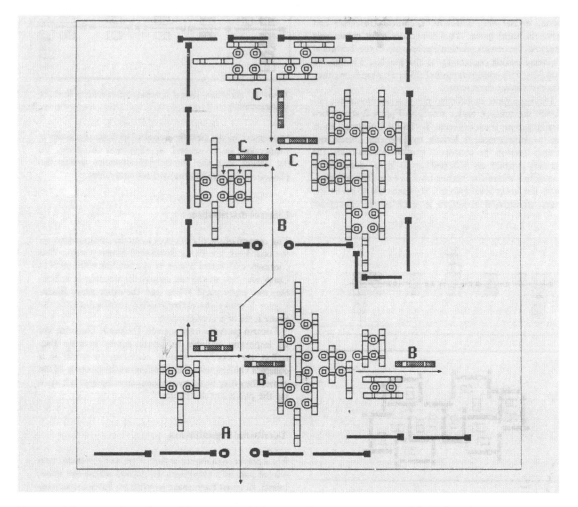

Figure 4 A fragment of one of one of the games in which territorial organization is part of the Technical Universe

fulfilled to complete the game. Without a program the individual goals of the players make for a competitive game. The program leads players to also cooperate and plan together.

Because design games have a program, they can never be purely competitive. Individual roles played in the games may compete with each other for reasons of scarcity of resources (pieces or space), or because of conflicting goals. But these must be reconciled with the common task and herein lies the source for negotiation and ultimate agreement and shared rulemaking. The pursuit of a common program can also bring tension where players interpret the program differently or advance different ways to achieve it. The program brings into the game many interactions we associate with designing.

In-play development

Another aspect particular to design games is that the game may be developed as much by the players as by the initial creator of the game. The variables mentioned so far – control distribution, territorial organization, and program interpretation – can be available to the players and indeed these represent typical variables to design teams in all design tasks.

We can therefore say that the work done by the game developer is continued by the team playing the game. This is only natural because both engage in a design process; the developer-designer setting the stage for the player-designers. It is the game developer, however, who determines the degree of freedom given to players to engage in these activities.

Many players, many pieces

Although some of our games can best be played with just two players, it is in the nature of design games that tasks and organizations can proliferate. In most games we can bring a larger number of players and increase the size of the board and the number of pieces accordingly.

Even when only two players play, they may find it of interest to work with large and complex configurations on the board. We are interested in interactive processes among designers because many design tasks today raise questions about controlling complexity. It is important that configurations on the board can, when needed, become sufficiently complex to reflect such conditions. To find the right balance between order and complexity, and between complexity and playability makes the game development a design challenge by itself.

Recording design play

Our main objective in developing a recording scheme was to assist game developers in analyzing game play. In the course of developing a game we would play it several times, then find ourselves unable to remember in detain how the game went. After playing, we would propose and discuss modifying the rules to improve the game, but we needed to know what actually had occurred. We tried recording game play by photographing the board after each move using an instant camera, but this proved difficult and distracting. We considered using a videotape recorder, but this, also, seemed to involve too much extra effort, both in recording the play, and again later, in viewing the tapes. Videotape might be a good way to record the games if one wanted to observe *all* events including those not directly pertaining to game play, but we merely wanted to record the moves made.

Games that forbid players from moving or removing pieces once places build, in effect, a partial record of game play. The board at the end of the play contains every move that was made. Tic-tac-toe is a simple example. In such games it may be possible to reconstruct the sequence of play, or at least plausible sequences of play, just by looking at the board at the end of the game. But our concept design games it is usually impossible to reconstruct the sequence of moves from the final state of the board. Hence our need for a means to record moves as the game is played.

From the start we thought to construct the game recorder as a computer program that could accept descriptions of game moves and display game states and histories on the screen. It was logical, therefore, to consider using the computer to develop and play the games as well as to record game play. Initially, however, we decided to develop our games outside the computer. We wanted to play with physical pieces on a physical site. We wanted to ensure that our games could also be played without a computer. We thought of the game recorder as a tool in a larger game development process.

Recording and reviewing

The game-recording tasks is minimally construed as keeping track of pieces placed: added, removed or moved. This includes recording:

- what piece
- where it is placed
- who placed it
- when it was placed

Recording just this information would be useful for post-game analysis. In an extended version of the game recorder we may also want to record why the piece was played, check whether the move was legal, and perhaps to keep score. Further, we may want the game recorder to keep track of rules, agreements and negotiations made among the players. Eventually we would develop the game recorder towards an environment for game play and game development.

The purpose of recording histories of game play are:

- to view and review previous game states, sequences of states, and entire histories of game play
- to restore previous game states
- to reply games from previous states

A history of a single instance of play is simply a sequence of moves and board states. When a game is replayed from an intermediate state, a branch is added from that state: the sequence becomes a tree. The history now represents a set of alternative ways the game was played; with every replay, the history tree becomes bushier.

Notation

Chess notation offers a model for our recording scheme. Three column-inches of newsprint suffices to record all the moves in a game. Chess notation describes a process – the sequence of moves from opening to endgame. The two players' moves are listed in order. Each move names a piece and describes its final board position: P-QB4, or, for a capture, it names the two pieces that engaged: P X P. Chess notation is space, as measured by the number of characters needed to record a move, or a game. It conveys each move using a small number of symbols.

In part, the elegance of Chess notation derives from assuming the reader understands the game rules. For example, to interpret the notation P X P the reader must know how pawns capture in order to determine which two pawns might be involved. If the notation did not presume this knowledge, it would need to describe the pawns' initial locations, and this would require more symbols. Thus, if we devise a different game using the Chess board and pieces, it is most likely that we cannot use Chess notation to record play in our new game.

This last observation relates directly to our problem. We wanted to devise a means to record play across a variety of different games. As mentioned above, in some of our games the rules change, are left unstated, or are invented as part of play. Unlike Chess notation, our recording scheme cannot rely on knowledge of the game rules.

Layout languages

From notation we came, therefore, to the idea of a layout or picture language. A layout language offers a means to describe and manipulate a two-or three-dimensional configuration of physical elements as a symbolic code. Once we have represented the layout in symbolic form, we can apply standard list-permuting and pattern-matching techniques, either to transform the layout, or to recognize, parse and classify its features. By using a layout language to describe the physical configuration on the game board, we avoid integrating the notation system with the game rules.

Layout, or picture languages, have been widely applied. Physicists devised picture languages to describe patterns of atomic particle scatter[4]. Layout languages are also used by VLSI designers in the layout phase of automated integrated circuit design[5,6]. The formal properties of layout languages have been studied[7]. A picture language can be recursive and purely functional[8]. The shape grammar formalism used in some studies of the built environment[9,10] to represent thematic variation in built environment is also related.

Writing form

We call our layout language "Writing Form," or 'WF' for short[11]. The game recorder uses WF to represent board configurations. It is implemented as an embedded language in an object-oriented dialect of Common Lisp[12]. WF nouns refer to material and space elements; WF verbs refer to operations for arranging these elements in space. WF's primitive arrangement operation strings elements along imaginary lines. Each WF sentence denotes a configuration of material and space elements; the most elemental descriptions of configurations are given in terms of edges and distances.

For example, the letter 'E' can be described in WF as a horizontal string of two elements: a vertical edge (e1) and a vertical string of three horizontal edges: two identical top and bottom edges (e2) and a middle one half as long (e3), with a distance (d1) between each pair of horizontal edges (see Figure 5). First, we define these edges and the distance; then we string them together to make the 'E' configuration.

```
(define    e1 (edge vertical 30))
(define    e2 (edge horizontal 20))
(define    e3 (edge horizontal 10))
(define    d1 (distance 10))
(define    E
(string    horizontal
e1
(string vertical e2 d1 e3 d1 e2)))
```

The names of the simplest elements – the edges and distances, are shown in the diagram (Figure 5). Note that each element is named uniquely, even the two instances of edge e2 that form the top and bottom horizontal edges of the E.

Concept design games 365

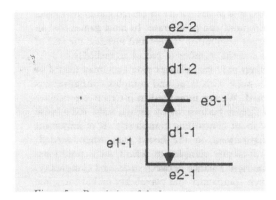

Figure 5 Description of the letter 'E' in WF

may be applied to. For example, players may define alignment, centering, equidistant spacing as well as more complex means and routines for positioning elements and configurations using parameters, conditionals and iteration.

We have built two interpreters for the WF language. The first – we all it the WF interpreter – translates WF expressions to layouts for display. The second – the WF reader – translates layouts entered with a graphic editor into WF expressions. For our present purposes it is sufficient for the WF reader to generate any WF expression that describes the layout. (Here we are not concerned with simplest or canonical forms.)

Writing Form users can extend the language in two ways. First, WF may be extended by defining new *element types*. Element types defined within WF are first-class WF objects: they may be composed and configured in the same ways as the built-in edge and distance elements. Second, users can define new operations for positioning elements relative to one another. These operations are independent of the elements they

A game recorder

The game recorder appears to the players as a graphic editor. Players record moves by directly manipulating pieces; they need not learn the WF language that the game recorder uses internally to represent board states.

The game recorder screen is divided into three parts (see Figure 6). One part contains a supply of elements

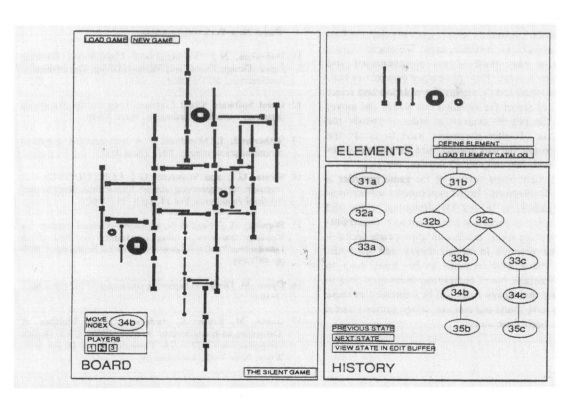

Figure 6 Game recorder screen

of various types. Each available element type appears as an icon; selecting the icon generates a new element instance that can be placed on the board. Another part of the screen contains the game board and the pieces in play. Most recently placed pieces are specially marked. A third part of the screen displays the game history.

Players take turns in making moves: selecting elements from the supply and placing them on the game board, moving elements already on the board or removing elements. The game recorder, using the WF reader described above, translates these moves into its internal representation and stores them in its history. Players can view game states by selecting items on the history and also explore the consequences of making alternative moves by playing games over again, beginning at intermediate stages.

The game board at any time is described, internally, by a WF expression. As we have seen, the physical configuration and the symbolic WF representation correspond directly. It follows that their transformations also correspond directly. Adding, deleting and moving pieces around on the board corresponds to (lexically) adding, deleting and replacing symbols and subexpressions in the WF expressions. The 'current board state' expression may also be viewed and edited in a text buffer. Changes made textually will alter the layout and this change will be recorded as a move.

Extending the game recorder

So far, the game recorder only records players' moves: the sequence of board states and transformations. Now we want to extend the game recorder to take account of rules. In particular, we want it to know about constraints on the selection, placement and dimensions of game pieces. Such constraints determine the 'behavior' of the game pieces. It must be possible for players as well as the game developer to write these constraints. Here are some examples of constraints we want the game recorder to be able to handle:

'washers only on grid crossings'
'pegs always perpendicular to nails'
'a washer must occur wherever a nail and a peg meet'

In games where a well-defined technical universe dictates allowed and forbidden arrangements of game pieces, we want the game recorder to check players' moves for validity. In games where players introduce rules during play, the game recorder should keep track of when rules are entered, rescinded, applied or violated. Once the game recorder can be taught rules, perhaps it could also suggest possible moves.

To achieve these goals, we are recasting the game recorder and the WF layout language within a constraint-based computing environment. Following well known work on constraints[13–15], we have developed constraint language[16, 17] and connected it with a package of interactive graphic routines. The constraint language interpreter maintains, manages, enforces, and solves relations among variables that describe attributes of a system whose behavior we wish to simulate. We can use constraints to describe both the geometry of our pieces and the rules about piece placement.

For example, we can define 'peg' as a special class of 'rectangular physical object,' with fixed dimensions, and certain position constraints with respect to other similarly defined objects, for instance, nails. We might require of pegs that they must always be connected and perpendicular to a nail. If we place a peg parallel to a nail, the game recorder can (1) report the violation and reject the move; (2) report the violation but accept the move; (3) rotate the peg 90 degrees in order to satisfy the constraint, or (4) offer alternative ways to satisfy the constraint (rotate the nail instead, turn the peg the other way, turn both peg and nail 45 degrees, etc.).

The constraint-based version of the game recorder is still under development. Initial experiments seem promising. In games, as in real-life designing, rules and constraints play an important role. Therefore, constraint-based computing seems to offer an appropriate technology for our research in design theory and methods. However, much work remains to be done, both to advance constraint-based computing techniques and to demonstrate that design rules can be expressed in these terms. We have found our concept design games a useful vehicle for both these aims.

References

1 Habraken, N. J. (1972). *Supports: An Alternative to Mass Housing*. New York and Washington: Preager Publishers.
2 Habraken, N. J., J. T. Boekholt, A. P. Thijssen and P. Dinjens (1976). *Variations – The Systematic Design of Supports* MIT Press, Cambridge, MA.

3 Habraken, N. J. (1983). *Transformations of the Site*. Aware Press, Cambridge, MA.
4 Shaw, A. (1972). "Picture Graphs, Grammars and Parsing." In *Frontiers of Pattern Recognition* New York: Academic Press.
5 Williams, J. D. (1977). *Sticks – A New Approach to LSI Design*. Master's Thesis, Massachusetts Institute of Technology, Cambridge.
6 Batali, J. and A. Hartheimer (1982). *Design Procedure Language Reference Manual*. Cambridge: MIT Artificial Intelligence Laboratory Memo #598.
7 Rosenfeld, A. (1974). "Multidimensional Formal Languages." In W. Spillers, ed. *Basic Questions of Design Theory*. New York: North-Holland, American Elsevier.
8 Henderson, P. (1982). *Functional Geometry*. Proceedings, 1982 ACM Conference on Lisp and Functional Programming, New York.
9 Stiny, G. (1980). "Introduction to Shape Grammars." *Environment and Planning B*, 343–351, July.
10 Flemming, U. (forthcoming). *The Role of Shape Grammars in the Analysis and Creation of Designs*. Proceedings, 1986 SUNY Buffalo Symposium on CAD – the Computability of Design, John Wiley, New York.
11 Habraken, N. J. (1983). *Writing Form*. Unpublished Working Paper; Design Theory and Methods Group, Department of Architecture, MIT.
12 Coral Software (1986). *Coral Common Lisp for the MacIntosh (Beta Test Version)*. Cambridge, MA: Coral Software.
13 Sutherland, L. (1963). *Sketchpad – A Man-Machine Graphical Communication System*. PhD Thesis, MIT, Cambridge.
14 Steele, G. L. and G. J. Sussman (1980). "Constraints – A Language for Expressing Almost Hierarchical Descriptions." *Artificial Intelligence*, vol. 14, 1–39.
15 Borning, A. (1977). *Thinglab – an Object-Oriented System for Building Simulations Using Constraints*. Proceedings Fifth International Joint Conference on Artificial Intelligence, New York, 497–498.
16 Gross, M. (1986). *Designing as Exploring Constraints*. PhD Thesis, MIT, Cambridge.
17 Gross, M., S. Ervin, J. Anderson and A. Fleisher (forthcoming). *Designing with Constraints*. Proceedings, 1986 SUNY Buffalo Symposium on CAD – The Computability of Design, John Wiley, New York.

2003

EMERGENT COHERENT BEHAVIOR OF COMPLEX CONFIGURATIONS THROUGH AUTOMATED MAINTENANCE OF DOMINANCE RELATIONS

Editors' Note: *The author jointly authored this paper with J. Willem R. Langelaan, Architect. It was published in the Proceedings of the ISARC 2003 Conference, Eindhoven, the Netherlands, pp 249–255.*

1. Introduction

Dominance has been explained as a pervasive relationship among objects in complex configurations like the built environment [Habraken 1998]. It is partly based on physical constraints like gravity and containment, but also to a large extent by convention of use and interpretation. The concept gives rise to algorithmic principles by which dominance can be understood by the computer. In general, use in practice precedes programming. The proposed interface may not only clarify the concept, but also illustrate use of dominance relations and stimulate their being incorporated in CAD programs. There are always many possible interfaces to deal with a certain design aspect. In this case we have tried to conceive of a simple formula to be used in conjunction with visual object representation on the screen. The interface is bi-directional in that changes in a relationship between objects show in the formula bar, while changes in the latter activate changes in the visual representation. Where terminology is needed, we have tried to keep it as close as possible to the practitioner's experience, avoiding unnecessary mathematical vocabulary.

2. An interface convention

2.1 Relations between objects

Given two objects in space, as shown in an on-screen design, a distance vector can be drawn from one object to the other. If drawn from A to B, it tells us about a relation of A relative to B. Many different vectors can be drawn from A to B each giving another relational aspect. The length of a vector will be calculated by the computer and may be seen next to it on the screen:

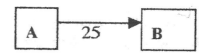

Figure 1 Relation of A towards B

Once a vector is drawn, a formula will appear in a formula bar:

$$A, B = 25 \qquad\qquad 1)$$

If we change the vector value to say, 20, object A will translate along the Vector towards B over a distance of 5. The Vector value can be changed in the formula as well as in the design. If we displace one of the objects, the Vector and the formula will adjust. If we draw another Vector between A and B or between two other objects, the first Vector will disappear.

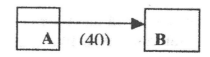

Figure 2 Negative vector value

By convention, Distance vectors running outward from an object have positive values; those drawn inward across the object will be negative.

2.2 Sides of objects

To identify sides of an object in the formula bar, a convention of names for the three pairs of opposite sides are proposed:

Head and Tail, Left and Right, Spine and Belly, or, respectively, H, T; L, R; and S, B.

For easy reading, a black dot will be shown at the head of an object when a Vector is drawn from or towards it.

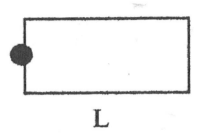

Figure 3 Identification of sides of an object

When the head is given, only one side of one other pair needs to be identified for all six sides to be known. For instance, when side L in Figure 3 is identified as well as the head, all other sides are identified. We will be free to establish the sides of an object as we prefer, or to follow generally accepted conventions.

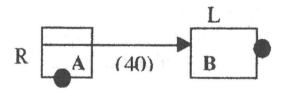

Figure 4 Relations by means of sides

Figure 4, for instance, specifies further Figure 2, and will show in the formula bar as:

$$Ar, Bt = (40) \qquad 2)$$

Here the sides are written in lower case because they specify the relation AB. Instead of drawing a
Distance Vector by hand, it can be efficient to let the computer choose a default Vector based on an orthogonal system, to be corrected later. Clicking on A first and B next would produce the Vector of Figure 1. But now the formula gives us the sides as well:

$$Al, Bt, = 25 \qquad 3)$$

We could next alter Al into Ar, and obtain the Vector in Figure 4 with the (negative) length of (40).

2.3 Behavior profile (1)

In formula 3) we may replace the value of 25 with x, and we would get:

$$A1, Bt, = x? \qquad 4)$$

The question mark asks for a specification of the constraints on x. Double clicking on it we get a window in which we may write, for instance:

$$A1, Bt, = x > 10 \qquad 5)$$

Saying in fact that the distance between the left side of A and the right side of B in Figure 4) must be more than 10. This amounts to a statement of the behavior of A relative to B. The window contains the behavior profile of A. Relations of A to other objects may be entered there as well.

2.4 Internal relations

Once the sides of an object are identified, we can transform the object by moving opposite sides relative to one another. In Figure 3, for instance, we can click Head and Tail, obtaining the corresponding default Vector:

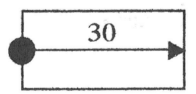

Figure 5 Relations of sides of an object

While the formula bar shows:

$$H, T, = 30 \qquad 6)$$

This time, the sides are written in capital letters because they are the objects in play. If we change the Vector value of 40 into 20, for instance, we will see the object shrink with moving toward T because we have clicked on H first. If we change formula 6) and write L instead of H, the computer knows relation LT makes no sense and will give us:

$$L, R, = 12 \qquad 7)$$

This is a general way to find out dimensions of objects and change them.

2.4 Dominance relation

If we want to establish a dominance relation in which A is to follow B, we must click A first and B later to obtain the default Vector of Figure 1, accompanied by formula 1). We next underline the formula obtaining:

$$A1, Br, = 25 \qquad\qquad 8)$$

Meaning that we want A to maintain that distance when B is displaced, or when the side to where the Vector points is displaced. If next we displace object A the Vector value will change (or the other way around.) But if we displace object B, we will see object A move as well to maintain its position relative to B. This is typical dominance behavior.

Suppose later in the design we return to objects A and B, but now we click on B first, we will see that nevertheless the Vector will point from A towards B. Because the computer remembers B dominates A, and we cannot move it relative to A. Similarly, when we have a window and the wall in which it resides in a dominance relation, we will only get Vectors from the window towards the sides of the wall. (Figure 6)

Once we underline a formula, the computer will maintain a dominance relation between the two objects for any Distance Vector that may be drawn or given constraints, maintaining the full behavior of the subordinate object relative to the dominant object. Removing the underlining in any statement will render subordinate behavior inactive.

2.5 Behavior profile (2)

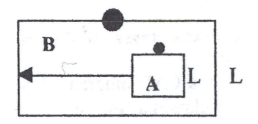

Figure 6 Window in wall

Suppose we now want to make sure the window stays within the wall. This requires a general statement about all possible relations between A and B. To make this, we click on A and B while keeping the shift key down, and get:

$$A, B, = BP? \qquad\qquad 9)$$

In which BP stands for behavior profile and the question mark indicates none is specified so far. To specify, we double click on BP and get a separate window in which A s BP, which specifies the dominance relation between A and B. We may type there, for instance:

Al, Bl, = x	and	x > 0
Ar, Br, = x	and	x > 0
Ah, Bh, = x	and	x > 0
At, Bt, = x	and	x > 0

We may summarize this statement with a heading: for instance, inside. Next time when we ask for the general AB relation we will get:

$$\underline{A, B, = BP\ inside} \qquad\qquad 10)$$

Without a summary title, only BP will appear, and by double clicking on it, the behavior profile window will open. With a summary title, we can quickly see what is going on and, in a second case of containment, the designer can simply write inside in the general formula to make two new objects relate in the same way. Readymade behavior profiles under summary titles may be available for the designer, who remains free to edit them. For instance, by changing the zero value in any of the four relations, the window may stay away a certain distance from the walls edge.

It may be that an object A is in relation with more than one other object. For each relation a BP can be written. When, in such a case, we click on object A only, holding down the shift key, we get:

$$A, = BP \qquad\qquad 11)$$

And by double clicking on BP we will get the behavior profile window of A, giving us the specifications and summary names of all relations A maintains in our design.

2.6 Relations between classes of objects

The database held by a CAD program yields lists of all kinds of object classes available in the object library. Referring to these, the designer may call for relations between classes:

$$Class\ A,\ class\ B,\ = BP? \qquad\qquad 12)$$

And may enter sub-ordinate behavior of A by underlining the formula, or specify the BP for class A. In this way relations may be settled for all high back chairs relative to all worktables and dining tables. Or for certain kinds of windows in certain kinds of walls. Instead of these functional relations we may distinguish classes according to levels of intervention [Habraken 1998] like, for instance, partitioning following a base building and dominating furniture, or buildings following the site, or a curtain wall following a steel frame.

A single instance of an object may belong to several classes and thus inherit a fully specified behavioral profile. Having access to the individual object s BP, (where s means specifies) the designer can at all times edit it.

3. Algorithmic aspects and bi-directional editing

Bi-directional editing implies freely editing a CAD database both deductively and inductively, and freely analyzing and evaluating a CAD database. In the current art, CAD application software can analyze a database on the basis of user specified criteria, such as square footage, building cost, etc. To evaluate a database on the basis of criteria and values is a manual and iterative editing process. Our proposal implies a structured approach towards automating such evaluation processes.

3.1 Objects

In object-oriented CAD application software, the objects range from low-level primitives such as vectors and text strings to high level complex 3D assemblies of primitives such as a door in a frame complete with hardware. All objects must be parametric. A parametric object is defined by an array of attributes and attribute values and may include encapsulated algorithms that lend it characteristic behavior. As already discussed, a specific object is an instance of a specific object class and has a specific set of attribute values for the attributes which it inherits from the parent class. The location of the instance is determined by the coordinates of its local origin in relation to the origin of the database. In what follows, object and object class are equivalent unless specifically indicated otherwise.

3.1.1 Object geometry

The geometry of an object is specified by its morphology and topology. The morphological attributes qualify the shape. For example, a curve. The topological attributes quantify the shape. For example, the radius of the curve.

3.1.2 Object space

The total space that can be allocated to an object is the union of its concrete and abstract space. The concrete space is the space filled by the object as a result of its geometry. The abstract space is the space to be added to make it function and to use it. For example, the object geometry of a door is given by its height, width, and depth. Its functional space is the space needed for the sweep of its door leaf. Its user space may be additional space on either side of the door to allow access.

(Functional space and user space by themselves can also be parametric objects. For example, a corridor can be a functional space element. The associated user space may be smaller and is embedded inside the functional space.)

3.1.3 Object intersections

In a design it may be found that the spatial relation between objects includes both their concrete and abstract spaces.

The Distance vectors in our proposal allow the maintenance of abstract space added to concrete space of an object. For instance, by setting a minimum distance from the object's concrete space to another concrete space or to an abstract space.

Relations will require editing. To automate such an evaluation requires that the geometric attributes of the abstract space are included with the parameters of each object. The nature of spatial relations may be an intersection of concrete space and another concrete space, concrete space intersecting with abstract space, and abstract space intersecting with abstract space.

3.2 Autonomous object behavior

Behavior can be described as a deterministic system with in-put, through-put, and out-put. In a digital system these 3 phases would be: data transfer, data analysis, and internal data transfer to an encapsulated method. In the behavior sub-system, the function of the data analysis phase is to determine to which encapsulated method the data should be passed. The encapsulated method may be an algorithm which edits the object geometry and/or edits the 6 parameters associated with the co-ordinates and orientation of the local origin within the cartesian coordinate system of the model's database and/or outputs data to a selection of objects. The data analysis phase makes the object autonomous and it seems to have a will of its own. On the other hand, if the data analysis phase is not included with the sub-system, received data is executed as instructed and object behavior is pre-determined.

3.2.1 Reactive agents

Attribute values about internal object space and global position can be transmitted as low-level data between objects. In that case an object behaves as a reactive agent [NWANA 1996] that gathers data, pulling data and transmits data to a selection of other objects pushing data. Reactive agents do not possess internal, symbolic models of their environment. They act and respond in a stimulus-response manner to the present state of the environment in which they are embedded. Reactive agent algorithms can be relatively simple as they interact with other agents in basic ways. Complex patterns of behavior emerge from these interactions between objects when observed as a group.

3.3 Dominance behavior

Relative behavior of objects can be symmetrical or asymmetrical. With symmetrical behavior, a transformation of object A results in transformation of object B and vice versa. With asymmetrical behavior a transformation of object B may not result in a transformation of object A, but may induce transformation of object C. The concept of dominance as illustrated in this paper captures this a-symmetrical behavior. A- symmetrical behavior was implemented in 1999 while developing new prototypes of high-level objects for a library of parametric objects [Langelaan 1999] for ArchiCAD [Graphisoft]. For example, a change in the section width of a doorframe results in a larger total width and height of the door object, but a change in the total width of the door object does not affect the width of the frame but implements a change of the width of the door leaf.

Dominance relations can be identified in different contexts. Although not always obvious, they are mostly conventional and therefore can be generalized with editable Behavior Profiles.

3.3.1 Design level sub-systems

These are generally governed by scale and construction sequence [Habraken 1998]. Customary design levels are those for Urban design, Site design, Building design, and Room design. More recently, a Fit-out design level has emerged in commercial and residential building [SAR 1978]. Dominance between levels is fairly obvious from design experience.

3.3.2 Group aspect system

Within each design level, objects with a common aspect can be related as logical groups, such as mechanical, structural, electrical, egress, furnishing, story, etc. Dominance is not obvious.

3.3.3 Class aspect system

This aspect system coordinates instances belonging to different classes. Class dominance is not obvious.

3.3.4 Custom relationships

Design intention may lend sets of objects a relationship with custom dominance. For instance, object A always remains at the center line of object B. Special geometric relationships could be specified with abstract relationship object classes.

3.4 Possible applications

Capacity to deal in a systemic way with dominance relations allows new ways of computer supported editing and design development:

3.4.1 Fuzzy choices

When the output of a logical process is discreet, the process can be automated with Boolean algorithms. If a process encounters an array of possibilities whose choice is not stochastic neither objective nor decisive following iteration but requires weighting and averaging, then the logical process is fuzzy. At such occurrences an automated process must be interrupted and the question with its array of choices must be presented in an input window on the screen. For example, questions about value sets of attributes, proportional relationships, dominance, etc. It must be noted that fuzzy logic reasoning algorithms may be possible to solve some of these problems.

3.4.2 Intelligent editing

This requires methods which maintain a geometric or positional relationship between discreet objects. The relationship can be inherited from the parent class or custom specified. The value of the relationship can be discreet: A on the centerline of B, or may be fuzzy: A near B, where near has the value set near={min(n), max(m)}. For example, when the geometry or position of a wall object is edited, the related doors and windows remain embedded in the wall. Or if a kitchen cabinet is placed on a floor plan it will automatically position itself against the nearest wall.

3.4.3 Bi-directional editing

This becomes possible because related attributes of an object can be reciprocally edited, such that any attribute value can be edited, and values of related attributes are automatically updated and implemented.

Moreover, in sets of related objects, any object can be reciprocally edited, and attribute values of related objects are automatically updated and implemented.

Finally, criteria can be selected for analyzing the model database; the result can be edited and attribute values of related objects in the database are automatically updated and implemented.

4. Conclusions

The proposed instrument performs in a uniform way a number of functions already available like certain groupings, containment, shrinking or stretching and translation of objects. In addition. it adds important new aspects having to do with relational behavior including dominance.

In design, basic relations are rather simple, but relational chains can become extremely complex. With the proposed instrument coherent control of this complexity may become possible, leading to greater efficiency and smoother coordination among parties in control of different sub-systems.

The instrument will render the computer relationally intelligent and capable of tracing strings of adjustment in case of local design change to check on possible conflicts between sub- systems; list object space violations; evaluate dominance of listed objects and generally monitor and help control dynamic relations among objects.

Because relational data are connected by an instance to instance chain, control of complex configurations can take place without global checking of relational data.

With the help of this instrument, we may learn more about behavior of complex systemic organizations by exercise and research. This, in turn, may enhance our theorizing on form behavior in general and building design in particular, and may lead to automated editing of a virtual building model.

References

Habraken, N. J. (1998). *The Structure of the Ordinary: Form and Control in the Built Environment*. Cambridge: MIT Press.

Nwana, H. S. (1996). *Software Agents: An Overview, Knowledge Engineering Review*, vol. 11, no. 3. Cambridge: Cambridge University Press.

Langelaan, J. W. R. (1999). *MasterLibrary 7.0*. unreleased prototype, Langelaan Architect.

Graphisoft (1982–2003). *ArchiCAD*. Budapest: Graphisoft R&D Rt.

Stichting Architecten Research (1978). "Levels and Tools." *Open House International*, vol. 3, no. 4.

2008
DESIGN FOR FLEXIBILITY
Towards a research agenda

Editors' Note: *This book review is, to our knowledge, the only published book review by the author. In it, he takes the opportunity to lay out a research agenda that reiterates and clarifies the substance of other essays and book chapters he has written, in the context of responding to the request from the editors of Building Research and Information for a review of the book Flexible Housing, Tatjana Schneider and Jeremy Till (2007), Architectural Press. The book review was published in Building Research Information, Vol. 36, No. 3, 2008.*

It takes courage to devote a book on the concept of flexibility in architecture. Words like "Adaptability", "Flexibility", and "Polyvalence" have multiple and often overlapping meanings, that make it virtually impossible to come up with a vocabulary acceptable to everybody.

Confusion in terminology is typical for architectural discourse. Other professions – those of medicine, law or engineering for instance – define themselves by a precise vocabulary employed for internal communication. Architects take pride in coining their own words to describe the world as they see it, aiming to promote a personal or tribal vision.

In the introduction to their book Schneider and Till discuss the issue of terminology to then decide to use the term 'flexibility' to cover the entire range of possible design decisions that aim to loosen rigid functionality. We therefore find, among their many examples, Auguste Perret's famous 1903 Rue Franklin apartments – where physically everything is fixed, including bathroom and kitchen, but none of the other rooms seem functionally determined – as well as the entirely empty territories offered the user by the brothers Arsene – Henry in the early seventies.

That sensible approach successfully highlights a problem peculiar to contemporary architecture: the desire among architects to recognize the spontaneous variety of user preferences and the unpredictability of future use.

A broad exposition

More than 160 projects are documented of which more than seventy are given a page each for 'case studies.' I found quite a few instances that were new to me but note a Western slant in the selection. The extensive Japanese record on flexible housing is poorly represented, about which more later.[1] But the author's selection of examples approaches completeness in a more important sense: designers inclined to "go flexible" will find it difficult to come up with an idea that is not already present in this book.

The book's title is somewhat misleading in that the contents are entirely about *design* of flexible housing and not about the broader interaction of interdisciplinary influences that shape it. Within that limitation, the first two chapters sketch the larger context. We are first introduced to major motivations leading designers to address flexibility such as the rise of the restricted and minimal dwelling in modern times, the industrialization of housing and the movement towards user participation.

Next, the case for flexible design is made. Here as well the authors are very well informed and mention most if not all relevant views and instances from various parts of the world[2], but the narrative, as far as I could check it by personal knowledge, is superficial. We hear, for instance, that house builders worldwide benefit from planned obsolescence in housing production by way of inflexible plans, but it is not mentioned that it is

DOI: 10.4324/9781003011385-42

technically much easier to modify the balloon framed suburban house in the US as well as the timber framed one in Japan, compared to the apartment or row house in Europe built in masonry or reinforced concrete. Nor do we hear in this context that homeowners will change their houses no matter what, even when the latter are functionally determined when bought, because ownership is empowerment; while units for rent tend not to be adapted to user's wishes even when technically flexible. As a promoter of Open Building I raised eyebrows when reading that apparently the "history of Open Building . . . suggests the dangers of allowing technical issues to over- determine the design of housing at the expense of an original intent to create housing that empowers the user . . ." (p. 48), as if technical innovation implies abandonment of user empowerment or that trying to technically facilitate such empowerment is to be frowned upon. It also does not clarify much to first cite criticism by a third party and then add that it is probably unfairly given (p. 47). Lapses like this in an overall sensible exposition show how an attempt to cover a complex subject by that many references in just about twenty pages requires disciplined editing.

Further chapters look upon the available selection of examples from the perspective of design: the organization of space and material each are reviewed and a final "manual" summarizes the many ways flexibility can be provided, such as by external addition, internal transformation, or the combination or subdivision of territories.

All in all, a designer who is new to the subject is served a full plate, including much that can help to avoid the first handful of mistakes.

The wide range of information, both historical and morphological, that Schneider and Till provide is conveyed in a clear and relaxed prose, devoid of jargon. The authors do not hesitate to give an opinion, usually sensible and illuminating, but they do not seek to provide the reader with criteria or guidelines by which to find a way in all this evidence. The approach is descriptive, not analytic. It reminds one of a design studio conversation, focused on ideas of form, and somewhat removed from a more complex world.

Questions arising

Schneider and Till expose, but do not probe. Obvious questions one might ask after perusing the vast amount of evidence offered remain unanswered. For example: why is it that, after more than a century of attempts by architects to design with flexibility in mind, the issue is still marginal to the profession at large? Which of the many design ideas thus documented had some broader or more lasting impact on the way housing is done in the world? What theories and ideologies have been advanced attempting to frame the topic? If, for practical reasons, such questions may best be addressed separately elsewhere, some recognition of their validity and some reference towards answers might have helped the skeptical reader to stay with the subject.

Most importantly however, for a book about design, one would like to know in what way flexibility might inspire the making of a new architecture. Is it simply a social service some of us feel morally bound to pursue, or does it imply a new and challenging kind of architecture? This question is not raised in the book either and there is no sign that the authors see an architectural perspective.

Taking such questions seriously also helps to find out how further study and experiments can advance the cause of flexibility. As always, questions lead to research, in this case not only for the architect but also for other professional parties involved in housing.

To begin with the matter of the architectural profession's involvement in design for flexibility, or lack thereof, consider the wide array of architects mentioned by Schneider and Till, some well-known, who all aspired to a new WAY OF DOING housing design. The long list, spanning about a century, may give the impression that flexibility has always been a serious occupation for the profession, but the opposite is true. Among the practicing architects indexed in the book I could only find Avi Friedman and Frans van der Werf who actually built a career on doing flexible housing. Lucien Kroll in Brussels certainly also belongs to that short list but does not feature in the book. Neither do we find Tatsumi and Takada in Kyoto who, for several decades, proposed and implemented their "Two Step Housing" approach. Others, like Nabeel Hamdi and Nicholas Wilkinson in the UK, did an influential project after which user participation subsequently dominated their entire career but removed them from architectural practice.

I must have missed names that could be added to the exceptions, but overwhelmingly the examples documented in the book are one-off cases, done by architects who managed to get their flexible project built, but then moved on, flexibility remaining marginal to their careers as it has been for the profession at large.

The good reason for this lack of engagement is that the pursuit of flexibility is a risky and cumbersome affair. It depends heavily on the cooperation of other parties in the process and is therefore difficult to get implemented. The ten architect's offices that initiated the SAR research foundation, who paid for its research in the sixties and seventies and took pride in its mission and publications, never acted in their own practice along the lines our research advocated. They sensibly did not want to jeopardize their business.

The bad reason for keeping flexible housing at arms-length was that, when participation came to the fore, many architects resented the idea that users would make design decisions. And many still do. I remember emotional reactions from colleagues, ostensibly in favor of participation who, when pressed, finally blurted out that users could not be allowed to make design decisions. Of course, user involvement, like motherhood, cannot be criticized, so the arguments put forward against flexibility in public debate tend to be about costs, technical difficulties, and also the notion that dwellers are incapable, and in need of guidance.

In this context Schneider and Till perceptively note two opposite tendencies among those who actually did design for flexibility. Architects prepared to let go, seek to provide a context that stimulates unforeseen results of user action. Others attempt to build in constraints intended to steer the user towards a 'good' result.

A sense of being invaded in their domain of expertise is shared among other professions involved in housing.[3] We are all the product of a culture, already more than a century old, in which the exclusion of the inhabitant is regarded as unavoidable and efficient. In that culture we only need to agree among ourselves as to what is to be done. A common methodology is applied: The design of any housing project begins with the floor layouts. Once these are known, everybody can do their part: consultants can design structure and services, builders can calculate, bankers can assess financing, developers can figure marketing. Without a predetermined floor plan the familiar system of mutual accountability and cooperation is destabilized. As a result, the indignation at infringement of expert territory is exacerbated by anxiety: one is asked to operate in an unknown world where responsibilities shift and risk mounts.

Developers and owners taking initiative

Indeed, what is there to gain by embracing flexibility and re-educating oneself for another methodology? But times change, and while the limitations of current habits and conventions become more evident, a new generation of professionals appears willing to explore more promising terrain. This is demonstrated in recent projects all of which, not surprisingly, were initiated by developers and owners of real estate. (These projects are not mentioned by Schneider and Till, presumably because they became known after the due date of their manuscript.) Avi Friedman and Witold Rybscynski may have been the first to successfully introduce a systemic and flexible new house type that found its way in the market[4], but as architect/academics they may turn out to have been the exception rather than the rule.

The city of Helsinki, for instance, called a competition for Open Building design. Sato Development Company built the first two buildings of the winning scheme designed by Architect Esko Khari in combination with Tocoman data processing group[5]. All units were sold, executed within budget, and completed in time, yielding a profit. As a result, Sato offered Khari and Tocoman an open-ended contract for several such projects each year.

In the Netherlands, Lingotto Developers[6] took the initiative to build a multi-function building in which both residential and commercial uses can find space in any desired proportion. They recovered the extra costs for making space flexible by selling the empty building to a client who saw advantage in exploiting it.

Frank Bijdendijk, director of the Amsterdam housing corporation Het Oosten, concluded that internal flexibility makes long-term investment feasible. Construction for an entire city block formed by nine story high buildings will start this year. Eventually, more than 40 thousand sq.m. of interior space will be rented out to, and filled in by, the leaseholder for whatever function she fancies.

In Moscow, with the rise of a wealthy class, buyers of expensive apartments instantly had their new homes gutted to have an architect of their own choice design the interior to their taste. Appalled at this waste of capital, developers asked their architects to design "empty buildings", blissfully unaware of any precedent. Today thousands of units have been built that way[7].

If developers and owners of real estate are the new pioneers in flexible residential construction, they were preceded as such by their peers in commercial real estate. In the US and increasingly in Europe, office buildings are designed with empty floors to be fitted out by tenants who hire their own architects and fit-out companies. Similarly, no shopping center will be built without offering free space to retailer occupants.

Design for flexibility

Finally, governmental bodies begin to take initiative as well. I already cited the open building competition called by the Helsinki municipality. A month ago, the town of Almere, in the Netherlands, concluded an overwhelmingly successful competition on flexible buildings for private home ownership among developers and housing corporations. The seven winners from more than sixty entrants each committed themselves to around 150 units each. The building department of the Canton of Bern, Switzerland decided on the separation of a 'primary system' from a 'secondary system' for the building of an intensive care hospital. First, a design competition was called for the primary system and only after the winning scheme was under construction, a second competition was held for the fit-out. This abrupt reversal of habitual procedures caused problems that took time to be ironed out, but the initiative caught the attention of major architectural firms specialized in hospital design in Europe and the USA. Project time can be reduced if the design of the interior can be done while the base building is being erected, and in the long run alterations will be less costly.[8]

In 1994, the Osaka Gas Company initiated what is known as the Next21 project in which a flexible building contains individually designed dwelling units.[9] Schneider and Till mention its many technical innovations (p. 106) but, in the context of flexibility, its major impact was that, after many years of open-building experiments in Japan and an enthusiastic public acclaim of this project, the government finally embraced the principle of separation of levels of control. Ministerial blessing of "SI building (skeleton-infill)" as it is known, stimulated innovation in areas other than in hardware, such as jurisprudence and financing. As I write, a government sponsored drive is afoot to promote the idea of the "long term building" by way of a competition on an urban scale. A two hundred-year building lifetime is mentioned and the SI approach will be mandatory.

Architectural challenges

Although architects cannot take the initiative, they too must develop an expertise in this new game. Some fresh approaches are indicative of what that may mean. Frank Bijdendijk[10] argues that without the love and pride of its users a building is not assured of a long life even when the requirement of flexibility is met. To earn the love of its inhabitants a building need not necessarily meet standards fashionable among architects. But it need not be in conflict with them either. Bijdendijk's choice of architects[11] proves that he does not recommend a retro architecture or a pandering of mediocrity. He declares himself inspired by New York City's Soho warehouses with their neo-classicist cast iron facades, occupied in various ways for centuries already. It is no doubt debatable what an architecture loved by its inhabitants must mean, but the requirement unmistakably connects architecture with the quality of everyday environment.

Between urban design and individual dwelling

Two more opportunities for a new architecture can be mentioned. Both flow from the consideration that a flexible building is not an empty skeleton, but an architectural environment shared by individual tenants. For the distinction between 'fit out' or 'infill' on the one hand, and the 'flexible building', or the 'support', or the 'base building' on the other, the primary criterion is *control*, not hardware. To make this point in the early days of Open Building I drew an "X" over Le Corbusier's famous picture of a skeleton for the Dom-i-no house[12] This act puzzled Schneider and Till (p. 166), but understanding it is crucial if we want to bring the user into the housing equation. The purpose of design for flexibility by whatever name is to enable individual control in an otherwise collective environment. The concept of distribution of control, therefore, is at the roots of flexible architecture. By itself such a distribution is not new. The analogy with urban design is compelling. The urban designer controls the shaping of public space and seeks to make an inspiring context for architects doing the buildings. In the same way a flexible building creates an environment for individual settlement the design of which is done on yet a lower level of control.

The flexible building, properly understood, becomes a collective form performing between urban space and individual inhabitation. As such, it has not yet inspired the profession. The ubiquitous commercial office building is still considered an unfinished building rather than the continuation of urban fabric in another way. Possibilities, created by a longer life span, for higher initial investment in public interior space and other public amenities have not yet been explored. This is remarkable because, freed from a senseless cobbling together of floor plans, architecture can return to what it always was good at: the making of public environment. For the architect the separation of control is a liberation, not an encroachment.

Two designers of residential flexibility fully grasped the potential for a new architecture that mediates between urban design and individual dwelling. "I want to do three-dimensional urban design" Yoshitika Utida, the chief architect for the already mentioned Next21 project told me when showing his plans. Consequently, he invited thirteen other architects to do the houses in the environment he had designed. Schneider and Till mention the project's systems approach but do not note this distribution of design control among architects which makes the Next21 project truly of interest.

When asked to design the 'dwelling of the future,' Utida took his Osaka client team to visit the Molenvliet project near Rotterdam done fifteen years earlier by Frans van der Werf. For Frans, a 'support structure' was not a building but a means to form a continuous three-dimensional urban fabric. He wanted to deploy a single structural and architectural principle at a neighborhood scale. It shapes major streets giving access to public courtyards while other courtyards offer space for gardens. The Molenvliet project as built is only a fragment of that initial competition entry, but it remains a compelling demonstration of the flexible building's potential for shaping extended urban fabric. Where, for Bijdendijk, the unit's flexibility allows long term investment, for van der Werf internal flexibility, including façade parts, enables urban scale continuity without uniformity. Frans van der Werf's project is still visited by flexibility devotees as a demonstration of what the future may hold.

The distribution of design control

The third architectural challenge to be mentioned also relates to the distinction between domains of control. Where should the flexible building stop and inhabitation's domain begin?

Each of the projects shown by Schneider and Till draws the line in its own way, but that variety only reflects architect's preferences. We lost our bearings here because professionals cannot determine the true boundary among themselves. Design control must first be delegated before the correct balance can be found by trial and error and post occupancy research. Moreover, there will be not just one solution.

In today's world the answer may vary with place and circumstances.

Several decades of Open Building experimentation have taught us however that, at the very least, bathrooms and kitchens must be under full user control. As industrially produced durable goods they have entered the millennia old tradition of human settlement only recently, somewhat in the way the car entered the world's historic road network.

Given that first separation, how much fixed material, in the form of columns and walls, should be found in a dwelling unit? The range between the proposals of Auguste Perret and the brothers Arsene-Henry, as noted earlier, is still wide open. Today, pre-stressed floor slabs make it easy to build large empty spaces, thus maximizing use of fit-out material. In the early days of rampant mass housing it was considered axiomatic that flexible parts were more expensive and had to be limited in number. We achieved perfectly flexible solutions with small span bays and a good deal of load bearing walls in each unit. Architecturally shaped human size dimensions need not be in conflict with freedom in user's settlement and can stimulate user decisions.

A similar question applies to the design of the façade. To what extent must it express inhabitation and to what extent must it help shape outside public space? This is a cultural issue as well. Georgian Londoners were quite happy behind monumental communal facades while the burghers of the Dutch republic wanted each house to have its own. Here too, long-term user feedback must teach us.

A research agenda

It is to be regretted that the commendable compilation by Schneider and Till does not draw attention to these architectural challenges and opportunities. This could have stimulated research and experimentation by architects. But the re- distribution of control, implied by the concept of flexibility, is not only of architectural import. It invites adjustment of method for all parties involved in housing, and as such opens new avenues for research. It suggests, for instance, a dedicated residential fit-out industry, delivering and installing the dwelling unit's fit-out as a single product. This industry-to-be has a potential comparable to the automobile industry. Separation between fit-out and collective building also asks consultants on utility systems to reconsider how main lines are best distributed in the flexible building to feed and drain a dwelling's territory at the boundary of which the fit-out contractor will take over and distribute lines to kitchens and bathrooms. Because the durable part of a housing estate will shift towards a much longer use-life, the division of design control is of interest to the economist as well. Whereas the flexible building becomes a truly long-term investment for collective use, the fit-out is more in league with durable consumer goods like the motorcar. (An installed fit-out kit, we learned, costs about as much as the occupant pays for his car.) New financing mechanisms are called for: long-term mortgage service on one side of the divide, short-term bank loans on the other. A sound legal framework for the separation of control must be worked out as well. All such issues are in need of closer study. In recent decades various ad-hoc suggestions have been made in the directions suggested here, but the field for a comprehensive research agenda is wide open.

Notes

1. There is a long track record on "flexible design" in Japan, both in terms of user participation and in terms of technology, initiated by public agencies as well as private companies. The approach is pragmatic and much less encumbered by ideology than is the case in Europe. Professor Katsuo Tatsumi and his younger colleague Mitsuo Takada have for several decades advocated what they call "Two Step Housing" which produced a number of projects over the years. The Japan Housing Corporation, a semi-governmental institution for subsidized middle-class housing has consistently experimented with the same idea. Professor Stephen Kendall in his (unpublished) 1995 report on "Developments Toward Open Building in Japan" mentions some 17 recent or ongoing initiatives. In the last ten years after the influential NEXT21 project was built, a spate of other projects has been done in Japan.
2. The search for a new professional methodology replacing the one based on predetermined floor plans, which was SAR's major research agenda item, is not mentioned at all. SAR (Foundation for Architect's Research) was founded in 1965 by ten architects' offices to investigate the implementation of the 'support-infill' idea.
3. Only recently I found myself in a conference of professional experts in the business of housing, when someone mentioned the need for more user participation. The response was one I have heard for half a century: "let's first deal with the shortage of houses before we address user participation." I could not resist raising my hand and ask: "Can you tell me what you have to gain from an end to the housing shortage?" After a painful silence the moderator of the meeting asked: "Prof. Habraken, are you accusing us of a conspiracy?" No, was my response, it is ignorance. If you do not know what there is to gain, why bother?"
4. At my request, Avi Friedman emailed me the following: "Of the Grow Home (which I designed with Witold Rybcsynski) by conservative estimate some 10.000 units have been constructed in the Montreal area by various private builders. The Next Home which I designed alone as part of a research project and which we constructed on our university campus was also adopted by builders. I estimate the number of built units at 1000."
5. Arabianranta (Arabian Shore) competition 2001. winning project completed 2005, Two different support structures, 80 apartments, SATO Development company, Esko Kahri & Co Architects, and ToCoMan Group cost, data, & Internet consultant: PlusKoti Arabian Kotiranta, PDF/Adobe Acrobat – HTLM version.
6. Multifunk project, Lingotto real Estate, 2005; concept by Bob Jansen, president and CEO, design by ANA Architecten, www.lingotto.nl.
7. Bart Goldhorn, *The Free Plan, Russia's Shell-and-Core Apartment Buildings, Project Russia 20*. Moscow and Amsterdam: A-Fond Publishers, 2003. ISBN 90-806207-3-4.
8. Giorgio Macchi, director of the Bern Canton (provincial) Building Department, has decided to make the distinction between a primary, secondary and tertiary system general policy in his department.
9. Osaka Gas Next21 project 1993, supervised by Yositika Utida with Kazuo Tatzumi, Mitsuo Takada and Seiichi Fukao, and executed by Shu-Koh-Sha Architectural & Urban Design Studio under Shinichi Chikazumi.
10. Frank Bijdendijk calls his flexible buildings 'Solids'. His contribution to Open Building theory lies in his emphasis on the building's 'lovability' as a precondition in conjunction with full interior flexibility for its long life. An English language book by him is expected to be published this year. www.solids.nl.
11. The eleven building, 40.000 square meters project for which construction will start this year is designed By Dietmar Eberle, Baumschlager & Eberle, www.baumschlager-eberle.com. An earlier 'Solids' building in Amsterdam West is under construction, and was designed by Tony Fretton.
12. In: "Three R's for Housing," originally published in *Forum*, vol. xx, no. 1, December 1966, bilingual reprint by Scheltema & Holkema, Amsterdam, ISBN 90 6060 014 2.

INTERMEZZO BY THE EDITORS

JH: As a student, I spent most of my time in the library. And I followed the professor in architectural history. I did not take other courses because I thought you could find it in books and I can just do the exam. This guy was an interesting professor. He was excited about the topics he taught. But other professors, you should not put that in the book, but you have to do your examination with them, but I didn't want to sit every week with their talking. So, I came from time to time. Everybody was always writing down, but I was just looking at the guy. Because I wanted him to remember my face.

SK/JD: That's great!

JH: But history – this thing I liked. This was a nice topic.

SK/JD: Because, I mean, the interesting thing is, and I understand that, too, because I like drawings, I like books which are well illustrated with variations on themes. You can look at those plans and read so much into them without at all being explicit because the patterns themselves and the fact that there are patterns that repeat but there are also variations is what makes it fascinating, right? So that's really interesting. That clearly is something that's shaped your work. Shaped the way you look at things.

JH: It is interesting that you mentioned that, because now that we talk about it, it was a very great, a strong influence. It was the world that helped me figure things out. Funny.

SK/JD: Yeah, but compelling, as well, I think. And then, you know, . . . your native country is also a country where there are very strong, traditional architectural patterns. There are forms that repeat there in many variations. The smaller cities have a relation to the bigger cities because of the canals and the row houses, forming a kind of continuity. You know, it went from Amsterdam to Delft. It was a different scale, but there were many common aspects to it.

JH: Yeah. Absolutely. I remember I took pictures of the canal in Delft, along with every house. . . . All the pictures, you could put them all together. I had to do a design for a townhouse on Delft Canal for somebody. He was one of the more interesting designers, architects, teachers. And it took me a long time to do that well, because I wanted it to be a new building. Not a copy of an old one. Because I figured out that, for instance, the fact that the canal houses have high spaces on the ground floor, they have a mezzanine inside. First you go up the steps, then you go to the high space of the mezzanine where business was conducted, and then, every other floor above is lower. It makes a beautiful facade. But I also did that, and the professor liked it very much. That professor was an interior designer. In those days, he did many of the expositions in the wax museum, and was very, very good, because you knew he had designed it. If you went to the space he had designed, you always ended up looking at the objects. He was so modest in his design that he made objects shine. So, I liked to work with him. His details were beautiful.

CULTIVATING BUILT ENVIRONMENT

1978
BUILD AS BEFORE

Editors' Note: *This essay was published in* SAR Open House, *Vol. 3, No. 1, 1978. The introduction was written by the author, shortly after he was appointed Head of the Department of Architecture at MIT (1975). The drawings were produced by the SAR office and summarize previous studies carried out there. The essay presages the historic preservation movement; it proposes a strategy as a basis for discussion on how to preserve existing urban tissues and yet to renew them.*

Introduction

Sooner or later, the extensive 19th century developments in our big cities will have to be rebuilt. The object of this report is to sketch a strategy – or rather a part of a possible strategy – for this task. It deals with the part of the strategy concerned with planning and building activities. We shall not discuss problems of finance, legal aspects, procedures for participation and right-of-say, rents and subsidies, or many other aspects which are correctly considered to be essential parts of the problem involved. It might be thought that such a restriction of our subject matter is irresponsible or even absurd, but we are convinced that this is not the case. We shall try to explain the reasons for this conviction briefly and would ask readers to be so kind as to suspend their judgement for a moment. After reading this introduction, readers are at liberty . . . to lay this report aside and to pass on to other matters.

One thing seems certain: there is as yet no clear, generally accepted strategy regarding the future of the 19th century developments in our cities. Indeed, so far there has been relatively little discussion about such a strategy. Now we cannot expect a strategy to be developed before we have a clear idea in our minds of what we want to do; and in the present case this should be an idea about which there is general agreement. The only common point that has emerged from the past decade of protests, failures and endless procedures is probably the following: no one believes anymore in a policy of knocking everything down and starting all over again.

No one wants mass housing – blocks of flats and terraced housing – in place of what we have at the moment.

The reasons are well known. The disintegration and disorganization in social structure in the districts in question which would result from mass demolition is unacceptable. The organization which would be needed for such an operation demands an authoritarian and paternalistic-bureaucratic apparatus which cannot be accepted by current norms. Moreover, the procedures of compulsory or voluntary purchase involved would take years, if they turned out to be possible at all. Empty gaps in the city structure would wait years for the completion of planning procedures, etc.

On the other hand, it has been established that the renovation of individual houses is not the solution either. This approach can be useful in many cases, but it is very expensive. When the renovation of an existing dwelling costs as much as or more than the building of a new one, it is difficult to defend this as a generally valid solution. If neither wide-scale development projects following after demolition, nor piecemeal renovation, is the solution, in which direction should we look for an answer to our problem? What is the *product* we should concentrate on as desirable and feasible? This brings us near to the heart of our problem. For we can only undertake joint action, finance, regulate, subsidize and produce if we have a picture – a concrete idea – of what we are aiming at. What is it that we want to make? What is the object, the kind of thing, to be produced?

Not until we know the answer to these questions can the designers start designing again, the builders building, the financiers financing, the bureaucrats administering, the authorities coordinating and the occupants looking forward to improved housing conditions.

The 19th century was a period of great expansion. The 19th century districts in our cities rose up in the space of a couple of generations. This enormous effort, giving rise to an enormous increase in building production, was possible because an image – right or wrong – existed of what had to be done. A street was a street; a house was a house. Certain types were developed, the work was carried out according to certain themes and patterns which there was little or no need to discuss.

This generally accepted image created a framework within which steps could be taken, plans made, work carried out. Of course, the picture could be varied and interpreted in countless ways. The rich merchant's house was one variant; the workman's dwelling on the third floor, reached by a steep flight of stairs from the street was another (in the Dutch situation). The construction of the sash window in the two types of dwellings did not differ all that much, however; nor did the construction of facades, floors, roofs and party walls. There were standard solutions for various problems and standard details.

There were indeed pattern books for plans, facades, window construction, decorations, etc. In short, at every level (from the street patterns in each district to the standard dimensions used in parceling out the ground, from the distances between party walls to the details on the facades) there were generally accepted starting points and general principles. Within such a framework, things can be done. Design, production, financing and administration can then be seen as separate problems which can be tackled separately because there is a basic coordination principle underlying the whole. As we said above, there was a picture of the product, a picture that was generally accepted by the people who made the decisions.

We do not wish to enter into argument about whether the norms and values of the 19th century were good or bad. What we are trying to say is that effective action and coordination of action are only possible when there is a generally accepted picture of what can and should be done.

We have no such picture today. We only know what we don't want. And the lack of such a picture means indecision and hence inertia. That is why, even though we have powers today which greatly exceed those known by past generations – powers of production, organization, administration, financing and coordination – we are powerless because we don't know what we want.

This is a paradoxical situation; but the paradox can be explained. What we really want to do is to preserve an existing urban tissue and yet to renew it. And that is a situation which has no precedents from the recent past in which all these great powers were developed.

The image on which all our operations have been based recently in the building world is that of mass housing – large-scale developments which ignore the existing structure of the tissue of our cities; the image of "new" neighborhoods which are supposed to be better than what they replaced. This image made it possible to develop new techniques, new forms of organization, new architectural concepts and new forms of land tenure and financing. And just when we thought that we had got everything running smoothly, the whole picture reversed: from the expansion of the city into virgin land back to small-scale, old, familiar, the complex use of space, the intermingling of functions and mixing of utilitarian forms and family types.

The image we need, to achieve coordination of our actions in the renewal of 19th century urban districts, can only be based on acceptance of what is already there: houses with spans of six meters on straight streets; front doors leading to the pavement, dwellings above shops and workshops. Buildings two to four, at most five stories high, closed blocks of houses enclosing an inner space. If we want to start from the existing situation, this is our starting point. Nevertheless, the choice of a starting point does not mean uncritical acceptance of a whole existing situation. But if we want to improve a situation, we have to start at the beginning; and the problem in the present case can be stated as follows: Is it possible to replace a single unit of terraced housing fast and effectively?

The key to the problem lies in the words "fast and effectively." If 19th century districts can only be

Build as before

renewed by preserving the tissue, that means that the tissue must be subject to a continuous process of renewal in which we replace cell by cell. Fast, because otherwise the neighborhood will be turned into a building site for years; effectively, because otherwise no improvement will be realized. The characteristic feature of living urban tissue is that every cell is different, although all cells are of the same sort; it must thus be possible for the new cells to be different, too, though of the same sort (just as they must be able to be different from the cells they replace).

Once again, the process of renewal must be fast, for it must be completed within 10–20 years. And it must be effective, for it must be carried out with the means available.

So, we see that our first question: how can a single house be replaced? hides a whole ambitious program. This question must be answered in such a way that a systematic program for design and production can be developed, a program in which financing and administration can be coupled to yield a coordinated strategy.

The following drawings represent a first attempt at sketching such a systematic program for design and production. The main reason for producing these drawings is to show that such an undertaking is possible. The 19th century developments in our cities show clear signs of a systematic approach. There are typical ways of parceling out the ground, typical styles of buildings, typical dwellings, etc. With the aid of analysis, we can distil rules from these types. However, these rules must not be a thoughtless regurgitation of what we have taken in. New rules will have to be added, reflecting present-day norms concerning living, building and decision-making. These <u>rules</u> can form the basis for the development of technical <u>systems</u> from which new building proposals can be generated. The main features of these proposals will be that they are general in character, i.e. they do not refer to a particular situation, to a gap to be filled in. Application of these <u>models</u> to existing situations will lead to certain adjustments; and in this way the final <u>plans</u> will be arrived at. This is the path that leads to the picture that provides the inspiration for action: the development of building systems and components which, combined in different ways in different houses, will give scores of different solutions depending on the situation involved and the wishes of the people concerned. The formulation of standards for financing and subsidies on the basis of the types developed; the development of procedures for participation and policy formation based on knowledge of the basic possibilities, etc.

In this way, we should be able to unleash forces leading to a development comparable to that which led to the 19th century building activity. It is this thought which was behind the choice of the title of this report: "Do it Again," or "Build as Before."

The drawings are basically summaries of the results of the studies carried out by SAR during the past years. They distil the findings embodied in various reports to a simple whole which is presented here as a basis for discussion, in the hope that it will be one more stimulus towards the creation of a coordinated renovation strategy.

RULES
from the context: 19th century building

1. supporting structure

1. number of storyes - max. 4, excl. basement and roof
2. floor to floor heights - grnd.flr. 28-42M, uppr.flrs 28M
3. access to upper dwellings - vertical, direct from street
4. private outside space - rear roof terraces
5. spans - for living rooms 39-66M, access/sleeping 24-30M
6. depth of building - always α-β-α zoning, corner situations α-β
7. internal stair openings - β- zone or αβ-margin
8. openings in structural walls - in zone 20M, in margin 11M
9. service ducts - β-zone or αβ-margin
10. facade floor projection - at 1st floor level
11. roof parapet - 6M-9M above floor

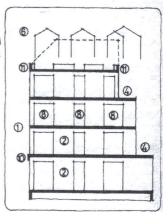

2. facade

1. front facade - always in one plane, recessed balcony or bay windows possible
2. rear facade - in one plane or recessed
3. ground floor facade - front facade open infill ad hoc. rear facade extension possible.
4. facades upper levels - windows and mullions
5. windows and balcony doors - breadth 8-11 and 14M, height n.M.
6. sill heights - upper floors max. 6M
7. mullions - breadth 4-7-10M, side mullions intermediate mullions
8. bay windows - max. 9M projection, 22M broad
9. facade infill upper floors - except for bay windows, all floors identical

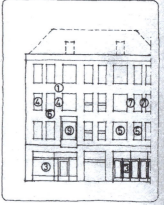

3. roof

1. roof line - perpendicular or parallel to facade
2. drainage - to rear facade
3. roof height - min. 30M
4. slope - 45o
5. dormer windows - on parapet, behind gutter 10-13M wide, height 13-16M
6. gables - in plance of facade, not on side facades

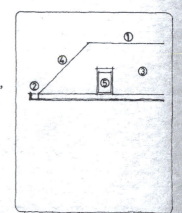

Figure 1 Rules from the context: 19th century building

from the decision levels: support-infill

1. levels

1. the planning levels - (tissue plan) support plan and infill plan
2. differentiation
   - in block dimensions - lot distribution tissue plan
   - in block subdivision - support plan variations
   - in dwelling dimensions - lot distribution support
   - in dwelling subdivision - dwelling plan variations
3. participation
   - of resident association - tissue plan and lot distribution tissue
   - of the inhabitant - support plan and lot distribution support
4. Right of say
   - residents association - support plan and lot distribution support
   - of the inhabitant - infill plan

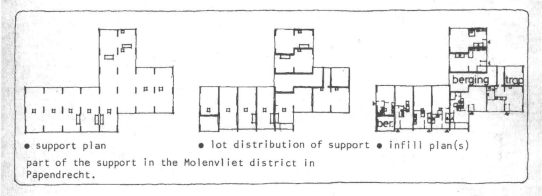

- support plan
- lot distribution of support
- infill plan(s)

part of the support in the Molenvliet district in Papendrecht.

The participation mainly has a relationship to a definate phase of the process - the model phase and to a definate aspect of the process - the physical planning.

2. phases

1. the plan phase - model phase and plan phase
2. model - non-situation bound
3. plan - situation bound

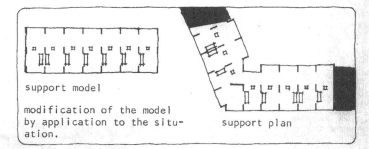

support model

modification of the model by application to the situation.

support plan

Figure 2 From the decision-levels: Support/infill

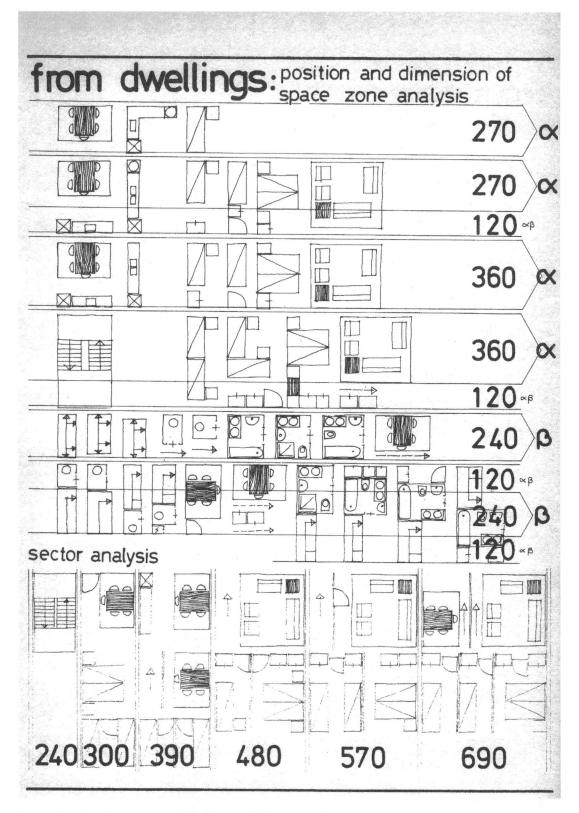

Figure 3 From Dwellings: position and dimensions of space/zone analysis

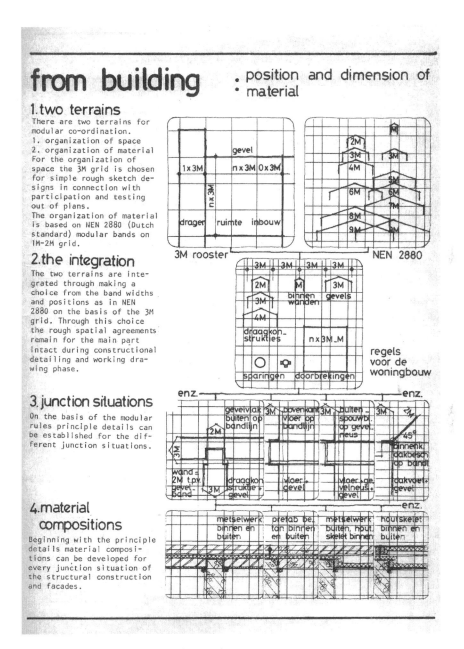

Figure 4 From building: position and dimension of material

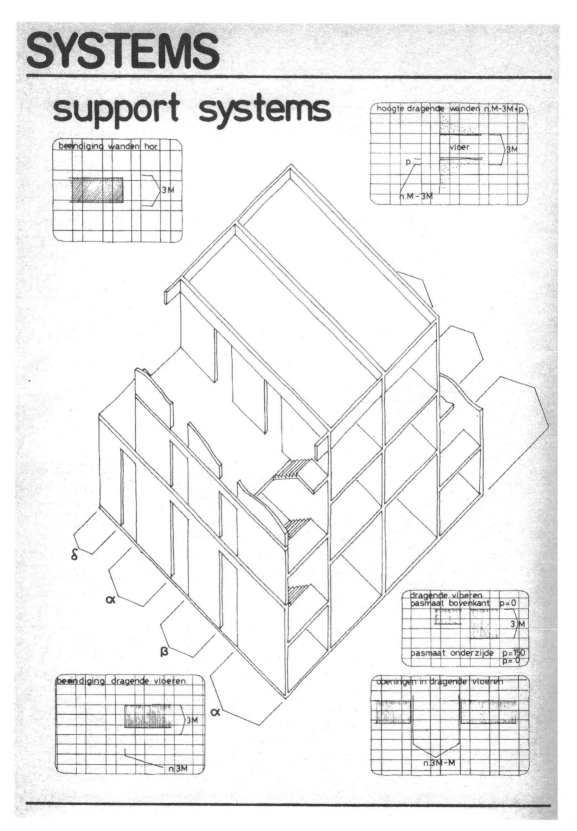

Figure 5 Systems: Support systems

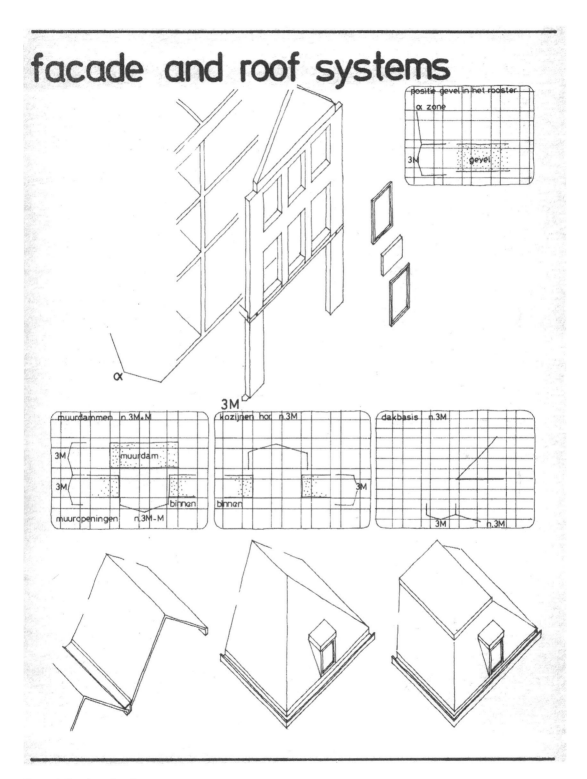

Figure 6 Façade and roof systems

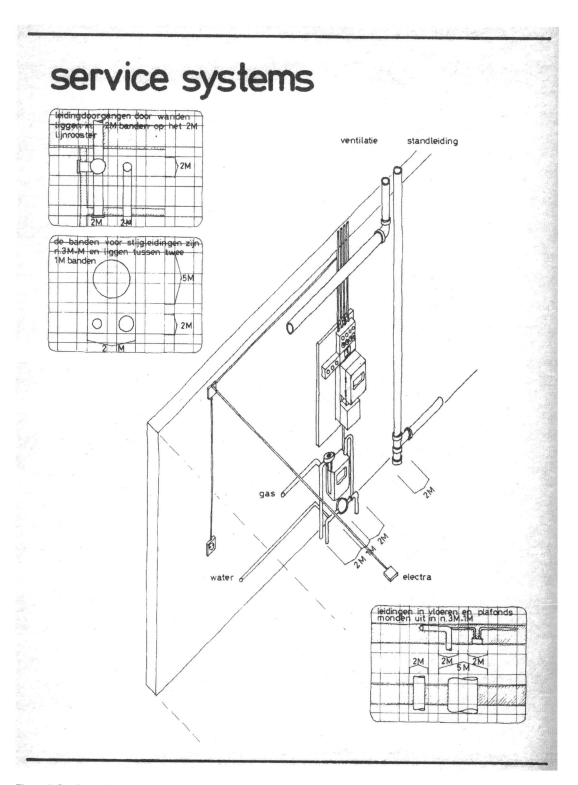

Figure 7 Service systems

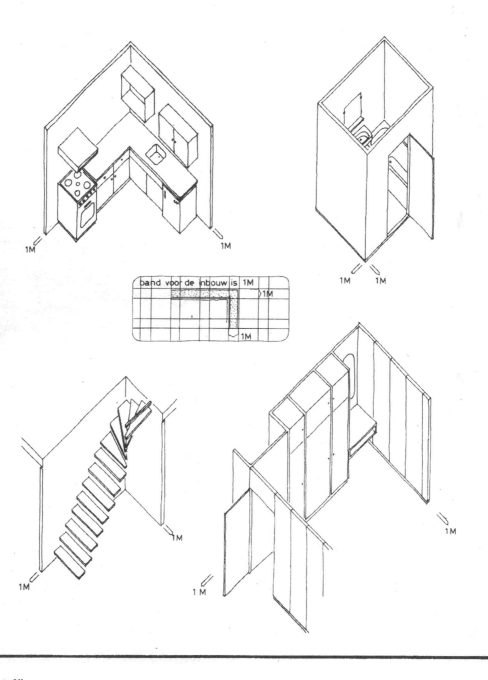

Figure 8 Infill systems

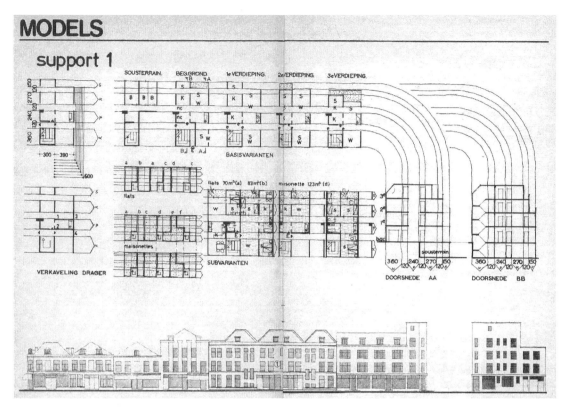

Figure 9 Models: Support 1

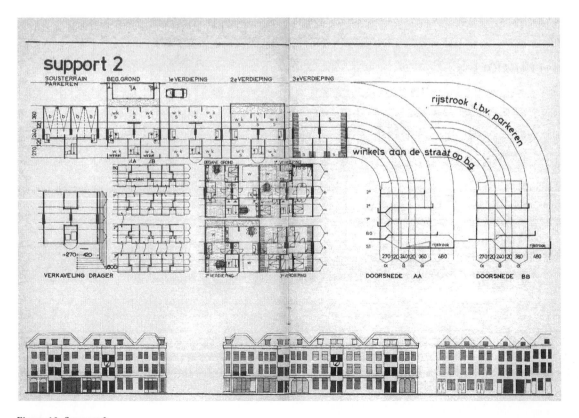

Figure 10 Support 2

Build as before

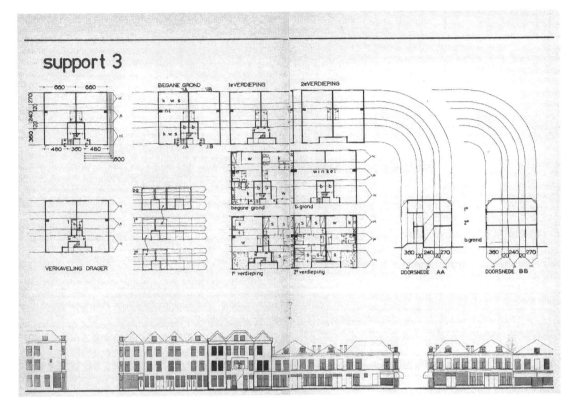

Figure 11 Support 3

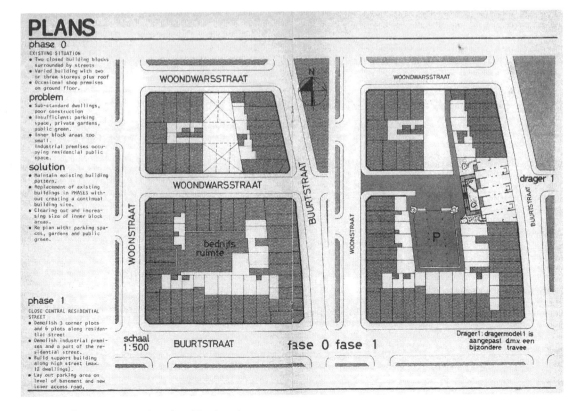

Figure 12 Plans – Support 1 introduced in phase 1

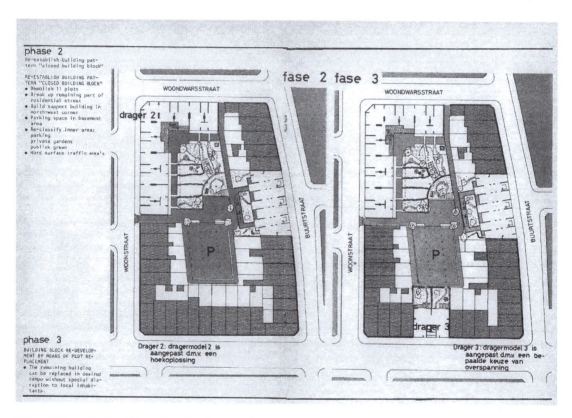

Figure 13 Supports 2 and 3 introduced in phases 2 and 3

1987
CONTROL OF COMPLEXITY

Editors' Note: *This paper was published in PLACES, Volume 4, Number 2, 1987. It continues the authors examination of complexity, this time using examples of the work of students under his direction at MIT as examples. The general principles laid out here were developed more fully around the same time in an informally published book The Appearance of the Form (later released as one of The Open Building Series in Routledge's Reissue Series) and in Conversations with Form, A Workbook for Students of Architecture (co-authored with Jonathan Teicher and Andres Mignucci), published by Routledge in 2014.*

How can we design large projects without necessarily imposing uniformity and rigidity where variety and adaptability overtime are desirable? How can big projects nevertheless do justice to the small scale?

There are good reasons to believe that variety and adaptability yield a better match between the built environment and the life it shelters. Moreover, the state of the art in building technology suggests that there is not necessarily a conflict between efficient production and variety of form. In fact, variety might be the logical outcome of efficient production.[1]

If neither the use nor the technical means dictate uniformity and rigidity of built forms, design skills may become the weakest link in the chain. The design of complex, varied forms that are adaptable over time and nevertheless easy to control and to build demands new methods and skills.

In turn, such new methods and skills must come from a good understanding of the structure of complex artifacts. And much can be learned from the study of environments with a high degree of spatial complexity to find out what their structure is and what processes could make them come about. In this context, the studies done by Fernando Domeyko are most valuable. His meticulous documentation of vernacular environments of high density in cities like Santiago (Chile); Madrid and Cordoba in Spain; Cambridgeport, Massachusetts; and others gives us a wealth of information to be interpreted and studied. An interest in these environments has nothing to do with a romantic yearning for past conditions. We are not looking at them to copy but to learn how today structures of similar sophistication and resilience may come about in accordance with the means we have today. In a similar way, Maurice Smith of MIT has studied the Portuguese hill towns and found consistencies in dimension and spatial organization that are useful for present day designing. What we took for and what we are interested in here are systemic properties from which complex environmental organizations can be built.

In what follows, I will discuss a number of issues that have to do with understanding complex environmental forms and their design manipulation. These are, if you like, areas of knowledge and skill of interest in a search for new methods. They have been the subject of discussion and experimentation in my course on design methods and theory in the post-professional degree program (M.S. Architecture Studies) at MIT.

Transformation

First, and possibly most importantly, it should be noted that architectural form may result from a process of transformation. Suppose we set up, by way of demonstration, two columns and a lintel spanning them. This primitive configuration, when studied, leads to a number of alternative next moves. We may expand with another column and beam. This may be done in alignment with the first beam or at an angle to it. Or we may repeat the portal at a distance parallel to the first, which would allow us to put planks from beam to beam and make a floor or roof. The choice of any of these steps leads to new alternatives.

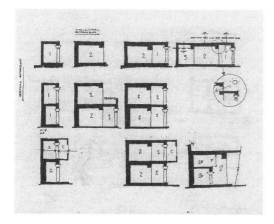

Figure 1 **Thematic development of a section following a growth pattern in which new kinds of spaces are developed.** *Starting from the upper left-hand corner, horizontal expansion is from left to right, and vertical expansion is from top to bottom. From a class assignment by Solomon Benjamin, M.S. Arch. Studies Program, Massachusetts Institute of Technology.*

This basic exercise gives us the ingredients of a design attitude. We see in the form at hand the moves available to us. We enter into a dialogue with the form. Our freedom is in choosing the next move; our skill is in choosing what leads us in the general direction we must take to satisfy a demand or a strategy; our knowledge and experience lie in being able to find many alternative moves.

The result of such a humble beginning, if the process is continued, can be very complex and very rich. But nothing in it needs to be done by happenstance, and all steps are accounted for technically as well as architecturally.

This very beginning is initially found difficult by many designers for a number of reasons: First, it can only be done from a knowledge of and interest in the way the building is actually built. Columns have certain properties, and these suggest next moves. There is a difference between a concrete portal or a steel one, or freestanding columns with a lintel on top. All three alternatives are interesting to work with, but the moves we can choose from them are different. When the design is too abstract, anything goes. There can be no dialogue with the form. In short, one can only work this way if one believes a building can only be designed when one knows how it is built. I should point out here that the same knowledge about building allows us to generalize. For instance, we may decide later whether to use concrete or steel portals while we reject early on the free-standing column. The requirement that we design from a knowledge of the building system does not mean that we must decide everything now or cannot change our mind as we go.

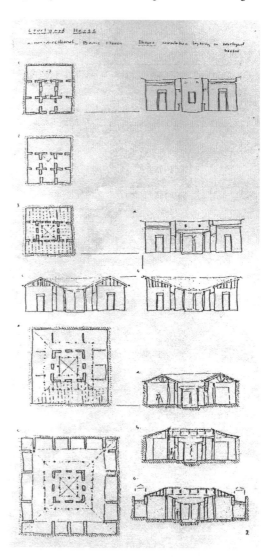

Figure 2 **Thematic exploration of a contained form.** *The study focuses on the transition from the outside space of the courtyard toward the inside spaces around it, resulting in a number of different concentric screens. From a class assignment by Sergio Palleroni, M.S. Arch. Studies program, Massachusetts Institute of Technology.*

A second difficulty students have with this exercise is that there is no program. They are asked not to think of any guiding functional demands. For those trained in a culture in which one justifies one's architecture functionally, this is difficult. Even designers who embrace the idea of an autonomy of the form find out how heavily their design reasoning depends on programmatic premises. In the approach suggested here, the function becomes a variable within a stable form. This relationship will be discussed separately later on.

It becomes evident when working without a program that we lack an appropriate vocabulary to talk form. Most of our language when discussing architectural form is related to use. A broader vocabulary is needed to discuss moves, directions of moves, developments of patterns, juxtapositions of spaces, relations of elements, and other aspects of form making.

The third barrier for the beginner is a feeling of lack of direction. "How can I design if I do not know what the end result will be like?" is a frequent complaint. "Why would you need to design if you already knew?" is my response. The need for a prior image is most keenly felt when we do not trust the form as something to work with. There is nothing wrong with having such an image, but it is not a prerequisite and may be a hindrance. When we speak with other people, we need not know what the result of the conversation will be either. We may come out of the conversation with a better sense of the issue; in fact, we may have changed our mind. When we are concerned about "doing our own thing" and feel we must be on top of the form all the time, we cannot relax and trust the process. Once students find out how one's dialogue with the form will always bear the imprint of one's personality – whether one likes it or not – the complaint is no longer heard.

Theme

Designing in dialogue with the form is like improvising on a theme. There can be variations and transformations of the initial pattern. We can elaborate, we can add subthemes, and we can shift the theme by changing some of the relationships among components or by introducing new components.

The concept of theme leads us to two important issues. First, the theme allows us to connect to others. Someone else, recognizing the theme, will know what we are trying to do. This link enables us to work together once the theme emerges in the process. The nice thing about the theme is that it makes us communicate through the form. Indeed, under ideal circumstances, thematic communication can be without words. One could simply supply a series of transformations, and someone else could continue the thematic development. Experimenting with thematic developments this way makes us appreciate the power of implicit conventions in designing. Much of what we do is based on unspoken understandings. We already share many common values and principles before a dialogue starts. Making form transformations in a thematic way establishes such implicit understandings and conventions. Once the mechanism is recognized, it can be used deliberately to foster teamwork and cooperation in the design process.

Second, the communicative power of a theme is also found in systems. A system gives us a choice of elements and their allowed relations in space. It emerges when we seek to establish rules. By approaching systems this way, we can see their thematic potential. A system always allows variations of form within the rules it imposes; it can support the thematic development of a configuration. Thus, systems thinking can be a means for generating variety by following rules.

Theme and system both set constraints on what we do. In the system, constraints are spelled out; in the theme, they are implicit. The system is rules, the theme is convention. A system usually allows for many

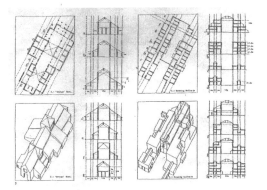

Figure 3 **Thematic transformations of a section**. *Inspired by the 'grange-type' of the Benedictine monasteries in France during the Middle Ages, the various sections join into a directional building organization. From there, the same zones serve a different section principle called 'housing galleria.' The two section principles also share the dominant central space relating to smaller spaces on the periphery. From a class assignment by John R. Dale, M.S. Arch. Studies program, Massachusetts Institute of Technology.*

themes, but a theme always implies something systematic. Both hold people together in that they imply a group of those who follow their constraints. Indeed, both are, in their own way, the product of people agreeing on a set of constraints. The explicitness of the system makes it more generally transferrable. The implicitness of the theme is bound more to social body.

By comparing themes and systems, we find how their rules and conventions give design a social context. They make people work together. Working only by ourselves, we may find implicit or explicit rules that can be used to master complexity. But if we want to work with others, rules become indispensable. Without systemic or thematic principles, delegation of work to others is very difficult and will soon lead to confusion. Moreover, if we want to divide responsibility among peers in a team, we must agree on such principles as well. By their use, thematic designing becomes a shared adventure.

Thus, by starting from the concept of theme, which lead us to the concept of systems, we begin to see designing as something happening among people. No one designs alone in architecture anyway. We will be less defensive if we can explain the thematic aspects of our work to others because it allows them to think along with us and it makes us free to change the elaboration of the theme or choose a different theme without loss of control.

The nonthematic

Once the thematic is understood as a means to guide our actions and connect to others, we realize we are also free to divert from the conventions we follow. At any point elements can be introduced and moves can be made that go outside the theme. The thematic and the nonthematic define each other because the special cannot exist without the conventional, and it is the tension between the two that brings out qualities of form. It is therefore important to understand that both the thematic and the nonthematic are part of the design effort and that both can be subject to agreements and rules. Since each one makes the other possible, we cannot argue which is more interesting. The way we orchestrate the thematic and the nonthematic is what designing is about.

Type

Once the thematic is understood as something we can share, the concept of type can be brought into focus. When we study house types from different places and cultures, we find how they represent very complex combinations of systems. The type can be described in many ways, as a spatial system, as a combination of technical systems, as a system of facades and decorations. All descriptions can be valid and yet they do not exhaust the type. There is always another way to describe a type merging in real life.

Types are shared properties within a culture. Everyone, builders, designers, users, is familiar with them. Yet, types, such as the Venetian Gothic palace, the Amsterdam renaissance townhouse, the Georgian terraced house, or the Pompeian courtyard house, were never formally described by those who made and used them. Types only exist in a social body. Once we realize this, we find how futile it is to discuss typology in terms of form only. The power of the type is that it is never explicated but allows a social body to produce very complex artifacts with a minimum of formal designing and a maximum of efficiency.

As shared knowhow within a social body, the type is known through acts, not through description. Indeed, I found that students have no difficulty making a reasonable instance of a type after studying a number of examples for a day. However, being asked to describe the type produces much labor, long disputes

Figure 4 **Pompeii as an example of a continuous architectural field.** The urban tissue shows variations of a house type. The house units are formed by the combination of atrium, peristyle, and garden, with cell – like rooms around them. Note how large houses have a larger atrium and peristyle, but that the size of the rooms is not much different with the size of the house; there are only more rooms. While all houses have an atrium, only the larger house a peristyle. Although their number may vary, the relations between the spaces that make the house is always the same, for instance the peristyle is always behind the atrium and both are surrounded by cell- type rooms.

and little conclusive results. Each observer stresses another aspect. Each description is inevitably a reduction and therefore destroys the holistic power of the type. The type exists as long as we follow the conventions it implies. The living type need not be explained because it is already shared knowledge; hence its efficiency and coordinating power.

This field can be read in both ways as discussed in the text. First, as a deployment of walls and columns, following certain continuous patterns across the whole field. See for instance the cells lining the streets. Second, as a combination of units. Closer scrutiny shows that the latter are not the same as the house units by which we recognize the type. Openings in party walls, for instance, suggest the combination of two or more "houses" into one territory. Irregularities in party walls also betray exchanges of spaces from one house to another in the course of time. Detail of the map in Overbeck, Pompeii, Leipzig. 1866.

Field deployment

Once the thematic development of forms is understood, we need not think of self-contained forms that grow and transform, but we can use the same approach for the creation of large continuous fields. The theme can work its way across the field, making instances and reiterations without ever repeating exactly the same form. In environmental design, urban tissues are examples of continuous thematic fields.

To control the deployment of such fields, a number of issues must be studied. One has primarily to do with tools: we need a formal geometry to help us organize such fields. The other has to do with a better under- standing of complex forms: we need to know about their hierarchical structure.

Geometry

Geometry in design has to do with the placement of parts. It organizes where things go. To make the position of each part in our field unambiguous but manipulable, we need placement rules. These rules should facilitate the thematic development itself, making a link between theme and field. The formulation of such placement rules is accomplished by means of grids.

A grid, by nature, is predominantly homogeneous and continuous. However, we may not want the field to be fully homogeneous. The introduction of zones to which we designate particular properties allows us to articulate distinctions in the whole. The zone, similar to the way it is used in urban legalization, is an abstraction of site conditions; it allows us to state what is, and what is not, allowed in a particular area. When our exercise is formal and not bound to a particular site, the zones themselves help us to establish "site conditions." By attaching various deployment constraints to zones, the field is no longer neutral and must be responded to. Of course, in real site cases, the zones and the rules attached to them are expressions of conditions we note in the site.

Zones and grids are tools developed for the specific needs of thematic development of larger fields. As such, their discussion is inevitably technical in nature and only of interest to those who engage in such deployments. Grids have a bad name in architectural circles mainly because they are confused with dull and repetitious grid like forms. But we must not confuse the tool with the form. As a tool, used with appropriate portion rules, grid allow for the generation of extremely complex and varied arrangements. It is the arrangement we ultimately see, not the grid.

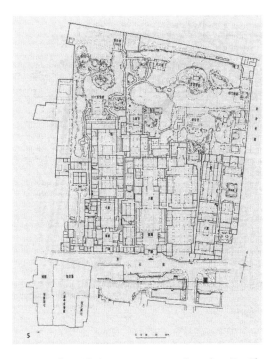

Figure 5 **Zhou Zheng Yuan estate and garden, Zu Chou China, example of a continuous architectural field**. From: Liu Dun Zhen. Zu Chou: Classic Chinese Gardens, China, Architectural Industrial Press. Beijing, 1979.

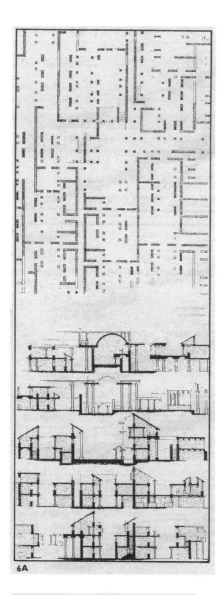
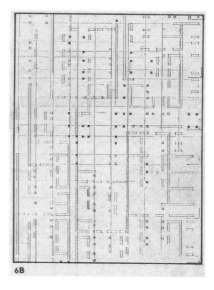
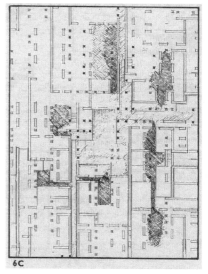
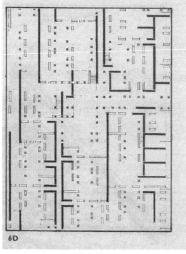

Figures 6A-D : **Study in continuous field deployment**. A) Plan and A2) section; B) The grid superimposed on the plan. Note that the two axes of the grid have different modules, producing a direction to the field; C) A territorial interpretation of the field; D) Distinguishing the different layers of the deployment; long walls, combined with shorter perpendicular ones, as given in black, make a first layer. Subsequent layers are made by strings of short walls or piers in two directions and two kinds of columns. From a class assignment by Margret Lew, M.S. Arch. Studies Program, Massachusetts Institute of Technology.

Control of complexity

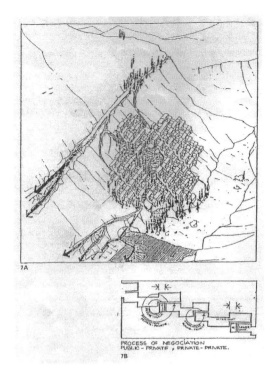
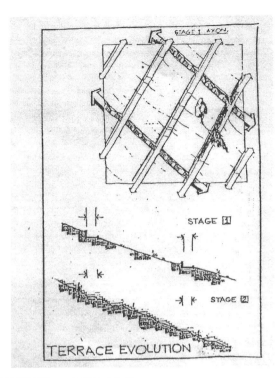
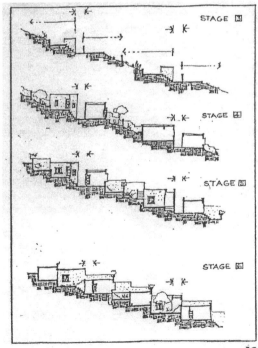

Figures 7A,B: **Study for a field deployment** inspired by the settlement type found in Ladakh, Northern India. A) Overview and B) Sections of the subsequent layers used in the development. Project by Solomon Benjamin, M.S. Arch. Studies Program, Massachusetts Institute of Technology.

In a broader context, zones and grids are of interest because they constitute a new geometry in design. Geometry has always been the hallmark of architectural skill. Where ruler and compass allowed the Renaissance architects to produce formal organizations of a predominantly self-contained kind, we seek a geometry of fields, and one that is by itself continuous – albeit varying from place to place – allowing us to make formal arrangements of a different nature.

Hierarchy

We are all familiar with the notion that rooms make the house and houses the neighborhood and neighborhoods the town. Large things are made out of small things, and complex forms are inevitably hierarchical in structure. But to make the idea of hierarchy useful in design, we need to be more precise about this concept. In the analysis of complex forms, two kinds of hierarchies must be distinguished. When we say that the small makes the larger, we refer to a part-whole hierarchy, a hierarchy of assembly. In building we may say that the bricks make the wall and the walls make the house. Here the wall is a part out of which a house may be built, and the bricks are the parts of which the walls are made. But when we say that the furniture makes the room or the houses make the neighborhood, we speak metaphorically. We cannot assemble a room out of furniture or a neighborhood from houses. We can, however, place and arrange furniture in a room, and we can build and demolish houses in a neighborhood.

Apparently, we have, in the latter example, terms for entities that contain one another rather than make up each other's constituent parts. Such an alternative hierarchical concept distinguishes realms of intervention. I can design a room, and you can design the arrangement of furniture in it. You can design a neighborhood and determine the context by the layout of streets and public places, and I can design a house in it. When complex forms are studied this way, we find that there is a hierarchy of discrete physical parts on different levels that constitute realms of control. Each design intervention takes place on at least one such level. Relative to the level on which we are designing we always find a higher level which is part of the physical context offered us. Similarly, a lower level will be accommodated by the design we make. This kind of hierarchy we may call a "control hierarchy," or "dependency hierarchy."

In control hierarchies we find two important aspects of designing combined. First, we see the complex form composed of systemic physical realms, or "levels," which are individually manipulable over time. The vertical relationship of such levels in control hierarchies is one of loose fit (in contrast with the part-whole hierarchy). The lower level can change without disturbing the higher level. In this way the highways make a network in which secondary roads can be deployed, and office buildings make structures in which partitioning systems constitute floor plans. It is this innate flexibility that enables complex artifacts such as cities to change and adapt over time and allows us to inhabit buildings in different ways.

Second, because the levels are realms of intervention, we find these hierarchies defined in terms of control. A level exists because there is a party out there that operates on it. In complex artifacts, we discover the levels of intervention by trying to change things. In fact, our general distinction between interior designers, architects, urban designers, and city planners reflects the reality of control hierarchies.

Knowledge of control hierarchies can be utilized in continuous architectural fields one level at a time. In urban design, we first make the road network and next arrange the buildings in the blocks. In building we first deploy, for instance, the larger structure of columns and floors and next distribute facades and infill walls. Each deployment on one level allows alternative deployments on lower levels. Once this principle is recognized, we can use it more fully. The large field need not be a juxtaposition of already vertically integrated entities, such as houses put next to one another, but can be the deployment of walls and columns over the whole field, followed by facades over the whole field, to be followed by infill walls over the whole field, followed by kitchens and sanitary equipment over the whole field. Thus, we begin to see the field as horizontally organized: layer after layer of distinct deployments. In each layer, we need not repeat the same combination ever but can stay with thematic variations. When all layers are in place, the result can be extremely complex and varied. Yet each instance is fully under control, and local changes are possible on each level, and each time we can test its impact on lower levels.

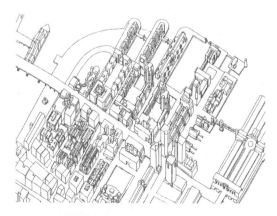

Figure 8A **Study for Fort Point Channel, Boston**, based on thematic field deployment of predetermined building types. Overview.

Control of complexity

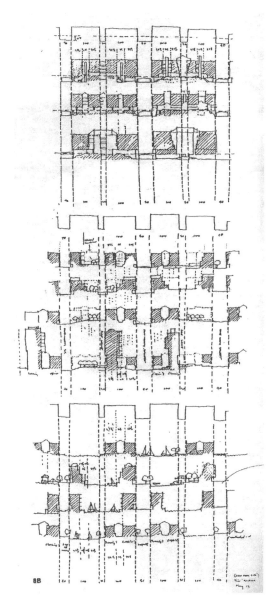

Figure 8B **Sketches for building sections arranged in the zoning of Figure 8A.** From the thesis project by John R. Dale, M.S. Arch. Studies Program, Massachusetts Institute of Technology.

Capacity

We recognize a room's function by the arrangement of furniture and equipment in it. Given the location and dimensions of a space, we may decide, for instance, that it can be used as a bedroom or as a study. We can test this by arranging the furniture in the same space in two different ways. This is how what we call the "function" of a configuration (in this case the configuration of walls making a room) can be expressed by another configuration of a lower level. The concept of "function" as it is used in architectural design is linked to the levels of intervention. We can explore the "capacity" of what we produce on one level to hold configurations on a lower level. In a similar way, the urban designer may demonstrate how buildings can be built by other parties in the context of the streets and public spaces he has laid out.

Seen this way, the concept of function becomes part of the transformational development of the complex form and we learn about function by the study of the relation between levels of intervention. When we decide that a certain space must have a certain function, we mean that this space, when it is designed, must be able to hold an arrangement of objects that stands for the use we have in mind. This arrangement must conform to norms we deem representative for this use. We may, for instance, call a space a "one-person bedroom" if it can hold a bed, a closet, a chair and a table, all arranged in appropriate relations.

Although we cannot make a lower level arrangement before the higher-level context is in place, the expectations we have for lower level use can guide higher level design. The function does not dictate the space, but we can demand that the capacity of the space hold a certain function and test it by inserting an appropriate lower level arrangement. Coming from the higher level, we may produce a spatial context first and ask ourselves what uses it may have: we explore its capacity by projecting in it a variety of alternative lower level arrangements representing different uses.

Thus, what we usually call "function" when discussing the uses of spaces is part of a more general concept called "capacity," which applies to all levels of the complex form. We can study the capacity of a facade to hold windows and doors, the capacity of an office floor to hold arrangements of partitioning walls, or the capacity of a lot to hold a building.

The concept of capacity can be applied to the layered field deployment discussed earlier. Each pass across the field with a lower level system is a comment on the capacity of what was already in place. When, for instance, we first lay out a field of bays using different bay widths in various combinations, we may next study the capacity of bay combinations in the field for holding subdivisions by infill wall and other elements and make such lower level decisions while we go across the field once more. Capacity studies, therefore, can be conducted locally for each part of the field.

It is easy to see, then, how we can work from the bottom up as well as from the top down. We might, for instance, start from lower level considerations and first determine the capacity of different bay widths before we choose two or three for deployment in the field. In most design processes, we combine the upward and downward approaches.

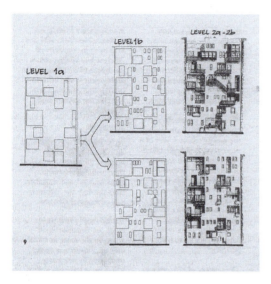

Figure 9 **Layered field deployment applied to a facade design.** Each stage serves as a constant "higher level" context for the next. From a study for an apartment building by Christina Gryboyanni, M.S. Arch. Studies program, Massachusetts

Territory

So far, we have only discussed the control of physical systems. Of course, we deploy them with architectural space in mind and transform them through the manipulation of material elements.

To distribute elements in space, we first must have access to the space in which they go. Territory is space controlled by one party, which must have the ability to keep things (and people) out. This is the basis of all use of space. We cannot dwell someplace unless we have certainty of some territorial control.

Territory, defined this way, is not the same as architectural space. The house, as an architecturally defined volume, for instance, may not define the territory of its inhabitants simply because it stands in a garden and the territorial boundary is at the curb where the lawn begins. A fence, to give another example, may be a territorial boundary but it can also be just a barrier to keep animals from wandering away.

Territory as a token of inhabitation is always an interpretation of a given physical organization. When a culture is familiar to us, we are very adept at reading territorial clues. We easily read signs of inhabitation such as plants placed on a doorstep, the room's door ajar, the towels and umbrellas arranged on the beach and avoid the embarrassment of trespassing. We know instinctively the difference between a ceremonial gate and one that defines a territorial boundary.

From a methodological point of view, territory is an independent variable relative to the physical arrangement it inhabits. Given such an arrangement we always can project a number of plausible territorial interpretations. This is true on all scales of environmental form because territories have their own hierarchy, distinct from the dependency hierarchies we discussed earlier. In each territory we find included territories. The common space is public space of the larger territory. Indeed, in all cases, a territory contains two kinds of spaces: those occupied by the included territories, which we call "private" spaces, and the space left free to be shared by the inhabitants, which we call the territory's "public" space.

Thus, we can have public space on all levels of the territorial hierarchy. For instance, the public space in the condominium is, in turn, private when we step out into the street. The concept of public space is therefore a relative one, and it is this relativity that accounts for the confusion of terms we often encounter such as "public," "semi-public," "private," and "semi-private."

This is not the place to elaborate on the theory of territoriality in environmental design, but enough has been said to make a few points. The territorial organization as a separate variable is methodologically useful. Once a territorial organization is determined in a given field, we can, within each territory, deploy lower level arrangements to serve this territory. Thus, territorial organization divides a field into self-contained areas guiding further deployment. Not all lower level development, given a first deployment as context, needs to be divided into territories, but each such division frames lower level arrangements.

Territorial structure reflects patterns of inhabitation. Seen this way, the territory is the most general expression of use and function, and it interprets indeed the given context in a manner similar to the way a lower level arrangement interprets it functionally. We could say that an arrangement of the furniture in a room is a functional interpretation, but it also reflects a territorial interpretation in the larger context of the house. Conversely, as we have seen, a territorial interpretation of the floor plan will "frame" the arrangement of furniture in the rooms.

In the design process, we should consider not only the territorial structure of inhabitation but territorial divisions among designers. The field can be given a territorial interpretation to guide the division of design responsibility within a larger team. Each designer will have a "territory" in which to make design decisions within the "public" space that is the joint responsibility of the team. Such divisions of design responsibility in a large project are most successful when the design territories correlate closely with the expected territories of use. This division of work is preferred to an arbitrary segmentation of a field where there is no "public" space to relate individual design efforts and interface conditions lack clarity. It is also an alternative to dividing the work in layers such that each design party is responsible not to a part of the field but to a level across the field. In the design of most complex environmental forms, a judicious combi- nation of such "horizontal" and "vertical" divisions of the form for the purpose of delegation of design responsibility is best.

Final remarks

This quick survey of methodological opportunities in the design of complex environmental forms can, of course, be no more than a sketch. What has been said may seem familiar to the extent that it gives more formal expression to concepts we deal with regularly: control hierarchies, territorial organization and division between public and private space, capacity analysis, type, and theme. Methodology should indeed always confirm what we already do in the sense that it can only be successful if it facilitates common practice and gives us power to deal with problems we are already confronted with.

At the same time, these familiar elements can be brought into a new perspective by applying two interrelated concepts not normally equated with design: change and control. By looking at the architectural form as an instance of a continuous process of change, we become interested in the mechanisms of transformation. That we can learn from change is not new. In all observations, scientific and otherwise, change and movement reveal the structure of what is observed. In our case, change is brought about by people designing, making, and inhabiting the environment. We have to deal with human constructs, and hence the complexities we observe are of our own making. Therefore, the structure we find is a reflection of patterns of control. We begin to see the complex form as a social artifact, and its hierarchical and territorial structure is, ultimately, a product of convention.

Such conventions we find reflected in the concepts of theme, system, and type. All three make us see form as shared, reflecting values we hold in common. A theme is what we design when we want others not only to understand what we do but participate in the development of the form. A system is the product of formal rules accepted by all who use it. A type, as we have seen is a complex form principle, containing many themes on various levels, which lives outside formal description in the social body that applies it.

Thus, the concepts on which rest the methodological tools discussed here run somewhat against the grain of traditional design attitudes. We tend to stress the constancy and immutability of the architectural form and do not readily take change into consideration when designing. We have not been taught how to share our designing with others. The myth of the master deciding everything confuses authority – based on skill and experience – with centralized control of decision-making. We need new attitudes that allow the qualities of daily life in the environment – variation in spatial development, thematic richness, and adaptability over time – to support our architecture in an efficient way. Without such qualities, environmental forms will maintain the poverty and rigidity we all deplore.

Note

1   Evidence of how efficiency can produce variety instead of uniformity can be found in recent developments in housing technology in the Netherlands. Builders, architects, and developers now cooperate for the introduction of infill systems. These systems comprise interior partitioning, kitchen and bathroom equipment and the plumbing and wiring that makes equipment work. Industrialized infill systems, if designed correctly, yield considerable savings in on-site labor and overall construction time. The dwelling's shell (called "support") and its infill are treated as separate, complementary, systems. The shell offers independent dwelling territories which can have their own infill configurations. The result is that no two dwelling plans need be the same for reasons of efficiency. See also N.J. Habraken, "Reconciling Variety and Efficiency in Large-scale Projects" in: Large Housing Projects; Design, Technology, and Logistics, ed. Margaret B. Sevcenco, pp. 46–53. Designing in Islamic Cultures, 5. Cambridge, MA: Aga Khan Program for Islamic Architecture.

1994
CULTIVATING THE FIELD
About an attitude when making architecture

Editors' note: *This essay is an adapted version of a text written at the invitation of the Faculty of Architecture and Town Planning at the Technion at Haifa, Israel for the graduation day address in 1993. It was later published in Places, Volume 9, Number 1, Winter, 1994. Pp 8–21. The essay as published in Places included a "Credo" which we have placed at the beginning of this book as a separate statement of principles.*

In the year 1748, Giambattista Nolli engraved a map of Rome. It shows not only streets and squares but also the interior of major buildings. The black mass out of which these public spaces are carved contains not only the ordinary buildings but also their courtyards and gardens. The public spaces and the monumental buildings are what architecture is about. But the map also shows how the white and black are inseparable. The one defines the other.

The wholeness of the urban fabric is the subject of my essay. I invite you to set aside the oppositions we so easily make: between architecture and vernacular, between monument and common building, between the large and the small, between the important and the unimportant. Let us consider the continuity of buildings and space – space covered and open, buildings of all kinds. This seamless continuous whole I call the 'built field.'

Nolli shows Rome's monuments as rooted in the black mass of the common fabric like plants rooted in the soil. But in the modern city, the common fabric is no longer self-evident. All of the built field is a professional product now. Where the everyday world used to be the context for architecture, it has now become the subject of architecture. The ordinary today has become elusive, perhaps more precious than the extraordinary.

For too long, architects have been preoccupied with the singular, individual statement. If we knew how to cultivate the ordinary, the field would be well. When the field is well, monuments will appear like flowers appear on a healthy tree.

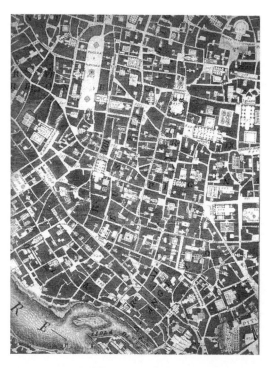

Figure 1 Details of Nolli's map of Rome, showing the Piazza Navona and the Parthenon. Giambattista Nolli, Planta Grande di Roma, 1748

Properties of the field

Built fields have bloomed for millennia all over the world. While there is a wide variety of forms and structures, all historic fields seem to share certain properties that are still valid in our day and age. To explain those, I will present a few examples.

Types and Patterns. First, we see the same types and patterns deployed consistently across a field. Indeed, we recognize a field by the types and patterns it holds.

In Pompeii, for instance, the same type comes in an extraordinary range of interpretations. The small house may not have as many rooms as the large one, but room size is fairly constant in all interpretations. A house may not have the full range of yards offered by the type, no peristyle, perhaps, and no garden, but each house has its atrium, each its own gate to the street. There is great dignity in the fact that all citizens, regardless of economic status, inhabit houses of the same type.[1]

Where a type comprises a number of similar elements combined into an organic whole, patterns are deployments of specific elements in the same relation across the field. Usually the elements forming patterns are either larger than the house, such as streets or squares, or smaller than the house, such as rooms and atria. In the example of Pompeii, we see cell-like spades opened to the streets. These are shops, workplaces, eating places. The artisan or shopkeeper may live in the mezzanine above. These spaces form continuous strings along the streets, almost independent of the houses behind them. From such primary patterns, fields are woven.

Venice is another example of a beautiful and complex field. The Gothic palaces of Venice are discrete, freestanding volumes several floors high. The type shows the interior hall facing the canal to catch the breeze, rooms aligned on both sides. These halls, repeated across the field, create a pattern seen in plan as well as in the facades. The facades align to make long elaborate walls. Rooftops and chimneys add another layer. As in most historic fields, public space is minimized and thus intensified. Alleys and streets are narrower than the private yards, narrower even than rooms, but all is of a scale and contributes to a unified, fine-grained tissue.

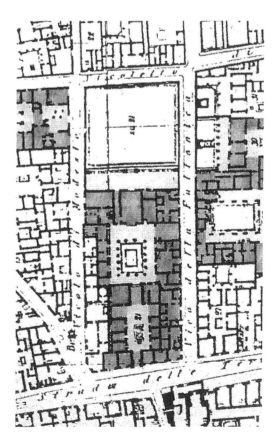

Figure 2 Detail of a map in Overbeck: Pompeii (Leipsig, 1866). Four houses are highlighted to show the range of types.

Figure 3 Part of the Gothic tissue of Venice, w/second floor plans of representative palazzi shaded. Map from Paolo Maretto, L'Ediliza Gotico Veneziana (Venice: Filippi Editore)

Figure 4 Facades of Gothic palaces along the Canal Grande, Venice (photo credit: Soren Popovich)

The Tunis courtyard house type belongs to the Middle Eastern tradition, within which it has its own characteristics. The field is very complex yet highly ordered. Rooms cluster around courtyards, houses cluster around dead-end ways that open to streets. Streets, in turn, may have their own gates facing major arteries. In the Middle Eastern field, hierarchy is elaborate and highly sophisticated.[2]

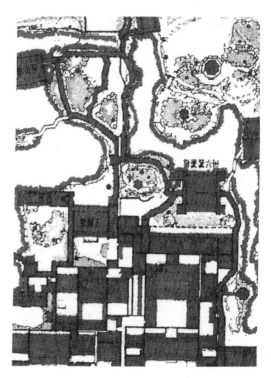

Figure 6 The spatial hierarchy of Tunis. Streets and courtyards are toned. (From Association Sauvegarde de la Medina, Tunis, 1968)

Figure 5 The Venetian fabric, consisting of water, land and buildings, combines different infrastructures. In this respect it precedes the modern urban structure. The network of canals, itself hierarchical, is meshed with the equally hierarchical network of streets and alleys radiating from squares and connected by bridges. (Bird's eye view of Venice by Jacopo De'Barberi, 1500)

Hierarchy. Each built field has its own way to make a hierarchical form.

Hierarchy is found in all fields. It assures flexibility and adaptability. Rooms are rearranged within the houses. Houses change themselves, either by building in their own lots or by trading territories with neighbors. All this happens without disturbing the higher-level organization of alleys and streets.

Once we are on the level of public space, we likewise find a hierarchy of alleys, residential streets, major streets and so on. This hierarchical organization preserves the health of a built field by allowing improvement and adaptation on each level with minimal disturbance of the larger context.

The hierarchy of the form is a hierarchy of intervention, starting with the room as the smallest cell of the living fabric all the way up to the major public

Cultivating the field

spaces. Everything changes and adapts on its own level, in its own time. In this way, complex built fields stay fresh and alive over centuries.

Intensification. The hierarchical nature of the field makes it grow denser and richer over time. There is a continuous process of intensification in living built fields.

We find this illustrated by the estate of a merchant clan in Soochow, China. The estate is a field by itself, and like all fields it is not a single creation but a collage of many interventions. When we try to define its structure, we find the pavilions to be the major elements. Pavilions form courtyards. A string of courtyards makes a house, which is separated from other houses by narrow service alleys. Pavilions also spill over into the garden, which is linked with the hills and the ponds by covered paths and curved bridges. The trees inhabit the hills and sometimes invade the courtyards; rocks inhabit the ponds. It is all artful and at the same time organic.

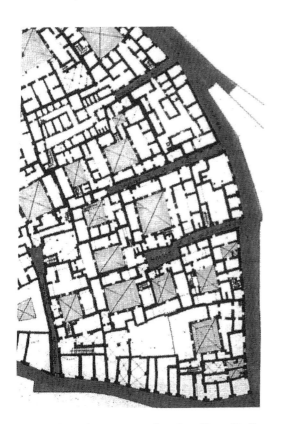

Figure 7 Zhou Zheng estate and garden. (From Liu Dun-Zhen, Zu Chou Classic Gardens, Beijing: Architectural Industrial Press)

Systematization. The student of built fields cannot escape the fact that these complex and ever-changing forms were always built in a systematic way. We find a consistent technology: the same parts, the same relations, are combined over and over again. But the combinations are always different; depending on site, size, use and plain personal preference. This produces endless variation.

The systemic properties of historic fields teach us that systems make variations possible; indeed, they are a precondition for variation and adaptation over time.

The power of the built field

The field is not only a form but also people taking action. Rooms are redecorated and newly equipped; houses are built, extended and taken down again; streets are widened or realigned; new infrastructure is inserted. Historic fields are fine-grained and wonderfully adaptable because powers of inhabitation operate at all levels.[3]

The tremendous powers of generation a healthy field can have are demonstrated by the well-known seventeenth-century extension of Amsterdam. It has two distinct parts, one built for the rich merchants along the major concentric canals, the other a separate neighborhood laid out for artisans and craftsmen. These two parts are topologically identical, not only to one another but also to the medieval field of the old city core.

In all three cases, we find major canals running parallel to each other and connected by secondary canals. The canals are lined by trees, streets and houses. The streets are connected by bridges and shorter perpendicular streets with back streets that run parallel to the major canals.

In the medieval core, this hierarchy emerged piecemeal; it follows the meandering course of the dikes alongside the river. In the extension it is done with geometrical precision: first, in a concentric sweep around the old core and in a monumental fashion, then orthogonal in more modest dimensions. So we find there was no innovation, but growth and transformation of what was already known into something much more extensive.

This explains why, remarkably, there is no evidence of anything we would call design in the modern sense of the word. Minutes of the meetings of the municipal government have been preserved. It turns out that the city's defense had priority; initial plans were for ramparts and fortresses around the growing city. Only in a later stage were surveyors instructed to lay out streets and canals in the terrain within the new walls. Without doubt the layout of canals and streets was the subject of deliberation, but no drawings have been preserved and there is no record of any discussion as to what the new extension should look like or of alternative concepts.[4]

Historians have praised Amsterdam's seventeenth-century extension as an early example of true urban design. There definitely was noting haphazard about the process. But it was not designed in the modern sense of the word. There was no need for design because everybody knew what the new city would be like.

A built field is not just a complex form, but an image shared by its inhabitants and builders. When the image is shared, then hierarchy, type, patterns and a multitude of details are self-evident and need not be discussed. From the beginning, all energy is channeled in the same direction; everyone can partake in the creation.

The professionalization of the built field

In the first half of the 20th century, a new class of professionals – bureaucrats, politicians, technologists and architects – emerged to make a new and dynamic world in its entirety. For the first time, the everyday environment in its full physical complexity was seen as a subject for architecture. Any building, no matter how humble, could be worth architectural attention.

The professionalization of the built field is perhaps the single most important issue to study when we seek to understand the Modern period in architecture and urbanization. We can see the results of the professional claim, and these lead to a conclusion of crucial importance: the process of professionalization went hand-in-hand with a gradual coarsening of the built field.

Amsterdam again is a good example. The Amsterdam South extension, designed by Hendrick Petrus Berlage and executed between 1920 and 1940, is the result of remarkable cooperation among professionals, between architects and the municipal bureaucracy and among architects themselves. The power of their work lies in the way architectural qualities – individual invention, exuberant expression and richness of detail – never became goals by themselves but were always put to the service of the field.[5]

Nevertheless, we also see how in this admirable built field the projects become larger; a whole city block could now be a single intervention. Behind the well-designed facades a much coarser and uniform fabric was hidden. This took its toll while the years went by; presently, Amsterdam South is being renovated at great cost. What is the product of large-scale intervention must be maintained by large-scale intervention. Meanwhile, the seventeenth-century city goes on living and renewing itself, house by house, as it has done over the centuries.

The next stage takes place after WWII. With freestanding blocks floating in space, we have arrived at the truly modernist city. Its coarseness is apparent when we consider the field and organic hole and ask ourselves what constitutes the living cell. In Amsterdam's seventeenth- century field, that cell is the canal house. In the modern city the cell is a freestanding apartment block floating in space and full of identical and inflexible apartments. A hectare of the new field has far fewer living cells than a hectare of the historic field.

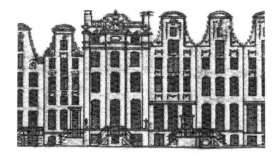

Figure 8 Elevations of the seventeenth-century canal facades in Amsterdam. From Caspar Philips. Grachtenboek, 1768–1771 (Amsterdam: Stadsdrukkerij, 1962)

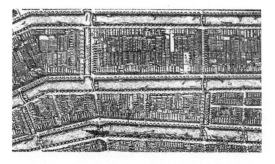

Figure 9 Part of the seventeenth- century extension of Amsterdam. Detail of map by Balthasar Florisz, ca. 1650.

It is sometimes said that uniformity and repetition are unavoidable because they are the result of modern mass production. But no building technology demands, by itself, the repetition of similar floor plans in one block and similar blocks in a neighborhood. Uniformity in the built field is the result of the centralization of design decisions, coupled with centralized project management seeking ever larger projects under the assumption of efficiency. If one party must decide on a hundred dwellings, they all will be the same. If a hundred parties each build their own, dwellings will all be different.

The centralization of designing, in turn, has led to a breakdown of the hierarchical organization of the field. As we have seen in the historic examples, hierarchy insures a smooth transition from large-scale design decisions to small-scale decisions and the other way around. In the modern city, hierarchy is lost not only in the buildings themselves, where all apartments together are inflexible parts of a single design, but also at the urban scale. No longer is public space designed first, to guide the subsequent deployment of buildings. In the modern way, urban design is done by arranging free-standing buildings, an artistic endeavor, but not a structuring one. The result is vulnerable: without the structuring power of predetermined public space, the alteration of a single building may upset the artistic arrangement of the whole. Because everything is equal to all else, everything also may impact everything else.

Toward the fine-grained field

It is possible to regard to modern housing and urbanism as the product of a period of transition. The monumental free-standing buildings of the early Modern period were seen by many as symbols of a new age. But they were the primitive product of an emerging professionalism operating without much sense of either the nature of the built field or the meaning of the fundamental change that was inflicted on the field.

Over time, design professions have become more sophisticated and we see a reappraisal of historic precedent. The urban block enclosed by streets is being reintroduced, as is the structuring quality of public space. But this return to tradition is largely intuitive and not yet supported by a good understanding of the properties of the field. So far it has been a return to the 1920's and '30's; the design may be more sensitive, but the rigidity is still there. The professionally controlled fine-grained field has not yet been achieved.

In order to reintroduce the hierarchical way of working in the modern built field, I have advanced a theory of levels. It holds that the scale of an intervention must match a certain scale of use. Hence, interventions cannot be arbitrarily sized, and a hierarchy of design activities must be introduced.[6]

Traditional neighborhoods have always been conceived this way. They are fitted within the higher-level structure of major roads and arteries. The neighborhood design itself would shape public space and allocate lots. Individual houses would be built on those lots and, finally, within each house, furniture and equipment could be modified.

However, if we want to regain the fine-grained nature of the field in large structures, we must introduce a new level distinction. This leads to she support/infill approach I have advocated for so long in housing. The idea is to design and install the individual house unit independently from the building it is part of, thus reestablishing for the dwelling unit the autonomy it has lost in the apartment building.

The concept is universal. Already we see in office buildings and shopping malls how space to be occupied by tenants is left undivided and empty. Tenants will hire their own interior architects to design and outfit their individual territories. The building itself constitutes one level; the units of use inside make another. This may seem a new idea, but it seeks to continue the age-old hierarchical organization of built fields in a context compatible with our time.

There is, obviously, an economical and technological side to all this. The concept of levels is related to the concept of 'open building,' which seeks to disentangle the many systems in a building (such as partitioning, sewage, electricity and electronics, sanitary and kitchen equipment) to make them less interdependent and therefore easier to install and replace. Years of trial and error have convinced a number of builders and developers in the Netherlands that the open building approach promises increased efficiency and better performance.[7]

The idea that variety and adaptability can be efficient and economically competitive sounds contradictory to those of us trained in the believe that uniformity and efficiency go together. But the more building practice is systematized, the more the many systemic parts can be combined and arranged in different ways without loss of efficiency. To respond to individual user demands, systematization must be pursued aggressively. This means that manufacturing will become increasingly important because it is the industrial entrepreneur who provides the systems that make buildings serve users.

After a century of professionalizing the built field, we are ready to come to grips with its full complexity. In a more sophisticated world, there is now a search for variety, adaptability and small-scale response to use. We may conclude that for purely commercial and technical reasons, the next quarter century will show a significant shift towards the fine-grained field. This will not be a romantic return to historical forms. In fact, the physical result will be different from anything that has ever been seen before. It will be a level-headed response to the conditions of the market by means of increased systematization.

An open architecture

The practice of open building responding to technical and commercial considerations will result in a more open architecture as well. Large projects will no longer be monolithic; they will offer fine-grained variation and adaptation. We have yet to explore the full architectural potential of the new level of distinction in office buildings, shopping centers and apartment buildings. Schools, hospitals, and laboratories could equally well use this approach. Indeed, any institutional building would benefit from the same strategy, as would all manner of mixed-use projects.

It is tempting to speculate about the architectural implications of the fine-grained approach. It does not mean that everything must be small-scale. On the contrary, when the small scale comes into its own, the large scale will be easier to design. Think of the monumental canals in Amsterdam that hold and guide the rich variation of individual houses alongside. It is more appropriate to see the large-scale, fine-grained project as a small-town design than as a big building design.

Being an addition to the built field, open architecture should not only offer flexibility at the small scale, but also stress the continuation of a larger fabric; it must invite a merging of public space networks from project to project. Public space would once more become an autonomous structure holding together interventions within a single field.

Open architecture will necessarily reinstate type and pattern as structuring elements. The variation of individual units works best if variation happens within a type. The merging of projects into a coherent whole needs patterns as a means to assure meaningful continuity.

The open architecture of which I am speaking will produce very different kinds of built fields that respond to local and cultural demands. These fields may, in fact, incorporate high-rise and large-scale interventions. But they will, whatever their form, have exactly the same properties we found in the historic fields: type, pattern and hierarchy will structure them; systematization will make them possible, intensification over time, driven by the powers of inhabitation will enrich them. Above all, these fields will endure because they have the power to renew themselves from day to day.

Sharing

The open architecture that is now emerging stems from a willingness to accept the complexity of the environment, a complexity so great that it cannot be controlled or shaped by a single agent. In the Modern era, architects have avoided recognition of this complexity. The strategy has been to simplify in order to get a difficult job done.

The time will soon come, however, when architects will be expected to play their part not by simplifying what is inherently complex but by applying new skills and knowledge that do justice to this complexity. An architect's ability to do this will depend on his or her willingness to share the field with others. The concept of levels calls for interdependence among autonomous designers, each operating on their own level of intervention, accepting what is done on the higher level and structuring what can be done on a lower level.

There need be nothing wrong with a designer wanting to do a chair one day and a city the other. But such a desire for universality should not be confused with total design control. The dynamic, fine-grained built field, as we have seen, is structured by types, patterns and other conventions. These are various ways of sharing, but the Modern tradition rejects them all. Therefore, we do not know the power of convention, or how to exchange patterns, or how to cultivate a type.

Yet convention, pattern and type do not contradict originality and innovation. After all, to say something new, one must first speak a common language. There need be no conflict between the constraints posed by the built field and the creativity and inventiveness of individual designers.

Sharing does not come easily to architects. From where this resistance? From where the obsession with originality and individuality? I believe it is because we never learned to enter into a dialogue with the built field. The Modern tradition is highly self-referential and delocalized and thinks it shameful to accept precedent and borrow from others. When we design, we do not speak to the field, but look over our shoulders to our peers elsewhere. There is little peer group prestige in working with the field.

Our inability to recognize the field has obstructed the development of professional knowledge and left architecture as the only profession without a knowledge base. Knowledge presumes the acceptance of what others have done, when proven useful. It develops best where sharing is perceived as beneficial.

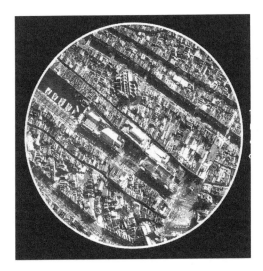

Figure 10 Amsterdam's historic core, of medieval origin (Photo courtesy of KLM Aerocarto)

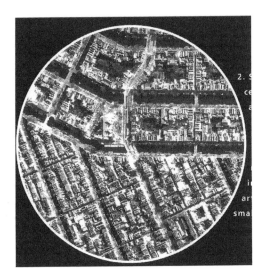

Figure 11 Amsterdam's seventeenth century canals around the core, with part of the smaller-scale Jordaan neighborhood, intended for artisans and small traders. (Photo courtesy of KLM Aerocarto)

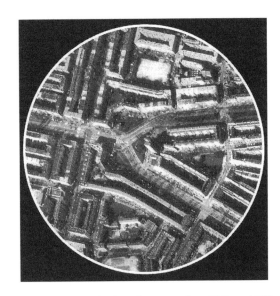

Figure 12 Amsterdam's Berlage extension, 1920's and '30's. (Photo courtesy of KLM Aerocarto)

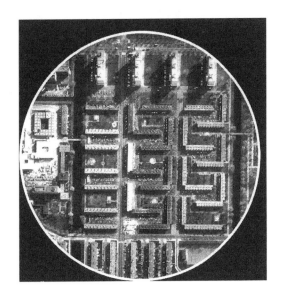

Figure 13 Amsterdam's van Eesteren extension, 1950's. (Photo courtesy of KLM Aerocarto)

The natural locus of architectural knowledge is the built field. We should study it, not necessarily as something designed but as something to be cultivated. We should seek to understand the nature of patterns and types; we should be able to explain the hierarchical structure of the field; we should know the design methods needed to deal with it; we should share with other professions the systemic organization of all built fields. The built field, in short, should be to architects what the law is to lawyers: it constitutes a domain of knowledge and expertise that, when studied, could pay off in many ways.

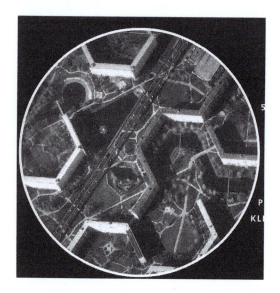

Figure 14 Amsterdam's Biljmeer extension, 1960's and '70's. (Photo courtesy of KLM Aerocarto)

Shared knowledge brings a common vocabulary, which allows its practitioners to share information and express understanding in a precise and effective way. In contrast to the engineer, the medical doctor and the lawyer, architects do not have a professional vocabulary. The language used by architects today seeks to stress what makes us different; it expresses personal meaning and intention. It is a language borrowed from the critic, whose task is to explain what buildings mean and to describe the impression they make on observers and users. We encourage our students to explain themselves freely but cannot offer them a vocabulary to address the field with any degree of accuracy or common understanding.

Open architecture breaks new ground because it seeks what we have in common. The avant-garde on the other hand rejects all forms of convergence. It is based on the romantic idea that creativity can only prosper outside the constraints of what is shared. It claims autonomy for the sake of art, but confuses the autonomy of the form, which is real, with the autonomy of the author, which is a fiction. It does not see that invention and originality need to grow from a common field.

Avant-gardism, in its heroic period, has achieved results that still move and inspire us because, at that time, it was utopian and sought to create a new world to inhabit. But now, deprived of its early idealism, it has lost its vigor and has become a liability. Insisting that all sharing must be rejected, the avant-garde attitude keeps us outside the built field; indeed, it makes us unable to see the field as a unifying force. What was a source of creativity and power early in the 20th century has now become an obstacle. What took courage in the beginning now has become an excuse for self-indulgence, a way to escape the realities of the world.

A new attitude

So, here is the dilemma we face: on the one hand, the demands of the field; on the other hand, a professional tradition at odds with it.

Sooner or later, each of us must choose. There is no such thing as artistic freedom. One can only choose which bondage one prefers. Will it be the avant-garde tradition, or will it be the constraints of the built field? Which will be more nourishing?

The built field, we can be sure, will go its way. It will be driven by the nature of the society inhabiting it – an increasingly sophisticated society, combining active and free individuals operating in larger and larger networks, ever more intertwined and interactive. The field will come to reflect these qualities.

Professional expertise will adapt to the fine-grained complexity of the society it serves. Technology based on true systematization will thrive on it. Lawyers will adjust to it. Politicians will soon know how to operate in it. Developers will exploit it. Bureaucracy will finally learn how to administer it. Will architecture adopt the new attitude needed to work with the built field?

As so often is the case, practice in the real world is ahead of theory and ideology. Today almost anything that can be built is also professionally designed; we are already deeply immersed in the built field. It is just that our self-image has not caught up with it. The new attitude I am speaking of will first manifest itself in practice. It is signs of that attitude that we want to look for.

Look not for buildings, but for coherence among buildings. Do not see an intervention as an autonomous act only but judge it as a voice in the ongoing dialogue in the field. Look for types, patterns and hierarchies. There will not be a single model to follow because that is not the way the field develops. But as we adjust to a new way of seeing, we will recognize more and more those with whom we share the field; we will not only find a new architecture but also friends and kindred spirits.

Notes

1. Pompeii's street-side shops and workplaces, called tabernae, have been described in Axel Boethius, *The Domestic Architecture of the Imperial Age and Its Importance for Medieval Town Building* (Ann Arbor, MI: The University of Michigan Press, 1960). See Chapter 4, "The Golden Houses of Nero."
2. My information comes from Jamal Akbar, who studied this neighborhood and discusses its transformations in his book *Crisis in the Built Environment: The Case of the Muslim City* (Leiden: E.J. Brill, 1988).
3. The phrase "powers of inhabitation" I borrow from Donlyn Lyndon, who, I believe, first coined it. It expresses very well what controls the form and makes built fields live.
4. A detailed history of the process leading to the new extensions is given in L. Jansen, De Derde Vergroting van Amsterdam (The Third Extension of Amsterdam) (Amsterdam: Amstelodanum, 1960). This publication is the 52nd yearbook of the Amstelodanum Society.
5. A good source for the history of the Amsterdam South scheme and the way cooperation was organized is the catalogue for the exhibition held to commemorate the first presentation of Berlage's plan 75 years ago, republished by the Amsterdam municipal archives in 1992.
6. For a brief exposition of the concept of levels, see my paper "The Uses of Levels," UNESCO regional Seminar on Shelter for the Homeless, Seoul, 1988. A more rigidly systematic description is given in *Control Hierarchies in Complex Artifacts*, proceedings of the 1987 Conference on Planning and Design in Architecture, International Congress on Planning and Design Theory, published by the American Society of Mechanical Engineers.
7. The Open Building Foundation is a non-profit organization that researches and develops the technical and organizational base of open building practice. It has a small research component at Delft Technical University. For information: Open Building Foundation, De Vries van Heyst Plantsoen 2, 1628 RZ Delft, The Netherlands.

2004
CHANGE AND THE DISTRIBUTION OF DESIGN

Editors' Note: *This essay was published in the Proceedings of the 10th International Conference of the CIB W104 Open Building Implementation network, Paris, CSTB, France, September 2004*

A two-level environment

In January 1699, Jules Hardouin Mansart, Superintendent of Buildings and "Premier Architect to Louis le Grand, King of France, put his signature to the design for what we now know as the Place Vendome. (Figure 1). His design included a monumental façade wall of exquisite proportions in the neo-classical manner. The square, including the façade wall, was subsequently built by the city of Paris on the request of the King. But no buildings were behind the façade. The land behind was for sale. In the next two decades, noblemen, bankers and other prominent and wealthy citizens who served the King in various administrative and financial functions built their houses there with their own architects. These buildings kept changing and adapting over time. But the façade as Mansart built it is still what we see today.

Mansart's scheme was a remarkable interpretation of what we may call a "two-level organization", by which we mean that one designer provides the spatial framework within which other designers subsequently can do their own thing. We have here an instance of time-based building in a very straightforward way. Mansart built what was to perform for a long time and to serve many. He thereby provided a context for what might change more frequently and serve individual clients. In general, such a distinction of levels of intervention separates what is relatively permanent from what

Figure 1 Place Vendome, Paris. Behind the uniform façade are different houses

is relatively changeable. But the way Mansart applied this principle challenged conventional notions. The façade of a building is normally seen as the expression of that particular building. Here it became part of the level of the urban design.

We are more familiar with a level distinction in which the façade of the building is part of the lower level architectural design. When, for instance, H.P. Berlage designed the new extension of Amsterdam in the first half of the 19th century, he designed public spaces like boulevards, streets and squares. He also determined the height of the buildings along these spaces, but architects designed them and produced the facades that made those spaces become real.

Another example

The Place Vendome was not a unique intervention. Earlier in the 17th century, King Henry IV initiated the building of the Place Royale (today known as Place des

Vosges). (Figure 2) Citizens could buy lots around it on the condition that the facades of their houses would be built according to a preconceived design, including an arcade on the ground floor. The Place des Vosges is larger than the Place Vendome and makes a more domestic space with its trees and flower beds and its more home-grown architecture. But the square's façade wall is clearly the result of a unified design, although in practice it was built one lot at a time.

Figure 2 Place des Vosges, Paris. Different interventions but (nearly) identical facades

Although both squares have uniform facades all around, the distribution of ownership is different. In the case of the Place Vendome, the facades were actually part of the urban infrastructure, like the pavement of the square or the statue in its center. But in Henry IV's Place des Vosges, the facades ere owned and erected by the private citizens.

Taken as examples of two-level thinking, the difference is significant, however. In case of the Place Vendome, designers only decided on their own level of control behind the already erected façade. In the case of the Place des Vosges, the higher-level designer put down rules to constrain lower-level design. He basically told the lower-level designer: 'do whatever you want, but make sure you do the façade my way.'

The latter case is more complicated but also more flexible because laying down rules for lower-level design can be done in many different ways. The set-back rule, for instance, telling architects to keep houses at a certain distance from the street, belongs to that mode of interaction. By the same token, an urban designer may impose a building height restriction, or stipulate that facades be done in a given material or that certain patterns should be followed for the sake of a consistent and well-conceived public space.

This way of working makes the urban designer reach across the level distinction to constrain lower-level design. It introduces a certain coherence in the lower level where normally variety is the inevitable result of different designers each doing their own thing.

A natural phenomenon

In history, such coherence in variety came about in a less formal manner. The 17th century facades along the canals of Amsterdam are all of a kind but no two of them are alike. That did not happen because a higher-level designer had laid down rules, but because the house type was familiar to both inhabitants and builders. Coherence resulted from the culture at work. Yet the level distinction was very clear. Each house could change, or be replaced, without disturbing the higher-level urban organization.[1]

Distribution of design responsibility along different levels of intervention comes naturally with complex form-making. We may shift the boundaries a bit, but life itself imposes the level distinction. When ignored, it will re-establish itself in the course of time.

The famous 'Crescents' in 18th century Bath, by father and son Wood, were originally designed as identical houses behind a common monumental façade. But since home ownership was dispersed, individual houses changed in time: expansions were made, and interior spaces were altered. But the facades remained unaltered by common consent.

The result, eventually, was similar to the Place Vendome distinction: variation behind an urban screen. Eventually, similar projects with unified facades came about in English domestic architecture. Most of them were built for speculation. Variations in the house plan might be made already when a house was sold before building started, but otherwise would surely come later.

The disappearance of levels

In Amsterdam, Berlage was the last to heed the level distinction in urban design. Cornelis van Eesteren's internationally renowned post-war extension of the city was not structured by urban space. Following CIAM ideology, he arranged building volumes within free-flowing space. Urban space was no longer structuring lower level design. As a result urban designer and architect both used the same medium, and it was no longer clear where urban design stopped and architecture began. This confusion still plagues the profession.

The disappearance of levels of intervention was not restricted to the distinction between urban design and architecture. It also took place within the building itself. Modernist architectural ideology claimed top down design control. The masters of the avant-garde like Corbusier, Mies von der Rohe and also Frank Lloyd Wright taught us by example that full vertical control, including even the design of furniture, was necessary to achieve good architecture. They lived in a time of fundamental change in which all design conventions and building habits were rendered obsolete. In such uncertainty it is understandable that those responsible for large projects insisted on full vertical control.

However, the upheavals of modernity only reinforced an attitude that already prevailed in the time when architects only did special buildings like churches, palaces, and grand houses. It goes back to Palladio whose marvelous villas we tend to understand as firmly controlled by a single hand. In that sense, Le Corbusier's Unité d'Habitation, fully controlled too and conceived as standing in a park, is very Palladian.

We have been educated in a tradition that was ignorant of the uses of levels in urban form. Mass housing in which inhabitants cannot influence the layout of their dwelling is part of that ignorance. Our present interest in time-based building seeks a remedy to the rigidity and uniformity that comes from excessive vertical control.

Learning from the past

As I have shown, level distinctions in complex environment may be achieved in different ways. Those we have noted so far: The Place Vendome, The Place des Vosges, Berlage's Amsterdam extension, and the Amsterdam canals, are architectural expressions of a primarily territorial level distinction. Yet a hierarchy of levels may result from technical conditions as well. In climates where protection from the cold, wind, or rain is important, the first act of building usually was to create a large envelope later to be subdivided. Medieval European architecture was based on a single large volume, defined by stone walls and a timber roof, erected as quickly as possible to provide sheltered space within which further subdivision could take place in a more protected environment. The English custom to refer to large buildings as "Hall" still comes from that practice.

So does the "grange", or barn, used in Medieval French agriculture: A timber frame held up a large roof that extended outward to low but heavy stone walls. This model was followed in buildings for a wide variety of purposes as we can learn from the 9th century document St. Gall design for a monastery.2

This way of building produced a large volume of interior space that was subsequently subdivided in response to practical needs. The same custom could still be witnessed a few generations ago in the New England tradition of "barn raising" where the agricultural barn's timber structure was prefabricated by the local carpenter to be erected in a single day with the help of many neighbors in a kind of festive ritual.

In China, about a decade ago, I saw a house just built in a country village. After materials had been amassed over a period of time, a solid brick masonry shell, some six by ten meters in surface area and two stories high with symmetrical façade had been built in a few weekends with the help of neighbors. Inside, the roof was supported by two timber posts, and the entire space was temporarily partitioned by a few bamboo screens just two meters high. The subdivision within the house had yet to be done in more solid materials once resources would allow (Figure 3). Similar examples are found in many other vernacular architectures.

Figure 3 Near Xi-an, China. Farmhouse shell just built

Once technically feasible, internal adaptability can achieve its own architectural expression. Most vernacular residential architecture has a dominant space in relation to which smaller scale change can take place.

The houses of Pompeii, preserved by volcanic ashes for almost two millennia, show us, for instance, that each house had an atrium: this large space with an inward sloping roof open in the center to let rainwater fall in a basin on the floor, was where guests were received and business was done. It was formed by walls two stories high behind which rooms were located. The ground floor rooms were open to the atrium and those on the upper floor had light coming in from above the atrium roof.

Pompeii's excavations show us irregular distributions of these surrounding spaces suggesting change and adaptation over time. In fact, we sometimes find that rooms have been turned around from one house to the neighboring house. The upper floors under a timber roof must have been even easier to subdivide. There is also evidence that these spaces could form suites for relatives within the extended family or could be rented out as separate apartments.

We see the atrium function the way a public space functions in a city: allowing change and adaptation behind surrounding walls. In this way atria were stable islands in the dense Pompeiian field, around which second order design decisions were made over time. (Figure 4). These were buildings without an exterior. The spatial sequence from street to atrium, with possible extension to a second courtyard behind, identified the house, while actual boundaries to neighboring houses behind the surrounding rooms remained invisible while the street front was occupied with shops and workplaces.

The Venetian Gothic palace is another example. It had on its main floor a large hall running from canal front to backyard, with open facades so that air could move through the house. On both sides of that central space were rows of rooms the arrangement of which allowed not only different uses but also change in size and decoration. Here again we find a two-level spatial organization securing permanence of the major space while allowing adaptation to inhabitation's second order preferences. (Figure 5)

Figure 5 Venice, Central hall on the main floor of Gothic houses (Drawn over a detail from Moretto, L'edilizia Gotica Venziana, 1978, Filippi)

From these two examples of major spaces in vernacular houses, it is only one step towards the courtyard house. The open courtyard too, is the 'public' space within the residential unit around which rooms are formed like houses around a square.

The Mediterranean courtyard house is also found in a variety of interpretations along the North African

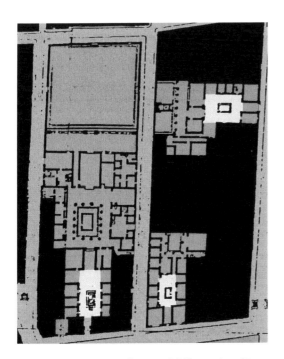

Figure 4 Pompeii, Atria in houses of different sizes. (Drawn over detail of the Overbeck Plan der Stadt Pompeii, 1866)

Figure 6 Left bank, Paris courtyard

coast and all the way East across the Arabian peninsula, and it traveled West from Spain to Latin America. Indeed, its influence extends as far North as Paris, (Figure 6) where gates give access from the street to courtyards surrounded by apartments. India and China have their own traditions of courtyard dominated urban fabric in many variations going back for millennia.

The Medina of historic Tunis (Figure 7) may serve as a case-in-point for many others. The rooms around the courtyards show a clear typology by themselves: they have a niche in the back wall facing the double courtyard door and two other niches to each side. This pattern is executed in endless variation of size and shape: even in one house no two of such rooms may be the same.

Figure 7 Tunis medina, courtyards and dead-end streets (Drawn over a base map by the Association Sauvegarde de la Medina, Tunis)

These few examples may show how vernacular architecture usually provides a dominant space that is stable relative to second order variety and change in response to day-to-day uses.

New ways of time-based building

As a counterpoint to these many historic examples we may note how large contemporary buildings tend to change their skin. The high-rise office building in the Hague, for instance, for which Michael Graves designed a new envelope is in many ways the opposite of Mansart's Place Vendome. Here the building, to prolong its life, sheds its skin when the urban environment changes. The curtain wall facade almost acquires autonomy; it may be part of the building, but it may also help shape urban fabric.

We begin to understand how the large contemporary building will, eventually, establish its own hierarchy of changeable subsystems. The very size and permanence of such extensive frameworks make their façade a relatively short-term garb. At the same time, interior flexibility must respond to a large and varied population. By their sheer bulk the high-rise and other large projects de facto become three-dimensional extensions of urban fabric. Inside, public space becomes increasingly important as a permanent framework around which day to day use, either residential or commercial or administrative, may settle. Seen in this way, we become aware of the latent architectural potential of such new environments without historic precedent.

A debilitating heritage

Modernist ideology did not know architecture in relation to levels, neither upward in urban design nor downwards in interior organization. Indeed, Modernist environment, for all its novelty, can be understood to a large extent as the reduction of complex urban fabric to a coarse single level product – hence its inability to make large things without imposing uniform repetition on inhabitation. In this respect the avant-garde movement was a regressive movement. It is truly ironic that our time, which calls itself dynamic and full of change and individuality, has produced an architecture more rigid in its articulation and less capable of dealing with the dimension of time than any period before in human history.

We still suffer the consequences of a functionalist tradition. We proudly rejected the Modernist's dogma of 'form follows function', but still expect each project we engage in to respond to a 'program' listing in some detail expected functions to be taken care of. A time-based architecture must assume functions to be largely unpredictable except in the most general of terms. Where architecture cannot follow function anymore it must take over by itself to establish a context for change and variety by inhabitation. This new initiative will lead to an articulation of levels of form-making. But that also implies distribution of design responsibility and we have not yet abandoned the modernist opinion that such distribution is a dilution of the architect's role. The dilemma renders academia clueless. Change and the distribution of design tasks are not yet subjects for architectural theory, nor do they feature in school's curricula.

A new architecture?

But practice already knows better and real life runs ahead of theory and teaching. Commercial office buildings offer empty floors for lease, to be filled in by specialized fit-out contractors executing designs by specialized fit out designers. Shopping malls leave retail space open for leaseholders to employ their own designers.

Residential architecture slowly follows suit. In the Netherlands the work of Frans van der Werf, spanning over some thirty years, has been the most extensive and the most advanced so far. His Molenvliet project in Papendrecht (Figure 8), done in 1974, was the first project ever to explore the architectural and urbanist potential of a distinction between a 'base building' designed by the architect and the subsequent 'fit-out' done by the user. Frans van der Werf developed an 'urban tissue' in which public courtyards giving entry to the dwellings alternate with garden courtyards to be cultivated by the users. Within this fabric, users chose the location and size of their units and designed their own floor plans. Van der Werf's most recent project in Zevenaar follows the same basic principles and received a prize for sustainable building. An international network for Open Building meets yearly somewhere in the world and in several other countries, most notably Japan and Finland, similar open residential projects have been executed.[2, 3]

Figure 8 Molenvliet project, Papendrecht, the Netherlands. Frans van der Werf, 1978.

It is now clear that in commercial architecture, workplace architecture, and residential architecture level distinctions serve the need for change and adaptation by day-to-day inhabitation. The dynamics of time-based building are already a fact of life and come naturally to the built environment, but as long as that reality is not fully embraced by the architectural profession as inspiring and challenging, a truly new time-based architecture will not take wings.

Notes

1 Actually, there were at least two types along the three major canals of Amsterdam. The type with a gabled façade similar to what had already been done in the medieval core of the city, and the broader façade with a cornice that was introduced in the 17th century.
2 See Walter Horn and Ernests Born, *The Plan for St. Gall*, 3 volumes (Berkeley: California Press, 1979). One volume brief version by Lorna Price, University of California Press, 1982.
3 See also S. H. Kendall and J. Teicher, *Residential Open Building* (London: Spon Press, 2000), which gives an overview of more than a hundred projects executed by that time.

2007
TO TEND A GARDEN
Thoughts on the strengths and limits of studio pedagogy

"What makes Good Art? Good Judgement. What makes Good Judgement? Bad Judgement."[1]

Editors' Notes: *This essay continues the author's focus on the education of architects and was published in In Design Studio Pedagogy: Horizons for the Future (ed) Salama, Ashraf and Wilkinson, Nicholas. Urban International Press, Gateshead, United Kingdom, 2007.*

Strengths

What is studio good for that cannot be done in another setting? Can we equate "studio teaching" with "design teaching?" Or are there aspects of teaching design that the studio cannot accommodate>

These questions I want to discuss here.

There is one thing that we all may agree on that studio is excellent for: as a social and organizational setting, studio is the ideal context to learn the art of good judgement. This important because analysis and logic reasoning, however important they may be, do not suffice for making architecture. We are talking about the ability to make wholes that are more than the sum of their parts, juggling multiple and elusive criteria in doing so.

To be sure, analysis and systemic development are more important today than ever before. But their application must be guided by something more comprehensive to make what is complex compelling, accessible and beneficial.

This is where good judgement comes in. It is the main subject of studio life: it permeates the teacher-student relation. It is the irreplaceable ability by which we can steer towards coherence, if not beauty, in the midst of a host of often conflicting demands and criteria.

Studio can be compared to a class in musical composition. The building and the symphony or sonata, simply by being there, tell us if their maker was able to bridle that wild impulse to shape things and has arrived at something standing on its own feet. Judgement makes the final form. That is why it can be argued that a jury need not know the student, or the path she followed while designing, or composing, to judge the quality of her work. In architectural education, we have recoiled from that harsh format and tend to structure reviews as conversations between student and visiting critic in an attempt to find a softer, gentler way of closure. Such meetings certainly have their educational merit, but every student knows the unspoken truth: in the end, your design must do the talking.

Because there is no recipe, learning to judge well must happen by trial and error and is best done in the shadow of a master of that elusive art, and in the company of peers who aspire to the same ability. It is in the presence of others that we must learn to do our own. Studios offer that essential social context.

What is lacking?

So far, so good. Now for what is missing. The judgement we talk about must encompass demands, criteria, and considerations that can be social, functional, political, fashionable, administrative and much more. From that broad array our decisions must lead to a form. Consequently, what we decide ultimately depends on our knowledge of form and our skill to make it. The broader our mastery of form, the greater our freedom of judgement will be. When we know only one solution, it will inevitably be to where our judgement leads, no matter what conditions must be met.

It is assumed that mastery of form is also taught in studio. There is no doubt that a good deal of architectural form making is going on there, but its range is limited by a teachers' preferences. The teaching is predominantly implicit and the learning imitative. In the times of the Beaux Arts, when building technology was much more homogeneous and teachers and students believed in general architectural principles that could be mastered under any Patron's guidance, that selective and implicit mode was enough. In our day and age, it is not.

To see what is lacking, we must remember where we came from and how Modernism has fundamentally altered our professional mission.

The architect we think ourselves to be emerged in the Renaissance. It was Alberti who first defined him, declaring he was no longer beholden to vernacular customs, and could, by his inventions and creativity, do buildings never seen before. And it was Palladio who established our professional role model along that vision. From then on, the architect did the special building: the castle, the place of worship, the palace and the villa, the town hall and the courthouse. Everything else, all that made urban and rural fields, took care of itself. Since time immemorial the craftsman and the master builder had made everyday environment and were made by it: their bondage being the very thing the new architecture escaped from.[2]

For centuries, the classicist courthouse and the town hall could grace the provincial town square. This fruitful complementary relationship between vernacular building and the art of architecture ended with Modernity, when everyday environment lost its organic autonomy. The reasons are familiar: the inability of vernacular habits to serve new uses, the introduction of new materials and ways of building, the emergence of formidable organizational power, impatience with historic examples and previous experience. The unprecedented growth of cities and much more – all this turned everyday environment into a problem. The profession, fully confident that a new world was to be shaped, believed it could solve that problem by *design*. Hence, everyday environment became architecture, too, and we got immersed in it. Urban layout and housing, as well as buildings for commerce and work, for learning and leisure, were newly minted and are now what most of us are busy with today.

It was, of course, inevitable, but nobody ever said: "Wait a minute, this has never happened before, maybe an involvement with everyday environment demands skills and knowledge we do not have."

We tend to see no lessons in what 'real architects' have not designed. Nonetheless, historic vernacular environments could often be amazingly rich and beautiful – as Amsterdam, Venice, old Beijing and so many other examples demonstrate – and were always dynamic, alive and full of qualities worth learning from. The same goes for contemporary environments grown beyond the claims of professional design, including suburban sprawl and informal settlements. Urban and suburban fields of all kinds are like gardens – some well-tended and some not – but always showing spontaneous and surprising thematic variation: human scale form is always in evidence and may happily coexist with the large size and the large number. Our instincts tell us that such environments cannot be 'made.' Indeed, they have a certain organic autonomy; to the extent that they can be designed we must think of a landscape or garden, and for their realization the concept of cultivation seems more appropriate than that of building.

If it is true, as I do believe, that the special and the large in human settlement always grew from the common and the small by irrepressible transformational energies making for increasing sophistication, we now must reexamine our mission in that light.

Three points of conflict

To make the case that we are out of touch with everyday environment, let me bring up three aspects of the latter that we continue to deny. None of them lends itself to the studio format of teaching. I will come back to that, but first let me mention them:

First of all, there is change: life keeps environment in a state of constant transformation. What is there must adjust to new ways of living. Cities endure by renewal and alteration. Change usually occurs partially – by growth, alteration or attrition. Its ways are complex but seldom irrational.

What resists life we will get rid of, but what we love we keep, often by adjustment and, so doing, make it last. Thus, change defines what lasts and vice-a-versa.

Secondly, partial change implies distribution of design control. All change comes from discrete interventions. No urban fabric, indeed, no large project, can result from a single design effort but always must, over time, allow inhabitation to act partially and in its own time, and thereby sustain the whole. Distributed design control renders large projects fine-grained and sustainable, allowing renewal part by part. Where no design is delegated, rigid uniformity is the inevitable result.

Thirdly, values are shared among actors. In spite of constant partial transformation and distributed design control, environments remain coherent to a remarkable degree. Historic fabrics and, indeed, all vernacular fields past and present, express shared values by thematic variation of type, patterns and habits of building and designing. When the desire to share is lacking, environments become sculpture exhibitions at best and at worst become a zoo, where different animals pace invisible cages ignoring one another.

In light of these three qualities, we can summarize our present ideology: We still find change an insult to our creative effort. We are convinced that good architecture demands a top-down, centrally controlled design proves. Our professional culture values being different and does not know how to share.

Consider, too, the Studio: It demands a static result usually responding to a fixed functional program, done by a single student who is encouraged to act unrelated to what others do.

You may retort that all that is a matter of intentions. If we wish, we surely must be able to change studio teaching to encompass change, distribution of design responsibility, and the sharing of values? Yes, in principle the social setting in studio could be adjusted accordingly. But that will only work when the participants already have mastered the necessary skills to deal with such new attitudes. Without such skills, and the knowledge that brings them forth, good intentions will fail.

A design curriculum

And here's the rub: Knowledge and skills go together and reinforce one another. Their acquisition demands a focused effort that should not interfere with the mission of studio. In studio, knowledge and skills must be applied but cannot be taught in any depth without seriously derailing studio's central purpose.

Knowing environment's complex behavior is indeed a prerequisite for good judgement, and skills in handling dynamic environmental for offer the necessary range of alternative solutions our judgement may consider. But to make them support studio work, they must be taught elsewhere first.

Having tried and failed the impossible combination when teaching studio at MIT, I launched an advanced course on "Thematic Design" in 1982 (and continued for a number of years), which was deliberately divorced from studio teaching. Students took to it with generous interest, which was a powerful incentive for me to persist in the experiment.

It was a very hands-on course. It started with exercises in form transformation. After all, designing can be seen as a generative process. As Louis Sullivan already told us, the healthy plant grows from a small seed. Students discovered how, by transformational 'moves' an initially simple form may grow into something rich and complex while remaining under full control. We discussed how environmental form has different levels of intervention (or change), each with its own physical attributes and its own lifecycle. The recognition of such

Levels, each under the control of a different agent, establishes a first distribution of design control. One must learn how to settle interface conditions among actors controlling different levels and different territories. One then must be able to assess the capacity of each form to contain variable lower level intervention. One must also know how to share types, patterns and systems among actors on a given level, and how to play with them for general advantage and specific identity. Students brought the skills and insights they had mastered to their studios and found them helpful, assuaging initially skeptical teachers.

Such a complementary relation between two teaching environments should not be a surprise. We can compare the studio setting with the composition class in a music school. No one will confuse composing a symphony with learning to play an instrument or studying musical structure. Both making a composition and playing an instrument demand a good ear, and a sensitive touch. The ability to play surely informs the ability to compose. But the distinction in terms of teaching and learning is clear.

A shrinking world

Looking at contemporary studio teaching in that light, we can see the limitations imposed by lack of design skills along the lines suggested above.

For instance, the present scope of design in studio is severely constrained. We typically find, on the students' screen, such subjects as the villa and sometime the urban house, the small library or a place of culture or one for retreat, a campus museum or an exhibition space: all examples of special functions that are supposed to deserve a special form. All limited enough in size to be controlled by a single designer and preferably situated far enough away from other architecture to avoid interference. Moreover, in spite of the demise of functionalism, a functional program usually shapes the exercise. When qualities of environmental field – their patterns of change, their typologies, their systems or their relation to the distribution of design control – are not brought into play, only function remains to help structure a task. I know that exceptions can be mentioned and that sometimes studios venture to do a small neighborhood for instance, or a multifunctional building, or attempt something collective (which does not necessarily imply a distribution of design control), but the general picture is clear: large parts of contemporary environment remain ignored.

Consequently, we seldom find, in studio, the kinds of subjects demanding fine-grained change in larger structures, or distribution of design control on different levels of intervention, or variations on shared formal constraints like types, patterns and systems. Think of such projects as the shopping mall, the suburban neighborhood, the high-rise workplace, the hospital, the airport terminal, or the apartment building: forms that are a chunk of environmental fabric rather than just big buildings. These are the kind of projects that architects work on in the real world but that are seldom found in studio. We sense full well that they demand a different game. Hence, while projects in the real world tend to get larger and larger, the world of the studio shrinks more and more, shying away from what most students will make a living from. As a result, those in the field remain unable to advance real-world practice, while the distance between that practice and academia is inexorably widening.

A professional language?

Another indication of our divorce from everyday environment's inspiration and discipline can be found in our use of language.

In the Beaux Arts days, when the studio emerged, the architects' world was confined to the special and the monumental building, while technical know-how and craftsmanship still were homogeneous. I that circumscribed world, it was believed that design followed general principles that, although admittedly implicit and mysterious, teachers could convey, and students could come to understand, by patient exercise. That world knew a generally accepted vocabulary that was shared among the profession at large.

In short, in those days, Architecture was like other professions. The lawyer, the medical doctor and the engineer all have their own language by which they discuss with clarity and precision what they are doing. Their vocabularies reflect what their professions are about. It is what they share and jealously guard. Today, architecture is the only profession that has no such language.

How do we use language today? Two aspects can be noted

First of all, each teacher seeks a personal vision of the built world. We like to explain how we, personally, see it. In that attempt, we coin our own words, avoiding those introduced by others. Our language does not reflect a search for common ground but serves a tribal purpose where each allegiance implies another language. In such a setting, it is inevitable that a thing gets different names by different groups, and meaningful distinction, so essential in a discourse that strives for excellence, is severely hampered.

Secondly, although vocabulary is no longer universal, teaching by conversation makes language more important than ever, since we rightly reject the Beaux Arts notion that criteria are universal, judgement can no longer be 'objective,' and it is reasonable to let the student explain. But how can she do so if there is no common vocabulary about the making of form anymore? What we hear is usually a declaration of intent and an explanation of what the building is 'trying to say,' what its 'meaning' is, and what we are supposed to feel when we experience it. Ironically, that is exactly what the building she speaks of should be able to convey by its very presence. Her audience, however, responds in the same vein. Visiting critics may elaborate on what *they* think the building is telling them, or ought to tell them. Consequently, there is little or no shoptalk about the making of architecture. Any naming of spaces or building parts is primitive and personal or tribal and almost always metaphorical. In short, the discourse is not professional: in fact, it borrows from the language of the critic. It is, after all, the critic's role to explain how the observer sees the building, what is experienced by him and how the meanings he finds and the feeling he notes, compare to those evoked by other buildings, etc.

A discussion among architects should not be about meaning or a putative observer's impressions, but about the work done and the decisions made: it must seek to achieve clarity about the form at hand and the process that brought it forth. Since the vocabulary for that kind of discourse is not available, we now speak among ourselves like those who are not us, lamely trying to convince others what they should feel or think when seeing our work.

Our source of knowledge

Lack of precise and common language betrays lack of a common knowledge base. Today, if architectural publications are to be believed, the profession mainly tries to think of something new, never before seen. An overriding desire for self-expression and originality is an invitation for ignorance, if not amnesia. The less one knows (as distinct from being informed about things), the less reference to precedent is possible, and the easier it is to think oneself original.

The Beaux Arts and Modernism are history now, and since Post Modernism, we have mercifully abandoned the idea that style must hold us together. But to justify its placer in the scheme of things, a profession must be able to declare loudly and proudly what skills and knowledge constitute its particular way of understanding the world. If we carry responsibility for everyday environment, we must study it. Where the medical doctor must know the human body for us to submit ourselves to her intervention, the architect must know everyday environment as a living and complex body for his intervention on it to be beneficial.

The three aspects already mentioned as characteristic for everyday environment can guide that quest for knowledge. Such a study will allow us to find, by patient and careful observation, certain morphological transformations subject to human intervention by which all environments live, however different they may be. It need not exclude the special and the monumental, but it can help us understand them as peculiar transformations of the common; in the way flowers emerge among the leaves of a bush. The methodology is not new; all knowledge of nature rests on observations of transformational processes. This is what I tried to clarify in my book *The Structure of the Ordinary*.[3] It is a first try, but the idea that our professional knowledge should be about the built environment, observed as an autonomous and living entity – something too complex to claim as a product, but subject to our cultivation – seems to be sound and promising. Such knowledge may, eventually, allow us to decide with confidence what can be taught in studio and what is best conveyed and learned in another way.

Notes

1 As quoted from the late Professor Hans Jaffe, Historian of Modern Art.
2 N. J. Habraken, *Palladio's Children*, ed. Jonathan Teicher (London and New York: Taylor and Francis, 2005).
3 N. J. Habraken, *The Structure of the Ordinary: Form and Control in the Built Environment*, ed. Jonathan Teicher (Cambridge, MA and London: MIT Press, 1998).

2012
CULTIVATING BUILT ENVIRONMENT

Editors' Note: *This is an updated and partly revised version of a chapter in the book Sustainable Urbanism and Beyond, edited by Tigran Haas and published by Rizzoli, 2012.*

Metaphors to work with

From the 1960's onward I have advocated adaptability in housing construction. The major reason for doing so was to reintroduce, in contemporary built environment, what I have called the 'natural relation,'[1] the age-old settlement process where inhabitation and built form were one. Sustainability in built environment has everything to do with that restoration.

The idea that built environment can be wasteful is peculiar to our times. For millennia, humanity has produced shelter that could be highly complex and endure for centuries. No one has ever argued that such fabrics wasted available resources.

The constant aspect of historic urban fabrics was their organic quality. The term is justified because by a slow but continuous process of renewal, improvement and adaptation of individual houses, they had a self-generating ability. Houses functioned like living cells of the fabric. There is a living cell where the nominal social unit interacts without mediation with the smallest material unit recognizable as a changeable whole. House types never were architectural inventions but came to full bloom by that very interaction. House typology being self-evident, acts of urban design were about providing context for a fabric to manifest itself; much in the way a gardener lays out the beds for plants to flower in.

Our contemporary built environment may look very different from past examples, but it is unlikely that humanity's settlement habits of more than five thousand years have suddenly evaporated. It is reasonable to assume that they have continued and that the degree in which that has happened may tell us something about present day environments' health.

Following up on that assumption, I will look at present day built environment by using the metaphors of 'living cell' and 'organism'. 'Living cell', as already stated, denoting those instances where occupancy interacts immediately with its material envelope. 'Organism' because a certain autonomy, a capacity for self-organization, is found in all built environment, which we must accept as intrinsic to it. These terms provide a shorthand that can help us to understand age old human settlement behavior and consider its continuation and interruption in contemporary environment. This may help us to find out why we worry about sustainability in the first place.

Built environment as organism

A traveler flying at night from Washington DC to Boston, Massachusetts, a distance of some 400 miles, sees a pattern of lighted roads and buildings that never darkens and which, following the Eastern seaboard, stretches inland to the Appalachian Mountains. There are spots where the network becomes vestigial while other places are ablaze with light. Already in 1961 geographer Jean Gottmann named it Megalopolis.[2] From the air, it appears as a giant weed on the surface of the earth with a life of its own, consuming energy and many other resources on a vast scale, day and night.

We know that today the world is replete with similar fields. The Mexican Federal District, the Nile delta

DOI: 10.4324/9781003011385-48

triangle including Cairo and Alexandria, the Guangdong area opposite Hong Kong, and many others come to mind. They are at least as complex and energetic and uncontrollable in their growth.

The living cell: change and disappearance

The living cell is where human settlement most immediately shapes physical form and decides on the use of resources and the rhythm of environment's metabolism. All infrastructures, particularly the many utility networks, serve to feed it. They also enable new innovations to reach that cell. Cells and infrastructure together make the organic whole.

In history, the house as living cell, under unified control, could encompass an extended family and might include servants and slaves. Spaces to work in were found in it as well: to do business, to sell merchandise, to process food or do handicraft. Its contents represented a culture at its most intimate scale. As such, the living cell could be large as the Venetian Gothic palace, extensive like the family compound in 18th century Beijing, hierarchically ordered like the Atrium house in Pompeii.

Today the house is still a living cell and still determines built fields that range from suburban sprawl including neighborhoods for well-to-do citizens to the 'informal settlements' surrounding most of the world's mega-cities. Of those, the latter most faithfully continue the age-old process of human settlement where the house as living cell, for all its improvisational emergence and slow growth, harbors extended families and often combines domestic and workspace. Informal settlement is now consuming materials like cement, glass and bricks; elements like tiles, window frames and doors; and all kinds of piping and wiring, bathroom and kitchen equipment and much more – partaking of the name nourishment as all other contemporary fabric.

In today's environment on the other hand, the house, inhabited by the nuclear family, contains only one of the many social clusters in need of a responsive envelope. Other social entities are found in the wide variety of workplaces, in retail stores, in the office of the therapist and consultant, the apartment building, and where else daily human intercourse takes place. The diverse and tightly packed social activities found in the historic house have escaped the domestic realm and, having diversified and multiplied, are found all across contemporary fabric: promising a richer and more diverse interaction between inhabitation and physical form.

In contrast to this rich diversity of ever smaller but dynamic social clusters, the smallest material unit recognizable as a changeable whole in the environmental fabric is no longer just the single house, but also the larger, sometimes very large building. The result is an increasingly coarse fabric, unresponsive to inhabitation of any kind and at worst oppressively deterministic. The one-on-one interaction between material form and social entity, so naturally manifest in historic fabric, is no longer evident. Many social clusters do not inhabit a form that lives by their care and initiative, and which in turn stimulates and facilitates their actions. The living-cell-that-could-be has been weakened or has entirely disappeared. Inhabitation for both work and living can now be found as a nomadic activity in an environment that is no longer its product or responsibility.

The fine-grained large project

This lack of reciprocity between an increasingly diverse and dynamic social body and a less and less agile material environment is not just inconvenient. It complicates and slows down the metabolism that sustains built environment and renders inhabitation passive and hence un-productive, leaving it incapable to stimulate innovation or to be stimulated by it. Only a fabric of living cells can be a truly self-generating system.

To be sure, pleading for the living cell is not a rejection of the large project, which is very much part of our world, is here to stay and most likely will be larger and more common. The challenge is to make it accommodate the living cell, help the cell to take care of itself. Such a new way of restoring the 'natural relationship' will produce what can be called the 'fine-grained large project.'

This challenge is intensified by the growing complexity of built form as such. Today's living cell, domestic or otherwise, must contain not only bathroom and kitchen equipment and replaceable partitioning, but also a host of conduits for sewage, water, electric power, data, ventilation, heating and more. These utilities are distributed throughout habitable space to serve every room or workstation. Today's entities of inhabitation, so widely diverse and dispersed, may be small or singular compared to the closely packed historical household, but the envelope they want to animate is technically far more complex.

Before we look at this lack of reciprocity as another professional problem to be solved, we should pause and remember that the degrading and outright disappearance of the living cell had much to do with the Modernist inclination to see all things environmental as a technical problem, or, at least, a design problem, and its belief in the economy of scale. Living cells cannot be designed or produced; we can only provide conditions by which they may come about. To meet today's environmental challenge, a strategy of cultivation is required, not a production program.

The return of the living cell

If built environment is an organism, and as such has a certain autonomy, it can be expected to seek to remedy what is ailing it. And indeed, our present environment has been moving already in that direction almost unbeknownst to its observers and theorists. A gradual introduction of the living cell in parts of our environment where it could not be found earlier on can be noted.

For instance, increasingly across the world, the commercial office building offers empty floors for lease to various occupant parties who are free to have them fitted-out by their own designers and fit-out contractors. There already, inside the large built volume, a clear separation of the collective environment on the one hand and the small-scale act of inhabitation on the other hand enables the living cell to return in a new way. In the same manner, an institutional client will expect a new office building to be able to respond to future mutation in work unit composition and location.

In the shopping mall, retail space is likewise left empty to be fitted out by specialized contractors familiar with the tenant retailers' house style.

So-called "open" residential projects have been done on an experimental basis for quite some time now,[3] but in the last decade or so, the approach has entered the commercial world. Residential Open Building projects initiated for profit can be found, among other countries, in Finland, Japan, the Netherlands and Finland.[4]

Where conditions are favorable, the living cell appears spontaneously. In Moscow, for instance, wealthy apartment owners would rip out the entire elaborately finished interiors of their newly bought apartments to start again with their own designers. Appalled by this destruction of capital, developers, unaware of any international network advocating such an approach, now routinely produce 'empty' apartment buildings, selling available floor space and collective facilities.

In hospital construction, the perennial need for partial and ad-hoc adaptation of space in response to changing demands of work units has triggered debate in professional circles and has led to various innovations. The most advanced project so far, is found in a new intensive care hospital for the City of Bern, where a radical separation of the so-called 'primary system' from the 'secondary system' led to separate design competitions for each.[5]

New opportunities: 3d urban design

All this leads to an awakening awareness of a new professional role implied in the design for the 'fine-grained large project.' This was perhaps first expressed when Professor Yositika Utida, the leader of the design team for the pathbreaking NEXT21 residential open building project in Osaka, Japan,[6] declared that he did not want to do a 'flexible' building but a 'three-dimensional urban design.' True to this statement, he invited thirteen other architects to custom design the eighteen dwelling units in the project, occupying himself with the design of the public spaces and the infrastructure for the living cells to settle in.

The NEXT21 project was not the first 'open building' residential project in Japan. For decades already experimental projects had been done to serve user preferences, but its exploration of new urban design made possible by the creation of an urban scale architectural structure was significant. It was also inspired by an earlier project in the Netherlands by architect Frans van der Werf, whose "Molenvliet" project demonstrated how a low-rise "Support" could form a continuous structure by which urban spaces like streets, public courtyards and alleys could be shaped to make an urban fabric.[7]

Figure 1 Molenvliet project, Papendrecht, the Netherlands, 1984

Figure 2 NEXT21 Experimental housing project, Osaka, Japan, 1994

Figure 3 'SOLIDS" project in Amsterdam West, the Netherlands

New opportunities: long-term investment

Once this new perspective on urban fabric unfolds, it becomes possible to point out some additional opportunities worth exploration.

The 'base building,' as it is already known in commercial development, now free from demands for individual inhabitation, can live a long time, just as streets tend to live longer than houses. This allows for long-term investment which, in turn, makes higher initial investment feasible for internal public spaces and external architecture. Right now, this approach is followed by a not-for-profit housing corporation in Amsterdam where two different projects offered such 'base buildings,' here called 'SOLIDS,' were completed in 2012. Empty space is rented by occupants who are free to take care of their interior fit-out for any purpose, domestic or otherwise, that is not disruptive to the community. The extra investment in high quality facades and exterior arcade and inside public spaces is expected to bring a profit in the long run.[8]

No doubt this initiative will be regarded with skepticism by many. However, it is in tune with a law, passed by the Japanese Diet (congress) in 2008, which encourages residential construction that can last up to two centuries. The law refers to detailed technical requirements in which subsystems are identified that must be replaceable with minimal disturbance of other parts of the building to ensure the long life of the whole. For some sub-systems, technical wear and tear force a shorter lifespan, while the use-life of other subsystems is limited by user preferences. If a building meets those requirements for partial renewal, the owner will receive substantial tax reductions.[9] This is the first time that formal legal recognition is given to the dimension of time in housing policy. The practical result, of course, is that rendering a long life to what can endure and keeping adaptable what must respond to inhabitation makes the living cell possible again.

The Japanese law applies to all residential construction. The single house as well will benefit if subsystems can be renewed and replaced with minimum disruption of more durable parts of the building. In present professional practice that is not now the case. The numerous utilities that have been added to buildings in modern times have led to a notorious entanglement of subsystems including piping and wiring. Although the free-standing house is the prototype living cell, this entanglement renders its metabolism sub-optimal. Here as well the new law's requirements will have a beneficial effect.

New opportunities: a fit-out industry

Bundling user related subsystems into a coherent 'fit-out system' is one of the major objectives of the global open building network which advocates enabling the living cell. Where the 'empty' base building provides space for the living cell to settle in, a dedicated fit-out system utilizes the full potential of that condition. As a composite of available subs-systems it is itself able to adopt the most efficient versions that enter the market. Experience has already shown that a dwelling unit can be fitted out by a team of two or three all-round installers in less than three weeks. The cost of such a fit-out is of the order of magnitude of the cost of the households' cars.

Developing a fit-out industry is not a matter of new manufacturing – the necessary hardware sub-systems being already available – but it does require sophisticated logistics and software supported pre-assembly and packaging. Well organized, such an industry will enable urban fabric to adapt smoothly and universally to more effective and less wasteful technology.

The first initiatives to a dedicated fit-out system on a commercial basis have been taken in Japan as well. The NEXTInfill company aims at serving new construction as well as renovation of existing stock. Its service is used also by a new breed of developers who buy old apartments that they entirely clean out and restore to then install new units for sale.[10]

A sustainable built environment needs a fit-out industry that has access to all parts of extant fabrics. Conversely, for a fit-out industry to reach full potential, existing stock must be made receptive to fit-out. Fit out industry can also offer such conversion. Its effective emergence needs support of a dedicated policy including legal and fiscal initiatives.

Professional attitude and political will

For environment to be sustainable, two major conditions must be met:

> Firstly, recognition of the time dimension must render long term what can endure and render adaptable what serves actual inhabitation.
>
> Secondly, recognition of user responsibility is needed to give feedback for development of more efficient means of inhabitation and to receive such means by rapid distribution across an entire fabric.

Only cultivation of the living cell can provide these conditions.

This in turn demands a reorientation of professional habits and political encouragement.

A fit-out industry needs new ways of management and logistics. It also needs legal recognition and formal certification to assure dependable performance.

A scrutiny of legal and management aspects as well as financial policy is also needed to make both the extant building stock and new construction receptive to customized adaptation.

In other words, to begin cultivation, new hardware is not a pre-condition although it will, of course, be a result. What is needed is something more difficult than technical invention: a new professional attitude, explicit methodology and the application of political will.

Notes

1. N. J. Habraken, *Supports: an Alternative to Mass Housing*, ed. Jonathan Teicher, English ed. (London: Urban International Press, Reprint of the 1972).
2. Jean Gottmann, *Megalopolis* (New York: The Urbanized Northeastern Seaboard of the United States, The Twentieth Century Fund, 1961).
3. Stephen Kendall and Jonathan Teicher, *Residential Open Building* (London: E & FN Spon, 2000).
4. For projects of the last decade: see the booklet by Prof. Jia Beisi at the Open Building website: http://www.open-building.org/archives/booklet2_small.pdf.
5. The INO project, Bern, Switzerland, Client: Office of Properties and Buildings of the Canton Bern, Giorgio Macchi, director.
6. Next21 housing project, Osaka, Japan, Experimental project commissioned by Osaka Gas Company. Prof. Yositika Utida project leader with prof. Kazuo Tatsumi, Seiichi Fukao, Mitsuo Takada, Shinichi Chikazumi. For English language documentation of the Next21 project: *GAJapan*, 6 January/February 1994; DOMUS, 891, October 1999.
7. Architect Frans van der Werf's housing project in the town of Papendrecht, the Netherlands, 1974 was the partial implementation of his winning scheme for an international competition for a new urban neighborhood. It was visited by the Next21 Client team at the initiative of Prof. Yositika Utida. Frans van der Werf did some eight other Open Building projects in the following years: www.vdwerf.nl/home.html.
8. Two 'Solids' Projects, by housing corporation *Stadgenoot*, Frank Bijdendijk, Director. The IJburg project designed by Baumschlager Eberle, architects. The Amsterdam Old West project designed by Tony Fretton.
9. The "Act for Promotion of Long-Life Quality Housing." Prof. Kazunobu Minami, *The New Japanese Housing Law to Promote the Longer Life of Housing*. Paper presented at the Open Building conference in Bilbao, Spain, 2010.
10. From an unpublished report by architect Shinichi Chikazumi, Tokyo.

INTERMEZZO BY THE EDITORS

SK/JD: Someone else that I remember you having a great sympathy with was Donald Schön (Professor of Urban Planning at MIT). Is that true?

JH: Yes.

SK/JD: You had a kind of collaborative relationship with him. Tell us a bit about that.

JH: Don was interested in creativity, also. So, he wanted to talk to architects to understand creativity. Where does it come from? He rightly criticized his colleagues in all the departments. He said, "You teach these kids all the rules, the systems, but you don't encourage their inventions. The freedom to think of things. And architects are the only ones who do that." And I said, "Yes, Don, that's right. But architects are the only ones who have no rules." So, we had these long discussions. And of course, he was a very smart guy, so we always had something interesting to talk about. And I asked him to read my STRUCTURE OF THE ORDINARY book which he did. And he had very good comments. He also pointed out that it was the terminology that bothered him.

SK/JD: He had a problem with your terminology?

JH: Yes, he did. . . . Form. Place. And the order of understanding. And he said, "What do you mean order of place?" And I said, "territory." "Why don't you say that?" Of course, he was right, but I didn't listen. That was nice. In the end, it was always a problem because he liked to smoke a pipe. But he couldn't do it in his own room because his secretary next door would smell it.

SK/JD: So, he came over to N-52

JH: I said, "You can always come to my room where you can smoke your pipe." No, he was an interesting guy, he had good understanding of the schools' running. What different people wanted to do.

SK/JD: Well also I know he did a kind of re-creation of a conversation session between a student and a teacher . . . he and his graduate students tried to understand the interactive processes of design studio which resulted in his little book THE DESIGN STUDIO. Later, these ideas developed in two books: "The Reflective Practitioner" and "Educating the Reflective Practitioner."

JH: Yes, he had a good sense of all that. He sensed that very well.

SUMMING UP

2013
METHODOLOGY AND IDEOLOGY IN ARCHITECTURE

Editors' Note: *This essay was published in Umbau 26, in 2013.*

A distinction to be made

Methodology is the study and knowledge of ways of working. Questions about how we do things and how we improve the way we do things are essential for all professions and deserve close study in professional theory and education. It is therefore remarkable that we architects seldom discuss the way we work.

This lack of interest is caused by a failure to distinguish between design ability and creativity. The creative act is essential in all professions, and perhaps more so in architecture. Creation is a mystery that escapes rational explanation. It does not necessarily need design: paintings and sculptures are usually created in direct interaction with the material that is shaped. Designing in architecture includes the creative act, but also entails conveying what is created to other parties who must approve or execute it. It also involves cooperation among designers working in the same location or in the same team. Most importantly, the distribution of discrete design tasks in large projects is a typical contemporary aspect of designing itself. These varied interactions demand shared ways and means of working, which is where method comes to the fore. In short, where creation is a lonely act, designing is a social one, and while creation is immediate and personal, designing involves working with others.

Of course, in real world practice architects do interact with others in many ways. But what needs to be shared and how that is best done is neither studied nor taught. When asked what architecture is about, we tend to refer to the creative act and are inclined to consider that necessary interaction an unwelcome constraint to our individual adventure. This not only makes for an ineffective profession, but also denies its practitioners a source of inspiration. It is in interaction with the world around us that creativity is sparked, and ideas are born.

A methodical evolution

In the early nineteen sixties, I suggested another way of working on housing projects. I proposed that architects make a distinction between the design of the individual floor plan of a single apartment and the design of the collective structure shared by all apartments. This was, in fact, a methodological proposal. There were varied reasons for it: one could point out that in a sophisticated modern society in which households and individuals had come to expect the freedom to decide what they needed residents should be granted control over their own dwellings. One can also argue that distinguishing the long lifetime of the collective building from the short lifetime of the individual 'infill' is an important condition for environmental sustainability. Another motivation, this time from the point of view of technology and production, is that kitchen systems, bathroom systems, partitioning systems, and all kinds of piping and wiring systems are best developed in direct exchange with a market of users, just like all other durable consumer goods. Last but not least, our recent inclination to retrofit outdated buildings implicitly embraces the proposed two-level design approach.

Whether they be social, technical, or political, these reasons are now all recognized and support one another,

DOI: 10.4324/9781003011385-49

but the proposal itself, for those of us who design, was a methodological one. Instead of considering an apartment building a single design object, we should proceed in a t wo-level manner: first design the collective part, and then have others design the individual units.

This way of working is not new in itself. A similar distinction is made between urban design, which shapes a collective framework, and architectural design, which takes care of the buildings in it. More recently, developers of commercial real estate routinely build large high-rise buildings within which individual companies can hire empty floors to be fitted out in response to their own needs by architects commissioned for that particular job and executed by specialized "fit-out" divisions that are owned by large general contractors. This approach is also followed in the design of institutional buildings. The large shopping center likewise offers a collective environment with- in which retail shops will have their own interior f it-out, taken care of by specialized companies who do both the design and the execution.

The increasing size of buildings reinforces the need for a t wo-step approach. With the help of contemporary technology, we now routinely create buildings that contain more people than lived in the average classical Greek town. Such projects can properly be considered three-dimensional urban design. But any collectively inhabited building always needs the same separation to have a healthy life.

Examples

The general examples cited above may show how hierarchical distribution of design tasks is increasingly a reality in contemporary practice. But the profession has failed so far to consider its potential for a new architecture. The large office building that allows lessees to construct their own interiors is still treated as an "empty building" rather than as a long-term, three-dimensional built environment with well-defined public spaces and well-conceived zones for private settlement. The large shopping mall – the icon of collective retail environment – never could decide if it should be a very large warehouse, a kind of extended hotel lobby, or an interior urban environment. In our profession, the architectural interaction between the individual and the collective is not the subject of theory or research. In the apartment building, likewise, the distinction between the two levels of design intervention is not yet generally recognized as a new paradigm. In most cases architects resist it and insist on their "right" to design the floor plan as an integral part of the whole.

Of course, the real world will prevail. The demand for sustainability, for response to user preferences, and for technical efficiency will eventually cause us to accept the two-level distribution of design control. Under the heading Open Building, a growing and dedicated group of designers, academics, and managers has been active on this front for decades[1], and hundreds of experimental projects are on record.[2] This is not the place to dwell on this development in any detail, but a few of the major stages are worth mentioning.

In the late eighties, Osaka Gas Company asked a prestigious team of designers to help it build the apartment building of the future[3]. In addition to numerous advanced technical innovations related to the use of energy and the management of waste, a clear distinction between the level of the collective environment and that of the individual inhabitation became the leading concept. Professor Utida, the leader of the design team, declared that he wanted to make a "three-dimensional urban design". True to that idea he invited thirteen different architects to design the eighteen residential units in the collective framework. A dedicated facade system was made available for them to use in the design of individual units. NEXT21, as the project was known, was by no means the first of its kind in terms of separation of design responsibility, but it stood out for its attempt to architecturally think through the distinction bet ween the individual and the collective and, most importantly, for its impact as a prestigious research effort initiated and conducted by a large institution known for its dedication to research in building technology.

Figure 1 The NEXT21 project in Osaka, Japan

From then on, the government in Japan took notice, and the concept gradually established a foothold in political circles. In 2008 the Japanese legislature enacted a law that provides a significant tax reduction to owners of durable dwellings. To earn the tax advantage, extensive technical requirements must be met. These basically demand that each subsystem can be replaced in due time, depending on wear and tear as much as on user preferences and changing lifestyles. Cast in technical terms, the law ensures the long-term maintenance of the collective environment, as well as the adaptability of the individual unit for inhabitation.[4] This is the first time this approach has attracted formal governmental support.

In the sixties and seventies, when the idea of separation of design responsibility was new and untested, many architects pursued the tenets of Open Building; some of them did pathbreaking work.[5] More recently, however, the initiative for the two-level approach has come predominantly from the client – not only from developers involved with commercial offices and shopping centers as already mentioned, but also from some government institutions and public housing corporations, the leadership of which decided that the separation of levels of intervention makes managerial and economic sense.

Figure 2 The Molenvliet project, Papendrecht, the Netherlands. Architect: Frans van der Werf, 1976. The first Open Building project in the Netherlands

The City of Helsinki, for instance, in cooperation with the national building research institute, held a competition for the Arabianranta housing neighborhood for designs done in the Open Building mode. It turned out that the result yielded a profit for the developer of the project, who subsequently offered the winning architect additional similar projects.[6]

Professionals in hospital development and management in the United States and Europe are studying the approach's potential to speed up hospital projects and to facilitate alterations to the building over time. The most advanced result to date is the new intensive-care hospital in Bern. Here the cantonal Office of Properties and Buildings that served as client called for a strict separation of a "primary structure" that could last a century and a "secondary system" that could change in a matter of decades. A first competition was held for the design of the primary system and, once construction had begun, a second for the interior layout.[7]

A Dutch development company renovates industrial and commercial buildings to make them accommodate a variety of private users. It also erected what it called a "Multifunk" building, which can hold separate residential and commercial fit-out territories in any proportion the market wants.

It demonstrated that the extra investment for that approach was acceptable to owners who saw the advantage of adaptability over time.[8]

Also in the Netherlands, a large not-for-profit housing corporation took the initiative to build several buildings, the empty floors of which were offered for hire in a public auction for any use, commercial or residential, with the inhabitants taking care of their own interior fit-out. The corporation's director, who initiated these projects, calls them "Solids", argues that a true Solid can live a long time, and that it can therefore bear a higher initial investment that will return a profit in the long run.[9] He mentions two major conditions that must be met to make a long-life building feasible: it must be internally adaptable and it must be loved by the inhabitants. The second requirement is an interesting new architectural criterion. He points to the survival of nineteenth century loft buildings with cast-iron facades in SoHo, New York City as evidence of its impact.

The fine-grained large project

These are just a few examples of a worldwide trend towards buildings that are made adaptable to small-scale occupation. While projects tend to be bigger and bigger and need to live longer, we are entering the era of the fine-grained large project. This trend will fundamentally alter the complex interactions among the many professionals involved in the creation and maintenance of the built environment. It will be a slow process, but one that is eminently compatible with a society that is increasingly becoming fine-grained itself: individual responsibility and the freedom to choose are already considered birthrights and are actively promoted by industrial manufacturers and, more recently, by new modes of communication.

The trend is slow, because changing a familiar way of working is painful and risky, and professionals therefore tend to avoid it as long as possible. Where the commercial and technical worlds can be expected to voluntarily reject habit when the opportunity for gain is clear, the architectural profession, locked in an ideological self-image, will remain unprepared until clients insist on the new way of working.

Of course, as architects we depend on client initiative and cannot single-handedly dictate change. But we claim to understand built environment and could therefore be expected to promote a vision for its long-term improvement and to educate clients and politicians. Most importantly for the profession itself, we should make sure to have the competence to operate successfully in the fine-grained built environment that we will be asked to design for.

Capacity, not function

The distribution of design control in increasingly large projects is in direct conflict with the idea that good design demands full top-down control. I remember being given a tour in downtown Chicago by a partner of a leading architectural firm who showed me the various high-rise buildings they had done. As evening descended upon the city, a variety of interior lighting fixtures on the ceilings became visible behind the geometric patterns of the curtain walls. My guide regretted the fact that he had not been allowed to control the arrangement of those fixtures and apologized for "the messy result." In those days, a powerful example of the architect's ideal of full top-down control was found in the Chicago Lake Shore Drive apartments by Mies van der Rohe. Here the architect's chairs graced the lobby, and the sunshades behind the windows were moved up and down in uniformity so as not to spoil the facade design.

The anecdote may seem incidental and outmoded, and it surely represents a degree of design control that is seldom granted, but we still consider a building's inside and outside an indivisible whole. For reasons that merit closer investigation than is possible here, architects implicitly adhere to the idea that the program, translated in a detailed layout, is mirrored in the building's exterior. Interior layout is often used to make interesting exterior shape or, even worse, is forced to follow exterior shape. In Hong Kong's high-rise urban fabric, a tendency can be noted to make a specific floor plan justify its more expressive exterior, thereby seriously limiting interior adaptability.

Figure 3 Example of the Parisian courtyard type building along the Haussmannian boulevards. A loose fit between the exterior and interior occupancy.

The idea that interior program must shape the exterior is clearly a remnant of modernist functionalism. The same mistaken ideology makes us think that without that match, a neutral architecture is called for. This is refuted by historical evidence. The Venetian Gothic palace, the Amsterdam canal house, and the Parisian courtyard building flanking the boulevards – to name just three examples – are far from neutral architectures; both their interior and exterior shapes are part of a typology that is always functionally open-ended. For that reason, these examples have endured for centuries.

Although functionalism has been rejected already by a previous generation, a new paradigm is still needed to replace the idea that architectural expression is driven by program and function. The overriding question to be answered addresses the variety of uses that can inhabit a single building. This is known as the question of capacity. Capacity assessment, a methodological tool, makes architecture balance a building's interior and exterior in the same open-ended way that we witness in historical examples.

Relations between designers on different levels demand attention in two directions. By necessity we have learned to accept a given 'site' as an inevitable constraint from above, but we continue to balk at the thought of releasing downward control. How the "site" we are making today may help or inspire designers who will work in it tomorrow is a new question that must be taken seriously.

This includes attention to the degree of control to be delegated. For instance, should a facade be the result of lower- level design or belong entirely to the collective building? Or how can the transition between interior collective spaces and interior private territories be given shape?

Interaction among designers

The vertical relation we have discussed so far is not the only feature of the contemporary built environment entrusted to us. Horizontal relations among designers operating in the same street or neighborhood are equally important today – another topic that has yet to receive serious attention in architecture. We tend to omit neighboring buildings in the pictures we show of our work. Historically, vernacular typology took care of local coherence. It was self-evident and unquestioned. Today, a more sophisticated way of working is needed to make an urban field in which the whole is more than the sum of the parts. The question as to what is to be shared is now a professional one.

There are familiar words for it: pattern, type and system are different means for sharing architectural values and can be the subject of negotiation and agreement among designers operating in a common urban fabric. These concepts offer thematic clues to be shared among designers. So far, the profession has shown little inclination to use them as professional tools.[10]

Thematic aspects need not be a limitation to self-expression. To express ourselves meaningfully we must employ a shared language. How you work with a given type will be significantly different from what another designer may do with it. In music as well, individual performers identify themselves by the variations they make on a shared theme. Architects have an innate ability to pick up thematic forms in a built environment. Without it no environmental coherence would be possible. But we do not talk about that ability nor is its use taught in schools. A fixation on originality and self-expression has put the subject out of bounds.

The idea that total freedom makes good architecture has perhaps been the most damaging force to the coherence of urban environments. There is no such thing as a blank slate. We always add to and change what has been done earlier. For a good designer, local constraints are a source of inspiration.

We tend to consider it a bureaucrat's task to regulate what needs to be shared. Something architects should not deal with. But regulations are powerless when designers are not willing to share form, and much less needed when they are. In absence of architectural cooperation, formal rules are the symptom of a pathology rather than its solution.

Our ideological heritage as makers of the exceptional monumental building, eschewing local thematics, seeking top-down control and idolizing self-expression is entirely outdated. It stems from the time when the Renaissance architect escaped the common field to create a new architectural tradition based not on local customs and habits but on general networks of style: from Palladianism of the sixteenth century onwards to the International Style in early modern times. For many generations it was a glorious liberation of creative powers in what became a global culture. But with the advent of modernity we were called upon to shape everyday environment for a new future, thereby returning to what we came from, five centuries ago – this time not to be subject to it, but to invent it anew. Unfortunately, we did so without realizing that this new task posed a formidable new methodological challenge, and that as builders of monuments we were not able to take it on.

Once we acknowledge this fateful misalignment, we understand why methodology remained outside the realm of architectural theory and education. Method comes to the fore when designers want to interact and cooperate. As long as we think of architectural design as an act of self-expression only, and believe that creativity is diminished rather than stimulated by interaction among designers, our profession will be stranded with an outdated self-image that keeps us poorly equipped for the cultivation of everyday environment.

Sources

1 The Open Building network was formed in 1996 as W104 under the umbrella of the CIB (International Council for Research and Innovation in Building and Construction).

2 For an overview of 132 projects, see Stephen Kendall and Jonathan Teicher, *Residential Open Building*. London: Spon, 2000. For a more recent record of projects, see the overview prepared by Professor Jia Beisi of the University of Hong Kong (http://open-building.org/archives/booklet2_small.pdf.)

3 NEXT21, an experimental project initiated by the Osaka Gas company. Design team: Professor Yositika Utida,

Meiji University; Professor Kazuo Tatsumi, Fukuyama University; Associate Professor Seiichi Fukao, Tokyo Metropolitan University; Associate Professor Mitsuo Takada, Kyoto University; Shinichi Chikazumi, Shukoh-Sha Architectural and Urban Design Studio.

4 Professor Kazunobu Minami, Shibaura Institute of Technology, Tokyo: "The New Japanese Housing Policy and Research and Development to Promote the Longer Life Housing," paper delivered at the CIB W104 Conference in Bilbao, Spain, 2010.

5 Among many others: Architect Frans van der Werf, Molenvliet project, Papendrecht, the Netherlands, 1974; Professor Kazuo Tatsumi's promotion of "t wo-step housing" in Osaka, Japan; Professor Ottokar Uhl, Dwelling of Tomorrow project, Hollabrunn, Austria, 1976; Georges Maurios, Les Marelles project, France 1975; Lucien Kroll, La Mémé student housing, Brussels, Belgium 1974; Arch. Nabeel Hamdi and Nicholas Wilkinson, PSSHAK, Adelaide Road project, London, UK, 1979.

6 Arabianranta compettition project, won by Esko Kahri Architects in close cooperation with Tokoman Data Co. Sato development company, investors, pilot project completed 2004, 78 units custom-designed for sale.

7 INO Intensive Care facility, Inspelspital Hospital, Bern, Switzerland, 45,000 m². Client: Canton Bern Office of Properties and Buildins, Giorgio Macchi, director. Primary system: Kamm Architekten; Secondary System: Itten + Brechbuehl; first half completed 2011. The two-system approach is now the standard at the Canton Bern Office of Properties and Buildings.

8 Multifunk Building, Ijburg, Amsterdam. ANA Architecten; developer: Lingotto Vastgoed; 2006.

9 Frank Bijdendijk, director of Het Oosten, a non-profit housing corporation in Amsterdam. The first phase of the Solids project in IJburg, Amsterdam, designed by Baumschlager & Eberle, was completed in 2011. Another Solid in Amsterdam West, designed by Tony Fretton, was built in 2011.

10 Despite its popularity with students, Christopher Alexander's Pattern Language did not lead to a methodical application of the concept in support of professional cooperation but has mainly been used as a catalogue to pick and choose from in individual design.

2016
CULTIVATING COMPLEXITY
The need for a shift in cognition

Editors' Note: *This is Chapter 4 in the book Complexity, Cognition, Planning and Design, Post-proceedings of the 2nd International Conference, editors Portugali, Juval and Stolk, Egbert. Springer Proceedings in Complexity, 2016.*

Abstract

Cities and towns are the result of acts like building, renovating, maintenance and adaptation that continue over time. This makes them behave like living organisms of considerable complexity.

Closer examination allows us to distinguish two kinds of complexity. Contemporary construction is about the combination of a large number of subsystems that not only enclose spaces and hold up loads but also, among other things, distribute power, water, and gas; cool, heat up and circulate air; remove waste and serve communication. Each subsystem is available in a variety of alternatives. This technical complexity has produced a professional culture that itself has become increasingly intricate and self-referential. By comparison, historic built environments were the result of much more constrained material conditions that could nevertheless produce very sophisticated solutions. Their complexity was not technical but the result of continuous small-scale change over time in direct response to inhabitation.

We live in a period of transition in which an entirely new material reality must learn to serve the millennia old ways of human settlement. This chapter argues that this is not a technical problem. It demands a re-examination of our professional culture.

1. Field control

The apparently effortless complexity of traditional human settlement patterns has always fascinated me. Evidence of their variety is still available. We are of course familiar with the urban fabrics of Cairo, Venice, Amsterdam and many other famous cities, and the 'vernacular' fabrics of Mediterranean hill towns have attracted architects for generations. Much can be learned from studies of the extremely complex Middle Eastern historic fabrics that emerged for millennia from bottom-up control processes by social consensus. Age old ways of settlement can still be visited today like those of the Indonesian and Malayan kampongs. The extensive spontaneous self-help urban growth around today's rapidly developing mega cities are worth serious attention exactly because they have much in common with historic processes.

Then there are old maps: those still available from historic cities in Europe, from the early settlements in North America, and the colonial cities in Latin America as well as the famous huge map of Beijing in 1748 where bays of every pavilion in every courtyard house are shown. And of course, records of the excavations of Pompeii and Herculaneum as well as Classical Greek towns present detailed evidence of towns inhabited more than two thousand years ago. All these examples of human settlement suggest a one-to-one compatibility of social and material structure; a marriage that recurs across a variety of scales and patterns, as well as across millennia; showing both longevity and resilience.

All these fields of settlement – or built environments, as we now call them – have an organic quality.

They follow implicit laws that nobody invented but which framed professional experience and innovation.

Contemporary built environments are so different from historic examples that Modernist ideology can be excused for thinking that comparison with them was no longer relevant. According to it, we just live in a new and fundamentally different world.

But history moves slowly and, while architectural styles change and building techniques develop, there is no reason to assume that patterns of human settlement which have persisted for millennia in spite of wars, migrations, natural disasters and very different cultural values, can suddenly be dismissed as no longer relevant.

My generation was probably the last to have personally experienced the seduction of Modernist ideology. After the Second World War architects and other professionals believed sincerely that built environments could be conceived from a blank slate. I remember how, when I was a student, one of our renowned teachers, whose name I will not mention, declared with passion in an academic meeting that if we failed to design the right city for the future a third world war would be inevitable. And nobody laughed . . .

Over five hundred years ago Leon Battista Alberti declared that a surge of 'wonderful creativity' had created a new professional – the Architect – free from ingrained habits, who could invent entirely new kinds of buildings. From the 1550s Palladio became the outstanding role model. The new professional designed villas for the rich and palaces for the nobility, the church, the town hall, the castle and other projects of public importance as products of a single creative individual. Meanwhile, the everyday environment took care of itself in the age-old way, using accepted typologies and growing according to collective values. Traditional master builders continued to operate as their fathers and grandfathers had done, adapting to new circumstances and social preferences in their own deliberate and unassuming way.

Modernity changed that happy co-existence. Industrialization brought workers in ever larger numbers to the rapidly growing cities. New ways of building and management rendered historic examples obsolete – or so, at least, was the generally accepted opinion. For the professional reared in the tradition of innovative artistic intervention, the everyday environment was no longer a stable background that would take care of itself: it became a design problem to be solved.

This remarkable shift was virtually completed after the Second World War. It is a safe bet that at least 95% of architecture students will spend their professional lives designing mostly, if not exclusively, for the everyday environment. This turn of the professional role never caused us to question our ability to deal with a fundamentally different task in terms of skills, knowledge and judgment. The result is a disturbingly contradictory ideology.

Today, anything that can be built can be "Architecture". Yet we cling to the idea that its task is to make the special thing in defiance of precedence. How can everything be special?

In the mid 1960's, my fascination with built environments, both historic and contemporary, made me ask myself what basic properties they all share. A quarter century later I published a first attempt to answer the question;[1] We need to understand what made built environments bloom and adapt to daily life for thousands of years. If we expect the medical doctor to know how the human body works before operating on it, we must equally understand how built environments live and stay healthy before we intervene in them.

In the book mentioned above I look at the built environment as the result of patterns of human control. Control of physical things is defined as the ability to change them, and control of space the ability to refuse entrance to it. Control, therefore, equals the ability to intervene, which makes the observation of change and movement the key to our study of environment.

This approach is not new. Observation of transformations is the most common way to study nature. Patterns of form behavior reveal an inner structure. We need not know the intentions and meanings of the agents who exercises control, but we must look at what happens to the built environment as a result of their actions.

In terms of control, inhabitation means both the control of a space and the control of things in it. This combination of control I will call a 'control field' or just 'field.' Thus 'field control' is the kind of control exercised by the inhabitant party over its space and the things in it.

The office worker's cubicle and the personal belongings brought into it make a control field. So do the homeowner's house and garden and their contents, the space in a rented apartment and the occupant's furniture and other belongings in it, as well as the public spaces and public buildings that a municipality is responsible for.

Control of space is territorial. It is about deciding who and what may enter it. Field control also includes control of material things. We do not only allow things to be brought in our space, but also determine their location within it as we combine them into larger configurations.

A control field is local by definition. As such, it constitutes environmental energy. The sum of a built environment's control fields makes it 'live' and 'behave'.

Of course, other modes of control are exercised in built environments: The homeowner who rents out a space for profit is not its inhabitant and does not control a field but reduces local inhabitant control of physical things to furniture and personal belongings. A *builder's control* is temporary and limited to manipulating material things within someone else's territory. He comes from outside and when the job is done leaves what he made where he made it. *Commercial control* is about buying and selling spaces or things and generally dislikes territorial boundaries as obstacles in its desire to move things to where customers are. It cannot constitute the integration of space, things and inhabitation that makes a *living field*. *Design control* is also temporary and can be exercised on behalf of a field control party or a commercial party. In an ideal world controlling parties feed, serve, and help improve fields.

Field control causes the environmental complexity that we admire in historic built environments. In its smaller scale manifestations, it represents the 'bottom up' process that is often considered desirable for environmental quality. It produces a complexity that is natural and spontaneous and, by definition, responds to inhabitant values and needs. No two individuals ever act in exactly the same way. Hence the more field control is distributed among many inhabitant parties, the greater the variation in form that results, and the more we will experience a built environment as complex. Also, the more these variations are thematically similar in their individual differences the more environmental complexity strikes us as the result of a coherent culture of inhabitation.

Historical complexity was achieved with extremely limited technical means and available materials. Yet it appears that our contemporary built environments, in spite of their undeniable technical and form making energies, are less complex than their historical counterparts. Compared to the natural and fine-grained variety exhibited by the historical examples that we know about, our most advanced contemporary environments appear repetitive and uniform: a sure sign of the absence of small-scale field control. However, the environments we produce today shelter a society that prides itself on individual freedom of choice and self-expression. This betrays a misalignment between our present social culture and its physical environment.

This misalignment is not universal. In most parts of the world people live and work in the age-old way of the single dwelling containing one or two families, often combined with a workplace or store. But in contemporary large-scale construction projects, built volumes must shelter populations the size of entire neighborhoods or small historic towns, and inhabitant initiative gives way to centralized professional control. The result is repetition of uniform windows, facades, floor plans and entire buildings. This cannot be the harbinger of a future culture. Why should small-scale field control have become so suddenly obsolete, after successfully serving human life for millennia? It is more reasonable to believe that we find ourselves in a period of transition in which we have yet to learn how to trigger fine grained patterns of field control with the managerial and technical abilities of our age, thereby producing truly complex environments that have never been seen before but nevertheless show kinship to historic examples.

2. Hierarchy of control fields

The examples of field control cited earlier suggest a hierarchical order among them. A member of a household may have a private room into which others have no unbidden access. Similarly, the room rented out to a boarder is a territory of its own included in the landlord's domain. That shared domain, in turn, is found within a larger one as well. An apartment building or a gated community or, less clearly defined, a street or neighborhood all are fields that contain a number of dwellings as smaller control fields which are included in, and contribute to, the whole. Such collectively inhabited entities are, in turn, part of the entire municipal field. Hence the spatial order of control is one of inclusion. A territory resides in a larger one and may contain smaller ones. As for material things, the control of access that comes with a territory means that what reaches the boarder's room must first cross boundaries of larger fields. The city may refuse the boarder the right to carry a firearm, while the landlord may forbid him to bring in cats and dogs.

The hierarchy of inclusion among control fields may differ in depth from one culture to another. To reach the front door of a suburban villa from the public street only one territorial boundary must be crossed, against two to enter a similar house in a gated community. The apartment in a high-rise building is two territorial crossings away from the street compared to one for the townhouse on that same street. Historic fields like those of Cairo and Beijing to mention only two, had gates that guarded access to entire streets and even neighborhoods making for deep territorial hierarchies.

The concepts of 'public' and 'private' turn out to be relative depending on the direction in which we move. The boarder leaves her private room to enter the house's hallway, stairwell and communal living space that make a 'public' space shared with other inhabitants of the house. Those who leave the house step out into the street which is the public space of a larger field relative to which the entire house is a private space. Hence in any territory we may find included spaces that we call private and a space which is 'public' to all territories that can be reached through it. But such a 'public' space is 'private' to the larger territory in which it resides. In other words, the space we find ourselves in is considered public relative to territories it gives access to and private relative to the 'outside' space it has access to. This phenomenon is reflected in the a-symmetric function of a gate: we can close it to what comes from outside but at all times it allows us to come out into that outside space.

The territorial hierarchy puts control fields in a 'vertical' relation to one another. Neighbors visit one another by way of two vertical crossings: out into the shared public space and down again into a private space. We avoid a direct 'horizontal' crossing of boundaries: it is generally 'not done' to step into a neighbor's backyard from one's own, and consequently no gate is found in the fence between the two.

But there are 'horizontal' relations among neighbors as well. The have to do with shared values. The material configurations that we control reveal our personal preferences, needs, and means, but also the values we share with neighbors. Shared forms, types and patterns, betray horizontal relations between inhabitants operating on a same level. They make an environment coherent and we identify ourselves by the way we personally interpret them.

3. Weakness of contemporary fields

Aspects of hierarchy

When we rent a unit in an apartment building, we are in full territorial control behind the front door but have material control only over the furniture. In a hotel room even, the furniture is part of higher-level control. If furniture is all we can manipulate our level of control is weak indeed. The owner-inhabitant of an apartment unit is able to knock out partitions, set up a new bathroom or change the kitchen. When we own and inhabit a villa with its own garden, our degree of material control is stronger still.

Even with a horizontal sharing of values no two control parties will act in the same way; the result will be variety from control unit to control unit. When all the doors in an apartment corridor are the same in shape and color, we know they are centrally controlled. The identity of a controlling party is not important. Central control can be collective: a board representing lower-level inhabitants can decide all front doors will have the same color.

When field control is widely distributed, variety is the natural result and is experienced as complexity. Centralized control makes for repetition. When operating on a single level of intervention it can frame lower level variety: An office tower can have a uniform curtain wall facade and a wide variety of occupant floor plans inside.

In residential projects, high-rise and low rise, central design control often stretches over several levels with repetition and uniformity of floor plans as result.

The proliferation of technical systems

It is often argued that contemporary construction is extremely complex and therefore needs centralized control to be successfully implemented. The complexity mentioned in such cases has nothing to do with field control. Over the past century building practice increasingly became the combination of numerous technical systems, including: different kinds of load bearing systems, facade systems incorporating a variety of environmental control techniques, diverse partitioning systems, an almost infinite choice of sanitary and kitchen equipment and, most complicating of all, a proliferation of options for service systems such as water, gas, heating, waste disposal, electric power and modes of communication. These service-systems are buried in walls and run above hung ceilings or under raised floors. Each sub-system had its own specialized workers coming into and leaving the construction site. Choreographing all these parties increasingly taxes the abilities of managers, rule makers, designers and other professionals.

The distribution and combination of the many new material sub-systems remains a technical coordination problem, and has created ingrained specializations the management of which, in turn, is the main excuse for centralized control. As a result, technical coordination (or rather, the lack of it) and management complexities (ever on the increase) prevent rather than stimulate true field control distribution. By definition, unsolved technical problems cause technical complexity – and thus a constraining kind of complexity. This must be distinguished from the complexity caused by distribution of field control which is a sign of freedom and opens up possibilities.

Invisible territorial control

Perhaps the most intriguing question arising from a comparison of historic and contemporary built environments is why the latter entirely lack architectural expression of gates and boundaries as means of territorial control. In the historic city the elaborate presence of gates – both functional and symbolic – was the pride of inhabitants and a major factor in defining its architecture. The present absence has nothing to do with absence of territorial control as such. The very fact that our contemporary environment is increasingly equipped with all manner of devices, electronic and mechanical – often hidden and always unassuming – to alert the fearful inhabitant is proof that today's citizen does not feel safer than his forbearers in history, yet expression of gates and boundaries is no longer part of our culture.

The modernist architectural ideology was one of total free space without boundaries. Of course, transitions from inside to outside and from light into darkness are aspects of architectural form that all schools teach, but these are mainly used to create a spatial experience rather than to express control. The means of closure and control of passage do not inspire the designer and their application is apologized for by the user as only a necessary intervention.

An explanation for this baffling observation remains to be studied but it may be relevant to note that among professionals it may come down to our own territorial instincts. We love 'public' space to be a product of our intervention in the city and tend to reduce open space that citizens take care of themselves because it reduces the scope of professional control. We prefer unfenced front yards to increase the public realm and prefer collective backyard space in urban blocks over its subdivision in private gardens. In the US, suburban culture front yard fences are frowned upon as 'not done' and, where allowed elsewhere, are rarely considered as means of urban coherence by designers. The historic environment however, as a bottom up product, sought to minimize public space as dangerous and costly to control, and guarded its backyards by placing buildings right at the edge of public space. The result was that streets and squares were full of people and enlivened by social interaction.

4. Spontaneous emergence of field control hierarchy

Human nature will eventually assert its ways, adjusting new technology and managerial skills to its preferences. An increase of territorial depth can be noted in contemporary environments wherever lower-level field control asserts itself. I cite five examples of this resurgence of depth in field control at a range of scales:

The two-level office building

When in nineteenth-century Chicago steel structures, the elevator and other technical inventions made the high-rise office tower possible, it soon became profitable for the building owner to rent out parts of the volume to various companies. In the course of time this distributed interior subdivision was perfected both technically and legally. In the US, and increasingly across the world, the occupant company rents empty floor space and has a designer of its choice design a layout while a designated fit-out contractor will install it. The building's owner remains in legal possession of the collective base building and (sometimes) the custom fit-out, but design control of the latter is delegated to the occupant thereby creating a two-level hierarchy.

The shopping mall

A similar development took place in the design and construction of the shopping mall in the mid-twentieth century. Its public spaces are centrally planned and maintained. Empty space is made available for retail to be fitted out by companies who are thoroughly familiar with their customer's needs.

Two-level apartment buildings

A network of academics, practicing architects, managers, and politicians has advocated and implemented the two-level approach in residential construction for decades. It was formalized in 1996 in Tokyo as the W104 Open Building Implementation, a commission within the CIB (International Council for Research and Innovation in Building and Construction). The group continues to meet every year in a different country to discuss research and executed projects.[2]

However, where professional power is weak, age old bottom up control re-asserts itself in new ways. In Moscow, in recent years, developers built upscale apartment buildings that were expensively equipped and decorated, ready to be occupied. They found that first buyers had their new property entirely emptied and new fit-out installed by a designer and builder of their choice. Appalled by this wasteful process, and seeing an opportunity to reduce costs and risk, they began to sell 'empty' or 'free plan' buildings, leaving their customers to take care of their own interiors. Hundreds of such 'empty' buildings for the upscale residential market are on record in Moscow and other Russian cities.[3]

The gated community

Hierarchical field control is found in the emergence of 'gated communities.' Worldwide, upmarket neighborhoods have fenced in their collective territory as a 'bottom up' response to municipal inability to offer security and service to its citizens. Urban designers tend to criticize the concept for reasons that are unclear. After all, a modern high-rise apartment building is no different in terms of field control hierarchy from the horizontal gated community. I suspect urbanists see the gated community as a partial privatization of what they consider to be their field of action. Moreover, as we have already seen, gates jar with the professional ideology of free-flowing space that leaves territorial ownership invisible.

The informal sector

Whenever the individual house is on its own lot, we have a unit of traditional field control. This is still the case for the majority of built environments across the world. Obviously, personal field control is alive and well where affluent citizens can afford to own both land and house. But much more significant are the extensive stretches of land around major cities in the less affluent areas of the globe where people build for themselves. In many cases, do-it-yourself production, often on land inhabited without legal ownership, encompasses more than half of the housing stock of cities such as, for instance, Cairo, Rio de Janeiro and Mexico City. This kind of settlement is labeled 'informal' by politicians and the professional world, and usually tolerated grudgingly if not actively opposed.

It is worth noting that these self-build processes make use of the latest technical products: cement, steel reinforcement rods, sanitary and kitchen equipment, sheet glass, roofing materials and all manner of piping and wiring find their way from the sophisticated industrial sector to the informal market, where products are bought piece by piece to be installed in a house that may take years to be completed – and will often be expanded repeatedly after completion to cater for a growing family. If any proof is needed that small-scale field control is compatible with contemporary industrial products we need look no further.

5. Fine grained field control and sustainability

Perhaps the most important argument for encouraging a hierarchy of field control is found in the recognition that it is the basis for environmental sustainability. The lower levels of such a hierarchy enable a fine-grained structure of small control units that can adapt efficiently and quickly to the latest technology, as well as to new social trends. The higher levels of the control hierarchy secure longevity and stability by taking care of what can endure. I cite three new initiatives that move in that direction:

Long term investment

Frank Bijdendijk, former director of a not-for-profit housing corporation in Amsterdam says that two conditions must be met to ensure long life for a building: that occupants are free to change and adapt their own units, and that they love the building they share.

Buildings that people love, he argues, will not go away. He calls such buildings 'solids.'

Bijdendijk decided that his company's long-term ownership of buildings justifies higher initial investment that will pay for itself over time. Assuming a use-life of a century allows initial investment in higher quality design, materials and detailing. An auction of empty floor space for rent in the first building they designed according to this policy yielded the necessary income for its upkeep,[4] supporting Bijdendijk's theory. Of course, how we can predict that people will love a building remains to be seen. We must learn about that over time when feedback from individual users will help us to find out what people really like in a given case. Without that feedback we will remain in a professional echo chamber.

The long-life housing act in Japan

In December 2009 the Japanese National Legislature passed a law to encourage a lifetime of up to two centuries for residential construction. The law includes a document listing the technical conditions that must be met by homeowners to receive a substantial tax break. These technical requirements are based on the view that a contemporary building is a composition of sub-systems that each have their own use-life. Ideally, these systems should be combined in such a way that each can be replaced over time with minimal disturbance of other sub-systems. The use-life of sub-systems is either determined by wear and tear or by inhabitants' preferences. Examples of the latter are kitchen and bathroom systems that must yield to the more attractive look and feel provided by newly available products. An example of a sub-system whose use-life is determined by wear is the vertical main drainpipe in an apartment building, rated by the 2009 Act as having an ideal lifetime of 50 years. To facilitate its replacement, an extra space must be available in the utility shaft for a new pipe to be put in place before the older one is taken out. Moreover, that shaft must be accessible from a public corridor or hallway near the apartment entrance because it belongs to the public realm of a collective building. In short, this law demands no technical innovation, but the sophisticated design and management needed for hierarchical field control.[5]

A fit-out industry

The drive for a truly sustainable environment has spawned a large number of inventions, as the industry searches for materials and sub-systems that perform according to current sustainability criteria. In order to have a meaningful impact on real world conditions such inventions must reach the existing stock of dwelling and work units. To make this possible, three conditions must be met: each such unit must have a replaceable fit-out, it must be a single control unit so that its renewal does not depend on a collective or centralized control, and it needs an industry that can replace its fit-out – in whole or in parts – efficiently and speedily. The first condition can generally be met with state-of-the-art systems. The second condition means that the larger apartment or office building must have at least a two-level control hierarchy that allows the single dwelling or work unit to change independently. The third condition, by and large, has already been met by most office buildings and retail stores, but for apartment buildings a new dedicated fit-out industry is needed.

The first Fit-out company dedicated to the renovation of extant housing stock is NEXTINFILL in Japan, initially part of Sekisui Heim housing division but now an independent company. Developers working on renovation projects have begun to sign contracts with this company to do the fit-out, one-at-a-time, when a unit changes hands. NEXTINFILL is also active in new projects, in which the units are usually identical. But clients who buy one for immediate occupancy will be able to adapt it over time when needed. Those who desire a custom fit-out design will prefer to buy space in an empty base building to have the fit-out industry serve them individually.

The potential market for this new industry is substantial. The cost of a fit-out replacement is roughly comparable to the cost of the cars owned by the inhabitants and a twenty-year use life for a fit-out package is generally assumed reasonable. That makes for a fit-out industry which is comparable with the car industry in terms of market size and financing of the product.

That fit-out industry makes a sustainable environment possible where each dwelling unit is individually capable to accept the latest technical improvement as soon as it is available. Such an environment will have a complexity comparable to historic examples.

6. Design for everyday environment

Everyday environments demand that architects and their clients accept conditions that are fundamentally different from those that framed their work in the past.

Whereas traditionally *change over time* has been the enemy of architectural creation, we now must embrace it as a fourth dimension to work with. It used to be the sign of avant-garde design to make each construction entirely different from any other one, while now the aim must be to share values with our peers to achieve coherence between designs and their larger environment. Full 'top down' control is seen as a necessary means to achieve quality but, as discussed earlier in this paper, a healthy living, built environment needs multiple levels of design control.

Various architects have decided that distribution of design control offers opportunities for a new kind of architecture. Their executed works encourage 'horizontal' variation and introduce new 'vertical' relations. For our purpose, stylistic considerations are not the issue and can vary greatly, but the methodological aspects exhibited by the following cases are of interest, and represent a new way of working:

The continuous base building

In the early 1970s architect Frans van der Werf built the 'Molenvliet' residential neighborhood following the two-level approach, separating a 'base building' for long term use from short term 'fit-out' of the individual dwelling units that made it up. He designed a single low-rise high-density base-structure that was deployed as a continuous urban framework with which he shaped a variety of urban spaces like streets and courtyards.

This could be done without monotonous repetition because the resulting urban spaces could vary in size and shape while the inside of the structure and parts of the facades could vary over time in response to user preferences. In this way of working the continuous base structure transcends the building level to become a design tool on the urban scale. It suggests a new way to do very large projects that are nevertheless fine grained and invites a new kind of urban design. The Molenvliet project in the city of Papendrecht, the Netherlands, was the first fully executed Open Building project for a not-for-profit housing corporation that made floor space available for rent. Inhabitants could determine the size and location of their unit and take care of its interior fit-out. Virtually unknown in the Netherlands the project is still visited by architects from abroad. Frans van der Werf has since executed some eight other Open Building projects.

3D Urban design

Today we build single buildings that house populations equal in size to a Classical or Medieval town. For all practical purposes these structures act as three-dimensional urban frameworks. In Japan, Professor Yositika Utida was asked by the Osaka Gas Company to lead a team to design the 'housing for the future.' Embracing the 'two-level' approach, he considered his urban block size base-building design to be what he called 'three dimensional urbanism.' His team conceived of a carefully worked-out scheme of public pedestrian circulation connecting a communal garden on ground level with another on the roof. The dwelling units could vary in size and be fitted out individually. In line with the urbanist analogy, Utida invited thirteen professional architects to design the individual residential units after the completion of the collective structure.[6] This division of design tasks, one directly serving individual households and the other the collective of inhabitants, nicely makes the point that inhabitant control is not necessarily a matter of do-it-yourself action.

The three-level institutional building

Architect Giorgio Macchi saw in the distinction of levels of intervention an opportunity for a radically new project management model. As Chief Architect of the Canton (province) Office of Properties and Buildings in Bern, Switzerland, he acted as client for the province's public buildings. When asked to lead the design and construction of a new intensive care hospital he introduced a rigorous separation between the 'primary system' that had to last a very long time, a 'secondary system' for interior spatial distribution that would remain unchanged for less than 20 years, and a 'tertiary' system for medical equipment to be used for up to 5 years. First, a competition for the primary system was called without any program given other than the amount of floor space needed. After the construction of the winning scheme had started, ten architecture offices with experience in hospital building were asked to compete for the design of the 'secondary' and 'tertiary' systems. The rationale for this approach was that designing and building a hospital takes an average of seven years, which renders any program written in the beginning obsolete halfway through the construction period. Moreover, during the lifetime of the hospital costly adjustments and changes were to be expected every few years. The separation of levels of intervention would reduce time and costs during both construction and renovation. On the experience of this project the entire Canton Building Office administration was turned around to routinely apply the separation of levels approach for all buildings under its supervision. So far more than twenty projects – university buildings, health care, housing and other types – have been realized using this strategy.[7]

Open building design management

When a developer wants to offer custom-designed apartment units, a well-conceived data management is vital to making the two-level system work well. In 2002 a competition was called by the Helsinki municipality for an Open Building project to be executed in a coastal extension known as "Arabianranta." The winning proposal was submitted by Esko Kahri Architects in close cooperation with Tocoman data processing company. Together they submitted a design and also a data processing system that could help would-be inhabitants to design and budget their individual units and pass on the necessary technical specification to the builder. The Sato real estate development company took on their winning scheme, most likely not expecting financial gain from an experimental design. However, when the project was completed – in time and within the budget, with all units sold and custom designed – Sato had made a profit and offered a contract to Kahri and Tocoman to continue this approach. Recently in 2013, architect Kahri was invited by Hartela Construction Company to participate in a competition as OB expert. Their proposal was selected for the very large and long term FINNOO urban development project which is expected to take 15–20 years to complete.

Sharing values

In the Netherlands a practice has emerged in which a coordinating architect is asked to work out an overall urban design and supervise the work of fellow architects invited to build parts of the scheme. The coordinator's task is to make sure that their cooperation produces a coherent result. This kind of 'horizontal' professional cooperation has mostly to do with establishing shared types, patterns and other qualities to frame the design of individual buildings.

A paradigmatic example of this approach is a neighborhood of 1500 houses for which the architect, Henk Reijenga, was asked to work out an initial general scheme and supervise its execution. For the architecture level of design, he defined twelve 'types' of houses to be built, including row houses, canal houses, free-standing houses and duplex houses of various dimensions. He then invited five architecture offices to design two variants for each of the twelve types, after which he distributed the resulting designs in the larger scheme, making sure to mix houses from different architects in a same cluster or a same street. They then collectively decided on seven colors for bricks, a single slope for roofs, three types of roof tiles, a number of entry doorway types and other details to be adhered to. The pre-selection of house types, components and materials made an efficient execution by the builder feasible, while no two of the 1500 houses are exactly the same. Each house has its own identity within a coherent, and sustainably built, urban fabric. In the middle of the recent recession the neighborhood was quickly occupied and financially successful.[8]

7. Cultivating complexity

Modernism's explosion of science and technology has unleashed tremendous energies and produced urban environments of unprecedented size and composition. But as configurations of control patterns, these environments are less complex, less socially grounded and less use-responsive than we might expect. The 'hardware' we are making for our cities appears to be in conflict with a society that prides itself on individual freedom of expression, action and choice. I have suggested that we find ourselves in the middle of a long period of transition in which design and management are slowly learning how to match technical power with social structure and stimulate the human energies of settlement that have always shaped our built environment. The examples in the previous section are evidence of new design processes that can lead to a more socially driven interaction between people and their habitat, resulting in a sustainable architecture that adequately serves contemporary social complexity.

It has often been pointed out that erecting a contemporary building of any size, given the variety of materials and the many subsystems it combines, is a demanding process. This is not to say that construction in past times was primitive. To the contrary, historic building techniques could attain marvelous levels of sophistication honed by generations of practice. Technical sophistication and social structure reinforced one another. Our forefathers would be amazed by the number of material sub-systems that must be brought together in even an ordinary contemporary building. They might well sympathize with our struggle to keep the technical job under control. It is therefore more correct to say that, so far, technical *complications* have prevented us from arriving at the *environmental complexity* that historic environments display so effortlessly.

The usual answer to the lack of inhabitant control is that we do not yet have the advanced technology to deliver a more responsive environment. But the new ways of working mentioned in this paper *are* already responsive to occupant intervention and desire for choice and have all been successfully executed with currently available technical means. However, they all required an overhaul of ingrained design and management habits. The problem is not the hardware, but the profession's reluctance to re-organize itself.

We instinctively resist change. We stick to our ways of working for the good reason that one becomes vulnerable and mistake-prone when we can no longer rely on the familiar. Inventing new technology is also much more attractive than dropping acquired habits and questioning procedural conventions. In building practice, moreover, every professional task is intimately connected to what others do, so changing how one works demands a willingness by other parties to cooperate in the new. Thus, the impulse is to continue working the way we are used to even when evidence shows a better alternative.

While society has progressed substantially, our management and design methods have become outdated. Early last century, when lack of decent shelter for a substantial proportion of the population challenged the professional world and labor was relatively cheap, solving the housing shortage relied on workers trained to handle a specific subsystem. Carpenters, plasterers, painters, plumbers, installers of heating systems or ventilation ducts, to name only a few of the sub-systems to be installed, moved from one unit to another repeating the one act they were familiar with. Each team was preceded and followed by other specialists doing something else on the same site. The choreography of these various actors, some of whom had to return at a later stage but none of whom saw through the entire end product, became a major management task. This repetitive and fractured mode of operation was erroneously inspired by the conveyor belt production of the original Model T-Ford automobile as the hallmark of an efficient industrial production.

Applied to building, it required the exclusion of direct inhabitant involvement, a prerequisite which has shaped professional thinking for more than a century. As a result, we struggle as a profession to imagine how inhabitant control could contribute to the quality of built environment.

It has been demonstrated that, with the more advanced subsystems available today, a team of two or three trained multi-skilled workers can fit out an entire dwelling unit in a couple of weeks. This was convincingly demonstrated in an Open Building renovation project for a not-for-profit housing corporation in the town of Voorburg, the Netherlands more than three decades ago. The new fit-out industry in Japan follows this more efficient and cost-effective way of working, using available hardware and up to date logistic capacity to do the job. Moreover, there is no need for the repetition of a single design since each dwelling unit is treated as a project in its own right, matching the basic control unit of the household, and can differ from any other one.

The fact that small-scale control in today's big projects demands first of all delegation of design control does not diminish the importance of industrial innovation. To the contrary, when the dwelling unit and the work unit are active control fields, they stimulate innovation, as well as reward it by individually absorbing technological advances without the controlling mediation of central management. User control does not depend on new technology, but successful technical innovation does depend on fine-grained user control.

Nevertheless, while wholesale adoption of this alternative is technically possible, it demands more than just yielding reluctantly to a new reality that can no longer be ignored. A fundamental – and willing – cognitive re-orientation of the profession is needed.

Design and technology cannot make built forms live; only occupancy can. Fine-grained field control at the scale of the household and the work unit will breathe life into the entire environmental body. Enabling the energy of occupancy to do its part must become an essential subject of professional skills. When we respect the built environment as a truly living entity, we can make it bloom. It will pay to see ourselves not only as builders who make environmental things but also as gardeners who know how to cultivate a living field.

Sources

1. Habraken N. J. (1998). *The Structure of the Ordinary: Form and Control in the Built Environment*, ed. Jonathan Teicher. Cambridge: MIT Press.
2. See "Residential Open Building" by Kendall and Teicher published by E and FN Spon, 2000, as well as a more recent series of about 80 executed projects collected by Prof. JIa, Beisi, of Hong Kong University, available online: (http://open-building.org/archives/booklet2_small.pdf).
3. Goldhorn, B. (2003). *The Free Plan, Russia's Shell-and-Core Apartment Buildings, Project Russia 20*. Moscow and Amsterdam: A-Fond Publishers.
4. This first 'Solids' is located in Amsterdam West and was designed by architect Tony Fretton for the not-for Profit Housing Corporation "Stadgenoot."
5. Prof. Kazunobu Minami of Shibaura Institute of Technology reported on the "Long Life Housing Act" at the Open Building conferences in Noordwijk, the Netherlands, in 2010 and in Bilbao, Spain, in 2011.
6. Osaka City Next 21 experimental housing project, 1993. Design: Prof. Yositika Utida, Prof. Kazuo Tatsumi, Associate Prof Seiichi Fukao, Associate Prof. Mitsuo Takada. Arch. Shinichi Chikazumi and his Shu-Ko-Sha Arch. & Urb. Design Studio.
7. INO intensive care hospital, Bern, Switzerland. Primary system 1997 by Peter Kamm and associated Architects. Secondary and tertiary systems by Itten Brechbuehl Architects. See also Kendall, S. (2008). "Open Building: Healthcare Architecture on the Time Axis." In *Sustainable Healthcare Architecture*, eds. Robin Guenther and Gail Vittori. New York: Wiley and Sons.
8. Westpolder-Bolwerk project, Lansingerland municipality, the Netherlands. Urban design and architectural coordination by Henk Reijenga Architecture and Urban Design bv.

2017
BACK TO THE FUTURE

Editors' Note: *This essay was published in AD: Loose-fit Architecture – Designing Buildings for Change (guest editor: Alex Lifschutz) 05/vol. 87 / 2017/. It was among the last invited essays the author wrote, and brilliantly summarizes many of the concepts, WAYS OF SEEING and ways of working that have occupied him over his career.*

When I visited Dammam, Saudi Arabia, in 1985, I was taken to a neighborhood of some 20 identical high-rise apartment buildings standing in open space with carefully designed parking facilities, playgrounds, lawns and flowerbeds. The entire project looked as if it had been finished just yesterday. No inhabitants could be seen anywhere.

I learned that it had been built a few years earlier to show the world that Saudi Arabia could do modern housing as well as Western countries could. When it turned out that no Saudi citizen wanted to live there, the project was fenced in and immaculately maintained to be proudly shown to foreign visiting professionals.

Here was the ideal modern housing project, exactly as it had been designed and not marred by the inevitable tokens of everyday life: laundry hanging from balconies, dirty stairwells nobody feels responsible for, public lawns partly turned into private vegetable gardens or invaded by fast-food sellers, parking lots used to take apart and repair vehicles, and so on. This pristine example demonstrated the way designers like to think of their work.

Today, the architectural profession makes a living by designing not only housing, but also workplaces, schools, facilities for sports and recreation and many other kinds of buildings that together make our everyday environment. Anecdotal experience suggests a fundamental difference between the everyday environment as a living organism and the desire of architects to make art.

Early in the past century – under the pressure of entirely new ways of building and unprecedented demographic changes – the everyday environment became a 'problem' to be 'solved' by design. But when architects turned towards these tasks, they did not change their ways of thinking and doing. Suddenly everything could be 'architecture.' They were driven by the rational functionalism of the Congrès Internationaux d'Architecture Moderne (CIAM) and had a profound disdain for historic examples of urban fabric.

We now worry about the rigidity and coarseness of contemporary environments, discuss long-life loose-fit and aspire to 'sustainability,' but remain largely unable to design for the social dynamics of the everyday environment. We have not yet learned how to do that.

It is true that, with the retreat of Modernist ideology, the architectural profession has slowly, albeit often reluctantly, tried to adapt its ways to a poorly understood reality. More explicit knowledge and particular skills are needed to successfully design attractive, healthy, adaptable and lasting urban environments. We are in the middle of a long period of transition towards a new professional role, and housing is at the heart of it.

In Renaissance times, Leon Battista Alberti first described the architect as the inventor of entirely new kinds of building, a person to be distinguished from the traditional master builder who was bound by customs and familiar typology. Andrea Palladio's genius most seductively applied this new attitude in his lifelong practice. His oeuvre was unprecedented and free from local typology. It could therefore be published and followed by foreign practitioners on an international scale. Architecture became the product of a professional class. Modernism's belief in an 'International Style' had its origins in the 16th century.

After the Albertian emancipation of architecture from the everyday context, two professional cultures coexisted. The everyday environment remained the product of local vernacular. Architecture with a capital 'A' became an international phenomenon and dealt mainly with houses of worship, castles, palaces and monumental villas. This separation was mutually beneficial. Architects could occasionally be inspired by a vernacular in the way an artist can be inspired by nature, but the profession created its own history, one that has been carefully recorded as a major expression of art.

Figure 1 *Neighborhood new Hamamatsu-cho station, Minato, Tokyo, 2008. An example of the countless state-of-the-art high-density everyday environments in the world that the majority of today's architects and urban designers depend on for a living.* Photo Credit © John Habraken

Modernism changed this peaceful co-existence. New techniques disrupted familiar ways of building, residential typology was considered outdated, and the emerging power of logistics and management developed in the Second World War to move and equip millions of soldiers promised efficient production at a very large scale. Soon the building professions decided that history did not offer any lessons for the new problems they faced. They aspired to design a New World.

That aspiration was irresistible. It promised huge profitable projects. Never before had the design profession held such hubris. As an architecture student at TU Delft in the early 1950s. I remember one of our prominent teachers calling out in a public meeting that if we failed to succeed in our mission to shape the future, a third world war might be inevitable.

At the same time, however, housing was not considered real architecture and could not be the subject of a design studio. Our teachers, among whom were Jacob Bakema, Jo van den Broek and Cornelis van Eesteren, were busy doing large housing projects that were never discussed in school. But designing a villa was considered a good task for beginners. I asked Van Eesteren to let me do a project for him, and he gave me a site, asking for a high-rise apartment building on it. This was, of course, a design lesson, not a housing exercise. Only in the late 1960s were a few radical students permitted to graduate on a housing project.

Learning from the past

Modernism's ideology allowed a romantic admiration for the coherent complexity of environments like Venice, 17th-century Amsterdam or Mediterranean hill towns. Aldo van Eyck's love affair with the Dogon settlements of Mali is legendary. However, this admiration did not lead to questions of comparison with contemporary practice. For instance, while architects generally admire the Georgian domestic fabric such as that at Bedford Square in London where the Architectural Association (AA) is found (see Clare Wright's article on the AA of this issue), the question of how eight former dwellings came to accommodate an entire professional school without disrupting the coherence of the local environment is seldom raised in discussions about loose-fit and flexibility. Modernist ideology kept us ignorant of specific qualities of the everyday environment. Some of those qualities are briefly mentioned in what follows.

Historic settlements could deal with partial change over time, allowing them to endure over centuries in a coherent manner. Function always was a variable in the life of an environmental fabric. Form did not follow it but had the capacity to accommodate functional change. Nevertheless, architectural education today takes it for self-evident that a studio task starts with a functional program. In short, the dimension of time is not part of architectural theory nor of education.

Several years ago, architect Andrés Mignucci and I ran an international workshop in Barcelona for young practicing architects and urbanists. As a warming-up exercise the class was divided into groups of five or six, and each was given an urban block in the city's celebrated 19th-century urban expansion, which was built following Ildefons Cerdà's proposal. The students were asked to identify what the buildings in their block had in common. As they were trained to look for something special, this turned out to be an entirely new and bewildering experience for them.

We discussed how even Antoni Gaudí's famous Casa Milà ('La Pedrera'/'The Quarry') building (1910) shares many thematic features with the other buildings in the neighborhood, such as the typical access by carriage to an internal stairway leading to the main floor, space for shops and workplaces animating the pavement, the structural bay size and story heights.

Figure 2 Antonio Gaudi, Casa Mila, Barcelona, Spain, 1910. Notable for its unconventional appearance, this building, also known as 'La Pedrera' – the Quarry – nevertheless fits thematically into the architecture of Ildefons Cerdà's famous 19th century plan for the extension of the city. Photo credit: © Thomas Ledl

Built environments follow particular architectural values that we identify as types, patterns, themes or systems. Yet today's dominant belief in invention and originality discourages designers from sharing these forms. Of course, refusing to observe an environment's thematic qualities is an accepted way of working, but to actually follow such qualities is not. Christopher Alexander's proposal to work with patterns in 1977[1] is still read by students but did not trigger any additional theory about sharing form, except, perhaps, the 'form-based codes' movement in the US and its advocates elsewhere. When the spontaneous desire to share types and patterns is absent, outside agencies seek to impose coherence by regulation, which in turn meets resistance by designers who dislike them.

Historically, thematic coherence was partly the result of a lack of technical alternatives, and local vernacular was the only language one could work with. In today's world, coherence of thematic variety does not come easily by itself. To achieve it, a deliberate choice must be made. We need to study how types, themes, patterns or architectural systems are shared, and must have the skills to apply that knowledge as part of normal practice.

The most striking difference between the urban fabrics that we make today and those of the past has to do with territorial markings. Gates and other means of territorial crossing abound in the historic fabrics of all cultures. They were important means of thematic architecture. Their absence today does not mean that territorial structure is no longer important. Indeed, the abundance of technical devices that protect and control 'our' space in the world, often deliberately kept invisible, is amazing. Contemporary territorial structure may well be different from any example from before the motorcar was introduced, but that does not explain why it is no longer a basis for architectural elaboration and a means of social identification.

Territorial control in the historic urban fabrics always led to minimal public space and maximal private space. The former was unsafe and expensive while the latter could be profitable. Buildings were put right at the edge of public space to make good use of backyard space, and to keep vegetable gardens and animals out of sight and well protected. This produced crowded public spaces and encouraged semi-public gated courtyards for social collectives, causing deeper territorial hierarchies. By contrast, contemporary designers like open space floating freely around buildings, and instinctively seek design control over the largest possible part of the earth's surface.[2]

Proper distribution of design control leads to variety. Shared typology, or patterns or systems, produce coherence. Control of all design decisions by a single party in a particular area soon results in repetition and uniformity. Partial change and variety come naturally when individual inhabitants control their own space. The question as to what can be decided individually and what should be held in common naturally arises. When we seek a neighborhood to settle in, we ask ourselves what we will share with our neighbors, and the answer to that question is often decisive. When many individual parties operate in a particular area without any sharing of values, incoherence will inevitably result. Finding a proper balance in the distribution of design control and the sharing of thematic form makes coherent variation possible.

All complex organizations distribute control on different levels. Traditional environments usually have public space, streets and squares, as the higher-level framework in which buildings find their place. Modernist urbanism distributed buildings into unshaped spaces and, if space was shaped, then this was only the by-product of the way that buildings had been located. Hierarchical clarity was lost, urbanists and architects found themselves making decisions on the same building for different reasons, causing confusion and design tension. On the other hand, advocates of bottom-up processes often fail to recognize the need for a higher-level party – be it one selected from among themselves or invited from outside – to shape and control a collective framework within which individuals 'can do their own thing.'

Everyday life seeks hierarchy. A commercial office building leaves the design of its interior space to the tenant's architect. The large 'building' becomes a two-level part of the continuous environmental hierarchy. The shopping mall is another example. Normally, increasing size and complexity trigger increased hierarchical depth.

Contemporary residential construction ignores that rule. In present housing design, dwellings, or as they are mostly known 'units,' have predetermined interior layouts. The layout defines the distribution of structural elements as well as of piping and wiring. It is also the basis of cost estimation and government approval. In other words, the floor plan must be there from inception to enable most other professions to play their part. Making all layouts the same saves work for everybody, whereas withholding the floor plan at the early stages of design disrupts a century-old professional culture and methodology.

In the Netherlands, this outdated philosophy was initially the result of revolutionary legislation in 1902 that made money available for low-income tenants via not-for-profit housing corporations. Governments, as well as investors such as pension funds, want to make sure their money is well spent, and the inhabitant was not considered a reliable party. This heritage has shaped an entire building industry that argues that allowing the inhabitant individual control is more expensive. The opposite is true, as has been demonstrated by recent open building projects discussed by Stephen Kendall in this issue of *AD*.

Working with the everyday environment

The everyday environment tells us that we must be able to deal with change and make time the fourth dimension of design; to encourage designers to share thematic forms; to appropriately distribute design control; to understand the relation between complexity and hierarchical depth; to give the inhabitants or users their own level of intervention within the environmental hierarchy; and, finally, to understand territorial structure, the control of space, and how to design for it.

It is a tall order, but professionals are slowly beginning to meet these demands.

The international Open Building Network promotes the idea of a level of intervention for residents or users in the environmental hierarchy. This network of academics and practitioners has about 350 members from some 30 countries. Kendall's article gives an overview of the most innovative projects over a period of four decades. It shows how in the last 10 years, initiatives in practice have come from clients who see economic advantage in the approach because short-term control by the user results in longer life and better long-term investment returns for a building. He also references Japan's Long-Life Housing Law of 2008, which recognizes the hierarchical nature of building construction.

In the Netherlands, a 'supervisory' architect is often appointed for the management of urban development to make sure his or her peers, who design the buildings, follow thematic forms to assure coherent variation in an entire neighborhood. There is also a trend to bring the user into the process. Some of these initiatives are taken by municipal governments, but many are taken by architects, developers, private investors and user groups. The trend is unmistakable, but poorly documented, which, in fact, is the traditional way for everyday environments to renew themselves.

Ultimately, well-informed and skilled designers will integrate several if not all aspects of the everyday environment into their projects.

Henk Reijenga's ongoing low-rise, high-density Westpolder Bolwerk project – an extension of the town of Berkel en Rodenrijs, the execution of which began in 2005 – has 1,500 dwellings. No two buildings are exactly the same, but design and implementation were nevertheless organized in an efficient manner. Early on, a handful of building types were defined by Reijenga, and the architects under his supervision collectively selected the materials, colors and details. For all three phases, a team of four or five architects each did several designs of each of the defined house types. The distribution of these varied designs was then decided by the supervisor. The urban design also shows a thematic variation in the combination of well-defined urban elements like streets and canals of different kinds. The project was implemented within budget, and the first part was successfully occupied in the middle of the 2008 recession.[3]

Figure 3 Henk Reijenga, Westpolder, Bolwerk, Berkel en Rodenriis, the Netherlands, 2005 – This is an example of a street within Reijenja's 1500 home residential extension of Berkel en Rodenrijs, with fine-grained distribution of design tasks and thematic architectural variation. No two buildings are exactly the same. Photo Credit: © Robbert H Reijenga

Sjoerd Soeters and his firm PP HP (Pleasant Places Happy People) carried out the urban design for the Copenhagen Slusenholmen waterfront renovation, for which they deliberately reduced the amount of public space by surrounding urban blocks on two or three sides with open water, and increased territorial depth by arranging houses around collective courtyard space over underground parking. As supervising architect for Sydhavnen, the southern part of this masterplan and the first part of it to be executed (in 2009), Soeters distributed the design of the facades for the terraced houses among some 30 architects, suggesting a few key thematic ingredients. To this day he still receives fan mail from residents.[4]

Figure 4 (Pleasant Places/Happy People), Sydhavnen, Sluseholmen Waterfront renovation, Copenhagen, 2009. Photo credit: © Sjoerd Soeters/ PP HP, photo Daria Scagliola and Stijn Brakkee. View of the Sydhavnen neighborhood showing the thematic variation of the facades. Note also the public space on only one side of each block, the vaulted bridges breaking the cubic space, an entryway to a courtyard inside of a block with cars going down into the sub-courtyard parking, and pedestrians entering the courtyard on level.

Challenging academia

Until now, the development and endurance of human settlement in harmony with social reality has always occurred in an implicit way. Yet, given our professional involvement today, a more explicit approach must be possible. Without educational programs, more generally accepted theories and more research, our arrival at a harmonious professional engagement with the everyday environment will take a very long time. In closing, I mention the three most important academic tasks we need to pursue to successfully cultivate it: study the built environment as the living organism that it is; increase its hierarchical depth to include the autonomous dwelling unit; and teach the specific skills needed.

We must build a body of knowledge. We seek help from a medical doctor because we trust he or she knows how the body functions. The medical profession collectively improves that knowledge by experience, research and careful documentation. Similarly, lawyers share knowledge of the law and seek to improve it by experience, debate, social consensus and careful formulation. The design professions lack collectively maintained knowledge of the way the built environment behaves over time because they do not see it as a living organism with its own laws. We are the only profession that has no formally documented body of knowledge about the subject of its interventions. Yet we do intervene.

Sustainability demands an increased hierarchical depth that allows each dwelling unit to adapt individually over time. This is not only advantageous for the inhabitant, but allows renovation whenever a single unit needs it, which, of course, is the case with any freestanding suburban house. In other words, the autonomous dwelling should be considered the living cell in the environmental organism, and its autonomy an essential requirement for keeping existing stock up to date. Environmental sustainability demands that every dwelling can be renewed, improved, accept new technology or follow new cultural priorities in direct relation to what the market has made available.[5]

Once transformation over time is recognized as the fourth dimension of design, professional education might begin by teaching students how to follow themes by making variations; how to propose types, patterns and architectural systems to be accepted by a peer group; how to determine the capacity of built spaces to hold a variety of functional arrangements; how to figure out the best way to distribute design control among peers; how to guide spatial design by territorial knowledge; and how to express identity by the design of territorial crossings.

There is nothing in these skills that inhibits outstanding design.

Notes

1 Christopher Alexander, Murray Silverstein and Sara Ishikawa, *A Pattern Language: Towns, Buildings, Construction* (New York: Oxford University Press, 1977).
2 Sjoerd Soeters illustrates this trend by examining Colin Rowe's comparison of Le Corbusier's design for Saint-Dié-des-Vosges (1945) with the historic fabric of the city of Parma, Italy. See his post from 4 April 2016 at: http://thematicdesign.org/sydhavnen-sluseholmen-copenhagen-harbour-renovation-project-2000-2009.
3 For a detailed description by Reijenga of the Westpolder Bolwerk design process, see his post from 3 May 2016 at: http://thematicdesign.org/the-westpolder-bolwerk-development-project/.
4 For a detailed description by Soeters of the Sluseholmen waterfront urban design and the execution of the Sydhavnen project, see his post from 4 April 2016 at: http://thematicdesign.org/sydhavnen-sluseholmen-copenhagen-harbour- renovation-project-2000-2009/.
5 For a well-researched argument that the autonomous dwelling unit is a necessary condition for a sustainable built environment, see Frank Bijdendijk's keynote paper at the Open Building Network Conference, ETH Zurich, 2015, titled *The Future of Open Building Resides in the Existing Built Environment* and available at: http://thematicdesign.org/the-future-of-open-building-resides-in-the-existing-built-environment-6/.

2018
THE LURE OF BIGNESS

Editors' Note: *This is an interview with the Habraken by Dirk van den Heuvel (Director of the Bakema Foundation and Prof. at TU Delft), as published in Dirk van den Heuvel (ed.), Jaap Bakema and the Open Society. Amsterdam: Archis Publishers, 2018, pp 298–300.*

John Habraken (1928) is best known for his groundbreaking study De dragers en de mensen (1961, translated as Supports: An Alternative to Mass Housing). Habraken also served on the editorial board of the journal Forum (1964–1971), after the renowned board with Jaap Bakema, Aldo van Eyck and Herman Hertzberger had stepped down. Habraken was also the first director of the Stichting Architecten Research (SAR), an architects' research foundation established by a group of Dutch architecture firms. In 1967 Habraken was appointed professor at Eindhoven University of Technology to establish a new architecture department there. In 1975 he moved to the USA to head the Architecture Department at MIT in Cambridge, Massachusetts. Throughout his career he has propagated the radical transformation of the power structures behind city planning and building production in order to hand more influence to the users.

Dirk van den Heuvel: In 1964 the SAR was established. It was an initiative of a dozen architectural firms leading in the field of housing, among others Lucas and Niemeijer for whom you worked yourself at the time, but also the offices of Van Embden, Groosman, Kraaijvanger, and Maaskant. Van den Broek and Bakema were also involved. It was pretty unusual for architectural practices to set up a joint organization for design research.

John Habraken: Yes, it was unusual in two ways in fact. Firstly, that it was an initiative of independent architects who felt that something had to be done for the future. And secondly that any research institute at all should have been set up. I think the SAR was the first formal research institute in architecture, because in those days research and architecture weren't combined at all. I only realized later on that it was the start of something new. Bakema, along with Van den Broek, was with that group from the very beginning.

DvdH: The SAR and its research program were very much tied to the social challenges of the day of course.

JH: Actually, it was a reaction. It was convened by Leo de Jonge, who chaired the BNA housing study group. De Jonge and his colleagues were concerned about the fact that prefab construction was taking off in a big way – along with the standardization of floor plans – and although architects had plenty of work, they

DOI: 10.4324/9781003011385-52

nonetheless felt they were being marginalized. They no longer had much influence over what would actually get built. Perhaps only the exterior was left to them. It was that concern, both for their own profession of course but also for housing in general, that led Leo de Jonge to call the group together. To see what they could do about it. Jan Lucas, for whom I was working at the time and who took me with him to the first meeting, proposed setting up a research office and said: "If each of us gives the equivalent of a draughtsman's salary that must surely be enough for some research." And that's how it developed.

DvdH: But that research interest, was that already present in the practices themselves? Because with Van den Broek and Bakema, you also see that they used competitions for a sort of investigation of possibilities.

JH: Yes, competitions have always been invitations to launch new ideas and to explore them. In itself, that's a very powerful and legitimate form of innovation in architecture, but you mustn't confuse it with research, where a general question is posed, and you try to find an answer to it. We can distinguish those two important ways in which architects work.

DvdH: So, when you look at Bakema's work, at that time as well, can you detect that interest in research in housing production in terms of systematization or optimization?

JH: I don't think so, because that's one generation too early. We can talk about it in that way now, but at the time it wasn't yet an issue. There wasn't even a vocabulary for it yet. Bakema's generation did have a very considerable ambition and urge to do innovative things. But that was done in, let's say, that very engaged but also pragmatic way of floating ideas and trying to implement them.

DvdH: And the idea of emancipation? Was user emancipation part of your research? Bakema talks about building for an open society, open to different walks of life, and your discourse on supports and people is also about making it possible for people to design their own living environment. That entails an aspect of emancipation, which was very important in those days.

JH: I took a very critical view of that back then. It was a time when mass housing, with its uniformity, worried everyone to some degree. And that's what gave rise to that discussion about emancipation and participation. But when I took part in such a discussion and at a certain moment brought up my point of view saying: "you can only change that if you give individuals the power to make decisions about their own houses," that was the end of it. You always met with opposition from the architects. There was a very strong emotional reaction to this notion: architects claimed they were obliged and had the right to design the floor plan for the sake of architecture. However, they were prepared to listen to the people. But we said: we're not talking about participation; we're talking about control. That is a political matter of course and it always caused a parting of ways. That also held for the architects who were members of the SAR's executive board, including Bakema. People felt that it went too far, they couldn't imagine how it would work. So that resulted in a rather ambivalent situation.

DvdH: So, in fact the idea behind Supports: An Alternative to Mass Housing was far more radical than the welfare state which was then in the process of being set up?

JH: Yes, it was actually formulated in direct opposition to it, because the approach to housing construction in those days, and even today to a large extent, was a top-down situation. The 1901 Dutch Housing Act had made it possible for money to flow from government downwards. Consequently, they wanted their money to be controlled by professionals, and the whole idea of the residents themselves being involved went by the board. So, the entire system was actually geared to total control of the project by the professionals.

DvdH: It seems as if there's a fundamental tension between democracy and architecture, it's something you hear from a lot of people. From Aldo van Eyck as well, as if at a certain moment, as the one who takes the decisions, he collides with full participation. Somewhere there's a limit.

JH: That's certainly true. I tried to address that in my book Palladio's Children. How is it that today's architect has difficulty working with the everyday environment? We come from a tradition of doing the exceptional buildings and in that tradition three things were important. The first: you were against change. The building should remain standing as it was. Second: You had to be able to control the process from the top down, because otherwise the quality would suffer. And third: You had to do your own thing and collaboration with other architects led to compromise. Before Modernism the architect has always been the maker of the exceptional building, the rest of the built environment took care of itself. And that tension is precisely what you are pointing to now. Everyday environment demands a fundamental change in the attitude of the architect which has never been clearly discussed.

DvdH: The other issue at play is hierarchy. As an expert in the design and construction process you know that it takes several steps to achieve realization. The 'support/infill' concept is in that sense itself a hierarchical model. But hierarchy and democracy are at odds. In the 1970s in particular, with the anti-authoritarian trend, hierarchy was just not accepted.

JH: Yes, but that was based on a misunderstanding. All complex and big organizations are hierarchical. It's inherent. There are always problems that relate to the whole and other problems that relate to smaller parts only. The built environment has always been hierarchical. We've always acknowledged it in our profession because you have planners, urban designers and architects and that's never been denied. Later on, when buildings got bigger and bigger, we started to say that you have architecture and infill which adds another level to the environmental hierarchy. So, the recognition that the built environment as an organism has a hierarchical structure has always played a role. And I think you muddy the waters by saying that that's not democratic. The point is that in the profession we divide our responsibilities on different levels to make the increasingly complex

DvdH: environment more flexible and manageable.

JH: Jaap Bakema wrote in the 1970s, because he went along to some extent with the participation business, about 'deciding from bottom-up'. He embraced it but also added, "it's going to make the whole process extremely complicated."

JH: Yes, that's typical of that generation. Participation is like motherhood, it's impossible to be against it. You can't say: I'm against people taking decisions, that people get involved and so on. It's just not on. So, all you can say is: "it'll get more complicated." Certainly, it'll get too complicated. Therefore, it means that the existing way of working as a professional has to change. Everybody finds that very difficult because it makes you vulnerable. And that's what it comes down to at a certain moment. We're not talking about technical matters; we're talking about a professional structure that needs to overhaul itself.

DvdH: There's another aspect, and that's the architect's artistry, or how the architect handles formal idioms, or gives a particular task visual form. That was part of what Bakema called the 'function of the form'. You see it very strongly for example in his monumental plan for Stadt on Pampus, in which the mass housing task is given a very strong visual expression. Where is the role of the architect in this new formulation of his position in the process?

JH: Yes. In my view, it becomes much more interesting, and the architectural possibilities are indeed much more interesting. I concede that a great many people think that it represents an impoverishment, but that is not the case. To show what I mean, I've just held a lecture in which I showed some ten projects worldwide by architects who worked according to this new approach. In other words, with change, with a division of powers of decision and with the introduction of variation.

DvdH: But to go back to that Pampus Plan, in the early 1960s, the heyday of the paternalistic welfare state, how did you view it back then and how might you view it today? You were also one of the Forum editors when it published a special issue devoted to Pampus.

JH: Bakema asked whether it could be published, and we felt we should do it, because of course it was something that would generate a lot of discussion. I had my own doubts about this approach; it struck me as typical of that generation, that on the one hand people saw and happily grasped the opportunities for very ambitious approaches and projects, and at the same time the question could be asked, as you yourself said, how that could be reconciled with the paternalistic top-down situation. This project was of course an illustration of that ambivalence. But we didn't doubt for a moment that it should be published, because it would also prompt this discussion.

DvdH: It was before the Bijlmermeer was built. That massive, megastructure-like district south east of Amsterdam comes closest to that kind of ambition.

JH: Yes, exactly, that is indeed in the same category. Once again, the ambivalence of those days, on the one hand the lure of the big project and the power, and on the

DvdH: other hand the debate about the user who falls by the wayside.

JH: Yes, the users were referred to as the 'anonymous client.'

DvdH: There were all kinds of nice formulas aimed at maintaining your way of working and at the same time responding to these concerns. Actually, that has always characterized the work of the architect with respect to the everyday environment.

JH: And to what extent did the fact that society as a whole was keen for new and modern architecture to play a role? Because Pampus was in a way a new concept for the Dutch landscape, for you see all kinds of affinities or continuities in it, with the famous Ruisdael Dutch landscape: the horizon, the ditches and the polders. But very modern and progressive.

DvdH: Yes, it was very much dominated by the notion of the 'clean slate.' That instead of trying to fit in with the existing, you started afresh. Making a new world. That was really typical of that generation.

JH: In what respect did the way SAR address the issue of mass housing differ from that of Team 10.

DvdH: In the last instance in the sense that we wanted to accommodate the idea of user control, the party of the resident, and that Team 10 persisted in beating around the bush. 'We all have to do it, but how do we do it so that people like it?' That sort of thing. The reason I didn't find it interesting was that it was a dialogue among architects. About how you're all busy improving the world or carrying on a CIAM tradition. To my way of thinking at that moment – and I was young, too, and then you tend to have very radical opinions about things – I didn't think it was relevant anymore.

JH: What I find most interesting about SAR, Supports and the Team 10 stories, and certainly Jaap Bakema and the open society, is that interest in open processes and the quest for a different relationship with the user.

DvdH: I totally agree with you there. When you look at it today in light of our post-postmodernist period, and in the wake of the star-architecture, you realize that back then there was a debate about society and architecture – whatever you might say about it and however different various opinions of it might be – that was ongoing, in which architects were involved. And that has vanished completely. Luckily, as you said yourself, there's renewed interest in it among the younger generation. In that sense the present period is interesting, as a whole and in all its nuances.

JH: When you look back, Bakema as architect succeeded not only in being very much engaged in thinking about those big social issues, but also in ensuring that the office worked on that kind of project and built a reputation for social engagement. In that sense he was not an avant-garde architect, but rather someone who could almost be said to have embodied the welfare state.

DvdH: That's right. Among those of his generation he was the one who struggled most with the ambivalence of that period: the forces in housing construction, professionalization and industrialization on the one hand, and architectural ambitions on the other hand.

2021
OPEN BUILDING
A professional challenge

Editor's Note: *This essay was published in a book titled Baumschlager Eberle Architekten, 2010–2021, edited by Dietmar Eberle and Eberhard Tröger and published by Birkhauser, Basel, Switzerland, in 2021.*

Introduction

When mass housing became a universal means to deal with both post WWII reconstruction and the relentless worldwide increase of urban populations, the obsessive uniformity of its products triggered the idea to separate the collective 'base building' from the inhabitant-controlled 'fit-out.'[1] Like motherhood, freedom for the user cannot be argued against, but professionals pointed out that it was complicated, too expensive, and inefficient and therefore decided that, regrettably, it could better be ignored. Designers often felt that Open Building limited the realm of architecture and inhibited its quality.

Generally, it was considered a radical concept without precedent. But some of us sought to learn from historic urban fabrics, attracted by their spontaneous sophistication. Examples that are still with us have maintained complexity and adaptability for centuries in an apparently effortless manner. We now know that the Open Building idea is not an avant-garde proposal but a return to what always was a basic condition for settlement: the dynamic interaction between dwelling unit and social unit. What we build today defies that form-to-inhabitation interaction to a large extent. We value individual freedom of expression and personal control more than any known culture in the past, but contemporary big projects offer shelter in rigid and unresponsive physical environments. Open Building wants to bring back a lost energy in the settlement process and do so in a way that is compatible with the means and needs of contemporary society.

Already in 2000, a book titled *Residential Open Building* by Kendall and Teicher[2] listed some 120 projects worldwide, the earliest of which is from 1975. No one has counted the many projects completed after that publication, but more importantly, the process of their emergence has changed. In the beginning, as experiments go, such projects were considered unfit for large-scale adaptation. In the past decades, however, the most interesting cases were initiated or approved by clients who expected economic benefit from their investments. Moreover, today I am alerted from time to time to projects done by people who never heard of an "Open Building" movement. This relieves me from once more arguing the inevitability of this approach and encourages me to write open building without capital letters. In this essay, I want to discuss the open building approach's potential for a new architecture in general, not just for housing, and for a better use of industrial production. I will show projects that enhance architecture's range, use technology well, and created fine-grained big projects. What follows reflects personal impressions. I hope to show that new and successful ways of working challenge professional skills.

New hierarchical organization

The separation of fit-out from base building creates a hierarchical relation. The base building is a stable form within which individual settlement can be introduced and change over time. We have here the introduction

DOI: 10.4324/9781003011385-53

of new levels of design intervention in the organization of built environments. Environmental hierarchy is familiar to us. Professional designers always identified themselves by it: urban designers make a higher-level context for architects to build buildings, in which interior designers work in spaces architects have designed. Highways and other transportation infrastructures create yet higher levels of form making. In general, more complex forms have deeper hierarchical organizations. The practice of open building splits the traditional building level into two autonomous levels of design. It enables the management of large projects of a fine-grained complexity. It also opens new kinds of environmental organization.

Frans van der Werf, the author of the first formally recognized open building project[3], completed in 1975, understood that a base building could, by itself, become a continuous three-dimensional framework with which urban spaces are shaped. He used the idea to make an arrangement of urban courtyards half of which were accessible from a street as collective territory of the residents who could access their units from them; the other half were collective backyard spaces subdivided and maintained by the residents living around them. This arrangement could make a continuous three-dimensional megastructure the size of a true urban field that nevertheless provided a human scale environment. It avoided monotony because it could produce a variety of sized and shapes for courtyards and dimensions for streets and alleys, while, on a lower level, van der Werf introduced wood-framed façade openings in the brick masonry exterior of the base-structure that inhabitants could subdivide to their personal preferences. These openings could contain windows, doors and wall elements filled with glass or opaque panels. In this way, the levels of fit-out and base-form came to meet in the exterior surface.

Frans van der Werf's project demonstrates two new levels of intervention. There is not only the fit-out level as such; but the base-form is neither a building nor an urban design in the conventional sense. Although of an urban design scale, it is an architectural presence while, at the same time, it pre-empts the building of free-standing buildings. In other words, his project does not only introduce a fit-out level but replaces the traditional building level with something else.

Architect Hans van Olphen was asked to turn an abandoned industrial harbor area into a high-density residential neighborhood.[4] The site sloped between the water's edge and a six-meter higher road at the periphery of the town center. A two-story garage got partly buried in the slope, its top surface level with the upper road. On the harbor side, at the edge of the garage, runs a two-story commercial strip with an arcade behind a four-story façade wall. This combination follows the water's edge for some 250 meters. On top of the garage and behind the facade wall were built apartment buildings, some four to six-stories tall, around various urban courtyards. These residential buildings and the courtyards that they share make for a conventional urban design that contains different buildings by different architects.

We can distinguish the different levels in the hierarchy of design intervention. The garage structure together with the arcade and arcade wall, designed by van Olphen himself, make for the highest level. The arrangement of the residential buildings and the urban courtyards is an example of conventional urban design that could be done n different ways in the given context. The apartment buildings themselves are the next lower level of design intervention with the fit-out level as the lowest level possibility. In this scheme, we find another urban framework of architectural presence, this time approaching the scale of infrastructure and allowing an infill of buildings and collective spaces.

These two examples demonstrate how new hierarchical organizations occur when we want the large project to result in a fine-grained living whole. There is no single good solution fitting all situations, but in all cases, we seek to link the lowest level of individual inhabitation to the highest level of environmental infrastructure by a number of intermediate levels of design intervention.

Not only must these levels be defined, but each time their boundaries need to be carefully considered anew. For instance, Frans van der Werf's façade solution created a meeting of fit-out and base building in a new way. Hans van Olphen predetermined the location of elevator shafts that allow residents to reach their units directly from the garage. This makes these shafts part of the higher-level framework and an extension of public circulation around which the actual buildings were designed. Apartment buildings behind the continuous urban wall interact intimately with it. A hierarchical environmental organization creates 'vertical' relations between designers operating on different levels. This does not tell us who may be the design agent. Fit-out can be designed by the user or a professional designer. Houses have been designed by their occupants, local builders, master craftsmen and, since the Renaissance, by architects.

Eventually, new hierarchical organizations may create new kinds of professional designers. Professor Yositika Utida, the leader of the design team for the famous NEXT21[5] experimental project for Osaka Gas Company, called his five-story base building which filled an urban block a 'three dimensional urban design' and he took the logical step to invite 13 other architects to design the dwelling units in it. In all cases, an environmental hierarchy makes a designer relate 'upwards' as well as 'downwards.' One must abide by the decisions made on a higher level and create space for design variations on a lower level. Top down full control of all details of the large project is replaced by a well-conceived delegation of design tasks on different levels and the management of their interactions.

Capacity

The open building distinction raises an interesting methodological problem. When confronted with two alternative proposals, how can a client for a base building know which one serves best a given target population? This question is also valid in any vertical design relation. Higher level decisions are always based on assumptions of lower level use. On the urban design level, plot size and setback rules are based on expected and desired types of buildings. On the residential building level, more than a century of housing design has yielded a range of familiar unit types that can help shape the base building. But in each type the designer of a base building must assess its capacity for a representative range of fit-out variations. Design studies have provided formal methodological means that can help a well-trained designer to analyze a buildings' capacity for fit-out variations of a desired quality.

There is no need in this essay to go into a methodological discussion, but the concept of Capacity must be mentioned because assessing it requires the ability to think in variations. On each level of the environmental hierarchy, we must generate a representative range of possible variants to assess what our design offers to those who inhabit what we created. The ability to think in variations is an empowering skill. We can no longer zero in on a single 'best' lower level solution and repeat it to shape our higher-level form but must consider thematic variations that we want to be possible. Types, patterns and systems are venerable concepts as themes with which we develop variations that can be sketched out or notated quickly. Any formal method to assess capacity is only a tool to use this basic skill more efficiently.

Shared values

So far, the discussion among open building advocates has focused mainly on enabling individual expression on the level of inhabitation, but people also care passionately about the values they share with others. Before we decide to settle somewhere, we scrutinize the physical and social qualities that our potential neighbors have in common. Sharing forms and doing your own thing are two sides of the same coin.

The question as to what forms should be shared on a lower level dominates higher level design, and this makes the judicious handling of patterns, types and systems of all kinds an essential design skill on any level. Dealing with this question is not only a matter of higher-level form making but can also lead to imposing rules on lower level design. In urban design, for instance, lower level themes are often translated in actual rules to be followed by architects. Set-back dimensions, height restrictions, façade patterns and materials as well as entryway patterns are translated in rules. Designers working on the same level of intervention may also seek consensus on shared thematic aspects to assure coherence of the whole. The same constraints imposed from a higher level can be the subject of horizontal agreement.

Architect urbanist Henk Reijenga did the urban design for a scheme for fifteen hundred houses in the Netherlands and supervised their design. The execution of the entire urban field[6][7] was done in three phases. While the streets, canals, parks and other public spaces of one phase were under construction, five architects were invited to do the buildings for it. Reijenga composed a list of a dozen 'types' of houses. These were actual variations on familiar concepts, like 'row-house,' freestanding single house,' 'duplex,' and so on that were further differentiated by variations in things like mode of access, size, height or parking. Each team member was asked to design two variants for each of the twelve 'types.' To achieve coherence of the whole, the team also agreed on a detailed list of constraints. For instance, roofs would have a slope of

45 degrees and a choice of three kinds of roof tiles. Six colors of brick were selected, and details, color and material of all window frames were standardized while their dimensions and subdivisions were free. A number of entry door frames would be chosen from as well as several colors for the front doors themselves. Another purpose of these constraints was that the builder of the entire project could expect a known limitation of details, materials and colors regardless of differences in their actual design. The result was a production of 1500 houses of which no two are the same, executed in an efficient building process without surprises. In spite of an ongoing recession, the entire new neighborhood was quickly occupied.

The success of the scheme was to a significant extent due to the fact that no design rules were imposed by the municipality or the developers but that architectural constraints were the result of teamwork under peer management and therefore were followed willingly and creatively.

Time

By and large, higher level forms last longer than lower level forms. Use life, particularly on the fit-out level, is not only the result of wear and tear but also a matter of preference. The use life of a base building can be much longer than that of a residential fit-out. Important economic and managerial consequences can be drawn from that fact. Frank Bijdendijik,[8] director of a not-for-profit housing corporation decided that the base building can last a century or longer. This makes a long-term investment feasible with a larger initial building budget which, in turn, allows for a higher quality of detailing and use of more expensive materials while still turning a profit over time. Two projects in Amsterdam[9] were initiated by him following this new investment strategy made possible by the 'levels' distinction.

A radical distinction of use life was applied with the design of a large intensive care hospital in the city of Bern, Switzerland.[10] Architect Giorgio Macchi, the director of the building office which acts as client for public buildings in the Canton Bern, initiated a competition calling for a 'primary system' which had to last a century. A functional program was only provided with the winning scheme was already under construction and a second competition was called. Ten experienced hospital design firms were invited to submit a design for the 'secondary system' which had to last no longer than twenty years and the 'tertiary system,' being the equipment, replaceable after five years. Convinced of the long-term efficiency of this approach, Macchi reorganized the entire Canton office to make this way of working standard requirement for all buildings it is responsible for.

In Japan, the importance of the dimension of time was confirmed in a national law, issued December 2009 to stimulate the erection and maintenance of housing that can last up to two centuries. A technical committee scrutinized the use life of the many subsystems that make a residential building and prescribed conditions that facilitated their replacement with minimal disturbance of other subsystems. Owners of dwellings that satisfy those requirements receive a substantial tax break.[11]

Process management

When the municipality of Helsinki called a competition for an 'open building' solution for some six hundred units in a new coastal extension the winning scheme was submitted by architect Esko Kahri in combination with the Tocoman building data processing company[12] They had decided that a base building design was just half the answer, the other half having to do with supporting the would-be owner in selecting the location and size of the dwelling units and the design of the fit-out including the selection of finishes and the accounting of the costs. From there, the data on materials and details had to be provided to the builder. In other words, a system of unified execution was made compatible with the inhabitant's personal preferences. Sato development company was found willing to take on the winning scheme and we can safely assume that they did so without expecting to make a profit of this unusual project. However, the entire job was completed at both levels on time and within budget. Sato and made a profit and offered Kahri a contract to repeat the experiment.

A fit-out industry

Yoshikazu Adachi in Tokyo founded NextINFILL, the first residential fit-out system formally put on the market. Its primary aim was the one-at-a-time renovation of privately-owned units in post-WWII apartment buildings. After cleaning out a to-be-renovated apartment unit it will install a carefully prepared, custom-specified fit-out package. Development companies who empty entire apartment buildings and fix up the remaining base building not necessarily getting inhabitants involved prefer the single-party service over subcontracting interior finishing in the traditional way. Demanding a variety of floor plans and easy adaptation in the future is an additional bonus. In new construction, it is similarly invited to do the fit-out.

There are now companies in the Netherlands who study so called 'cyclic' fit-out where the fit-out company leases the custom-made package remaining responsible for maintenance and responsive to demands for change. It is in such a company's interest that the product needs little maintenance and that used components and materials are recycled.

The potential fit-out market is comparable in size and unit cost to the personal car market, with likely a somewhat longer turn-over time. A fit-out industry's investment pattern and management structure including a bank supporting loan system will also be more comparable to the car industry than any building industry.

An institutional challenge

Examples like those cited above can be dismissed as incidental and have so far failed to attract a mainstream dialogue. But for those who are familiar with the open building approach, a point of no return seems to have been passed. I already noted that the two-level distinction is repeatedly reinvented by parties who do not know of any formal open building network. In Moscow, for instance, developers of expensive apartment units found that units were cleaned out after purchase by their residential owners and fitted out anew to suit their personal preferences. Appalled by this waste of capital they asked their architects to design 'empty' buildings. Some of those complained and said they expected to do the floor plans again when Russia had caught up to the West. What is still revolutionary in residential construction is already customary in commercial architecture. Owners of commercial office buildings increasingly offer free floor space to be fitted out by office tenants who hire their own architect. In the U.S. large building companies already have their own dedicated fit-out divisions to execute commercial fit-out jobs. The ubiquitous shopping mall of course has institutionalized the two-level separation for more than a half-century and retail companies have their specialized fit-out firms that can renovate a shop's interior in a weekend.

Nevertheless, the building industry, the design professions as well as the financing institutions and government bureaucracies have yet to adjust their ways of thinking and acting to fully use the potential of a hierarchical reality. Top-down thinking dominates, and separation of levels is considered a complication rather than a liberation. In big projects, public/private distinctions are often obscure and confusing. At best, architects are expected to deliver 'empty' buildings rather than 3D urban structures. Real estate investment knows no long-term strategies. We are at the tail end of a more than a century of professionalism that has become outdated. A slow and painful institutional turn-around is setting in. The signals are clear but remain unseen.

Advocates of sustainability have the most to gain. Any new technical invention, new material, or new systematization will be outdated before it is widely applied as long as innovation is limited to new construction and beholden to the control of institutions that are still thinking in terms of massive top-down renovation projects. A true fit-out industry needs to reach the autonomous residential unit without intermediate parties so that inhabitation can respond individually to what is offered. If the transportation industry would be organized like the present building industry, we would have only buses and roads but no private cars.

The introduction of a new level in the contemporary environment is basically a political issue. But a political body can only act on what it learns from the professions. So far, the earlier mentioned Japanese Long-Life Housing Law is the only example where the problem has been addressed on a national level. The international housing establishment has yet to express interest in this half-a-decade old precedent.

Another way to unleash the fit-out level's rejuvenating responsiveness might be certification of fit-out companies somewhat in the way plumbers and electricians are certified. If individual households would know that a custom-made fit-out can be installed quickly by a single party certified to deliver on time and within the agreed price, the fit-out market might come into its own. It would basically do what the handyman is already doing. But the development of the necessary management skills and the accompanying software and logistics knowledge could be enhanced, stimulated and made available by government policy.

We do live in interesting times.

Notes

1. I will use the expression 'fit-out' and 'base building' following an already established terminology in the US as equivalent for the earlier used infill' and 'support' which were the literal translation of the Dutch terms *inbouw* and *drager*.
2. Stephen Kendall and Jonathan Teicher, *Residential Open Building* (London: E&FN Spon, 2000) ISBN 0-419-23830-1.
3. Molenvliet project, city of Papendrecht, Netherlands. Frans van der Werf, Architect, completed 1975.
4. Town of Katwijk, the Nertherlands; renovation of the inner harbor, completed 2002. Hans van Olphen, masterplan and overall design supervision.
5. NEXT21 Project, Osaka, Japan. Client: Osaka Gas Company. Professor Yositika Utida, with Kazuo Tatsumi, Seiichi Fukao, Mitsuo Takada, and Shinichi Chikazumi design office, 1994-present.
6. Westpolder project, Town of Berkel RSodenrijs, municipality of Lansingerland, the Netherlands. First two phases completed in 2013; Henk Reijenga, master planner and design supervisor.
7. The title of "Supervisor' in Dutch urban and architectural practice means a formal appointment to supervise and organize the architectural implementation of a new urban scheme. The supervisor has a say in the selection of architects in coordination with the municipality, developers, and other investors, and can formulate design rules and constraints; in general, to steer designs and deliver a coherent environment. The way that role is interpreted differs widely and depends to a large extent on the supervisors' ability to chair a peer group effort.
8. Frank Bijdendijk, director of the not-for-profit housing corporation Stadgenoot, Amsterdam. He promoted the concept of "SOLIDS," base buildings of high architectural quality that would last at least a century and allow inhabitation for any function, residential and commercial. He is now retired but acting as a general consultant.
9. The 'Furore' SOLID, a 7000 m2 project, was designed by architect Tony Fretton; it's fit-out space was auctioned off in 2011 to a wide variety of occupants, including a small hotel. Two 'Iburg' SOLIDS of 9 stories were built as part of a 7-building project filling an entire city block, designed by Baumschlager Eberle and still in construction when Bijdendijk retired.
10. The INO Intensive care project at the Inspital Hospital, Bern, Switzerland. Primary system design by Kamm and Kundig Architects; secondary system designed by Itten & Brechbuehl architects. For general information about the Canton Office of Properties and Buildings, see Grundstucke & Gebaube (www.be.be.ch).
11. The Law is not yet translated into English. My information is from architect Professor Kazunobu Minami, SMARCHS student, MIT, Professor of Architecture, Shibaura Institute of Technology who was a member of the committee that set up the technical requirements.
12. Location of the 2002 competition building: Arabiantranta coastal section, Helsinki. Kahri & Company (ArkOpen Ltd.), architects with Tokoman data processing company. In 2013, Kahri was invited by Hartela Construction Company to join them as open building expert in a competition for the FINNOO Urban Development project expected to take 15–30 years to complete, which this team won.

2022
OPEN BUILDING AND GOVERNMENT
Lessons Learned

Editor's notes: *This brief essay was written as part of Habraken's long-term commitment to the emergence of an infill or fit-out industry. It sums up his views given recent developments in PR China. At the time of its writing (March 2022) he was in communication with leading architects in the Netherlands, including a past "State Architect" (a former student of his) as well as the new Minister of Housing of the national government, in an effort to inform them about HENENGHOME "industrialized Interior Decoration Company" and its successes in PR China. His intention was to encourage them to learn more by a visit to China and for a Board to make an invitation to this company to visit the Netherlands and to consider expanding to the European market. Information about this development in China initially came to Habraken from Stephen Kendall who visited the company in 2014 and wrote about it in his recent book RESIDENTIAL ARCHITECTURE AS INFRASTRUCTURE: OPEN BUILDING IN PRACTICE. Routledge, 2022).*

In this present essay, Habraken takes what readers may think of as a sharp departure from his long-term concept of user control of the infill. In fact, that is not the case. He now says very clearly that the most important thing to emphasize is the efficient separation of the Base Building and the Infill, and the emergence of a certified industry capable of saving developer's money by delivering one-unit-at-a-time infill. This, he believes, will set the stage for eventual control by users of the infill of their own dwellings leading eventually to an Open Building environment: "Inhabitants are able to take care of their own units of occupancy in time. They can change their dwellings with the help of the fit-out company that installed the unit they currently live in, or they can replace what they have now by an entirely new design, possibly by another fit-out company."

Background

In the European context after WWI, governments decided to make money available to subsidize not-for-profit residential construction. The Netherlands was far ahead of its time, and was one of the first to do this, even before WWI, in 1902. Before that date workers sometimes started to collectively save money to build houses that were made available to participants by lottery. Churches and socialist parties made money available as well, but all that effort did not match the rapid growth of cities, especially in the post-WWII era. To make sure that government money was well spent, bureaucrats, being asked to distribute the subsidy money, wanted professionals to be responsible for its use. Inhabitants were not invited into the process, and this shaped a well-established professional mass-housing culture which became wide-spread in many countries around the world.

About a decade ago the Japanese government issued the Long-Life Housing Law based on the initiative of a now retired minister. It created a new certification system for residential buildings classified as excellent long-term housing.

The law assumed that a building is a combination of technical subsystems that each has their own use life, depending on wear-and-tear or user preferences. The most adaptable building is one where each subsystem can be changed or replaced with minimum disturbance of other subsystems

The law offered technical solutions on the basis of which certification would be based. An easy to remember example is the requirement that vertical drainpipes must be renewed after about thirty years while the building is expected to live more than a century. To meet the requirement, the law suggests that an empty space next to the functioning drain is made available during initial construction, in which to install the replacement pipe. When a building meets all such conditions (including a certain floor-to-floor dimension) the owner gets a predetermined tax break. It turned out that many single-family homeowners took advantage of the law, but so far few if any of the large developers building large multifamily condominium projects have done so, and the Law is considered unsuccessful at least for the latter market. The Ministry of Land, Infrastructure, Transport and Tourism (MLIT), which administers the certification process, is frustrated with the excellent long-term housing system, as only 2% of the 800,000 condominiums for sale between January 2010 to December 2020 have been certified.

Although the tax break in theory enables the producer to ask more money from the owner there is no appreciation or incentive among the professionals to change their ways of working. Japan was the first where various fit out companies were founded, but to judge from what we know, while it promoted change, the law did not encourage innovation. Instead, it told the professions what solutions to implement.

Something very much like this happens presently in most countries around the world, even where the role of government is minimal and the role of private developers is dominant. The inhabitants are not part of the decision-making process, except in the luxury market, and even there it is rare to invite inhabitants to take control because the habits of the industry continue to ignore the value of full independence of individual dwelling units in large projects.

The housing industry worldwide is now a purely professional culture in which now, a full century later, government agencies and private developers negotiate with architects, bankers, sociologists, politicians and other professionals but not the inhabitants.

Addressing housing uniformity and rigidity

From its beginnings, Open Building re-introduced the inhabitants in that culture by proposing that they become responsible for the design and execution of their individual dwelling interior with everything needed to make it habitable. This never happened except in a relatively few well-documented instances.

From its beginning, Open Building has always focused on the role of the inhabitant. This came from a reading of history that tells us that complex living environmental fields always were bottom-up technical results. Small scale initiatives could become rich and beautiful environments that could live and renew themselves for centuries. Uniformity always was the result of top-down visions and belonged for the most part to the special monumental projects.

Only contemporary technology produced everyday uniformity. **We believe that that is a temporary problem that the Open Building approach can deal with.** The fact that everyday uniformity is only happening in the worlds richest and technically most advanced cultures (and not in informal settlements) tells us that the thrust of the original Open Building approach was not basically a technical but a political one.

Introducing the Open Building approach as a technical innovation without getting the inhabitant involved was a brilliant thing to do. This has allowed a new industry to demonstrate how it deals with each dwelling unit as an independent job in which all parts are defined, produced, packaged, shipped on time and delivered on site and installed by a multi-skilled team. This is the case even when the design is repeated many times. At the same time, it does not demand any change in the larger project design, execution, or political ideology, operating like any other subsystem company hired by the familiar project management.

We have learned that an Open Building company has two agendas it can deal with:

- THE FIRST IS TO MAKE THE DWELLING USER THE AUTONOMOUS INDIVIDUAL ACTOR IN AN ENTIRELY NEW MARKET.
- THE SECOND AGENDA IS TO DEVELOP AND ESTABLISH AN INDUSTRIAL FIT-OUT TECHNOLOGY.

We now see that fit-out system companies (called 'industrialized interior decoration' companies) in PR China are entering their market making the second agenda demonstrate its power (albeit not without problems). These companies, encouraged and incentivized by various methods of governmental 'pushing,' are serving both rental social housing and the market of condominium homebuyers. They deliver everything to make an empty space habitable, in one integrated process, from factory to multi-skilled installation team. One of these companies (www.henenghome.com), has delivered more than 100,000 units in less than three years, in both new construction and the renovation of older buildings. Inhabitants have not been part of the decisions. These companies save their clients money, reduce waste, deliver a completed unit in 7 days and offer a multi-year warrantee. They are now beginning to meet the market of individual buyers in their showrooms, for both new construction and the reactivation of existing buildings.

Given this information, we believe that in time, the first agenda noted above is inevitable.

Based on what we now see, it is not a prerequisite to consider the social and political management of a market of autonomous inhabitants; it is not important to talk about user control. Inhabitants remain outside the professional network. But the result is nevertheless an Open Building environment.

Because of the separation of design tasks (one to design the base building and another to design and deliver the infill, thereby severing the dependency between building and floor plans, even use), technically speaking, inhabitants are able to take care of their own units of occupancy in time. They can change their dwellings with the help of the fit-out company that installed the unit they currently live in, or they can replace what they have now by an entirely new design, possibly by another fit-out company.

Over time, the century old professional network will adapt and be able to serve a true Open Building environment.

All this suggests a straightforward government policy:

- ENCOURAGE THE DEVELOPMENT OF NATIONAL OR INTERNATONAL INDUSTRIAL FITOUT SYSTEMS.

These will be product/service system companies that do not need to argue for user control. Instead, they can compete with ongoing housing companies for fitting-out of new or existing housing projects (or conversion of buildings to residential use) with economically competitive services.

If they become available, the market for autonomous fit-out units will develop by itself.

That market will potentially be comparable in size to the automobile market. The cost of a basic fit out unit will eventually become comparable to what a family pays for the cars that it uses.

SHORT WORKS
Conclusions

The words, drawings and diagrams in these 'short works' stand on their own and retain their relevance across decades of original, seminal thinking. We conclude with the following 'end' note from the informal publication in 1988 of *Transformations of the Site* (Awater Press). That book laid out the basic structure of thinking that was later to become *The Structure of the Ordinary: Form and Control in the Built Environment* (MIT Press, 1998).

End?

One cannot visit the site without feeling a troubled consciousness emerge. It is not that oppression can take place through control in the environment, although this is by itself an undeniable reality. Freedom and coercion are part of the human condition and we must here, as in other aspects of our life, take position as our conscience dictates. Nor is it that todays' power can be wielded on so much vaster a scale than ever before in the history of human settlement. This capacity can be used for good as well as for bad causes and the opportunity for its use in support of life is not yet lost. The most troublesome aspect is that we have not even begun to understand the relation of the operating powers to the environment that is their product and their context at the same time.

This ignorance we can ill afford. When it does not trouble the mind, it will in the end render ineffective the motivations of the heart. So many of us have already pursued the good environment with patience and intelligence to become, ultimately, disappointed. Love for the environment must be the indispensable basis for our efforts, but by itself, as it binds us by self-identification, it will be ineffective.

When we see blind forces operating all over the world, be they those of habitation as well as those called professional, creating environments on an unprecedented scale, the complexities of which are clearly outside human comprehension, there is no other choice but to step back and think.

Having visited the site, we must look at it for a while with the eyes of a detached observer . . .

How to account for years of bearing in mind a single subject? Or to do justice to the context in which gestation took place? What is truly studied acquires a life of its own, escaping our desires for self-identification. Therefore, I do not feel I own what I learned to see, but bear responsibility for this attempt to point it out.

WAYS OF SEEING/WAYS OF DOING – A TIMELINE

NJH Life Events	NJH Writing		Contemporaneous Events
1928 Born in Bandung, Indonesia **1943–1945** Japanese internment camp **1955** Completed architecture studies at TU Delft **1955–1957** Architect, Building Division, Dutch Air Force **1958–1960** Instructor, TU Delft			1928 – CIAM Founded 1933 – Plan Obus for Algiers – Le Corbusier 1956 – Yona Friedman's 'Ville Spatiale' 1957 – Kristalbouw project by Jan Trapman 1959 – Team 10 founded in Otterlo 1959 – Metabolism introduced at a CIAM meeting 1961 – *The Death and Life of Great American Cities* by Jane Jacobs
1960–1965 Architectural practice	• **Supports: An Alternative to Mass Housing** (Dutch edition - 1961) • **Dragers '63** • Quality & Quantity: • The Industrialization of Housing • **The Tissue of the Town** • **Man and Matter** • **SAR Principles and Methodology** • **SAR Rules for Design** • 3R's For Housing • Supports: An Alternative to Mass Housing (First English edition – 1972) • **Housing-The Act of Dwelling** • **Supports, Responsibilities and Possibilities** • **You Can't Design the Ordinary** • **The Pursuit of an Idea** • **Involving People in the Housing Process** • **Playing Games** • **SAR Design Method for Housing** • **SAR73**	   	1962 – First Design Methods Conference / London 1962 – <u>Systematic Method for Designers</u> by Bruce Archer 1963 – Candilis, Josic, Woods and Schiedheim - The Free University of Berlin 1964 – *Notes on the Synthesis of Form* by Christopher Alexander 1967 – PREVI Housing Competition 1971 – <u>Architecture versus Housing</u> by Pawley 1972 – John Turner's <u>Freedom to Build</u> 1972 – Kata Mass Housing by Kiyonori Kikutake 1968–75 – Bijlmermeer built in Amsterdam 1970 – Design Methods by John Christopher Jones 1970-6 – Lucien Kroll's student housing in Leuven 1973 – Operation Breakthrough's Townland scheme 1973 – Schumacher's *Small is Beautiful*
1965–1975 Director, Stichting Architecten Research **1967–1975** First Chair and Professor, Department of Architecture TU Eindhoven			

1975–1989
Professor Department of Architecture, MIT (Head of Department – 1975–81)

Architectural Systems Consultant – 1987–90

1990-2001
President, CEO Matura International

- Limits of Professionalism
- Build as Before
- Around the Black Hole
- Notes of a Traveler
- General Principles about the Way Built Environments Exist
- The Leaves and the Flowers
- ANGEL Project
- Grunsfeld Variations
- Conventional Form
- Notes on Hierarchy in Form
- On Writing Form
- The General from the Local
- The Appearance of the Form: Four essays on the Position Designing Takes between People and Things (Awater Press, 1988)
- Towards a New Professional Role
- Architecture & Agreement: Report on Design Methods (originally published in Japanese)
- Control Hierarchies in Complex Artifacts
- Control of Complexity
- Control Relations in the Built Environment
- Shell Infill House
- Concept Design Games
- The Uses of Levels
- Transformations of the Site (Awater Press, 1988)
- Lives of Systems
- Type as a Social Agreement
- Interventions- Professional and User Inputs
- An Efficient Response to User's Individual Preferences
- Samarkand Competition
- Cultivating the Field - About an Attitude When Making Architecture
- An Infill Industry
- Making Urban Fabric Fine Grained

1977 – *A Pattern Language* by Christopher Alexander
1977 – Molenvliet/Papendrecht Built
1978 – SMARCH degree program established, Department of Architecture, MIT
1980 – *How Designers Think* by Bryan Lawson
1983 – *The Reflective Practitioner* by Donald Schon
1987 – EDRA Founded

1987 – *Design Thinking* by Peter Rowe

1987 – Allan Jacobs & Donald Appleyard: *Toward an Urban Design Manifesto,*

1989 – SITE's 'vertical real estate' scheme
1991 – Housing without Housing by Nabeel Hamdi
1991 – IDEO Design Process from Stanford Curriculum
1993 – Founding of the Congress for New Urbanism
1994 – NEXT 21 built in Osaka

1996 – CIB W104 formed in Tokyo

2002–2022
Retired, Living in Eindhoven, NL

- **NEXT21 in the OB Perspective**
- **The Open Building Approach – Examples & Principles**
- **The Power of the Conventional**
- Tools of the Trade - Thematic Aspects of Designing
- **Forms of Understanding**
- Form Sheet
- *The Structure of the Ordinary: Form and Control in the Built Environment* (MIT Press)
- **The Power of the Conventional**
- **Notes on a Network Profession**
- **What Use Theory**
- **Memories of a lost future**
- **Emergent Coherent Behavior of Complex Configurations**
- **Open Building as a Condition for Industrialized Construction**
- **Change and the Distribution of Control**
- **Palladio's Children: Seven Essays on Everyday Environment and the architect**
- Practice & Everyday Environment
- **To Tend A Garden- Design Studio Pedagogy**
- **Design for Flexibility-A Research Agenda**
- On Designing, Inhabitation and morphology
- **Conversations with Form: A Workbook for Students of Architecture** (with Andres Mignucci and Jonathan Teicher)
- **Cultivating Complexity**
- **Cultivating Built Environment**

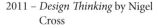

2000 – *Housing for the Millions: John Habraken and the SAR (1960 – 2000)* (NAi Publishers, 2000)

2000 – Rotman School of Management Integrative Thinking for Solving Wicked Problems

2005 - Design school established at Stanford University

2008 – Japanese Law on Long-Lasting Housing

2011 – *Design Thinking* by Nigel Cross

2014 – HENENGHOME (Chinese infill company)

2017 – Council on Open Building founded

- **Back to the Future**
- **The Lure of Bigness**
- **Open Building – A Professional Challenge**
- **Open Building and Government**

2018 – Chinese guidelines on Long-lasting housing
2018 – OpenBuilding.co-founded in the Netherlands
2021 – Discovery Building, Santa Monica High School opened

Timeline figures

Note: WRITINGSS IN BOLD are included in this book.

1938 (ca) First family car in Indonesia
1955 Habraken (standing) giving the Almanac speech to fellow students at TU Delft
1961 House for his mother in Apeldoorn
1965 Habraken (on the right) with colleagues at the SAR
1967 Habraken with graduating students at TU Eindhoven
1967 Entry to the Amsterdam Town Hall Competition
1975 Habraken as Head of Department at MIT with students celebrating his birthday
1998 The Structure of the Ordinary (book cover)
2010 Habraken with architect Frans van der Werf at Molenvliet/Papendrecht
2015 Habraken (left), Kendall (center) and Dale (right) at the Future of Open Building conference, ETH Zurich
2021 Habraken in his house

COMPLETE LIST OF EXPERIENCE, HONORS AND WRITINGS OF JOHN HABRAKEN

Professional education

- Bouwkundig Ingenieur, BI, Technical University, Delft, The Netherlands; 1955

Professional experience

- NUSS Rotating Professorship, National University of Singapore; 12 January–12 February 2004
- Colin Clipson Fellow, Taubman College of Architecture and Urban Planning, University of Michigan, Fall Semester, 2002
- Consultant to the Rijksbouwmeester (Architect of the Netherlands Government); 2003–5
- Professor Emeritus, Department of Architecture, MIT; 1989–present
- President and CEO, Matura International BV, Delft, The Netherlands; 1990–4
- Board Member, Infill Systems BV (A corporation for the development of infill systems in housing); Delft, the Netherlands; 1986–99
- Patron, STOA Annual review of EAAE, European Association of Architectural Education; 1996–present
- Member, contributing board, *Places: A Quarterly Journal of Environmental Design*; 1984–present
- Principal Advisor, *Open House International*: Magazine on housing and the built environment, theories, tools, and practice; 1975–98
- Architecture Systems consultant (with Prof. A van Randen); 1987–90
- Professor of Architecture, Department of Architecture, MIT; 1975–89

Developed courses for students in advanced degree programs (MArch, MsArchS, PhD):
- Thematic Design, Theory (spring semester)
- Thematic Design, Methods (fall semester)
- Seminars on: Rule Making in Design (spring 1988); Concept Design Game Development (spring 1987); Urban Tissue Model development (1983, 1985); Support type development (1984)
- Taught design studio in the MArch program; 1982–5

- Head, Department of Architecture, MIT; 1975–81
  - Initiated Master of Science in Architecture Studies program (SMArchS), a research-based program for students with professional degrees in architecture or urban design; 1978
  - Initiated Master of Science in Visual Studies program (SMVisSt) for advanced studies in visual imaging
- Professor of Architecture, Department of Architecture and Urban Design, Technical University Eindhoven, Eindhoven, the Netherlands; 1967–75
- First Chairperson, Department of Architecture and Urban Design, Technical University Eindhoven. Oversaw creation of educational and organizational structure and selection of teaching staff of the newly established department; 1967–70
- Director, Stichting Architecten Research (SAR – foundation for architectural research). A non-profit research organization, financed through contributions by architects and other parties

involved in the building process, SAR was charged with the development of design methods to facilitate implementation of the 'support/infill' approach in housing; 1965–75
- Architect, project architect, Lucas & Niemeyer, Architects, Voorburg, the Netherlands; 1962–5
- Freelance Architectural Designer; 1960–2
- Instructor, Interior Design Section, Department of Architecture, Technical University Delft; 1958–60
- Architect, Building division, Noncommissioned officer, Dutch Royal Air Force; 1955–7

Honors received

- Honorary doctorate, Technical University Eindhoven, April 2005
- BNA Kubus, award "for advancing the standing of Architecture" from the Society of Dutch Architects, 2003
- Knight of the "Orde van de Nederlandse Leeuw" ("Order of the Dutch Lion") 2003
- Oeuvres Award for Architecture 1996, Fonds BKVB (The Netherlands Foundation for Art, Design, and Architecture) The Netherlands
- Architectural Institute of Japan, Honorary member, 1994
- Association of Collegiate Schools of Architecture (ACSA) Creative Achievement Award, 1989
- King Fahd Award for Design & Research in Islamic Architecture, 1985–6
- David Roell Prize, Prince Bernhard Fund, the Netherlands. 1979 – Bi-annual prize for total work of a living Dutch artist; second architect to receive this award since its inception in 1963

Publications

Books

Conversations with Form; A Workbook for Students of Architecture. Co-authored with Jonathan Teicher and Andres Mignucci. London: Routledge, 2015.
Palladio's Children; Seven Essays on Everyday Environment and the Architect. Edited by Jonathan Teicher. London and New York: Taylor and Francis, 2005.
The Structure of the Ordinary: Form and Control in the Built Environment. Cambridge: MIT Press, 1998.
The Appearance of the Form: Four Essays on the Position Designing Takes between People and Things. Cambridge: Awater Press, 1985. Private edition; second edition 1988; Routledge Revivals Open Building Series, 2019.
Transformations of the Site. Cambridge: Awater Press, 1983. Private edition. Second edition 1988.
General Principles About the Way Built Environments Exist. Open House BCB series. Eindhoven: SAR, 1979.
Variations, the Systematic Design of Supports. With J. T. Boekholt, A. P. Thyssen, P. J. M. Dinjens. MIT Laboratory for Architecture and Planning; distributed by MIT Press, Cambridge, USA and London 1976. English translation by W. Wiewel and Sue Gibbons from the original Dutch publication: *Denken in Varianten*, Alphen a/d Rijn, Samson, 1974.
- Spanish translation: *El Diseno de Soportes.* Ed. Gustavo Gili, Barcelona.
- Chinese translation by Prof. Wang, Ming Hung, Natl. Cheng Kung University, Tainan, Taiwan 1989.
- Korean translation, 2010.

Three R's for Housing. Amsterdam: Scheltema & Holkema, 1970; originally published in Forum, vol. XX, no. 1, 1966.
- Spanish translation: *Tres Notas Sobre Vivienda*, in AUCA, no 29/30, Santiago de Chile, 1975; and *Tres Principios Fundamentales para la Vivienda*, in *Summarios*, no. 8, 1972, Buenos Aires, Argentina.
- Italian translation: *A Come Abitare*, in N. J. Habraken ed il gruppo SAR, Instituto di Composizione Urbanistica, Venezia, 1973.
- Norwegian Translation: *Bolig byggingens ABC*, in Byggekunst, vol. 52, no. 2, Norway, 1970.
- French translation: *Pour Qui, Pour Quoi: Reflexion a propos de l'Habitat*, in Environnement No. 3, 1970. Belgium.

Supports: An Alternative to Mass Housing. London: The Architectural Press and New York: Praeger, 1972. First English-language edition. Originally published in Dutch under the title: *De Dragers en de Mensen.* Amsterdam: Scheltema en Holkema, 1962.
- Italian translation: *Strutture per una Residenza Alternativa.* Milano: Il Saggiatore, 1973.
- Spanish translation: *Soportes: una alternativa al alojamiento de masas.* Madrid: Alberto Corazon, 1976.
- Korean translation, 2010.
- U.K., Urban International Press, edited by Jonathan Teicher, reprint of the 1972 English edition; Rutledge Revivals Open Building Series, edited by Stephen Kendall, 2019.

Major published research reports

With Mark D. Gross and James Anderson, Nabeel Hamdi, John Dale, Sergio Palleroni, Ellen Saslaw and Ming-Hung Wang: *Concept Design Games: Book One: Developing. Book Two: Playing.* A report submitted to the National Science Foundation. Cambridge: MIT Department of Architecture, 1987.
With J. A. Aldrete-Haas, R. Chow, T. Hille, P. Krugmeier, M. Lampkin, A. Mallows, A Mignucci, Y. Takase, K. Weller

and T. Yokouchi: *The Grunsfeld Variations: A Demonstration Project on the Coordination of a Design Team in Urban Design.* Cambridge: MIT Laboratory for Architecture and Planning, 1981.

With Joop Kapteyns and John Carp: *Deciding on Density: An Investigation into High Density, Low Rise, Allotment for the Waldeck Area, the Hague.* Eindhoven: SAR, 1977.

With Henk Reyenga and Frans van der Werf: *SAR 73, The Methodical Formulation of Agreements in the Design of Urban Tissues.* First publication on basic principles of SAR method on urban tissue design; Eindhoven: SAR, 1973.

Principal Investigator, With Hans van Olphen, *SAR 65, Proposals by the Foundation for Architect's Research.* First publication of the basic principles of SAR method for support design. Eindhoven: SAR, 1965.

Papers, chapters and articles

- *Open Building and Government.* Essay addressed to Dutch colleagues supporting a role for government in stimulating an infill industry.
- *Open Building: A Professional Challenge.* Published in a book titled *Baumschlager Eberle Architekten, 2010–2021*, edited by Dietmar Eberle and Eberhard Tröger and published by Birkhauser, Basel, Switzerland, in 2021.
- *The Lure of Bigness.* Interview with Dirk van den Heuvel (Director of the Bakema Foundation and Prof. at TU Delft), as published in Dirk van den Heuvel (ed.), *Jaap Bakema and the Open Society*. Amsterdam: Archis Publishers, 2018, 298–300.
- *Back to the Future. AD: Loose-fit Architecture – Designing Buildings for Change* (guest editor: Alex Lifschutz) 05/vol. 87 / 2017.
- *Cultivating Complexity: The Need for a Shift in Cognition.* Chapter 4 in the book *Complexity, Cognition, Planning and Design*, Post-proceedings of the 2nd International Conference, editors Portugali, Juval and Stolk, Egbert. Springer Proceedings in Complexity, 2016.
- *Methodology and Ideology in Architecture*, Umbau 26, 2013.
- *Cultivating Built Environment* (pp. 204–7) in Sustainable Urbanism and Beyond: Rethinking Cities for the Future, edited by Tigran Haas (Rizzoli, 2012).
- On Designing, Inhabitation, and Morphology, in *Urban Morphology*, vol. 13, no. 2, October 2009.
- *Coda/Reflections Afterward*, in Supports: Housing and City, N. J. Habraken and Andres Mignucci, Experiancias 1, Master Laboratorio de la Vivienda del Siglo XXI, Universitat Polytecnica de Catalunya, 2009.
- *Learning from the INO Experience*, Essay in Systems Separation, Open Building at the Inselspital Bern, INO Project, Amt für Grunstücke und Gebaüde (AGG) Kantotn Bern, Schweiz, 2008.
- *Towards a Research Agenda.* Review of "Flexible Housing," by Tatanja Schneider and Jeremy Till. London: Arch. Press, in 'Building Research Information,' vol. 36, No. 3, 2008.
- *To Tend a Garden – Thoughts on the Strengths and Limits of Studio Pedagogy.* Invited essay in: *Design Studio Pedagogy, Horizons for the Future*, Ashraf M. Salami and Nicholas Wilkinson editors, The Urban International Press, 2007.
- *Palladio's Children*, Chapter 3. in FOLIO 06, Documents of NUS architecture, March 2005, Editors: Li Shiqiao and Belinda Ho.
- *Werken aan het Gewone.* Chapter in: Beter bouwen en bewonen, een praktijkgerichte toekomstverkenning, Redactie: drs. Michiel D.J. van der Well, Stichiting Toekomst der Techniek, STT/Beweton, 2004.
- *Lectures Fall 2003 in Tokyo University and Kyoto University with Discussions.* Jusoken housing research fund report No. 0325, Fall 2004. Kazunobu Minami, editor. Japanese/English.
- *On Comments on Clinton J. Andrew's Interview.* Posted online for readers of the IEEE Society and Technology Magazine, Fall 2004.
- *Security and the Built Environment.* Interview with John Habraken, by Clinton J. Andrews in: IEEE Society and Technology Magazine, Fall 2004.
- *Open Building as a Condition for Industrial Construction.* The Future Site – Proceedings 20th International Symposium on Automation and Robotics in Construction, ISARC 2003, Delft, Editors, Ger Maas and Frans van Gassel.
- *Emergent Coherent Behavior of Complex Configurations Through Automated Maintenance of Dominance Relations.* With J. Willem R. Langelaan. In: *The Future Site* – Proceedings 20th International Symposium on Automation and Robotics in Construction, ISARC 2003, Delft, Editors, Ger Maas and Frans van Gassel.
- *Die Umsetzung einer Einfachen Idee, Das SAR-Konzept von Trager und Ausbau.* Interview August 2002 in: HIER ENTSTEHT, Strategien partizipativer Architectur und Raumlicher Aneignung, Jesko Fezer and Mathias Heyden, Berlin: B-Books 2004.
- *Questions That Will Not Go Away: Some Remarks on Long-Term Trends in Architecture and Their Impact on Architectural Education*, in Shaping the European Higher Architectural Education Area, Transactions in Architectural Education No. 18, Editors: Constantin Spiridonidis and Maria Voyatzaki, ISBN 2-930301-14-7.2003.
- *Making Urban Fabric Fine Grained*, in *Dense Living Urban Structures*, proceedings of the International Conference on Open Building, 23–26 October 2003, Hong Kong, Editor: Dr. Jia Beisi.
- *Memories of a Lost Future.* Chapter in: Back from Utopia, The Challenge of the Modern Movement, Hubert Jan Henket and Hilde Heynen, editors, 010 Publishers, Rotterdam, September 2002.
- Shared Forms and the Role of Designers, in *Open House International*, vol. 24, no. 4, 1999.

- *Comments on Open Building in Relation to the Next 21 Project*, Osaka, Japan, in Domus 819, October 1999.
- Notes on a Network Profession in *Places*, vol. 12, no. 3, 1999.
- *Woningbouw en het Probleem van de Architectuur.* LisA, Architectuurtijdschrift, jaargang 1, no. 2. 1998.
- *Werken met Complexiteit.* Chapter in: De Onvermijdelijke Revolutie, Konstable et.al. Editors, Stichting Maatschappy en Onderneming, SMO, 1998. Revised translation of The Control of Complexity, 1987.
- *Werken met Complexiteit.* Zeezucht, no. 4, 1998.
- *Forms of Understanding.* Chapter in: The Education of the Architect, Post Renaissance, Post-Modern. Martha Pollak, Editor. MIT Press in 1997.
- *The Power of the Conventional*, paper in: Rethinking XIXth Century City, Attilion Petruccioli, Editor. Aga Khan Program. Proceedings of the international symposium sponsored by the Aga Khan Progra for Islamic Architecture at Harvard University and the Massachusetts Institute of Technology. MIT, Cambridge, April 1996.
- *Tools of the Trade.* Discussion paper for the Department of Architecture, MIT, February 1996.
- *Around the Black Hole. Stoa*, annual review of EAAE, reprint of 1980 article, January 1996.
- *Open Building: Principles and Practice.* Invited Paper for the Instituto de tecnologia de la Constuccio de Catalunya, Barcelona, 1995.
- *Support and Infill, Design and Implementation.* Proceedings, Seminar on Urban Housing Towards the 21st Century, Tainan, Taiwan, 1994.
- *The Open Building Approach, Examples and Principles.* Seminar on Urban Housing Towards the 21st Century, Taipei, Taiwan. 1994.
- *Infill Systems A New Industry.* Slide presentation at the Seminar on Urban Housing Towards the 21st Century, Taipei, Taiwan, 1994.
- *NEXT21 in the Open Building Perspective.* SD25, Japan.
- Cultivating the Field: About an Attitude When Making Architecture, *Places*, vol. 9, no. 1, 1994.
- *Open Building and Efficiency: Recent Developments in the Netherlands.* Paper presented at the International Symposium on Frontline Issues on Research and Development, Housing for a World in Need. Israel: Faculty of Architecture and Town Planning, Technion Institute of Technology, May 1993.
- *Cultivating the Field: About an Attitude When Making Architecture.* Faculty of Architecture and Town Planning, Technion Institute of Technology. May 1993; *Places*, vol. 9, no. 1, Winter 1994, 8–21.
- *An Efficient Response to Users' Individual Preferences.* Housing Design 2000 Conference, September 1992.
- *Operations: The Designer's Tools.* Seminar paper MIT, draft for presentation, 1989.
- *Type as a Social Agreement.* Seoul, Korea: Third Asian Congress of Architects, November 1988.
- *The Uses of Levels.* Proceedings of the UNESCO Regional Seminar on Shelter for the Homeless, Seoul, Korea, November 1988. *Open House International*, vol. 27, no. 2, 2002.
- With Mark Gross, *Spatial Coordination Program*. Tokyo. Research report for the Shimizu Corporation.
- With Mark Gross, Concept Design Games. *Design Studies*, vol. 9, no. 3, July 1988.
- The Control of Complexity. *Places*, vol. 4, no. 2, 1987.
- *Shell Infill House: A Study of the Application of the Open Systems Approach in Housing Design.* Japan, May/June 1987.
- *Control Hierarchies in Complex Artifacts Proceedings.* Conference on Planning and Design in Architecture. Protzen, Ed. Boston: International Congress on Planning and Design Theory, 1987.
- With Mark Gross, *Concept Design Games: Design Games for Experimentation in Design Theory and Methodology.* Waldron, Ed. Oakland, CA. Proceedings, NSF Workshop in Design Theory and Methodology, 1987.
- *Architecture and Agreement* – A Report on Research for New Design Methods. (Overview of my work on design methods 1965–1985). *Kenchiku Bunka*, vol. 42, no. 486, April 1987.
- *Three WAYS OF SEEING the Built Environment.* London: Pidgeon Audio Visual Series, 1985.
- *Towards a New Professional Role. Design Studies*, vol. 7, no. 3, 1986.
- *Design Coalition Team.* Behesti, Ed. Who Is Participating? International Design Participation Conference Proceedings, vol. 1, 1985. Also published in: "Occasional Paper" UK: University of Strathclyde, Dept. of Arch. and Building Science, 1985.
- *To Share an Architecture.* Die Aesthetic der Stadterneuerung. Fassbinder and Fuhr, Eds. Published as Materialien No. 2. Berlin: Hochschule der Kunste, 1985.
- *Reconciling Variety and Efficiency in Large Scale Projects.* Large Housing Projects; Designing in Islamic Cultures 5. Cambridge: The Aga Khan Program for Islamic Architecture, 1985.
- Turkish translation: "Liyum Degisim ve Kullanici Katilimi" in Rusen Keles, ed., Konut ve Gelisme. Ankara: Ankara University, 1987.
- On Writing Form. *Design Studies*, vol. 5, no. 3, July 1984.
- *Notes on Hierarchies in Form.* Working paper, FALL 1983–Winter 1984.
- *The General from the Local.* Architectural Education 2, 1983. Also published in *Open House International*, vol. 8, no. 2, 1983, and in *Places*, vol. 3, no. 5, 1985; German translation in: Trialog: Zeitschrift fur das Planen und Bauen in der Dritte Welt. no. 3, 1984.
- *Writing Form, a Formal Way to Describe Form Transformations.* Working Paper, August 1983.
- *Notes on Lay-Out Methodology; VLSI Design.* Working Paper, 1983.
- *Notation of Position of Elements in Thematic Systems.* Working Paper, 1982.

- *Comment on: Hierarchical Design Methodologies and Tools of VLSI Chips, a Paper by C. Niessen*. Eindhoven: Philips Physics Research Lab Working Paper, 1982.
- *Conventional Form*. Seminar on Convention and Canons, MIT, 1982.
- *Angel, the Designer's Guardian: On the Role of the Computer in Architectural Design: A Computer Program Development Proposal*. Working paper, 1982.
- With Ming-Hung Wang: *Notation of the Design Process: The Six Operations*. Working Paper, 1982.
- *Signs of Structures*. Chapter of Transformations of the Site. Reprinted in *Space and Society*. Cambridge: MIT Press, 1982.
- With Mark D. Gross: The Turtle Tissue Project: Use of the Computer in the Design of Urban Tissues. *Open House International*, vol. 7, no. 2, 1982.
- *Methods for Efficient Housing Design*. International Colloquium on Low-Cost Housing Financing, INFONAVIT, Mexico City, 1982. Spanish translation: "Metodo Para un Deseno Aficaz de la Vivienda." Eure. Santiago de Chile, 1982.
- *Lower Housing Costs Through Design for Adaptability*. International Colloquium on Low-cost Housing Financing, INFONAVIT, Mexico City, 1982.
- *Thematic Systems Theory and Communication Among Those Who Investigate the Built Environment*. ARCC, Ann Arbor, MI, 1981.
- *Notes of a Traveller: On Dilemmas of the Researcher in Architectural Design Methodology*. Journal of Architectural Education, 1980.
- *Around the Black Hole: Critique of Ideology in Architectural Education*. Plan. Cambridge: MIT School of Architecture and Planning, 1980.
- *The Leaves and the Flowers*. Design study for town hall in Amsterdam. VIA, Culture and the Social Vision, Arch. Journal of the Graduate School of Fine Arts, University of Pennsylvania. Cambridge, MA: MIT Press, 1980.
- With E. Dluhosch: The Role of Industrial Production for Increasing Housing Production in the Low-Income Sector in Egypt. *Ekistics*, vol. 47, no. 280, January/February 1980.
- *The Built Environment and the Limits of Professional Practice*. Chapter in R. Plunz, Ed., Housing Form and Public Policy in the US. New York: Praeger Press, 1980.
- Interventions: Professional and User Inputs. *Open House*, vol. 5, no. 4, 1980.
- L'Ambiente Construito e i Limiti della Practica Professionale. *Spazio & Societa*, vol. 1, no. 1, 1978. Italian translation of "The Built Environment and the Limits of Professional Practice"
- *Housing Cultivation Instead of Mass Housing*. Seminar on Development of New Approaches to Housing Policy and Production in Egypt. TAP Report 78-4. Cambridge, MA: MIT, 1978.
- Foreword to Wampler, Jan, *All Their Own: People and the Places They Build*. Cambridge, MA: Schenkman, 1977.
- Creation Architectural et Industrie, Intervention au Colloque d'Yerres. *Techniques et Architecture*, no. 311, October/November 1976.
- Ten Years of SAR. *Open House*, no. 1, 1976.
- *New Design Concepts? Professional Roles and the Existence of Built Environments*. Proceedings EDRA7, Vancouver, 1976.
- Fragments, quotations from a lecture at Portoroz, Yougoslavia, 1975. In *Dossier SAR*. Techniques et Architecture, no. 303, March 1976.
- *Grenzen van de Vakbeoefening*. Plan, no. 5, 1976.
- *Over de Gebouwde Omgeving en de Grenzen van de Vakbeoefening*. Lecture, Eindhoven University, published by same. Also published in: *Weg en Waterbouw*, vol. 35, no. 7 and 8, 1975.
- *Experiences and Practical Application of SAR Methods in Design and Production of Houses*. Paper Europrefab Conference, Paris, 1975.
- The Limits of Professionalism. *Architectural Association Quarterly*, vol. 8, no. 1, 1976 Edited version of the First John Dennys Memorial Lecture, the AA, London, 1975.
- With Rinus van den Berg, *Het ontwerp van het Inbouwpakket*. Rotterdam: Bouwcentrum Rotterdam, 1974.
- *Objectifs de l'Habitat et de son Industrialisation*, contribution to B. Hamburger, Ed., CORDA-DGRST, Paris, 1974.
- SAR Design Method for Housing: Seven Years of Development in the Real World. *DMG-DRS Journal for Design Research Methods*, vol. 7, no. 3, July/September 1973.
- *De SAR Methodiek*. Woningraad, no. 4, 1973.
- *Support Structure and Detachable Units on the Basis of Industrialization and Participation*. Toshi – Jutaku Urban Housing No. 55, 1972.
- Involving People in the Housing Process. *RIBA Journal*, November 1972.
- Playing Games. *Architectural Design*, no. 4, 1972.
- Das Ende Des Wohnbauprojectes. *Architese*, no. 1, 1972.
- *SAR Methodiek; reorganisatie bouwproces*. Series of three articles in Industrieel Bouwen, nos. 5–7, 1971.
- *Individu en Industrialisatie*. Lecture at Congress on Housing and Planning, published by Stichting Werkgemeenschappen Bergeyk, 1966, Republished, 1971
- You Can't Design the Ordinary. *Architectural Design*, April 1971.
- L'Habitat, l'Homme, et l'Industrie. *L'Architecture D'Aujourd'hui*, February/March 1970.
- *De Integriteit van de Stad*. Chapter in De Mens in de Stad van de Mens; The Netherlands: Samson N.V. 1970.
- The Pursuit of an Idea. *Plan*, no. 3, 1970.
- With Ir. M. F. Th. Bax: Systematische Ontwikkeling van Plattegronden in een gegeven Woonstruktuur met Behulp van de Computer. *Bouw*, vol. 25, no. 31 and 32, 1971.
- *Kommunikatie in Het Ontwerpproces*. Lecture at PDOB post-graduate course. Delft Tech. University, 1970. Published by the Dept. of Arch. Tech. U. Eindhoven.

- Supports, Responsibilities and Possiblities. *Architectural Association Quarterly*, Winter 1968-69. French translation: *Supports, responsabilites et possibilites*, in Bruno Fortier, Ed. *L'Habitat comme Pratique*. Paris: Institute de l'Environnement, 1974.
- *Stichting Architecten Research: Industrialisierter Wonungsbau*. Bauwelt, Heft 10, 1968.
- *Het Alledaagse, over het Ontstaan van de Omgeving van Alledag*. Initiatory Lecture at Dept. of Arch., Tech. U. Eindhoven. Rotterdam: Lemniscaat, 1967.
- *Individual en Industrialisatie in de Drager Woningbouw*. Lecture at conference on SAR in Bergeyk, the Netherlands. Published by Stichting Werkgemeenschappen Bergeyk, 1966.
- *Stichting Architecten Research*. A series of four articles in *Misset's Bouwwereld,* nos. 2-5, 1966.
- Man and Matter. *Forum*, vol. XVIX, no. 1, 1965.
- Quality and Quantity: The Industrialization of Housing. *Forum*, vol. XVIII, no. 2, 1964.
- The Tissue of the Town: Some Suggestions for Further Scrutiny. *Forum*, vol. XVIII, no. 1, 1964.

A partial list of publications on N. J. Habraken

- Palladio's Children, review by Ivor Samuels, in: Urban Design, 112, 2009.
- Montaner, Josep Maria, *John Habraken y el sistema de los 'soportes*. In: La Vanguardia, 28 September 2008.
- Lüthi, Sonja. "Democratiserung der Architectur." In: *TEC21/39*, 2008.
- Ole Bouman, *John Habraken*, Foundation for Arts, Design, and Architecture, Amsterdam, 1996.
- Fassbinder, H. and J. van Eldonk, "Flexibilität im Niederlaändischen Wohnungsbau." *Architecture Plus*, 100-1, 65-73, 1998.
- Buch, J., *De Sociale matrix: Blom, Habraken en de planning van de jaren zeventig*. Rotterdam: Een eeuw Nederlandse Architectuur, 1993, 329-33.
- Grunhagen, Harm, interviewer, *Open Bouwen is meer dan Liefdewerk voor Bewoners*. Woningraad, no. 12, June 1989.
- Luchinger, Arnolf, Article in *Altagliche Architectuur*. The Hague, 1985.
- Prins Bernhard Foundation. *Habraken*. The Hague: Prins Bernhard Foundation, 1984.
- Kendall, S. H. "The Netherlands: Distinguishing 'Support' and 'infill.'" *Architecture; the AIA Journal*, 10, 1986, 90-4.
- Barbieri, Unberto, ed. "Profile." In *Architectuur en Planning. Nederland 1940-1980*. Rotterdam and Amsterdam: Uitgeverij 010, 1983.
- *Habraken: SAR 73*. Special issue of Parametro, June 1982.
- Yoshida, Masahiro, ed., "Open Housing." special issue, *Toshi-Jutaku*, no. 135, 1979.
- Dossier SAR, Henri Bonnemazou, Jean Louis Cohen, Bruno Fortier, in: *Techniques et Architecture*, 311, 1976.
- Dluhosch, Eric, Involving People in the Housing Process; The Story of Habraken's Supports and Detachables. *Industrialization Forum*, no. 1, 1976.
- Taylor, B.B. Nicolaas Habraken: Du regne de la quantite a l'ordre de la qualite? *L'Architecture d'Aujourd'hui*, July/August 1974.
- Mamoli, Marcello et al., *N. J. Habraken e il Gruppo SAR: matgeriali di ricerca sulla progrettazione della residenza*. Venice, 1973.
- Uyeda, Makato, *SAR. Toshi-Jutaku*, September 1972.
- Pawley, Martin, *Mass Housing: The Desparate Effort of Pre-Industrial Thought to Achieve the Equivalent of Mass Production*. Architectural Design, January 1970.
- Pawley, Martin, *The Perfect Barracks and the Support Revolution*. Interbuild Arena, October 1967.
- *Mass Housing*, Prof. M. J. Granpré Moliere, Translation of an article on the book 'Supports' in the Dutch 'Bouwkundig Weekblad' no. 14, 1962.

EDITORS' BIOGRAPHIES

Stephen H. Kendall, PhD

BArch University of Cincinnati
MAUD, Washington University in St. Louis
PhD, Massachusetts Institute of Technology

Dr. Kendall is a registered architect with a professional degree from the University of Cincinnati, a Master of Architecture and Urban Design from Washington University in St. Louis, and a PhD in Design Theory and Methods from the Massachusetts Institute of Technology. Prior to starting his academic career, he was a carpenter building houses in the US and Puerto Rico. He joined an architectural office in St. Louis, Missouri, where he designed hospitals, schools and residential buildings as a registered architect. He has taught architectural design and urban design studios, and courses in building technology and design theory in the US, Taiwan, Italy, Indonesia, South Africa, Japan and PR China. He has experience in guiding professional, post professional and PhD studies at US and several foreign universities.

His research focuses on the theory and practice of open building. This work has roots in recognition of challenges to the profession as we guide transformation of the built environment under conditions of change and distributed decision-making. His research and writing focus primarily on housing and health care architecture, facing several major challenges. First is the increasing size and complexity of buildings. Second is the dynamics of the living environment, the workplace and the marketplace where use is increasingly varied and changing. Third is the availability of, and demand for, an increasing array of equipment and facilities serving the inhabitant user.

He has written more than 45 papers and book chapters; is the co-author (with Jonathan Teicher) of <u>Residential Open Building (Routledge, 2000)</u>, available in English, Japanese, Chinese and Korean; and has authored many technical reports and funded research projects. He has lectured widely to university and professional audiences around the world. His edited book <u>Healthcare Architecture as Infrastructure: Open Building in Practice</u>, was published by Routledge in 2019. Another edited book – <u>Residential Architecture as Infrastructure: Open Building in Practice</u> – was published by Routledge in 2021. Both are part of the Open Building Series of books published by Routledge.

With John Dale, he co-founded the Council on Open Building in 2017, with the mission to make the Open Building approach normal across all sectors of practice in improving the quality of the everyday built environment.

Stephen H. Kendall, PhD
Emeritus Professor of Architecture, Ball State University
Philadelphia, PA, 19119
Vice President, Council on Open Building (www.councilonopenbuilding.org)

John R. Dale, FAIA, LEED APBArch, University of Toronto
SM Arch S, Massachusetts Institute of Technology

John Dale has been planning, programming and designing educational environments for over 35 years. In 2008, he was named a Fellow of the American Institute of Architects (AIA) for this focus. By defining small learning communities which boost student achievement and galvanize community involvement, he creates high performance learning environments that are widely recognized models of regional and national significance. Mr. Dale also promotes green schools. Building on evidence-based research, he puts in practice the theory that students are healthier and learn more effectively in well-ventilated, acoustically balanced, naturally lit spaces with strong connections to the outdoors.

As Principal, and Pre-K12 Studio Leader for Harley Ellis Devereaux (HED), a national Architecture and Engineering firm, John's projects have been honored with numerous awards at national, state and local levels. He has taught at USC, MIT, UCLA, California State Polytechnic University, Pomona and participated in symposia, design reviews and competition juries. His articles and projects have appeared in books and journals, including Green Technology Magazine, LA Architect (Form Magazine), Learning by Design, Spazio e Società, Architectural Record, Fast Company, Faith & Form, Transitions 19 and the LA Forum for Architecture and Urban Design Newsletter (online).

John completed a term as Chair of the Leadership Group of AIA's National Committee on Architecture for Education (CAE) in 2016 and then served on the Board of the CAE Foundation. He is also a member and Past-President of the Board of Directors of the A+D (Architecture and Design) Museum, Los Angeles; is a member of the Advisory Board of the Armory Center for the Arts in Pasadena and also advises Abode Communities in Los Angeles, having served on its Board. John is President and Co-Founder of the Council on Open Building.

John R. Dale, FAIA, LEED AP
Principal and Studio Leader
HED (Harley Ellis Devereaux)
Los Angeles, CA 90017
President, Council on Open Building – www.councilonopenbuilding.org

INDEX

Note: Page numbers in *italic* indicate a figure on the corresponding page.

abandoned territories 178–180
academia 460–461
adaptability 161–162
adaptation 301
agents 103
agreements 48
Alexandria (Egypt) *196*, 432
algorithmic aspects 373–375
Amsterdam (Netherlands) 19, 210, 442, 445, 450, 457, 465, 470; the built field 32, *33–36*, *38*, 39, 43, 48, 50, 74–76; control 91–94, *92–93*, 101, 117–119; cultivating built environment 402, 413–418, *414*, *417–418*, 420–422, 427, 434; examples of WAYS OF DOING 233–244, *234–243*; Open Building approach 328; tools 378, 382; role of the architect 158–160, *158*, *160*, *163*, 182, 185, *194*, 203; sharing forms 135
apartment buildings 450
architect, emergence of 193–194; *see also* role of the architect
architectural education: "Questions that Will Not Go Away" (2006) 193–199, *193–196*
architecture: architectural challenges 379; "Cultivating the Field: About an attitude when making architecture" (1994) 410–418, *410–414*, *417–418*; in denial 22–23; in everyday practice 183–184; immersion in the everyday world 21–22; local 181–182; new 122; open 416; "Questions that Will Not Go Away" (2006) 193–199, *193–196*
architecture, students of: "Attitudes towards the Built Field" xxi–xxii
"Around the Black Hole" (1980) 2, 172–180
art 182
artifacts *see* complex artifacts
assembly hierarchies 102, 104

attitude: "Cultivating the Field: About an attitude when making architecture" (1994) 410–418, *410–414*, *417–418*; professional 435
automated maintenance of dominance relations: "Emergent Coherent Behavior of Complex Configurations through Automated Maintenance of Dominance Relations 2008" (2003) 370–375, *370–372*
autonomy: autonomous environment 184; of built environment 21
avant-garde 126–128

"Back to the Future" (2017) 3, 456–461, *457–458*, *460*
balloon frame house *64*
Barcelona (Spain) 457–458, *458*
base building 452
bi-directional editing 373–375
book reviews: "Design for Flexibility: Towards a research agenda" (2008) 376–381
"Build as Before" (1978) 385–398, *388–398*
buildings, disappearance of 183–184
built environment: autonomy of 21; beginning to look at 24; "Build as Before" 385–398; "Change and the Distribution of Design" 420–425; "Control of Complexity" 399–409; "Control Relations in the Built Environment" (1987) 2, 113–116, *113–116*; "Cultivating Built Environment" (2012) 431–435, *433–434*; "Cultivating the Field: About an attitude when making architecture" 410–418; "General Principles About the Way Built Environments Exist" (1979) 45–57; and powers 153–154; study of 20; as subject for expertise 20–21; "To Tend a Garden: Thoughts on the strengths and limits of studio pedagogy" 426–430
built field: "Attitudes towards the Built Field" xxi–xxii; "The General from the Local" (1984) 58–62; "General Principles About the Way Built Environments Exist"

(1979) 45–57; Habraken's contribution to a theory of xviii–xix; "Lives of Systems" (1988) 63–73; "Making Urban Fabric Fine Grained – A Research Agenda" (2003) 74–79; power of 413–414; professionalization of 414–415; "The Tissue of the Town: Some suggestions for further scrutiny" (1964) 2, 29–41, *29–31, 33–41*; "You Can't Design the Ordinary" (1971) 2, 42–44, *43*

capacity 77–78, 203–204, 407–408, 469
change 46, 169, 179–180, 196–197; "Change and the Distribution of Design" (2004) 2, 117–122, *117–122*, 210, 420–425, *420–425*; and the living cell 432
"Change and the Distribution of Design" (2004) 2, 117–122, *117–122*, 210, 420–425, *420–425*
choice 282–283
classic order *63*
cognition: "Cultivating Complexity: The need for a shift in cognition" (2016) 210–211, 445–455
commercial dimensions 303
commercial Open Building 324–325
common ground 125–126
communication 165–166, 171
complex artifacts: "Control Hierarchies in Complex Artifacts" (1972) 102–112, *105–112*
complex configurations: "Emergent Coherent Behavior of Complex Configurations through Automated Maintenance of Dominance Relations 2008" (2003) 370–375, *370–372*
complexity: "Control of Complexity" (1987) 210, 399–409, *400–408*; "Cultivating Complexity: The need for a shift in cognition" (2016) 210–211, 445–455
Complexity, Cognition, Planning and Design: "Cultivating Complexity: The need for a shift in cognition" (2016) 210–211, 445–455
"Concept Design Games" (1988) 210, 359–368, *360, 363–364, 367*
conduits: re-ordering of the deployment of 305
configurations 103; "Emergent Coherent Behavior of Complex Configurations through Automated Maintenance of Dominance Relations 2008" (2003) 370–375, *370–372*; territorial interpretations of 110–111
conflict 76–77, 427–428; reconciliation of 304
consensus 46–48
consultation 46–47
consumer product 325
contradictions 195
control: "Change and the Distribution of Design" (2004) 2, 117–122, *117–122*, 210, 420–425, *420–425*; "Control of Complexity" (1987) 210, 399–409, *400–408*; control distribution 108–109, 362–363; "Control Relations in the Built Environment" 2; distribution of design control 380; field control 445–447, 449–451; hierarchy of control fields 447–448; invisible territorial control 449; "Involving People in the Housing Process" (1972) 90–101, *92–100*; "Playing Games" (1972) 88–89; re-distribution of design control 326–327; spontaneous emergence of field control hierarchy 449–450; "Supports, Responsibilities and Possibilities" (1968) 83–87

control distribution 108–109
control hierarchies: "Control Hierarchies in Complex Artifacts" (1972) 102–112, *105–112*
"Control of Complexity" (1987) 210, 399–409, *400–408*
control relations: "Control Relations in the Built Environment" (1987) 2, 113–116, *113–116*
conventional, the: "The Power of the Conventional" (1998) 145–148
conventions: interface 370–373
cooperation *see* professional cooperation
coordination 77; of parts 326
Copenhagen (Denmark) 460, *460*
costs: balance of 307; labor 307
creativity 86–87, 197–198
credo: "Attitudes towards the Built Field" xxi–xxii
cultivating built environment: "Build as Before" (1978) 385–398, *388–398*; "Change and the Distribution of Design" (2004) 2, 117–122, *117–122*, 210, 420–425, *420–425*; "Control of Complexity" (1987) 210, 399–409, *400–408*; "Cultivating Built Environment" (2012) 431–435, *433–434*; "Cultivating the Field: About an attitude when making architecture" (1994) 410–418, *410–414, 417–418*; "To Tend a Garden: Thoughts on the strengths and limits of studio pedagogy" (2007) 426–430
"Cultivating Built Environment" (2012) 431–435, *433–434*
"Cultivating Complexity: The need for a shift in cognition" (2016) 210–211, 445–455
"Cultivating the Field: About an attitude when making architecture" (1994) 410–418, *410–414, 417–418*
cultivation 185; "Cultivating Built Environment" (2012) 431–435, *433–434*; "Cultivating Complexity: The need for a shift in cognition" (2016) 210–211, 445–455; "Cultivating the Field: About an attitude when making architecture" (1994) 410–418, *410–414, 417–418*
curriculum: design curriculum 428

demand *see* supply and demand
denial, architecture in 22–23
dependence 106–108
dependency control: relations between territorial control and 112
dependency hierarchies 102, 106
design 361; "Change and the Distribution of Design" (2004) 2, 117–122, *117–122*, 210, 420–425, *420–425*; design curriculum 428; "Design for Flexibility: Towards a research agenda" (2008) 376–381; design net 184; design research 167; design responsibility 197; design rules 344–345; for everyday environment 451–453;

instance design 327; Open Building design management 453; recording design play 365; re-distribution of design control 326–327; "SAR: Rules for design" (1965) 331–337, *331, 334, 336–337*; systems design 327; teaching design 172–175; three-dimensional urban design 312, 433; users designing 323

designers, interaction among 204

"Design for Flexibility: Towards a research agenda" (2008) 376–381

detachable units 83–85

developers 378–379

developing countries *72*

development, in-play 364

dimensions 305–307

distribution: "Change and the Distribution of Design" (2004) 2, 117–122, *117–122*, 210, 420–425, *420–425*; control distribution 108–109, 362–363; of design control 380; of design responsibility 197; of material 55–56; of power 56–57; re-distribution of design control 326–327; of territory 55

Dokkum (Netherlands) *37*

dominance 105; "Emergent Coherent Behavior of Complex Configurations through Automated Maintenance of Dominance Relations 2008" (2003) 370–375, *370–372*

dwellings 379–380; as dual unity 288–289; "'Grondslagen' – Basic Principles for the Building of Supports and the Production of Support Dwellings" (1963) 210, 215–231, *217–231*; "Housing: The act of dwelling" (1968) 14–19

economization of labor 157

editing *see* bi-directional editing

education *see* architectural education

efficiency 356; "An Efficient Response to Users' Preferences" (1992) 298–309, *299–300, 303, 305–306*

"Efficient Response to Users' Preferences, An" (1992) 298–309, *299–300, 303, 305–306*

elements 48–49

"Emergent Coherent Behavior of Complex Configurations through Automated Maintenance of Dominance Relations 2008" (2003) 370–375, *370–372*

essays: "Around the Black Hole" (1980) 2, 172–180; "Back to the Future" (2017) 3, 456–461, *457–458, 460*; "Build as Before" (1978) 385–398, *388–398*; "Change and the Distribution of Design" (2004) 2, 117–122, *117–122*, 210, 420–425, *420–425*; "Cultivating the Field: About an attitude when making architecture" (1994) 410–418, *410–414, 417–418*; "Forms of Understanding: Thematic knowledge and the modernist legacy" (1997) 125–142, *129–130, 132–134, 136–139*; "General Principles About the Way Built Environments Exist" (1979) 45–57; "The Leaves and the Flowers" 210, 233–244, *234–243*; "Making Urban Fabric Fine Grained – A Research Agenda" (2003) 74–79; "Man and Matter" (1965) 9–13; "Memories of a Lost Future" (2002) 2, 187–191, *188–189, 191*; "NEXT21 in the Open Building Perspective" (1994) 310–318, *313–314, 316–317*; "Notes on a Network Profession" (1999) 181–186; "Notes of a Traveler" (1980) 165–171; "Open Building: A professional challenge" (2021) 3, 467–472; "Open Building and Government: Lessons learned" (2022) 473–475; "Playing Games" (1972) 88–89; "The Power of the Conventional" (1998) 145–148; "Quality and Quantity: The industrialization of housing" (1964) 281–297, *287, 289, 291, 293–295*; "Questions that Will Not Go Away" (2006) 193–199, *193–196*; "Supports, Responsibilities and Possibilities" (1968) 83–87; "To Tend a Garden: Thoughts on the strengths and limits of studio pedagogy" (2007) 426–430; "The Tissue of the Town: Some suggestions for further scrutiny" (1964) 2, 29–41, *29–31, 33–41*; "What Use Theory?: Questions of purpose and practice" 20–25; "You Can't Design the Ordinary" (1971) 2, 42–44, *43*

everyday environment 194–195; design for 451–453; working with 459–460

everyday practice 183–184

everyday world, immersion of architecture in 21–22

examples of WAYS OF DOING: "'Grondslagen' – Basic Principles for the Building of Supports and the Production of Support Dwellings" (1963) 210, 215–231, *217–231*; "The Leaves and the Flowers" 210, 233–244, *234–243*; "The Samarkand Competition Submission" (1994) 268–276; "Shell-Infill House" (1987) 245–267

expenses *see* voluntary expenses

experimentation 170

expertise 168; built environment as subject for 20–21

façade system 314–315, 322

field control 445–447, 449–451

field deployment 403

flexibility 85–86; "Design for Flexibility: Towards a research agenda" (2008) 376–381

form and forms 360–361; *see also* sharing forms

"Forms of Understanding: Thematic knowledge and the modernist legacy" (1997) 125–142, *129–130, 132–134, 136–139*

freedom 86–87

function 203–204, 343–344, 360–361

game box 361–362

games: "Playing Games" (1972) 88–89

gardens *see* private gardens

gated community 450

general, the: "The General from the Local" (1984) 58–62

"General from the Local, The" (1984) 58–62

"General Principles About the Way Built Environments Exist" (1979) 45–57

geometry 403–406
government: "Open Building and Government: Lessons learned" (2022) 473–475

Habraken, John xv–xvi
Haussmann 39, 43–44, 134–135, *134*, *138*, 145–148, 203, 442
heritage 121–122
hierarchies 406, 412–413, 448; of control fields 447–448; "Control Hierarchies in Complex Artifacts" (1972) 102–112, *105–112*; new hierarchical organization 467–469
Hong Kong *196*, 203, 312, 324, 432, 442
housing and houses: core 353–354; house type 338–343; "Housing: The act of dwelling" (1968) 14–19; "Involving People in the Housing Process" (1972) 90–101, *92–100*; long-life housing act 451; "Quality and Quantity: The industrialization of housing" (1964) 281–297, *287*, *289*, *291*, *293–295*; "Shell-Infill House" (1987) 245–267; uniformity and rigidity 474–475
"Housing: The act of dwelling" (1968) 14–19

ideas, implementation of xix–xx
identification 46
ideology 23, 167–168, 197; "Methodology and Ideology in Architecture" (2013) 200–204, *201–203*
independence: industrial product as 292–294; relations as 289–290; of the systems 340–341; what is built as 290–292
implementation of Habraken's ideas xix–xx
inclinations 156–158
industrial construction: "Open Building as a Condition for Industrial Construction" (2003) 210, 319–327, *320–324*
industrialization 18–19; "Quality and Quantity: The industrialization of housing" (1964) 281–297, *287*, *289*, *291*, *293–295*
industrial product 285–288; as independent 292–294
infill 299, 355; commercial dimensions 303; separation of 'support' and 301, 304; technological dimensions 304
informal sector 450
infrastructure 325
inhabitation 184–186
in-play development 364
installations 307
instance design 327
institutional building 452–453
institutional challenge 471–472
institutions *see* network institutions
intensification 413
interface convention 370–373
intermezzos 1, 26, 149–150, 277–278, 328, 382, 436
international values 160–161
interviews: "The Lure of Bigness" (2018) 462–466

investment, long-term 434, 450–451
"Involving People in the Housing Process" (1972) 90–101, *92–100*
isolation 165–166

knowledge 198–199; source of 430; *see also* thematic knowledge

labor *see* economization of labor; labor costs
labor costs 307
language *see* professional language
layout languages 366
"Leaves and the Flowers, The" 210, 233–244, *234–243*
lectures: "The Limits of Professionalism" (1975) 153–164, *158*, *160*, *163*; *see also* talks
levels 52; disappearance of 118–119; of intervention 179; relations on different levels 53–54; relations on the same level 52–53; "The Uses of Levels" (1988) 348–358, *350–355*
"Limits of Professionalism, The" (1975) 153–164, *158*, *160*, *163*
"Lives of Systems" (1988) 63–73
living cells 76, 414, 431–435, 461
local, the: "The General from the Local" (1984) 58–62; local architectures 181–182
location 166
London 145–146
long-life housing act 451
"Lure of Bigness, The" (2018) 462–466

"Making Urban Fabric Fine Grained – A Research Agenda" (2003) 74–79
"Man and Matter" (1965) 9–13
mapping 170
masonry *72*, 228, 231
material and materials 45, 175–178; distribution of 55–56
matter: "Man and Matter" (1965) 9–13
"Memories of a Lost Future" (2002) 2, 187–191, *188–189*, *191*
metaphors 431
method and methodology 77, 168, 198; "Methodology and Ideology in Architecture" (2013) 200–204, *201–203*
"Methodology and Ideology in Architecture" (2013) 200–204, *201–203*, 439–443, *440–442*
modernist legacy: "Forms of Understanding: Thematic knowledge and the modernist legacy" (1997) 125–142, *129–130*, *132–134*, *136–139*
Molenvliet (Netherlands) *441*, 452; the built field 74–75, *75*; control 122; cultivating built environment 425, 433, *433*; Open Building approach 311–312, 315, 323–324; tools *355*, 380; role of the architect *202*
morphological systems 48
moves 103

Nash, John 145–146
national values 160–161
natural phenomenon 118
'natural relationship' 17–18
network inhabitants 185–186
network institutions 181–182
network profession: "Notes on a Network Profession" (1999) 181–186
new construction 303
NEXT21 74, *75*, 201, *201*, 319–323, 379–380, 433, *434*, 440, 469; "NEXT21 in the Open Building Perspective" (1994) 310–318, *313–314*, *316–317*
"NEXT21 in the Open Building Perspective" (1994) 310–318, *313–314*, *316–317*
nomad 16–17
nonthematic 402
notation 366
"Notes of a Traveler" (1980) 165–171
"Notes on a Network Profession" (1999) 181–186

office building 449
Olynthus *31*, *32*
open architecture 416
Open Building: design management 453; "An Efficient Response to Users' Preferences" (1992) 298–309, *299–300*, *303*, *305–306*; "NEXT21 in the Open Building Perspective" (1994) 310–318, *313–314*, *316–317*; "Open Building: A professional challenge" (2021) 3, 467–472; "Open Building as a Condition for Industrial Construction" (2003) 210, 319–327, *320–324*; "Open Building and Government: Lessons learned" (2022) 473–475; "Quality and Quantity: The industrialization of housing" (1964) 281–297, *287*, *289*, *291*, *293–295*
"Open Building: A professional challenge" (2021) 3, 467–472
"Open Building and Government: Lessons learned" (2022) 473–475
"Open Building as a Condition for Industrial Construction" (2003) 210, 319–327, *320–324*
open systems 304, 325–326
ordinary, the: quality of 128–131; "You Can't Design the Ordinary" (1971) 2, 42–44, *43*
organisms 54–57; built environment as 431–432
Osaka (Japan) *see* NEXT21
owners 301, 378–379

Papendrecht (Netherlands) *75*, 122, *122*, *202*, 311, 323, 425, 452
papers: "Concept Design Games" (1988) 210, 359–368, *360*, *363–364*, *367*; "Control of Complexity" (1987) 210, 399–409, *400–408*; "Control Hierarchies in Complex Artifacts" (1972) 102–112, *105–112*; "Control Relations in the Built Environment" (1987) 2, 113–116, *113–116*; "An Efficient Response to Users' Preferences" (1992) 298–309, *299–300*, *303*, *305–306*; "Emergent Coherent Behavior of Complex Configurations through Automated Maintenance of Dominance Relations 2008" (2003) 370–375, *370–372*; "Open Building as a Condition for Industrial Construction" (2003) 210, 319–327, *320–324*; "Type as a Social Agreement" (1988) 338–347, *338–346*; "The Uses of Levels" (1988) 348–358, *350–355*
Paris: the built field 39, 43–44, *43*; control 117, *117–118*, 120, *121*; cultivating built environment 420, *420*, *423*, 424; examples of WAYS OF DOING 241–242; Open Building approach 311; role of the architect 163, *203*; sharing forms 134–149, *134*, *136–139*, 145–148
participation 161–162
past, the: learning from 119–121, 457–459
patterns 411
pedagogy *see* studio pedagogy
physical organizations 340, 343–344, 360, 362, 408
"Playing Games" (1972) 88–89
policy 327
Pompeii *30*, 119–120, *120*, 141, 445; cultivating built environment *402*, 411, *411*, 422–423, 432
position 46, 305–307
positioning 78
possibilities: "Supports, Responsibilities and Possibilities" (1968) 83–87
post-modern self-indulgence 24–25
power and powers 49–51; and built environments 153–154; of the built field 413–414; distribution of 56–57; "The Power of the Conventional" (1998) 145–148; power-relationship 162
"Power of the Conventional, The" (1998) 145–148
practice: "What Use Theory?: Questions of purpose and practice" 20–25
preferences: "An Efficient Response to Users' Preferences" (1992) 298–309, *299–300*, *303*, *305–306*
principles: "General Principles About the Way Built Environments Exist" (1979) 45–57
private gardens 313–314
private territory 158–160
process management 470
product *see* consumer product; industrial product
production 307
professional attitude 435
professional cooperation 312–313
professionalism 182; "The Limits of Professionalism" (1975) 153–164, *158*, *160*, *163*
professionalization: of the built field 414–415
professional language 429–430
professionals 154–156
program 363–364

public territory 158–160
purpose: "What Use Theory?: Questions of purpose and practice" 20–25

"Quality and Quantity: The industrialization of housing" (1964) 281–297, *287, 289, 291, 293–295*
"Questions that Will Not Go Away" (2006) 193–199, *193–196*

recording: game recorder 367–368; recording design play 365; and reviewing 365
regulations 178
relations 51–54, 284–285; "Control Relations in the Built Environment" (1987) 2, 113–116, *113–116*; "Emergent Coherent Behavior of Complex Configurations through Automated Maintenance of Dominance Relations 2008" (2003) 370–375, *370–372*; independent 289–290; power-relationship 162; between territorial control and dependency control 112
renovation 299
repetition 185
reports: "SAR: Rules for design" (1965) 331–337, *331, 334, 336–337*
research 171, 198–199, 361, 380–381; "Design for Flexibility: Towards a research agenda" (2008) 376–381; design research 167; "Making Urban Fabric Fine Grained – A Research Agenda" (2003) 74–79; Open Building research laboratory 315–317
residential Open Building 324–325
responsibilities: design responsibility 197; "Supports, Responsibilities and Possibilities" (1968) 83–87
retreat 182–183
rigidity, housing 474–475
role of the architect 347; "Around the Black Hole" (1980) 2, 172–180; changing 22; "The Limits of Professionalism" (1975) 153–164, *158, 160, 163*; "Memories of a Lost Future" (2002) 2, 187–191, *188–189, 191*; "Methodology and Ideology in Architecture" (2013) 200–204, *201–203, 439–443, 440–442*; "Notes on a Network Profession" (1999) 181–186; "Notes of a Traveler" (1980) 165–171; "Questions that Will Not Go Away" (2006) 193–199, *193–196*
Rome (Italy) 29, *32*, 39, 69, *70*, 410, *410*
Rotterdam (Netherlands) *39–41*, 40, 94, 188, 311, 323, 380

"Samarkand Competition Submission, The" (1994) 268–276
"SAR: Rules for design" (1965) 331–337, *331, 334, 336–337*
Schiedam (Netherlands) 40, *41*
self-indulgence *see* post-modern self-indulgence
shape 106–108
sharing 416–418

sharing forms: "Forms of Understanding: Thematic knowledge and the modernist legacy" (1997) 125–142, *129–130, 132–134, 136–139*; "Power of the Conventional, The" (1998) 145–148
sharing values 195, 453, 469–470
"Shell-Infill House" (1987) 245–267
shopping mall 450
site 45–46, 179, 353
skills 198
social conventions 326
social dimensions 299
social support 166–167
space 45, 175–178, 343–344
spatial organization 339
St. Gall (Switzerland) 119, 128, *129–130*, 422
structure 49; and power 50–51
students of architecture *see* architecture, students of
studies: "Shell-Infill House" (1987) 245–267
studio pedagogy: "To Tend a Garden: Thoughts on the strengths and limits of studio pedagogy" (2007) 426–430
submissions: "The Samarkand Competition Submission" (1994) 268–276
supply and demand 303–304
support and supports 355; "'Grondslagen' – Basic Principles for the Building of Supports and the Production of Support Dwellings" (1963) 210, 215–231, *217–231*; separation of 'infill' and 301, 304; "Supports, Responsibilities and Possibilities" (1968) 83–87
"Supports, Responsibilities and Possibilities" (1968) 83–87
survival 126–128
sustainability 450–451
Sustainable Urbanism and Beyond: "Cultivating Built Environment" (2012) 431–435, *433–434*
systems 48–49, 354–355; independence of 340–341; "Lives of Systems" (1988) 63–73; open 304; and power 51; systems design 327; technical 448–449

talks: "The General from the Local" (1984) 58–62; "Involving People in the Housing Process" (1972) 90–101, *92–100*; "The Limits of Professionalism" (1975) 153–164, *158, 160, 163*
teaching: teaching design 172–175; teaching formats 198
technical studies: "Housing: The act of dwelling" (1968) 14–19
technical systems 448–449
technology 182, 304, 322
territorial control: invisible 449; relations between dependency control and 112
territorial hierarchies 102, 109–110
territorial interpretations of configurations 110–111
territorial organization 363

territory and territories 408–409; abandoned 178–180; distribution of 55; public and private 158–160

thematic knowledge: "Forms of Understanding: Thematic knowledge and the modernist legacy" (1997) 125–142, *129–130, 132–134, 136–139*

theme 401–402; nonthematic 402

theory: Habraken's contribution to a theory of the built field xviii–xix; understanding Habraken's theories xvii–xviii; "What Use Theory?: Questions of purpose and practice" 20–25

three-dimensional urban design 312, 320, 433, 452

three-level institutional building 452–453

time 170, 470

time-based building 121

tissue: Amsterdam *33–36, 38, 43*; Dokkum *37*; Forma urbis *31*; Olynthus *31*; Pompeii *30*; Rome *29, 70*; Rotterdam *39–40*; Schiedam *41*; "The Tissue of the Town: Some suggestions for further scrutiny" (1964) 2, 29–41, *29–31, 33–41*; Ur *31*

"Tissue of the Town: Some suggestions for further scrutiny, The" (1964) 2, 29–41, *29–31, 33–41*

Tokyo 311–312, 320, 450, *457*, 470

tools: "Concept Design Games" (1988) 210, 359–368, *360, 363–364, 367*; "Design for Flexibility: Towards a research agenda" (2008) 376–381; "Emergent Coherent Behavior of Complex Configurations through Automated Maintenance of Dominance Relations 2008" (2003) 370–375, *370–372*; "SAR: Rules for design" (1965) 331–337, *331, 334, 336–337*; "Type as a Social Agreement" (1988) 338–347, *338–346*; "The Uses of Levels" (1988) 348–358, *350–355*

"To Tend a Garden: Thoughts on the strengths and limits of studio pedagogy" (2007) 426–430

transformation 196–197, 399–401; *Transformations of the Site* (1988): "Lives of Systems" (1988) 63–73

Transformations of the Site (1988): "Lives of Systems" (1988) 63–73

travel: "Notes of a Traveler" (1980) 165–171

Tunis (Tunisia) 120, *121*, 412, *412*, 424

two-level apartment buildings 450

two-level environment 117

two-level office building 449

type 402–403, 411; "Type as a Social Agreement" (1988) 338–347, *338–346*

"Type as a Social Agreement" (1988) 338–347, *338–346*

understanding: "Forms of Understanding: Thematic knowledge and the modernist legacy" (1997) 125–142, *129–130, 132–134, 136–139*

uniformity 156–157; housing 474–475

unity: dwelling as dual unity 288–289

Ur *31*, 32

urban design 78, 117–121, 201, 292, 312, 379–380, 468–469

urban fabric 323; "Making Urban Fabric Fine Grained – A Research Agenda" (2003) 74–79; *see also* tissue

users: "An Efficient Response to Users' Preferences" 298–309; users designing 323

"Uses of Levels, The" (1988) 348–358, *350–355*

values and value systems 157, 160–161, 169–170, 175–178, 181–183; sharing 195, 453, 469–470

variants: and power 50; relations of 51–52

Venice (Italy) 457; control *120*; cultivating built environment 411–412, *411–412*, 423, 427; role of the architect 193, *195*; sharing forms 131, *132–133*, 135

Vicenza (Italy) *193*

voluntary expenses 301

"What Use Theory?: Questions of purpose and practice" 20–25

writing: understanding Habraken's writing xvii–xviii

writing form 366–367

Xi-an (China) *119, 422*

"You Can't Design the Ordinary" (1971) 2, 42–44, *43*

Zhou Zheng estate and garden (China) *403, 413*

zones 78–79